ISBN 978-0-656-68188-4
PIBN 10520369

FB &c Ltd, Dalton House, 60 Windsor Avenue, London, SW19 2RR.
Company number 08720141. Registered in England and Wales.

For support please visit www.forgottenbooks.com

[H. S. T. A. BULLETINS 29-46]

EFFICIENCY IN HIGH SCHOOLS

Studies, 1911-14, in the Application of the Principles of Scientific Management to High School Problems

made by the

HIGH SCHOOL TEACHERS' ASSOCIATION
OF NEW YORK CITY

Under Direction of

WILLIAM T. MORREY, President

Monograph

PREFACE

The Representatives of the High School Teachers' Association voted, May 26, 1914, that "copies of our BULLETINS be bound and furnished to the High School, College and Public Libraries of the City."

The President generally printed more BULLETINS than were distributed, and reprinted many of the important early articles, so that the bound volumes beginning with BULLETIN No. 34 are practically complete. The last eight pages of BULLETIN No. 46 are to be detached in binding. They contain for the bound volume of BULLETINS: Title Page, this Preface, and the contents of BULLETINS Nos. 29 to 46. The BULLETINS beginning with No. 35 are paged consecutively up to page 372, the end of the alphabetical index.

The 444 pages of BULLETINS contain announcements of General, Section or Department, and Representatives' Meetings; Minutes of the same; Reports of Committees; Addresses, and Statistics.

Through this routine work there was the central purpose to devote the energies of the Association, in so far as the President could direct these energies, to the study of "Efficiency in the High Schools through the Application of the Principles of Scientific Management" as enunciated in the industrial world. To a person desiring to study this central theme, the following analytical outline will serve as a key:

SCIENTIFIC MANAGEMENT OR HIGH SCHOOL EFFICIENCY

PREFACE

In conclusion, I wish to thank my friends in the Association for three elections without opposition. These years have given me the opportunity to attempt many things for the inspiration of high school teachers and for their improvement along lines purely professional. I have felt it my duty to keep out of controversies, although I have endeavored to post myself thoroughly from both sides in controversy.

I have been able to form the acquaintance of a great many of the high school teachers, men and women, and also of the elementary school people, for my work for the la four or five years has been in the same buildings with elementary schools.

I have prized the right to make and unmake such committees as I saw fit. As far I know but one person ever suggested in vain that a committee be appointed, and dropped the matter when I asked him to submit to me in writing definite proposals exactly what he wanted done.

I have thoroughly enjoyed the monthly meetings with the Representatives from tl various high schools. I have appreciated their uniform kindness, courtesy, and co-opera tion, and, above all, the intimate knowledge I have obtained of the workings of the various schools.

Finally, Fellow High School Teachers of the City of New York, I prize among m most cherished recollections that of the great esteem and confidence you have show in me. Renewing my thanks, I am, Sincerely,

WILLIAM T. MORREY.

December 7, 1914.

Brown Bros., Printers, 225 West 39th Street, New York

CONTENTS H. S. T. A. BULLETINS 29-46—1911-1914

June 30, 1911—December, 1914.

ISSUED BY WILLIAM T. MORREY, PRESIDENT, 1911-1914.

CONTENTS H. S. T. A. BULLETINS 29-46—1911-1914

// Official Bulletin
of the High School Teachers Association of New York City

No. 29 FRIDAY, JUNE 30 1911

The Board of Representatives, on May 23, 1911, empowered the Executive Committee to issue a Bulletin monthly, instead of four times a year.

May 23, 1911, Meeting

The last meeting of the Board of Representatives of the H. S. T. A. for 1910-11 was the first meeting under the newly elected officers of the Association for the year 1911-1912. It gave an opportunity for a retrospect over the work of this last year and for a prospect over the year to come.

Mr. Aaron I. Dotey, Chairman, reported that the Teachers' Interests Committee had taken up the *Excessive Clerical Work Demanded of Teachers,* and had dropped it because of the pedagogical value of this work. *The 25-Hour Schedule* was dropped because of impending investigations. *The Right of the Board to Teachers' Time after 2:30* is covered by a By-Law giving the Board of Education the right over teachers' time to an average of 6½ hours a day. *The Time of Regents' Examinations and the Frequency of School Examinations* are to be investigated further.

The Committee recommended putting all energy into opposing the political control of schools. Mr. Dotey was reappointed chairman of the committee.

Copies of the resolutions adopted May 6 in the General Meeting of the H. S. T. A. in opposition to educational provisions of the Gaynor Charter were ordered to be given to The Globe, The Evening Post, The New York Times, School, and The Brooklyn Eagle.

Mr. Frederick H. Paine, Chairman of Committee on Retirement Legislation, reported on the status of the pension question. He was reappointed chairman.

Mr. Emberson E. Proper, Chairman of the Promotion Committee, reported the resolution of the High School Committee of the Board of Superintendents, "No nomination to the position of first assistant in any high school, except where a vacancy exists—and then in no case where the number of teachers employed in said department is less than five."

The recommendation of Mr. Proper's committee was amended and passed as follows:

The Board of Representatives of the High School Teachers' Association recommend:

1. That first assistants be appointed on the grounds of efficiency in teaching and administrative work without regard to chairmanship of a department.

2. That it be desirable that one first assistant be appointed in high schools for every 150 pupils registered."

Mr. Clarence D. Kingsley, Chairman of the Committee on Increase of High School Accommodations, reported that three new high schools are promised in the next two years—one at Bay Ridge, one in the Bronx, and one in East New York.

The Committee on Secondary Education reported that its work was completed and would go to press this week.

Mr. Benjamin C. Gruenberg, Chairman of the Committee on Child Welfare Exhibit, was granted permission to publish his report in other periodicals before its appearance in the Year Book.

Mr. Clarence D. Kingsley, Chairman of the Committee on Conference with Colleges, reported that the "Committee of Nine" would report at the San Francisco meeting of the N. E. A. a definition of a well-planned high school course. Such a course to consist of 15 units, of which 11 are to be devoted to academic subjects and 4 to electives. The schools to have small classes, adequate equipment, and suitable teaching force. To protect the interests of sound education, 2 majors of 3 units each should be required. National efficiency would be promoted and the moral standard raised by devoting more time to technical study and less to general education. Mr. Kingsley was continued as chairman.

Dr. Loring B. Mullen, the Treasurer, reported a membership of 670 and a balance in the treasury of $723.73.

The president suggested that committees be formed on the Relations between Elementary and High Schools, on Statistics and Directory, and on Efficiency in the High Schools. The Efficiency Committee and its sub-committees could profitably consider such topics as School Ideals, what they are in the various schools, and who determines them; Planning, Co-ordinating, and Checking Up; Standardization of Instructions for Admission, Transfers, Promotions, etc.; Records, Standardized, Reliable, Up to Date, Accessible; Discipline, Common Sense, Judgment, Competent Counsel for Pupils and Teachers; The Fair Deal and Efficiency Reward for Pupils, and for Teachers; Relations between Teachers and their Principals and Superior Officers; Professional Etiquette.

All members and all prospective members of the Association and all interested in High School problems are cordially invited to send written suggestions as to lines of work and as to composition of committees, to the president, W. T. Morrey, 535 West 111th St., New York City.

Mr. Arthur L. Janes, President for 1910-1911, announces that the Year Book will be ready for members on their return to school in the fall.

Passed by Board of Representatives Jan. 7

Whereas the teachers in New York City High Schools constitute the largest body of secondary school teachers in any city on this continent; and

Whereas many of the most far reaching educational and social problems must be worked out during the next few years within the high school; and

Whereas the High School Teachers Association of New York City is already engaged in some of the most important of these problems: and

Whereas this Association needs the support and counsel of every high school teacher in New York City;

Therefore be it resolved that this Association invite and urge all high school teachers in New York City to unite with it; and

Be it further resolved that this Association pledges itself to take no part in any salary proposition.

General Officers for 1911-1912

President,
William T. Morrey, Bushwick

Vice President,
L. Louise Arthur, Bryant

Secretary,
Agnes Carr, Morris

Treasurer,
Dr. Loring B. Mullen, Girls'

Additional Members of Executive Committee:
H. Elizabeth Seelman, Girls'
Aaron I. Dotey, DeWitt Clinton
Clarence D. Kingsley, Manual Training

Department Chairmen for 1911-1912

Ancient Languages,
Mr. E. C. Chickering, Jamaica

Bookkeeping,
Miss Emma M. Skinner, Eastern District

Biology,
Dr. Henry R. Linville, Jamaica H. S.

Drawing,
Mr. Raymond Carter, H. S. of Commerce

History,
Miss Antoinette Lawrence, Jamaica H. S.
Miss Florence L. Beeckman, Sec.

Mathematics,
Mr. Albert E. King, Erasmus Hall H. S.
Sec., Miss Emily M. Jennison, Far Rockaway H. S.

Mechanical Arts,
Mr. George W. Norton, Bushwick H. S.

Modern Languages,
Nannie G. Blackwell, Washington Irving H. S.

Physical Science,
Mr. Joseph S. Mills, H. S. of Commerce

Physiography,
Mr. Willard B. Nelson,
Manual Training H. S.

Stenography and Typewriting,
Mr. E. J. McNamara,
Jamaica H. S.

Representatives for 1911-1912

(Senior Representative first)

Boys—Charles E. Oberholser
Francis T. Hughes
Frederick B. Jones
S. Ridley Parker
William W. Rogers
Alfred A. Tansk

Bryant—Carolyn P. Swett
Mary Elizabeth Reid

Bushwick—George M. Falion
Maud E. Manfred

Commercial—Edwin A. Bolger
George W. Harman
Benj. C. Gruenberg
A. Franklin Ross
Robert P. St. John

Curtis—James Shipley
Mabel G. Burdick

DeWitt Clinton—
Donald C. MacLaren
Oscar W. Anthony
Aaron I. Dotey
Ellen E. Garrigues
Fayette E. Moyer
Charles E. Timmerman

Eastern District—
James P. Warren
Emma M. Skinner
John A. Bole
Maude L. Calkins
Jeannette Trowbridge

Erasmus Hall—
Preston C. Farrar
George E. Boynton
Abigail E. Leonard
William F. Tibbets
Kate E. Turner

Far Rockaway—
Eldon M. Van Dusen

Flushing—Paul R. Jenks

Girls—Loring B. Mullen
H. Elizabeth Seelman

H. S. of Commerce
Horace G. Healey
Alfred H. Lewis
George H. Van Tuyl

Jamaica—Benjamin H. Thorp
Lydia F. Root

Manual Training—
Arthur L. Baker
Sidney Edwards
Mary A. Hall
Clarence D. Kingsley
Frederick A. Peters
Elizabeth Schütze
J. Clarence Smith
Carlton C. McCall
Caroline M. Dithridge

Morris—Gilbert S. Blakely
Harriet L. Constantine
Paul B. Mann
Anna S. Thompson

Newtown—
George H. Kingsbury
Alex E. W. Zerban

Richmond Hill—
Charles Robert Gaston
Gertrude M. Leete

Stuyvesant—T. Harry Knox
Clayton G. Durfee
Joseph L. Beha
Stanley A. Gage
Charles F. Moore
Ernest S. Quimby
Walter M. Smith

Wadleigh—Helen E. Bacon
Florence Middleton

Washington Irving—
Idelette Carpenter
Jessie A. Beach
Emma F. Lowd

Official Bulletin

of the High School Teachers Association of New York City

No. 31 SATURDAY, DECEMBER 9 1911

GENERAL MEETING, DECEMBER 9, 1911.

The next quarterly meeting of the High School Teachers Association for the year 1911-1912 will be held on Saturday morning December 9, at the High School of Commerce at 10 o'clock.

The general meeting precedes the Department meetings and should be over by 11:30. The subject for discussion is:

THE PRINCIPLES OF SCIENTIFIC MANAGEMENT AND HOW THEY WOULD AFFECT SCHOOL EEFICIENCY BY MR. HARRINGTON EMERSON,

Consulting Engineer.

Tne Association is fortunate in securing one of the best expounders and one of the most successful practitioners of the application of these principles to great Industrial Plants.

Mr. Emerson's experience enables him to apply his principles to school problems and conditions in a way that should prove stimulating and helpful to every teacher, to every principal, and to every superintendent.

DEPARTMENT MEETINGS

At 11:30 A. M. Department meetings will be called. The following is a partial list of programs:

Ancient Languages. Room 217. Miss Ruth M. Prescott, Far Rockaway H. S., Chairman. "Classical Clubs in the High School" by Dr. Arthur Alexis Bryant, De Witt Clinton. Discussion led by Mr. W. E. Foster, Stuyvesant; Mr. W. F. Tibbetts, Erasmus Hall; Dr. E. San Giovanni, Manual Training.

"A Latin Play Given in England by Children," Miss Theodora Ethel Wye, Teachers' College.

The recent performance of "Phormio" at Normal College, Dr. Jane Gray Carter.

Biology. Room 301. Dr. Henry R. Linville, Jamaica H. S., Chairman. "1911 Textbooks in Biology in Relation to Recent Movements in Biology Teaching." A Discussion of the following books: Atkinson's High School Botany, Bigelow's Applied Biology, Hunter's Essentials of Biology, Kellogg's The Animals and Man.

Bookkeeping. Room 303. Chairman, G. H. Van Tuyl, H. S. of Commerce, The New Course of Study for Commercial Departments. Principal Fairley of Commercial H. S. Leader.

Chemistry. Teachers' Club. President, Roland H. Williams, Horace Mann School; Secretary Reston Stevenson, College of City of N. Y.

The next meeting will be held at the Chemists' Club, 8 P. M., Dec. 9, 1911.

Drawing. Room 206. Morris Greenberg, Commercial H. S., Chairman.

Meeting of the Exhibition Committee of the H. S. A. T. A. to arrange for a Teachers' Exhibit.

English Teachers' Association of N. Y. City High Schools. President, Edwin Fairley, Jamaica H. S.; Secretary and Treasurer, C. R. Gaston, Richmond Hill H. S.

At meeting held Nov. 25, Mr. G. S. Blakely of Morris H. S., gave report of Committee on Uniform

Nomenclature in Grammar.

B. A. Heydrick of H. S. of Commerce reported on College Entrance Requirements.

Theodore C. Mitchell sent as Delegate to National Convention at Chicago, Dec. 1 and 2, 1911.

German. The New York Association of High School Teachers of German. President, Henry Zick; Secretary, Chas. E. Oberholser.

Next Meeting, 11 A. M., Saturday, Dec. 16, at Gregorian Hotel, 42 West 35th St.

Dr. Stuart H. Rowe, "Habit Formation and the Teaching of Modern Languages."

Luncheon after the lecture.

History and Economics. Room 205. Miss Antoinette Lawrence, Jamaica H. S. Chairman. The Use Notebooks in History, by Principal Sullivan, Boys.

Mathematics. Room 304. Mr. Albert E. King, Erasmus Hall, Chairman. "Outline Recitations in Geometry to Show Economy in Time and Efficiency in Work."

Mechanical Arts. Mr. George W. Norton, Chairman. Meeting, Friday evening, Dec. 15, 1911. Notice of hour and place to be sent later.

"Relative Merits of the Individual Motor Drive and the Line-Shaft Drive for High School Shops."

Modern Languages. Room 401. Miss Nannie G. Blackwell, Washington Irving H. S., Chairman. "Uniform Grammar Terminology" by Mr. Coleman D. Frank, De Witt Clinton H S.

Physical Science. Ben. M. Jaquish, Erasmus Hall, Chairman. Meetings of section as a whole at call of Chairman. Members belong to other departments or associations. See under Chemistry Club, Physics Club, Physiography Department.

Physics Club. President Raymond Brownlee, Stuyvesant H. S.; Secretary F. W. Huntington, Erasmus Hall H. S. Next meeting at Pratt Institute, 10 A. M. Dec. 9. General Topic Mechanics Problems, Demonstrations.

Physiography. Room 105-B. Chairman, Kirk W. Thompson, Jamaica H. S. 'Recent Textbooks in Physiography." Comparisons of Treatment of Topics: Earth as a Planet, Miss Mary E. Reid, Bryant H. S.; The Atmosphere, Miss Miriam L. Taylor, Wadleigh H. S.; The Sea, Mr. Rupert H. Hopkins, Curtis H. S.; Rivers, Mr. F. M. Surrey, Morris H. S.; Glaciers, Mr. Charles A. Miller, Morris H. S.; The Land Forms, Mr. Willard B. Nelson, Manual Training H. S.

Shorthand. Room 216. Mr. Horace G. Healey, H. S. of Commerce. "Teaching of Shorthand in the Public Schools" by E. H. Craver, H. S. of Commerce.

Discussion by Miss Elizabeth Roche, Washington Irving H. S., and David J. O'Keefe, Jamaica H. S.

A large attendance is desired, as several business matters of importance will come up, among them being the proposed license for First Assistant in Stenography.

GENERAL MEETING.

October 21, 1911.

The meeting was called to order in the High School of Commerce at 10.07 o'clock by President W. T. Morrey. The minutes of the last meeting were read and approved. The President made a brief address, stating that the chief work of the year would be the study of High School Efficiency, and urging all who were willing to serve on the committees organized to make known their preference at once.

Mr. Kingsley reported for the Committee on Conference with Colleges that printed bulletins of the work accomplished would be issued in the near future.

The speaker of the morning was

then introduced, Prof. Chas. H. Judd Director of the School of Education of Chicago.

In an interesting and enlightening talk Professor Judd showed the results of detailed study in some of the cities in the Middle West, of the relations existing between Elementary and High School, and between High School and University. These results were pictured on carefully prepared charts, on some of which the progress of the pupil was traced as to his position in the upper, middle or lower third of his class, rather than by his individual rating in per cent. One chart which proved especially interesting to the audience illustrated the widely differing values given the same papers when rated by several different persons.

According to a new plan, the general meeting was adjourned at 11.30, and the members then went to their respective section meetings.

WM. T. MORREY,
President.

AGNES CARR,
Secretary.

OCT. 31 MEETING.

The representatives were called to order at 4 P. M.. Miss C. P. Swett of Bryant was appointed secretary *pro tem* The report of the May meeting was read, corrected and accepted

The Treasurer reported a balance of $358.73.

The various Senior Representatives then reported on the membership of their various schools.

Reports of Department Chairmen.

Mr. Norton of Bushwick discussed the policy of his Section announced as the main topic for the year's work in Mechanic Arts, "Motive Power for Running Machines."

Miss Blackwell of Washington Irving made a report for the Modern Language Section.

Mr. Weaver reported for the Students' Aid Committee that 200 pupils had been assisted; that the promise that this work be recognized in the Budget had failed; that an effort is now being made to obtain outside help, and legislative action for establishing in each city a bureau to give employment. The committee has been active as usual in distributing pamphlets on different occupations.

Mr. Kingsley of the Committee on Increase in High School Accommodation reported the promise of new buildings, and suggested that the question of greater accommodation be taken up with the Board of Education.

Mr. Greenberg believed that this committee should do more work in emphasizing need for more high school accommodation. He also criticized the administration of High School annexes, and thought that the effort should be made towards eventual elimination of annexes as a part of the system.

Miss Seelman of Girls' High, Mr. Mann of Morris, and Mr. Falion of Bushwick declared that in their annexes neither pupils nor teachers were discriminated against.

Mr. Kingsley reported for the Committee on Conference with Colleges that of the six members forming that committee, five are in favor of adopting as a whole the report of the "Committee of Nine." Dr. Sullivan believes that both mathematics and a foreign language should be required for entrance to college.

New Business.

Motion carried that chairman be empowered to appoint a Committee on Conference of Relations Between Elementary and High Schools.

Motion carried that chairman be empowered to appoint a Committee on Efficiency, and such other committees as he sees fit to call.

Meeting adjourned.

(Signed) AGNES CARR,
Secretary.

NOV. 28 MEETING.

Representatives were called to order about 4 P. M.

Miss Maud B. Manfred of Bushwick appointed Secretary *pro tem.*

The minutes of the Oct. 31 meeting were read, corrected, and then adopted.

The Department Programs for the Dec. 9 meeting were read and revised.

Mr. Janes reported the Year Book for 1910-1911 all ready for weeks, except one report.

The question of merging the lists was discussed in an informal way by everyone present, bringing out the advantages and disadvantages. No formal action taken.

Miss Alice Higgins, appointed by former President Janes, reported by letter her meeting with Dr. James Sullivan's committee. There was a general discussion of the propriety of teachers taking part. No formal action taken.

The investigation of the status of the position of librarian was at the suggestion of Mr. Oberholser referred to the Teachers' Interests Committee.

AGNES CARR,
Secretary.

PROFESSOR JUDD ON EFFICIENCY.

Dr. Judd claimed that percentages are unreliable as a basis of comparisons, and that the relative standing, or his positional rank of a student in his class is a much more reliable and constant quantity.

Some of the charts showed the differences in marks given in different departments in the same school, in different years in the same department, and by different teachers in the same department. In the English departments in one or two schools there has been a great tendency to grade the students just a little above passing, very few students receiving high marks, and very few receiving penalizing marks. This practice was contrasted with that of some other departments in which there was a normal distribution. In every case where there was a marked variation from the normal distribution, a question was raised as to the cause of the disturbing factors, and in many cases these causes were ascertainable.

Professor Judd emphasized the idea that deductions drawn from such statistics were to be regarded not as conclusive, but as raising fruitful subjects for inquiry.

A set of charts showed how many students from the highest third of a lower school maintained their rank in the highest third of an upper school, and how many dropped to the middle third, and how many to the lowest third; and, similarly, how many from the middle third maintained that rank, or went up or down; and similarly for the lowest third. This method of comparing the rank of students as they pass from one institution to another is to be used in the Middle West in the attempt to establish objective standards for measuring the efficiency both of the various high schools and of the colleges, and of studying out problems of articulation both of the institutions themselves and of the various departments in the lower and higher institutions.

Students in the middle and even lowest divisions in the elementary schools occasionally awoke later on and secured a better rank in high school and college. One chart showed the progress of 158 students who went from the elementary school through the high school and college. He claims that this method of study seems more satisfactory than reports dealing only with failures; a school receiving students from the highest third of a lower school is not discharging its duty when those students maintain merely a passing mark; on the other hand, a student coming up from a lower school, from the lowest third of his class, and maintaining a passing mark in the higher school, is doing well.

Professor Judd urged the desirability of keeping careful records of the positional rank of students as they go from one school to another, extending over a series of years, carefully analyzed and available to those engaged in the work in the various schools.

Official Bulletin

of the High School Teachers Association of New York City

No. 32 TUESDAY, JANUARY 30 1912

The next meeting of the Board of Representatives will be held, Tuesday, January 30th, at 4 P. M., at Washington Irving H. S. 34 1-2 E. 12th Street.

Chairmen of Committees are invited to be present and to report progress.

Dr. Edward A. Fitzpatrick, Chairman of Committee on Scientific Management, will outline proposed work of the Committee: Topic ' On the Reorganization of an Existing High School in accordance with the Principles of Scientific Management." All interested are invited.

Dr. Fitzpartrick, Chairman of the committee, on Principles of Scientific Management, will outline in a general way, the problem that he believes the committee should discuss and investigate. He will take up a few topics. indicate the method of treatment, and state the recomendations he would make at the present time. Suggestions and criticisms are welcomed by the committee now and hereafter. Please send them to the Chairman, Dr. Edward A. Fitzpatrick, High School of Commerce, 155 West 65th Street, New York City.

GENERAL MEETING, DEC. 9

The December Meeting of the High School Teachers' Association was called to order by the President, W. T. Morrey, in the H. S. of Commerce at 10:10 on the morning of Dec. 9.

Mr. Frederick C. Paine, Chairman of the Pension Committee discussed the bill prepared and sent to Albany by Mr. Best. This bill provides for a one per cent deduction from salaries $3500 and less, and during service up to 20 years and more, and for salaries more than $3500 a deduction of two per cent is proposed.

Mr. Bryan of the High School of Commerce moved that it be Resolved, that this Association is opposed to any change in the present pension law creating an increase over the present one per cent deduction on salarlies $3500 or less, and that it is opposed to the proposition to make a deduction of two per cent on salaries when the length of service has been twenty years or more.

This motion was carried.

To Mr. Gruenberg, Mr. Paine stated that no actuarial investigation of pensions had been made, but the printed record of what had been done was obtainable.

The speaker of the morning Mr. Harrington Emerson, a Consulting Engineer, was then introduced. Mr. Emerson had had six years of experience in the University of Nebraska, so that he was in sympathy with school room matters, though he presented his topic "The Principles of Scientfic Managemen," in the terms of the industrial world.

It is not often that we are privileged to feel so close a kinship between our problems and those of the world of business surrounding us. That the subject was of vital interest was amply proved by the eager attention of the audience, and the evident reluctance with which at last, with a rising vote of thanks to Mr. Emerson, the Association adjourned to the Section meetings at 11:40.

Signed,

AGNES CARR, Secretary

[Mr. Emerson left for Bermuda that afternoon and returned early in January. He is revising his address]

REPRESENTATIVES MEETING

DECEMBER 19th

Miss E. A. Roche, W. I. H. S. was appointed Secretary *Pro Tem*

Minutes of Nov. 28th meeting were read and adopted.

Reports on membership.

Mr. Crossley of Teacher's Interests Committee opened an informal discussion of meaning of "A Teacher of Superior Merit; all present participated.

Mr. Quimby, of Stuyvesant, spoke of work of Hanus Committee.

On a motion of Mr. Kingsley, the Secretary was empowered to ask the Building Committee of the Board of Education to see that in the new building for the Washington Irving High School there is provided a committee meeting room suitable for the meeting of this association and other associations.

The President announced that he hoped to make the meetings of the Board of Representatives of educational value, by arranging definite topics for discussion.

For the January 30th meeting the chairman of the Committee on Scientific Management will talk "On the Reorganization of an Existing High School in accordance with the principles of Scientific Management."

Chairmen of Committees, Members of Scientific Management Committees, all Delegates should attend or send Proxies who are interested in school efficiency.

E. S. Roche, Secretary *Pro Tem*

COMMITTEE ON CONFERENCE WITH THE COLLEGES.

The committee of this Association has unanimously endorsed the main part of the report of the Committee of Nine of the National Education Association. One member of our committee believes that under no circumstances should a student be admitted to an academic college without foreign language and mathematics. But the five other members of the committee endorse the entire report, including the recommendation "that provision should be made by many of the larger colleges to continue the education of students of whom it has been discovered that the requirement of mathematics or the requirement of foreign language is an obstacle to the continuation of their education." Complete copies of the report may be secured from the Chairman of the Committee of Nine, Clarence D. Kingsley, Manual Training High School, Brooklyn.

Pamphlet "Articulation of High School and College"—50 pages—contains Statement of the New York High School Teachers' Association, Replies from Superintendents and College Presieents, and Resolutions adopted at the Boston Meeting of N. E. A. 1910

The Department of Mechanical Arts held a most successful meeting on Friday evening, Dec. 15, 1911, with 23 present. After an informal dinner there was an interesting and instructive address by Mr. Herbert Lester, of the firm of Manning, Maxwell & Moore, on the Relative Merits of the Line Shaft Drive and the Individual Motor Drive for Manual Training Shops. There was a lively and interesting discussion. Mr. Kingsley of the Manual Training High School spoke of the advisability of this department's formulating a statement of policy as to what should be the content of the manual training work of the future so as to receive the same credit as other high school subjects. Some discussion followed after which it was voted that the chairman should appoint a committee of five to study this question and formulate such a statement.

It is expected that Associate Superintendent, E. L. Stevens, will address the next Departmental Meeting which will be held Friday evening, March 1st, 1912. His subject will be "The Function and Place of the Mechanic Arts in the Secondary Schools of New York City.

JANUARY 1, 1912

RANK	HIGH SCHOOLS	TEACHERS	PUPILS
1	Washington Irving	144	3769
2	Morris	122	3208
3	De Witt Clinton	111	3076
4	Erasmus Hall	128	3060
5	Manual Training	128	2848
6	Wadleigh	122	2717
7	Girls	116	2639
8	Eastern District	92	2498
9	Commercial	100	2169
10	Stuyvesant	92	2002
11	Commerce	66	1936
12	Boys	74	1709
13	Bushwich	42	1074
14	Bryant	46	885
15	Jamaica	42	845
16	Curtis	(37)	797
17	Newtown	31	765
18	Richmond Hill	26	694
19	Flushing	29	501
20	Far Rockaway	14	233
	(Bay Ridge Annex of E. H. H. S.)	22	567

EFFICIENCY THROUGH PUPIL CO-OPERATION

(As Posted)

PUPILS IN CHARGE OF 2K, ROOM 413.

Representative of The General Organization: Miss Bloss (also order at recess).

Class Representative: Miss Luhrs (daily report, order at recess and in absence of teacher, etc.).

Vice-Representative: Miss Mahler (order at recess, also all duties of Class Representative in her absence).

Leader in Fire Drill: Miss Rohde (to lead and hold line).

Leader in Setting-up Exercises: Miss Steeg.

Substitute Leader: Miss Rohde (in Miss Steeg's absence).

Girls that erase boards at close of period: Miss Specht, Miss Rohde.

Ventilation: Jacob Weber (to see that windows are opened at top).

Wardrobe Doors: Miss Beer (to see that doors are kept closed).

Front Closet Door: Miss Hallote (to see that door is kept closed).

Song Books: Miss Saladino. (to distribute them and see that none are lost).

Uncovered Books and Scissors: Miss Horr (to confiscate and lock up all books found uncovered, until paper be brought to cover them; also to see that scissors are returned to teacher's desk).

Ink Wells: Miss Spengler (to see that they are kept filled).

Erasers, Chalk, etc.: Jacob Weber.

Every Pupil is responsible for *the condition of floor around his or her desk*, also for the *turning up of his or her seat at the close of school.* Care taken in both these matters will make the task of the Janitress a much easier one.

MISS MANFRED, Prefect.
Term beginning September 11, 1911.

Mr. Arthur L. Janes, President for 1910-1911, announces that the Year Book is in press.

The Board of Representatives, on May 23, 1911, empowered the Executive Committee to issue a Bulletin monthly, instead of four times a year.

The Board of Representatives of the High School Teachers' Association recommended:

1. That first assistants be appointed on the grounds of efficiency in teaching and administrative work without regard to chairmanship of a department.

2. That it be desirable that one first assistant be appointed in high schools for every 150 pupils registered."—May 23, 1911.

This Association pledges itself to take no part in any salary proposition.—Jan. 7, 1911.

NOTICES.

The next meeting of the Board of Representatives will be February 27, 4 P. M., at Washington Irving H. S. 34½ E. 12th St. N. Y. City.

Committee appointments will be considered as declined if before Feb. 15th the President is not notified of their acceptance.

Chairmen of Departments who have not already submitted their plans for the remainder of the year, should do so at once.

Persons desiring to do committee work should notify the President of their preferences.

The one dollar for the current year should be collected by the Senior Representative and forwarded to the Treasurer, Dr. Loring B. Mullen, Girls' High School, Brooklyn.

DIRECTORY FOR 1911-1912
GENERAL OFFICERS.

President,
William T. Morrey, Bushwick

Vice President,
L. Louise Arthur, Bryant

Secretary,
Agnes Carr, Morris

Treasurer,
Dr. Loring B. Mullen, Girls'

Additional Members of Executive Committee:
H. Elizabeth Seelman, Girls'
Aaron I. Dotey, DeWitt Clinton
Clarence D. Kingsley, Manual Training

REPRESENTATIVES.

(Senior Representative first)

BOYS'. Charles E. Oberholser, Francis T. Hughes, Frederick B. Jones, S. Ridley Parker, William W. Rogers, Alfred A. Tansk.

BRYANT. Carolyn P. Swett, Mary Elizabeth Reid.

BUSHWICK. George M. Falion, Maud E. Manfred.

COMMERCIAL. Edwin A. Bolger, George W. Harman, Benj. C. Gruenberg, A. Franklin Ross, Robert P. St. John.

CURTIS James Shipley, Mabel G. Burdick.

DeWITT CLINTON. Donald C. MacLaren, Oscar W. Anthony, Aaron I. Dotey, Ellen E. Garrigues, Fayette E. Moyer, Charles E. Timmerman.

EASTERN DISTRICT. Minnie K. Pinch, Katherine Meigs, Lou Helmuth, Charlotte Crawford, Henry E. Chapin, Franklin H. Smith

ERASMUS HALL. Preston C. Farrar, George E. Boynton, Abigail E. Leonard, William F. Tibbets, Kate E. Turner.

FAR ROCKAWAY. Eldon M. Van Dusen.

FLUSHING. Paul R. Jenks

GIRLS. Loring B. Mullen, H. Elizabeth Seelman,

H. S. OF COMMERCE. Horace G. Healey Alfred H. Lewis, George H. Van Tuyl

JAMAICA. Benjamen H. Thorp, Lydia F. Root.

MANUAL TRAINING. Arthur L. Baker, Eleanor R. Baker, Sidney Edwards, Marion Hackedorn, Mary A. Hall, Clarence D. Kingsley, Charles Perrine, Frederick A. Peters

MORRIS. Paul B. Mann, Harriet L. Constantine, Frederick C. White.

NEWTON. Geoge H. Kingsbury, Alex E. W. Zerban.

RICHMOND HILL. Charles Robert Gaston, Gertrude M. Leete.

STUYVESANT. T. Harry Knox, Clayton G. Durfee, Joseph L. Beha, Stanley A. Gage, Charles F. Moore, Ernest S. Quimby, Walter M. Smith.

WADLEIGH. Helen E. Bacon, Florence Middleton.

WASINGHTON IRVING. Idelette Carpenter, Mary C. Craig, Elizabeth S. Rose.

COMMITTEE ON SECONDARY EDUCATION.

Henry R. Linville; Jamaica, Chairman; L. Louise Arthur, Bryant; M. Ellen Barker, Girls' Colman D. Frank, DeWitt Clinton; Clarence D. Kingsley, Manual Training; A. E. Peterson; Morris; Ernest E. Smith, Boys' Louise Thompson, Morris.

COMMITTEE ON TEACHERS' INTERESTS.

A. I. Dotey, DeWitt Clinton, Chairman; A. L. Janes, Boys; Sidney Edwards, Manual Training; Ida G. Galloway, Washington Irving; Margaret L. Ingalls, Girls'; James P. Warren, Eastern District; A. L. Crosley, Stuyvesant.

PROMOTION COMMITTEE.

Albert E. King, Eramus, Chairman; Michael D. Sohon, Morris, Lillian M. Elliott, Wadleigh James A. Fairly, Commercial, Mary A. Hall, Manual Training; Claude F. Walker, Commerce; Emma F. Pettengill, Girls'; John L. Tildsley, De Witt Clinton; Jesse Haley, Morris.

STUDENTS AID COMMITTEE.

E. W. Weaver, Chairman, Brooklyn Evening High School for Men; Gilbert J. Raynor, Commercial; Paul J. Abelson, DeWitt Clinton; A. L. Pugh, Commerce; Jennie M. Jenness, Girls' Henrietta Rodman, Wadleigh; George K. Hinds, Washington Irving; Philip Dowell, Curtis; O. F. Ferry, Erasmus Hall; John P. Cahill, Jamaica: Charles Perrine, Manual Training; E. M. Wiliams, Morris; H. B. Slater, Newtown: Edward F. Lewis, Bryant; Charles S. Hartwell, and Mabel Skinner, Eastern District; E. S. Augsbury, Stuyvesant; M. B. Lambert, Richmond Hill; Etta E. Southwell, Bushwick; P. R. Dean, Curtis Evening; F. H. J. Paul, New York evening; Marie Gurnee and Meriel Williad, Washington Irving; Kate Turner, Erasmus Hall.

COMMITTEE ON INCREASE OF HIGH SCHOOL ACCOMMODATIONS

Clarence D. Kingsley, Manual Training, Chairman; Woodward A. Anderson, Washington Irving; John A. Bole, Eastern District; George E. Boynton, Erasmus Hall; Bertha F. Courtney, Bryant; Charles S. Estes, Erasmus Hall; Margaret L. Ingals, Girls'; Paul R. Jenks, Flushing; J. Herbert Low, Manual Training; Harry K. Monroe, Bryant; Hawley O. Rittenhouse, Eastern District; Henrietta Rodman, Wadleigh; Robert P. St John, Commercial; Elizabeth Schutze, Manual Training; H. Elizabeth Seelman, Girls'; Louis B. Semple, Bushwick; Gilbert S. Blakely, Morris; I. A. Hazen, Man. Tr'ng; Philip R. Dean, Curtis.

COMMITTEE ON CONFERENCE WITH COLLEGES.

Clarence D. Kingsley, Manual Training, Chairman; William McAndrew, Washington Irving; James Sullivan, Boys'; James F. Wilson, Stuyvesant; Alexander L. Pugh, H. S. of Commerce; John L. Tildsley, DeWitt Clinton.

COMMITTEE ON RETIREMENT LEGISLATION.

Frederick H. Paine, Eastern District, Chairman; L. Louis Arthur, Bryant; A. C. Bryan, H. S. of Commerce.

COMMITTEE ON SCIENTIFIC MANAGEMENT (EFFICIENCY)

Edward A. Fitzpatrick, Commerce, Chairman; Arthur L. Janes, Boys; Harold E. Butterick, Brooklyn Evening H.S; L. Louise Arthur, Bryant; Geo. M. Falion, Bushwick; A. L. Pugh, W. S. Schlauch, S. P. Koopman, Commerce; B. C. Gruenberg, Commercial; W. R. Hayward, Curtis; H. B. Penhallow, Clinton; Minnie Ikelheimer, Eastern District; Kate E. Turner, Erasmus; A. G Belding, Far Rockaway; Paul R. Jenks, E. C. Hood, Flushing; M. Ellen Barker, Girls; B. H. Thorp, Jamaica; I. A. Hazen, A. C. White, Chas. Perrine; Mary J. Bourne, E. M. Williams, H. C. Laughlin, Morris; J. J. Klein, Richmond Hill; A. G. Crossley, E. S. Quimby, Stuyvesant; Helen E. Bacon, Rose M. Barton, W. W. Clendenin, Wadleigh; David L. Arnold, Washington Irving.

COMMITTEE ON ABSENCES OF TEACHERS

Charles R. Fay, Erasmus, Chairman, Frank H Miller, Flushing, William R. Lasher, Erasmus, J. Herbert Low, Manual Training.

COMMITTEE ON GRAMMAR: UNIFORM NOMENCLATURE FOR HIGH AND ELEMENTARY SCHOOLS, FOR FOREIGN LANGUAGES AND FOR ENGLISH

Charles Perrine, Manual Training, Chairman, Committee is not completed. Send suggestions to the Chairman or to the President.

General Meetings are planned for March 2 and May 4, 1912.

The Board of Representatives meets on the last school Tuesday of the month. The dates are October 31, November 28, December 19, 1911 and January 30, February 27, March 26, April 30, and May 28, 1912. No meetings in September and June.

BIBLIOGRAPHY.

Teachers will find much of interest and inspiration in the following books on Industrial Efficiency:

Carpenter, Charles U,—Profit Making Management.

Gantt—Work, Wages, and Profit.

Gilbreth—Motion Study.

Gillette & Dana—Cost Keeping.

Emerson, Harrington—Efficiency.

Taylor, Frederick Winslow—Principles of Scientific Management.
—Shop Management.

Official Bulletin

of the High School Teachers Association of New York City

No. 33 SATURDAY, MARCH 16 1912

WHAT CONSTITUTES THE TEACHER OF SUPERIOR MERIT?

This question will be answered by Examiner George J. Smith and Superintendent Edward L. Stevens, and the Principals of our High Schools at the general meeting of the Association, 11 A. M., Saturday, March 16, 1912, at the High School of Commerce.

This meeting will be the third of the year devoted to the study of efficiency. In the first, Professor Judd discussed the methods of testing efficiency. In the second, Mr. Harrington Emerson discussed the principles of scientific management. This meeting will consider the ideals of the teacher and of the school. For the last general meeting we announce with pleasure that

On May 28 Prof. Paul H. Hanus, chairman of the Committee of School Inquiry, will address us.

WILLIAM T. MORREY, *President.*

AGNES CARR, *Secretary.*

DEPARTMENT MEETINGS.

Department meetings, beginning at 10 A. M., precede the general meeting.

Ancient Languages—Room 217, Miss Ruth M. Prescott, Far Rockaway. H. S., Chairman. Latin Composition—"What the Colleges Haye a Right to Demand." Prof. Gonzales Lodge will speak informally and there will be general discussion.

Biology—Room 301, Dr. Henry R. Linville, Jamaica, H. S., Chairman. C. W. Hahn, Secretary. Review of recent text-books in Biology.

Dr. A. J. Grout, Atkinson's High School Botany.

Miss Florence W. Slater, Bergen and Caldwell's Practical Botany.

Miss Kate Hixon, Bigelow's Applied Biology.

Miss Carolyn P. Swett, Hunter's Essentials of Biology.

Other text-books if time permits.

Bookkeeping—Room 303, G. H. Van Tuyl, Chairman. Dr. Edward J. Clapp of the New York University School of Accounts and Finance will speak on "The Teaching of Salesmanship." There will also be an exhibition of maps and other illustrative materials for use in Commercial Geography.

History and Economics—Room 205, Miss Antoinette Lawrence, Jamaica H. S., Chairman. "How the Modern History Course Actually Works Out in Practice." A discussion of experiences.

Mathematics—Room 304, Mr. Albert E. King, Principal P. S. 83, Brooklyn, Chairman. "Efficiency in the Geometry Room," by A. Latham Baker, Manual Training H. S.

Modern Languages—Room 401, Miss Nannie G. Blackwell, Washington Irving H. S., Chairman.

Tests of efficiency in modern language teaching in New York City High Schools.

Symposium—A contribution asked for from Modern Language Department of each High School.

Physiography—Room 105B, Mr. Kirk W. Thompson, Jamaica H. S., Chairman.

Mr. Anthony Fiala, Secretary of the Arctic Club of America will talk on plotting positions geographically on the Polar ice. He will bring with him a sextant, an artificial horizon and an ephemeris with which to illustrate his talk.

Shorthand—Room 216, Mr. Horace G. Healy, H. S. of Commerce, Chairman.

Mr. Chas. E. Smith of the Underwood Typewriter Co. will discuss "Methods of Teaching Touch Typewriting in High Schools."

CONTENTS OF THIS BULLETIN.

"Principles of Scientific Management" by Harrington Emerson.

Recommendations of the Conference Committee on the Course of Study to the Hanus Committee of School Inquiry.

Report of Students' Aid Committee.

MEETING OF REPRESENTATIVES, JANUARY 30, 1912.

The minutes of the previous meeting were read and approved as read.

Report of membership by schools.

Dr. Mullen reported a balance in treasury of $382.91. Total number of members, 381, with nine high schools to hear from. Membership exceeds by 76 that at the same time last year, which reached 670.

Mr. Payne, Chairman of Committee on Retirement Legislation, outlined the details of the pending pension bill. Questions and discussion followed. Mr. Paine suggested that the representatives present ascertain the sentiment in their respective schools and report the same to him.

Mr. Kingsley, Chairman of the Committee on Increase of High School Accommodations, reported that high schools were in sight for East New York and the Bronx, as recommended in Superintendent Steven's annual report.

President Morrey announced that this committee would be reorganized.

Mr. Kingsley, as Chairman of the Committee on Conference with the Colleges, read an extract from the report of President Burton of Smith College, advocating more flexible high school courses and the acceptance of such by the colleges.

Mr. Weaver, Chairman of the Students' Aid Committee, reported. (See elsewhere in this bulletin.)

Dr. Fitzpatrick, Chairman of the Committee on Scientific Management, outlined in a clear and interesting manner, the topics his committee would deal with in their discussion and investigation of high school efficiency. Discussion followed.

It was affirmed that the Hanus Committee desired a committee of the High School Teachers' Association to confer with it in its present investigation. It was moved, seconded and carried that a committee be formed at the discretion of the President, to represent the High School Teachers' Association before the Hanus Committee.

The meeting adjourned at 6 P. M. H. E. SEELMAN, *Secretary Pro Tem.*

MEETING OF REPRESENTATIVES, FEBRUARY 27, 1912.

Minutes of the January meeting were read and approved.

President Morrey announced that Mr. Emerson's address would appear in the next bulletin instead of waiting to be issued in the Year Book. Attention was called to this policy.

Mr. Dotey, Chairman of Teachers' Interest Committee, resigned from chairmanship on account of pressure of school work and illness. His resignation was accepted.

The program of general meeting was referred to whether department meetings should precede or follow the meeting of the entire body. No action taken.

Mr. Kingsley reported for Conference Committee on Course of Study appointed to confer with the Hanus Committee on Scientific Investigation of Schools. At the first conference sixteen were present. A number of questions were discussed resulting in entire agreement on the need of greater flexibility in high school course. No desire was expressed to cut out subjects already in course but several more seemed urgently needed. The committee was enlarged to fifty-seven, of whom forty were present at the second meeting. At this meeting a sub-committee was appointed to put its recommendations into shape to be submitted to full committee. Mr. Kingsley read to the Representatives his preliminary draft of the report of the sub-committee. There was much discussion with regard to five-subject or four-subject courses, and requirements for high school work.

Meeting adjourned at 5:50 P. M. AGNES CARR, *Secretary.*

DIRECTORY FOR 1911-1912.

President—William T. Morrey, Bushwick.

Vice-President—L. Louise Arthur, Bryant.

Secretary—Agnes Carr, Morris.

Treasurer—Dr. Loring B. Mullen, Girls.

Additional Members of Executive Committee—H. Elizabeth Seelman, Girls; Aaron I. Dotey, DeWitt-Clinton, and Clarence D. Kingsley, Manual Training.

CHAIRMEN OF COMMITTEES.

Absences of Teacher—Charles R. Fay, Erasmus Hall.

Conference with Colleges—Clarence D. Kingsley, Manual Training.

Grammar Uniform Nomenclature—Charles Perrine.

Increasing High School Accommodations—Gilbert S. Blakely, Morris.

Promotion Committee—Harold E. Buttrick, Boys.

Retirement Legislation (Pensions)—Frederick H. Paine, Eastern District.

Scientific Management—Dr. Edward A. Fitzpatrick, H. S. Commerce.
Secondary Education—Henry R. Linville, Jamaica.
Standardization of Reports, Forms and Blanks—Harry B. Penhallow, DeWitt Clinton.
Students' Aid—E. W. Weaver, Boys and Brooklyn Evening School.
Teachers' Interests—Paul B. Mann, Morris.

SCIENTIFIC MANAGEMENT AND HIGH SCHOOL EFFICIENCY.

By Harrington Emerson, Efficiency Engineer.

December 9, 1911

Ladies and Gentlemen of the High School Teachers' Association:

I regard it as one of the most fortunate events of my life that when I was very young, and perhaps ought still to have been going to school, I had the opportunity to become a teacher in one of the younger western state universities. What I there learned in managing boys and girls has stood me in good stead ever since. Your president was kind enough not to mention that my career as a university professor came to a sudden and permanent end. The faculty was divided into two sides: the younger men and the older, the radicals and the conservatives. The radicals were very strenuous, but the older men were more skillful, and at one of the meetings of the regents all the younger men were requested to depart. I was one of them, another is one of the most famous professors at Columbia; others have since made their way in name and fame. I am proud to say that as a result of the work of men, of whom I was one, that state university has become one of the great institutions of our country.

I also regard it as fortunate that when I was still young I was forced out into a cold world and made to earn my living in competition with others. I found that what I had learned in the management of boys and girls was applicable to the management of men and women in every walk of life, that the fundamentals of organization which underlie the development of a great state university apply equally to the management, administration and development of all institutions of learning. They apply not only to schools and universities, but also throughout all life. Those fundamental principles are universal.

There are certain fundamentals that underlie our whole life. Each living animal must breathe or the individual dies in a short time. Each individual must have rest or it dies at the end of a very short time. Each individual must have food, or it will die. Each individual must not exceed very narrow temperature limits or its life ceases. One can spend a life time and not know all there was to know about any individual animal or insect.

You know the practice of teaching far better than I do. I shall talk only about the fundamentals of those educational matters which are similar to all other activities, and I shall have succeeded if I make each one of you realize that this is a part of the universal problem, and that if you grasp these essentials you can apply them everywhere, not only here to school life, but to everything human.

I am to talk on efficiency, and I shall begin by telling you three things that efficiency is not. Nine-tenths of the people who have heard of efficiency confound it with one of the three things that efficiency is not.

First—*Strenuousness* is not efficiency. Strenuousness is the accomplishment of a slightly greater result by a very much greater effort. Efficiency is the accomplishing of a very much greater result by very much less effort.

A man can walk easily three miles an hour. If I were to assign a task for the man, about the maximum that he could perform, I would say four miles an hour, for perhaps six hours a day, and give him a choice of walking three miles an hour for eight hours a day, making a total of twenty-four miles a day. That is quite enough for any man to walk day in and day out. Let us consider the case of a postman or a messenger. Suppose that I place a piece rate of ten cents a mile. The normal daily wage of the walker would be $2.40, and this would encourage some man to walk five miles an hour during the six hours, accomplishing thirty miles in the course of the day, thus earning $3.00. Five miles an hour is too much for anybody to walk. If I should walk five miles an hour I would want to rest a week.

When the man wants to walk more than four miles an hour, I would give him a bicycle, the slow speed of which is ten miles an hour. This speed is more than twice as great as the most strenuous speed for the walker. The man on the bicycle can speed up to twelve miles an hour, then to fifteen miles an hour. There is one man who rode 390 miles in less than twenty hours, more than twenty miles an hour for the whole time he was on the road, the extreme of human endurance. He had prepared months in advance and rested weeks afterward. That is strenuous riding of the bicycle. But by the time my bicycle rider had come up to twelve or fourteen miles an hour, I would give him a motorcycle, and I would station policemen at the cross roads to prevent him from exceeding the speed limit. The difference between strenuousness and efficiency is thus indicated.

I have seen Egyptian girls digging the earth with their bare hands, the only implements being their fingernails, and it took a long hard day's work to accomplish a very small result. I have seen also on the western prairies, several modern engines dragging a gang plow of fifty-one shares, turning over a section of land in thirty-six hours. That plow could do more work in thirty-six hours than ten thousand girls could accomplish with their fingernails in the period of their lives, and yet the girls with their fingernails were working strenuousnessly, and the men with the plow were doing what might be called gentlemen's work.

Recently I went to see a series of bee-hive ovens, with openings in the top. They were red hot. The soft coal was dumped down into them, the ovens were sealed, and the soft coal was distilled. It leaves only the coke behind. When the poisonous gases are driven out it is necessary to empty the ovens by manual labor. The ovens are still very hot, and poisonous gases are yet being driven from the coke. After I saw this they took me to see ovens on one side of which was a machine that leveled the coal with two or three strokes. When the coal had been distilled and the poisonous gases driven out, another machine pushed the whole lot of coke out at one push, and then the other machine pushed in and loaded the coke. I asked the tender of this engine what the men who were working on the first ovens received for their work. He said that they received $1.50 a day. I asked him what these men got who tended the machines. He said this was gentleman's work, and that they received $2.50 a day. It was gentleman's work, work I would have found pleasure in doing. Here is another example of the difference between strenuousness and efficiency.

The rooster, when you chase him, flutters from his dung hill over a low neighboring fence and is easily caught in some corner. He is strenuousness. It his ancestors ever knew how to fly, they forgot it long ago. The eagle, who soars hour after hour, in the blue air and never flutters a pinion, is efficient.

The Chinese woman who bears ten children and only raises two of them to maturity is strenuous. The condor who lays a single egg once in several years and brings up each of its young, until it knows how to fly, is efficient.

Secondly—Efficiency is not *system*. There is very much confusion regarding efficiency and system. I illustrate this by a story of the Spanish-American War.

A young doctor was sent to Cuba. He went to a hospital and found men dying of wounds, of typhoid, of yellow fever. There was no quinine or other medicine, and no dressings, and in a frenzy of anxiety and eagerness he wrote a requisition and sent it to Washington, and paced up and down waiting for the return of the vessel with the supplies which would save the lives of these soldiers. When the vessel came he could not find his package. He could scarcely believe it. He hunted around and after a while went back to his office. He found there an official envelope awaiting him. He opened it. The letter stated: "What you ordered requires Form 23 and you have written the requisition on Form 25. Please make it out again on the correct form and send it to us."

For the second time he made out his requisition and sent it in, this time with no such anxiety, with less eagerness, with less hope. He awaited the return of the vessel. At the end of the two weeks he was not surprised as much as the first time when he found no package. He went back to his office and found an official envelope, and read: "If you had properly observed the regulations, you would have found that you should have summarized your figures in column 5, not in column 7. Please correct the requisition and send it in and we will fill it." And after that, the young doctor lived not to save the lives of the soldiers in the hospitals but solely to make out requisitions in accordance with the red tape of the government. He had been diverted from an efficient surgeon to a systematized one.

Efficiency has made it possible to meet new conditions in a new manner. System therefore should always be subordinated to efficiency. Throughout the world it is not. Disorderly souls have been guided by strenuousness, and system has taken a hand and accomplished a great deal, but to-day efficiency has to make its way against the opposition of the strenuous, and against the much more dangerous opposition of the systematic.

Thirdly—Efficiency does *not primarily rest upon intensified use of* such crude instruments as *land, labor and capital;* but it rests upon ideas and the use of imagination. Efficiency is therefore imaginative, not strenuous and not systematized. Efficiency is that gift which enables us by intensified thinking to accomplish a maximum with the least effort and the least waste.

Is your work as teachers strenuous? If so it is not efficient.

Is your work as teachers systematized? If it is it cannot be efficient.

Does it depend on your school buildings, on the toil and labor of many teachers, on your books? If it does it cannot be efficient.

Now let me tell you how I work when I am called into a plant to give them the benefits of efficiency. There are four essentials that apply in every plant.

1. The first are the aims or the ideals that must be definite and clear, but not strenuous, systematized or materialized.

2. There must be an organization, to attain or maintain all the ideals.

3. Equipment, with which the organization can attain and maintain these ideals.

All these mean but very little unless the plant has:

4. A strong executive, who is able to carry them out.

So the first thing we do is to ask the manager: "What are your aims? *What are you trying to do?* Shall I tell you or will you tell us what you are trying to do?"

Usually when we go into a new plant we find that the ideals are not clear. One man may be trying to do three or four different things at the same time. He may be trying to sell the largest quantity of mediocre goods, a perfectly legitimate aim. Another time he may change his mind and try to sell a small quantity of high quality goods. But we want his statement of what he is trying to accomplish, because the whole management of the business will depend upon these ideals.

Now we come to the *organization*. We generally find that the organization is haphazard. Like Topsy, it growed. We find that it is lop-sided, imperfect, that certain men are trying to do a great many things that do not belong to their department. Other men have been misplaced. We may find that the organization is dominated by relatives, with no reference to their ability or integrity, and that the organization can neither maintain nor attain the best ideals.

We next investigate the equipment. *What is the equipment that has been given to the organization* with which to accomplish results? The equipment consists of men, materials, money, machines and methods. If for instance I were expecting to start an automobile factory in Argentine, I would first get up an organization that would carry on the business, and then, what is far less important, would provide the equipment. To do this we must have money, men, and materials. These we must get, or we cannot do business.

Finally we come to the *main requirement—a strong, able executive*, an individual, or it may be a board or a committee. A strong executive maintains the aim, and inspires the organization.

In these matters plants are generally defective, and the conditions cannot be rapidly changed. Assuming, however, that we find a satisfactory condition, we next apply the twelve principles of efficiency.

Take, for instance, a bank burglar. I tell him that the first principle is that of a *high ideal*. I ask him if his ideal is compatible with the first principle of efficiency, a high ideal.

The second principle of efficiency is *common sense*, good judgment. I ask him if it is compatible with common sense to choose as a profession bank burglary.

The third principle of efficiency is *competent counsel*. I ask him where he got counsel to the effect that the business of breaking into banks is a good one.

The fourth principle is *discipline*, which means the welfare of society. I ask him whether breaking into banks is compatible with discipline. Discipline plays a part only when the burglar is caught red-handed and sent up.

The fifth principle is the *fair dealing*. I ask him whether breaking into a bank is a fair deal.

If at the very start of his business a man neglects the five first principles, how can we apply for him the other *practical principles*:

(6) *Standard records.*
(7) *Planning.*
(8) *Standard conditions.*
(9) *Standardized operations.*
(10) *Standard instructions.*
(11) *Standard schedules.*
(12) *Efficiency reward.*

Then we come down to organization, and we apply to each part the same test of the twelve principles. We apply it to the aim. We apply it to every man and to every movement, and after we finish with the organization we apply the same twelve principles to the equipment—to each machine, to all the materials, to all the methods. Then we go to the executive, and we apply to him the twelve principles.

By the time we have made this survey, the whole organization looks to us like a sieve. There are holes in it everywhere, some of them large, some of them small. The first thing to do is to stop the larger leaks, then we stop the lesser leaks, and we keep busy until all the leaks are stopped. Trying to increase the efficiency of a plant with a sieve-like organization is like carting water in a pail filled with holes. You cannot carry it very far. This is the manner in which the principles of efficiency are initially applied.

We consider the rest of the problem under three simple categories:

(1) Materials or supplies.
(2) Personal services.
(3) General charges.

In your school work the materials do not count for very much in money.

The personal service bill is the largest element, and the equipment charges might amount to a considerable item. Now for every item of material, for every item of personal service, and for every item of equipment charges, there are four different efficiencies. These four different efficiencies stand to one another in a dependent sequence and this results in efficiency being tremendously low in the end.

If a man should lose in Wall Street half his fortune, and to-morrow he should lose the half of what remains, and the next day half of that, he would very soon come to a very small number of dollars.

I went to England to sell a large Western mine in which some of my friends were interested. A man had cabled to me to come over at once. I had been offered a large commission ($100,000) if I should succeed in selling the mine. I met the young man at the railroad station. He asked me about the mine. He said, "I have a friend. He is a solicitor. I will introduce you to him and he will immediately place the mine. Do I get half the commission?" I said. "Yes." So now I was down to a $50,000 basis. He took me down to the solicitor. All the papers were looked over. A new statement was prepared, and he said, "Now, next week, Monday, I will meet you in London. I have a friend who puts these things through. By the way, do I get half the commission?" I said, "Yes, I will give you half of what is coming to me. I was down to $25,000. I met him in London and he took me to another solicitor, who punched a number of holes in the proposition, showed me that there were other better mines for sale in New Zealand, in Australia, in all parts of the world, and that my proposition was no better than the others. He then said: "We can put this proposition through; it looks favorably to me. By the way, do I get half the commission?" I said, "Yes." I was now down to a $12,500 basis. Two days afterward he took me down to see Mr. Wright, one of the great promoters in England. Mr. Wright said to me, "Mr. Emerson, you are wasting your time in London. You cannot float the best gold mine. There is no market for American securities. I advise you not to wait a day. Take this up some day in the future, not now." I came back with the mine unsold. Had he taken me up my commission would have shrunk still further. This illustrates dependent sequence, half and half and half.

For every article and material equipment there are four efficiencies. There is:

(1) Efficiency of *Price*. (2) Efficiency of *Supply*. (3) Efficiency of *Distribution*. (4) Efficiency of *Use*.

I can illustrate this best by railroad time tables. One of the great railroad purchasing agents said that by proper looking around he had been able to reduce the cost of the printing of the time tables 30 per cent. Therefore, the efficiency of that printing was only 70 per cent. A great many more time tables are printed than there is necessity for. Many of the time tables are not taken away from the printer. I remember looking over some of the books. There was an over-supply. The amount of the bill was very high. We will assume that the efficiency of the supply was 80 per cent. Now, these time tables were distributed everywhere. When you only wanted a leaflet, you had to take the whole time table. This illustrates inefficiency of distribution. That is found to be as low as 50 per cent. I frequently forget what I have looked up and get another time table. I always take two or three. The efficiency of use of the time table is extremely low. Multiply 70x80 (the first two efficiencies) and that brings you down to 56 per cent. Multiply that by 50 and you get down to 28 per cent., and thence to 14 per cent. Remember, too, that the cost of making time tables amounts to as much as the bill for the renewal of steel rails.

The same principles of efficiency apply to labor.

I went to a New England textile mill, and they took me through the machine shop and through the departments of textile work. When I returned the superintendent said, "What do you think of it?" I said, "I do not think that your machine shop is very efficient." Immediately they took offence. The master mechanic said, "This is a repair shop. Do you realize its purpose? It is our duty to repair all the machinery that breaks down. It does not make any difference what it costs. We cannot put in a lot of records, planning and efficiency rewards, and all that stuff. We must keep the mill going."

Before I had a chance to reply, the president said, "Let us go into the machine shop, that you may show me what you mean."

It is naturally not easy to point out a concrete case of inefficiency, but I went with him and stopped at the first machine. I watched it for a minute or so. There was a little steel plate to be shaped, and the tool was making a long stroke back and forth, cutting air three-quarters of the time and metal one-quarter of the time. The efficiency of the stroke was only 30 per cent. The tool was moving very slowly back and forth. There was no reason why it should not have been going like a sewing machine. The efficiency of speed was only 33 per cent. They had a diamond-pointed tool that was taking off only a sixty-fourth of an inch, almost as fine as a human hair. I could not see why they could not take off an eighth of an inch. The efficiency of feed was only 25 per cent. They were taking four cuts where two cuts would have been sufficient, a roughing cut and a smoothing cut. The efficiency of the number of cuts was 50 per cent. You multiply 33x30 and you get 10 per cent.; multiply that by 25 and you get 2½ per cent.; then multiply that by 50 and you get 1¼ per cent. In this repair shop a machine was taking eighty times as long as it had any business to take. I then said, "The way you are running this shop makes anything possible. In your shop the machines are cutting air three-quarters of the time, the tool is taking off but one sixty-fourth of an inch and taking four cuts where two would be sufficient." This illustrates the dependent sequence as related to machine labor.

This is a general outline of the modern teaching of efficiency. We are just on the threshold of the work. When we go into a plant, we properly and rightly tell the proprietor that we know the state of the art up to the present, that we can give him the best help that modern knowledge affords in putting his plant on an efficient basis. But when we come back to our own office and we face the other way and look at the problem as it stretches out before us, we see that we are just on the threshold of knowledge, that the fog is gradually lifting.

The efficiency of the material, the efficiency of the wage earner, the efficiency of the equipment, the efficiency of the ideals of organization, and of the executive—may not be as important in the future as certain dawning possibilities. We are just beginning to study the difference between energizing work and enervating work, and particularly the difference between men and women taking up work they are not fitted for, and taking up work for which they are fitted.

Let us begin with the latter problem. Suppose that I wanted to develop a race horse. If I should supply the best kind of kite track, if I should bank the curves and elevate them mathematically, if I should construct the best kind of a sulky, and if some skillful blacksmith would make the proper kind of shoes, and a harnessmaker the best harness, and if I should have the best kind of a stop-watch, that would record the one-hundredth part of a second, *if I were working on some ordinary plug of a horse*, I should not accomplish as much as if I had no track but a country road, no wagon but a spring wagon, no harness but an ordinary harness, but had *a thoroughbred to begin with*. The difference between what a man can do when he is adapted to his work and what he can do when he is not adapted to his work is almost infinite.

There is an old German saying that every barber is a conservative and every tailor a radical. The barber, shaved each customer's face, dressed the customer's hair, fixed his wig, looked after his dress, and bled him, acting as surgeon as well as barber. He was busy on his feet all day, talked about the latest news, and discussed topics of the day. When a man of that kind went home he was thoroughly satisfied to become a peaceful citizen. But the tailor, who sat all day long with his legs crossed sewing, when he finished his work, had to go out and raise a disturbance of some sort to let out the accumulation of the fatigue poisons he accumulated in his work. The tailor's work is enervating.

A man from Cincinnati went into a mill in New England, and said to the owner: "There is the department from where all the troubles begin! Those men are disorderly. They start up the strikes. They are bad family men." The owner of the plant said, "That is perfectly true, but how do you know." The reply was: "The condition of the work is such that it is impossible that they will be otherwise. It is so noisy that these men cannot even hear each other. Necessarily, they have accumulated such an amount of fatigue poison that it is impossible for them to settle down and lead peaceful lives." Their work instead of being energizing was enervating.

To close, I shall tell you an anecdote in which efficiency work is shown. I went into a large mill in Cincinnati in which the girls had been very difficult to discipline. They left; they did not stay. They were troublesome; they were disorderly and the superintendent, who was wise, one morning put a large Maltese cat in the room and when the girls came around they did not know how the cat got there and adopted it as a pet. The superintendent said that the cat had better be removed. The girls wanted to keep the cat. When I came in I saw the cat on a shelf and the cat jumped off and went to one of the girls. The girl stopped her work and gave the cat to the next girl and passed it all around. This gave the girls a rest of two or three minutes. Then the cat went back to her place. This time had been sufficient to stop the accumulation of the fatigue poisons. This difference of two or three minutes made all the difference in the world.

This subject is tremendous. You must feel it for yourselves.

SUMMARY OF ANSWERS TO QUESTIONS.

The success of a school depends on the executive, and executive ability in the highest authority is more important than lower down the line. Executive ability is always and everywhere valuable.

The executive must have definite aims and must have a suitable organization, he must have equipment. The child, the parent, the teacher, the principal, the superintendent is each an executive as to respective parts of the work, and the clashes between different ideals caused tremendous loss.

Shall the type of management be strenuous, shall it be systematic, shall it be efficient? Consider the possibilities of waste of the child who is efficiently trying to pursue the ideal of a good time and the teacher who is with systematized strenuousness pursuing the ideal of a curriculum.

Schools are tremendously inefficient, not because everybody does not work, but because there is no accepted ideal for any executive from child up to superintendent to play and work up to.

BIBLIOGRAPHY.

"Profit Making Management," Charles U. Carpenter; "Work, Wages ,and Profit," Gantt; "Motion Study," Gilbreth; "Cost Keeping," Gillette & Dana; "Efficiency," Emerson, Harrington; "Principles of Scientific Management—Shop Management," Frederick Winslow **Taylor.** The subject is also discussed by Benjamin C. Greenberg in the January and February numbers of *The American Teacher*.

THE STUDENTS' AID COMMITTEE.

The Committee in conjunction with the Department of Sociology of the Brooklyn Institute and the Brooklyn Teachers' Association has arranged for a general conference on Vocational Guidance on March 19th at 8 P. M., at the Academy of Music, Brooklyn, near Flatbush Avenue Subway Station.

The committee has in the hands of the printer the following

"Choosing a Career for Boys," fourth edition.
"Choosing a Career for Girls," second edition.
"Occupations Connected with the Domestic Arts."
"Industrial Chemistry for Girls."
"The Effect of Education on Earning Capacity."

Copies of these will be furnished free to members of the association applying before printing. Those in excess are for sale. The receipts from outside sales have paid for the printing of these bulletins.

Small quantities of the following can be secured:
"Accountancy and the Business Profession," 10 cents.
"The Civil Service," 5 cents.
"Opportunities for Boys in Machine Shops," 2 cents.
"Applying for Work," 2 cents.
"Country Vacation Work," 2 cents.
"Vacation Excursions for Young People," 2 cents.
"List of Special Training Schools," 1 cent.
"The Vocational Adjustment of School Children," 10 cents.

The following can no longer be supplied:
"Does an Education Pay?"
"Report on School Incentives."
"Reports of the Work of the Committee."
"Directing Young People in the Choice of a Vocation."

The United States Department of Labor reprints an interesting bulletin on Vocational Guidance from the twenty-fifth annual report of the department. Copies can be secured free by early applicants.

E. W. WEAVER, *Chairman.*

25 Jefferson Avenue, Brooklyn. 'Phone, 1377-M-5 Prospect.

REPORT OF CONSULTATION COMMITTEE OF SIXTY. HIGH SCHOOL TEACHERS' ASSOCIATION.

To the Committee on School Inquiry:

In accordance with your request, we submit herewith a statement of our recommendations concerning the "General Course" of study for the high schools of New York City:

1. We commend to your consideration the detail suggestions contained in the final report of the "Committee on the Revision of the High School Course of Study" (Dr. W. H. Eddy, High School of Commerce, Chairman), as contained in the Year Book for 1910-1911, just issued. This report is the result of three years of careful study by a large committee of our Association.

2. REQUIREMENTS FOR GRADUATION. We recommend that the requirements for graduation be substantially those contained in the report of the Committee of Nine of the National Education Association, including the recommendation contained in the supplementary part of said report.

3. FLEXIBILITY. We recommend that far great flexibility be introduced into the general course. To this end we recommend that no subjects now given be eliminated and that the following subjects be introduced as electives: Introductory Social Science, Economics, Manual Training, Commercial Subjects, Household Economics, Theory of Music, Elements of Engineering, Advanced Drawing, and, in general, under proper restriction, such other subjects as may be demanded by a reasonable number of students, and for which there are qualified teachers in the school.

We further recommend that the subjects introduced shall be made equivalent in intensity and in amount of work required, to that required in the other subjects in the general course.

4. INTENSITY. We concur in general with the present tendency in educational theory favoring greater concentration upon fewer high school subjects. At present many of our students are required to carry six or more subjects at once. This leads to distraction, superficiality, and the violation of many principles of "efficiency." Among the objections to fragmentary courses occurring two or three periods per week, we would mention:

(1) Personal contact of teacher and pupil is very superficial.
(2) Excessive strain is imposed on teacher by reason of the large number of different students with whom the teacher must become acquainted, and this strain is not sufficiently recognized in the assignment of work to teachers.
(3) Programs are very complicated and often impossible, and the equalization of classes is retarded or prevented.
(4) Clerical work is increased.
(5) Discipline is weakened.

To obviate the above difficulties, it is sometimes proposed to adopt a FOUR SUBJECT PLAN whereby each student would take only four subjects each term and each subject would occur each day in single prepared or double unprepared periods, or a combination of the two. This plan would overcome all of the foregoing difficulties. It is substantially the plan in practice in many of the best high schools of the United States. It makes possible the offering of many electives without entailing as much difficulty as is found under our present heterogeneous time allotment. But serious difficulties would arise under this four subject plan, for one subject must be English, and a second subject for most students would be a foreign language, thus restricting a student to the choice of two subjects from Mathematics, History, Science, Mechanic Arts, Commercial Branches, and Household Economics. All but two of these subjects would have to be omitted from each student's program, or one subject taken one year and one subject another, thus breaking continuity. Among these subjects, Mathematics and Science would be given most of the field, History would suffer, and the election of Mechanic Arts, Commercial Branches, and Household Economics would be unduly discouraged.

There is, however, a practical means of escape, namely, the adoption of a FIVE-SUBJECT PLAN, whereby each student would take five subjects and each subject would be allotted four hours of prepared work or a correspondingly larger number of hours where part or all of the work is unprepared. Under this plan the student who takes a vocational subject would also take four academic subjects. A larger number of subjects would then occur in uninterrupted sequences. Moreover, a student deciding to specialize in vocational work, could then take two-fifths of his work vocational and still keep three academic subjects. The five subject plan with 32 periods in the week permits more flexibility in the program than can be secured in the four subject plan with 30 periods in the week. The double laboratory period is less obstructive under the five subject plan than under the four subject plan.

WE THEREFORE RECOMMEND THE FIVE SUBJECT PLAN.

5. FIRST YEAR SUBJECTS. We recommend that students of the first year be *required* to take:

		No. of Periods.
(1)	English	4 prepared
(2)	Introductory Social Science. This course should include: Local Government, Local Industries, Study of Vocations, and Current Topics. This course should make specifically for good citizenship, assist the student when he comes to select a vocation, and emphasize the value of a thorough schooling.	4 prepared

and be allowed to choose three of the following:

(3)	Introductory Natural Science, based largely on Biology	4 prepared
(4)	Algebra	4 prepared
(5)	Latin or a Modern Language	4 prepared
(6)	Household Economics (for girls), including Freehand Drawing as applied to the decoration of the home—equivalent to	4 prepared
(7)	Mechanic Arts (for boys), including Shopwork, supplemented by recitation and Mechanical and Freehand Drawing—	8 unprepared (or equivalent in prepared and unprepared)
(8)	Commercial Subjects (for boys and girls), including Freehand Drawing as related to commercial interests—	8 unprepared or equivalent.

The committee recommends that the student be advised to elect Introductory Natural Science.

In addition to the above all students should be required to take two periods of Physical Training, one period of Music, and one period of Oral English.

Students not taking either (6) Household Economics or (8) Commercial Subjects, should probably be required to take two periods of general Free-Hand Drawing.

If this plan is adopted and the number of hours in first-year English, Algebra, and Foreign Language is reduced from 5 to 4, of course it would be necessary that the amount of work required of students in each of these subjects in the first year, should also be materially reduced.

6. SECOND, THIRD AND FOURTH YEAR SUBJECTS. English should be required throughout the course, four periods per week. In the last year students taking Commercial Electives might well be offered an alternative course in Commercial English. Four years of work should be offered in each of the following:

(1) Latin and German.

(2) Mathematics. Surveying or the Elements of Engineering should be offered with ample opportunity for field practice and office computations.

(3) Natural Science, including electives in Physics two years, Chemistry, Physiography, Agricultural Science and Household Chemistry for Girls.

(4) Social Science, including History of last 150 years, History up to last 150 years, American History and Civics, Economics.

(5) Mechanic Arts (including Shopwork, supplemented by recitations and lectures) and Mechanical and Freehand Drawing. In this department opportunity should be offered in the last two years for special students to take double the usual amount of Mechanic Arts.

(6) Household Economics, including recitations on Household Accounts, Purchasing and Dietetics; and Freehand Drawing and Art Appreciation as applied to the decoration of the home.

(7) Stenography, Typewriting, Bookkeeping, Office Practice, Salesmanship, Advertising, Accountancy, etc.

In addition, electives should be offered in Advanced Drawing and in the Theory of Music.

CLARENCE D. KINGSLEY, *Chairman.*

CONFERENCE COMMITTEE ON COURSE OF STUDY.

The preliminary report was read to the Board of Representatives February 27, revised by Sub-Committee appointed to draw up recommendations, and finally amended and adopted by the Committee March 5, 1912.

Bay Ridge—Mabel R. Benway.

Boys—E. W. Weaver, Charles E. Oberholser.

Bryant—Carolyn P. Swett, Mary Elizabeth Reid.

Bushwick—Mary P. Green, Josephine A. Dempsey, Geo. W. Norton, Etta E. Southwell and W. T. Morrey.

Commercial—Edwin A. Bolger, Benj. C. Gruenberg.

Commerce—Edwin A. Fitzpatrick, Alexander L. Pugh, Benj. A. Heydrick, Walter G. Eddy, Horace G. Healey.

Curtis—James Shipley, Mabel G. Burdick.

De Witt Clinton—Aaron I. Dotey, Ellen E. Garrigues, Donald C. MacLaren, Fayette E. Moyer.

Eastern District—Frederick H. Paine, Minnie K. Pinch.

Erasmus Hall—Charles R. Fay, Kate E. Turner, Preston C. Farrer, John B. Stocker.

Far Rockaway—Eldon M. Van Dusen.

Flushing—Paul R. Jenks, Frank H. Miller.

Girls—Loring B. Mullen, H. Elizabeth Seelman, M. Ellen Barker.

Jamaica—Benjamin N. Thorp, Henry R. Linville.

Manual Training—Clarence D. Kingsley, Chairman; Charles Perrine, Arthur L. Baker, Eleanor R. Baker, Marion Hackedorn.

Morris—Paul B. Mann, Hugh C. Laughlin, Otis C. Skeele, Josephine A. Davis, Abby B. Bates, Helen M. Storey, Michael D. Sohon.

Newtown—George H. Kingsbury, Alex E. W. Zerban.

Richmond Hill—Charles R. Gaston, Gertrude M. Leete.

Stuyvesant—T. Harry Knox, Clayton G. Durfee, Charles B. Howe.

Wadleigh—William W. Clendenin, Helen E. Bacon, Florence Middleton.

Washington Irving—Idelette Carpenter, Mary C. Craig.

OFFICIAL BULLETIN

of the High School Teachers' Association of New York City

No. 34 APRIL-MAY 1912

REPRESENTATIVES SHALL BE ELECTED by ballot during the week preceding the regular May meeting.—Constitution, Art. V, Sec. 2.

LAST REGULAR MEETING for 1911-1912 will be held Saturday, May 25, at the High School of Commerce, beginning at 10 A. M.

DEPARTMENT MEETINGS will begin at 10 A. M., in usual rooms, for the report on the work and attendance for the year, FOR THE ELECTION OF OFFICERS for 1912-1913, and to prepare plans and the budget for next year.

GENERAL MEETING will begin at 10:30 A. M. for the ELECTION OF OFFICERS for 1912-1913, and for the reports of Chairmen of Committees and Departments.

ADDRESS BY PROFESSOR PAUL H. HANUS ON THE RESULTS OF THE INVESTIGATION OF THE NEW YORK CITY HIGH SCHOOLS BY THE COMMITTEE ON SCHOOL INQUIRY.

Numerous definite suggestions will be made, many of which, no doubt, can be tested next year by this Association.

WILLIAM T. MORREY,
President.

AGNES CARR,
Secretary.

MINUTES OF GENERAL MEETING, MARCH 16.

The third meeting of the High School Teachers' Association in the Efficiency Series was held in the High School of Commerce on March 16. Section meetings preceded the general meeting called for 11 A. M. Between six and seven hundred members were present—the largest meeting of the year, probably the largest meeting ever held.

The minutes of the December meeting were read and adopted as read.

Mr. Paine, of the Pension Committee, presented a new proposition in the pension bill, viz: All salaries up to $3,000 be taxed 1%; of the salaries above that sum, 1% be deducted on amounts up to $3,000, and on the sum above that amount, 2% be paid.

An exhibit of Commercial Maps and Commercial Geography was announced as being in progress in rooms of the building devoted to that purpose.

Mr. Weaver, of the Students' Aid Committee, stated that the work of his committee had attained national importance, and called attention to the General Conference to take place in Brooklyn on March 19, noting that this Association has always taken the lead in this matter.

The President then introduced as the first speaker of this meeting, devoted to "What Constitutes the Teacher of Superior Merit," Mr. George J. Smith of the Board of Examiners.

Mr. Smith was followed by Associated City Superintendent Edward L. Stevens, and Principals John Holley Clark of Flushing High School, John H. Denbigh of Morris High School, William Fairley of Commercial High School,

William L. Felter of Girls' High School, Charles D. Larkins of Manual Training High School, William McAndrew of Washington Irving High School and John L. Tildsley of DeWitt Clinton High School.

[These addresses were stenographically reported by A. Rosenblum, revised by the speakers, and are all published elsewhere in this Bulletin.]

The meeting adjourned at two o'clock.

WILLIAM T. MORREY,
President.

AGNES CARR,
Secretary.

A COMMUNICATION.

March 24, 1912.

To the Honorable Committee on High Schools, Board of Education, New York City.

Gentlemen:—May we, in the name of the High School Teachers' Association of New York City, urge you to request the By-Laws Committee of the Board of Education to formulate rules for the guidance of the Board of Examiners and the Administrative Officers of the Board;

(1) To rate as of Superior Merit, all teachers marked as B+ or higher; **superior** being a comparative term and not superlative, not equivalent to supreme.

(2) To rate as of Superior Merit, those who prior to January 1, 1912, were receiving the **Maximum salaries** of their grades. We believe that such was the not unreasonable expectation not only of such teachers but also of those officers of the Board who estimated the cost of new law. This eliminates the **Ex Post Facto** feature.

(3) To rate as approved for **twelve** years, such teachers as have been approved for **nine years** and have in addition received **credit for three additional** years in the adjustment of the Junior Teacher Question.

The Executive Committee of the High School Teachers' Association.

WILLIAM T. MORREY, President.

[Reported to Board of Representatives March 28, 1912, and adopted by them.]

MARCH 28, MEETING OF REPRESENTATIVES.

The March meeting of the Representatives of the High School Teachers' Association was held at the Washington Irving High School, March 28, with President W. T. Morrey in the chair.

The minutes of the previous meeting were read and accepted. The Treasurer reported $365.48 in the treasury, with several large schools not yet heard from.

[The communication of March 24, 1912, from the Executive Committee of the Association to the Committee on High Schools of the Board of Education was read and adopted.]

Mr. Penhallow, of DeWitt Clinton, Chairman of the Committee on Forms and Blanks, described the work undertaken by his committee. He said it was necessary to find out first the kind and amount of information required from Fifty-ninth Street, and then to have blanks prepared to gain that information and nothing else. In that way reports from various schools will be uniform, and can be easily tabulated.

Mr. Dotey, of DeWitt Clinton, gave an interesting and detailed account of the meeting of the High School Committee of the Board of Education held March 27. This gave rise to much discussion, and suggestions were made that while the subject is still fresh in mind, but after salaries have been adjusted, the matter of an advance grade be presented; and also that protest be made against method of rating teachers on five-minute inspection and on basis kept secret from teacher.

Mr. Oberhoalzer was appointed Chairman of committee to consider the status of librarians with power to form his own committee.

Meeting adjourned.

AGNES CARR,
Secretary.

APRIL 30, MEETING OF REPRESENTATIVES.

The April meeting of the Representatives of the High School Teachers' Association was held on the thirtieth at 34 East Twelfth Street. The Secretary's report was read and accepted. The Treasurer reported in the treasury $132.62, with one large school still to be heard from. The net cost of printing the Year Book of 1910-1911 had been $244.27.

Mr. Fay, Chairman of the Committee on Teachers' Absences, gave a report of the work done by his committee, which was unanimously approved and adopted for recommendation to the Board of Education.

[This report is printed elsewhere in this Bulletin.]

This report covered two fields of work:

(a) Investigation of practice in other cities in reference to loss of salary for absence due to illness or other causes.

(b) Study of methods prevailing in this city.

For the first of these, investigation was mde of 224 cities of 25,000 inhabitants or over, and the results gained by a carefully planned questionnaire were tabulated.

A study of methods prevailing in this city revealed that in most cases the attitude of the city towards the teacher is most generous; and the pension fund is so inextricably bound up with legislation in regard to pay during absence that the change does not seem necessary or expedient.

The committee offered, however, six constructive recommendations as follows:

1. Allowed absence for death in family be made more specific.
2. Full pay for attendance at court be allowed for two days in all cases.
3. Allowed absence without pay for purpose of travel.
4. Pay granted for absence due to quarantine be for entire time, not ten days only.
5. Discretionary power be granted to Board of Superintendents to allow absence with pay in "emergency cases"—cases equally compelling with illness.
6. Sabbatical year be allowed for study on half pay.

A vote of thanks was given to the committee for this report.

Mr. Penhallow, Chairman of Committee on Standardization of Forms, gave a brief account of the work of his committee. He suggested that if the teachers would send to him copies of their individual programs, with size of classes, his committee would compile a report on comparative size of classes, and periods of work.

Mr. Penhallow was authorized to obtain such material as he desired for use in the work of his own committee, and also in that of the Efficiency Committee.

Dr. Fitzpatrick, Chairman of the Committee on Efficiency, read a part of the report of his committee. The first recommendation in regard to teachers' ratings by principals was tabled. There seemed so much material for discussion, that, as the hour was late, it was noved to adjourn until May 7, when this report could be taken up at length.

(Signed) AGNES CARR,
Secretary.

MAY 7, MEETING OF REPRESENTATIVES.

On May 7, an adjourned meeting of the Board of Representatives of the High School Teachers' Association was held at the Washington Irving School to consider the report of Dr. Fitzpatrick, Chairman of the Committee on Efficiency.

Minutes of the previous meeting were read.

In the absence of President Morrey, Mr. Dotey, of DeWitt Clinton, was asked to take the chair.

In presenting his report for a second time before the Board, Dr. Fitzpatrick referred to its publication in "The Globe" of May 7, saying he had thought it would simplify matters to have a printed copy of the propositions in the hands of those present. He suggested that the propositions be voted on singly.

Objection was made to this method of procedure by Mr. Jenks.

Reference was made by Mr. Dotey, who asked permission to leave the chair for this purpose, to the resolution passed two years ago that the High School Teachers' Association is opposed to all discussion of questions relating to salary.

Further objection was made that too small a number was present to take action on any subject of so great importance to the Association as a whole.

Objection was made to the publication of a report which had not yet been acted upon by the Board of Representatives, and under a caption very misleading to the casual reader.

A resolution was then passed that the report of the Committee on Efficiency be tabled, and that the public press be informed of that fact.

It was resolved further that it is unwise to enter into any discussion of "superior merit" at the present time.

Mr. Jenks suggested a constructive plan of inspection of work; that a teacher be relieved of work in his special field for a period of six months at a time, and spend the time in inspecting work done throughout the city, and reporting upon it.

The meeting adjourned at 5:35 P. M.

(Signed) AGNES CARR,
Secretary.

WHAT CONSTITUTES THE TEACHER OF SUPERIOR MERIT?

Addresses by Examiner George J. Smith, Superintendent L. Stevens and Principals Clark, Denbigh, Fairley, Felter, Larkins, McAndrew, and Tildsley

[Stenographically Reported by A. Rosenblum]

ADDRESS BY EXAMINER GEORGE J. SMITH

Mr. President, Ladies and Gentlemen:—Mr. Morrey will bear witness that I consented with some reluctance to speak at this time upon the subject, "What Constitutes a Teacher of Superior Merit," in the meaning of the new law. Not that I was unappreciative of the honor of the invitation to address you, but because of the difficulty of the subject. We are still crossing the stream, and, in a sense, it is really impossible as yet to discuss this question with definiteness. At any rate we cannot appeal to the results of the investigation now in progress; and the phrase "superior merit" is in a state of vagueness and ambiguity which, I am afraid, I cannot hope to clear up. It is somewhat like the phrase "reasonable restraint of trade" which the Supreme Court has made popular or unpopular. Nobody knows what a reasonable restraint of trade is; and about all that the commercial world can do is to await the successive decisions of the United States courts upon that question.

We are all aware of the provisions of the law which it is now attempted to put into effect. I will read the law, however, so that we may have a foundation to start from in this discussion. After setting forth the salary schedules, the law states "None shall advance beyond the salary of the sixth year, unless and until his service is approved as fit and meritorious by a majority vote of the Board of Superintendents." And in the next paragraph, "None shall advance beyond the salary of the ninth year, unless after investigation and inspection he is declared, on the report of a committee, consisting of an associate superintendent, a district superintendent and a principal, by a majority vote of all the members of the Board of Examiners, the district superintendent and the principal having a right to vote, to be a teacher of superior merit."

Now, in the first place, "fit and meritorious" are the adjectives used for the first approval, the sixth year approval. And, in the second place, the words for the ninth year, and similarly for the twelfth year, are "superior merit." Now the question is, of course, simply what the intention of the framers of that law was, what distinction was intended between "fit and meritorious" and "superior." It is evident that if the framers of that law had wished to make the terms the same, they would have done so.

There is no new principle involved in this law. The passing of a certain inspection in order to advance in the salary schedules has been a fact, has been in force for several years. Some teachers, not a very large proportion, just what proportion I do not know,—some teachers have found that the provision that they must be declared fit and meritorious has not been a mere empty form. I presume, however, that the number of teachers, the proportion of teachers, who have been held up in the salary advances by that provision of the old law has been rather small. However, the establishing of certain tests as a condition prerequisite to advancing in the salary schedule is not a new thing in this city.

Now the question is, what is the meaning of this phrase "superior merit?" I shall address myself first to a general, or perhaps theoretical, consideration of that point. The Board of Examiners, when this matter came up last fall, addressed inquiries to a large number of prominent educators, from associate superintendents down to college presidents. (Laughter.) We got a considerable number of answers, some of them rather illuminating. It is evident that this law established three new maximums for high school teachers,—$2,050, $2,500 and $2,650; that is to say, all teachers found to be fit and meritorious would advance to the $2,050 salary in due course. At that point there is another hurdle to jump, the declaration of superior merit. If that is granted for the ninth year, the teacher advances to the second maximum of $2,500. And then in case of approval again as a teacher of superior merit, to the final maximum of $2,650.

Now one of the persons to whom we addressed these inquiries, not a high school principal, but a teacher in one of the high schools, said that such a differentiation was just and desirable, "It is about time that something besides mere existence should count for salary increases." Superintendent Stevens said he took the words to mean better than the average. Another said, in his judgment the teacher who, after nine years' experience, had not been rated **B** plus or better was not a superior teacher, and that no teacher should be declared superior on the twelfth-year approval unless rated **A.** Another high school principal had apparently the same idea, that a rating of **B** plus should be required for any declaration of superior merit. One of the principals said the words "superior merit" meant more than excellent, they meant possessing exceptional merit. He added, however, that it would make great trouble in the high schools to attempt to put into effect this meaning. Another said, "Certainly more than fit and meritorious,—the highest type." Another, "Better than the general run of teachers,—getting more substantial results." Another spoke of the duty of drawing a line between merely satisfactory and superior work. "Results superior to those of the ordinary teacher," said another. "The tendency of teachers to become perfunctory in their work is without question. Few workers in any line are of surpassing excellence." I am quoting again from a statement of a high school principal in this city. Nicholas Murray Butler, of Columbia University, said he was glad an attempt was going to be made to discriminate between the rank and file and the teachers of superior merit; he thought that the term meant more than either satisfactory or excellent. The superintendent of schools in a nearby city said that in his judgment it meant the discrimination of the few from the many. He suggested from his experience in one city he would consider about one teacher in ten of superior merit. Another said about one teacher in twenty.

Now, I am quoting these statements for a purpose which I will explain in a moment. I am trying to show you the general feeling of high school principals and other prominent educators as to the natural meaning of these words. One high school principal said he would divide teachers into three classes: first, those unquestionably superior; second, those unquestionably inferior, and third, to quote his words, "the great mass of teachers who are conscientious, faithful and fairly successful."

Now, it is evident from these statements that a great many educators who answered the question had the opinion that the intent of the law was to grant the maximum increases of salaries to, I would say, a comparatively small proportion of the teachers. I think that is a fair conclusion from the quotations I have given. It perhaps is not necessary to go into the analysis, which in some cases was made with great care, of the qualities that constitute, or should constitute, superiority. However, I can briefly sum up what some seventeen persons offered in answer to that question: "How would you analyze the meaning of superior merit, that, what qualities should be found in teachers who are declared to be of superior merit?"

A considerable majority of that number mentioned mastery of subject-matter and interest in subject-matter as among the first points.

Second, mastery of methods, skill and science in the conduct of the recitation; this was mentioned by practically all as a test which must be used. Under that head, ten out of seventeen emphasized the importance of preparation of lessons and making of plans of work, the organizing the subject-matter, the ability to place the emphasis in the subject-matter where it belongs,—upon the important points; in a word, organization of subject-matter and planning of daily work. Considerably more than a majority believed that that was an important element. I have heard it said that comparatively few high school teachers prepare the daily lessons in a minute or careful way before entering the classroom. Under mastery of methods of teaching, the following was mentioned by nine out of seventeen, securing the self-activity of the pupils and leading pupils to exercise judgment and reasoning power. Maintenance of interest, holding attention of all the pupils,—was mentioned as another mark of the superior teachetr. Attention to the individual was emphasized by a considerable number; the backward pupil, the average pupil, and the proficient pupil. Skill in exposition and illustration (these are subheads under the mastery of methods of teaching), were urged by several as important points; thoroughness and skill in drill and review, by an equal number. Skill in questioning was mentioned by only three, nevertheless it seems a somewhat important point.

Now, I have mentioned two general heads, mastery of subject-matterand mastery of methods. The third head is results. About half of those who answered the question thought that the results of a teacher's work as measured by any possible standard, the more concrete and definite the better, should be an important element. And that included not only the percentage of pupils promoted by the individual teacher, and the percentage of his promoted pupils who proved able to sustain themselves in the advanced work, but also the holding of pupils in school, the prevention of the high mortality rate in the high schools. Somebody must be responsible for that in a degree. There are teachers on whose account pupils desire to remain in school, and there are other teachers on whose account some pupils are anxious to leave school.

Nearly all mentioned in one form or another, the fourth point,—that of excellent character and personality in the teacher. That, of course, is indefinite. It includes such things as the power to inspire pupils with respect to character, taste, culture, love of study; it includes self-control and politeness on the part of the teacher, and his influence upon the pupils. It includes breadth of mind, a sane attitude, knowledge of youth, sympathy with youth, qualities of leadership, inventiveness, and resourcefulness. And of course a great many other things might be included under this general head.

A certain number of those who answered the questions included this fifth point,—of proving what might be called the accumulation of efficiency, the increased efficiency of the teacher, which might be evidenced by the pursuit of studies in some form, or by writings, observation, travel, study of schoolroom problems, contributions to pedagogical progress generally. Nearly all mention service to the school at large as one of the essential points, outside of mere classroom routine work. Promptness and accuracy in making reports, etc., was mentioned by only two. Discipline in the classroom and out was mentioned by six. Punctuality and attendance were mentioned by a small proportion. And finally physical health and endurance was urged by four as an essential mark of a superior teacher; that is as much as to say that if a teacher is unfortunate in respect to health he is to be sympathized with, but not declared superior.

Now, it is evident from this analysis which I have tried to sum up, that the meaning of "superior" is very complex, very inclusive and, on the whole, vague. There are so many elements to take into account that it at once becomes a serious and difficult question how to take these elements into account, how to weigh them, what plan to follow, what data to secure, and then how to act upon the data.

The superintendent of schools in Chicago said that she thought the whole thing was a joke; it could not be done. That was what I gathered from her very brief letter. I think some similar attempt has been made in Chicago, with more or less unsatisfactory results.

The great difficulty is to secure one standard, not in any one school, but in all the schools. One principal said, and perhaps truly, that the teachers in his school would all, or nearly al of them, rank as superior if they were working in other schools he knew of. Now, how was he to know that, how was anybody to know that? A principal stated recently, orally, that he believed that 80% of his teachers, or at least 80%, were of superior merit. Now that is considerably different, you see, from the point of view we started out with, the preliminary point of view, as shown in the answers given, you remember by the persons questioned as to the natural and proper meaning of the words "superior merit." Instead of a few being selected as superior, some principals now appear to think that 80% or 90% should be regarded as superior. Another principal suggested that there should be comparative tests of some sort as among the various high schools; that there should at least be inspections and visits for this special purpose. A good many high school principals thought that the members of the Board of Examiners ought to go about and inspect the teaching in the classrooms, and pass upon the work. Others thought that examinations should be held to settle the matter.

Supt. Brooks of Boston wrote that in Boston no teacher can advance beyond the sixth year salary who has not passed the promotional examination. That consists first of an examination in some academic subject; second, some professional subject; and third, success in teaching. A college professor thought the way to get at it was to have a ranking list of teachers prepared by each high school principal. Perhaps he would say a list of the teachers in each subject arranged according to rank in the opinion of the principal as to their degrees of merit. That suggestion was discussed, but it was not adopted; at any rate no written list of that sort was asked for.

One high school principal said that he thought the thing ought to be done mathematically. Let us have a thousand points, and let us divide the thousand into ten parts of a hundred each, and each teacher shall be rated on a scale of one hundred to each of these ten parts, and those teachers who get 900 points or over shall be regarded as superior.

Now certain practical considerations decided how this thing should actually be done. There was need of haste. The time was very short. The new schedules went into effect January 1, and we did not desire to be acused of holding up the increases of teachers any further than was absolutely necessary. Hence these night sessions, and Sunday sessions, and the sessions still going on.

Unfortunately one important member of the committee fell seriously ill. We have not had the benefit, expressed orally, of the judgment of Supt Bardwell since near the beginning of the work. Our plan was simply to get all the information possible in the time at our command and with the means at our command, and then to use our best judgment, in view of all the facts brought forth, in our voting. It is a little like the working of a breath-testing machine; the indicator rises jut so far; in some cases it rises high and in others it does not. All the factors are taken into account. We listen to the statements of the principals, of the first assistant, if any, and we look at the written report of the principal. We consider the rating of the teacher during his whole career in the high schools. We take into account the memoranda on the cards made by Supt. Bardwell. We take into account the attendance record, the punctuality record, the ratings, of course, given by the principal and by the superintendent, and the results of the teaching so far as they can be ascertained not only from the reports made by the principal but from the results of Regents' examinations. Not much weight, of course, was given to the last, but still it was one element taken into account.

Now the net result was that here was a body of six; sitting at headquarters, who all but one had in most cases no personal knowledge of the teacher's work; and that body was obliged under the law to consider all the facts that it could get at either in the form of written answers or by direct questioning, oral questioning. You have attended auctions some of you, and you may have observed how things find their level in auctions. Mr. A's picture, for example, which he regards as a masterpiece, the auctioneer succeeds in selling after much effort for exactly eight dollars; while Mr. B's picture of precisely the same dimensions brings two hundred and fifty dollars. Now that is very annoying and embarrassing for A if he happens to be present, but there is something impersonal about it, fateful about it. It is a fascinating thing to see how in an auction articles find their natural level most times. Of course there are auction flukes, and we hope to profit by them when fortune favors. But, generally speaking, all the elements that enter into the worth of the article put up are considered by those present, and the price obtained is the result of a sort of consensus. In a somewhat analogous way, the committee passing on "superior merit" has endeavored to reach a fair consensus, a just decision, in view of all the elemeents entering into each teacher's case.

Now how has this plan worked so far? It is evident that the working out of a plan is primarily and for the most part dependent upon the mental and, I may add, the moral attitude of the high school principals. The bulk of the evidence comes from them; the most telling judgments come from them. The principals have seen the teachers and are better acquainted with their daily or weekly or monthly work and results than anybody else who can give us information. The high school principals, as of course were to be expected, have not all adopted the same attitude, the same mental attitude. I say that was to be expected, simply because no set of men will be identical in their feelings or views in a matter of this sort or of any other sort. Some principals were undoubtedly endeavoring to be judicial minded, they were not holding back any derogatory elements, or vice versa. Others were rather, as it would seem, in the position of advocates. They were desirous of getting a large proportion of their teachers declared of superior merit, and that notwithstanding their declarations in the preliminary inquiry as to the actual and intended meaning of the phrase "superior merit." In other words while a principal might, in the initial inquiry, suppose that maybe 10 or 20 or 30% of his teachers ought to be declared of superior merit, as he understood the phrase then, when it came to the "pinch" his opinion got to be that 80% or 90% ought to be declared of superior merit; and I believe there have been cases on record in which a principal refused to vote against a declaration of superiority for any teacher in his school. Now that attitude is of course the easy attitude, the gratifying attitude from the point of view of the teachers. It is not, as it seems to me, the right attitude; and it is not a defensible attitude. It tends to nullify the purpose of the law, which, in the opinion not only of the makers of the law but of most of the educators consulted, was a just and proper purpose, namely, to limit the advances to the highest salaries to a comparatively small proportion of the teachers. Just how small, of course nobody knows, but let us suppose that 50% of the teachers coming up for this declaration, those eligible for it, should be declared of superior merit; that would have seemed at the outset, not only to the examiners and the city superintendent but to the high school principals themselves, a liberal interpretation of the law. Well, we have gone much beyond that in my opinion. I have not the results in figures(but I think the proportion of those declared superior among those who are eligible for such declaration has been considerably over 50%. I wish I could give you the exact figures, but I was unable to get them; it would take some time and the office is very busy, and the clerks could not be spared to look them up. Everybody knows that some good things can be said about any teacher; there is nobody who is so hopelessly bad that he has not some merit; and a principal could by dilating upon such merits, however obscure and limited, produce an impression—also by silence, of course, as to certain faults or short-comings—could produce an impression favorable to a teacher, almost any teacher. Of course I do not say this in a spirit of criticism, but in order to show the difficulty of the task, and the practical impossibility of performing it with absolute equality and fairness.

You know, perhaps, the anecdote of the Scotch gardener who stole so much truck from his master's garden that finally the master was obliged to dismiss him. But he came to his master nevertheless for a recommendation, and the master wrote: "Sandy McGraw got more out of my garden than any gardener I ever employed."

Now will you excuse a personal word. My votes in this body of seven, or practically six, in the absence of Supt. Bardwell, my votes have been without doubt in more cases adverse for a declaration of superior merit than the votes of any other person sitting in the body. I say that not in an apologetic spirit, but in order that I may explain my point of view. I believe that the term "superior merit" was intended to mean more than faithful or satisfactory or good or willing or industrious. In voting against a considerable number of teachers who were rateed **B plus** and in some cases even **A** by the principal, while Supt. Bardwell after two or three visits had made some adverse comments and had never rated higher than B, I felt justified, and more than that; I felt it to be my absolute duty, as I understand the purpose of the law, to attempt the discrimination. In the first place not only does it reduce to a question of what I conscientiously believe to be the meaning, the intended meaning, of the word "superior"; but in the second place, bear in mind that that withholding of the declaration of superiority is in every case only of temporary effect—every teacher's case will come up annually at least, and on appeal might come up more frequently; and in the third place every teacher obtains under the new law an advance of salary—I am speaking of the women teachers. Of course the men teachers continue to advance too, under the old law temporarily, even before the recent decision of the Board of Education granting an absolute increase of three years in the salary schedule all round. Consequently, it appeared to me that it was only reasonable and necessary that the examiners before being expected to vote should have positive and conclusive evidence of superiority. Well, the net result has been that by this leniency, in my judgment many more teachers—I do not know what proportion, but many more than should have been at this time, on the evidence before us, with an investigation so limited and so hasty, declared of superior merit—have been so declared. Perhaps it is just as well. It is not advisable to attempt to go too far or too fast at the first introduction of an innovation like this. It is better to err on the side of leniency than on the side of severity. I am glad the error has been in that direction. I am sorry it has gone so far. In some cases I feel sure the effect of having declared certain teachers superior will be rather bad; and, may be, if the effect becomes cumulative, it will be found to be very bad in the long run.

However, let me say in conclusion, that we have done the best we could. There is no telling how to get inside the minds of all people. I have been astonished at the way some of my colleagues have voted, and I have no doubt they have been astonished at the way I have voted, in many cases. After all, we are human. Here is a human machine set to perform a certain task; it has great limitations; it is not in the best working order, one of the superintendents being absent; and the material, the data, has been not of a kind rationally desirable for this work. Nevertheless, in the face of all these difficulties, I believe, I certainly hope, the net result in the schools will be good, will be beneficial. That, of course, is a point that only time can decide. The problem is too complex for any one to be prophetic about it at this stage.

I have tried to make clear, first, the point of view of prominent educators as to the intent of the law; second, what these same persons thought ought to constitute superiority in a teacher; third, the difficulties of the tack; fourth, how the work has actually been done; and finally what the net result has been as well as I could state it up to this time.

ADDRESS BY SUPERINTENDENT EDWARD L. STEVENS.

Associate Superintendent E. L. Stevens then addressed the meeting as follows:

Mr. President, Ladies and Gentlemen:—Usually on Saturday mornings you come to see me. I am very glad indeed that I am permitted on this Saturday morning to come to see you. I congratulate you Mr. President, that there are so many here today. I hope that past issues have become events of a dead past, and that the high school teachers can meet with common interests and for a common purpose, and will not be divided into teachers of the second year, who are over forty years old, and teachers of the first year, who are men, and the teachers of the graduating class who are women, and every other imaginable kind of faction. If equal pay will bring about unity in the teaching force in the various high schools of this city it will be the greatest benefit which the law has conferred upon us.

I am permitted occasionally by the grace and favor of the Board of Examiners to enter the room in which they are cerebrating. Those of you who have read those remarkable enactments called "schedule conditions" will find that while it is necessary for the associate city superintendent to transmit a report to the Board of Examiners, he is not given a vote in that body,—one of the duties which I am very glad to escape from. But you will permit me to say that if the Board of Superintendents in any way or manner has, as Kim said, acquired merit, I think I am qualified to bear evidence at this time that the Board of Examiners has acquired superior merit.

It is undoubtedly true that the Board of Examiners has gone about this very difficult task in the most careful way and manner; that the Board itself and its several members have exhibited a calm, dispassionate, and judicial attitude; and I believe that they have done and that they will do substantial justice to the teachers of this city. And I am glad to know from one of its members that the new schedules went into effect on the first of January. (Laughter.) Now the immediate effect of the passage of this law, when all its formalities have been complied with, will be the readjustment of salaries, resulting in many cases in substantial increases, which you all deserve and which I hope that you will expend wisely. Its ultimate effect, however, will be helpful because it will bring about I think (and I am not saying this in any complaining or critical manner at all), it will compel a more careful organization and supervision of the work of teachers, it will compel principals of schools to make life miserable for me until I give them more clerks. It will bring about the establishment of certain administrative positions in the high schools, occupied by persons of experience and intelligence who can undertake the discharge of administrative duties which now crowd the principal's time until the limit of fatigue is almost reached. And it will bring about the careful organization of departments of instruction in which the first assistants and the chairmen of departments will find that it is incumbent upon them to make good teachers out of poor ones, which is the great aim and object of organization and supervision in a school, any way.

Now concerning the statute itself I have little to say because I do not want to be quoted. It is a very good example of what we call vicious satute making, that is, it is full of holes,—it is full of inconsistencies. Samuel J. Tilden would never have written a statute like that. And that great statute drafter here in New York for many years,—Judge Hoffman, would never have written a statute like that, nor a statute like the Davis Law. Take a man like the draftsman of our first Charter, Pinney of Richmond, J. Hampton Dougherty, they would not have drafted a law in these terms. There is talk of what the effect of the law is to be, or what the result will be. I maintain that no man has a right, nor a woman, nor a body of men or of women, to draft a law which will lead to litigation. Take the Davis Law, Section 1901, under which we have been living for a number of years. As you know a large number of inconsistent and contradictory clauses were written in there. There was a clause written into the Davis Law to the effect that junior teachers should receive a certain salary with certain increments; and then some one in the hurry of passage wrote in, "And none of the perons named therein" (namely persons in high schools) "shall receive a salary less than that which they would have received for service in the aforesaid elementary schools." Just think of the inconsistency of that when in the aforesaid elementary schools they might have received an annual increment of a hundred or more dollars, whereas according to the schedule written in another sentence in the same section the annual increment was only fifty dollars. Now when these schedule conditions were adopted by the Board of Education,—they have since been given the effect of law by the enactment of Chapter 902 of the Law of 1911—I don't know whether it was ever intended that they should or should not in that form become law. I think that if it had been intended of expected that they should become law they would have been more carefully framed. But I am not practicing; and I do not want to be the legal adviser of anybody. I urge all of you to abide in faith, knowing that the appropriate committee of the Board of Education is endeavoring to eliminate every ambiguous construction of these schedule conditions, and is endeavoring to reconcile apparently inconsistent features, and that ultimately we will be able to discover what the working interpretation of these schedule conditions really is. The recent amendments which the Board of Education has adopted to its by-laws, by which the law is now interpreted as it was intended to be interpreted originally, is evidence of the wish on the part of the authorities to do what the law intended should be done.

Now I am goinng to talk about what constitutes a teacher of superior merit. I shall use that text as a point of departure, and I have the right to speak to you, perhaps, as a pastor to his flock. The act of a board or body in declaring fitness or merit is an act affirming the quality of service. The fixation of salary is a ministerial act which can be performed by an administrative officer or a clerk in acordance with certain salary schedules. There is a mistaken notion that the act of the Board of Superintendents or of the Board of Examiners is taken only and solely for the purpose of giving somebody an increase in salary. Now please note the distinction I make: The declaration of fitness and merit in a teacher is an affirmation or certification of the quality of service. It then becomes and remains only a ministerial or administrative act for some ministerial officer to affix opposite the teacher's name the appropriate salary. I want that clearly understood by the teachers of this city. If you have not received an increase to which perhaps you became entitled when the Board of Examiners declared you of superior merit, it is because the ministerial act has not yet been performed of putting the appropriate salary against your name upon the certificate or payroll. That cannot be very well done, my friends, until the schools as units, have been finished, and the schools as units have been surveyed, and all the cases of all the teachers in these scools, gone over by the appropriate board or body. It is quite evident that it will be idle for the clerks or ministerial officers of the Board of Education to go on with a certain high school, and raise the salaries upon certain payrolls of fifty teachers, when the casees of forty others are still under adjustication. As rapidly as these schools and the service of the teachers in these schools may be determined and rated, then just as rapidly the certificates and payrolls will be amended accordingly.

I have said that the Board of Examiners is proceeding with zeal and with inteligence, with industry, and an industry which extends into the evenings and over Saturdays, and sometimes into the day following, to determine the quality of service of the teachers in the high schools of this city. Of course when it extends to the day following it is made more or less solemn and religious rite; sometimes they take up a collection; sometimes it depends on who is present whether or not it opens with prayer. (Laughter).

There are some things that follow this law, my friends, that you must realize. Equality of task follows upon equality of salary. It that plain? Equality of quantity of duty and service follows upon equality of pay. None of you who are wearing hats can claim special privilege for lateness or absence any more. (Laughter). Well, I will withdraw that words "any more."

Now as to the text to which I was asked to speak. I do not know how I should determine superior merit. If I were an autocrat, and had full power, with me it would be simply a matter of intuition. I confess it. I believe that as a principal I should know a good teacher and a better teacher. But intuition alone cannot prevail in a system of this size any more than it could prevail as a standard for examinations for admission to the profession. There must be tests for the credential which entitles you to teach in the high schools of this city; there must be a method and examination of some kind in order that it may be discovered whether there is fitness of personality and merit in your work. This task has been given to the Board of Examiners, as has been said, and it is an unexpected task. In the future there will be more data at the service of that board. In the future principals and others will be more certain in the statements which they wish to make or which they are able to make in regard to the character and service of teachers.

In the final analysis I should say that that teacher is superior who is not only able and willing to teach, but also to lead, to interest, and to inspire boys and girls; and that is the final test. I am grateful for this opportunity of meeting you this morning, and wish you God-speed in your work. (Applause).

ADDRESS BY PRINCIPAL JOHN HOLLEY CLARK.

Mr. John Holley Clark, Principal of Flushing High School addressed the meeting as follows:

Mr. President, Ladies and Gentlemen:—I had supposed that the first speaker called from amongst the principals would be the principal of one of the largest high schools; but the president of the association for some reason has called upon the principal of the oldest public high school in the city and perhaps the oldest of the principals.

This question of superior merit has been presented with great clearness by Examiner Smith; and from my experiences before the Board of Examiners I can bear the highest testimony to the carefulness and the conscientiousness and the thoroughness with which the Boad of Examiners has taken up the question in reference to all teachers whose cases have come before it.

The views of the principals and others, as expressed in the answers to the letter sent out by the Secretary of the Board of Examiners, were perhaps influenced by certain suggestions that were made in that letter; and perhaps at first it would appear that, in order that a teacher may be of superior merit, the quality of that teacher's service should be "better than excellent" or should be "of the highest type." That, however, is an extreme view.

Another view, which perhaps might be supported with equal force, is that all teachers have some degree of merit; those whose work is not found satisfactory are **inferior merit**, and those who are rendering satisfactory service are of **superior merit**, whether rated **B, B plus** or **A.** An objection, however, to this view, as it seems to me, is the relation of this particular section of the law to other sections of the law.

One section of the law requires the Board of Superintendents to determine whether a teacher's service is "fit and meritorious." The words "superior merit" would therefore seem to imply a somewhat higher degree of merit than that described by "fit and meritorious." In fact that is the meaning of the word **superior,**—higher; and that must mean higher than something else. Now what is that something else? "Superior" in the sense in which it is used in this law would see to mean superior to **B.**

On the blanks that are sent out to the principals for rating teachers, three grades of service are said to be meritorious. These are **A, B plus** and **B. B** is a grade of service considered meritorious and it may be called the positive degree of merit. Any higher degree of merit may properly be said to be "superior." **B plus** satisfies this requirement; **A** is not required, according to my idea. It is not supreme or superlative merit that is required; it is **superior** merit or the comparative degree of merit. Consequently all those teachers should be determined to be of superior merit who are justly rated as high as B plus this being a grade of merit higher than another meritorious grade which is designated as **B.**

I know how many there are, Mr. President, to speak upon this subject; I therefore will not take further time.

ADDRESS BY PRINCIPAL JOHN H. DENBIGH.

Principal John H. Denbigh of the Morris High School addressed the meeting as follows:

Mr. Chairman, Ladies and Gentlemen of the High School Teachers Association of New York City:—There is one thing that as a principal I should like to say. I think that Mr. Smith is wrong in believing that the high school principals had made up their minds at first that 20 or 25 or 30% of their teachers were of superior merit. I do not believe that any such impression or opinion had taken shape in their minds; and I think there is on file at the Board of Education a document of about the same date as our letters to the Board of Examiners, to show I am right in that conclusion. I do believe that at the time these letters were writen we were all engaged in making a sort of standard in our own minds as to what a superior teacher or superior teaching might be.

I tried to do it somewhat in this way, and I gave a good deal of time and thought to it. If I had a school of my own in which I were able by some fortunate combination of circumstances to secure the kind of teachers I should like to have in order that superior work might be done there and superior training given, I would ask myself what I ought to expect to find of value in the classroom, and then in the personality of the teacher.

I will begin with the classroom. In the first place I should expect to find when I went there to see a recitation, scientific conduct of that recitation. I should expect to find that the lesson had been prepared, not perhaps in every detail, because I am not wholly a believer in such preparation, but at least prepared in its general plan. I should expect to find that teacher was proficient in the art of questioning. I should expect to find a nice balance between those questions which should train the thought of the student, in other words questions which might belong to the Socratic method, and questions which were merely tests of memory and which trained the memory,— quizzing. Then I should expect to find a constant training of the pupil to use his own judgment; no direct information conveyed to the pupil if possible, but that the student might be made by skilful questioning to form his own judgment, and to form a correct judgment. I should expect to find also unmistakable proofs of awakening interest in the subject, and of maintenance of interest in it, if the teaching were of superior order. I should expect to find cultivation of self-activity on the part of the student, and this implies a good deal more than would appear at first sight.

Divide your class roughly, and you will have three classes of students. You will have those who are distinctly more gifted in mental ability than their fellows, those who are distinctly less gifted and slow, and a large group who do not appear to fall into either of the other groups. A skilful teacher knows how to take care of each member of each one of these groups; and the degree to which he or she knows how to take care of these individuals, marks the degrees to which that teacher has attained superiority in discrimination of individual power and of individual ambition. I think there should be persistent and relentless exaction of the best effort of the student both in oral and in written work.

I think there should be quick perception on the part of the teacher of the failure of close attention on the part of the student. Now the student may appear to be very attentive indeed and have his thoughts a thousand miles away from anything that is going on in the classroom. Inattention does not necessarily mean a deliberate attempt to break a window or the throwing of crayon about a room. The teacher should, I repeat, have quick ability to recognize loss of attention on the part of the individual, and marked ability to regain it through something in the lesson. You cannot regain it by mere command that the student shall attend. You may whip up apparent attention for an instant in that way, but you do not regain it permanently in that way.

It is of vital imporance, I think, that the teacher should be kindly, good-humored, self-controlled, and exceedingly courteous in class. If the teacher is courteous, rigorously, consistently courteous, no matter what the provocation may be—and I know as well as the rest of you, because I am gifted with a hot temper, that it is an extraordinarily difficult thing to be self-controlled—he will control well and be at an immense advantage in dealing with either teachers or students.

Next, a superior teacher should use good judgment in rating pupils' work, good judgment in rating oral work, good judgment in rating written work. And last, but not least, in my judgment there should be good results both in school examinations and tests, and in outside examinations. Now I do not believe that results in examinations are final tests of good teaching; I do not believe that to teach for mere results in examinations would be good teaching. I do believe, and am ready to maintain it, that good teaching will produce good results in examinations, that is, in examinations that are fairly set and well conducted; and therefore, to some extent, results in examinationse are a test of superior teaching.

I think we may turn now to the qualities that the superior teacher should show in his own make-up and personality. In the first place I should put as the most important quality of all, the possession of good health. I should like to have some provision made by which teachers who are not in good health could be removed from work, made comfortable and happy, and kept somewhere until their health was recovered, and have no teacher who is not comfortable, happy and cheerful in the classroom.

I think the superior teacher must show superior scholarship in his special subject. I think he should show habits of punctuality and of regular attendance. While I sympathize with all my heart with those who are compelled to be out of school much of the time during the term, I still think that no one can, in honesty to the city, rate the services of such teachers as efficient. You know and I know what an interruption it is to be continually changing from one teacher to another, from a regular teacher to a substitute, and from the substitute back to the regular teacher.

I think, moreover, that the superior teacher should display accuracy and promptness in making reports, and accuracy in keeping records; and I have absolutely no sympathy at all with the teacher who declares that such work is not to be expected of a teacher, or with one who belittles the importance of such work. Such work is vastly important, such work cannot be wholly removed from the province of the classroom teacher, and it should be well done. It is such important work that I think is should be rated in estimating the superior personality of the teacher.

A superior teacher should show some executive ability. He should display cheerful willingness for extra service of any kind, such as censorship of a society or, if he is gifted that way, the care of some branch of athletics, or as class adviser to a group of students,— boys or girls. He should have ability to see fields of usefulnes for himself. I was very much astonished by having two teachers come to me recently and say "You have never given me an opportunity to be useful in this school." Now, ladies and gentlemen, I lay it down as a true proposition that the teacher who has been five or six or seven years in the school and then comes to the principal and says "you have never given me an opportunity to be useful in this school," will never be very useful in that school.

A superior teacher should possess qualities of tact, good temper, justice, humor, sympathy and patience. He should display, in my opinion, willingness to be present at school conferences, commencement exercises, and all such gatherings. And I think he should display, and I feel this strongly, though I may be wrong, I think he should display serenity in times of stress. I do not believe that a superior teacher suffers very acutely from the mysterious and painful malady that is known as nervous strain. The people who talk most about nervous strain never are and never will be superior teachers. He should possess ability to deal with any ordinary case of laziness and small breaches of discipline in his own class without having to bring the offender to the office. He ought to be unwearying in his effort to bring laggards up to better standards. The teacher who promptly disappears every day at 2:30 can never be a superior teacher in my judgment. He should display an active interest in each member of his official class because the interest of the official teacher means frequently success or failure to a very large number of students in his particular group. It is n ot sufficient that the biology teacher in charge of a group of students should merely be interested in the biology lessons of his students. The official teacher of that group of students ought to be interested in what the students may have done in English or in algebra or in any other subject; and a little interest displayed at the right time early in the term will very often change the whole attitude of a class and mean success instead of failure to a large group of students. I have seen that happen frequently. The good class teacher exercisees a tremendous influence up his group of students by encouragement, by little personal inquiries as to difficulties, and by a little prodding in his own classroom of the lazy.

Perhaps after all this you will imagine that the last thing necessary for the superior teacher is a pair of wings. Now I am not sure but that a really superior teacher is a person who is almost in possession of a pair of wings. I think that none of the qualities that I have named are qualities I would willingly omit, and yet I do not think that any individual teacher can measure up to all of them. I do not suppose any one of us, or anyone in the whole system, could measure up to the standard which I have presented; and yet, in some degree, the superior teacher should possess all the qualifications mentioned. If there are any qualities which he should not possess I am sure the speakers who come after me will tell you what they are. (Applause).

ADDRESS BY PRINCIPAL WILLIAM FAIRLEY.

Mr. Fairley, Principal of Commercial High School, Brooklyn, addressed the meeting as follows:

Ladies and Gentlemen:—I think we shall all have to be brief, I will make what I have to say very brief. Some one stated that going over all these blanks which we have been requested to sign for the rating of so many teachers, and applying the questions personally, and asking, "Mr. Present Principal, how would that have hit you three years ago?" would be a rather humbling exercise.

I think I shall limit what I have to say to two considerations, and I will begin by saying that all my remarks are colored by the fact that I have to do only with men in a boys' school, and that certain phases of the problem which would be incidental to the mixed or girls' school do not come within my view at all.

I read some time ago that in some petty German state,—call it the Grand Duchy of Mechlenburgh-Schwerin,—there was great agitation among the teachers for a very needed increase of salary; and in Germany, if not in New York, as those who are familiar with German teachers' pay know there is a chronic need of increase of salary.

Well, the benevolent administration decided, as other benevolent administrations have decided, that a substantial change looking toward an increase of salary was not at that time feasible; but it did decree to all the teachers of Mechlenburgh-Schwerin a very gorgeous and dazzling uniform, with a lot of braid and gilt buttons. I don't know whether the ladies had tassels or not; but there are not many ladies in the German schools.

Now if this rating of men in my school was to give them another stripe down the trousers, or another row of buttons down the front of the coat, or an extra tassel on the head, or something of that kind, and didn't go into the question of a needed and promised and merited increase of salary, it could be done in a much more cold-blooded way.

Associate Superintendent Stevens differentiated very justly and keenly between the rating function and the salary-fixing function. To make out one of these volumnious blanks, to discuss it with the other six members of the Board, to decide whether a teacher is really of superior merit or not, if you could seperate it entirely from the underlying, burning question of the need of increased money to meet increasing bills, that would be relatively simple, and my work would be easier. I have confessed that before the examiners and before the superintendents.

I would answer a remark that was made by one of my colleagues on this problem. Let me quote from a resolution of the High School Principals, framed by a committee of which I was a member. This statement was made in a report of such committee: "That it is the judgment of the High School Principals that all teachers who are at the maximum should automatically pass to the new maximum," That was the position of that committee, and I believe it was unanimously supported, or all but unanimously supported, by the principals.

If I am asked what is my definition of "superior teacher," I should agree with Mr. Stevens that it is largely a matter of intuition. You could not define it any more than we men teachers could pick out wives, or women teachers pick out husbands, by an advertised catalogue of virtues. I have made out these lists for fifty or sixty men; and according to that catalogue a man may be not a superior teacher;

and yet I am persuaded that he is one, because I have found out the good things about him. But he is not a superior teacher according to the catalogue of excellencies; and in committee meeting I might be compelled to vote seemingly against my own statements, in black and white. Again I feel I may have been obliged in many cases to chronicle some very serious fault on the part of the teacher who on the whole is more than fit and meritorious,—who is superior.

Now, let me in closing voice the sentiment of a number of teachers with whom I had the pleasure of journeying over here in the subway this morning. Expression was given to this,—that this rating and this salary fixing should not be for the purpose of keeping down the expenses of the city, and keeping as many as possible away from the increase, but that it should be for the benefit and uplift of the teaching force. And as an end to that, this was strongly urged, as from the defendant's point of view, by the teachers,—if we principals, if we visiting superintendents, marked and kept records of deficiences, then the teacher should know it in every case, and the statement of the fact should be used as a basis by the superior for endeavoring to help the teacher to a higher standard by correction of his faults. (Applause).

ADDRESS BY PRINCIPAL WILLIAM L. FELTER

Principal Felter, Girls' High School, addressed the meeting as follows:

Examiner Smith has indicated that the new law is a method of separating the sheep from the goats; and every man and every woman who has not learned of favorable action by the Board of Examiners is asking the question, "Am I the goat?"

Let me say that I believe that the result of the law will be a decided improvement in high school teaching. I believe, however, that those who have fought so well and so long for an increase in salary should have that increase in salary, the law to the contrary notwithstanding. I believe that the strict provisions of the law, or the strict interpretation of the provisions of the law, should apply to those who come up in the future. And I heartily agree with the remarks last made that every teacher should be appraised of his shortcomings to the end that the needed improvement may be made.

Now let me say that every principal, of course, looks on these matters from his own point of view. Personally I am inclined to put emphasis in superior merit upon work done in the classroom. I agree that social activities are desirable, I agree that every teacher should be interested in every activity of the school, I agree that the teacher should be a paragon; nevertheless the great burden of emphasis should beplaced upon this: What does this teacher do in the classroom? (Applause.)

Now then one question to be asked is, What use is made of the time,—only 45 minutes to a recitation,——how long does it take that teacher to get down to business? The second is, Is he so wound up with the machinery of his instruction that he can never divorce himself from it? Is he such a cut-and-dried pedant that he has outlined that lesson exactly as he wants it, and never thinks of deviating from that plan by a hair? Or, on the other hand, does he go in there and say, "I have taught this subject for 10 years; what need have I to make any special preparation?" Then he wonders why pupils are not interested in his subject. He had better go back and read Matthew Arnold.

Or does he say, "Why there is nothing for me to do put to hear the recitation." Is that making the best use of the time? There are teachers who unconsciously repeat every answer a pupil gives, and cut the recitation time in half by doing this.

You ask a teacher of that kind, "Are you strving to get attention?" "Certainly; I insist on everybody looking right at me." And yet that teacher's efforts are always putting a premium on inattention. A teacher ought to know the Socratic method, and ought to know when that method should be used and used wisely; ought to know when it is time to give questions which call simply for information from the pupil, and then ought to know when it is time to use power questions that will test the real instruction that has been given in the subject. I do not know one high school teacher out of a hundred who in my judgment ever begins to get out of a pupil what there is in him. I will give you an illustration. In the elementary school the teachers have dictation in English, and they will dictate a little group of words, three in number; and the attention of pupils is never cultivated to take more than three words at a time. We have the same thing in high school work. We will ask a question, even in English. If we get back an answer of two or three words we are satisfied. Our standards are too low. We have never yet as teachers devised methods that will enable us to develop the powers that lie dormant in every child before us. Why? Because we have been pedants and not teachers. It is because we have been too willing to walk on in these paths they are good enough for us. It is high time we woke up to the problem before us, and began to use the material before us day after day. Take the mater of employing the self-activity of the child. Do we do it? No.

My great fault with teachers is that they make the recitation turn around themselves and not around the child; and the teacher in planning a lesson says, "What am I to do?" instead of saying, "How am I going to arrange this work so as to get the maximum of self-activity from the pupil?" It is the wrong point of view in the conduct of the recitation. Of course the implication is that the teacher who knows how to question skilfully, who knows how to utilize every minute of the 45, who is skilful in devising methods for utilizing the self-activity of the child, is on the high road to being a teacher of superir merit.

But so long as we study psychology, and know the terms in the book, and talk glibly about the self-activity of the child; and of acomplishing the maximum result with the minimum of effort, and then fail to exhibit these things in the classroom in our daily work, thus demonstrating that we have our psychology at our tongue's end and not at the end of our fingers, until we have done that, why we should not make very serious claims to be teachers of superior merit. It is the younger ones I am talking to now.

Now mark you, do not misunderstand me, do not think for a moment that I infer or imply that the older teachers do not now exemplify the very things of which I am speaking. They do in many instances. I am speaking of the young ones, who, instead of spending ten minutes at the end of the day looking back upon the way in which they have gone through the day, spend their time in reading books of psychology. These are the persons I am talking about. I have in mind some of the older teachers who have precious little to say during the 45 minutes; and problems of attention, and problems of interest, and all other problems, disappear because the pupil is kept so busy he has no time to think of anything else. (Applause).

ADDRESS BY PRINCIPAL CHARLES D. LARKINS.

Dr. Larkins, Principal of Manual Training High School, addressed the meeting as follows:

We have heard so much said about what constitutes a superior teacher, that I wish to present some things that appear to me positively to prevent a person's being rated as a teacher of superior merit.

We often hear quoted the expression: "A sound mind in a sound body." It seems to me that no one can be considered a superior teacher who has not reliable health and a reliable head. I shall illustrate some of my remarks by concrete examples.

First, I know one man whose health is so unreliable that when his girl "went back" on him he went to bed and stayed there for two weeks. A physician gave a certificate of illness, and I was requested to sign it. I felt a good deal like editing the physician's certificate, and wrting into it the disease was "weak knees."

No person can be a superir teacher, of course, who has not intelligence. But to that there must be added sympathy with the stupid and with one's associate. In other words, no one can be a superior teacher who is hard and unyielding, nor can a person be a teacher of superior merit who lacks stamina, who has not the ability to "stay put." The person who decides to do one thing to-day and another to-morrow cannot possibly be a teacher of superior merit, or so it seems to me.

A teacher to be of superior merit must have a fund of useful and usable information. I taught in a school with a man whose reading seemed to be governed by the size of the book. He told me he was in love with small books because he could carry them in his pocket. And after knowing him some years I came to the conclusion that he knew nothing except what he could get from small books. He had the most varied mass of facts of any man I ever knew, and he knew more things not worth knowing than any man I ever knew. On the other hand there were many things an intelligent man ought to know of which he seemed to be ignorant. He knew enough facts, but they were neither useful nor usable; they seemed to have been dumped into his mind as they dump bricks to the sidewalk; and he never seemed able to use the thing he needed just at the time that he needed it. That chap, as I view it, cannot become a teacher of superior merit.

Again, a teacher cannot be superior who is not reliably conscientious—now notice the adjective—who is not **reliably conscientious.** A woman told me not long ago about how conscientious she was in doing her work; and, yet, when I assigned her to certain work, she said if I insisted on her doing it, she knew it would make her ill. On the following Monday morning she didn't show up—pardon the slang—and she didn't for a week. When she did come to school she brought a physician's certificate. I do not think that her conscience was reliable. The man before mentioned, who went to bed for several weeks, did not have a reliable conscience, although possibly it was a case of heart failure instead of weak knees.

Again, a superior teacher must be dependably self-controlled. I know teachers who for three or four months at a time are reliable and straight and dependable until the test comes; then they lose themselves completely. One man has never brought a boy into the office without announcing at the very start: "This boy is the worst boy I ever saw." And apparently all the boys that come to him are in ascending degrees, in arithmetical progresion, of badness; each one is worse than all the rest. I remarked when he said it the last time that he must have had an awful experience.

A teacher of superior merit must have patience and take infinite pains. I believe we fail in our teaching more often because we are not careful enough than for any other cause. We are not definite enouh in what we mean, in just exactly what we want. The ability to be patient and to take infinite pains must be inherent in us, to make it appear in our insrtuction.

Of course, it goes without saying that no one who fails in unlimited and untiring industry can be a successful teacher, and the same may be said of perserverance. If we decide to do anything, we must look after it until it is finished. I went into a gymnasium, two or three days ago. The teacher was giving an exercise to a large class. I had spoken to her fequently about a practice she had of giving the first part of a command—the command of warning—then interpolating a little speech, and after that giving the command of execution. I had spoken of it so many times that I think my presence disturbed her more or less. She gave a command of warning, had the class at attention,—and they were in the position of exact attention! then she interpolated a little speech; then she said, "In place rest"; then she finished her speech; then she gave a different command of attention and quite a different command of execution from what she had started with. That type of teacher is easily shunted from her course. Of course, if we lack perserverance we cannot be superior teachers.

Again, a superior teacher must have an engaging personality; and that covers a multitude of things. For example, there are two women teachers, that I know, to whom, if they should meet me on the way out of the school building and should say to me, "If you are going up the street I will walk with you," I think I should say, "Let us go back into the office and talk it over." It is incumbent on a teacher to dress well, to look well on the street. "The apparel oft proclaims the man."

Lastly, a successful teacher must have a broad and abiding love for his fellow-men. And the ladies will understand that I do not mean a broad and abiding love for some particular fellow, but they shall love mankind in general.

Now this catalogue of virtues, as Dr. Fairley called it, would seem to indicate, as Mr. Denbigh has said, that a person needed wings to be rated as a superior teacher. I feel rather sorry that the discussion of this morning has taken the direction it has,—an attmpt to interpret the law. There ought to be a committee of legal lights to do that. In my practice in the matter of rating teachers I have been satisfied wtith a good many fewer than the points I have indicated. Before I tell you how I felt when I went before the Board of Examiners, I wish to say that the attitude of the Board was an attitude of perfect fairness and squareness. I think they made mistakes some times. I think occasionally they rated a person as superior who ought not to have been so rated. I think occasionally perhaps they rated teachers below superior who ought not to have been so rated. Nevertheless, in every such instance, it was a mistake of judgment, due entirely to a lack of knowledge of the facts. They were trying to be perfectly fair and square and they were administering the law as they understood it, and in the most liberal way. My own attitude was that of attorney for the applicant. I thought every teacher was entitled to representation in that board. The teachers of the Manual Training High School are all my personal friends, and I know all about them. Who was to speak a good word for them in that board if not I?

That was my attitude, and I think it was the attitude of every principal in the system. That will be my attitude in the future. I am the one who knows the teacher more intimately than any one else. I know many good points in the teacher that the superintendent does not discover in a short inspection. Personally I think that so far as the Manual Training High School is concerned, the law has been a good thing; because as soon as that law was enacted and discussion upon it began, I discovered that certain teachers can teach much better than I ever suspected they could.

ADDRESS BY PRINCIPAL WILLIAM McANDREW.

Wm. McAndrew, Principal Washington Irving High School:

Ladies and Gentlemen:—Considering the time of day and the amount of talk you have endured you are superior in one quality, beyond all doubt. That is in courtesy and politeness.

Mr. Smith has told us of the difficulty in getting at the purpose of the law. Those of us who were in the system in 1898 and who have watched with economic interest the matter of salary schedules since then recognize one intent of the law which Mr. Smith has not very largely touched upon. In 1898 the high school schedules proposed clearly defined rates of pay for high school teachers. Annual increments were provided. A man could look forward pretty definitely as to what he could expect. But a remarkable depreciation in the value of money has gone on until what was a dollar in 1898 is not worth more than 60 cents in 1912. The $2000 salary looked forward to, proves when you reach it to have shrunk to $1200. Never for a moment during the discussion of the need of a better salary law did anyone lose sight of the fact that the depreciation of high school salaries needed correction. I can not bring myself to believe that there was any intent or purpose so important as that of making the salaries of 1912 equal in value to what they were in 1898. The main proposition admitted by those who advocated this law, and by those who passed it was, the high school salaries should be corrected; they should be

Now, to bring into this law another purpose: that of rewarding superior merit, may be all right. We are all in favor of getting a relation between pay and value received. But that was not, I believe, the primary purpose of this act. Until the corrective effort of it is satisfied; until the people of 1898 and 1899 and 1900 have the value of the schedules restored why be so decidedly negative in refusing to adjust the salaries of those who do not shine in the precise particular way the examiner demands.

We could learn something from Pittsburgh in this regard. The Teachers' Association convinced the authorities that the deterioration of money values had left the teachers underpaid.

New and advanced schedules were passed. Then the good people who wanted to be sure of a bargain got a commission of merit established to examine all the teachers. A suit was brought by a taxpayer to prevent the subjection of his children to the instruction of underpaid teachers. The judge decided not only that the law should not be vitiated by the injection of a new device but he wiped the examining board off the slate. (Applause). No; please don't cheer. This is a simple business proposition.

I noticed here the allusion to the action of the principals before the Board of Examiners: that the principals seemed to feel themselves called upon to act as attorneys for the teachers. Really, Mr. Chairman, such an attitude would be inevitable if a principal found reason to believe that the investigation were searching too insistently for negative qualities and was too little marked by a disposition to see the superiority of the sum of all the characteristics of a teacher. Two deficiencies and eight superiorities can easily make an excelling combination. Examiners may not always be able to see that.

I think, too, there should be borne in mind that this is a new scheme. One can not be so cocksure of things as some wish to be. To be given an analysis of a teacher into thirty parts, most of which have not ever been recorded or officially suggested, and to be asked to summarize a teachers' work for three years under those heads is extremely difficult. A failure of a teacher to show perfection in one of those points is not a serious thing. Teachers should be given to understand in a fair advance what the peculiar virtues are to be rated.

I do not feel so doubtful as Mr. Smith about the considerable number of teachers who are superior. We must remember that these are picked people, already branded superior by the Board of Examiners when the best applicants were passed; branded superior again when they were picked from the head of an eligible list and sent into the schools; scrutinized by superintendents, rated by principals and judged meritorious by a board before advancing beyond the sixth year of service. There ought to be a large proportion of superior persons among people guarded like that.

I hardly think the attorneyship of principals before the examiners has done any harm. No principal would boomerang himself by urging the elevation of an unfit teacher.

There is no reason for any harshness in the superior merit agitation. Better pay for better service is all right. We are all agreed on large purposes, but it is not necessary to threaten the whole question of superior merit, as they did in Pittsburgh by over-doing the exclusion act. Remember, the salary schedules have been deeply cut by the rise of prices. It is hardly desirable to prevent even ordinarily good teachers from getting this cut made good. Those who reach the ninth and twelfth year hereafter will no doubt improve under the stimulus of the law. But there are many of us, I am sure, salary-raise or no salary-raise, who know better than we did before what superior teaching is and who are going into our class rooms to do it.

ADDRESS BY PRINCIPAL JOHN L. TILDSLEY.

Principal John L. Tildsley, DeWitt Clinton High School, addressed the meeting as follows:

Mr. President, Members of the High School Teachers' Association:—You ask me the question, "What is a superior teacher?" I ask in return "What do you pay?" In other words, I believe the term "superior" can only be defined on the basis of salary paid.

I came down in the train this morning with a teacher who is working for the City of New York, but not in the regular school system. I asked him if he knew of any available drawing teachers. He said,

"What do the high schools pay?" I did not tell him the whole truth. I said we were paying $2,650 for assistants, and $3,150 for first assistants. I should have said, "If you are very fortunate, they will pay you $2,650, provided you have a long list of qualifications." Now as to these qualifications I am in agreement with Mr. Denbigh and the other principals, provided you pay what they are worth.

It is not necessary for me to read the list of qualifications given by Examiner Smith and by the principals. Turn over to me the payroll of DeWitt Clinton High School, amounting to $220,000 a year, and I will very gladly rate teachers in that school on this basis of superior merit. And if I found a teacher who approached within gunshot of the superior teacher as defined by the Board of Examiners, I would pay him about $4,500 a year. I would not pay him $5,000, because that is all I get myself, and I feel that my dignity requires that I get more than my teachers. I would take the next class, those whom the Board of Examiners would not allow to pass for the twelfth year but for the ninth, and I would pay them $3,500. I would take those who have a scheme that would work well. Possibly I should not need any more money than is paid out at the present time, for there are some teachers whom I could secure in the open market for much less than is paid under our present salary system.

Now this Grady law, that is the name given to it I believe, has two aims, with one of which I am in sympathy and with one of which I am not. The one with which I am in sympathy is the increase of the salaries of the teachers for the purpose of securing a better supply of teachers. The other aim is a very manifest one; since it is the law, it should be realized in the fairest possible manner. The object of the Board of Examiners, together with the associate city superintendent, the district superintendent, and the principal, should be so to administer that law as to secure what I regard as one of the two great objects of that law, namely, an adequate supply of teachers. At the present time in DeWitt Clinton High School there are twenty-six vacancies. If I had my way there would be more. What do I mean by that last statement? I mean we have among our corps of teachers, some I won't say whether they are recent or old, whom I would not have there if I were running a private school. There are twenty-six vacancies there, and many in other schools. The Board of Examienrs and the other members of this committee, having a certain measure of discretion provided for in the law, are administering that law so as to cut down the supply of teachers. And in the future, I see it in "The Globe." I don't know whether it is true or not, the Board of Superintendents proposes to increase the qualifications for assistant teachers, and that with twenty-six vacancies in the DeWitt Clinton High School.

There is but one common sense way to administer the law. The fundamental need at the present time is teachers, and good teachers. We do need to improve the teaching of those now in the system; but the most serious difficulty confronting us at the present time is that we cannot get any teachers at all. I cannot obtain even substitutes. What is going to be the effect on the supply of teachers in the City of New York when word goes about that only very exceptional teachers can secure the magnificent salary of $2,650? And what is to be said to the person who comes to you as a candidate for a teaching position when he asks, "What are my prospects for the future?" As this law is administered in the case of the teachers in the DeWitt

Clinton High School, I could not say to that person that the chances are good for securing a salary of $2,650, because the law is administered very strictly.

I will give the Board of Examiners credit for desiring to administer the law justly. I do not always agree with them. I think they have made one fundamental mistake in the administration of that law; but that belongs to another part of the discussion. If I am right in saying that the effect of the present administration of the salary law will be to seriously cut down the supply of teachers in the next few years, or to result in a steady degeneration in the quality of the applicants for licenses, then in my judgment there ought to be a change in the administration of the law or, if necessary, a repeal of th elaw.

I had occasion, last Sunday, to give a talk on the high schools of New York, and I made the prophecy that a generation from now would find an inferior lot of teachers in the high schools of New York. At the present time we need to stretch every salary law to the utmost so as to secure the greatest maximum to every teacher possible. We need the greatest number of first assistants merely that a great number may receive the higher salary. We ought to pay every teacher the highest salary, for only in that way can we secure an adequate supply of teachers. And if the present system does not do that, it must inevitably come that we shall have a new law.

Now, just one more point, with regard to the definition of "superior," my one and only criticism of the Board of Examiners in the administration of the law. From the standpoint of passing on teacher's qualifications, I think they are making one very serious mistake. A very wise principal once said to me that if a teacher had one serious defect, he did not see how a teacher could be rated "excellent." But some two years later he stated to me that he had made a serious mistake in the judgment thus expressed. I find a tendency on the part of the Board of Examiners to lay too much emphasis on mere methods of teaching in the classroom. I visited, yesterday, the recitation of a teacher who, inside of ten minutes, violated many rules of good teaching as laid down by the Board of Examiners and the writers on pedagogy. He did the things he ought not to have done. Nevertheless, I regard him as one of the most valuable teachers of the DeWitt Clinton High School. He had what I regard as the most valuable element in superior teaching,—a strong, effective, positive personality. I regard superior teaching as the projection of a strong personality modified by a study of right methods. If the choice were to arise between methods and personality, I should choose personality every time.

You were told this morning that it was the function of the principals and heads of departments to make good teachers out of poor teachers. If the Board of Examiners will supply us with young men and women without experience in teaching, but who have character, who have culture, who have breeding, I will guarantee that the heads of departments and the principals can make out of them good teachers; methods can be acquired, and almost everything else can be acquired, provided your raw material is good. But I believe it is absolutely impossible to make good teachers out of some of the material now sent to us by the Board of Examiners. And the reason that such material is sent to us by the Board of Examiners is that they cannot furnish us with anything else. I do not blame the Board of Examiners, because they send us the best of what they get. Some 400 or 500 candidates for teaching positions in the New York high schools took the examinations in the DeWitt Clinton High School auditorium last fall. Up to date I doubt if fifty have survived, and I would not want some of the fifty.

The salaries paid in the New York high school are not high enough to longer induce young men of education, of culture, of breeding to enter our ranks. Why, in such a condition of things, administer the salary law, when you have discretion, in such a way as to make it impossible for even the less ambitious to enter our high school system in the future.

THE TEACHING OF SALESMANSHIP AND ADVERTISING.

An Address Before the Bookkeeping Section of the High School Teachers' Association.

By DR. EDWARD J. CLAPP,
New York University School of Accounts and Finance.

Gentlemen:—Mr. Pugh has written and asked me to speak to you on the subject of teaching salesmanship and advertising. At my request I have been excused from discussing the propriety or possibility of teaching such subjects in commercial high schools—of which I know little—and have been allowed to describe my own course in Selling and Advertising at the School of Commerce, Accounts and Finance of New York University. About one year's experience on the road in all parts of the country, and a pretty thorough study of selling literature was the preparation I had for my salesmanship course. All I know about advertising is what I have learned from books, from observation and from friends in the advertising business.

There is one certain way not to give a course in selling and that is to have the course given by outside lecturers, eminent specialists, who have been a success in the sales department or on the road. It must have been the sad experience of every teacher of commercial subjects that rarely can a business man tell you a simple, round, unvarnished tale of how he does it. To him it is a huge mass of detail in which he instinctively finds his way about, but which he never has stopped to classify. Not in all cases has he the education and the knowledge of related business subjects to enable him to carry out this classification if he tried. You will usually do better if you call on him, get him to tell you what you want to know and then present it to the class in condensed, logical form.

If you do have the sales specialist come before your class the chances are that he will come and give advice. It is always assumed that the young want this, and need it. They are told to go to bed early, to hustle and never give up, to remember that the good of the House is also their own good, to be neat, industrious, honest and what not. But that is not teaching them salesmanship. It is merely bad preaching. Indeed, of all classes of men, not excepting even the clergyman, salesmen are most addicted to giving advice. Those who have perused sales literature will bear me out when I say that it contains little else than more or less good precepts.

Even when, in other courses, such as Transportation, men of broad grasp and wide vision can be persuaded to speak to the class, the result is not usually satisfactory. None of them will stick to his last; the various lectures overlap and contradict; the whole series is without beginning and end. A one-man course, provided that man has thought through the subject, has a chance of being a complete and coherent whole.

At the beginning of the course I warned the men that I should not teach them how to be salesmen. The attempt was made to teach them the science, not the art, of salesmanship. There is no point in teaching them the details of selling, which are different with each firm. We must teach them the principles which are unvarying. My first lecture consisted of a skeleton of the development of trade, the mediaeval organization of production and trade, the change wrought by the industrial revolution with its wide separation of producer and consumer and its need for a new distributing mechanism for the surplus which factory turned out. They were told of the rise of the traveling salesman and his place in that mechanism, of the probable changes in distribution that would affect him in the future.

Then we treated the Psychology of Selling. They were told, for instance, what psychology was, something of the nervous system and its operation, something of the nature of Attention, Interest, the Association of Ideas, of Argument and Suggestion and the respective parts which they played in persuasion.

Next we considered Traveling Salesmanship and all that pertains to it. They were told what qualities a salesman should have and we investigated the old charge that "salesmen are born, not made." We saw what equipment he should have and what modern aids he could use, such as a card catalogue of his customers. We saw that, as prices were pretty equal under ordinary conditions, the salesman's hold on his customers was dependent on the care he took of them: the service he gave them. We discussed price maintenance, methods of salesman's compensation, the reports a salesman should render to the house, etc.

We then examined Sales organization. Such subjects were considered as: Planning a Selling Campaign, Salesmen's Training Schools, Salesmen's Demonstration Meetings, the Sales Committee in the Factory, the Standard Selling Record, Keeping Track of Salesmen on the Road, Cost Accounting to Find the Salesman's Values, etc.

From this point on the course dealt rather with the broad questions of distribution. We took up first the usual channels of distribution and discussed the place and the workings of the commission man, the wholesaler and the retailer. We investigated in detail the new developments in the field of selling: the department store, the mail order house, the chain store, the-operative buying and selling association. We examined carefully the advantages and disadvantages of selling direct.

Foreign Selling was the next subject. We glanced at the direction and nature of our foreign trade and decided where and wherein the field of expansion lies. Through many examples we saw the need of a better study of foreign markets by our exporting industries. We discussed the various forms which the organization of export sales can assume. We considered the preparation which a young American salesman should make before launching forth in the foreign field.

Finally, we took up the matter of Credits and Collections, not because it necessarily belongs in a course on Selling, but because it can more easily be tacked on there than anywhere else. We ascertained the nature and the basis of credit and discussed the problem of the credit man, the rating books and reports of the commercial agencies, credit clearing houses, credit insurance, salesmen's reports on persons of doubtful credit. We investigated the methods of ascertaining the credit of foreign buyers and methods of foreign collection. Next year the subject of Installment Selling will be treated under the head of Credits and Collections. It belongs here rather than among the strictly selling problems.

But I do not anticipate that there will be many changes in the next year's course. In general it seems to me that the ground is fairly well covered. Only one outside lecturer was called in for the course and he was a success. He was a traveling salesmen's instructor of the National Cash Register Company, of Dayton, Ohio. He happened to be east while I was on the subject of Traveling Salesmanship. He brought up to the classroom a heroic-sized cash register and one evening sold it to another National Cash Register man who accompanied him and impersonated the recalcitrant merchant to the great amusement and edification of us all.

As regards Advertising, I shall tell a shorter tale. Like Salesmanship, I am giving it this year for the first time, and am arranging it from notes which I have collected from reading, observation and conversation with many advertising men. But the Salesmanship course is behind me; the Advertising course is just fairly in swing.

Thus far we have discussed the history of advertising, its place in the scheme of distribution, the main classes of men engaged in the advertising business, the main mediums by which we advertise. We have just been engaged in the subject of the Psycholofy of Advertising, wherein we cover briefly the same ground which we covered in Selling, and in addition consider what optics teaches us to observe in advertising practice. We shall then consider the relation of Art to Advertising and state principles of good advertising.

Next we take up in detail the work of the three main classes of men in the advertising business; the advertising agent, the advertising manager and the advertising solicitor.

Then we shall learn to know the tools of advertising: type, copy, layout, border, illustrations, colors, etc.; consider rates, keying and checking up advertisements. Next we study the laying out of an advertising campaign for national advertiser, retail advertiser, mail order advertiser, etc. Here we come to a consideration of the relative value of various mediums for various purposes and the value of "circulation" statements. We discuss the purpose and the principles governing the make-up of newspaper, magazine, trade paper, mail order, poster, street car, booklet, window display, house organ and letter advertisement. Finally, we shall discuss the move to purify advertising, including statutes passed.

In this Advertising course we plan to have three outside lecturers: one an advertising agent, one an advertising manager and one the proprietor of a mail order house. They are all friends of mine and will not resent my telling them just what ground they are to cover. We expect to use considerable illustrative matter. Monday night I lectured on the relation of art to advertising, using slides loaned me by the New York Advertising Men's League and reading a lecture they loaned me, prepared to go with these slides. Plenty of illustrations can be cut from the newspapers and pinned up. A reflectoscope would be a splendid help to an advertising class, and we shall have one next year.

A few details of the way in which these courses were given may interest you. There were about sixty in either class. We meet every Monday night, from 7:45 to 9:45. It is a straight lecture punctuated by questions when I see anyone falling asleep. We mark entirely by the examinations at the end of the term. At the end of each lecture I give a ten-minute dictated abstract of what has been said during the two hours. This frees them from paying attention to their note books rather than to me while I am talking. It is a practice which I brought back from Germany, and which, for many reasons, I thoroughly believe in. I keep my notes all on 5x8 sheets and the notes for each lecture, with the dictation, in a manila envelope that just holds them. There they lie, ready for use next year.

I shall not weary you with a lengthy bibliography. In Selling it would not be possible to give a long bibliography, conscientiously, anway. I know of no good book on Selling, none worthy to be used as a text-book. On the Psychology of Selling consult the standard text-books on Psychology, especially James, and see Walter Dill Scott's "Influencing Men in Business." For Sales Organization the best thing is the chapters thereon in Carpenter's "Profit-Making Management." For Selling Practice the best thing in existence is the manual which the National Cash Register Company gets out for the salesmen. They sent me one. Such a sly dissection of fallible human nature you never read.

On Mail Order Selling there is much in recent volumes of "Printer's Ink" and "Advertising and Selling." The leading mail order houses will send you their catalogues and some of the proprieors talk freely with you, though they will write little. There is a great deal about department stores in the report of the Industrial Commission. Their doors are always open; they welcome investigation and are a fascinating study. On "Credits and Collections" the best thing I have seen is Volume I of the Business Man's Library, published by the System Company. Regarding Foreign Selling you can use the Daily Consular and Trade Reports, the Monthly Summary of Commerce and Finance, and the very numerous publications of the Bureau of Manufactures, Department of Commerce and Labor sent free to teachers. A valuable manual is the "Exporters' Encyclopedia," published here in New York.

With regard to Advertising, there is much to choose from. We adopted as text-book Calkins & Holden's "Modern Advertising." Close competitors are French's "Science of Advertising" and a book of the same name by Balmer. There is an excellent history of advertising in the May issue of the Quarterly Review for 1855. For Psychology see Walter Dill Scott's "Theory of Advertising." Scott's three later books are merely restatements of what he said here. A very suggestive study, pointing the way to the application of Psychology to Advertising, is the thesis of Dr. Strong, of Columbia, "The Relative Merits of Advertisements."

With regard to the entire field of advertising practice there is no text-book like the volumes of "Printer's Ink," the leading trade paper of advertising men. It will pay you to glance over the recent volumes, catalogueing under single headings the many excellent articles on "Mail Order Lists," "Advertising Agencies," "Copywriting," etc. It will give you a complete text-book on Advertising.

The "I. C. S. Handbook for Advertisers" and Mahin's "Advertising Data Book" are convenient compendiums of advertising information.

Finally, as to the value of these courses to the students. I am not fully sure what the value is. I know I am not trying to turn out salesmen or advertising experts. I have been a salesman, but not an advertising man. Yet I find it as easy to teach Advertising as to teach Selling. This indicates to me that my hope is being fulfilled, that I am teaching them principles.

Their particular sales manager or their advertising boss will show them his individual system, his practice of selling or advertising. I cannot show them that. Nor can he give them what I have to give, because I am a teacher,—the power to interpret, to understand, to see their activity in its proper relationship to their business and to business in general, now and then even to think.

In the narrow sense this is no "practical" course. A man who has taken it can earn nothing more than if he had not; he will show no startling sign of precocity when beginning his career. But I believe that such men are the ones who are likely to be advanced when advancement is to be made. I believe they are the sort of man the sales manager will call home to be his assistant, the sort the advertising agency will some day take into the firm. From to-day's point of view they have not had a practical education; from the point of view of ten years hence perhaps they have. I believe that my men will, if they become manufacturers or merchants, be able to follow and check up the work of their advertising departments. The course is for those who want to understand Advertising, whether they are to be employed in it or not.

In view of the cry for practical education we teachers of Commercial Education need to keep in mind that a practical commercial education does not consist of cramming the students with tasteless facts and details. The poor man will get enough of those later. Let us teach him strength, grasp, breadth of vision, which teach him to interpret and classify the facts when he sees them. We have no business to show the student how to fill out order blanks, to memorize type kinds and sizes or proof-correcting terms. To my mind, the only excuse in the world for including commercial subjects in High school and University Curricula is that they are becoming real sciences, real disciplines. Now that they are such, they have the advantage over the older subjects that they are disciplines which the student can carry with him through life. But let us consider them as true disciplines. We should busy ourselves with hatching out not stuffed, but live birds.

REPORT OF COMMITTEE ON ABSENCES.

To the High School Teachers' Association of New York City:

Ladies and Gentlemen:—Your committee on Teachers' Absences has had the matter referred to them under advisement, and beg herewith to submit for your consideration the following report:

In studying the subject of teachers' absences we have carried on two lines of investigation: (1) we have gathered together detailed information in regard to the policy pursued by other American cities in this regard; (2) we have studied the conditions that exist in our own system.

I.

OTHER CITIES.

In reference to our investigation of conditions existing in other American cities, we desire to point out at the outset that we did not have in mind any desire to blindly imitate what we might find working successfully in other places; we are fully aware of the peculiarities of our own system that grow out of its immense size; and we have not sought to graft features of other systems onto our own. Our notion is that as a preliminary to intelligently studying our system, nothing could be more helpful than a knowledge of methods existing elsewhere. Accordingly, we sent out to every one of the 224 American cities, containing 25,000 or more inhabitants a questionnaire by which we endeavored to learn the systems in vogue in those cities. For detailed information of the results of our inquiries we refer you to the various appendices to this report; the summaries of the tabulation of the various reports are as follows:

A.

PAYMENT OF SALARIES.

Cities of 25,000 or more	224
Reporting this item	179
Twelve payments annually	19
Eleven payments annually	7
Ten payments annually	135
Nine payments annually	20
Eight payments annually	1
Semi-monthly payments	8
Weekly payments	6
Optional with teachers	12

(See Appendix A)

B.

DEDUCTIONS FOR ABSENCES DUE TO ILLNESS.

Cities of 25,000 or more	224
Reporting this item	192
No deductions	3
Some allowance with full pay	70
Deduction of ¼ pay	2
Deduction of 3/10 pay	1
Deduction of ½ pay	32
Deduction of 2/3 pay	6
Deduction of ¾ pay	5
Deduction of 80% pay	3
Deduction of $1 to $3 per day	5
Deduction for one day	1
Deductions for all day	21
Deduction of substitute's pay	37
High and elementary schools treated differently	2
Men and women treated differently	1
Allowed absences cumulative	2
Unclassified	9

Full pay allowed:

½ day allowed	2
2 days allowed	1
3 days allowed	9
4 days allowed	1
5 days allowed	14
1 day per month	1
10 days allowed	24
12 days allowed	1
15 days allowed	5
2 days per month	2
20 days allowed	5
3 days per month	1
30 days allowed	2
40 days allowed	1
95 days allowed	1
	70

(See Appendix B)

C.

ABSENCES FOR REASONS OTHER THAN ILLNESS.

Cities of 25,000 or more	224
Reporting this item	191
Pay allowed for illness alone	42
Full pay for death in family	100
Full pay for illness in family	14
Deduction for death in family	11
Allowance for family illness	16
Other than personal illness treated alike	8
Other than personal illness or death treated alike	1
Quarantine	18
Court attendance	5
Visiting schools	52
Teachers' meetings	19
Special permission	14
For study or travel	2
Tardiness counted as absences	2
Provision against "soldiering"	2
Attendance at weddings	2
Study or health; 1 year no pay	1
"Sabbatical year"; ½ pay	1
Unclassified	8

(See Appendix C)

In Appendix D will found some information as to miscellaneous systems, those of the state of new corporations, National government, the City of New York, and private corporations.

To the various city superintendents of schools, officials of State and city governments, and officials of corporations who have so kindly furnished to the committee information we desire to extend our thanks, and an expression of our appreciation of their kindness.

II.

THE CITY OF NEW YORK.

We have had brought to our attention documentary proof that for a long time the city has suffered from the dishonest practices of some of the teachers; its generosity has been abused in a manner little short of scandalous. We endeavored to find a remedy for these abuses. It is, however, a relief to learn from the responsible financial officers of the Board of Education that, through the co-operation of the Board of Superintendents and the Auditor, these delinquencies have been uncovered. punished and eliminated. The evils and injustice suffered by the city have ceased to exist. That simplifies the task of your committee. We have to deal only with the teachers and their side of the problem.

The rules that at present govern absences in our system are found in section 44 of the Manual of the Board of Education of the City of New York for 1911, pp. 54-57. Briefly summarized, they are as follows:

1. Without loss of pay to visit schools, three days.

2. Without express permission, no absence on account of legislation.

3. Absence without pay allowable with approval of the Board of Superintendents.

4. Absence with pay:
   - (a) For serious personal illness.
   - (b) For death in the immediate family, three days.
   - (c) For compliance with the requirements of a court; if it concerns the administration of the schools, full pay; otherwise, half pay.
   - (d) Because of quarantine: 10 days full pay, then half pay.

5. No refund for absence of more than ninety-five days in any school year.

6. For illness:
   First day, no refund.
   Second day, ¼ pay.
   Third day, ¾ of a day's pay.
   Fourth day, 1½ days' pay.
   Full pay for 5 to 95 days.

7. Absence without pay for one year for study or health.

8. Extraordinary delays in transportation: lateness may be excused by vote of the Board of Superintendents.

Let us take up these items seriatim:

As to (1):—We learn from the facts gleaned from our questionnaire that these fifty-two cities in the United States that allow the privilege of visiting schools with pay; of these in twenty no specific number of days is mentioned; in nine cities one day is so allowed, twenty-one cities two days are allowed, and in one city five days are allowed; New York allows three days. We have no suggestion to make for a change in this particular.

As to (2):—We have no suggestion to make for a change in this.

As to (3):—We have no suggestion to make for a change in this.

As to (4a) and to (6):—These relate to allowed absence for personal illness. From our questionaire we learn that there are in the United States seventy cities that allow full pay for personal illness; of these two grant it for a half day, one for two days, nine for three days, one for 4 days, fourteen for five days a month, one for one day per month, twenty-four for ten days, one for twelve days, five for fifteen days, two for two days per month, five for fifteen days, two for two days per month, five for twenty days, one for three days per month, two for thirty days, one for forty days and one, New York, for ninety-five days. Such being the case, we cannot but express our appreciation of the generosity of the city in this particular. As to the arrangements that obtain with us in reference to the five days, we should feel like asking for a slight modification were it not that in our system the pension fund has in practice become inextricably bound up with the deductions for absence during those periods. Any suggestion for a change in these respects would fall on deaf ears in the Board of Education; accordingly we do no advise any suggestion along these lines.

As to (4b):—We suggest that the provision in regard to allowed absence for death in the family be made slightly more specific, and that the three days be allowed for the death of any relative living in the immediate family, or of a grandparent, parent, husband, wife, children, brother or sister.

As to (4c):—We suggest that the present provision as to allowed absence for compliance with the requirements of a court be made a little broader, so as to read for compulsory attendance at court in consequence of a subpoena, and that the full pay be allowed for two days.

As to (4d):—In as much as we see no reason for limiting the allowed number of days to ten, we suggest that for purposes of quarantine that full pay be allowed for the full time that quarantine is established. Of the eighteen American cities that make any provision for quarantine, eleven grant it for the full time.

As to (7):—To the allowed absence without pay for study or health, we should add "or travel." It seems to us that if any teachers are willing to travel, and forego their pay, that the advantages to their work that will result from the added culture and enthusiasm will be such that they should go with the full consent of the Board of Education.

As to (8):—We have no suggestions to make in regard to this.

In addition to the allowed causes for absence, we wish to make two suggestions:

1. Many cases have come to our notice that could not possibly be included in any list that could be drawn up; life is so unexpected in its realities that it seems to us that somewhere there should be lodged discretionary power to act in what in the report of the Superintendent of Schools of Waltham, Mass., is called emergency cases. By this he means any cause equally compelling with illness. At present there is no discretionary power lodged anywhere in our system, and cases of severe injustice have arisen in consequence; we therefore suggest as an additional case for full pay "emergency" cases favorably reported on by the District Superintendent, and also by the Board of Superintendents:

2. We desire to call your attention to the fact three cities make provision for allowed absence with partial pay for study and travel, viz: Cambridge, Gloucester and Boston, Mass. Cambridge allows one-third pay after ten years of service, Gloucester allows full pay less the pay of a substitute, and Boston grants a "Sabbatical year" on half pay. We are indebted to William T. Keough, Esq., Business Agent for the School Committee of the City of Boston for full particulars of the system as it is in vogue in that city. This information is found in section 317, paragraphs 1, 2, 3 and 4, and paragraph 2 of section 344 of the Rules of the School Committee and Regulations of the Public Schools of the City of Boston (School Document No. 11, 1910, Boston Public Schools).

"Section 317. 1. Applications for leave of absence to study and travel shall be for a period not exceeding one year, shall state the definite purpose for which such leave of absence is desired, and, if recommended by the superintendent, shall be submitted by him to the Board for approval.

"2. A member of the supervising staff or teacher receiving leave of absence to study and travel must have completed seven years of service in the public school of the City of Boston, part of which may be in the parental school. He may be granted such leave of absence more than once, but not to exceed one year in any eight consecutive years.

"3. The teacher shall make to the superintendent at such times and in such form as the latter may specify, reports as to the manner in which the leave of absence is employed; and for failure on the part of the teacher to comply with any part of this section, or to pursue in a satisfactory manned the purpose for which leave of absence was granted such leave may be terminated at any time.

"4. The teacher shall file with the Secretary of the Board an agreement in writing, binding the teacher to remain in the service of the Board for three years after the expiration of such leave of absence, or, in case of resignation within said three years, to refund to the Board such proportion of the amount paid him for the time included in the leave of absence as the unexpired portion of said three years may bear to the entire three years. The provisions of this agreement shall not apply to resignation on account of ill health, with the consent of the Board, not to resignation at the request of the Board."

"Section 344. 2 The salaries of members of the supervising force, teachers, etc., absent from duty on leave granted by the Booard, shall be subject to a deduction for each day's absence equal to one four-hundredth part of the annual salary of the absentee——" As the pay of teachers in Boston is made in ten monthly installments, each day of school is paid for at the rate of 1/200 of the annual salary; hence as this deduction is at the rate of 1/400, the teacher receives one-half pay for the year. In reply to an inquiry as to how generally the Boston teachers avail themselves of this opportunity, Mr. Keough informs us that in 1906-7 there were twenty; in 1907-8, thirty-four; in 1908-9, twenty-nine; in 1909-10, thirtyone; in 1910-11, twenty-four; in 1911-12 to date, March 19, there were fifteen.

We recommend that the Boston plan be put in force here. The cost to the city would be negligible as the difference between a substitute's pay and half pay for a teacher is small.

We have made six constructive suggestions: (1) allowed absence for death in the family is made more specific; (2) we would allow full pay for attendance at coure in response to a subpoena for two days in all circumstances; (3) to the allowed absences without pay for study or health, we would add "or travel"; (4) we would allow full pay for the entire time that quarantine is established; (5) we would give discretionary power to the Board of Superintendents to grant pay in "emergency" cases; and we urge the adoption of the plan of a Sabbatical year for purposes of study and travel on half pay. These changes can be instituted without any appreciable expense to the city, and they will, we are confident, serve to improve the efficiency of the teaching staff of the city schools.

All of which is respectfully submitted.

CHARLES R. FAY,
Chairman, Erasmus Hall High School.
W. R. LASHER,
Erasmus Hall High School.
J. HERBERT LOW,
Manual Training High School.
F. H. MILLER,
Flushing High School.

New York, N. Y., April 16, 1912.

APPENDIX A.

PAYMENT OF SALARIES.

Cities of 25,000 or more	224
Reporting this item	179
Twelve payments annually	19
Eleven payments annually	8
Ten payments annually	134
Nine payments annuallly	20
Eight payments annually	1
Semi-mnthly payments	8
Weekly payments	6
Optional with teachers	11

Twelve Payments Annually.

Augusta, Ga.; Baltimore, Md.; Bayonne, N. J.; Denver, Col.; Hoboken, N. J.; Jersey City, N. J.; Los Angeles, Cal.; Memphis, Tenn.; Mobile, Ala.; Nashville, Tenn.; Oakland, Cal.; Passaic, N. J.; San Francisco, Cal.; San Jose, Cal.; Tacoma, Wash.; West Hoboken, N. J.; Yonkers, N. Y.; Watertown, N. Y.; San Diego, Cal....................19

Eleven Payments Annually.

Boston, Mass.; Cambridge, Mass.; Kalamazoo, Mich.; Milwaukee, Wis.; Paterson, N. J.; Seattle, Wash.; Superior, Wis.; New York, N. Y..........8

Ten Payments Annually.

Albany, N. Y.; Atlantic City, N. J.; Bay City, Mich.; Binghamton, N. Y.; Bridgeport, Conn.; Brockton, Mass.; Buffalo, N. Y.; Canton, O.; Chattanooga, Tenn.; Chelsea, Mass.; Chester, Pa.; Chicago, Ill.; Cincinnati, O.; Cleveland, O.; Columbus, O.; Council Bluffs, Ia.; Covington, Ky.; Davenport, Ia.; Dayton, O.; Des Moines, Ia.; Detroit, Mich.; Dubuque, Ia.; Duluth, Minn.; Elizabeth, N. J.; Elmira, N. Y.; Erie, Pa.; Evansville, Ill.; Fitchburg, Mass.; Fort Wayne, Ind.; Gloucester, Mass.; Grand Rapids, Mich.; Hamilton, O.; Harrisburg, Pa.; Indianapolis, Ind.; Jackson, Mich.; Joliet, Ill.; Jacksonville, Fla.; Kansas City, Mo.; Knoxville, Tenn.; LaCrosse, Wis.; Lancaster, Pa.; Lexington, Ky.; Lincoln, Neb.; Louisville, Ky.; Lowell, Mass.; Lynn, Mass.; Madison, Wis.; Malden, Mass.; Manchester, N. H.; Meriden, Conn.; Minneapolis, Minn.; Mobile, Ala.; Newark, N. J.; New Bedford, Mass.; New

Britain, Conn.; New Haven, Conn.; New Orleans, La.; Newton, Mass.; Niagara Falls, N. Y.; Norfolk, Va.; Oklahoma City, Okla.; Omaha, Neb.; Pawtucket, R. I.; Perth Amboy, N. J.; Philadelphia, Pa.; Pittsburgh and Alleghany, Pa.; Portland, Me.; Portland, Ore.; Providence, Rd.; Pueblo, Col.; Quincy, Mass.; Racine, Wis.; Rockford, Ill.; Rochester, N. Y.; Rutland, Vt.; Saginaw, Mich.; St. Joseph, Mo.; St. Paul, Minn.; Schenectady, N. Y.; Scranton, Pa.; Sioux City, Ia.; Somerville, Mass.; South Bend, Ind.; Spokane, Wash.; Springfield, Ill.; Springfield, Mass.; Syracuse, N. Y.; Taunton, Mass.; Terre Haute, Ind.; Topeka, Kan.; Trenton, N. J.; Troy, N. Y.; Utica, N. Y.; Waltham, Mass.; Washington, D. C.; Waterbury, Conn.; Wheeling, W. V.; Wilkes-Barre, Pa.; Wilmington, Del.; Woonsocket, R. I.; Worcester, Mass.; Youngstown, O.; Berkley, Cal.; Brookline, Mass.; Chicopee, Mass.; Clinton, Ia.; Colorado Springs, Col.; Danville, Ill.; Decatur, Ill.; Easton, Pa.; East Orange, N. J.; Elgin, Ill.; Everett, Mass.; Flint, Mich.; Green Bay, Wis.; Kingston, N. Y.; Lansing, Mich.; Lima, O.; Loraine, O.; Mt. Vernon, N. Y.; Newport, R. I.; Norristown, Pa.; Ogden, Utah; Orange, N. J.; Portsmouth, Va.; Poughkeepsie, N. Y.; Sheboygan, Wis.; South Omaha, Neb.; Stamford, Conn.; Warwick, R. I.; Watertown, N. Y.; Zanesville, O.; Akron, O......134

Nine Payments Annually

Altoona, Pa.; Cedar Rapids, Ia.; Charleston, S. C.; Dallas, Tex.; Houston, Tex.; Huntington, W. V.; Johnstown, Pa.; Kansas City, Kan.; Little Rock, Ark.; Mongomery, Ala.; Newcastle, Pa.; Pasadena, Cal.; Savannah, Ga.; Shenandoah, Pa.; Wichita, Kan.; Williamsport, Pa.; Waterloo, Ia.; York, Pa.; Waco, Tex.; Muskogee, Okla..20

Eight Payments Annually.

St. Louis, Mo. 1

Semi-Monthly Payments.

Albany, N. Y.; Brockton, Mass.; Buffalo, N. Y.; New Bedford, Mass.; Springfield, O.; Waterbury, Conn.; Woonsocket, R. I.; Pawtucket, R. I....8

Weekly Payments.

Fall River, Mass.; Gloucester, Mass.; Lawrence Mass.; Lynn, Mass.; Worcester, Mass.; Pittsfield, Mass. 6

OPTIONAL WITH TEACHERS.

Ten or Twelve Payments.

Mobile, Ala.; Watertown, N. Y.—2.

Ten Payments or Semi-Monthly Payments.

Albany, N. Y.; Brockton, Mass.; Buffalo, N. Y.; Gloucester, Mass, New Bedford, Mass.; Pawtucket, R. I.; Waterbury, Conn, Woonsocket, R. I.—8.

Ten Payments or Weekly Payments.

Worcester, Mass.—1.

Total 11

CITIES EMPLOYING 1,000 OR MORE TEACHERS.

Ten Payments Annually.

Buffalo, N. Y.; Chicago, Ill.; Cincinnati, O.; Cleveland, O.; Detroit, Mich.; Kansas City, M.; Newark, N. J.; New Orleans, La.; Philadelphia, Pa.; Pittsburgh, Pa.; Washingtn, D. C. 11

Eleven Payments Annually.

Boston, Mass.; Milwaukee, Wis.; New York, N. Y.......................3

Twelve Payments Annually.

Baltimore, Md.; Denver, Col.; Los Angeles, Cal.; San Francisco, Cal...4

APPENDIX B.

DEDUCTIONS FOR ABSENCES DUE TO ILLNESS.

Cities f 25,000 or more	224
Reporting this item	192
No deductions	3
Some allowance with full pay	70
Deduction of ¼ pay	2
Deduction of 3/10 pay	1
Deductin of ½ pay	32
Deduction of 2/3 pay	6
Deduction of ¾ pay	5
Deduction of 80% pay	3
Deduction $1 to $3 per day	5
Deduction of all pay	22
Deduction of substitute's pay	37
High and Elementary Schools treated differently	2
Men and women treated differently	1
Allowed absences cumulative	2
Unclassified	5

Full pay allowed:

½ day	2	
2 days	1	
3 days	9	
4 days	1	
5 days	14	
1 day per month	1	
10 days	24	
12 days	1	
15 days	5	
2 days a month	2	
20 days	5	
3 days a month	1	
30 days	2	
40 days	1	
85 days	1	
Total		70

No Deductions.

West Hoboken, N. J.; Wichita, Kan.; Muskogee, Okla.—3.

FULL PAY ALLOWED.

Half Day.

Chattanooga, Tenn.; Meriden, Conn. (then substitute's pay deducted).—2.

Two Days.

Duluth, Minn. (then ½ for 2 months)—1.

Three Days.

Atlantic City, N. J. (then ½ for 20 days); Binghamton, N. Y. (3 consecutive; 5 in year); Boston, Mass. (for masters); Cambridge, Mass. (then deduct 2/3 for 12 weeks); Elgin, Ill.; Lynn, Mass. (then deduct ¾ for 5 weeks); New Castle, Pa.; Pittsfield, Mass. (1 per term); South Bend, Ind. (then ¾ for 7 days)—9.

Four Days.

Warwick, R. I. (1 each term of 10 weeks)—1.

Five Days.

Canton, O.; Denver, Col. (cumulative; then deduct substitute's pay for 15 days); Houston, Tex. (then ½ for 10 days); Kansas City, Kan. (then "part" for 15 days); Lincoln, Neb. (15 half days additional); Mobile, Ala. (if no substitute is employed; sub gets ¾ salary for 1 month, then all); Niagara Falls, N. Y. (then ½ for 35 days); Pawtucket, R. I.; Quincy, Mass. (then ½ second 5 days); Rockford, Ill. (and 5 half days); Springfield, Mass. (3 consecutive, 5 in year); Chicopee, Mass. (deduct ½ second 5, ¾ third 5); Danville, Ill.; South Omaha, Neb.—14.

One Per Month.

Brockton, Mass. (then deduct substitute's pay ½ year)—1.

Ten Days.

Akron, O.; Cleveland, O.; Columbus, O. (5 days each half year, then deduct sub. pay); Grand Rapids, Mich.; Joplin, Mo.; Madison, Wis.; Malden, Mass.; New Orleans, La.; Newton, Mss. (3 a month, then deduct sub. pay); Omaha, Neb.; Perth Amboy, N. J.; Pueblo, Col.; Racine, Wis. (5 in each half year, then deduct ¾ next 10); Schenectady, N. Y. (5 each semestre, special action then); Superior, Wis.; Taunton, Mass. (5 each semestre); Utica, N. Y.; Waltham, Mass. (3 consecutive a month, 10 per year); Colorado Springs, Col. (cumulaitve); Hazelton, Pa.; Ogden, Utah; Orange, N. J. (then sub. pay deducted for 30 days); Waco, Tex.; St. Joseph, Mo. (then deduct ½ for 30 days).—24.

Twelve Days.

Mt. Vernon, N. Y. (2 per month).—1.

Fifteen Days.

Bayonne, N. J. (then ½ deducted for 45 days); East St. Louis, Ill.; Hoboken, N. J. (then deduct sub. pay for 1 month); Covington, Ky.; Somerville, Mass. (5 in 1 month).—5.

Two Days Per Mnth.

Elmira, N. Y.; Oklahoma, Okla. (then deduct ½ for 20 days).—2.

Twenty Days.

Kansas City, Mo.; Lexington, Ky. (10 each semestre); Wilmington, Del. (then deduct ¾ the rest of the year); Yonkers, N. Y.; Clinton, Ia.—5.

Three Days Per Month.

Newport, R. I. (not continuous with each other, then deduct 2/3 for 4 weeks).—1.

Thirty days.

Joliet, Ill.; Newark, N. J. (then sub. pay).—2.

Forty Days.

East Orange, N. J.—1.

Ninety-five Days.

New York City.—1.

Total 70

Deduction of Quarter Pay.

Lacrosse, Wis.; Quincy, Ill. (20 days) 2

Deduction of Three-tenths Pay.

Knoxville, Tenn. 1

DEDUCTION OF HALF PAY.

For Five Days.

Jackson, Mich. (¼ second week); Green Bay, Wis.—2.

For Seven Days.

Dubuque, Ia.—1.

For Ten Days.

Cedar Rapids, Ia.; Chester, Pa. (¾ second week); Rutland, Vt.; Spokane, Wash.; Syracuse, N. Y.; Williamsport, Pa.; Davenport, Ia.; Harrisburg, Pa.—8.

For Fifteen Days.

Dallas, Tex.; Stamford, Conn. (then ¾ for 15 days).—2.

For Twenty Days.

Atlanta, Ga. (10 in one month, 20 in a year); Des Moines, Ia.; Little Rock, Ark.; Erie, Pa.; Kalamazoo, Mich.; Lowell, Mass.; Milwaukee, Wis.; Minneapolis, Minn.; New Haven, Conn.; St. Paul, Minn.; Sacramento, Cal.; Seattle, Wash.; Tacoma, Wash.; Reading, Pa.—14.

For Thirty Days.

Charleston, S. C.; Montgomery, Ala.—2.

For Forty Days.

Brookline, Mass.—2.

For Five Weeks.

St. Louis, Mo. (then special arrangements).—1.

For Sixty-five Days.

Baltimore, Md.—1.

Total 32

Deduction of two-thirds Pay.

Everett, Mass. (1 month); Evansville, Ind. (until $50.00 has been paid sick teacher); Hamilton, O. (12 weeks); Passaic, N. J. (20 days); Providence, R. I. (then special action); Woonsocket, R. I. (1 week)...........6

Deduction of Three-quarter Pay.

Bridgeport, Conn. (3 weeks); Louisville, Ky.; Lansing, Mich. (2 weeks); Lewiston, Me. (3 weeks); San Diego, Cal....................................5

Deduction of Eighty Per cent. Pay.

Salem, Mass. (2 months); Waterloo, Ia.; Wheeling, W. Va. (as long as ill) 3

Deductions $1 to $3.00 Per Day.

Jersey City, N. J. ($1 per day for 10 days, ½ for 90 days; after 10 years' service, same for the rest of the year); Chicago, Ill. (H. S. $2, E. S. $1.50 for 10 days; sub. for 10 weeks); Manchester, N. H. ($1.50 to $2.00); Kingston, N. Y. ($2.00); Portland, Me. ($3.00 for 90 days)......................5

Deduction of All Pay.

Altoona, Pa.; Bay City, Mich.; Berkley, Cal.; Council Bluffs, Ia.; Easton, Pa.; Fall River, Mass. (revising rules); Jacksonville, Fla.; Johnstown, Pa.; Indianapolis, Ind. (sick allowance not in excess of $50 to $100); Lima, O.; Oakland, Cal.; Pittsburgh, Pa.; Poughkeepsie, Pa.; Rochester, N. Y.; San Francisco, Cal.; San Jose, Ca.; Scranton, Pa.; Sioux City, Ia.; Washington, D. C.; Youngstown, O.; Shenandoah, Pa.................................22

Deduction of Substitute's Pay.

Albany, N. Y.; Augusta, Ga.; Buffalo, N. Y.; Chelsea, Mass. (for 1 month); Cincinnati, O. (for 40 days); Dayton, O.; Detroit, Mich. (20 days); Elizabeth, N. J. (for 2 months); Fitchburg, Mass. (for 20 days); Gloucester, Mass.; Lancaster, Pa.; Lawrence, Mass. (1 week); Nashville, Tenn.; New Bedford, Mass. (for 4 weeks); Norfolk, Va. (½ to substitute); Pasadena, Cal.; Paterson, N. J. (10 days); Philadelphia, Pa. (1/400 for each day); Portland, Ore.; Saginaw, Mich. (special arrangements in meritorious cases); Springfield, O. (for 2 months); Terre Haute, Ind.; Topeka, Kan.; Troy, N. Y.; Waterbury, Conn. (first and fourth, 5 days; no deduction for second and third 5 days); Wilkes-Barre, Pa.; York, Pa.; Alleghany, Pa. (minimum for 5 days; worthy cases special action); Charlotte, N. C. (½ sub. pay); Flint, Mich.; Huntington, W. B. (2/3 given to sub.); Nashua, N. H.; Loraine, O. (minimum for sub.); Norristown, Pa. (2/3 for sub.); Portsmouth, Va.; Sheboygan, Wis.; Zanesville, O. (sub. pay for 40 days) 37

High Schools and Elementary Schools Treated Differently.

Fort Wayne, Ind. (no deductin in high school for 1 month; none in E. S. for 3 days); Trenton, N. J. (no deduction in H. S.; for sub. in E. S. for 35 days) 2

Men and Women Treated Differently.

Boston, Mass. (no deduction for masters for 3 days; no allowance to women) 1

Allowed Absence Cumulative.

Colorado Springs, Col. (10 days in 1911-19, 5 days thereafter, and absences are cumulative); Denver, Col. (5 days each, and absences are cumulative) 2

Unclassified.

Springfield, Ill. (no rule; each case by itself); Memphis, Tenn. (1/60 deducted if physician's certificate is presented, otherwise 1/30); New Britain, Conn. (no deduction for "short," only for "protracted" periods); Watertown, N. Y. (deductions made in excess of an "occasional" day, then for sub. pay); Worcester, Mass. (1-9 years' service, deduct ½ first, ¾ for 3 weeks, 3 to 9 years ½ for 4 weeks, 20-29 years' service ½ for 5 weeks, 3 to 9 years ¼ first week, ½ for 5 weeks) 5

APPENDIX C.

ABSENCES FOR REASONS OTHER THAN PERSONAL ILLNESS.

Total number of cities	224
Number reporting this item	191
Pay allowed for no other cause	42
Full pay fr death in family	100
Full pay for illness in family	14
Deductin for death in family	11
Allowance for family illness	16
Other than personal illness treated alike	8
Other than personal illness or death treated alike	1
Quarantine	18
Court attendance	5
Visiting schools	52
Teachers' meetings, etc.	19
Special permission granted	14
For study or travel (pay)	2
"Sabbatical year"	1
Tardiness counted as absence	2
Provisions against "soldiering"	2
Attendance at weddings	2
No pay; study or health; 1 year	1
Unclassified	7

Pay Allowed For No Other Cause.

Akron, O.; Atlantic City, N. J.; Augusta, Ga.; Bay City, Mich.; Butte, Mon.; Chattanooga, Tenn.; Charlotte, N. C.; Chicopee, Mass.; Council Bluffs, Ia.; Elizabeth, N. J.; Jacksonville, Fla.; Johnstown, Pa.; Lansing, Mich.; Little Rock, Ark.; Lima, O.; Loraine, O. (revising); Madison, Wis.; Mobile, Ala.; Nashua, N. H.; New Britain, Conn.; Norristown, Pa.; Oakland, Cal.; Pasadena, Cal.; Pittsburgh, Pa. (not even for illness); Quincy, Ill.; San Francisco, Cal. (not then); Savannah, Ga.; Scranton, Pa.; Sioux City, Ia. (not then); Spokane, Wash.; Sheboygan, Wis.; Shenandoah, Pa.; Springfield, O.; Tacoma, Wash.; Terre Haute, Ind.; Warwick, R. I.; Washington, D. C. (not then); Waterloo, Ia.; West Hoboken, N. J.; Wichita, Kan.; York, Pa.; Zanesville, O. 42

Full Pay Caused by Death in Family—Full Pay for One Day.

Indianapolis, Ind.; Kansas City, Mo. (not close relative); Oklahoma City, Okla.; Taunton, Mass.—4.

Full Pay for Two Days.

Altoona, Pa.; Charleston, S. C.; Decatur, Ill.; Duluth, Minn.; Kalamazoo, Mich.; Memphis, Tenn.; St. Louis, Mo.; Seattle, Wash.—8.

Full Pay for Two Days—Death of a Relative.

Bayonne, N. J.—1.

Full Pay for Three Days—Death in Family.

Atlanta, Ga.; Baltimore, Md.; Canton, O.; Cedar Rapids, Ia.; Cleveland, O.; Davenport, Ia.; Dayton, O.; Des Moines, Ia.; Easton, Pa.; East St. Louis, Ill.; Elgin, Ill.; Elmira, N. Y.; Hazelton, Pa.; Hoboken, N. J.; Kansas City, Mo.; Louisville, Ky.; Lynn, Mass.; Malden, Mass.; Milwaukee, Wis.; Minneapolis, Minn.; Newport, R. I. (per month); Portland, Ore.; Orange, N. J.; St. Paul, Minn.; Somerville, Mass.; South Bend, Ind.; Springfield, Mass.; Waltham, Mass.; New York, N. Y.—29.

Full Pay for Four Days—Death in Immediate Family.

Bridgeport, Conn.; Brookline, Mass.; Everett, Mass.; Jersey City, N. J.; Meriden, Conn.; Newark, N. J.; New Haven, Conn.; Passaic, N. J.; Paterson, N. J.; Philadelphia, Pa.; Salem, Mass.; Stamford, Conn.; Worcester, Mass.; Grand Rapids, Mich.—14.

Full Pay for Five Days—Death in Immediate Family.

Bayonne, N. J.; Boston, Mass.; Chester, Pa.; Colorado Springs, Col. (cumulative); Detroit, Mich.; Houston, Tex. (and 10 days on half pay); Danville, Ill.; East Orange, N. J. (or more); Kingston, N. Y.; Niagara Falls, N. Y.; Pawtucket, R. I. (½ secnd week); Racine, Wis. (¼ next 10 day); Rockford, Ill.; South Omaha, Neb. (alternating with sick leave); Topeka, Kan.; Trenton, N. J.; Utica, N. Y.—17.

Full Pay for No Specified Time—Death in Immediate Family.

Clinton, Ia.; Lawrence, Mass.; Lincoln, Neb.; New Castle, Pa.; Newton, Mass.; Portland, Me.; Rutland, Vt.; Schenectady, N. Y.; Poughkeepsia, N. Y.; New Orleans, La.; Woonsocket, R. I.; Hamilton, O.—12.

Full Pay for One Day—Death of Near Relative.

Joplin, Mo.; New Orleans, La.; Paterson, N. J.; Perth Amboy, N. J.; Portland, Ore. (1 day).—5.

Full Pay—Death of a Distant Relative.

St. Louis, Mo.—1.

Full Pay for Any Funeral a Teacher Wishes to Attend.

Newton, Mass.; Worcester, Mass.—2.

Full Pay to Attend a Funeral of a Teacher.

Milwaukee, Wis.—1.

Full Pay Ten Days—Death in Family or of a Near Relative.

Joplin, Mo.—1.

Full Pay to Attend a Funeral.

San Jose, Cal. (1 day); Ogden, Utah.—2.

Total full pay for absence due to death 100

DEDUCTIONS FOR ABSENCE DUE TO DEATH.

Substitute's Pay Deducted for Death in Family.

Lancaster, Pa.; Nashville, Tenn.; New Bedford, Mass.; Quincy, Mass.—4.

Substitute's Pay Deducted for Death in Family, Two Days.

Brockton, Mass.—1.

Deduct Half for Three Days—Death in Immediate Family.

Harrisburg, Pa.; Williamsport, Pa.—2.

Deduct Half for Five Days—Death in Family.

St. Louis, Mo.; Lowell, Mass.; Reading, Pa.; Syracuse, N. Y. (10 days).—4.

Total deductions for death 11

ILLNESS IN FAMILY.

Full Pay for Illness in Family.

Clinton, Ia.; Colorado Springs, Col. (5 days, cumulative); Danville, Ill. (5 days); East Orange, N. J. (1 week); Elgin, Ill. (3 days); Houston, Tex. (5 days); Newport, R. I.; Rockford, Ill. (5 half days); Pueblo, Col. (10 days, immediate family); Schenectady, N. Y.; Waltham, Mass.—11.

Partial Pay for Illness in Family.

Binghamton, N. Y.; Lacrosse, Wis. (¼ pay deducted); Lowell, Mass.

(½ pay deducted for 5 days); Syracuse N. Y. (½ for 5 days); Waterbury, Conn. (substitute's pay deducted).—5.

Total allowance for illness in family 16

ABSENCES FOR CAUSES OTHER THAN PERSONAL ILLNESS TREATED ALIKE.

$1.50 Deducted for Five Days.

Manchester, N. H.—1.

Substitute's Pay Deducted.

Albany, N. Y.; Binghamton, N. Y. ("partial pay"); Brockton, N. Y.; Fitchburg, Mass. (less than 5 days); Flint, Mich.; Troy, N. Y.—6.

Deduct Two-thirds Salary for Ten Days.

Providence, R. I.—1.

Total 8

ABSENCES DUE TO OTHER CAUSES THAN PERSONAL ILLNESS OR DEATH TREATED ALIKE.

Deduct Substitute's Pay.

Canton, O. 1

QUARANTINE.

Full Pay Allowed.

Cleveland, O.; Hoboken, N. J.; Jersey City, N. J.; Newark, N. J.; Kingston, N. Y. (contagious contracted at school); New Bedford, Mass; Paterson, N. J.; Perth Amboy, N. J.; Portland, Me.; St. Louis, Mo. (head of family, others half pay); Yonkers, N. Y.—11.

Full Pay for Two Weeks.

Chicago, Ill.; New York, N. Y. (then ½).—2.

Full Pay for One Week.

Utica, N. Y.—1.

Full Pay for Two Days.

Duluth, Minn.—1.

Full Pay for Three Days.

Cambridge, Mass.—1.

Half Pay for Twenty Days.

Milwaukee, Wis. (longer time for old teachers); St. Paul, Minn.—2.

Total 18

COURT ATTENDANCE.

Full Pay Allowed.

Chicago, Ill. (certain cases); Jersey City, N. J.; Louisville, Ky.; Portland, Me.; New York, N. Y. (certain cases).—5.

VISITING SCHOOLS.

No Specific Number of Days Named.

Buffalo, N. Y. ("occasionally"); Berkeley, Cal.; Chelsea, Mass. (special action); Cleveland, O.; Covington, Ky.; Dayton, O.; East Orange, N. J.; Erie, Pa.; Fort Wayne, Ind.; Hazelton, Pa.; Hoboken, N. J.; Huntington, W. Va.; Lexington, Ky.; Newark, N. J.; Norfolk, Va.; Omaha, Neb.; Pittsburgh, Pa.; San Diego, Cal.; Waco, Tex.; Pittsfield, Mass.—20.

One Day for Visiting Schools.

Davenport, Ia.; Hamilton, O.; Minneapolis, Minn.; Oklahoma, Okla.; Portland, Me.; South Bend, Ind.; Springfield, Mass.; Superior, Wis.; Worcester, Mass.—9.

Two Days for Visiting Schools.

Boston, Mass.; Cincinnati, O.; Denver, Col.; Dubuque, Ia.; Elmira, N. Y.; Fall River, Mass.; Grand Rapids, Mich.; Houston, Tex.; Jackson, Mich.; Knoxville, Tenn.; Kingston, N. Y.; Mt. Vernon, N. Y.; Muskogee, Okla.; Orange, N. J.; Rochester, N. Y.; St. Joseph, Mo.; Springfield, Ill; Troy, N. Y.; Wheeling, W. Va.; Wilmington, Del.; Youngstown, O.—21.

Three Days for Visiting Schools.

New York, N. Y.—1.

Five Days for Visiting Schools.

Meriden, Conn.—1.

Total 52

ATTENDANCE ALLOWED AT EDUCATIONAL INSTITUTES OR TEACHERS' MEETINGS.

Boston, Mass.; Charleston, S. C. (2 days); Cleveland, O.; Davenport, Ia.; Decatur, Ill.; Dubuque, Ia.; Evansville, Ill.; Joplin, Mo.; Lancaster, Pa. (1 day); Lexington, Ky.; Montgomery, Ala.; Muskogee, Okla.; Omaha, Neb.; Springfield, Ill.; Superior, Wis. (2 days) 19

ABSENCE WITH PAY SOMETIMES GRANTED BY SPECIAL ACTION OF SUPERINTENDENT OR OTHER OFFICIALS.

Binghamton, N. Y. ("partial pay"); Buffalo, N. Y.; Cincinnati, O.; Columbus, O.; Dallas, Tex. (irregularly cases); Mt. Vernon, N. Y.; Newport, R. I.; Portland, Ore.; Saginaw, Mich.; Stamford, Conn.; Watertown, N. Y.; Wilkes-Barre, Pa.; Alleghany, Pa.; New York, N. Y. (without pay)..............14

LEAVE OF ABSENCE FOR STUDY OR TRAVEL.

Cambridge, Mass. (after 10 years' service, on 1/3 pay); Gloucester, Mass. (substitute's pay deducted) 2

"SABBATICAL YEAR."

Boston, Mass. (½ pay) 1

TARDINESS COUNTED AS ABSENCE.

Five Unexcused Absences and Tardinesses Counted as ½ Day's Absence.

Newark, N. J.; Orange, N. J. 2

PROVISIONS AGAINST "SOLDIERING."

St. Louis, Mo.; Chicago, Ill. 2

St. Louis:—"A teacher who has been absent for five weeks, or nearly five weeks, on account of illness, and who has received half pay for such time, shall not be entitled to further half pay for absence on account of illness, unless she has taught for at least five weeks consecutively, subsequent to her return from the period of absence for which half pay has already been allowed."

Chicago:—"Compensation shall cease after an absence of two weeks, and when teachers are absent nearly two weeks and then return to their schools temporarily, for the apparent purpose of avoiding the effect of two weeks' continuous absence, and immediately thereafter absent themselves again, the period from the first day of absence to that of the final return shall be treated as continuous."

ABSENCE WITH PAY ALLOWED FOR A MARRIAGE.

Newark, N. J.; Paterson, N. J. (in both cases, the marriage of a parent, brother or sister) (1 day) 2

UNCLASSIFIED.

Lewiston, Me. (bad weather); Oklahoma City, Okla. (taking required examinations); St. Louis, Mo. (accidental injury received in school); Waltham, Mass. ("emergency cases"); Cambridge, Mass. (unassigned teachers after 65); Kansas City, Kan. (deduct 1/360 for reasons other than illness, for 20 days); Reading, Pa. (absence at pleasure of the teacher, all pay forfeited)..7

APPENDIX D.

MISCELLANEOUS SYSTEMS, NATIONAL, STATE AND LOCAL.

UNITED STATES GOVERNMENT.

The action in reference to absence in the various executive departments is governed by the Act of March 15, 1898 (30 stats. 316), which authorized thirty days' annual, and thirty days' sick leave. Heads of departments must act within these limits, and accordingly, in some departments only fifteen days' sick leave is allowed. The Department of the Interior has this provision:

"48. Penalties for deception. All employees will be held to a strict accountability for statements made by them of inability to perform duty. When sick leave has been granted and subsequent developments prove that it was obtained by misrepresentation, it will be charged to leave without pay, even if the offender has annual leave still due. A second attempt to mislead or deceive official superiors, directly or indirectly, in regard to absence on account of alleged illness, will be deemed sufficient cause for dismissal."

THE STATE OF NEW YORK.

The State Water Supply Department apparently makes no deduction for illness. The Public Service Commission for the first district allows to its employees hired by the month, about a week for this purpose; if this is not taken for illness it can be added to the yearly vacation.

The State Insurance Department allows a week a year for "personal business engagements" in addition to the annual vacation of three weeks. For brief illnesses no deduction is made; for protracted illnesses, excuse is granted without pay.

The Tenement House Department allows two weeks vacation; in addition, to employees who are not absent more than one day in a quarter, an extra seven days' vacation is allowed; for every absence over the four so allowed two days is deducted from the extra seven; these are allowed for illness or any other cause.

CITY OF NEW YORK.

The Department of Correction makes no deductions for illness; the employee asks for it for vacation without pay.

The Fire Department apparently follows the same rule. It also grants absence with pay for "personal bereavement, and for important personal business."

PRIVATE CORPORATIONS.

The Commercial Cable Co. has this rule:—"Employees must furnish medical certificate from period of illness. The company's physician visits the invalid, from time to time, at the company's expense, to verify illness, and to see that employee is receiving medical attention. Full pay allowed during absence due to illness."

PUBLICATIONS OF THE H. S. T. A. OF NEW YORK CITY.

To be obtained from Agnes Carr, Secretary, Morris High School, 166th Street and Boston Road, New York City.

Year Books for 1909-1910 and 1910-1911; Arthur L. James, President; 20 cents each.

Bulletins for 1911-1912, No. 31, 5 cents; No. 32, 5 cents; No. 33, 10 cents; No. 34, 10 cents.

Partial contents are: Summary of Prof. Chas. H. Judd's address on Test of High School Efficiency, ¾ page, No. 31; Efficiency Through Pupils' Co-operation in Classroom, ½ page, No. 32; Scientific Management and High School Efficiency; an address by Harrington Emerson, Efficiency Engineer, 7 pages, No. 33.

Five-Subject Plan in High Schools, Report of Consultation Committee in Course of Study, Clarence D. Kingsley, Chairman; 2 pages, No. 33.

High School Teachers' Association of New York City.

TREASURER'S REPORT.

May 6, 1911—May 16, 1912.

RECEIPTS.

	1911	1912	
Balance	$406.98		
Ads. in Year Book	66.47		
Contribution, "Committee of 40"		4.78	
Dues from 1910-1911	74.00		
Dues to date, 1911-1912		637.00	
Total	$547.45	$641.78	$1189.23

EXPENSES.

	1911	1912	
Sections—			
Biology	$4.00		
Bookkeeping	3.00		
History	5.75		
Mathematics		1.00	
Mechanic Arts		5.00	
Committees—			
College Conference	146.00		
Student Aid	14.00		
Secondary Education		6.00	
Teachers' Absences		20.50	
School Efficiency		6.03	
Meetings—			
Janitor Service	11.50	27.00	
Board of Representatives	8.00	4.00	
October, Speaker		76.75	
December, Speaker		50.00	
Printing—			
Official Stationery		15.00	
Board of Representatives		6.00	
Circulars	2.00		
Official Bulletins	16.00	111.01	
900 Year Books	243.24		
1400 Year Book "Separates"	67.50		
Postage and Expressage—			
Official Bulletins	4.75	27.15	
Year Books	8.32		
Exhibits		3.11	
Total	$534.06	$358.55	$892.61
To Balance	13.39	283.23	296.62
			$1189.23

Respectfully submitted,

LORING B. MULLEN, Treasurer,
Girls' High School, Brooklyn.

May 16, 1912.

This is to certify that we have examined the above account of Loring B. Mullen, Treasurer of the High School Teachers' Association of New York City, and find the same to be correct.

JOSEPH J. KLEIN,
Richmond Hill High School.
H. ELIZABETH SEELMAN,
Girls' High School.
Auditing Committee.

NEW YORK CITY HIGH SCHOOLS, APRIL 30, 1912.

1, Rank; 2, Names; 3, Number of First Assistants; 4, Men Teachers; 5, Women Teachers; 6, Total Teachers; 7, Boys; 8, Girls; 9, Total Pupils; 10, Pupils per Teacher; 11, Pupils per First Assistant; 12, Teachers per First Assistant.

1	2	3	4	5	6	7	8	9	10	11	12
			Teachers.			Pupils.					
Rank.	Names.	1st Asst.	Men.	Women.	Totals.	Boys.	Girls.	Totals	Pupils per Teacher.	Pupils per 1st Asst.	T'ch'rs per 1st Asst
1	Washington Irving	7	23	134	157	—	4396	4396	28.0	628	22
2	Morris	8	53	80	133	1286	2400	3686	27.7	461	17
3	De Witt Clinton	9	104	15	119	3587	—	3587	30.1	399	13
4	Manual Training	9	72	61	133	1655	1592	3247	24.4	361	15
5	Wadleigh	7	10	115	125	—	3005	3005	24.0	429	18
6	Erasmus Hall	7	47	65	112	954	1816	2770	24.7	396	17
7	Eastern District	7	30	64	94	899	1822	2721	29.2	359	23
8	Girls	8	11	99	110	—	2588	2588	23.5	323	14
9	Commercial	9	99	—	99	2455	—	2455	24.7	273	11
10	Commerce	9	72	—	72	2327	—	2327	32.3	259	8
11	Stuyvesant	7	92	—	92	2324	—	2324	25.2	275	13
12	Boys	7	73	—	73	1816	—	1816	24.7	259	10
13	Bushwick	3	26	30	56	514	1070	1584	28.3	528	19
14	Bryant	2	10	36	46	461	574	1035	22.9	517	23
15	Curtis	6	17	22	39	425	530	955	24.5	159	7
16	Jamaica	7	19	22	41	293	617	910	22.2	130	6
17	Newtown	1	12	21	33	395	505	900	27.3	900	33
18	Richmond Hill	3	14	23	37	297	483	780	21.1	260	12
19	Bay Ridge	1	4	20	24	203	447	650	27.1	650	24
20	Flushing	5	13	16	29	186	373	559	19.3	120	6
21	Far Rockaway	1	6	9	15	106	153	259	17.3	259	15
		123	807	832	1639	20183	22371	42554	25.3	346	13.3

CONTENTS OF H. S. T. A. BULLETIN NO. 34.

OFFICIAL BULLETIN

of the High School Teachers' Association of New York City.

No. 35. SATURDAY, NOVEMBER 9, 1912

The Board of Representatives, on May 23, 1911, empowered the Executive Committee to issue a Bulletin monthly, instead of four times a year.

THE FIRST REGULAR MEETING FOR 1912-1913 will be held Saturday, November 9, 1912, at the High School of Commerce.

DEPARTMENT MEETINGS begin at 10 A. M. Programs are given below.

GENERAL MEETING begins at 11 A. M. in Auditorium. Topic: MORE EFFICIENT ORGANIZATION OF OUR HIGH SCHOOL.

MAIN ADDRESS AND ANNOUNCEMENTS OF NEW POLICY. —ASSOCIATE SUPT. EDWARD L. STEVENS.

Brief Addresses are expected from:

Dr. James Sullivan, Principal of Boys' High School on "How a Principal may increase the Efficiency of his School.

Dr. Alfred C. Bryan, High School of Commerce, President of Associaton of High School First Assstants.

Miss Elizabeth Seelman, Girls' High High School, Grade Adviser.

Miss Lina E. Gano, Wadleigh High School, President of Women's High School Teachers' Association, or her representative.

Mr. Robert H. Keener, Bushwick High School, President of Men's High School Teachers' Association.

General Discussion.

WILLIAM T. MORREY, President.

AGNES CARR, Secretary.

DEPARTMENT MEETINGS, 10 A. M.

ANCIENT LANGUAGES—Room 534, Mr. Walter E. Foster, Stuyvesant High School, Chairman.

"Caesar's Campaigns in Gaul," illustrated by 100 lantern slides taken by Mr. Frank A. Reynolds of the Stuyvesant High School.

BIOLOGY—Room 301, Dr. Henry R. Linville, Jamaica High School, Chairman.

"New Theories of Ventilation," by Prof. C. E. A. Winslow, Profssor of Biology, College of City of New York.

Recent experiments in ventilation reopen questions of great practical importance to the schools. Come and bring your principal with you.

BOOKKEEPING SECTION—Joseph J. Klein, Richmond Hill High School, Chairman.

"Standardization of Methodology, or What Teaching Methods Lead to Greatest Efficiency.

Discussion:—Dr. Joseph J. Klein, Leader.

DRAWING—Room 206, Mr. Morris Greenberg, Commerce High School, Chairman.

Election of officers.

Discussion of Report of Committee of Fifteen on Exhibit of Drawings.

HISTORY AND ECONOMICS—Room 205, Miss Antoinette Lawrence, Jamaica High School, Chairman.

"Use of the Museum in Connection with the Course in Modern History." Mr. H. W. Kent, Assistant Secretary of the Metropolitan Museum of Art.

MATHEMATICS—Room 304, Elmer Schuyler, Bay Ridge High School, Chairman.

Topic:—What Mathematical Proficiency should the High School Teachers expect of Graduates of the Elementary Schools?

By Mr. Leslie M. Locke of the Brooklyn Training School.

Elementary School Teachers welcomed.

MODERN LANGUAGES—Room 401, Miss Nannie G. Blackwell.

"Uniform Grammar Nomenclature—English, German, French, Spanish."
"What Has Been Done, What Ought to be Done in New York City."

PHYSICAL TRAINING—Room 305, Otis C. Skeele, Morris High School, Chairman for organization.

All teachers of Physical Training in our public high schools are invited to meet and to consider their special interest, and the organization of a department.

PHYSIOGRAPHY—Room 105B, Mr. Kirk W. Thompson, Jamaica High School, Chairman.

Mr. Anthony Fiala, Secretary of the Arctic Club of America, will talk on plotting positions geographically on the polar ice.

He will bring with him a sextant, an artificial horizon, and an ephemesis with which to illustrate his talk.

Elementary School Teachers wll be welcomed to this practical talk.

SHORTHAND—Room 216, Miss Harriet K. Smith, Morris High School, Chairman.

Discussion of the Preliminery Report on Shorthand Teaching by Edward J. McNamara.

The recent examination for First Assistant.

PRESIDENT'S REPORT.

INTRODUCTION.

According to Mr. Harrington Emerson, the leading efficiency engineer, the four essentials in every **plant** are: definite and clear **aims** and high ideas; **organization** to attain and maintain all the ideals; equipment for the organization and a strong **executive.**

The twelve **principles of efficiency** are:

(1) High ideals.
(2) Common sense, good judgment.
(3) Competent counsel.
(4) Discipline.
(5) Fair dealing.

The practical principles:

(6) Standard records.
(7) Planning.
(8) Standard conditions.
(9) Standardized operations.
(10) Standard instructions.
(11) Standard schedules.
(12) Efficiency reward.

THE PLANT.

This Association, in 1911-1912, enrolled 15, or 72%, of the 21 high school principals; 94, or 76% of the 123 first assistants; and 622, 42%, of the 1,495 teachers—a total of 731, or 49%, of the 1,639 high school teachers, first assistants and principals.

THE ORGANIZATION.

The 731 members are represented by about seventy-one representatives in the **Board of Representatives,** which meets on the last school Tuesday of every school month, excepting September and June, with "power to act upon all matters affecting the association."

All schools are advised to send all their representatives or substitutes duly accedited to every meeting, bringing some idea as a contribution.

The **Executive Committee** consists of the President, Vice-President, Secretary, Treasurer, and three other elected members. It has the power to "approve all appropriations of funds and shall audit and direct the payment of all bills."

Standing Committees—Teachers' interests and Secondary Education, each with nine members, including the President.

Such other Committee as may be ordered or as may be appointed by the President, who may also remove chairmen and members.

AIMS.

The President has tried:

First. To bring about as friendly relations as possible between the men and women in the high schools and between their various organizations.

Second. To devote the year's work to a practical examination of the Principles of Scientific Management and their use in increasing High School Efficiency.

COMPETENT COUNSEL.

The second aim has been carried out in the **general meetings**. The principles were enunciated and discussed by their ablest exponent, Mr. Harrington Emerson, in the December 9 meeting. (His address is reprinted in this Bulletin.)

Prof. Hanus in his address, published in this Bulletin, has furnished us an address to be thoroughly "chewed and digested." It combines **common sense and good judgment**, in a discussion of the **definite and clear aims** of education. This address clarifies the situation.

The addresses on "Superior Merit," by Superintendent, Examiner and Principals, discuss the ideals of the teacher rather than of the aims of the organization. There are embodied in these speeches, **"high ideals," common sense and good judgment** and **competent counsel**, with an undercurrent of thought about **fair dealing** and **efficiency reward.**

Prof. Judd's address furnished **competent counsel** on the tests of efficient teaching.

Superintendent William H. Maxwell, and all school officials, have been most obliging. Superintendent Edward L. Stevens has been particularly suggestive and helpful. Examiner George J. Smith kindly consented to discuss for the Association the porcupine question of "Superior Merit."

All High School **Principals** were invited to make suggestions, especially with reference to persons well qualified to do good committee work. Their prompt and hearty participation in the discussion of "Superior Merit" made that meeting the most interesting and best attended meeting in the history of the Association.

The **first assistants** have the higher percentage of membership, and about 25% of them took active part in the committee or department work of the Association.

Competent counsel for the teacher was furnished in the general meeting to discuss "Superior Merit." The fundamental problem was that of **fair dealing** and **efficiency reward**, but the discussion of **ideals, common sense** and good judgment.

Competent counsel for the pupil has been, in so far as this Association is concerned, in the hands of Mr. Eli W. Weaver and his committee, The Students' Aid Committee.

PLANNING.

The most important piece of constructive work done by the Association was that of the Consultation Committee of Sixty, Mr. Clarenc D. Kingsley, Chairman. This committee, formed at the suggestion of the School Inquiry Committee, submitted recommendations: (1) Great flexibility; (2) the introduction into the general course "under proper restrictions, such subjects as may be demanded by a reasonable number of students, and for which there are qualified teachers in the school; (3) greater concentration upon fewer subjects; (4) the five-subject plan per week, each subject allotted four hours per week of prepared work, enabling those desiring to specialize to take two-fifths of his work vocational and three-fifths academic.

FAIR DEALING.

One phase of this question was taken up with reference to Absences by Mr. Charles R. Fay, Chairman of Committee on Absences of Teachers. The report is the result of careful conscientious investigation. It is well-balanced and conservative. The Association should actively support the six constructive recommendations:

1. More specific allowance for absence for death.
2. Full pay for two days' court attendance.
3. Absence without pay for travel.
4. Pay for entire time lost by quarantine.
5. Discretionary power to Board of Superintendents to allow for "emergency cases."
6. Sabbatical year on half pay, for study.

YEAR BOOK.

It has been the custom to issue annually a Year Book. This year the reports of committees, the addresses and other matter worth presenting has been put into the **Bulletin**, which may be issued every month.

This **Annual Report** number of the Bulletin with Bulletin No. 34, containing the addresses on Superior Merit, Report of Committee on Absences, Talk on Salesmanship, etc., constitute what may be considered a Year Book. If enough ask for it, copies of the two will be bound uniform with previous Year Books and issued to members. Those desiring a Year Book should notify the Secretary before December 1, 1912.

CONCLUSION.

It will be seen that many of the principles of Scientific Management have not been taken up by the Association this last year.

In 1912-1913 the Association should continue its studies in Efficiency, especially with reference to the so-called Practical Principles enumerated by Mr. Emerson. The year begins November 9, with a meeting devoted to Greater Efficiency in Line and Staff Organization. The December meeting is to be devoted to Greater Efficiency in the Recitation.

WILLIAM T. MORREY.

MEETING OF REPRESENTATIVES OCTOBER 29, 1912.

The Board of Representatives of the High School Teachers' Association met on October 29, at the Washington Irving High School. The meeting was called to order at 4:10 by President Morrey. The minutes of the May meeting were read, and adopted as read. The treasurer reported the membership of the association in June as 731, larger than at any previous time. The treasury begins the year with a balance of $281.96.

Mr. Payne, of Eastern District High School, Chairman of the committee on pensions, spoke of the present situation in pension legislation. As the matter is in the hands of actuaries, no definite action can be taken until that investigation is completed. Four broad recommendations, endorsed by the committee, were offered for discussion and criticism by the schools:

1. Retirement after 30 years of service to be voluntary.
(The term "30 years of service" was purposely left vague to be settled in detail later.)

2. City should pay a fair share of the retirement fund.
(Suggestions that 50 per cent., instead of approximately 30 per cent. as now, would be "fair share".)

3. If necessary to increase rate of deduction from salaries, that this be a uniform rate: 1½ per cent. suggested.

4. All persons to receive half-salary pensions.

Discussion of these points followed, and the question was presented, whether the city's share of the retirement fund might not be obtained from budget appropriation instead of excise tax. Disapproval was expressed of a method by which many pay for the pensions of a few, and by which a teacher retiring before the end of the 30-year's term of service, or the heirs of a teacher who has died, gets no return from an outlay extending perhaps over many years. Informal votes were taken of those present; the vote was more than two to one in favor of a uniform rate, and against half-salary pensions.

Mr. Dotey reported a suggestion offered for one method of rating teachers. All pupils reciting to a given teacher are to be examined at the beginning of a term, and again at the end. By comparing the average per cent. gained in the first examination with that of the later test, the rate of progress of this set of pupils can be determined. Comparing this with the rate of progress made by other groups of pupils under other teachers will give a standard for rating of teacher's ability.

A letter was read from Mr. Clarence D. Kingsley in which he tendered his resignation from the Executive Board of the High School Teachers' Association, as he had accepted the position of Agent of the Massachusetts Board of Education. With great regret it was voted to accept this resignation.

The meeting adjourned at 5:30 o'clock.

(Signed) AGNES CARR, Secretary.

DIRECTORY FOR 1911-1912 GENERAL OFFICERS.

President—William T. Morrey, Bushwick.
Vice-President—L. Louise Arthur, Bryant.
Secretary—Agnes Carr, Morris.
Treasurer—Dr. Loring B. Mullen, Girls'.
Additional Members of Executive Committee—H. Elizabeth Seelman, Girls'; Aaron I. Dotey, DeWitt Clinton; and, Clarence D. Kingsley, Manual Training.

REPRESENTATIVES.

(Senior Representative First).

BOYS': Charles E. Oberholser, Francis T. Hughes, Frederick B. Jones, S. Ridley Parker, William W. Rogers, Alfred A. Tansk.

BRYANT: Carolyn P. Swett, Mary Elizabeth Reid.

BUSHWICK: George M. Falion, Maud E. Manfred.

COMMERCIAL: Edwin A. Bolger, George W. Harman, Benjamin C. Gruenberg, A. Franklin Ross, Robert P. St. John.

CURTIS: James Shipley, Mabel G. Burdick.

DeWITT CLINTON: Donald C. MacLaren, Oscar W. Anthony, Aaron I. Dotey, Ellen E. Garrigues, Fayette E. Moyer, Charles E. Timmerman.

EASTERN DISTRICT: Minnie K. Pinch, Katherine Meigs, Lou Helmuth, Charlotte Crawford, Henry E. Chapin, Franklin H. Smith.

ERASMUS HALL: Preston C. Farrar, George E. Boynton, Abigail E. Leonard, William F. Tibbets, Kate E. Turner.

FAR ROCKAWAY: Eldon M. Van Dusen.

FLUSHING: Paul R. Jenks.

GIRLS': Loring B. Mullen, H. Elizabeth Seelman.

HIGH SCHOOL OF COMMERCE: Horace G. Healey, Alfred H. Lewis, George H. Van Tuyl.

JAMAICA: Benjamin H. Thorp, Lydia F. Root.

MANUAL TRAINING: Arthur L. Baker, Eleanor R. Baker, Sidney Edwards, Marion Hackedorn, Mary A. Hall, Clarence D. Kingsley, Charles Perrine, Frederick A. Peters.

MORRIS: Paul B. Mann, Harriet L. Constantine, Frederick C. White.

NEWTON: George H. Kingsbury, Alex E. W. Zerban.

RICHMOND HILL: Charles Robert Gaston, Gertrude M. Leete.

STUYVESANT: T. Harry Knox, Clayton G. Durfee, Joseph L. Beha, Stanley A. Gage, Charles F. Moore, Ernest S. Quimby, Walter M. Smith.

WADLEIGH: Helen E. Bacon, Florence Middleton.

WASHINGTON IRVING: Idelette Corpenter, Mary C. Craig, Elizabeth S. Rose.

DEPARTMENT CHAIRMEN FOR 1911-1912.

Ancient Languages—Ruth M. Prescott, Far Rockaway.
Bookkeeping—G. H. Van Tuyl, High School of Commerce.
Biology—Dr. Henry R. Linville, Jamaica High School.
Drawing—Mr. Morris Greenberg, Commercial High School.
History—Miss Antoinette Lawrence, Jamaica High School; Miss Florence L. Beeckman, Secretary.
Mathematics—Mr. Albert E. King, Erasmus Hall High School; Miss Emily M. Jennison, Far Rockaway High School, Secretary.
Mechanical Arts—Mr. George W. Norton, Bushwick High School.
Modern Languages—Nannie G. Blackwell, Washington Irving High School.
Physical Science—Mr. Joseph S. Mills, High School of Commerce.
Physiography—Kirk W. Thompson, Jamacia High School.
Stenography and Typewriting—Horace G. Healey, High School of Commerce.

CHAIRMEN OF COMMITTEES.

Absences of Teacher—Charles R. Fay, Erasmus Hall.
Conference with Colleges—Clarence D. Kingsley, Manual Training.
Grammar Uniform Nomenclature—Charles Perrine.
Increasing High School Accommodations—Gilbert S. Blakely, Morris.
Promotion Committee—Harold E. Buttrick, Boys.
Retirement Legislation (Pensions)—Frederick H. Paine, Eastern District.
Scientific Management—Dr. Edward A. Fitzpatrick, H. S. Commerce.
Secondary Education—Henry R. Linville, Jamaica.
Standardization of Reports, Forms and Blanks—Harry B. Penhallow, DeWitt Clinton.
Students' Aid—E. W. Weaver, Boys and Brooklyn Evening School.
Teachers' Interests—Paul B. Mann, Morris.

COMMITTEE ON SECONDARY EDUCATION.

Henry R. Linville, Jamaica, Chairman; L. Louise Arthur, Bryant; M. Ellen Barker, Girls'; Colman D. Frank, DeWitt Clinton; Clarence D. Kingsley, Manual Training; A. E. Peterson, Morris; Ernest E. Smith, Boys'; Louise Thompson, Morris.

COMMITTEE ON TEACHERS' INTERESTS.

A. I. Dotey, DeWitt Clinton, Chairman; A. L. Janes, Boys'; Sidney Edwards, Manual Training; Ida G. Galloway, Washington Irving; Margaret L. Ingalls, Girls'; James P. Warren, Eastern District; A. L. Crosley, Stuyvesant.

PROMOTION COMMITTEE.

Albert E. King, Eramus, Chairman; Michael D. Sohon, Morris; Lillian M. Elliott, Wadleigh; James A. Fairly, Commercial; Mary A. Hall, Manual Training; Claude F. Walker, Commerce; Emma F. Pettengill, Girls'; John L. Tilrsley, De Witt Clinton; Jesse Haley, Morris.

STUDENTS AID COMMITTEE.

E. W. Weaver, Chairman, Brooklyn Evening High School for Men; Gilbert J. Raynor, Commercial; Paul J. Abelson, DeWitt Clinton; A. L. Pugh, Commerce; Jennie M. Jenness, Girls'; Henrietta Rodman, Wadleigh; George K. Hinds, Washington Irving; Philip Dowell, Curtis; O. F. Ferry, Erasmus Hall; Chas. C. Vosburgh, Jamaica; Charles Perrine, Manual Training; E. M. Williams, Morris; H. B. Slater, Newtown; Edward F. Lewis, Bryant; Charels S. Hartwell and Mabel Skinner, Eastern District; E. S. Augsburg, Stuyvesant; M. B. Lambert, Richmond Hill; Etta E. Southwell, Bshwick; P. R. Dean, Curtis Evening; F. H. J. Paul, New York Evening; Marie Gurnee and Meriel Williad, Washington Irving; Kate Turner, Erasmus Hall.

COMMITTEE ON INCREASE OF HIGH SCHOOL ACCOMMODATIONS.

Clarence D. Kingsley, Manual Training, Chairman; Woodward A. Anderson, Washington Irving; John A. Bole, Eastern District; George E. Boynton, Erasmus Hall; Bertha F. Courtney, Bryant; Charles S. Estes, Erasmus Hall; Margaret L. Ingals, Girls'; Paul R. Jenks, Flushing; J. Herbert Low, Manual Training; Harry K. Monroe, Bryant; Hawley O. Rittenhouse, Eastern District; Henrietta Rodman, Wadleigh; Robert P. St. John, Commercial; Elizabeth Schutze, Manual Training; H. Elizabeth Seelman, Girls'; Louis B. Semple, Bushwick; Gilbert S. Blakely, Morris; I. A. Hazen, Man. Training; Philip R. Dean, Curtis.

COMMITTEE ON CONFERENCE WITH COLLEGES.

Clarence D. Kingsley, Manual Training, Chairman; William McAndrew, Washington Irving; James Sullivan, Boys'; James F. Wilson, Stuyvesant; Alexander L. Pugh, High School of Commerce; John L. Tildsley, DeWitt Clinton.

COMMITTEE ON RETIREMENT LEGISLATION.

Frederick H. Paine, Eastern District, Chairman; L. Louis Arthur, Bryant; A. C. Bryan, Migh School of Commerce.

COMMITTEE ON SCIENTIFIC MANAGEMENT (EFFICIENCY).

Edward A. Fitzpatrick, Commerce, Chairman; Arthur L. Janes, Boys'; Harold E. Butterick, Brooklyn Evening High School; L. Louise Arthur, Bryant; George M. Falion, Bushwick; A. L. Pugh, W. S. Schlauch, S. P. Koopman, Commerce; B. C. Gruenberg, Commercial; W. R. Hayward, Curtis; H. B. Penhallow, Clinton; Minnie Ikelheimer, Eastern District; Kate E. Turner, Erasmus; A. G. Belding, Far Rockaway; Paul R. Jenks, E. C. Hood, Flushing; M. Ellen Barker, Girls'; B. H. Thorp, Jamaica; I. A. Hazen, A. C. White, Chas. Perrine; Mary J. Bourne, E. M. Williams, H. C. Laughlin, Morris; J. J. Klein, Richmond Hill; A. G. Crossley, E. S. Quimby, Stuyvesant; Helen E. Bacon, Rose M. Barton, W. W. Clendenin, Wadleigh; David L. Arnold, Washington Irving.

COMMITTEE ON ABSENCES OF TEACHERS.

Charles R. Ray, Erasmus, Chairman; Frank H. Miller, Fluhsing; William R. Lasher, Erasmus; J. Herbert Low, Manual Training.

COMMITTEE ON GRAMMAR: UNIFORM NOMENCLATURE FOR HIGH AND ELEMENTARY SCHOOLS, FOR FOREIGN LANGUAGES AND FOR ENGLISH.

Charles Perrine, Manual Training, Chairman. Committee is not completed. Send suggestions to the Chairman or to the President.

GENERAL MEETING—OCTOBER 21, 1911.

The meeting was called to order in the High School of Commerce at 10.07 o'clock by President W. T. Morrey. The minutes of the last meeting were read and approved. The President made a brief address, stating that the chief work of the year would be the study of High School Efficiency, and urging all who were willing to serve on the committee organized to make known their preference at once.

Mr. Kingsley reported for the Committee on Conference with Colleges that printed bulletins of the work accomplished would be issued in the near future.

The speaker of the morning was then introduced, Prof. Chas. H. Judd, Director of the School of Education of Chicago.

In an interesting and enlightening talk Professor Judd showed the results of detailed study in some of the cities in the Middle West, of the relations existing between Elementary and High School, and between High School and University. These results were pictured on carefully prepared charts, on some of which the progress of the pupil was traced as to his position in th upper, middle or lower third of his class, rather than by his individual rating in per cent. One chart which proved especially interesting to the audience illustrated the widely differing values given the same papers when rated by several different persons.

According to a new plan, the general meeting was adjourned at 11.30, and the members then went to their respective section meetings.

WM. T. MORREY, President.

AGNES CARR, Secretary.

GENERAL MEETING DECEMBER 9.

The December Meeting of the High School Teachers' Association was called to order by the President, W. T. Morrey, in the H. S. of Commerce at 10:10 on the morning of December 9.

Mr. Frederick C. Paine, Chairman of the Pension Committee discussed the bill prepared and sent to Albany by Mr. Best. This bill provides for a one per sent deduction from salaries $3500 and less, and uuring service up to 20 years and more, and for salaries more than $3500 a deduction of two per cent is proposed.

Mr. Bryan of the High School of Commerce moved that it be Resolved, that this Association is opposed to any change in the present pension law creating an increase over the present one per cent deduction on salaries $3500 or less, and that it is opposed to the proposition to make a deduction of two per cent on salaries when the length of service has been twenty years or more.

This motion was carried.

To Mr. Gruenberg, Mr. Paine stated that no actual investigation of pensions had been made, but the printed record of what had been done was obtainable.

The speaker of the morning Mr. Harrington Emerson, a Consulting Engineer, was then introduced. Mr. Emerson had had six years of experience in the University of Nebraska, so that he was in sympathy with school room mattere, though he presented his topic, "The Principles of Scientific Managemen," in the terms of the inductrial world.

It is not often that we are privileged to feel so close a kinship between our problems and those of the world of business surroundnig us. That the subject was of vital interest was amply proved by the eager attention of the audience, and the evident reluctance with which at last, with a rising vote of thanks to Mr. Emerson, the Association adjourned to the Section meetings at 11:40.

(Mr. Emerson left for Bermuda that afternoon and returned early in January.

Signed,
AGNES CARR, Secretary.

MINUTES OF GENERAL MEETING, MARCH 16.

The third meeting of the High School Teachers' Association in the Efficiency Series was held in the High School of Commerce on March 16. Section meetings preceded the general meeting called for 11 a. m. Between six and seven hundred members were present—the largest meeting of the year, probably the largest ever held.

The minutes of the December meeting were read and adopted as read.

Mr. Paine, of the Pension Committee, presented a new proposition in the pension bill, viz: All salaries up to $3,000 be taxed 1 per cent; of the salaries above that sum, 1 per cent be deducted on amounts up to $3,000, and on the sum above that amount, 2 per cent bepaid.

An exhibit of Commercial Maps and Commercial Geography was announced as being in progress in rooms of the building devoted to that purpose.

Mr. Weaver, of the Students' Aid Committee, stated that the work of his committee had attained national importance, and called attention to the General Conference to take place in Brooklyn on March 19, noting that this Association has always taken the lead in this matter.

The President then introduced as the first speaker of this meeting, devoted to "What Constitutes the Teacher of Superior Merit," Mr. George J. Smith of the Board of Examiners.

Mr. Smith was followed by Associated City Superintendent Edward L. Stevens, and Principals John Holley Clark of Flushing High School, John H. Denbigh of Morris High School; William Fairley of Commercial High School; William L. Felter, of Girls' High School; Charles D. Larkins, of Manual Training High School;

William MsAndrew, of Washington Irving High School, and John L. Tildsley, of DeWitt Clinton High School.

(These addresses were stenographically reported by A. Rosenblum, revised by the speakers, and are all published elsewhere in this Bulletin).

[This Bulletin, No. 34, will be sent by Secretary Miss Agnes Carr, Morris High School, for five cents in stamps.]

The meeting adjourned at two o'clock.

WILLIAM T. MORREY,
President.

AGNES CARR,
Secretary.

GENERAL MEETING OF MAY 25, 1912.

The fourth and last meeting of the High School Teacehrs' Association in the Efficiency Series was held at the High School of Commerce on May 25. Section meetings were called for 10:00 a. m., and the general meeting opened at 10:45.

The minutes of the March meeting were read and adopted.

The first business before the meeting was the election of officers for the next year, which resulted as follows:

President: Wm. T. Morrey, Bushwick.
Vice-President: Henrietta Rodman, Wadleigh.
Secretary: Agnes Carr, Morris.
Treasurer: Dr. Loring B. Mullen, Girls'.
Executive Board: Aaron L. Dotey, DeWitt Clinton; H. Elizabeth Seelman, Girls'; Clarence D. Kingsley, Manual Training.

The treasurer reported 677 members to date.

Dr. Fitzpatrick, of Commerce, presentd a short report from his committee on efficieny, making a plea for co-operation from the teaching force, and offering some suggestions for the work of another year.

Mr. Kingsley, for the committee on conference with colleges, reported that he had been in Washington for two months, tabulating the entrance rekuirements of about 200 colleges. 48 of these will accept 4 points of vocational work, and rebuire but one foreign language.

Dr. Linville, chairman of committee on Secondary Education, read a report of the work of his committee dealing with the mortality in the schools. The investigations were based on the records of three of the large high schools, and included many of the reasons given by the students for preferring to leave school.

Mr. Fay, of the committee on Teachers' Absences, stated that the report of his committee embodying some recommendations with regards to absence with pay had received favorable support.

Mr. Keener, of Bushwick, made a motion:

That the President by instructed to send a communication to the High School Committee of the Board of Education asking them to request the By-Laws Committee of the Board of Education to formulate a rule for the guidance of the Principals, Examiners, Superintendents and other Administrative Officers of the Board that all adverse rating and reports be made in writing and that the teacher be furnished with a copy of such rulings and reports.

This motion was carried.

It then developed that reports on teachers' ratings are in a very unsatisfactorfy condition, as different kinds of ratings are filed on different floors of the building at 59th Street, and that a teacher desiring to consult those records may find only one of two or three sets. It was therefore further resolved that,

WHEREAS; In the course of the proceedings of the Board of Examiners of the Board of Education in the matter of Superior Merit, it has been shown that a part of a teacher's record is kept in a file on the fourth floor of the hall of the Board of Education; that another part of the record, consisting of the term or yearly ratings given by the Principal and District Superintendent is kept upon cards on the fifth floor, and that another part of a teacher's record may be found upon supplementary reports made to the Board of Examiners, as required by the provisions of Chapter 902, of the Laws of 1911, and,

WHEREAS; In addition to these, the Board of Examiners, in passing upon Superior Merit, has accepted oral statements from First Assistants, Principals, Superintendents, and others; therefore, be it

RESOLVED; That it is the sense of the High School Teachers' Association that the records of all teachers should be consolidated, that they should be in one place., and accessible to the inspection of each teacher concerned; furthermore that any statements made orally by First Assistants, Principals, Superintendents, and others, which influence or determine the action of the Board of Examiners of the Board of Superintendents, in passing upon merit, should be reduced to writing and should be included in the file, so that these allegations may also be accessible to and known by a teacher.

This motion was carried unanimously.

Prof. Hanus, the speaker of the day, was then introduced, after whose address the meeting was adjourned at 1:05 o'clock.

(Signed) AGNES CARR, Secretary.

MAY 23, 1911, MEETING.

The last meeting of the Board of Representatives of the H. S. T. A. for 1910-11 was the first meeting under the newly elected officers of the Association for the year 1911-12. It gave an opportunity for a retrospect over the work of this last year and for a prospect over the year to come.

Mr. Aaron I. Dotey, Chairman, reported that the Teachers' Interests Committee had taken up the *Excessivt Clerical Work Demanded of Teachers*, and had dropped it because of the pedagogical value of this work. *The 25-Hour Schedule* was dropped because of impending investgations. *The Right of the Board of Teach-* is covered by a By-Law giving the Board of Education the*ers' Time after 2:30* right over teachers' time to an average of 6½ hours a day. *The Time of Regents' Examinations and the Frequency of School Examinations* are to be investigated further.

The Committee recommended putting all energy into opposing the political control of schools.Mr. Dotey was reappointed chairman of the committee.

Copies of the resolutions adopted May 6, in the General Meeting of tht H. S. T. A. in opposition to educational provisions of the Gaynor Charter were ordered to be given to The Globe, The Evening Post, The New York Times, School, and The Brooklyn Eagle.

Mr. Frederick H. Paine, Chairman of Committee on Retirement Legislation, reported on the status of the pension question. He was reappointed chairman.

Mr. Emberson E. Proper, Chairman of the Promotion Committee, reported the resolution of the High School Commttee of the Board of Superintendents, "No nomination to tne position of first assistant in any high school, except where a vacancy exists—and then in no case where the number of teachers employed in said department is less than five."

The recommendation of Mr. Proper's committee was amended and passed as follows:

The Board of Representatives of the High School Teachers' Association recommend:

1. That first assistants be appointed on the grounds of efficiency in teaching and administrative work without regard to chairmanship of a department.

2. That it be desirable that one first assistant be appointed in high schools for every 150 pupils registered.

Mr. Clarence D. Kingsley, Chairman of the Committee on Increase of High School Accommodations, reported that three new high schools are promised in the next two years—one at Bay Ridge, one in the Bronx, and one in East New York.

The Committee on Secondary Education reported that its work was completed and would go to press this week.

Mr. Benjamin C. Gruenberg, Chairman of the Committee on Child Welfare Exhibit, was pranted permission to publish his report in other periodicals before its appearance in the Year Book.

Mr. Clarence D. Kingsley, Chairman of the Committee on Conference with Colleges, reported that the "Committee of Nine" would report at the San Francisco meeting of the N. E. A. a definition of a well-planned high school course. Such a course to consist of 15 units, of which 11 are to be devoted to academic subjects and 4 to electives. The schools to have small classes, adequate equipment, and suitable teaching force. To protect the interests of sound education, 2 majors of 3 units each should be required. Natonal efficiency would be promoted and the moral standard raised by devoting more time to technical study and less to general education. Mr. Kingsley was continued as chairman.

Dr. Loring B. Mullen, the Treasurer, reported a membership of 670 and a balance in the treasury of $723.73.

The president suggested that committees be formed on the Relations between Elementary and High Schools, on Statistics and Directory, and on Efficiency in the High Schools. The Efficiency Committee and its sub-committees could profitably consider such topics as School Ideas, what they are in the various schools, and who determines them; Planning, Co-ordinating, and Checking Up; Standardization of Instructions for Admission, Transfers, Promotions, ttc.; Reords, Standardized, Reliable, Up to Date, Accessible; Discipline, Common Sense, Judgment, Competent Counsel for Pupils and Teachers; The Fair Deal and Efficiency Reward for Pupils, and for Teachers; Relations bttween Teachers and their Principals and Superior Officers; Professional Etiquette.

All members and all prospective members of the Association and all interested in High School problems are cordially invited to send written suggestions as to lines of work and as to composition of committees, to the president, W. T. Morrey, 535 West 111th Street, New York City.

OCTOBER 31 MEETING.

The representatives were called to order at 4 P. M., Miss C. P. Swett of Bryant was appointed secretary pro tem. The report of the May meeting was read, corrected and accepted.

The Treasurer reported a balance of $358.73.

The various Senior Representatives then reported on the membership of their various schools.

Reports of Department Chairmen.

Mr. Norton of Bushwick discussed the policy of his Section, announced as the main topic for the year's work in Mechanic Arts, "Motive Power for Running Machines."

Miss Blackwell of Washington Irving made a report for the Modern Language Section.

Mr. Weaver reported for the Students' Aid Committee that 200 pupils had been assisted; that the promise that this work be recognized in the Budget had failed; that an effort is now being made to obtain outside help, and legislative action for establishing in each city a bureau to give employment. The committee has been active as usual in distributing pamphlets on different occupations.

Mr. Kingsley of the Committee on Increase in High School Accommodation reported the promise of new buildings, and suggested that the question of greater accommodation be taken up with the Board of Education.

Mr. Gruenberg believed that this committee should do more work in emphasizing need for more high school accommodation. He also criticized the administration of high school annexes, and thought that the effort should be made towards eventual elmination of annexes as a part of the system.

Miss Seelman of Girls' High, Mr. Mann of Morris, and Mr. Fallon of Bushwick declared that in their annexes neither pupils nor teachers were discriminated against.

Mr. Kingsley reported for the Committee on Conference with Colleges that of the six members forming that committee, five are in favor of adopting as a whole the report of the "Committee of Nine." Dr. Sullivan believes that both mathematics and a foreign language should be required for entrance to college.

New Business.

Motion carried that Chairman be empowered to appoint a Committee on Conference of Relations between Elementary and High Schools.

Motion carrid that Chairman be empowerd to appoint a Committee on Efficiency, and such other committees as he sees fit to call.

Meeting adjourned.

(Signed) AGNES CARR, Secretary.

NOVEMBER 28 MEETING.

Representatives were called to order about 4 P. M.

Miss Maud B. Manfred of Bushwick appointed secretary pro tem.

The minutes of the October 31 meeting were read, corrected, and then adopted.

The Department Programs for the December 9 meeting were read and revised.

Mr. Janes reported the Year Book for 1910-1911 all ready for weeks, except one report.

The question of merging the lists was discussed in an informal way by everyone present, bringing out the advantages and disadvantages. No formal action taken.

Miss Alice Higgins, appointed by former President Janes, reported by letter her meeting with Dr. James Sullivan's committee. There was a general discussion of the propriety of teachers taking part. No formal action taken.

The investigation of the status of the position of librarian was at the suggestion of Mr. Oberholser referred to the Teachers' Interests Committee.

AGNES CARR, Secretary.

REPRESENTATIVES MEETING. DECEMBER 19th.

Miss E. A. Roche, W. I. H. S. was appointed Secretary *Pro Tem.*

Minutes of November 28th meeting were read and adopted.

Reports on membership.

Mr. Crossley of Teachers' Interests Committee opened an informal discussion of maning of "A Teacher of Superior Merit; all present participated.

Mr. Quimby, of Stuyvesant, spoke of work of Hanus Committee.

On a motion of Mr. Kingsley, the Secretary was empowered to ask the Building Committee of the Board of Education to see that in the new building for the Washington Irving High School there is provided a committee meeting room suitable for the meeting of this association and other associations.

The President announced that he hoped to make the meetings of the Board of Representatives of educational value, by arranging definite topics for discussion.

For the January 30th meeting the chairman of the Committee on Scientific Management will talk "On the Reorganization of an Existing High School in accordance with the principles of Scientific Management."

Chairman of Committees, Members of Scientific Management Committees, all Delegates should attend or send Proxies who are interested in school efficiency.

E. S. ROCHE, Secretary *Pro Tem.*

MEETING OF REPRESENTATIVES, JANUARY 30, 1912.

The minutes of the previous meeting were read and approved as read.

Report of membership by schools.

Dr. Mullen reported a balance in treasury of $382.91. Total number of members, 381, with nine high schools to hear from. Membership exceeds by 76 that at the same time last year, which reached 670.

Mr. Payne, Chairman of Committee on Retirement Legislation, outlined the details of the pending pension bill. Questions and discussion followed. Mr. Paine suggested that the representatives present ascertain the sentiment in their respective schools and report the same to him.

Mr. Kingsley, Chairman of the Committee on Increase of High School Accommodations, reported that high schools were in sight for East New York and the Bronx, as recommended in Superintendent Steven's annual report.

President Morrey announced that this committee would be reorganized.

Mr. Kingsley, as Chairman of the Committee on Conference with the Colleges, read an extract from the report of President Burton of Smith College, advocating more flexible high school courses and the acceptance of such by the colleges.

Mr. Weaver, Chairman of the Students' Aid Committee, reported. (See elsewhere in this bulletin.)

Dr. Fitzpatrick, Chairman of the Committee on Scientific Management, outlined in a clear and interesting manner, the topics his committee would deal with in their discussion and investigation of high school efficiency. Discussion followed.

It was affirmed that the Hanus Committee desired a committee of the High School Teachers' Association to confer with it in its present investigation. It was moved, seconded and carried that a committee be formed at the discretion of the President, to represent the High School Teachers' Association before the Hanus Committee.

The meeting adjourned at 6 P. M. H. E. SEELMAN, *Secretary Pro Tem.*

MEETING OF REPRESENTATIVES, FEBRUARY 27, 1912.

Minutes of the January meeting were read and approved.

President Morrey announced that Mr. Emerson's address would appear in the next bulletin instead of waiting to be issued in the Year Book. Attention was called to this policy.

Mr. Dotey, Chairman of Teachers' Interest Committee, resigned from chairmanship on account of pressure of school work and illness. His resignation was accepted.

The program of general meeting was referred to whether department meetings should precede or follow the meeting of the entire body. No action taken.

Mr. Kingsley reported for Conference Committee on Course of Study appointed to confer with the Hanus Committee on Scientific Investigation of Schools. At the first conference sixteen were present. A number of questions were discussed resulting in entire agreement on the need of greater flexibility in high school course. No desire was expressed to cut out subjects already in course but several more seemed urgently needed. The committee was enlarged to fifty-seven, of whom forty were present at the second meeting. At this meeting a sub-committee was appointed to put its recommendations into shape to be submitted to full committee. Mr. Kingsley read to the Representatives his preliminary draft of the report of the sub-committee. There was much discussion with regard to five-subject or four-subject courses, and requirements for high school work.

Meeting adjourned at 5:50 P. M. AGNES CARR, *Secretary.*

A COMMUNICATION.

March 24, 1912.

To the Honorable Committee on High Schools, Board of Education, New York City:

Gentlemen:—May we, in the name of the High School Teachers' Association of New York City, urge you to request the By-Laws Committee of the Board of Education to formulate rules for the guiadance of the Board of Examiners and the Administrative Officers of the Board;

(1) To rate as of Superior Merit, all teachers marked as B+ or higher; *Superior* being a comparative term and not superlative, not equivalent to supreme.

(2) To rate as of Superior Merit, those who prior to January 1, 1912, were receiving the *Maximum salaries* of their grades. We believe that such was the not unreasonable expectation not only of such teachers but also of those officers of the Board who estimated the cost of new law. This eliminates the *Ex Facto* feature.

(3) To rate as approved for *twelve* years, such teachers as have been approved for *nine years* and have in addition received *credit for three additional* years in the adjustment of the Junior Teacher Question.

The Executive Committee of the High School Teachers' Association.

WILLIAM T. MORREY, President.

(Reported to Board of Representatives March 28, 1912, and adopted by them.)

MARCH 28, MEETING OF REPRESENTATIVES.

The March meeting of the Representatives of the High School Teachers' Association was held at the Washington Irving High School, March 28, with President W. T. Morrey in the chair.

The minutes of the previous meeting were read and accepted. The Treasurer reportd $365.48 in the treasury, with several large schools not yet heard from.

(The communication of March 24, 1912, from the Executive Committee of the Association to the Committee on High Schools of the Board of Education was read and adopted.)

Mr. Penhollow, of DeWitt Clinton, Chairman of the Committee on Forms and Blanks, described the work undertaken by his committee. He said it was necessary to find out first the kind and amount of information required from Fifty-ninth Street, and then to have blanks prepared to gain that information and nothing else. In that way reports from various schools will be uniform, and can be easily tabulated.

Mr. Dotey, of DeWitt Clinton, gave an interesting and detailed account of the meeting of the High School Committee of the Board of Education held March 27. This gave rise to much discussion, and suggestions were made that while the subject is still fresh in mind, but after salaries have been adjusted, the matter of an advance grade be presented; and also that protest be made against method of rating teachers on five-minute inspection and on basis kept secret from teacher.

Mr. Oberhoalzer was appointed Chairman of committee to consider the status of librarians with power to form his own committee.

Meeting adjourned.

AGNES CARR, Secretary.

APRIL 30, MEETING OF REPRESENTATIVES.

The April meeting of the Representatives of the High School Teachers' Association was held on the thirtieth at 34 East Twelfth Street. The Secretary's report was read and accepted. The Treasurer reported in the treasury $132.62, with one large school still to be heard from. The net cost of printing the Year Book of 1910-1911 had been $244.27.

Mr. Fay, Chairman of the Committee on Teachers' Absences, gave a report of the work done by his committee, which was unanimously approved and adopted for recommendation to the Board of Education.

(a) Investigation of practice in other cities in reference to loss of salary for absence due to illness or other causes.

(b) Study of methods prevailing in this city.

For the first of these, investigation was made of 224 cities of 25,000 inhabitants or over, and the results gained by a carefully planned questionnaire were tabulated.

A study of methods prevailing in this city revealed that in most cases the attitude of the city towards the teacher is most generous; and the pension fund is so inextricably bound up with legislation in regard to pay during absence that the change does not seem necessary or expedient.

The committee offered, however, six constructive recommendations as follows:

1. Allowed absence for death in family be made more specific.
2. Full pay for attendance at court be allowed for two days in all cases.
3. Allowed absence without pay for purpose of travel.
4. Pay granted for absence due to quarantine be for entire time, not ten days only.
5. Discretionary power be granted to Board of Superintendents to allow absence with pay in "emergency cases"—cases equally compelling with illness.
6. Sabbatical year be allowed for study on half pay.

A vote of thanks was given to the committee for this report.

Mr. Penhallow, Chairman of Committee on Standardization of Forms, gave a brief ccount of the work of his committee. He suggested thit if the teachers would send to him copies of their individual programs, with size of classes, his committee would compile a report on comparative size of classes, and periods of work.

Mr. Penhollow was authorized to obtain such material as he desired for use in the work of his own committee, and also in that of the Efficiency Committee.

Dr. Fitzpatrick, Chairman of the Committee on Efficiency, read a part of the report of his committee. The first recommendation in regard to teachers' ratings by principals was tabled. There seemed so much material for discussion, that, as the hour was late, it was moved to adjourn until May 7, when this report could be taken up at length.

(Signed) AGNES CARR, Secretary.

MAY 7, MEETING OF REPRESENTATIVES.

On May 7, an adjourned meeting of the Board of Representatives of the High School Teachers' Association was held at the Washington Irving School to consider the report of Dr. Fitzpatrick, Chairman of the Committee on Efficiency.

Minutes of the previous meeting were read.

In the absence of President Morrey, Mr. Dotey, of DeWitt Clinton, was asked to take the chair.

In presenting his report for a second time before the Board, Dr. Fitzpatrick referred to its publication in "The Globe" of May 7, saying he had thought it would simplify matters to have a printed copy of the propositions in the hands of those present. He suggested that the propositions be voted on singly.

Objection was made to this method of procedure by Mr. Jenks.

Reference was made by Mr. Dotey, who asked permission to leave the chair for this purpose, to the resolution passed two years ago that the High School Teachers' Association is opposed to all discussion of questions relating to salary.

Further objection was made that too small a number was present to take action on any subject of so great importance to the Association as a whole.

Objection was made to the publication of a report which had not yet been acted upon by the Board of Representatives, and under a caption very misleading to the casual reader.

A resolution was then passed that the report of the Committee on Efficiency be tabled, and that the public press be informed of that fact.

It was resolved further that is is unwise to enter into any discussion of "superior merit" at the present time.

Mr. Jenks suggested a constructive plan of inspection of work; that a teacher be relieved of work in his special field for a period of six months at a time, and spend the time in inspecting work done throughout the city, and reporting upon it.

The meeting adjourned at 5:35 p. m.

(Signed) AGNES CARR, Secretary.

REPRESENTATIVES MEETING OF MAY 28, 1912.

The last meeting of the Board of Representatives of the High School Teachers' Association was held at 34 East 12th Street, May 28, with President Morrey in the chair. The secretary's report was read and accepted. The treasurer reported 680 members, and a balance in the treasury of $166.11.

It was reported from the committee on teachers' absence that a petition is being sent to the schools to be signed by individual teachers. President Morrey suggested the advisability of getting the co-operation of as many associations of teachers as possible. It was stated that it is the unanimous opinion of the Board that the suggestions offered by this committee should be followed.

In the absence of Dr. Fitzpatrick, an outline of the work of his committee was presented by Mr. McNamara. A detailed report with suggestions for work of next year was promised for later publication.

Mr. Overholser reported for his committee on status of librarians that the standard of requirements as well as character of examination are changing, which will naturally produce a modification in salary adjustment. Raising standard of work should raise salary. A committee will be formed to investigate the conditions in libraries of other cities.

Mr. Weaver, of the Students' Aid Committee, gave an interesting account of the movement for vocational guidance, of which the first matter published in this country, appeared in the 1907 bulletin of the High School Teachers' Association. This report figured later in a hearing before the Assembly. The funds appropriated to the use of the committee have been used for agitation. A brief for the establishment of an employment agency for children when leaving school has been presented before the Chambers of Commerce which body will provide funds for carrying on the work. An administrative body which will command the confidence of the people is necessary. Much interest has been arosed, but the problem requires business enterprise.

A motion was carried that:

WHEREAS; There is pending before Congress a bill known as Senate Bill No. 3, on the Page Bill in support of vocational education, providing for an appropriation of $14,000,000 to vocational schools, therefore,

RESOLVED; The High School Teachers' Association of New York City urges the senators and representatives in Congress to give to the bill their favorable consideration.

The secretary was directed to send this request to the members of Congress.

Mr. Dotey moved that the President be empowered to appoint chairman and members of such committees as he sees fit to form, and to remove such as he feels are not working in accordance with the best interests of the Association. Carried.

Mr. Baker moved that a special committee be requested to see what can be done to abolish the grading of teachers (in part even) upon the percentage of promotions, and to make recommendations to that end.

Amended by Mr. Dotey that this special committee be appointed by the president. Carried.

A report of the work done by the Modern Language Section of the Association, of which Miss Blackwell is chairman, was then read. This report embodied a request that the Regent's Examinations in Modern Languages might not always fall upon the last day of the week of examinations.

Meeting adjourned at 5:45 o'clock.

(Signed) AGNES CARR, Secretary.

(Conclusion of Prof. Hanus's Address from Page 32)

just the kind of theoretical work that can be made the basis of satisfactory experimentation.

This Association seems to me to be in a fair way to do more increasingly effective work of the kind you are now doing. You can promote and you are promoting self-examination; and in the end you are certain to succeed, if you have not already succeeded in establishing experiments to appraise results—to test such conclusions as you may reach. It seems to me then that you are in a fair way to promote educational progress; for the secret of good schools and good school systems is co-operation of this sort under proper leadership.

SCIENTIFIC MANAGEMENT AND HIGH SCHOOL EFFICIENCY.

By Harrington Emerson, Efficiency Engineer.

Ladies and Gentlemen of the High School Teachers' Association:

I regard it as one of the most fortunate events of my life that when I was very young, and perhaps ought still to have been going to school, I had the opportunity to become a teacher in one of the younger western state universities. What I there learned in managing boys and girls has stood me in good stead ever since. Your president was kind enough not to mention that my career as a university professor came to a sudden and permanent end. The faculty was divided into two sides: the younger men and the older, the radicals and the conservatives. The radicals were very strenuous, but the older men were more skillful, and at one of the meetings of the regents all the younger men were requested to depart. I was one of them, another is one of the most famous professors at Columbia; others have since made their way in name and fame. I am proud to say that as a result of the work of men, of whom I was one, that state university has become one of the great institutions of our country.

I also regard it as fortunate that when I was still young I was forced out into a cold world and made to earn my living in competition with others. I found that what I had learned in the management of boys and girls was applicable to the management of men and women in every walk of life, that the fundamentals of organization which underlie the development of a great state university apply equally to the management, administration and development of all institutions of learning. They apply not only to schools and universities, but also throughout all life. Those fundamental principles are universal.

There are certain fundamentals that underlie our whole life. Each living animal must breathe or the individual dies in a short time. Each individual must have rest or it dies at the end of a very short time. Each individual must have food, or it will die. Each individual must not exceed very narrow temperature limits or its life ceases. One can spend a life time and not know all there was to know about any individual animal or insect.

You know the practice of teaching far better than I do. I shall talk only about the fundamentals of those educational matters which are similar to all other activities, and I shall have succeeded if I make each one of you realize that this is a part of the universal problem, and that if you grasp these essentials you can apply them everywhere, not only here to school life, but to everything human.

I am to talk on efficiency, and I shall begin by telling you three things that efficiency is not. Nine-tenths of the people who have heard of efficiency confound it with one of the three things that efficiency is not.

First—*Strenuousness* is not efficiency. Strenuousness is the accomplishment of a slightly greater result by a very much greater effort. Efficiency is the accomplishing of a very much greater result by very much less effort.

A man can walk easily three miles an hour. If I were to assign a task for the man, about the maximum that he could perform, I would say four miles an hour, for perhaps six hours a day, and give him a choice of walking three miles an hour for eight hours a day, making a total of twenty-four miles a day. That is quite enough for any man to walk day in and day out. Let us consider the case of a postman or a messenger. Suppose that I place a piece rate of ten cents a mile. The normal daily wage of the walker would be $2.40, and this would encourage some man to walk five miles an hour during the six hours, accomplishing thirty miles in the course of the day, thus earning $3.00. Five miles an hour is too much for anybody to walk. If I should walk five miles an hour I would want to rest a week.

When the man wants to walk more than four miles an hour, I would give him a bicycle, the slow speed of which is ten miles an hour. This speed is more than twice as great as the most strenuous speed for the walker. The man on the bicycle can speed up to twelve miles an hour, then to fifteen miles an hour. There is one man who rode 390 miles in less than twenty hours, more than twenty miles an hour for the whole time he was on the road, the extreme of human endurance. He had prepared months in advance and rested weeks afterward. That is strenuous riding of the bicycle. But by the time my bicycle rider had come up to twelve or fourteen miles an hour, I would give him a motorcycle, and I would station policemen at the cross roads to prevent him from exceeding the speed limit. The difference between strenuousness and efficiency is thus indicated.

I have seen Egyptian girls digging the earth with their bare hands, the only implements being their fingernails, and it took a long hard day's work to accomplish a very small result. I have seen also on the western prairies, several modern engines dragging a gang plow of fifty-one shares, turning over a section of land in thirty-six hours. That plow could do more work in thirty-six hours than ten thousand girls could accomplish with their fingernails in the period of their lives, and yet the girls with their fingernails were working strenuousnessly, and the men with the plow were doing what might be called gentlemen's work.

Recently I went to see a series of bee-hive ovens, with openings in the top. They were red hot. The soft coal was dumped down into them, the ovens were sealed, and the soft coal was distilled. It leaves only the coke behind. When the poisonous gases are driven out it is necessary to empty the ovens by manual labor. The ovens are still very hot, and poisonous gases are yet being driven from the coke. After I saw this they took me to see ovens on one side of which was a machine that leveled the coal with two or three strokes. When the coal had been distilled and the poisonous gases driven out, another machine pushed the whole lot of coke out at one push, and then the other machine pushed in and loaded the coke. I asked the tender of this engine what the men who were working on the first ovens received for their work. He said that they received $1.50 a day. I asked him what these men got who tended the machines. He said this was gentleman's work, and that they received $2.50 a day. It was gentleman's work, work I would have found pleasure in doing. Here is another example of the difference between strenuousness and efficiency.

The rooster, when you chase him, flutters from his dung hill over a low neighboring fence and is easily caught in some corner. He is strenuousness. If his ancestors ever knew how to fly, they forgot it long ago. The eagle, who soars hour after hour, in the blue air and never flutters a pinion, is efficient.

The Chinese woman who bears ten children and only raises two of them to maturity is strenuous. The condor who lays a single egg once in several years and brings up each of its young, until it knows how to fly, is efficient.

Secondly—Efficiency is not *system.* There is very much confusion regarding efficiency and system. I illustrate this by a story of the Spanish-American War.

A young doctor was sent to Cuba. He went to a hospital and found men dying of wounds, of typhoid, of yellow fever. There was no quinine or other medicine, and no dressings, and in a frenzy of anxiety and eagerness he wrote a requisition and sent it to Washington, and paced up and down waiting for the return of the vessel with the supplies which would save the lives of these soldiers. When the vessel came he could not find his package. He could scarcely believe it. He hunted around and after a while went back to his office. He found there an official envelope awaiting him. He opened it. The letter stated: "What you ordered requires Form 23 and you have written the requisition on Form 25. Please make it out again on the correct form and send it to us."

For the second time he made out his requisition and sent it in, this time with no such anxiety, with less eagerness, with less hope. He awaited the return of the vessel. At the end of the two weeks he was not surprised as much as the first time when he found no package. He went back to his office and found an official envelope, and read: "If you had properly observed the regulations, you would have found that you should have summarized your figures in column 5, not in column 7. Please correct the requisition and send it in and we will fill it." And after that, the young doctor lived not to save the lives of the soldiers in the hospitals but solely to make out requisitions in accordance with the red tape of the government. He had been diverted from an efficient surgeon to a systematized one.

Efficiency has made it possible to meet new conditions in a new manner. System therefore should always be subordinated to efficiency. Throughout the world it is not. Disorderly souls have been guided by strenuousness, and system has taken a hand and accomplished a great deal, but to-day efficiency has to make its way against the opposition of the strenuous, and against the much more dangerous opposition of the systematic.

Thirdly—Efficiency does *not primarily rest upon intensified use of* such crude instruments as *land, labor and capital;* but it rests upon ideas and the use of imagination. Efficiency is therefore imaginative, not strenuous and not systematized. Efficiency is that gift which enables us by intensified thinking to accomplish a maximum with the least effort and the least waste.

Is your work as teachers strenuous? If so it is not efficient.

Is your work as teachers systematized? If it is it cannot be efficient.

Does it depend on your school buildings, on the toil and labor of many teachers, on your books? If it does it cannot be efficient.

Now let me tell you how I work when I am called into a plant to give them the benefits of efficiency. There are four essentials that apply in every plant.

1. The first are the aims or the ideals that must be definite and clear, but not strenuous, systematized or materialized.

2. There must be an organization, to attain or maintain all the ideals.

3. Equipment, with which the organization can attain and maintain these ideals.

All these mean but very little unless the plant has:

4. A strong executive, who is able to carry them out.

So the first thing we do is to ask the manager: "What are your aims? *What are you trying to do?* Shall I tell you or will you tell us what you are trying to do?"

Usually when we go into a new plant we find that the ideals are not clear. One man may be trying to do three or four different things at the same time. He may be trying to sell the largest quantity of mediocre goods, a perfectly legitimate aim. Another time he may change his mind and try to sell a small quantity of high quality goods. But we want his statement of what he is trying to accomplish, because the whole management of the business will depend upon these ideals.

Now we come to the *organization*. We generally find that the organization is haphazard. Like Topsy, it growed. We find that it is lop-sided, imperfect, that certain men are trying to do a great many things that do not belong to their department. Other men have been misplaced. We may find that the organization is dominated by relatives, with no reference to their ability or integrity, and that the organization can neither maintain nor attain the best ideals.

We next investigate the equipment. *What is the equipment that has been given to the organization* with which to accomplish results? The equipment consists of men, materials, money, machines and methods. If for instance I were expecting to start an automobile factory in Argentine, I would first get up an organization that would carry on the business, and then, what is far less important, would provide the equipment. To do this we must have money, men, and materials. These we must get, or we cannot do business.

Finally we come to the *main requirement—a strong, able executive*, an individual, or it may be a board or a committee. A strong executive maintains the aim, and inspires the organization.

In these matters plants are generally defective, and the conditions cannot be rapidly changed. Assuming, however, that we find a satisfactory condition, we next apply the twelve principles of efficiency.

Take, for instance, a bank burglar. I tell him that the first principle is that of a *high ideal.* I ask him if his ideal is compatible with the first principle of efficiency, a high ideal.

The second principle of efficiency is *common sense,* good judgment. I ask him if it is compatible with common sense to choose as a profession bank burglary.

The third principle of efficiency is *competent counsel.* I ask him where he got counsel to the effect that the business of breaking into banks is a good one.

The fourth principle is *discipline*, which means the welfare of society. I ask him whether breaking into banks is compatible with discipline. Discipline plays a part only when the burglar is caught red-handed and sent up.

The fifth principle is the *fair dealing.* I ask him whether breaking into a bank is a fair deal.

If at the very start of his business a man neglects the five first principles, how can we apply for him the other *practical principles*:

(6) *Standard records.*
(7) *Planning.*
(8) *Standard conditions.*
(9) *Standardized operations.*
(10) *Standard instructions.*
(11) *Standard schedules.*
(12) *Efficiency reward.*

Then we come down to organization, and we apply to each part the same test of the twelve principles. We apply it to the aim. We apply it to every man and to every movement, and after we finish with the organization we apply the same twelve principles to the equipment—to each machine, to all the materials, to all the methods. Then we go to the executive, and we apply to him the twelve principles.

By the time we have made this survey, the whole organization looks to us like a sieve. There are holes in it everywhere, some of them large, some of them small. The first thing to do is to stop the larger leaks, then we stop the lesser leaks, and we keep busy until all the leaks are stopped. Trying to increase the efficiency of a plant with a sieve-like organization is like carting water in a pail filled with holes. You cannot carry it very far. This is the manner in which the principles of efficiency are initially applied.

We consider the rest of the problem under three simple categories:

(1) Materials or supplies.
(2) Personal services.
(3) General charges.

In your school work the materials do not count for very much in money. The personal service bill is the largest element, and the equipment charges might amount to a considerable item. Now for every item of material, for every item of personal service, and for every item of equipment charges, there are four different efficiencies. These four different efficiencies stand to one another in a dependent sequence and this results in efficiency being tremendously low in the end.

If a man should lose in Wall Street half his fortune, and to-morrow he should lose the half of what remains, and the next day half of that, he would very soon come to a very small number of dollars.

I went to England to sell a large Western mine in which some of my friends were interested. A man had cabled to me to come over at once. I had been offered a large commission ($100,000) if I should succeed in selling the mine. I met the young man at the railroad station. He asked me about the mine. He said, "I have a friend. He is a solicitor. I will introduce you to him and he will immediately place the mine. Do I get half the commission?" I said. "Yes." So now I was down to a $50,000 basis. He took me down to the solicitor. All the papers were looked over. A new statement was prepared, and he said, "Now, next week, Monday, I will meet you in London. I have a friend who puts these things through. By the way, do I get half the commission?" I said, "Yes, I will give you half of what is coming to me. I was down to $25,000. I met him in London and he took me to another solicitor, who punched a number of holes in the proposition, showed me that there were other better mines for sale in New Zealand, in Australia, in all parts of the world, and that my proposition was no better than the others. He then said: "We can put this proposition through; it looks favorably to me. By the way, do I get half the commission?" I said, "Yes." I was now down to a $12,500 basis. Two days afterward he took me down to see Mr. Wright, one of the great promoters in England. Mr. Wright said to me, "Mr. Emerson, you are wasting your time in London. You cannot float the best gold mine. There is no market for American securities. I advise you not to wait a day. Take this up some day in the future, not now." I came back with the mine unsold. Had he taken me up my commission would have shrunk still further. This illustrates dependent sequence, half and half and half.

For every article and material equipment there are four efficiencies. There is:

(1) Efficiency of *Price*. (2) Efficiency of *Supply*. (3) Efficiency of *Distribution*. (4) Efficiency of *Use*.

I can illustrate this best by railroad time tables. One of the great railroad purchasing agents said that by proper looking around he had been able to reduce the cost of the printing of the time tables 30 per cent. Therefore, the efficiency of that printing was only 70 per cent. A great many more time tables are printed than there is necessity for. Many of the time tables are not taken away from the printer. I remember looking over some of the books. There was an over-supply. The amount of the bill was very high. We will assume that the efficiency of the supply was 80 per cent. Now, these time tables were distributed everywhere. When you only wanted a leaflet, you had to take the whole time table. This illustrates inefficiency of distribution. That is found to be as low as 50 per cent. I frequently forget what I have looked up and get another time table. I always take two or three. The efficiency of use of the time table is extremely low. Multiply 70x80 (the first two efficiencies) and that brings you down to 56 per cent. Multiply that by 50 and you get down to 28 per cent., and thence to 14 per cent. Remember, too, that the cost of making time tables amounts to as much as the bill for the renewal of steel rails.

The same principles of efficiency apply to labor.

I went to a New England textile mill, and they took me through the machine shop and through the departments of textile work. When I returned the superintendent said, "What do you think of it?" I said, "I do not think that your machine shop is very efficient." Immediately they took offence. The master mechanic said, "This is a repair shop. Do you realize its purpose? It is our duty to repair all the machinery that breaks down. It does not make any difference what it costs. We cannot put in a lot of records, planning and efficiency rewards, and all that stuff. We must keep the mill going."

Before I had a chance to reply, the president said, "Let us go into the machine shop, that you may show me what you mean."

It is naturally not easy to point out a concrete case of inefficiency, but I went with him and stopped at the first machine. I watched it for a minute or so. There was a little steel plate to be shaped, and the tool was making a long stroke back and forth, cutting air three-quarters of the time and metal one-quarter of the time. The efficiency of the stroke was only 30 per cent. The tool was moving very slowly back and forth. There was no reason why it should not have been going like a sewing machine. The efficiency of speed was only 33 per cent. They had a diamond-pointed tool that was taking off only a sixty-fourth of an inch, almost as fine as a human hair. I could not see why they could not take off an eighth of an inch. The efficiency of feed was only 25 per cent. They were taking four cuts where two cuts would have been sufficient, a roughing cut and a smoothing cut. The efficiency of the number of cuts was 50 per cent. You multiply 33x30 and you get 10 per cent.; multiply that by 25 and you get 2½ per cent.; then multiply that by 50 and you get 1¼ per cent. In this repair shop a machine was taking eighty times as long as it had any business to take. I then said, "The way you are running this shop makes anything possible. In your shop the machines are cutting air three-quarters of the time, the tool is taking off but one sixty-fourth of an inch and taking four cuts where two would be sufficient." This illustrates the dependent sequence as related to machine labor.

This is a general outline of the modern teaching of efficiency. We are just on the threshold of the work. When we go into a plant, we properly and rightly tell the proprietor that we know the state of the art up to the present, that we can give him the best help that modern knowledge affords in putting his plant on an efficient basis. But when we come back to our own office and we face the other way and look at the problem as it stretches out before us, we see that we are just on the threshold of knowledge, that the fog is gradually lifting.

The efficiency of the material, the efficiency of the wage earner, the efficiency of the equipment, the efficiency of the ideals of organization, and of the executive—may not be as important in the future as certain dawning possibilities. We are just beginning to study the difference between energizing work and enervating work, and particularly the difference between men and women taking up work they are not fitted for, and taking up work for which they are fitted.

Let us begin with the latter problem. Suppose that I wanted to develop a race horse. If I should supply the best kind of kite track, if I should bank the curves and elevate them mathematically, if I should construct the best kind of a sulky, and if some skillful blacksmith would make the proper kind of shoes, and a harnessmaker the best harness, and if I should have the best kind of a stop-watch, that would record the one-hundredth part of a second, *if I were working on some ordinary plug of a horse*, I should not accomplish as much as if I had no track but a country road, no wagon but a spring wagon, no harness but an ordinary harness, but had *a thoroughbred to begin with.* The difference between what a man can do when he is adapted to his work and what he can do when he is not adapted to his work is almost infinite.

There is an old German saying that every barber is a conservative and every tailor a radical. The barber, shaved each customer's face, dressed the customer's hair, fixed his wig, looked after his dress, and bled him, acting as surgeon as well as barber. He was busy on his feet all day, talked about the latest news, and discussed topics of the day. When a man of that kind went home he was thoroughly satisfied to become a peaceful citizen. But the tailor, who sat all day long with his legs crossed sewing, when he finished his work, had to go out and raise a disturbance of some sort to let out the accumulation of the fatigue poisons he accumulated in his work. The tailor's work is enervating.

A man from Cincinnati went into a mill in New England, and said to the owner: "There is the department from where all the troubles begin! Those men are disorderly. They start up the strikes. They are bad family men." The owner of the plant said, "That is perfectly true, but how do you know." The reply was: "The condition of the work is such that it is impossible that they will be otherwise. It is so noisy that these men cannot even hear each other. Necessarily, they have accumulated such an amount of fatigue poison that it is impossible for them to settle down and lead peaceful lives." Their work instead of being energizing was enervating.

To close, I shall tell you an anecdote in which efficiency work is shown. I went into a large mill in Cincinnati in which the girls had been very difficult to discipline. They left; they did not stay. They were troublesome; they were disorderly and the superintendent, who was wise, one morning put a large Maltese cat in the room and when the girls came around they did not know how the cat got there and adopted it as a pet. The superintendent said that the cat had better be removed. The girls wanted to keep the cat. When I came in I saw the cat on a shelf and the cat jumped off and went to one of the girls. The girl stopped her work and gave the cat to the next girl and passed it all around. This gave the girls a rest of two or three minutes. Then the cat went back to her place. This time had been sufficient to stop the accumulation of the fatigue poisons. This difference of two or three minutes made all the difference in the world.

This subject is tremendous. You must feel it for yourselves.

SUMMARY OF ANSWERS TO QUESTIONS.

The success of a school depends on the executive, and executive ability in the highest authority is more important than lower down the line. Executive ability is always and everywhere valuable.

The executive must have definite aims and must have a suitable organization, he must have equipment. The child, the parent, the teacher, the principal, the superintendent is each an executive as to respective parts of the work, and the clashes between different ideals caused tremendous loss.

Shall the type of management be strenuous, shall it be systematic, shall it be efficient? Consider the possibilities of waste of the child who is efficiently trying to pursue the ideal of a good time and the teacher who is with systematized strenuousness pursuing the ideal of a curriculum.

Schools are tremendously inefficient, not because everybody does not work, but because there is no accepted ideal for any executive from child up to superintendent to play and work up to.

BIBLIOGRAPHY.

"Profit Making Management," Charles U. Carpenter; "Work, Wages ,and Profit," Gantt; "Motion Study," Gilbreth; "Cost Keeping," Gillette & Dana; "Efficiency," Emerson, Harrington; "Principles of Scientific Management—Shop Management," Frederick Winslow Taylor. The subject is also discussed by Benjamin C. Greenberg in the January and February numbers of *The American Teacher.*

WHAT IS THIS SCHOOL SYSTEM FOR?

A RE-EXAMINATION OF EDUCATIONAL COMMONPLACES.

An Address Before the High School Teachers' Association of New York City on May 25, 1912.

By

Prof. Paul H. Hanus of Harvard University.

Mr. President and Fellow Teachers:—

I am very glad indeed to have this opportunity to meet you together. I am, however, sorry that both you and I are sure to be disappointed in this meeting. It is quite contrary to my understanding that I should speak to-day of the results of the School Inquiry. The misunderstanding on that matter is due partly to me and partly, I think, to your President. In any event the announcement that I was to do so is an error. One the other hand, I could not refuse the invitation of your President to meet, at least once, this Association, even if in what I have to say I represent only myself and not the School Inquiry.

I shall also anticipate another possible disappointment; I do not intend to deal specifically with high school problems as such. In what I have to say I wish to call your attention to certain high school problems in relation to some larger or related ,educational problems; which I think it is not uncommon for high school teachers to neglect, even to ignore; at any rate high school teachers very commonly give comparatively little attention to them.

With that general statement as a preamble, I beg you to bear with me while I call your attention to certain very important educational commonplaces, which, it is desirable we should remind ourselves of from time to time lest we lose ourselves in the details of our work and fail to realize, or at last to appreciate, its significance. Now, I do not hesitate to talk about these commonplaces because, after all, to get a fresh view of the significance of the commonplaces of which our lives are greatly made up is to gather renewed inspiration for effort; and that has to be often repeated if we are not to be enslaved by these commonplaces themselves.

I referred a moment ago to the fact that secondary school teachers —high school teachers—sometimes fail to recognize, and sometimes absolutely ignore, important educational questions with which they might well concern themselves. I mean that it is not uncommon for high school teachers to regard themselves as the "Corps d'elite" of the school system with but little relation to the rest of the school system. They are the Olympians seated on high, and they look down with more or less compassion, more or less tolerance, sometimes with a little contempt, on the humanity at the foot of the hill—the humanity being the elementary school teachers.

I want to call your attention, then, to the significance of this very comprehensive, complex, expensive public school system and ask you what it is all about—what it is all for. I am all the more encouraged to do so, because in conversation with a high school teacher the other day, he said to me: "What is this school system for?" That seemed to me to be significant, because, as I have already said twice, I think high school teachers do not often ask themselves that question, and it seems to me to be decidedly important.

In other words, nothing less than one's conception of his work will be determined by his conscious aims. His conscious aims will determine the selection of the material with which he works; it will also determine the distribution of his emphasis on this, that, or the other aspect of his work. That is to say, they will make his work significant—will prevent it from degenerating into mere routine. My observation leads me to believe that a very large portion, if not the majority, of high school teachers are merely conscientious workers in a routine, concerning themselves but little with its significance, and sometimes even wilfully ignoring that significance. I want, then, to direct your attention, as I say, to certain fundamental commonplace principles which underlie our whole public school activity. I want to direct your attention to its fundamental aims.

UNDERLYING PRINCIPLES.

I think the principles underlying contemporary provision for, and the tendencies in, public education may be formulated as follows:

1. Public education should train efficient citizens. It should arouse and develop all the worthy interests and the corresponding powers of each pupil, so far as his ability and stage of development permit, to the end (1) that the common interests of our democratic society may be recognized and appreciated and their progressive development provided for, and (2) that the interests of all individuals may be promoted so far as they are not mutually exclusive. These interests are, spiritual (intellectual, moral, aesthetic), hygienic, economic, civic or political. They are also religious; but since experience has shown that religious interests are inseparable from ecclesiastical interests, and society has an institution for fostering both at once, a democratic society very properly delegates the preservation and transmission of religious interests as such to the church.

2. Public education should strive to gradually emancipate each pupil from external restraint and guidance, and thus render him self-directing—intellectually, morally, and physically stable, alert, vigorous and active. Together with the instruction public education offers, it should, therefore, insist throughout on discipline that is wise, kindly and firm, including appropriate punishment when it is needed—a discipline that insists upon progressive conformity of conduct to insight, including habits of steady application and reasonable achievement.

3. Public education should endeavor to prepare each pupil to make the best use of his leisure, as well as of his working hours. Satisfactory diversions and good recreative habit are important for both the individual and society. Without disparaging harmless diversions and amusements, public education should therefore strive to develop an appreciation of, an a demand for, the serious pleasures our civilization affords.

4. Public education should strive to render each pupil economically intelligent and efficient. It should direct each pupil's attention to a vocation to which he may reasonably aspire; that is, every pupil

should be led gradually to realize that a suitable vocation accessible to him and adapted to him is indispensable to a useful and happy life; and as he approaches the end of his school career, whatever his age may be, he should come to see that his vocation will be not only the means of satisfying his personal wants and ambitions, but, because it is the chief means of establishing significant relations between himself and his fellow men, it is also the source of such public service as he is capable of and may be called upon to render. Public education should, therefore, provide for the development of vocational purposes based on vocational enlightenment; and it should offer each pupil appropriate training for the vocation of his choice—so far, at least, as the non-professional vocations are concerned.

CONTEMPORARY AIMS OF ELEMENTARY SCHOOLS.

The contemporary aims of the public elementary schools of a progressive city should be, accordingly:

1. To enable every pupil to read the English language intelligently, and to speak and write it correctly and with reasonable facility; and, so far as his capacity and stage of development permit, it should enable him to appreciate the literature of the English language as a source of guidance and inspiration in all the relations of life.

Further, for ambitious and able pupils, together with those pupils who intend to continue their systematic education in the high school, to provide instruction (elementary, but serious so far as it goes) in the three modern foreign languages—French, German and Spanish—of most use to Americans; thus laying the necessary early foundation for an ultimately satisfactory command of the resources of at least one of those languages in addition to English.

(I am not, you see, making specific application of these principles to any particular city. It seems to me that specific application of such principles as these must be worked out by each city. In what respects they may need modification is a matter which each community must determine for itself. In general, these principles seem to me those which underlie the large proportion of all American public education.)

2. To enable the pupil to acquire a command of the fundamental operations of arithmetic sufficient for the ordinary affairs of life and for further progress in mathematics; that is, it should lead the pupils to acquire the habit of correctness and reasonable rapidity in addition, subtraction, multiplication and division of whole numbers and simple fractions, both common and decimal, together with percentage and its simplest applications to interest and trade discount.

If these principles seem to you to run counter to progressive educational theory they should be experimentally tested, and the fruits of those experiments should be carefully collected and appraised. I, personally, have no doubt that the amount of mathematics which I have here set down for the elementary schools is sufficient for the ordinary affairs of life and for all further progress in mathematics. The point is, however, that such contentions as these require experimental verification.

3. To enable the pupil to acquire a knowledge of the earth and its products in relation to man—to man's distribution and occupations; that is, of geography, and particularly of the geography of North America and of his own State.

4. To give each pupil training in the elements of natural science on which our contemporary civilization so largely depends—science that can be assimilated by pupils of elementary school age.

5. To give each pupil the leading facts of the development of nations, and gradually enable him to understand the relation of these facts to each other; and particularly it should lead him to see the progress which the world has made toward democratic Government and the conditions on which the stability and further progress of our own democracy depends in city, state and nation.

6. To lead the pupils, by instruction and experience, to understand the significance of the industrial and commercial activities whereby society keeps itself going; that is, the public elementary school should offer instruction in the manual arts, domestic arts and agriculture where that is appropriate, accompanied by laboratory or practical experience, so far as local conditions permit; in order to give the pupil a real insight into industrial occupations and a practical acquaintance with their materials, tools and processes. Similarly, the pupils should be led to appreciate the significance of commerce so far, at least, as to enable him to understand the part played by commerce in the progress of society and in the world of to-day.

It is easy to misunderstand me here—I am still speaking of the elementary school. I have no expectation that children under fourteen years of age can be trained to be merchants or artisans, and I have of course no desire that they should be; on the contrary, I have every desire that they should not. My point is that the way to awaken understanding and appreciation of the significance of these things in modern life is to incorporate them into the training of children in the elementary schools in such a way that that significance can not be missed. The ordinary manual training does not do that at all.

It is sometimes expected that manual training will have an immediate vocational value; nothing is farther from the truth. As a matter of fact, it could have more vocational value than it has; but in the elementary schools the children are too young to be taught a vocation—they are too young to be turned into a particular channel.

I referred a moment ago to the necessity for the development of vocational purposes, and that means vocational enlightenment. I ought, perhaps, to say that the development of vocational purposes, and vocational enlightenment—or vocational guidance, as it has come to be called—does not mean prescribing a vocation. It does not mean abridging the pupil's education; it does not mean choosing a vocation for A, B or C. It does mean pointing out to A, B or C that a vocation is a necessary ultimate goal; pointing out to him also the conditions under which that goal is to be attained—pointing out to him, therefore, among other things, the advantages of further education to a realization of the purpose; then to help him to achieve his purpose, and plan his educational career accordingly.

Let me emphasize, once more, that the object of vocational guidance is not to prescribe an occupation; the object of vocational guidance is not to abridge the pupil's education. The object of vocational guidance is to bring to bear on the pupil all the information which he needs in order that ultimately he may choose his career deliberately and that he may prepare for that career in the most effective and desirable way.

7. To give the pupil an incipient command over the aesthetic resources of to-day, so that his own life may be enriched and sweetened thereby, and the appreciation of beauty in nature and in art may be generally disseminated. The public school ought, therefore, to give instruction in art.

8. To teach the pupil to take care of his body and how to promote its normal growth and vigorous development, to the end that he may possess the physique and endurance commensurate with the demand and opportunities of modern life, and that he may come to appreciate the reasonableness and the necessity of the provision for public, as well as for private health; that is, he should not only receive instruction in physiology, hygiene and biology, but he should be led to insist on the conditions that determine good health in private and community life.

AIM OF PUBLIC VOCATIONAL SCHOOLS.

The aim of public vocational schools is to teach skilled vocations to persons over fourteen years of age who do not aim at a high school education. Such schools combine both theory and practice, and offer their instruction as: (a) Full-time day schools to those children, fourteen to eighteen years of age who can attend continuously during the day; such schools alone, however, would fall far short of realizing the aim of vocational education. (b) Day co-operative schools for those children fourteen to eighteen years of age whose employers are willing to co-operate with the schools to the extent of allowing the pupils to alternate between work and school, the pupils being organized in pairs or in groups for the purpose, and receiving pay for the work they do. (c) Day continuation schools for those persons, fourteen years of age and upwards, whose employers are willing to release them from their work in order to attend school for several hours—perhaps for six to ten hours—per week without loss of pay. (d) Evening schools for persons over eighteen years of age who aim at general culture, or who desire to improve themeslves in their several callings.

Not long ago I was discussing with a considerable number of teachers the feasibility of establishing co-operative and continuation schools and the general trend of the discussion was that while it might be desirable to establish such schools, it was impossible in New York City, because industry and commerce would not co-operate. This same subject was discussed also at a meeting of employers—manufacturers and business men in New York City—and they were heartily in accord with such a general project, but said: "You cannot get such a thing as that going in this city, because the teachers will not co-operate." In other words, it is clear that what is needed is a propaganda for enlisting the co-operation of the teachers on the one hand and the business world on the other, so that they may work together for the consummation of this very desirable thing—the thing they both want.

It seems to me that the real solution—the only solution now in sight, whatever we may find possible by-and-by—of providing vocational education for the great mass of children over fourteen years of age is the continuation and the co-operative school; and the darkest area in the problem of vocational education is the education that should be provided for the automatic workers, those whose tasks tend to lethargize body and mind. Every community which is alive to its responsibilities should seriously study that problem.

It is not so difficult to establish appropriate school courses in the trades requiring the exercise of intelligence, or variety in the exercise of intelligence; but the occupations requiring that kind of activity on the part of the worker are diminishing and the automatic operations are increasing; and it is, therefore, a problem every school system, every community must face—what to do with the great army of automatic workers, so that they may not degenerate—grow more sophisticated, to be sure, but less intelligent than they were when they left school at fourteen or fifteen years of age.

Industry and commerce have not hitherto recognized their responsibility for the education of the youth by whose labors they profit. They have hitherto been willing to throw the responsibility of the education of the youth entirely upon the school; but the school cannot carry that responsibility alone.

It is certainly true that without the co-operation of industry and commerce, the education of the workers of the world—I use that term, for convenience, to designate the non-professional classes—without the co-operation of industry and commerce that education cannot be successfully carried on. If I had time I should like to dwell longer upon that point, but I must pass on.

So much for elementary education, including the vocational education, which a democratic society must provide if it is concerned about the dissemination of general well-being—about progressive satisfaction in the society in which the people live.

If we look upon the function of the school as the conservation, the improvement, and the transmission of the resources that society has developed, we shall be able to throw into their proper perspective the particular functions of the elementary school, the secondary school, and the vocational school.

AIM OF PUBLIC HIGH SCHOOL EDUCATION.

The aim of public high school education—public secondary education—in this country is to elevate the general level of intelligence, character and efficiency of all who are able to take advantage of the opportunities it offers. Unlike most secondary education abroad, secondary education in this country is not merely for the well-to-do and socially superior classes, with incidental opportunities for a few of the most gifted of the less fortunate classes. Our secondary education aims to reach the "masses" as well as the "classes." It does not recognize social segregation as such; and so far as its administration is concerned, it is, therefore, equally accessible to all, or should be.

High school education aims to secure for each pupil an approprlate extension of his acquaintance with the resources and problems of our civilization begun in the elementary school, and at the same time to fix and strengthen his command over them so far as his capacities and the time limits of his education permit.

To this end education in this country is free in the high school, as well as in the elementary school, and the transition from the elementary school to the high school should be as easy and natural as from grade to grade in the elementary school. Indeed, except for the grouping of pupils in separate buildings for the convenience of instruction and management, it ought to be impossible to say, in well-organized school systems, where the elementary school ends and the high school begins.

Remembering that one fundamental object of all American education is to disseminate common interests and a good mutual understanding of them among all the people, it is important that the studies and activities of the high school should cover all the interests of our civilization so far as they can be rendered interesting, intelligible and accessible to children and youths of high school age. In other words the scope of high school education should be as broad as human interests.

Every one will admit these general principles. I am dwelling on them, however, in order that we may measure the work we are doing by them. I am asking you to consider whether the work we are doing is really tending towards the realization of the purposes these principles embody—whether the teacher of manual training, for example, is really helping to achieve these purposes; whether the teacher of Latin is doing it, and whether the teacher of mathematics is doing it, and to what extent.

A little while ago I reminded you that the conception which each teacher entertains of his work will determine the significance of that work for his pupils. For example, suppose the teacher's conception of mathematics is that it is a bit of organized human experience, and teaches his subject from that point of view; the effect on the pupils will be far more vital than if he merely regards mathematics as a science for the pupils to assimilate if they can. Also, the value of history depends on the way in which the facts are selected, organized and related to life. Suppose one of your underlying principles in teaching history is that the pupil shall gain from that subject a deeper understanding of, and greater respect for, the best ideals of democratic government, obviously your teaching will be profoundly influenced thereby; and history may thus become, through your teaching, a means of enabling the pupil to assimilate at least one valuable portion of human experience for his own good and the good of society.

It is possible for a teacher to teach commercial subjects so that they have a real bearing on real commerce. In any subject—mathematics, history, commerce, manual training, and all the rest—if the teacher teaches his subject, so that it really serves to interpret contemporary life in a significant way the fundamental aims of the pupli's education are likely to be at least approximately realized. Otherwise they cannot be.

Just now I said that high school education aims to secure for each pupil an appropriate extension of his acquaintance with the resources and problems of our civilization begun in the elementary school. To conserve, improve, and transmit these interests of society in the most effective way, it is important that each pupil during the period of adolescence should be led to self-discovery in respect to his dominant tastes and capacities. He should shape his educational career progressively in harmony with that discovery in order that his work may be most fruitful of results for his own growth in knowledge and power while in school and subsequently; and to equip him to become a thoughtful and an active member of the society of which he is to be a part. Under other circumstances he can hope for only mediocre achievement both during his school life and thereafter. If he does achieve more it will not be because of his education but rather in spite of it.

It is important that all the resources which society possesses shall be preserved, improved and transmitted; it is not important, it is not possible, it is not desirable that any one pupil shall attempt the task of assimilating all of these resources himself, and of being effective in dealing with them. My point is that it is in the interests of the individual, as well as of society that he should choose to deal with that aspect, with those resources, in which he can be most competent.

The pupil's high school education, therefore, should include a training in choice, primarily the choice of studies; and to accomplish this end it must offer a considerable range of elective studies and insist on satisfactory achievement in all that the pupil undertakes. To prevent undue narrowness and premature specialization in the pupil's education, the public high school should also insist on attention to a considerable variety of studies, as well as on concentration of effort in a single field.

A good deal has been said, at various times and in various places, with respect to the purpose of a general high school or of general courses in the high school. Whatever else its purpose may be I suppose it aims at what is called general culture. Now, what is general culture? I should like to offer for your consideration, for the time being, this definition which looks upon general culture as a force and not as mere possession. General culture is the capacity to appreciate the resources and the problems of our civilization, and the power to deal effectively with some of them. It is a definition which covers both interest and power. It would find its exemplification in curricula for individual pupils which should emphasize a particular field of study and touch others; i.e., that is, each pupil aiming at general culture would in the high school both concentrate and disperse his attention during the entire four years of his course.

That definition of general culture, however, provides training for general social service only; it does not provide for specific social service, which means vocational service.

I have already said that our public high schools aim to elevate the general level of efficiency, as well as of intelligence and character. The discussion thus far, however, has referred only to general efficiency. But training for specific efficiency—for progressive usefulness in partcular vocations—is equally important, and is also a task which the secondary school must perform as well as it can.

Owing to the bad tradition imported from Europe—that secondary education is primarily for pupils of the well-to-do and professional classes, and hence aims only at general culture, including preparation for college vocational aims in high schools were, for a long time, looked at askance by teachers and school officers. They were looked upon as an unworthy concession to the commercial spirit of the age. They were treated with scant sympathy, and since they were merely tolerated it was natural that vocational courses should be inferior to other courses or departments. They were, and often are now, inferior; and too commonly the teachers of the vocational courses were and still are likewise inferior. This inferiority of course led to inferiority of pupils; and so we had an inferiority of courses, pupils, and teachers that was, and often still is, conspicuous.

The demand for suitable vocational education of high school grade has, nevertheless, persisted, and during the last quarter of the nineteenth century and since there has been a growing recognition of its value—at first for boys only, but later for girls as well. This recognition has become the most potent cause for the establishment of separate vocational high schools. It was believed that in such high schools the vocational aim would develop at least as keen an interest and as satisfactory work on the part of pupils, teachers, and administrative officers as prevailed in the non-vocational schools. This result has been partially realized. Vocational high schools have grown in number, variety and efficiency, particularly during the last decade. They now include technical high schools for both sexes, high schools of commerce, and agricultural high schools.

These schools meet an important demand. High school pupils wish to prepare for directve positons; they distinctly intend to rise above the level of the rank and file of the industrial army. The boy who goes to a high school looks forward not to work at the bench but to a directive position, no matter whether his course in school consists largely of shop work or not. In other words, technical high schools have the task of properly developing vocational education of secondary grade—an education that equips for directive activity in the world's work, on the basis of technical insight and practical experience.

The great defect of most technical high schools—I should like to emphasize this—is that the relation between the industrial work, or the commercial work, as the case may be, and the other work of the school, is not close. In other words, the specific vocational work of the school is not illuminated, strengthened, extended, by the so-called academic studies. Suppose it is the dominant purpose of a school to send boys out into the world of commerce equipped to deal with the commercial problems of to-day. If that be true, it certainly is true that the dominant note of a high school of commerce would be appropriate provision throughout its activities for realizing its aim; that is, the mathematics of such a school, it seems to me, would be appropriate to the dominant purpose which the school has; the English taught in that school—its subject matter and methods—would be such as are appropriate to the purpose of that school; the history too would be not only tinctured but would be controlled in the selection of material and methods, by the dominant purpose of the school.

Now I should also like to point out in passing that such a school in realizing its vocational purpose need not, and in my opinion does not wholly miss general culture. Its immediate object would be vocational efficiency; but if we agree that general culture is the power to appreciate and to deal effectively with some of the resources of the civilization of to-day, I think a vocational school that does its work well would incidentally also provide for general culture. It goes without saying that those young people who can defer their preparation for a vocation until they are more than eighteen years of age have the great privilege of pursuing general culture itself as an aim. But we are dealing specifically now with the mass of young people who go into the vocational school because they realize or believe that they must go into a vocation at the age of eighteen or thereabouts; we are dealing with the mass of pupils who go to a vocational high school because at the end of the secondary school they must enter at once on their life career. I would like to dwell longer on this point but I must pass on, otherwise I shall not fulfill my promise not to overstep my time.

It was to be expected that the success of the vocational schools would affect fundamentally the character of the vocational courses in the general high schools, and this has actually happened. Whereas it was once true that satisfactory commercial courses, for example, could not be obtained by pupils seeking such instruction in general high schools, it is now true that such courses are found in many schools. Vocational aims have accordingly already attained the recognition they deserve in many public high schools throughout the country, and that recognition is growing.

I should like to point out too that for the full realization of these aims, or of others that may commend themselves to you as teachers, co-operation under proper leadership is necessary. It is true that the problem of each school is, in a large sense, a peculiar problem, and that it ought to have the opportunity to solve its problem in accordance with the insight it develops and the industry, devotion and intelligence of its teachers.

I know of no better task for this association to undertake than to assign to some one of its committee—perhaps your committee on secondary education is the committee—the difficult duty of defining clearly the function of the public high schools of this city. Such a definition must be a series of definitions because the problem of the education which each school has to solve differs in important particulars from that which every other school has to solve.

In general, I am convinced that the efficiency of any school or school system depends upon habitual self-examination, and a careful appraisal of the results which that self-examnation brings to light. We now all take too much for granted, not only in education, but in life's activities in general; and the only way in which we can bring ourselves face to face with the realities with which we have to deal is by rigorous self-scrutiny. Then we must face squarely the results that that examination may bring to light and govern ourselves accordingly.

And finally, the way to make progress in education as in everything else, is by experiment. At the present moment experiments are going on everywhere, but the fruits are not gathered. Experiments to confirm or refute educational opinion is the watchword of contemporary educational progress. If we believe, for example, that English grammar is fundamental—a thorough-going drill five times a week for three or four years—to a satisfatcory progress in a foreign language in the high school—if we believe that that drill is necessary to satisfactory progress, there is a way to settle that by experiment. If we believe that pupils who are studying the classics get a better training in English than pupils not studying the classics, there is a way to find out—try it and see.

In conclusion, I wish to congratulate heartily the committee on secondary education for its painstaking and suggestive report; also I want to congratulate the committee that submitted a report on the relation of high schools to colleges. Both these committees are doing

(For Conclusion of Prof. Hanus's Address see Page 15)

(Reports will be continued in the next Bulletin)

OFFICIAL BULLETIN

of the High School Teachers' Association of New York City.

No. 36. SATURDAY, DECEMBER 7' 1912

The Board of Representatives, on May 23, 1911, empowered the Executive Committee to issue a Bulletin monthly, instead of four times a year.

THE SECOND REGULAR MEETING FOR 1912-1913 will be held Saturday, December 7, 1912, at the High School of Commerce.

DEPARTMENT MEETINGS begin at 10 A. M. Besides the programs as given below, there should be discussion of Questionnaire for Directory and Account of Aim, Scope and Equipment of Departments in the Ideal or Typical High School.

GENERAL MEETING begins at 11 A. M. in Auditorium.

MAIN ADDRESS BY DISTRICT SUPERINTENDENT BARDWELL.
EFFICIENCY IN RECITATION }
Discussion

WILLIAM T. MORREY, President.

AGNES CARR, Secretary.

DEPARTMENT MEETINGS, 10 A. M.

ANCIENT LANGUAGES—Room 534, Dr. Walter E. Foster, Stuyvesant High School, Chairman.

"Literary Allusions in Plautus," by Prof. Charles Knapp of Columbus University.

BIOLOGY—Room 301. Mr. Harvey B. Clough, H. S. of Commerce, Chairman. Frank Merrill Wheat, De Witt Clinton H. S., Secretary.

"Efficiency in Biology Teaching," by Prof M. A. Bigelow, Teachers' College.

BOOKKEEPING SECTION—Room 303, Joseph J. Klein, Richmond Hill High School, Chairman.

Dr. Albert Shiels, Superintendent in charge of Evening Schools of New York City, on Need of Standardizing Teaching Methods for Greater Efficiency.

Morgan J. Goldsmith, Washington Irving High School, on First Lessons in Bookkeeping.

Frank P. Baltz, Chairman Commercial Department ,Eastern District High School, on Controlling Accounts.

Dr. Joseph J. Klein, on the Introduction of Special Books.

The meeting starts at ten promptly in order to afford ample time for thorough discussion before the General Meeting.

ELOCUTION—Room 201' Mr. Raymond W. Kellogg, Morris High School, Chairman for Organization.

All teachers of Elocution, Voice Culture, and Oral Expression are cordially invited.

HISTORY AND ECONOMICS—Room 205, Miss Antoinette Lawrence, Jamaica High School, Chairman.

Tests of Efficiency, History Recitation, Dr. A. M. Wolfson, De Witt Clinton High School.

MATHEMATICS—Room 304, Elmer Schuyler, Bay Ridge High School, Chairman.

How to reach the individual Student in Mathematical Instruction, by Edward A. Hook, of Commercial High School.

Discussion Ralph B. Bliss, Commercial H. S.; Mr. Merle L. Bishop, Boys' H. S.

Elementary School Teachers welcomed.

MODERN LANGUAGES—Room 401, Colman Dudley Frank, De Witt Clinton High School, Chairman.

Modern Language meeting will be addressed by five Heads of Modern Language Departments who will give short talks on what they expect to find in thoroughly efficient recitations in the class-rooms under their jurisdiction.

Our meeting will thus be practical, pointed and a fit forerunner to the later General Meeting for the day.

PHYSICAL TRAINING—All teachers of Physical Training in our public hibh schools are invited to meet and to consider the organization of a department.

PHYSIOGRAPHY—Room 105B, Mr. Kirk W. Thompson, Jamaica High School, Chairman. Preparation of Questionaire.

"Some New Laboratory Experiments in Physiography," by Frank L. Bryant, Erasmus Hall High School.

SHORTHAND—Room 216. There was so much for discussion and so much critcism of the address on November 9, that it was voted to continue the discussion of Mr. MacNamara's Report.

CONTENTS OF THIS H. S. T. A. BULLETIN 36

HISTORY DEPARTMENT 1911-1912.

During the past year the Division of History of the High School Teachers' Association gave its attention mainly to two topics:—The new course in modern European history, and the supplementary readings required by the Board of Regents.

The first topic was discussed informally, and then, at another meeting, it was arranged to have reports, on the practical workings of the modern history course in the City High Schools, given by Dr. Sullivan, Dr. Wolfson, Miss Dixon, and by a representative of the Board of Regents. The necessity of a time limit prevented as long a discussion as we desired.

The members of the division expressed themselves strongly in favor of the adoption of this course in modern European ihstory. The chief difficulty seeming to be the lack of a text book that fully meets all the requirements of the situation.

As regards the question of supplementary reading for the history courses, a lively discussion early in the season started a consensus of opinion that the various city high schools were not then satisfactorily equipped with the books required for the aforesaid reading, nor was it certain that they would be so equipped before the January examinations. Accordingly a letter was sent by the department, asking the Regents to make the question on required readings on the examination papers optional with the students, and not obligatory, until the said books could be placed in sufficient numbers where the students could have access to them. This request was not granted.

FLORENCE L. BEEKMAN, Secretary.

ANTOINETTE LAWRENCE, Chairman.

MINUTES OF GENERAL MEETING, NOVEMBER 9, 1912.

The members of the High School Teachers' Association gathered at the High School of Commerce on November 9 for the first meeting of the year 1912-1913. The minutes of the May meeting were read and adopted as read.

President Morrey announced the time of the second meeting as December 7, when the principal speaker would be Superintendent Bardwell on the topic, "Greater Efficiency in the Classroom." The President called attention to the general subject of the work of last year. Principles of Scientific Management Applied to Efficiency in High Schools," stating that all activities had dealt with the ideals involved: that the discussions of the current year will deal with the practical application of these ideals. Speaking of the committees through which the work of the Associatio.. is done, President Morrey suggested that the various chairmen communicate with the members of their committees, outlining work and asking for co-operation.

Superintendent Stevens, the chief speaker of the morning, was then introduced. He took as his text John Fiske's phrase, "the lengthening period of infancy." He referred to the law requiring all children to remain in school until of age to go to work, thus increasing greatly the problem of the high schools. He stated emphatically that the high schools exist for all, without regard to mental calibre, their task involving the co-ordination of different races, of which fifty-two are reported as being represented and the maintenance of their position in spite of reluctant acceptance on the part of the community of Manhattan at least of their right of existence. (Stenographically reported by Mr. Horace G. Healey, and published in this Bulletin.)

As no one representing the Women's Association of High School Teachers was present to report for that body, Mr. Keener, President of the Men's Association of High School Teachers, was the next speaker. He began by suggesting that the President use his prerogative of committee-making by appointing a special committee of all members present, each to bring to the next meeting two members beside himself. This suggestion was acted upon at once. Mr. Keener mentioned the subjects discussed in his Association. (These are given in full in the Bulletin of his Association. Address R. H. Keener, 510 West 124th Street, New York City.

The work of the grade-advisers was presented in an interesting paper by Miss H. Elizabeth Seelman, of Girls' High School. Mr. Bryan, of High School of Commerce, spoke for the First Assistants. Dr. Sullivan, Principal of Boys' High School for the Principals. Dr. Stevens closed the discussion with a word of sympathy for democracy in the schools, but with the added statement that in spite of the best efforts in that direction, the constant tendency of a big organization is towards centralization.

(Miss Seelman's address found elsewhere in this Bulletin. The other addresses in next Bulletin.)

After a rising vote of thanks for the speakers, the meeting adjourned at 1:15.

(Signed) AGNES CARR,
Secretary.

ADMINISTRATION FOR EFFICIENCY.—ADDRESS BY ASSOCIATE SUPERINTENDENT EDWARD L. STEVENS.

(Reported by Horace G. Healey, Association Stenographer.)

Mr. Chairman: The remarks that I shall make on this occasion will be characterized, I hope, by breadth, but I also hope by neither length, nor thickness. I am glad to meet from time to time, as I have the opportunity and good fortune, the High School teachers of this city. I sometimes wish you might hold your meetings on some other day than Saturday; perhaps on Saturday afternoon, or Sunday morning, because then I would not be obliged to leave so many of your number waiting in the hall over at 59th street, anticipating my return. I begin to feel as if I were in a fatherly relation to a great many of you, because, as I look back on the lapse of years, I can recall sending in the appointments of about half or perhaps more than one-third of the High School teachers in this city. I have had the pleasure of rejoicing with you when you rejoiced, and of grieving with you when you grieved. I hope I have sympathized with you when sympathy was helpful. I have no doubt given admonition sometimes when admonition may have been unnecessary. With this assurance of interest based upon this long acquaintance, you will therefore accept my explanation and apology, if I say I have no address, as addresses are generally understood. But I shall speak to you freely, and I hope intelligently, concerning certain things which we, you and I, all of us, must bear in mind not only in the year to come, but in the years to follow.

Once upon a time, a man named John Fiske, formulated a theory which is generally known as that of **the lengthening period of infancy.** I know of no people to whom this particular hypothesis or this particular formula is of greater interest than to the High School teacher, because it is in the High School that we discover that this theory is probably true. There are certain things that go to prove it. One is the practice of the business world—the practice of the people here in this vicinity, where you and I live—who employ the boys and girls who come from our schools. We learn for example, that the New York Central Railroad does not care for apprentices under eighteen years of age. We know that most of the business houses do not care to employ boys and girls under sixteen. The time has come when the boy of ten, or the girl of eleven can no longer go to work. There is no opportunity for him or for her to labor. There is no demand for that particular kind or quality of work, which this boy or this girl at this particular age can perform; and this theory is also proven and demonstrated by the will of the people as it is formulated in statutes, and we discover that the boy or girl may not leave school before the age of sixteen, unless engaged in certain kinds or a certain character of employment.

But I need not dwell upon this, because it is a matter known to all of you. The thought in my mind is this: that this condition has imposed upon us an entirely different duty from that which was imposed upon the High School and High School teachers where you and I, in our generation, were prepared. We all can remember the time when the High School was a college preparatory school; but, it is no longer a preparatory school, either in this city or in any other city. It is a school for the boy and the girl, who is sent to us during this longer period of infancy—and this boy and this girl may be mediocre, dull or even stupid, but society in its wisdom has imposed this stupid, and this mediocre boy and girl upon us, and the care and the training and the education of such has become our duty and our obligation, just as much as the preparation of the boy and girl who has brilliant intellectual development and gives great promise of future scholarship, whom we hope shall leave our doors and enter a higher institution.

Now it is difficult for us, students of education, to realize this. It is far more difficult for the layman to realize this, and no wonder that if the layman does not recognize this great and remarkable change, he should from time to time criticise us for retardation, for High School mortality, for dropping back in classes, and for the failure of this pupil, and of that pupil or another. I think it may be safely stated that while we know that a great revulsion of feeling happened here in the United States lately, which has resulted, I am told, in the election of a President—a great revulsion of feeling to the extent that a party which at one time seemed in absolute control of the nation can only exhibit eight electoral votes for its candidates—there has been no general recognition, there has been no general sentiment exhibited in response to the proposition which I am so imperfectly endeavoring to submit to you; namely, **that the child of eleven or twelve, the child of sixteen or seventeen years of age, has become our care** and we may no longer say, "you and you may come to our school," and to the rest "you must go to work."

The time has come when we must accept this obligation; namely, that these people are our care, and for these boys and these girls of this particular age we must labor.

What does this mean? It means an entirely new definition, an entirely new circum-scription, an entirely new frame-work for the secondary school. As I have said, it is no longer a college preparatory school; my friends, it is no longer a school in which is taught only algebra or plain geometry or Latin or German or history. I think no greater service has been rendered by Stanley Hall than that in which he defies the High School as the school of adolescence. Let us begin to think about that. Let us begin to think about it and let us begin to make other people think about it, too. During the eight or nine years I have had the most intimate connection with the secondary schools of this community there has been no greater care, there has no greater trouble come to me than the correction of the understanding so usually common that the High School is not a High School for all. There has been no greater care, there has been no greater worry, there has been no greater difficulty than the criticism that has come to us, particularly to me, because the High School today is not doing what the college preparatory school of 1850 or 1860 or 1870 did. So I say the definition of a High School is entirely changed. Think of what an obligation and responsibility and what a duty this imposes upon us. The administration of a High School of this community, the direction and organization of its work, is made difficult because of this new condition of which I have spoken. It is also made difficult by the fact that in these schools are gathered the races of the world. I have told you on a previous occasion on this platform that in our schools there are 52 different races of the world represented, and this factor of difficulty is one which you and I may appreciate, but the layman has not yet begun to understand. The layman and the press have not yet begun to give us credit for teaching English as a foreign language. Yes, I mean that to many pupils of your schools the English language is as foreign as the imperfect knowledge of French or German, that I have, is to me.

The third point to which I ask attention is this: that the administration of the High School in this community is made difficult, because of the reluctant acceptance by the community of the secondary school. Now when I say "reluctant acceptance," of course I make it with certain reservations. I am perfectly willing to state in confidence that that part of the city known as Brooklyn has accepted the High School as an appropriate institution for a great many years, but I am telling no secret, and I am betraying no confidence, when I tell you that by many hundreds and thousands of people in Manhattan and the Bronx, the High School is not yet accepted. No longer than last week a prominent citizen of this community said he believed that the High School should be a place where boys and girls whose parents were able to pay tuition might attend, but he did not believe in any appropriation for High Schools, neither did he believe in supplying free books or teachers in any of these places. I think that one of our duties is not only as I have said, to work in our schools along the lines I have indicated, but to build up sentiment. I wish that in the five or ten years to come, those of you who belong to clubs, those of you who are interested in Sunday Schools, or those of you who have means of forming public sentiment would bear this in mind. Do not go into your club, or Sunday School, and talk about this "lengthening period of infancy," because not many would know what you meant, but let us begin to try to have the people realize that our boys and girls on the average must go to school until they are fourteen or fifteen or sixteen or seventeen, and that the High School is not alone for the bright boy or girl, but for the boys and girls of all capacities.

Now, my friends, it is common to state or to assert that the High School course is a course of four years. It is, on paper. There are 50,000 pupils in the High Schools of this city to-day. For 25,000 of the 50,000 the High School course will be of two years in length. I do not propose so long as I have anything to do with High Schools to recommend the establishment of two-year courses or three-year courses; but I do intend to state, to admit, to confess, if you would have me, that the High School course for half of the pupils who attend in your class rooms is of two years in length, and it seems to me that we, all of us, must sit up and take notice. Not that we will advise a two-year course, not that we will prescribe a two-year course, but let us make the work of the first two years in High School of such character and quality that the boy or girl who leaves at the end of the two years will be prepared for something definite; that there will be some definite and respectable work accomplished by the pupil at the end of that period. Not that I would want you to go into the school and class room and say we will give you a certificate at the end of two years, but let us have work so planned and of such quality and character that these 25,000 of our pupils will have done something worth while. I want to have the two-year boy feel when he has left at the end of two years, he has done something worth his time; that the three-year boy will feel at the end of three years he has accomplished something. He must not feel that the whole time has been wasted or lost if he should be compelled to leave before reaching the final or ultimate goal.

Therefore, do not repine; therefore, do not complain; therefore, do not resist or rebel, my friends, if because of your excellence as a teacher, your principal assigns you to classes of the first and second years: that is my exhortation to you. Do not feel that you have been demoted; do not come to 59th street and complain and appeal, if your principal finds that because of your excellence and ability and success as a teacher you have been assigned to classes of the first and second, or perhaps, third year. Remember that the great test of work is quality and excellence and efficiency of service, and if, because of your excellence and capacity and ability as a teacher you can be of great service, of great help, of great inspiration to this body, 50 per cent in number of all our pupils, be glad to have the opportunity to serve and to serve so abundantly.

It was my privilege last spring to speak to you from this platform concerning the statute which became a law in January and familiarly known as the "Equal Pay Law". Some of you have discovered how it operates. I do not expect it will be repealed very quickly. We discovered some years ago there were discrepancies and improper clauses in the "Davis Law", but twelve years elapsed before that law was amended or repealed. I doubt very much if the present salary law will be amended, repealed or changed very materiallv in the next ten years, and you and I will live under it.

I do not know of anything that has appealed to me more than the fact that this law has distinctly accelerated—if I may use that term—it has accelerated, or accentuated endeavor on the part of a large number of teachers. And it has led me to the belief that the key-note of the situation now, particularly in our High Schools, is the organization, the more efficient organizatino, of the departments of instruction. We cannot expect a principal who has one hundred teachers to know much about history and other subjects in our course. We cannot expect him to know much about modern languages, although he may have been excellent and very superior in his particular line of work as a teacher. It frequently happens that colonels of regiments forget the tactics, in what we call the school of the soldier, and we cannot expect a man who has charge of several thousand children to keep in mind the details which are necessary for proficient instruction in every subject in the corriculum. For a good many years the first assistant was regarded as a salary grade. In Brooklyn prior to the consolidation, there were "heads of departments." The two positions were consolidated in the "Davis Law," and the first assistant while retaining that title, has become "head of the department."

The first assistant, while he may retain that title, is going to become "head of department." The organization of the work for instance in classical languages or mathematics is going to depend in a large school very largely upon the ability, the skill, the capacity and the advice of the head of department. The head of department needs certain qualities. He needs scholarship—sufficient—not too much. The head of department needs to have a sense of proportion. I do not need to dwell on that; it means that you must be as wise as a serpent in dealing with people; it means that you must talk to a man one way and to a woman another way. We all know that.

All of you good people who took the last examination, if you are to be successful administrative heads of departments, if you are to have charge of, direction of, and care of other people, cultivate this faculty. To some people you can say "close that door", to others, "will you please close the door". And so I talk to you about this matter, for some of you may have trouble and you may want me to help you.

The principal of a High School once came to me and said, "I want to have you take this teacher out of my school, she is no good; she cannot teach at all." I said, "How long has she been there?" He said, "Two years." I said to him, "Do you know that that teacher has as much right to stay in your school as you have?" Now I said to him, "My dear sir, do you know what you are there in that school for?" He said, "What?" I said, "You are there to make good teachers out of poor ones; to make strong teachers out of weak ones, to make efficient teachers out of inefficient ones."

Now as I have said, the colonel of a regiment cannot help to forget the tactics in the school of the soldier, and these great schools we have in this community are too large, I regret to say, are too large for one individual to direct, but the duty remains nevertheless, that the poor teachers must be made good ones, and this duty is coming to fall more and more upon the heads of the departments. I hope the time will come when they do not need to teach so many periods as they do now—eighteen, twenty or twenty-four a day.

As to equipment, adequate equipment is a necessary thing. But remember the story told of Mark Hopkins, by James A. Garfield, that, "Mark Hopkins on one end of a bench, and a boy on the other, made a university." That is true of a college, and it is equally true of schools; but my friends, I do not want to have you forget in your effort to train the dull, the stupid and mediocre pupil, to have you forget the bright pupils. It seems to me, the point of attack in the secondary education of to-day is the conduct of the recitation. That is one on which our elementary school friends attack us very frequently, and perhaps with more reason, because the High School teacher as much as the College teacher is all too much in the habit of making the recitation period, the class period, a period for question and answer. Do you know what a lady investigator found in our schools as she went about with a stenographic note book in her hand? She found in certain class rooms that, of the entire time given to the recitation, forty-five minutes of the sixty were occupied by the talking of the teacher, and that twenty minutes of the time was devoted to answers by the pupils. I am compelled to believe that we talk altogether too much.

Of course, you may, if you wish to do so, adopt the lecture method. It was my privilege to attend not long ago some sessions in a medical college. I found that the physician devoted his entire time to the reading of notes which he had prepared for the purposes of the lecture, but the pupils were reading newspapers carefully folded and inserted in their note books. They knew that one of their number was taking notes and that he would manifold and supply them at three dollars each. How many of us have availed ourselves of the lists of questions usually to be found at the end of the lesson, especially in the older text books? Take for instance, geography and the lesson on South America. It was the finest thing in the world for the teacher, for he could turn to them and the pupils were expected to prepare their answers on those questions. Let us discover what the recitation is really for and what we can make out of it.

I recognize that this talk has been somewhat desultory—it has covered a number of subjects. I congratulate you on your opportunity for work, and I give you my best wishes that your work for the coming year may be efficient, that your hours may be happy. If there is any way that I may serve you in your schools. I shall be glad to do so.

HOW THE GRADE-ADVISER CAN PROMOTE HIGH SCHOOL EFFICIENCY.

By Miss Miss H. Elizabeth Seelman, of Girls' High School.

The honor of a place in this morning's program I owe not to any broad knowledge of the subject assigned me, but rather to a trap into which I unwittingly fell in conversation with President Morrey less than two weeks ago. My inability to acquire any wisdom since that time must be my apology for using, as the basis of my remarks, my own experience as grade adviser in the Girls' High School. I have written them down to save time, as I've had no experience with boys. What I have to say is of necessity deduced from my experience with girls.

I take it that the happy adjustment of the social life within the school to the more serious business of study is a problem common to all schools, but especially to girls' schools. Art, literary and debating clubs furnish social life to but a limited number. How are we to do for the majority not represented in these smaller circles, or how are we to keep these small groups from cutting themselves off socially from the larger whole? Out of this need for social reorganization after the abolition of school fraternities grew up the system of grade advisership in the Girls' High, but, strange to say, its immediate institution three years ago originated in an attempt to bind the Alumnae more closely to the school.

Alumnae did not return in large numbers on the evening set apart yearly for their reception. We learned, upon casual investigation, that a girl might attend the first year, but, failing to find the class-mates she sought, she spent a lonely evening and the following year remained away. To meet this situation, the Principal called together some of the old graduates of the school who had returned to the teaching force, discussed the matter with them, and concluded by appointing them advisers of respective grades. As such, the teacher was to organize the division to which she was assigned, look after its class meetings, guide it through parliamentary conflicts and presidential contests, be to the girls individually and to the division as a whole a general help in time of trouble, and share their fortunes and misfortunes, from grade to grade, right down to graduation and beyond. The beyond, you see, takes us back to our Alumnae problem, for the grade adviser keeps in touch with the girls after graduation, arranges for their reunions, and is present Alumnae evening to gather them together as of old. Thus, does she justify her existence.

Her contact, however, with these several hundred girls has led her a-field from the very beginning. She finds that she must take note of and guide the emotions of the growing girl into wholesome channels, or, as Jane Addams writes from her deep experience, the girl will have recourse to the more dangerous pleasures of the world outside. As I have suggested, the problem of grade recreation comes within the range of the adviser. She must help the girls to a normal democratic social life to supplant the old narrow fraternity clique. In the G. H. S. each grade is allowed three "large" affairs a term outside of school hours. These take the form of dances, salmagundi parties, theatre matinees and other amusements of a social nature. In addition to this, each grade in turn or in combination with another, is privileged to use the gymnasium one noon-period a week. The program of the grade-adviser is so arranged that she may be with her girls during this noon period. This is her opportunity of getting better acquainted with the individual girl and of talking over matters in general. At such a period earlier this term, my 3A girls evolved with me a scheme for raising money to help the Students' Aid Fund of the school. We put the scheme into operation this week. The girls are enjoying the work and fun together and at the same time learning the meaning of service. The grade adviser may in time help in the solution of the high school "mortality" problem. A new regulation in the G. H. S. requires that every girl who contemplates leaving school shall first confer with her grade-adviser. Last term, an impulsive, big-hearted little girl came to bid me good-bye. She had been conditioned in geometry. Summer was at hand, her father could use her in his store, and she was going to leave school to help him. We talked the matter over and I found that the condition was due to a shiftless method of home-study. We schemed out a plan to correct the same, she applied herself to geometry during the summer and passed off her condition in September. She is happy in this term's work, reports to me once a week after school, and together we confer most profitiably on matters at home and in school. Her case is but one of several of a like nature.

The problem of the girl who does not contemplate leaving school, but who has difficulties of another kind also comes within the range of the grade-adviser for solution. The other day a girl of good scholarship, sense, and dignity, who had been honored by her class-mates in various ways, asked if she might drop in to see me after school. The poor girl was tired of being dubbed trustworthy and dignified. She wished she were stupid like Grace Hunt who wasn't afraid to talk and walk in friendly fashion with Miss James. With the memory of my own girlhood in the same school, though somewhat past, still vivid, I suggested an hour's walk with a particular teacher one sunshiny afternoon. The way was easy, other walks are to follow, and that disheartened maiden now simply radiates happiness.

The gradeadviser has an opportunity, too, to extend her province into effective vocational guidance. A word in the class-room about the opportunities open to women and the need for a wise choice sets a class thinking to such an extent that for weeks afterward an adviser's time after school for other things is at a premium. If I but had the time, I could unfold many a tale in this connection.

Again, in the G. H. S. we are working out a co-operative student government organization. The grade-adviser belongs in an advisory capacity to the faculty board. It is easy to realize how her interest, her enthusiasm, and her knowledge of individual girls may relate her helpfully to this school organization that tends by supplanting the old police system of discipline to develop responsibility and moral courage. Further, in the Arista—the Phi Beta Kappa as it were of the high school—her first hand knowledge of the girls in her division lends weight to a fair choice of honor girls.

As the adviser moves on with her students from grade to grade, she is graduated a-new with them, for it is her's to help plan their class-day and commencement. Thus she supplants the functionary of old who must have spent many weary nights in trying, term after term, to evolve something original for each new occasion. In this way a different teacher is responsible each term with the Principal for these final functions, but a teacher who by this time ought to know her girls and how to use them.

Thus, the grade-adviser in a large high school may become a link between the necessary **impersonal** organization and the **live girl.** She does not supplant the **class-teacher,** for there is still need of all the personal interest the class-teacher can take, but whereas the latter works with a small group, she welds these groups into a social whole. She might further be likened to the "Big Sister" of the juvenile court probation movement, obviously, however, working with a law-abiding group, but coming in contact with them in the same helpful, motherly spirit. This, too, the class-teacher may do, but very often a girl, realizing how well her class-teacher seems to **know her,** naturally turns to a friendly intimate, just as the child will talk more freely to one outside the home.

I believe myself that the office of grade-adviser should be separate from any **formal** discipline or program-making functions. These, it seems to me, should be lodged in separate class-teachers or other officials.

The class-adviser in the Girls' High School has an official class and as full a teaching program as any other teacher. Her work with the girls is in excess of her regular classes. Herein lies a great limitation, for though she tries to accomplish something of what she seeks to do, how much more might she do if she were privileged to have some time for conferences with the individual girl in school hours?

In conclusion, let me say that I have avoided mentioning the reaction on the teacher of all this inspiring intercourse with the girls, for it does not seem to belong to the reorganization phase of the subject; but I should like to add that a Principal must be blind, indeed, who does not see how such personal contact with growing girls serves, unconsciously it may be, to reorganize most helpfully the growing teacher.

METHODS OF TESTING SCHOOL EFFICIENCY.—An address before the High School Teachers' Association by PROF. CHARLES H. JUDD, Director of School of Education, University of Chicago.

Dr. Judd claimed that percentages are unreliable as a basis of comparisons, and that the relative standing, or his positional rank of a student in his class is a much more reliable and constant quantity.

Some of the charts showed the differences in marks given in different departments in the same school, in different years in the same department, and by different teachers in the same department. In the English department in one or two schools there has been a great tendency to grade the students just a little above passing, very few students receiving high marks, and very few receiving penalizing marks. This practice was contrasted with that of some other departments in which ther was a normal distribution, a question was raised as to the cause of the disturbing factors, and in many cases these causes were ascertainable.

Professor Judd emphasized the idea that deductions drawn from such statistics were to be regarded not as conclusive, but as raising fruitful subjects for inquiry.

A set of charts showed how many students from the highest third of a lower school maintained their rank in the highest third of an upper school, and how many dropped to the middle third, and how many to the lowest third; and, similarly, how many from the middle third maintained that rank or went up or down; and similarly for the lowest third. This method of comparing the rank of students as they pass from one institution to another is to be used in the Middle West in the attempt to establish objective standards for measuring the efficiency both of the various high schools and of the colleges, and of studying out problems of articulation both of the institutions themselves and of the various departments in the lower and higher institutions.

Students in the middle and even lowest divisions in the elementary schools occasionally awoke later on and secured a better rank in high school and college. One chart showed the progress of 158 students who went from the elementary school through the high school and college. He claims that this method of study seems more satisfactory than reports dealing only with failures; a school receiving students from the highest third of a lower school is not discharging its duty when those students maintain merely a passing mark; on the other hand, a student coming up from a lower school, from the lowest third of his class, and maintaining a pasing mark in the higher school, is doing well.

Professor Judd urged the desirability of keeping careful records of the positional rank of students as they go from one school to another, extending over a series of years, carefully analyzed and available to those engaged in the work in the various schools.

THE REPORT OF CHAIRMAN OF THE COMMITTEE ON SCIENTIFIC MANAGEMENT (EFFICIENCY).

[This report expresses the personal opinions of Dr. Fitzpatrick. It was never submitted to all the members of his committe.]

PART I.

THE WORK OF THE COMMITTEE TO DATE.

THE SUB-COMMITTEE.

President Morrey appointed Committee on Scientific Management (Efficiency) in January (?), 1912. Soon thereafter the following sub-committees were appointed by the Chairman, and attempts were made to secure chairmen for other committees:

Superior Merit—The Chairman, Edward A. Fitzpatrick.
Stenography—Edw. J. McNamara, Jamaica.
Typewriting—David H. O'Keefe, Jamaica.

Supplies—Alex. L. Pugh, Commerce.
Supervision—Mary J. Bourne, Morris.
Cost of High School Education—Sieste Koopman, Commerce.
Visiting Schools—The Chairman, Edward H. Fitzpatrick.
Relation of High and Elementary Schools—
Relation of Day and Evening High Schools—
Program-Making—Henry B. Penhollow, De Witt Clinton.

THE PROPOSED UNION OF THE EFFICIENCY AND STANDARDIZATION COMMITTEES.

This committee was planning an investigation into various phases of the business side of school administration, and such topics as assignment of teachers. But upon learning of the appointment of the Standardization Committee, this work was stopped.

Standardization being the culmination of the series of Efficiency investigations, ought to be made the work of a sub-committee of the Efficiency Committee itself. Such a union of the committees is recommended.

THE REPORT ON SUPERIOR MERIT.

The Efficiency Committee submitted to the representatives a report on Superior Merit, which was tabled.

THE METHOD OF ATTACKING PROBLEMS WHEN INVESTIGATING COURSES OF STUDY.

I have asked Mr. McNamara to prepare report on series of the problems proposed by the Chairman and others, which he has solved in his stenography report, stating the problem and the method of attack which brought solution.

HIGH SCHOOL LIBRARIES.

In answer to a series of questions proposed by the Chairman of this committee, Miss Mary E. Hall, librarian in the Girls' High School, Brooklyn, and Chairman of the Committee on High School Libraries of the National Education Association, prepared an excellent report from the viewpoint of a high school librarian. We have asked Mr. Hill or the Brooklyn Public Library to place at our disposal his report on the "Co-operation between the Public Libraries and the Public Schools," read at the conference of Outside Agencies at the Colony Club on Friday. May, 1912. As yet we have not heard from Mr. Hill.

It is recommended that the report be printed in full for purposes of discussing.

NEW SUB-COMMITTEES.

The following new sub-committees should be appointed:

1. On general organization of schools.
2. Relation to colleges.
3. For each of the subjects taught in the high schools.
4. A special publicity committee.
5. On the hygienic aspects of secondary education.
6. On co-operation with outside agencies.
7. Adequate system of reporting.
8. Esprit-d'corps in the system.
9. The high school library.

THE STENOGRAPHY REPORT.

A preliminary report on Stenography will be ready for publication by June 30. The report is worthy of publication. The report on Typewriting may be ready by June 30, 1912.

THE REPORT ON VISITING.

Superintendent Stevens placed at the disposal of the committee the reports of visits to school written by the teachers in accordance with the by-laws. These reports were classified by subjects by Mr. McNamara of the Jamaica High School. These reports are being assigned to various teachers of the subjects for comment and report. Miss Nellie P. Hewins of Newtown, Mr. Norton of Bushwick, Mr. McNamara and Mr. O'Keefe of Jamaica have agreed to read the reports in their subjects. The others will be assigned by June 1.

THE INVESTIGATION OF RATINGS.

An investigation into the ratings of teachers was planned but was not permitted by the Board of Representatives.

OUTSIDE CO-OPERATION.

The Chairman of the committee has submitted to the President, apropos of the Committee on co-operation the report of the Bureau of Municipal Research with this subject, and recommended a new standing committee for this work. He has also suggested a conference with other teacher associations to secure a clearing-house for the expression of school needs as the teacher sees them.

PART II.

In accordance with the request of President Morrey, the plans of the Efficiency Committee for the next year are stated:

I. PUBLICITY.

The question of publicity was discussed at the last meeting of the committee, and there was a unanimous spontaneous opinion in favor of it. No committee such as this can succeed unless it secures the active co-operation of the teaching staff generally. The easiest and most economical way of securing this co-operation is through the columns of the newspapers. The question is not merely a question of publicity but of the success of the work itself. "Ye shall know the truth and the truth shall make you free."

II. "FOLLOW-UP" OF THE HANUS REPORT.

Probably the most important work of the committee during the next year—and its great opportunity—is the follow-up" of the recommendations of the Hanus Report. Though the teachers could arrange to have conferences with the experts who prepared the reports, nevertheless, it must be done without such conference, though there is liability to misunderstanding. The work of the committee will be to commend and perhaps to condemn. It should sharply distinguish between the facts and the inferences from those facts. It will seek to determine how far the recommendations meet the situations revealed by the facts. It will mark the omission of important problems, or the merely theoretical discussion of them, as well as the more important discovery of new problems by the investigators. If the results of the investigation are valuable, then the methods by which the results were derived should be fruitful of suggestion for the Efficiency Committee in its own work.

III. "FOLLOW-UP" OF THE REPORT OF THE CITY SUPERINTENDENT.

Another valuable source for the location of problems is the report of the City Superintendent of Schools. A number of problems are suggested in the last report.

FOLLOW-UP OF THE WORK OF THE ORGANIZATION ITSELF.

The follow-up idea points to a serious deficiency in the work of the organization itself. It is spending considerable time, energy and money on the preparation and publication of reports without any adequate system of "follow-up." What avails it to point out desirable improvements without an adequate effort to put these improvements into effect or to create a public opinion to compel such reconstruction as is desirable. As an illustration, take the report of the Committee on Revision of the High School Course of Study.

In his introduction to the report, the Chairman of the committee, Dr. Walter H. Eddy of the High School of Commerce, says:

"It must be made clear that the problem from the start was purely an academic one, and not an attempt to revise existing courses actively, except as the results of our research might influence local authorities in their decisions concerning courses of study."

It is almost naive to assume that local authorities will accept suggestions that are merely printed in reports. Unless there is a vigorous publicity campaign in support of the new propositions, there is little likelihood of local authorities anywhere (and local school authorities are especially conservative) accepting them, unless the authorities themselves are nominally responsible for them.

Take another illustration. The Biology Section of the High School Teachers' Association made a report in 1907 and again in 1909 for the creation of a new position: laboratory helper. This position was distinct from the positon of junior teacher. The incumbent was not in trainng for the positon of teacher. The report was an excellent one: its facts were pertinent and its reasoning cogent. But what was the result. It was submitted to the authorities and "filed," and there it rests. Is that efficiency?

Probably the only real argument against the adoption of a system of "follow-up" is the fear of candidates for promotion or election to a higher position that they will thus arouse the enmity of the authorities on whom their election or promotion depends. There is no doubt that such fear is general among the candidates, and there is some foundation for it. But there are many persons in authority in our school system who not only tolerate but encourage independence of thought and action, and personally I have always been under the supervision of such persons. I dislike to think that my case is exceptional.

I trust that the Efficiency Committee will be more successful in every way next year, especially in stimulating the interest of all the high school teachers in the problems of the high school.

Respectfully submitted,
(Signed) EDWARD A. FITZPATRICK.

NOTES OF DEPARTMENT MEETING ON EFFICIENCY.

The topic assigned for the conference was: "To what extent can the principles of scientific management be applied in the work of the Department of Biology?" (Morris High School, March 6, 1911.)

The following general characteristics of "Scientific Management" were suggested by members of the department:

1. Conservation of individual energy through co-operation with a minimum of friction.
2. Elimination of unnecessary effort.
3. Use of time-saving devices.
4. Well defined plan—head saving the heels.

The application of these principles to class recitations and laboratory work was then discussed as follows:

ABSTRACT OF MRS. PINGREY'S PAPER.

A. Purpose or object of "Scientific Management."
   1. To increase the efficiency of the laborer, *i. e.*, the pupil.
   2. To increase quality of product, *i. e.*, the pupil.
   3. Thereby to increase the amount of output and the value to the capitalist.

B. Comparisons between schools and mercantile establishments:
   1. The teacher obviously corresponds to planning department, superintendent, manager of a factory.
   2. The elements in the enterprise (the workman, the raw material, and the finished product) are combined in the pupil. The other elements (tools, etc.), are the text-books, charts, and apparatus.

C. The teacher should study and know thoroughly all these materials.

D. The final responsibility must be put on the pupil, and he should be trained and made to feel this responsibility. The teacher's system of grading a pupil helps him to realize the amount of his progress.

E. Difficulties in the way of making exact applications of scientific principles:
   1. So many different elements are combined in one (*i. e.*, the pupil).
   2. The raw material (pupil) is affected by so many outside conditions.
   3. Poor raw material cannot be exchanged for good.
   4. Teacher never sees or deals with a finished product.

ABSTRACT OF MISS MERCHANT'S PAPER.

A. Parallels. The output is the student. What, therefore, are the methods that will develop a desirable product? What will develop *quality* in pupils, *i. e.*, skill, grasp of subject, and power of accomplishment. *Quantity*, also, an aim.

B. Means. Printed outlines, seating plans of classes, recitation cards, attendance sheets, and other devices are labor saving, and hence aids. Lessons should be definitely assigned. Pictures, reference books are aids in fixing facts. Perfected business methods mean that better quality of work should be obtained with less expenditure of energy.

ABSTRACT OF MR. MANN'S PAPER.

A. Material different from that used by artist or artisan, in that "education is a mental process" and therefore we are working for mental improvement. Teachers should not be discouraged if they do not bring all members of a class to same level. If individual cases are improved in a relative degree, improvement should be regarded as generally satisfactory to all concerned; *i. e.*, the character of each pupil should be higher than it was before.

B. The relationship between the teacher and the pupil is all important, if the product is to have a high standard. *Joyous co-operation* of teacher with pupils at all times, and the creating of a healthful atmosphere should be the aim.

C. Aids in applying the principles of "Scientific Management":

1. The problem of discipline for the term should be solved during the first two weeks. An extra amount of energy specifically applied early saves constant drain of energy later. Mutual understanding with firmness clears the atmosphere.
2. Use boys and girls for errands and mechanical work wherever and whenever possible, without interfering with definite program of student. Have student monitors for passing paper, pencils and materials, for stamping note-books, for helping in various duties of the school. Pupils are always pleased to help and the responsibility is always good.
3. Short, quantitative examinations can often be given and the papers handed back to other students to be corrected by them under teacher's supervision.

The discussion is to be continued at the next meeting.

PAUL B. MANN, *Secretary*.

JAMES E. PEABODY, *Chairman*.

EFFICIENCY THROUGH PUPIL CO-OPERATION.

(As Posted)

PUPILS IN CHARGE OF 2K, ROOM 413.

Representative of The General Organization: Miss Bloss (also order at recess).

Class Representative: Miss Luhrs (daily report, order at recess and in absence of teacher, etc.).

Vice-Representative: Miss Mahler (order at recess, also all duties of Class Representative in her absence).

Leader in Fire Drill: Miss Rohde (to lead and hold line).

Leader in Setting-up Exercises: Miss Steeg.

Substitute Leader: Miss Rohde (in Miss Steg's absence).

Girls that erase boards at close of periods: Miss Specht, Miss Rohde.

Ventilation: Jacob Weber (to see that windows are opened at top).

Wardrobe Doors: Miss Beer (to see that doors are kept closed).

Front Closet Door: Miss Hallote (to see that door is kept closed).

Song Books: Miss Saladino (to distribute them and see that none are lost).

Uncovered Books and Scissors: Miss Horr (to confiscate and lock up all books found uncovered, until paper be brough to cover them; also to see that scissors are returned to teacher's desk).

Ink Wells: Miss Spengler (to see that they are kept filled).

Erasers, Chalk, etc.: Jacob Weber.

Every pupil is responsible for the condition or floor around his or her desk, also for the turning up of his or her seat at the close of school. Care taken in both these matters will make the task of the Janitress a much easier one.

MISS MANFRED, Prefect.
Term beginning September 11, 1911.

REPORT OF CONSULTATION COMMITTEE OF SIXTY. HIGH SCHOOL TEACHERS' ASSOCIATION.

To the Committee on School Inquiry:

In accordance with your request, we submit herewith a statement of our recommendations concerning the "General Course" of study for the high schools of New York City:

1. We commend to your consideration the detail suggestions contained in the final report of the "Committee on the Revision of the High School Course of Study" (Dr. W. H. Eddy, High School of Commerce, Chairman), as contained in the Year Book for 1910-1911, just issued. This report is the result of three years of careful study by a large committee of our Association.

2. REQUIREMENTS FOR GRADUATION. We recommend that the requirements for graduation be substantially those contained in the report of the Committee of Nine of the National Education Association, including the recommendation contained in the supplementary part of said report.

3. FLEXIBILITY. We recommend that far great flexibility be introduced into the general course. To this end we recommend that no subjects now given be eliminated and that the following subjects be introduced as electives: Introductory Social Science, Economics, Manual Training, Commercial Subjects, Household Economics, Theory of Music, Elements of Engineering, Advanced Drawing, and, in general, under proper restriction, such other subjects as may be demanded by a reasonable number of students, and for which there are qualified teachers in the school.

We further recommend that the subjects introduced shall be made equivalent in intensity and in amount of work required, to that required in the other subjects in the general course.

4. INTENSITY. We concur in general with the present tendency in educational theory favoring greater concentration upon fewer high school subjects. At present many of our students are required to carry six or more subjects at once. This leads to distraction, superficiality, and the violation of many principles of "efficiency." Among the objections to fragmentary courses occurring two or three periods per week, we would mention

(1) Personal contact of teacher and pupil is very superficial.
(2) Excessive strain is imposed on teacher by reason of the large number of different students with whom the teacher must become acquainted, and this strain is not sufficiently recognized in the assignment of work to teachers.
(3) Programs are very complicated and often impossible, and the equalization of classes is retarded or prevented.
(4) Clerical work is increased.
(5) Discipline is weakened.

To obviate the above difficulties, it is sometimes proposed to adopt a FOUR SUBJECT PLAN whereby each student would take only four subjects each term and each subject would occur each day in single prepared or double unprepared periods, or a combination of the two. This plan would overcome all of the foregoing difficulties. It is substantially the plan in practice in many of the best high schools of the United States. It makes possible the offering of many electives without entailing as much difficulty as is found under our present heterogeneous time allotment. But serious difficulties would arise under this four subject plan, for one subject must be English, and a second subject for most students would be a foreign language, thus restricting a student to the choice of two subjects from Mathematics, History, Science, Mechanic Arts, Commercial Branches, and Household Economics. All but two of these subjects would have to be omitted from each student's program, or one subject taken one year and one subject another, thus breaking continuity. Among these subjects, Mathematics and Science would be given most of the field, History would suffer, and the election of Mechanic Arts, Commercial Branches, and Household Economics would be unduly discouraged.

There is, however, a practical means of escape, namely, the adoption of a FIVE-SUBJECT PLAN, whereby each student would take five subjects and each subject would be allotted four hours of prepared work or a correspondingly larger number of hours where part or all of the work is unprepared. Under this plan the student who takes a vocational subject would also take four academic subjects. A larger number of subjects would then occur in uninterrupted sequences. Moreover, a student deciding to specialize in vocational work, could then take two-fifths of his work vocational and still keep three academic subjects. The five subject plan with 32 periods in the week permits more flexibility in the program than can be secured in the four subject plan with 30 periods in the week. The double laboratory period is less obstructive under the five subject plan than under the four subject plan.

WE THEREFORE RECOMMEND THE FIVE SUBJECT PLAN.

5. FIRST YEAR SUBJECTS. We recommend that students of the first year be *required* to take:

	No. of Periods.
(1) English	4 prepared
(2) Introductory Social Science	4 prepared

This course should include: Local Government, Local Industries, Study of Vocations, and Current Topics. This course should make specifically for good citizenship, assist the student when he comes to select a vocation, and emphasize the value of a thorough schooling.

and be allowed to choose three of the following:

(3) Introductory Natural Science, based largely on Biology	4 prepared
(4) Algebra	4 prepared
(5) Latin or a Modern Language	4 prepared
(6) Household Economics (for girls), including Freehand Drawing as applied to the decoration of the home— equivalent	4 prepared
(7) Mechanic Arts (for boys), including Shopwork, supplemented by recitation and Mechanical and Freehand Drawing—	8 unprepared (or equivalent in prepared and unprepared)

(8) Commercial Subjects (for boys and girls), including Freehand
Drawing as related to commercial interests—8 unprepared or equivale

The committee recommends that the student be advised to elect Introductory Natural Science.

In addition to the above all students should be required to take two periods of Physical Training, one period of Music, and one period of Oral English.

Students not taking either (6) Household Economics or (8) Commercial Subjects, should probably be required to take two periods of general Free-Hand Drawing.

If this plan is adopted and the number of hours in first-year English, Algebra, and Foreign Language is reduced from 5 to 4, of course it would be necessary that the amount of work required of students in each of these subjects in the first year, should also be materially reduced.

6. SECOND, THIRD AND FOURTH YEAR SUBJECTS. English should be required throughout the course, four periods per week. In the last year students taking Commercial Electives might well be offered an alternative course in Commercial English. Four years of work should be offered in each of the following:

(1) Latin and German.

(2) Mathematics. Surveying or the Elements of Engineering should be offered with ample opportunity for field practice and office computations.

(3) Natural Science, including electives in Physics two years, Chemistry, Physiography, Agricultural Science and Household Chemistry for Girls.

(4) Social Science, including History of last 150 years, History up to last 150 years, American History and Civics, Economics.

(5) Mechanic Arts (including Shopwork, supplemented by recitations and lectures) and Mechanical and Freehand Drawing. In this department opportunity should be offered in the last two years for special students to take double the usual amount of Mechanic Arts.

(6) Household Economics, including recitations on Household Accounts, Purchasing and Dietetics; and Freehand Drawing and Art Appreciation as applied to the decoration of the home.

(7) Stenography, Typewriting, Bookkeeping, Office Practice, Salesmanship, Advertising, Accountancy, etc.

In addition, electives should be offered in Advanced Drawing and in the Theory of Music.

CLARENCE D. KINGSLEY, *Chairman*

CONFERENCE COMMITTEE ON COURSE OF STUDY.

The preliminary report was read to the Board of Representatives February 27, revised by Sub-Committee appointed to draw up recommendations, and finally amended and adopted by the Committee March 5, 1912.

Bay Ridge—Mabel R. Benway.

Boys—E. W. Weaver, Charles E. Oberholser.

Bryant—Carolyn P. Swett, Mary Elizabeth Reid.

Bushwick—Mary P. Green, Josephine A. Dempsey, Geo. W. Norton, Etta E. Southwell and W. T. Morrey.

Commercial—Edwin A. Bolger, Benj. C. Gruenberg.

Commerce—Edwin A. Fitzpatrick, Alexander L. Pugh, Benj. A. Heydrick, Walter G. Eddy, Horace G. Healey.

Curtis—James Shipley, Mabel G. Burdick.

De Witt Clinton—Aaron I. Dotey, Ellen E. Garrigues, Donald C. MacLaren, Fayette E. Moyer.

Eastern District—Frederick H. Paine, Minnie K. Pinch.

Erasmus Hall—Charles R. Fay, Kate E. Turner, Preston C. Farrer, John B. Stocker.

Far Rockaway—Eldon M. Van Dusen.

Flushing—Paul R. Jenks, Frank H. Miller.

Girls—Loring B. Mullen, H. Elizabeth Seelman, M. Ellen Barker.

Jamaica—Benjamin N. Thorp, Henry R. Linville.

Manual Training—Clarence D. Kingsley, Chairman; Charles Perrine, Arthur L. Baker, Eleanor R. Baker, Marion Hackedorn.

Morris—Paul B. Mann, Hugh C. Laughlin, Otis C. Skeele, Josephine A. Davis, Abby B. Bates, Helen M. Storey, Michael D. Sohon.

Newtown—George H. Kingsbury, Alex E. W. Zerban.

Richmond Hill—Charles R. Gaston, Gertrude M. Leete.

Stuyvesant—T. Harry Knox, Clayton G. Durfee, Charles B. Howe.

Wadleigh—William W. Clendenin, Helen E. Bacon, Florence Middleton.

Washington Irving—Idelette Carpenter, Mary C. Craig.

THE STUDENTS' AID COMMITTEE.

The Committee in conjunction with the Department of Sociology of the Brooklyn Institute and the Brooklyn Teachers' Association has arranged for a general conference on Vocational Guidance on March 19th at 8 P. M., at the Academy of Music, Brooklyn, near Flatbush Avenue Subway Station.

Copies of these will be furnished free to members of the association applying before printing. Those in excess are for sale. The receipts from outside sales have paid for the printing of these bulletins.

"Choosing a Career for Boys," fourth edition.
"Choosing a Career for Girls," second edition.
"Occupations Connected with the Domestic Arts."
"Industrial Chemistry for Girls."
"The Effect of Education on Earning Capacity."

Small quantities of the following can be secured:
"Accountancy and the Business Profession," 10 cents.
"The Civil Service," 5 cents.
"Opportunities for Boys in Machine Shops," 2 cents.
"Applying for Work," 2 cents.
"Country Vacation Work," 2 cents.
"Vacation Excursions for Young People," 2 cents.
"List of Special Training Schools," 1 cent.
"The Vocational Adjustment of School Children," 10 cents.

The following can no longer be supplied:
"Does an Education Pay?"
"Report on School Incentives."
"Reports of the Work of the Committee."
"Directing Young People in the Choice of a Vocation."

The United States Department of Labor reprints an interesting bulletin on Vocational Guidance from the twenty-fifth annual report of the department. Copies can be secured free by early applicants.

E. W. Weaver, *Chairman*.

25 Jefferson Avenue, Brooklyn. 'Phone, 1377-M-5 Prospect.

COMMITTEE ON CONFERENCE WITH THE COLLEGES.

The committe of this Association has unanimously endorsed the main part of the report of the Committee of Nine of the National Education Associations. One member of our committee believes that under no circumstances should a student be admitted to an academic college without foreign language and mathematics. But the five other members of the committee endorse the entire report, including the recommendation "that provision should be made by many of the larger colleges to continue the education of students of whom it has been discovered that the requirement of mathematics or the requirement of foreign language is an obstacle to the continuation of their education." Complete copies of the report may be secured from the Chairman of the Committee of Nine, Clarence D. Kingsley, Manual Training High School, Brooklyn.

DEPARTMENT OF MECHANICAL ARTS.

The Department of Mechanical Arts held a most successful meeting on Friday evening, December 15, 1911, with 23 present. After an informal dinner there was an interesting and instructive address by Mr. Herbert Lester, of the firm of Manning, Maxwell & Moore, on the Relative Merits of the Line Shaft Drive and the Individual Motor Drive for Manual Training Shops. There was a lively and interesting discussion. Mr. Kingsley of the Manual Training High School spoke of the advisability of this department formulating a statement of policy as to what should be the content of the manual training work of the future so as to receive the same credit as other high school subjects. Some discussion followed after which it was voted that the chairman should appoint a committee of five to study this question and formulate such a statement.

List of Members of H. S. T. A. September 1911—June 1912.

BAY RIDGE HIGH SCHOOL (4)
86th Street, near 18th Avenue, Brooklyn

ANNEX

92d Street and Gleston Avenue (P. S. 104)

Allee, Winifred
Benway, Wahl R.
Buchnan, Louis
Lolling, Hela

BOYS' HIGH SCHOOL (60)

Marcy and Putnam Avenues and Madison Street

ANNEXES
Bedford and Jefferson Avenues

Berriman Street, Belmont and Atkins Avenues (P. S. 64)

Sullivan, James, Principal
Alden, Henry T.
Andrews, William H.
Bates, Clifton W.
Boyd. Maurice C
Brill, Abraham
Brummer, Sidney D.
Buttrick, Harold E.
Clark, Clinton
Cohen, A. Broderick
Crandall, Ernest L.
Downing, George B.
Edwards, William H.
Esselstyn, Henry H.
Fairchild, Ralph P.
Fisher, William W.
Flint, Ehomas
Fontaine, Andre C.
Flint, George C.
France, Sanford D.
Freeborn, Frank W.
Gemson, Irving
Hale, Albert C.
Handrich, Paul
Houson, P.
Hobson, George F.
Hopkins, Walter D.
Hughes, Charles E.
Hughes, Francis T.
Janes, Arthur L.
Jeffords, Clyde R.
Jenner, William A.
Jones, Frederick B.
Lewis, Frederick Z.
Levine, H. B.
Mattes, W. H.
Munson, Daniel G.
Overholser, Charles E.
Parker, S. Ridley
Parsons, Edward B.
Parsons, Herbert H.
Pasternak, Nathaniel
Proper, Emberson E.
Raiman, Robert I.
Reynolds, James I.
Reynolds, Lewis G.
Richardson, Roy S.
Riess, Ernest
Rogers, William W.
Smith, Ernest E.
Spaulding, Frank B.
Stone, Limond C.
Swenson, John A.
Tausk, Alfred A.
Tressler, Jacob C.
Weaver, Eli W.
White, Walter L.
Wilson, Henry E.
Wood, George C.
Yoder, Arthur L.

BRYANT HIGH SCHOOL (25)
Wilbur Avenue, Academy and Radde Streets, Long Island City

Arthur, L. Louise
Byrne, Margaret C.
Carll, Lydia A.
Carter, Bertha A.
Courtney, Bertha F.
Dickinson, Tenny V.
Evans, Ethel
Grubman, Adolph J.
Heermance, Emma W.
Joseph, Myrtle J.
Jones, Frances E.
Lewis, Edward F.
Loewy, George J.
McIntyre, Edith R.
Munroe, Harry K.
Price, Anna G.
Reid, Mary E.
Riblet, Mary V.
Rothberg, Meta
Schaffer, Rachel E.
Snow, Ella M.
Swett, Carolyn Patten
Vincent, Charlotte M.
Vogt, Charles R.
Waldman, Mark
Welch, Alberta M.

BUSHWICK HIGH SCHOOL (42)
Evergreen Avenue, Ralph and Grove Streets

ANNEXES

St. Nicholas and Willoughby Avenues and Suydam Street (P. S. 162)

Ryerson Street, near Myrtle Avenue (P. S. 69)

Quincy Street, near Stuyvesant Avenue (P. S. 129)

Rollins, Frank, Principal
Averill, Steve
Bonotaux, Henriette
Conant, M. Sybel
Cohen, Morris
Collier, Katherine B.
Cohen, Bertha
Dempsey, Josephine A.
Falion, George M.
Foley, Henry J.
Gilbert, Clara M.
Green, John C.
Green, Mary P.
Goldsmith, Elizabeth
Humphries, G. F.
Howley, Elizabeth
Humason, T. A.
Johnson, Julius M.
Keener, Robert H.
Levine, Maurice
Littig, M. Josephine
Leyenberger, Harry W.
MacDermott, Ada A.
Miller, Charles
Mohan, Lucy F.
Morrey, William T.
Miller, Grace Helene
McDonald, Milo F.
Norton, George W.
Putz, Edward H.
Semple, Lewis B.
Smith, L. Brewster
Smith, Marguerite
Southwell, Etta E.
Stanton, Anna E.
Smith, Louise
Taylor, A. W.
Townsend, Chas. W.
Townsend, May E.
Travers, Caulin
Tufts, Anna

CURTIS HIGH SCHOOL (18)
Hamilton Avenue and St. Mark's Place, New Brighton

ANNEX

Academy Place, Tottenville (P. S. 1)

Towle, Harry F., Principal
Abbott, Frances H.
Benjamin, Claude T.
Blanspied, Ethel
Brewer, Francis E.
Close, M M.
Dean, Philip R.
Gallagher, Ellen M.
Goodwin, M. W.
Grout, Abel J.
Haywood, William R.
Hopkins, Rupert H.
McMillan, Harlow
Shepherd, Florence D.
Shipley, James H.
Whitmore, Clara

COMMERCIAL HIGH SCHOOL (44)
Albany Avenue, Dean and Bergen Streets
ANNEX
Conover, Sullivan and Wolcott Streets (P. S. 30)

Fairley, William, Principal
Bagenstose, Harry L.
Bickmore, Frank L.
Bliss, Ralph P.
Bolger, Edwin A.
Chestnut, Howard D.
Conant, Fred L.
Cushman, Earl L.
Dann, Matthew L.
Denenholz, Alex.
Donovan, Herbert D. A.
Eells, Burr G.
Failing, Wilson R.
Finnegan, William E.
Fleischer, Edward
Flint, George C.
Greenberg, Morris
Gross, Henry I.
Gruenberg, Benjamin C.
Harmon, George W.
Harrison, Earl S.
Hook, Edward A.
Joseph, Samuel
Lee, Joseph B.
Loughran, John
Meehan, Wm.
Nanes, Philip
Newman, Joseph
O'Ryan, William P.
Proctor, Robert H.
Raynor, œilbert J.
Reser, Edward N.
Sawyer, George A.
Scarborough, Andrew J.
Schuyler, Elmer
Shea, John J.
Shearer, Robert J.
Smith, Joseph H.
Sternberg, George
St. John, Robert P.
Teeter, Charles H.
Van Buskirk, Edgar F.
Watson, Elba E.
Zeiner, Edward J. A.

DeWITT CLINTON HIGH SCHOOL (63)
10th Avenue, 58th and 59th Street

Tildsley, John L., Principal
Adams, Milly E.
Anthony, Oscar W.
Barber, Harry G.
Baylis, Sara
Bedford, Edgar A.
Benshimol, Alfred L.
Bierman, Henry M.
Boylan, Arthur A.
Broadhurst, Philip H.
Bryant, Arthur A.
Call, R. Ellsworth
Clark, Randolph C.
Currie, Thomas H.
Donnelly, John P.
Dotey, Aaron I.
Dudek, Alice E.
Erwin, Edward J.
Foote, Carleton A.
Foote, Edmund W.
Frank, Colman D.
Frank, Maude
Garrigues, Ellen E.
Gollomb, Joseph
Graw, Frederick S.
Haas Arthur
Haug, Emanuel
Herzog, Charles Carl
Hirsch, James A.
Hunter, George W.
Kelley, Frank B.
Knox, Jaxon
Krause, Arthur K.
Lucey, Michael M.
Lyon, Lorenzo G.
Lorevinthau, Albert
MacLaren, Donald C.
Mirsky, Israel
McCarthy, John D.
McKernan, Thomas
Monteser, Frederick
Miles, Dudley H.
Morse, Charles F.
Moyer, Fayette E.
Newman, Charles
Osborn, Ralph
Parelhoff, Benard M.
Patterson, Samuel W.
Penhollow, Harry B.
Perry, Edward O.
Phillips, Gertrude
Pickelsky, Frank
Rosenthal, Daniel C.
Sharpe, Richard W.
Sherman, Frederick D.
Salzano, Francis
Strauss, Julius
Timmerman, Charles E.
Whitsit, Jesse E.
Wolfson, Arthur M.
Wright, Herman H.
Works, Austin M.

EASTERN DISTRICT HIGH SCHOOL (66)
Marcy Avenue, Rodney and Keap Streets
ANNEX
Havemeyer, North 6th and North 7th Streets (P. S. 143)

Vlymen, William T., Principal
Adler, David
Anderson, Mary E.
Ayres, Mary S.
Baltz, Frank P.
Beeckman, Florence L.
Beitel, Helen S.
Blumenburg, Frieda
Bole, John A
Bowman, Nina
Bruce, Walter A.
Burlingham, Gertrude T.
Calkins, Maud L.
Campbell, Harold G.
Carey, Margaret E.
Chapin, Henry E.
Crawford, Charlotte H.
Dixon, Charles E.
Ennis, Mary G.
Faulkner, Eunice F.
Genung, Ina E.
Greenburg, Henry
Griffiths, Anna B.
Hartwell, Charles S.
Hazen, Annah P.
Hellin, Esther B.
Helmuth, Lou
Rerendeen, Jane E.
Higbee, Anna M. (Mrs.)
Hughan, Jessie W.
Ikelheimer, Minnie
Illich, Louis L.
Kauffman, Wm. A.
Mayo, Marion J.
McDermott, Annie
Meigs, Katherine H.
Meyer, Florence E.
Model, Charles
Myers, Willard L.
Kelly, Wm. H.
King, Helen L.
Kuhn, Adelina
Lanz, Jeanne
Lemowitz, Nathan H.
Manahan, Mary G.
Martin, Paul
Maynard, Ernes A.
Paine, Frederick H.
Phillips, Anna L.
Pinch, Minnie A.
Pond, Pearl F.
Read, Mary A.
Rittenhouse, Hawley O.
Rosmaren, Michael
Schradieck, Helen E.
Seamans, Mary A.
Smith, Franklin H.
Sperling, Harry
Stratford, Aline C.
Sullivan, Mary
Trowbridge, Cornelia B.
Warren, James P.
Watson, Alice D.
Wilson, Stuart
Wyckoff, Harriet E.
Zollinhofer, Sophie

ERASMUS HIGH SCHOOL (64)
Flatbush Avenue, near Church Avenue
ANNEXES
Avenue G, East 23d and East 24th Streets (P. S. 152)
92d Street and Gelston Avenue (P. S. 104)
Avenue T, East 12th Street and Homecrest Avenue (P. S. 153)
86th Street, near 18th Avenue (P. S. 101)

Gunnison, Walter B., Principal
Arnold, Frank J.
Barber, Cora L.
Beardsley, Frank J.
Boynton, George E.
Brickelmaier, Alice G.
Bryant, Frank L.
Burnham, R. Wesley
Campbell, Joseph A.
Cashman, Joseph A.
Chesley, Mabel L.
Connell, J. Wesley
Crane, Ella E.
Crockett, Esther M.
Cunningham, Maud M.

Doggett, Allen B.
Earle, Willis
Edgell, Frank D.
Estes, Charles S.
Everett, Edith M.
Farrar, Preston C.
Fay, Charles R.
Feldman, Daniel D.
Foster, Sarah P.
Habermeyer, Louise C. M.
Hancock, W. J.
Harley, Walter S.
Hewitt, Helen F.
Hodgdon, Katherine I.
Holmes, Mary H.
Howe, Alice C.
Huntington, Frederick W.
Jaquish, Ben M.
Johnston, Wm. H.
Keck, Frederick R.
King, Cyrus A.
Knowson, Walter S.
Lasher, William R.
Lauder, Mary A.
Leman, Geo. W.
Levy, Harry A.
Merchant, Manton E.
Neiswender, Ida B. C.
Peabody, Susan P.
Raynor, Geo. C.
Scovil, Florence M.
Scott, Izora
Simmons, Isabel
Sparks, Minnie E.
Sprague, Laura E.
Stocker, John H.
Strong, Wm. M.
Strout, Geo. M.
Talbot, A. May
Tibbetts, William F.
Tredick, Helen F.
Turner, Kate E.
Valentine, Henry D.
Volentine, Mary F. (Mrs.)
Whitney, N. Belle
Wight, Walter A.
Wilder, George F.
Williams, Lewis C.
Young, Charlotte S.
Young, Mabel A.

FAR ROCKAWAY HIGH SCHOOL (1)

State Street and Roanoke Avenue, Far Rockaway

Jennison, Emily M.

FLUSHING HIGH SCHOOL (9)

Sanford Avenue and Union Street, Flushing

Clark, John Holley, Principal
Barnwell, Walters
Baumeister, John
Hood, Edward C.
Jenks, Paul R.
Killen, Arthur H.
Miller, Frank H.
Nearing, Elena P.
Read, Warren W.

GIRLS' HIGH SCHOOL (16)

Nostrand Avenue, Halsey and Macon Streets

ANNEX

St. Mark's and Classon Avenues (P. S. 42)

Felter, William L., Principal
Babcock, Maude R.
Carter, Effie A.
Cochran, Mary
Gardner, Maudè
Higgins, Alice
Holmes, Abby B.
Jenkins, M. M.
Jenness, Jennie M.
Keyes, Rowena K.
Lee, Marguerite T.
Lyle, Edith K.
Mullen, Loring B.
Seelman, H. Elizabeth
Sullivan, Bessie
Wright, Mabel

HIGH SCHOOL OF COMMERCE (52)

65th and 66th Streets, West of Broadway

Sheppard, James J., Printipal
Aldinger, Harry E.
Barbour, William C.
Beatman, Augustus S.
Blume, Julius
Brennan, Alfred T. V.
Bryan, Alfred C.
Clough, Harvey B.
Eddy, Walter H.
Fitzpatrick, Edward A.
Flatow, Jacob
Flynn, Oscar R.
Foster, Wilfred L.
Grant, Forest
Greene, Russell T.
Hahn, Clarence W.
Mall, Henry M.
Cohen, Harry
Hall, Gamble
Hartwell, Frank W.
Hance, William
Hartung, Ernest
Healey, Horace G.
Heydrick, Benjamin A.
Kahn, Joseph
Koopman, Sietse B.
Lewis, Alfred H.
Lewis, Ernest D.
Lindsey, Frederick B.
Long, Reuben L.
Mills, Joseph S.
McGrath, William J.
Minnick, John D.
Montross, Charles G.
Norden, Norris L.
O'Neil, William R.
Porter, George H.
Pugh, Alexander L.
Renig, Alfred
Roessler, Erwin M.
Rosenblum, Abraham
Rotherham, Phillip
Schlauch, William S.
Schultze, Arthur
Sinagnan, Leon
Skinner, Herbert C.
Sprague, Charles H.
Van Deusen, Edwin W.
Van Tuyl, George H.
Walker, Claude F.
Woodman, Irving L.
Whiffen, Edwin

JAMAICA HIGH SCHOOL (22)

Hillside and Union Avenues, Jamica

Cahill, John P.
Chickering, Edward C.
Delger, Marie
Fairley, Edwin
Fennebresque, Louis
Gay, Laura S.
Gilliland, Alice M.
Hoadley, Harwood
Krause, Carl A.
Lawrence, Antoinette
Linville, Henry R.
McNamara, Edward J.
O'Keefe, David H.
Quick, Oscar
Root, Lydia F.
Root, Minnie R.
Starkey, Warren L.
Thompson, Kirk W.
Thorp, Benjamin H.
Vosburgh, Charles H.
Ward, Ada Webster
Wilkin, Josephine D.

MANUAL TRAINING SCHOOL (74)

7th Avenue, 4th and 5th Streets

ANNEXES

11th Avenue, Windsor Place and Sherman Street (P. S. 154)

Prospect Avenue, opposite Receve Place

Duffield, Johnson and Gold Streets

Larkins, Charles D., Principal
Abbott, Frederick B.
Aldridge, Vincent
Allen, J. Trevette
Bachelder, Mary A.
Baker, Arthur L.
Baker, Eleanor R.
Baldwin, Walter J.
Barasch, Morris
Bawden, Sarah E.
Beebe, Dee
Bloom, Isidore
Boecker, Alexander
Boole, Emily R.
Boole, Florence A.
Brockerant, May E.
Coan, Charles W.
Colony, M. Elizabeth
Dickinson, Henry N.
Dickler, Nathan N.
Dickman, Mary B.
Dithridge, Caroline N.
Edwards, Sidney
Fanning, Grace M. W.
Foster, Edwkin G.
Freeberg, Sigrid C.
Green, Florence (Mrs.)

Hackedorn, Marion
Hall, Mary A.
Harris, Lena
Heyer, Ella G.
Holly, Harold A.
Holzman, Abraham
Hunt, Arthur E.
Jacobson, Harry
Kingsley, Clarence D.
Leonard, Howard C.
Low, J. Herbert
Luther, Edith M.
MacKay, Alfred
Mageworth, J. Otis
Maginn, Elizabeth
McArdle, John P.
McCall, Carleton C.
Meneely, John H.
Murphy, Margaret L.
Nelson, Willard B.
Odell, Louis S.
O'Donnell, Emmett
Perrine, Charles
Peters, Frederick A.
Ping, Louise M.
Richardson, William C.
Robinson, Alfred T.
Robinson, John T.
Schaible, Godfrey C.
Schutze, Elizabeth
Shinn, Victor I.
Smith, J. Clarence
Smith, M. Helen
Snow, Minnie R.
Snyder, B. Louis
Stone, Mabel
Taylor, Nettie
Terrel, Lilian A.
Vail, Clarence W.
Vanderpoel, Edwin C.
Van Olinda, James E.
Volkarets, Marie
Walker, Alice J.
Weed, Henry T.
Wikel, Henry H.
Wolcott, Henry G.
Wright, Helen S. (Mrs.)
Yarrington, Adrian M.
Yerbury, Charles S.

MORRIS HIGH SCHOOL (43)

166th Street, Boston Road and Jackson Avenue

ANNEXES

Mott Avenue and 144th Street (P. S. 31)
Matilda Street, Wakefield (P. S. 16)

Denbigh, John H., Principal
Ames, Jessie I.
Blakely, Gilbert S.
Bogart, Elmer E.
Bogart, Sarah H.
Bridgman, Anne T.
Burt, Clara M.
Carr, Agnes
Clarke, Helen Mac G.
Constantine, Harriet L.
Coster, Silvie de G.
Davis, Josie A.
Diedrich, Marie M.
Evans, Austin H.
Hager, E. M.
Harding, Helen E.
Hixon, Kate B.
Knowlton, Mary E.
Lifschitz, Berthold
Mann, Paul B.
Mendum, Georgiana
Miller, Charles A.
Parker, Margaret B.
Peabody, James E.
Peterson, A. Everett
Pyne, Henry R.
Read, Edith
Sampson, Ezra W.
Schwartzenbach, P. A.
Scott, Cora A.
Scudder, John O.
Shannahan, Willard D.
Spencer, Estella
Story, Helen M.
Surray, P. M.
Eurray, P. M.
Thompson, Annie S.
Wahl, Emanuel M.
White, Fred C.
Williams, Joseph S.
Williams, Sarah P.
Winslow, Isabel G.
Zeizer, F.

NEWTOWN HIGH SCHOOL (2)

Chicago Avenue, Elmhurst

Kingsbury, George H.
Zerban, Alexander H. W.

RICHMOND HILL HIGH SCHOOL (26)

Elm Street and Stewart Avenue, Richmond Hill

Failor, Isaac N., Principal
Allen, Ralph W.
Beard, Stella S.
Beers, Florence E.
Chapin, Jennie E.
Conrow, Elizabeth
Emery, Stephen G.
Finnigan, James J.
Fuerstenan, Daisy M.
Gaston, Charles Robert
Golde, Margaret D.
Henderson, Royal L.
Hubbard, Ruth E.
Johnson, Esctelle M.
Kilburn, Florence M.
Klein, Joseph J.
Knapp, Annie M.
Lmbert, Marcus B.
Landers, Leland L.
Leete, Gertrude M.
Root, Eva R.
Stewart, Charles A.
Stilson, William E.
Vlentine, Morris C.
Voorhees, Sophia
Wolcott, Emily P.

STUYVESANT HIGH SCHOOL (55)

15th and 16th Streets, West of 1st Avenue

von Nardroff, Ernest R., Principal
Andrews, Richard M.
Augsbury, Earl A.
Beha, Joseph L.
Breckenridge, William E.
Brandan, George C.
Brownlee, Raymond B.
Bruce, Murray
Cheney, Thomas C.
Corbett, Jos. S.
Crossley, Arthur
Drury, Horation N.
Durfee, Clayton G.
Ellard, Charles H.
Elmer, Clement G.
Fink, Frederick W.
Foster, Walter E.
Fritz, Henry E.
Fuller, Robert W.
Gage, Stanley A.
Greenberg, Abraham
Gardner, Frank A.
Goodrich, Moses F.
Griswold, Edward D.
Hanford, Clarence D.
Hein, Henry E.
Henriques, Maurice
Hopkins, William C.
Howe, Charles B.
Klafter, Simeon
Knox, T. Harry
Lavers, Earl R.
Law, Frederick H.
Leavitt, William M.
Leonard, Theodore S.
Lipsky, Abram
Maier, Augustus
Marston, Charles W.
Mott, Howard W.
Mehrtens, Henry E.
Mersereau, Samuel F.
Messenger, John, Jr.
Neumarker, John G.
Norris, John
Oswald, Frederick W., Jr
Quimby, Ernest S.
Ross, Franklin A.
Sanford, Clarence H.
Smith, Seymour L.
Smith, Walter M.
Smith, W. Palmer
Steinert, John B.
Uhlig, William C.
Wilson, James F.
Worth, William A.
Weiser, Samuel

WADLEIGH HIGH SCHOOL (26)

114th and 115th Streets, West of 7th Avenue

ANNEX

138th Street, West of 5th Avenue (P. S. 100)

Rowe, Stuart H., Principal
Bacon, Helen E.
Bass, Bertha
Clendenin, William W.
Coman, Caroline
Cornish, Robert H.
Davis, Cornelia A.
Eaton, Mary P.
Elliot, Lillian M.
Ford, Jessie Frances (Mrs.)
George, Auguste
Griffith, Priscilla
Haefeln, Fanny
Harris, Gertrude B.
Hodges, Archibald L.
King, Elizabeth Edwards
Kupfer, Elsie M.
Newcomer, Harvey
Rodman, Henrietta
Syms, Louis
Taylor, Jane I.
Tefft, Mary B.
Tweedy, Grace B.
Womack, Mary D.
Zick, Henry

WASHINGTON IRVING HIGH SCHOL (19)
34 1-2 East 12th Street
ANNEXES
146 Grand Street — 60 West 13th Street — 140 West 20th Street
82nd Street and West End Avenue (P. S. 9)
88th Street, East of 1st Avenue (P. S. 66)

McAndrew, William, Principal
Ammerman, S. Lewis
Beach, Jessie A.
Blackwell, Nannie G.
Carpenter, Idelette
Cohen, Helen L.
Craig, Mary C.
Goodman, Annie
Hodgkins, Georgiana
Hurlbut, Martha A.
Lowd, Emma L.
Roche, Elizabeth A.
Sage, Lillian B.
Skinner, Emma M.
Slack, E. B.
Tuttle, Edith M.
Videre, Leontine
Welsh, John C.
Willard, Florence

CONTENTS OF YEAR-BOOK 1908-1909, JOHN L. TILDSLEY, PRES.

CONTENTS OF YEAR-BOOK 1909-1910, ARTHUR L. JANES, PRES.

CONTENTS OF YEAR-BOOK 1910-1911, ARTHUR L. JANES, PRES.

CONTENTS OF H. S. T. A. BULLETIN NO. 34.

[Year-Books 20c. each, Bulletins 10c. each—Miss. Agnes Carr, Secretary, Morris High School.]

OFFICIAL BULLETIN

of the High School Teachers' Association of New York City.

No. 37. SATURDAY, MARCH 1, 1913

The Board of Representatives, on May 23, 1911, empowered the Executive Committee to issue a Bulletin monthly, instead of four times a year.

THE THIRD REGULAR MEETING FOR 1912-1913 will be held Saturday, March 1, 1913, at the High School of Commerce.

DEPARTMENT MEETINGS begin at 10 A. M. Besides the programs as given below, there should be discussions of Questionnaire for Directory, of Account of Aim, Scope and Equipment of Departments in the Ideal or Typical High School, and of Questionnaire for Hanus' Reports.

GENERAL MEETING begins at 11 A. M. in Auditorium.

MAIN ADDRESS BY HON. FRANK MOSS, Assistant District Attorney.

TOPIC: HIGH SCHOOLS AND MORAL EFFICIENCY.

DISCUSSION led by DR. WALTER L. HERVEY of the Board of Examiners.

This is the seventh meeting in the series devoted to "Efficiency in the High Schools. Professor Hanus has discussed for us What the Schools are for; Mr. Harrington Emerson, Efficiency Engineer, the Principles of Scientific Management; Associate Superintendent Stevens, More Efficient Organization and the New Point of View; District Superintendent Bardwell, The Recitation; Professor Judd, Ways of Testing Efficiency in Teaching; and Examiner Smith and Principals Clark, Denbigh, Fairley, Felter, Larkins, McAndrew and Tildsley have discussed what constitutes the Teacher of Superior Merit.

But in the final analysis, in the last test, we must remember that our schools are not truly efficient unless they arouse a zeal for that "Righteousness that Exalteth a Nation."

WILLIAM T. MORREY, President.

AGNES CARR, Secretary.

DEPARTMENT MEETINGS, 10 A. M.

ANCIENT LANGUAGES—Room 534, Dr. Walter E. Foster, Stuyvesant High High School, Chairman.

A Round Table Discussion of the following questions:

Is it worth while for pupils in our High Schools to study Latin for a single year?

If it is worth while, what are the benefits?

If it is not worth while, what of the fact that from thirty to fifty per cent. of those who begin Latin do not carry it beyond the first year?

In your opinion, is it possible so to modify our first year work that the returns from one year's study will be decidedly more profitable?

BIOLOGY—Room 301, Mr. Harvey B. Clough, H. S. of Commerce, Chairman; Frank Merrill Wheat, DeWitt Clinton H. S., Secretary.

"Artificial Parthenogenesis," by Prof. Charles Packard, Assistant in Zoology, Columbia University.

BOOKKEEPING SECTION—Room 303, Joseph J. Klein, Richmond Hill High School, Chairman.

At 10 A. M. Sharp Examiner James C. Byrnes will address the Section. Subject to be announced later. Watch the papers.

At 10:30 A. M. Discussion: "The Formation of a Commercial Teachers' Club or Association."

The meeting starts at ten promptly in order to afford ample time for thorough discussion before the General Meeting.

ELOCUTION—Room 201, Mr. Raymond W. Kellogg, Chairman; W. Palmer Smith, Stuyvesant High School, Secretary.

Report on and discussion of the Questionaire recently sent out.

All teachers of Elocution, Voice Culture and Oral Expression are cordially invited.

HISTORY AND ECONOMICS—Room 205, Miss Antoinette Lawrence, Jamaica High School, Chairman.

Conference on how pupils should be properly started in the history work.

MATHEMATICS—Room 304, Elmer Schuyler, Bay Ridge High School, Chairman.

"Geometrographie: the Art of Geometrical Constructions."

An address by Mr. David L. MacKay, of the Bay Ridge High School.

Elementary School Teachers welcomed.

MODERN LANGUAGES—Room 401, Colman Dudley Frank, DeWitt Clinton High School, Chairman.

Mr. W. T. Morrey, Pres. H. S. T. A.,
New York City.

My Dear Mr. President:—

I believe it is quite unnecessary to announce the subject for the discussion of the Modern Language Conference for this meeting, as all the live language teachers of the System have already heard of it and will be on hand. We even expect it to resurrect some of the dead ones, so inspiring will it be. Yours enthusiastically,

COLMAN D. FRANK, Chairman.

PHYSICAL TRAINING—All teachers of Physical Training in our public High Schools are invited to meet and to consider the organization of a department.

PHYSIOGRAPHY—Room 506, Mr. Kirk W. Thompson, Jamaica High School, Chairman. Preparation of Questionaire.

Prof. Joseph E. Woodman, Professor of Geology, New York University, will discuss the Adirondack Water Supply. Lecture illustrated with stereopticon views.

Elementary School Teachers welcomed.

"Some New Laboratory Experiments in Physiography," by Frank L. Bryant, Erasmus Hall High School.

SHORTHAND—Room 216, Edwin A. Bolger, Commercial High School, Chairman.

"The Proposed Modification of the Regent's Examination in Shorthand II."

GENERAL MEETING OF DECEMBER 7, 1912.

The second meeting of the High School Teachers' Association for the year 1912-1913 was held at the High School of Commerce, December 7, at eleven o'clock, section meetings preceding the general meeting.

President Morrey announced that the other General Meetings of the year would take place March 1 and May 3. The president asked for an increase in membership, stating that only as the income of the Association warrants it, can the important reports submitted be published in the Bulletin.

Dr. Darwin L. Bardwell, Superintendent in charge of High Schools, was then introduced as the speaker of the morning. He gave a most interesting and inspiring address on "Efficiency in Recitation," a report of which appears in this Bulletin.

After an informal discussion, and a rising vote of thanks and appreciation to the speaker, the meeting adjourned at 12:50 o'clock.

(Signed), AGNES CARR, Secretary.

EFFICIENCY IN THE RECITATION.

By Superintendent Darwin L. Bardwell, December 7, 1912, Before the High School Teachers' Association of New York City.

From Stenographic Notes by Mr. Horace G. Healey.

Ladies and Gentlemen:

I approach this question this morning with two very strong impressions in my mind. The first one is this: I have no notion that I can treat this subject at all adequately. Moreover, I am not attempting to treat it in what may be called a learned fashion. I am to quote no so-called authority or pedagogical writer. I do not anticipate using long or scientific terms; not that you would be unable to understand them, but because they are rather foreign to the purpose which I have in mind.

The second conception which is strong and has been strong in my mind in preparing and thinking of this theme, "Efficiency In the Recitation," is this: The work of the recitation is the most important and the most vital work in the school. It is not the only work of the school. It is not the only important work of the school. There are many teachers who are called upon to perform and do perform exceedingly valuable services outside of the classroom. That must always be. But to my mind none of these services, invaluable though they are, can for a single moment excuse a lack of the maximum efficiency in the recitation. Nothing can take the place of it. There, as nowhere else, teacher and pupils are brought into close contact; and there, as nowhere else, the greatest and most important work of the school under the present organization must be done.

Briefly I wish to bring to your mind the purpose of the recitation, a double purpose as I conceive it. In the first place in the recitation new matter is taught. There is in every subject a progression in information; something new is to be learned, if not daily, at least at frequent intervals. The recitation is the place wherein part of this is done; and guidance is given by means of which the pupil shall obtain the rest for himself, by his own individual preparation and effort.

The test of efficiency in this direction, the learning of new matter, is not difficult. The test naturally comes in simply ascertaining whether or not the new matter is learned. Suitable examinations will test the acquirement of new knowledge. It is not the province of the morning's subject to discuss what suitable examinations are, how they are prepared, or of what they shall consist; that is quite enough of a theme for discussion by itself. But I think it will be generally agreed that whether or not knowledge has been obtained by the pupils, can be tested by a suitable examination.

The acquisition of knowledge is not to be minimized. It is exceedingly important that the boys and girls of High School age shall know certain things beyond peradventure: that they be sure, absolutely sure, of their ground in these particulars. It is often said, it is often thought, it is believed most heartily, that the amount of new matter which is to be learned by pupils in most High School subjects is enormously great. In my own opinion that is a serious error. The amount of really new information to be learned is not so very great; and the major purpose of the recitation is not the transmission and the acquiring of new matter. It is quite another: it is drill and practice, in order that certain things other than the simple acquisitian of information may be obtained. Among these other things there should be acquired a habit of correct thinking: using facts which have been learned, and using them in arriving at correct conclusions, in short, **in thinking.** Now two habits are fundamental in this process: first, the habit of keeping one's mind upon the topic or sequence which should be in mind until some conclusion is reached—this is **"concentration;"** and, second, is the habit of close and voluntary attention. These two are of course very closely related, and each includes the other; but I mention them separately because in the machinery of the recitation, now one, and now the other will, and must, be uppermost in the mind of the teacher. Not only must power of thinking be acquired in the classroom, skill in operation must also be obtained. For instance, in subjects like commercial arithmetic, geometry, and algebra a certain amount of skill of operation is essential. The same thing is true of shopwork, stenography, typewriting, and kindred subjects. But ability to do rapidly is of no value unless the doing is an accurate doing. A person who can add a column of figures of a given length in half the time that another person can add them is much more valuable, provided his addition is correct. His work is of no value, however, if it is not correct. An apparent skill at the sacrifice of accuracy is little short of a pedagogical crime.

Again, the ability to express oneself tersely and accurately should be acquired in the recitation room.

During this growth comes the gradual acquirement of an appreciation of that which is good; of a discrimination between clear and well-expressed and beautifully expressed work, and that which is not; between that which is skillful and accurate, and that which is neither. Appreciation of these things is growing quite rapidly; this, too, is a part of the function of the recitation.

Certain other products I will mention very briefly; they are largely by-products, but like other by-products of great industries, very valuable. Most important of all are courtesy, good breeding, gentlemanly and ladylike behavior. In the recitation more than anywhere else in the school are these to be fostered. I shall not stop to dwell upon the steps by means of which the development of these qualities may be known—not so much to the principal, to the first assistant, to the superintendent, as to the teacher himself. There is no incentive so great as the seeing of one's own advancement and the fruitage of one's own labors as they develop in one's pupils. Teachers ought to be able to see these things. Is it true that as time goes on the pupils are acquiring a power of clear and logical thought, and vivid, exact expression? Are they acquiring the power of accurate and skillful operation? Are they courteous, gentlemanly, and ladylike in their behavior and bearing? The tone and voice and manner and expression; do all these indicate that within the heart and mind, there are growing the most important fruitages of a refined and cultured manhood and womanhood?

I have said these things more at length, perhaps, than is necessary. There are two great functions of the recitation, the teaching of new matter and drill and practice in the various ways which I have mentioned.

How then is the efficiency of the recitation to be realized in both of these directions?

There are two conditions which I think must prevail, whether new matter is being taught, or drill and practice are being had.

There is a fundamental law of growth which must not be forgotten in the recitation room, namely, the law of subjective activity. If one is to grow, the activity must be his own; it is never vicarious. The teacher who makes a brilliant recitation possibly grows himself, but his pupils do not. They grow by their own efforts to do something and they do not grow in power in any other way. It is only by what they do themselves. Absolutely fundamental as a condition is constant, uninterrupted activity in the right directions by the pupils themselves to the highest possible maximum.

Secondly, this activity on the part of the pupils must be progressive or it is of very little value. A form of exercise which is not progressive will develop a certain sort of mechanical skill, and then stop. That is as far as it goes. This idea I shall try to emphasize towards the close.

Let me turn now to efficiency in the recitation when new matter is taught. I have already said that in my opinion the amount of really new matter is not so large as is commonly supposed. Let me sav what pretty nearly everybody knows, but what pretty nearly everybody forgets: telling a thing is not teaching it. If it were, we should all be out of a job because the phonograph is cheaper than we are! The test of teaching is in the learner. It is what he acquires that is taught. Constant telling doesn't do it. It is the constant effort of the pupil to give back to you, that does it.

Again whatever is done in this teaching of new matter, we must have constantly in mind that old law which we all have heard from the first day that we began to think about being teachers: the relation between the old and the new; the new must grow out of the old. Every development of a new subject, or a new topic, is an occasion for review, taking up here and there the items, the points, the facts, the principles, which have been mastered, and bear a direct relation to the building up process of that which is new.

The teacher who fails to keep this in mind and to use it, is failing very largely to convey a connected whole, which gradually grows in the minds of the pupil.

When I was a boy I studied, among other things, a topic which was exceedingly formidable to me; namely, profit and loss. You smile. Well, I do not wonder! I was taught there were many different cases. I have forgotten now how many different cases but they were all bewildering to me. Thus in case No. 1, certain things were given and certain things were required; in no sense practical at all. Case 1, Case 2! How many cases were there? I do not know, but profit and loss was a horrible thing to my mind. I did not realize any connection between profit and loss as presented in Greenleaf's Old Common School Arithmetic and Business Affairs, and that there were not a dozen cases, but only one, until I was put up against the proposition of teaching it, and then, in studying it, how easy it seemed, how natural! It was simply a matter of terms and the understanding of conditions and conclusions to be reached. When we try to separate into component parts things which are not separate we make a very great mistake. If we teach effectively there is a growth right through from first to last. Hence, in the introduction of the new, these old things need to be brought out and emphasized and the thing that is important in this emphasis is not what the teacher says about it. The teacher guides the thought of the pupils, and they make their own connections between the new and the known old. Except in matters which are outside the range of knowledge of the pupils and without their possibility of acquiring for themselves, the pupils should do the work of the mastery of the new and not the teacher do it for them.

There is a great temptation for the teacher, after having prepared his lesson, to say, "I know it thoroughly; I can make a fine recitation. The pupils blunder and they are slow. I do not get over the ground, and so I will make the recitation for them in order to save time." The trouble is, ladies and gentlemen, it doesn't save time! It appears to save time, but it doesn't, because when you have made that recitation you have robbed the pupils of the time which was theirs. There is no saving in this direction.

These things need to be kept in mind: make clear, explicit, brief statements, slow enough so that they may be grasped, and then stop. To ask the pupils whether they understand or not is giving the thing away, for of course they will say they do.

Rather ask them to tell you, then you will find out! The assignment of an advanced lesson, instead of being repeated by the teacher should be repeated by the pupil for most obvious reasons. I do not know how it may be with you, but I have, on a great many occasions, heard a preacher in announcing a hymn repeat it two or three times, and I have been interested to watch people about me during that process, and have come to this conclusion: The preacher who is in the habit of repeating the hymn number has an audience which never hears the number of the hymn the first time he says it. They are going to hear it again and they wait until he gets through the preliminary before they listen. Let there be no such preliminary. There is no time for it.

A recitation of forty-five precious minutes needs to be used for something that is worth while, and there is no time for the teacher to repeat any more than just enough to be sure that what he says is thoroughly understood.

Then the development of this matter needs to follow the law of the development in the child's mind, and not in the teacher's—in other words, the pedagogical rather than the logical order. For we all know when we stop to think of it that the pupil, a beginner, an inexperienced person, never sees anything in the same way that the experienced person sees it. A person who knows nothing about a topic cannot look at it is th same way, from the same angle at all, that the person who knows, does.

May I illustrate? In German we say there are certain so-called classes of declensions of nouns and adjectives. The teacher knows them for he naturally gathers together his great range of knowledge and makes the classification. But what about the poor pupil? He hasn't anything yet to classify, and to bring the classification to him at this time is useless; I will use no stronger term.

He needs to know a few things and then a few more things and then more things, and then, by and by, when he arrives at the possession of a good bit of knowledge it may be of use for him to gather together and to systematize, but not in the first place! In the first place it is a hindrance, by and by it becomes a help; but be quite sure that the by and by is deferred until there is matter in hand with which to make a classification.

Here is a constant temptation, especially for the person who is well informed and has mastered the subject, and has, perhaps, taken post graduate courses, and all that sort of thing. There is a constant temptation for that person to be trying to get the pupil to look at things from his standpoint, whereas he ought to be trying constantly to look at things from the pupil's standpoint.

Let us take any subject you like. In science—this is obvious! Let us take another, English, for instance. The outlining of an English classic—that is obvious, too! An outline and analysis, a series of logically arranged topics in the study of Ivanhoe, for instance, if they deserve any place at all, deserve a place only after Ivanhoe is inside the brains and hearts of the boys and girls, not before.

Perhaps I have made my meaning sufficiently clear in this connection, when I refer to these illustrations and say that the order of development in the teaching of new matter shall be pedagogical, from the pupils' standpoint, rather than logical.

Let me turn now to the other side. Now for the great problem, the problem of practice and drill; for to my mind, that is the big problem. The major part of the time in most recitations is devoted to practice, to drill, and all of the time in not a few recitations is and must be devoted to that purpose. We have something that is very important here, and upon the successful working of which will depend in no small measure the real efficiency in the recitation.

I have stated that the fundamental law of growth is activity on the part of the grower. It follows then that in practice and drill as in the teaching of new matter, it is fundamental that all of the pupils shall be busy all the time, on the subject in hand. There are two "alls," neither one of which can be forgotten, **all** of the pupils **all** of the time.

To this end a few things are absolutely essential. We must use questions more or less. When we call upon Mary Smith to answer a question, Mary is doing some thinking. But what about the others? Someone says: "I have sufficient control of my class, so that I know everybody is thinking, even when I call upon Mary Smith to answer a question before I ask it."

Good friends, don't delude yourselves, you are strong, you do have a tremendous power and influence over your pupils; you compel them, you control them, but don't forget there is a fundamental law of inertia in the human mind.

I remember a college recitation room back in the days of the past, presided over by a very genial, kindly gentleman who always asked his pupils to recite in regular order, running across the benches, back and forth. You do not know, of course, what I know about what was happening in that recitation: Mr. A. was on the **qui vive** at the beginning of the recitation and Mr. W. could wait until nearly the end of it, before giving any attention to the subect under discussion, because he knew he was safe.

You smile, as proper, perfectly proper. You don't do that? No? Maybe. Sometimes? Maybe. But when you do, you say you control, and I say "maybe." If you think, ladies and gentlemen, that even (and I am not sarcastic) the skillful teachers in the schools of New York can run counter to human nature, you are deluding yourselves. You cannot do it for any great length of time.

The question first—the announcement of the topic first, and not one of the forty in the recitation knows who is going to be called upon for the answer. Everybody is thinking about it, and when the attention has been on that sufficiently long, so that everybody has at least got some thought in his mind, then ask somebody to answer.

A certain principal and I tried an experiment the day before yesterday; it worked exceedingly well and favorably to the teachers. But I am suspicious that in a less heralding of the obvious purpose of the experiment it would not have worked so well. He said to me, "Let's try it." We went to eight different classrooms in rapid succession, and he asked the teacher in each class to give a thought question to be answered immediately. It is not easy for the teacher who is interrupted in this way, but though there was a little hesitation now and then—the most natural thing in the world—seven of the eight asked the question, got the attention, and then asked somebody to answer it. I am not giving a general rule of procedure which must never be broken. There is John Jones over there; he is a little rascal, and he is doing things that he has no business to do. You may jump on John Jones if you want to, because it does not do the other boys and girls any harm, and it does him a lot of good, probably; but what I am saying, is this, as a general rule of procedure, if you announce the topic or your question, and hold the attention of everyone until you are through and then call upon somebody to recite, you are getting the kind of attention that an efficient recitation needs.

Now that carries with it a number of things. The machinery of conducting the recitation shall not be obvious; the order of calling upon pupils shall not be obvious; if the questions which you ask or the topics which you propound are not arranged so as to be progressive and cumulative, you are falling short of the measure of efficiency which is most necessary. The promiscuous kind of question means but very little. It does amount to something because it does call for attention, and response; that is a good deal, but why be promiscuous when there is plenty of material to utilize which will leade to some place that you will have to get to? When you are going in that direction let the order be one of progress. I refer briefly to the use of questions. It is a topic big enough for an hour's discussion. I shall refer very briefly to one other element of efficient questioning. Let the questions be those which really provoke thought and not simply acquiescence.

Again I am reminded of old days. Not very many miles from the college that I attended, was another college for young ladies. The president of this college for girls conducted every Saturday morning for a good many years a course in Bible study and Bible history. I do not know why, I cannot understand it; I could if it had been a boys' college; I am not trying to account for it, but these girls sometimes did not pay very close attention, and one morning, he thought he would try an examination. Now the poor, innocent creatures had not been thinking about an examination, and they flunked, most deplorably flunked. The story goes that one of them on the next Monday morning met the dignified professor in one of the corridors, and, grieving at her failure, fell upon his neck and wept! I do not vouch the truth of this, but certain it is that that professor turned over a new leaf; he never tried that mean trick again, and every time, so the story goes, that he asked a question in the Bible history class, it was after this order: "Moses wrote the Pentateuch, did he not?" and I tell you it is an honest fact that Moses always wrote the Pentateuch! If you want to say a thing, ladies and gentlemen, why not say it. But what is the use of saying it and asking if it is not so? That is not a thought question. Neither is one which rehearses the facts and within itself gives the form and substance of the desired answer. Young people are quite naturally accommodating and always willing to please; if they know that a certain answer is wanted, don't you suppose you will get it?

There are some other things that I want to say, but the time is passing. What I have been trying to dwell upon so far in this matter of drill, is that all of the pupils all of the time are to be kept busy in thinking of the matter in hand.

If we take an exercise in rapid addition, which at the same time is to be accurate addition, obviously enough in a class of thirty or forty, some will be much more rapid than others. Do you think it is a profitable form of exercise to give four or five columns to be added, and then wait until the slow ones—they must have the time for it—have added them, while in the meantime the rapid ones are through and are waiting? Is that fair to the faster ones. Is there any serious difficulty, anything unfair or improper in giving, say twenty or twenty columns, devote the length of time you want to give to that exercise, and then let the test be the number of columns that they have to add accurately? Perhaps Mary Jones can add ten or twelve columns in the time that it takes John Smith to add four columns and get them right. Give each an opportunity to do that which he can do.

In drill and review we need to use a great deal of topic work; that is perfectly obvious, of course, but these topics must be presented in such a way as to lead somewhere; and the pupil must be held to giving the matter of the topic clearly and with reasonable completeness, both oral and written—and don't forget the oral. People talk very much more than they write, at least most people do, and while it is important that they should learn to write, it is also important that they should learn to speak. Am I old-fashioned and too particular? I don't mind being old-fashioned; but am I too particular when I say that, as a general rule, when a pupil is asked to recite, he shall stand, and when he stands that he shall stand, and then that he shall speak, so that he can be heard by every member of the class without difficulty, so that it is possible to hear what is said and at the same time grasp the significance of what is being said? Is it too much to say that these things should be done? Is it too much to say that in this type of recitation or in the brief statement, that the statement shall be reasonably complete; that the pupil shall be trained to organize all of his thoughts which bear upon that particular subject and give them in their logical, clear, and definite way? Let us take something very simple by way of illustration. We give in Latin drill in syntax construction, and the pupil speaks glibly of "ablatives of means," and "datives of possession," and "ablative absolutes," and "purpose clauses," and "result clauses." Quite too often that's all that we hear from the pupil. Grammatically considered, an "ablative absolute" is "absolute," but every one of these "ablative absolutes" has a purpose in the sentence; and the purpose is to be stated if you are to know that the pupil knows what he is talking about. A "result clause" or a "purpose clause" tells precious little.

Take another very simple form of drill. In exercises in French and German it has become a most desirable habit not to give synopsis with simply the subject and the verb but to include with the subject and the verb enough other words to have a little statement; not simply, "he ran," but he ran in some sort of a way, or to some place, or something of the kind. The pupil goes to the board and he writes the first form right through, but in the second form he simply changes the form of the verb, and uses ditto marks for the rest. The purpose of that exercise is to train that pupil, not to think of the form of the verb, simply, but to think of it in the context and to use it in the context. Now ditto marks do not help him to think. A college classmate of mine, now president of one of the universities in the State of New York, has the reputation, and reservedly so, of being one of the finest masters of English, oral and written, in the State and in the country. In a conversation, some years ago, without any reference to his reputation in the matter, he said to a number who were discussing certain pedagogical things, that he attributed his ability to speak correctly to the habit which he was required to form in a Brooklyn school when he was in his preparatory course: his teacher of English and the other teachers in the school compelled him to make complete statements every time he said anything.

In drill and practice, is it necessary that all of the pupils shall be working together all of the time? Most decidedly not. In my humble opinion if one person can do more let him do more. If one person needs to do something different it makes a little more trouble, but what of it? Yes, ladies and gentlemen, that's what we are here for: to give all the pupils all the opportunities and chances for drill that they can possibly get.

There must be a sufficient amount of variety in a recitation of forty-five minutes to insure the attention and the co-operation of all the pupils in the class. It is well enough to say that pupils need to be trained to give close attention to one topic for forty-five minutes without variation. It is well enough to say that, but you and I know in our hearts that they won't and that they can't do it. Courteous as you have been all this time that I have been talking I know in my heart, as you know in yours, that you haven't been giving close attention to what I have been saying all the time.

Other things being approximately equal, that teacher is the most efficient who seems to be doing the least, because the pupils are doing the most.

Years ago when I was in charge of certain elementary schools there was a kindergartner in the corps who was one of the most skillful kindergartners that I ever knew, but who didn't seem to do anything. The emphasis is on the **seem.** The children were spontaneous during all the period of the kindergarten, from 9 to 12. Over and over again I have sent kindergarten teachers who were busy bodies to watch that teacher. Some found what I hope they would find, and others didn't find it at all.

To put yourself apparently into the background, at least enough to get the maximum amount of work on the part of the pupils, is high art in teaching. And that can't be done if you are occupying the centre of the stage all the time. That don't do; **you** should be the more or less hidden but compelling force behind, influencing their self-activity.

What about these other items to which reference has been briefly made, courtesy, good breeding, the formation of right, and of high ideals? These are by-products which come only under certain conditions.

Am I, are you, courteous in tone, in bearing, in manner? There can't be that atmosphere existing in a recitation room for 190 forty-five-minute periods in a year without that influence becoming permanent and getting into the minds and hearts of the children.

You remember the story of the contest of strength between the sun and the wind. It is an old story. It runs something like this. The wind challenged the sun to a contest; they were to determine which was the stronger by finding out which one of the two could more quickly take off a certain man's overcoat, as he was walking along the road. The wind blew and the man shivered. And the wind blew and blew some more. The man buttoned up his overcoat and it blew with greater ferocity, and with a keener edge; and the man thrust his hands into his pockets and pulled his coat around tighter.

When the wind gave it up, the sun came out and smiled, that's all, just looked down and smiled at the man. Pretty soon his coat collar came down, and then he unbuttoned his coat, and the sun smiled some more; then the coat came off. That kind of an influence is the kind which is tremendously powerful.

All of these things, when transplanted into heart and soul, grow into the best kind of manhood or womanhood.

What about the teacher's preparation,—just a word. The teacher's preparation must first be comprehensive; not simply a day-by-day preparation, and second, **and don't forget the second,** it must be daily. The preparation which is not daily, which is not fresh, is far short of what is absolutely necessary.

I know I am speaking platitudes but sometimes platitudes are the very things that we need most. I remember the years when I was a class teacher and I remember how I used to have a little memorandum in my hand as I stood in the hall waiting for classes to pass that I might get a last quick glimpse of the things that I wanted to present,—the things I wanted to have the pupils do, so that these things were not in the back part of my mind but away up in the front, when the pupils and I got together. It is absolutely essential, ladies and gentlemen, that preparation must be not only broad and comprehensive, but also fresh and daily and immediate. And then again it must be from the pupil's standpoint and not the teacher's. Every review if it is effective is a new view, and every view must be from the pupil's standpoint if the pupil is to be the gainer.

EFFICIENCY OF THE FIRST ASSISTANT.

By Alfred C. Bryan, President of Association of Male First Assistants, Before the High School Teachers' Association of New York City.

There is an opportunity for a many-sided usefulness of the office in New York schools, if desired.

A. As general administrative aids of the principal.

B. As heads of departmental organization.

A.—1. In the generl activities of the school there are many functions which might to advantage be placed under the eye of the first assistants, thereby concentrating general oversight of these activities and bringing them in closer touch with the principal; e. g. athletics, literary clubs, debating clubs, school paper, etc.

2. The first assistant and the departmental organization are a convenient means of distributing information and instructions to teachers and of assembling reports, etc., where sufficient clerical help is not available.

3. Matters of discipline are assigned to first assistants in some schools.

B.—Departmental Management.

1. Systematize the business side, the provision of proper equipment, to economize the time and effort of all.

2. Departmental records, which may become of value, should be carefully preserved. While seemingly valueless, these departmental records in the aggregate become a mass of most important first-hand material. The Hanus Committee asked for just this sort of material ,and the superior merit test requires detailed evidence of a teacher's work extending over six terms.

3. The course of study should receive constant attention. The adaptation of the course to locality, to special school, to sex, to particular class and to advances of scholarship is really never completed, and this attitude toward the course assists in breaking down the idea that a text-book is a course of study. This subject may well be discussed at length in the departmental meeting and experiment arranged.

4. The supervision of classroom work seems to transcend in importance all other features of the first assistant's work. There is little provision for supervision of the teacher's work in New York City. Obviously, the superindents and principals cannot do it.

(a) Again in America there is little suitable training for the secondary school teacher. Compare with this condition the work of the German and Scandinavian Gymnasial Seminar. The New York City examination aims to correct this by requiring experience. Deficiency of knowledge is not so common as faults in class management, definiteness of aim, skillful questioning, versatility in classroom devices and approaches.

With our rapid changes in personnel the task of developing the immature teacher to efficiency is a great one, and it would seem that the burden in the main must fall to the first assistant.

(b) The improvement or maintenance of efficiency, if provided for at all, rests on the casual visit of the first assistant and frequently bears little result. Why should not the first assistant hear an entire recitation of every teacher at least once a month? and why should not the first assistant be ready with devices to make tests, from time to time, which result in some conclusion of value—such tests as of definiteness of lesson assignment, character of questioning, stimulation of thought, emphasis in teaching, summarizing, drill, interest and attention of class, reaching all the class, use of time, use of illustrative material, teaching how to study, etc., if these are fundamentals of method and management? The results of such tests would form the basis of free and helpful discussion in the departmental meeting, and they should, moreover, be made accessible to the principal in convenient form.

5. The departmental meeting seems to lack vitality and to play no part outside the dull routine of departmental business.

(a) May it not become the center of self-analysis and of departmental analysis, and therefore the place for suggestion and discussion, the starting point of experimentation and the final proving ground of real advance?

(b) Do the departmental head and every teacher contribute constructive suggestions frequently? and do they always have in progress at least one experiment relating to the course of study, class management or method?

(c) The departmental meeting may be a stimulus to growth and to the development of professional spirit. Consideration of school and departmental problems, new educational or scientific tendencies, research work by members, critical reviews of writers, timely questions, and the educational magazines are some suggestions for accomplishing these ends.

II.

The usefulness of this office seems to be impaired by vagueness in the definition of its functions and lack of uniformity in practice. Therefore, inasmuch as the whole range of duties of the first assistant lies, by the rule of the Board of Education, in the hands of the principal, subject to approval by the Board of Superintendents, and no definition of these duties has ever been made, as far as we can learn, would it not promote the efficiency of the first assistant and of the teaching staff as a whole, if:

(a) Some definition of their status and duties were laid down, and

(b) A plan of greater uniformity were adopted in the schools which would make the first assistant an organic and vital part in the organization of the school?

Such a plan would at least offer opportunity for effective departmental organization.

ELOCUTION TEACHERS.

The Elocution teachers of the High Schools of Greater New York met for organization in Room 201, High School of Commerce, at ten o'clock A. M., Saturday, December, 7, 1913. Nine teachers, representing eight different schools, were present.

Mr. Raymond N. Kellogg, of Morris High School, was elected Chairman, and W. Palmer Smith, of Stuyvesant High School, as Secretary. A program committee was elected, consisting of Mr. Kellogg, Mr. Smith and Miss Ada Webster Ward, of Jamaica High School.

These elections were followed by an informal discussion of: (1) uniformity of the Oral English work in the New York High School, (2) how to meet the new Regents requirements, (3) the outlook for making Oral English a distinct department in the New York City High Schools.

Respectfully submitted, W. PALMER SMITH.

DIRECTORY OF HIGH SCHOOLS OF NEW YORK CITY.

School	Telephone	Location	Principal or Teacher in Charge of Annex.
Bay Ridge	711 Bath Beach	86th st., near 18th av. (P. S. 101)	Harry A. Potter.
Annex	1273 Bay Ridge	92d st. and Gelston av. (P. S. 104)	
Boys'	690 Bedford	Marcy and Putnam avs. and Madison st.	James Sullivan.
Bryant	40 Astoria	Wilbur av., Academy and Radde sts., L. I. City	Peter E. Demarest.
Annex	1146-W Astoria	Van Alst av., near Flushing av., L. I. City (P. S. 7)	
Bushwick	13 Bushwick	Evergreen av., Ralph and Grove sts. (P. S. 75)	Frank Rollins.
Annex	5055 Wmsburg	St. Nicholas and Willoughby avs. and Suydam st. (P. S. 163)	William T. Morrey.
Annex	7411 Prospect	Ryerson st., near Myrtle av. (P. S. 69)	Julius M. Johnson.
Annex	3514 Bushwick	Quincy st., near Stuyvesant av. (P. S. 129)	Lewis B. Semple.
Commercial	3732 Bedford	Albany av., Bergen and Dean sts.	William Fairley.
Annex	7736 Bedford	Bedford and Jefferson sts.	William E. Doggett.
Curtis	351-J Tompkinsville	Hamilton av. and St. Mark's pl., New Brighton	(Vacant).
Annex	922-J Tottenville	Academy pl., Tottenville (P. S. 1)	
De Witt Clinton	4175 Columbus	10th av., 58th and 59th sts.	John L. Tildsley.
Eastern District	4565 Wmsburg	Marcy av., Rodney and Keap sts.	William T. Vlymen.
Annex	1715 Greenpoint	Havemeyer, N. 6th and 7th sts. (P. S. 143	Anna L. Phillips.
Erasmus Hall	288 Flatbush	Flatbush av., near Church av.	Walter B. Gunnison.
Far Rockaway	95 Far Rockaway	Far Rockaway	Sanford J. Ellsworth.
Flushing	321 Flushing	Sanford av., Flushing	John Holley Clark.
Girls'	372 Bedford	Nostrand av., Halsey and Macon sts.	William L. Felter.
Annex	5926 Prospect	St. Mark's and Classon avs. (P. S. 42)	M. Ellen Barker.
H. S. of Commerce	2658 Columbus	65th and 66th sts., west of Broadway	James J. Sheppard.
Annex	8114 Bryant	120 West 46th st. (P. S. 67)	Alfred C. Bryan.
Jamaica	165 Jamaica	Hillside av., Jamaica	Theodore C. Mitchill
Manual Training	1380 South	7th av., 4th and 5th sts.	Charles D. Larkins.
Annex	24 South	Prospect av., opp. Reeve pl.	Charles Perrine.
Annex	2627 Main	Duffield, Johnson and Gold sts.	Arthur L. Baker.
Morris	605 Melrose	166th st., Boston rd. and Jackson av.	John H. Denbigh.
Annex	2360 Melrose	Mott av. and 144th st. (P. S. 31)	Irving A. Heikes.
Annex	643 Westchester	Randolph, St. Lawrence, Hammond Aves. (P. S. 47)	Gilbert S. Blakely.
Annex	5634 Tremont	196th st., Bainbridge and Driggs avs. (P. S. 46)	
Newtown	40 Newtown	Elmhurst	James D. Dillingham.
Annex	122 Newtown	Elmhurst (P. S. 89)	
Richmond Hill	26 Richmond Hill	Elm st., Richmond Hill	Isaac N. Failor.
Stuyvesant	3739 Stuyvesant	15th and 16th sts., west of 1st ave.	Ernest R. von Nardroff.
Wadleigh	1892 Morningside	114th and 115th sts., west of 7th av.	Stuart H. Rowe.
Annex	4865 Harlem	138th st., west of 5th av. (P. S. 100)	Katherine A. Speir.
Washington Irving	3292 Stuyvesant	Irving pl., 16th and 17th sts.	William McAndrew.
Annex	2446 Stuyvesant	34½ East 12th st.	Helen L. Cohen.
Annex	3332 Spring	146 Grand st.	Idelette Carpenter.
Annex	4666 Schuyler	82d st. and West End av. (P. S. 9)	Rachel Bergamini.
Annex	4061 Chelsea	60 West 13th st.	Mary V. Linden.
Annex	5809 Lenox	88th st., east of 1st av. (P. S. 66)	Ida G. Galloway.
Annex	1612 Chelsea	140 West 20th st. (P. S. 55)	Eleanor Nightingale.

Brooklyn Training School for Teachers	1601 Bedford	Park pl., west of Nostrand av.	Emma L. Johnston.
Jamaica Training School for Teachers	1630-J Jamaica	Flushing and Highland avs., Jamaica	Archibald C. McLachlan.
Manhattan Trade School for Girls	3791 Gramercy	209 East 23d st.	Florence M. Marshall.
New York Training School for Teachers	1332 Harlem	119th and 120th sts., west of 7th av.	Edward N. Jones.
New York Nautical School		Foot of East 24th st.	Harry M. Dombaugh, Supt.
Vocational School for Boys		138th and 139th sts., west of 5th av. (P. S. 100)	Charles J. Pickett.

OFFICIAL BULLETIN

of the High School Teacher's Association of New York City. No. 38

No. 38. SATURDAY, MAY 3, 1913

The Board of Representatives, on May 23, 1911, empowered the Executive Committee to issue a Bulletin monthly, instead of four times a year.

THE FOURTH GENERAL MEETING FOR 1912-1913 will be held Saturday, May 3, 1913, at the High School of Commerce.

DEPARTMENT MEETINGS begin at 10 A. M. Besides the programs as given below, there should be in each Section an election of Chairman for 1913-1914.

GENERAL MEETING begins at 11 A. M. in Auditorium.

ORDER OF BUSINESS:

ELECTION OF OFFICERS FOR 1913-1914.

REPORT OF OFFICERS.

REPORTS OF CHAIRMEN OF COMMITTEES.

DISCUSSION OF RECOMMENDATIONS OF HANUS COMMITTEE.

LARGE vs. HIGH SCHOOLS OF 1500.

SPECIALIZED vs. COSMOPOLITAN HIGH SCHOOLS.

DISCUSSION opened by Mr. Frederick Paine, Eastern District H. S.

NEW BUSINESS.

WILLIAM T. MORREY, President.

AGNES CARR, Secretary.

DEPARTMENT MEETINGS, 10 A. M.

ANCIENT LANGUAGES—Room 534, Dr. Walter E. Foster, Stuyvesant High School, Chairman. Discussion of question:

In your opinion, is it possible so to modify our first year work that the returns from one year's study will be decidedly more profitable?

What should be the work of this department for 1913-1914?

Election of Chairman for 1913-1914.

BIOLOGY—Room 301, Mr. Harvey B. Clough, H. S. of Commerce, Chairman; Frank Merrill Wheat, DeWitt Clinton H. S., Secretary.

"Activities in Hygiene at Columbia," by Prof. George L. Meylan, Head of the Department of Physical Education in Columbia University.

In the light of recent agitation toward sex hygiene, come and hear Dr. Meylan tell what is being done in Columbia for undergraduates, in this and other lines of Physical Education.

Election of Department Officers for 1913-1914.

BOOKKEEPING SECTION—Room 303, Joseph J. Klein, Richmond Hill High School, Chairman.

"The Formation of a Commercial Teachers' Club or Association."

The meeting starts at ten promptly in order to afford ample time for thorough discussion before the General Meeting.

Election of Chairman for 1913-1914.

ELOCUTION—Room 201, Mr. Raymond W. Kellogg, Chairman; W. Palmer Smith, Stuyvesant High Schoool, Secretary.

All teachers of Elocution, Voice Culture and Oral Expression are cordially invited.

Report of committee of five on New Syllabus. General discussion.

Election of chairman and secretary for 1913-1914.

HISTORY AND ECONOMICS—Room 205, Miss Antoinette Lawrence, Jamaica High School, Chairman.

Plans for treating the Ancient History portion of the New History Syllabus.

Report by Alfred C. Bryan, Head of Department of History, High School of Commerce.

Election of Department Officers for 1913-1914.

MODERN LANGUAGES—Room 401, Co'man Dudley Frank, DeWitt Clinton High School, Chairman.

This section this year has broken all the Association records for attendance. At the first meeting of the year there were 68 in attendance, and at the second the number present was 73. The May meeting should prove as interesting and as inspirational to just as large a number, for there will be a practical discussion of the subject:

"The Auxiliaries in Modern Language Teaching and how to get the greatest good from them." The "Auxiliaries" include dramatic productions, clubs, newspapers, international correspondence, etc.

Actual experiments will be described by Miss Moskovits, of Washington Irving; Miss Hall, of Morris; Miss Kuhn, of Eastern District; Mr. Bierman, of DeWitt Clinton, and Dr. Zick, of Wadleigh.

Discussion will follow.

Election of Chairman for 1913-1914.

PHYSIOGRAPHY—Room 506, Mr. Kirk W. Thompson, Jamaica High School, Chairman. Preparation of Questionaire.

Time. How it is gotten at Washington and how it is distributed through the United States.—Kirk W. Thompson, Jamaica High School.

Election of Chairman for 1913-1914.

SHORTHAND—Room 216, Edwin A. Bolger, Commercial High School, Chairman.

Paper on History of Shorthand, by Dr. Frederick Beggrau.

Election of Chairman for 1913-1914.

MATHEMATICS—Room 304, Elmer Schuyler, Bay Ridge High School, Chairman.

"What use shall we make of the History of Mathematics in the High School Course?"

Election of Chairman for 1913-1914.

MINUTES OF THE GENERAL MEETING, MARCH 1, 1913.

The High School Teachers' Association met at the High School of Commerce on March 1, the general meeting following the section meetings called for ten o'clock.

The minutes of the January meeting were read and adopted. The treasurer reported 431 members, and balance in the trasury,$401.29.

President Morrey announced from the February meeting of the Board of Representatives that action had been taken favoring the resolution presented by th Principals' Association that rank and pay of first assistants in high schools depend on successful passing of examinations, and not upon subsequent appointment to position; and authorizing the publication of the Hanus reports for members of the association.

The president then referred to the meetings of the last two years which have been devoted to the study of various forms of efficincy, by means of which the association has been prepared to discuss in this meeting its highest type—moral efficiency. For the presentation of this subject the association wsa most fortunate in having present the Hon. Frank Moss, Assistant District Attorney.

Mr. Moss's address was so encouraging, sympathetic and inspiring, so illumined by his warm and genial and helpful spirit, that it was with a deep sense of gratitude the audience expressed its apprecation by a rising vote of thanks. [Printed in this Bulletin.]

Dr. Harvey, of the Board of Examiners, followed with a survey of the methods pursued in many schools for attacking this problem with organized effort. [Dr. Harvey's address will be published in the Bulletin.]

Some discussion followed Dr. Harvey's paper, and Mr. Moss than closed the meeting with a splendid picture of civic righteousness.

(Signed) AGNES CARR, Secretary.

HIGH SCHOOL AND MORAL EFFICIENCY.

An Address Delivered Before the High School Teachers Association of New York City March 1, 1913, by Hon. Frank Moss, Assistant District Attorney.

Reported by Mr. Horace G. Healey, High School of Commerce, Official Stenographer of the H. S. T. Association.

We love to state the greatness and the richness of our city, and we do it usually in terms of finance. The figures hardly suffice to show the financial greatness of our city. Officials of this city meet and their intelligent activities are co-ordinated to increase the resources and the powers of the city. Chambers of commerce and boards of various kinds unconnected with the city government meet together to consider the problems of commercial supremacy, and their thought and action are in co-ordination with the thought and action of the city fathers. The statistics pile up, and as we read them we are filled with enthusiasm—stocks and bonds, railroads and terminals, streets and waterways, harbors and docks. The Department of Docks has a program—not official as yet—but looking ahead for one hundred years, for the development of the harbor and the mantaining of New York as the principal seaport. Studies have been made concerning the harbors of other cities. Statistics have been obtained to show how certain improvements have resulted in the enlargement and the material growth of those cities. The true wealth of the city is not in its material resources. The hope of the city is not in those things; the hope of the city is in the character of its citizens. The hope of the city is in the ideals of its citizens. The hope of the city is in the creation and maintaining of civic pride. The hope of the city is in the creating and maintaining of civic patriotism. Patriotism we understand well in its application to the nation; quickly it is apprehended by the children in our schools who salute the flag every morning; but it must be applied to the city. We must learn and we must teach the truth that patriotism which is nation-wide is defective unless it burns the warmest and the truest in the city where we live. The program for he enlargement of our city's greatness, the foundation for the building of the greatness that is and that is to come, must be in the lives of the children and the youth of our city. Our boys and girls, our young people, are our chief asset. In the development of that asset we should put the best of our thoughts, give the best of our endeavors. To combinetions and co-ordination of effort, to develop material resources, there should be added combination and co-ordination of city officials. societies, Sunday-schools, and educators; co-ordination of thought, of effort, and of planning, looking and reaching far into the future, for the building up of our children and our youth in efficiency and in ethical and patriotic ideals; not only that they may be able to make money, and to carry on business, but that they have a love for their city and a devotion to its best interest, that will make them defenders of its honors, and maintainers of its goodness. It is of these matters that we are the least thoughtful. I do not say this, so much of you, for you are working with and for our youth all the time. I can go into many gatherings in this city and exonerate the people, those people from this criticism. Though there are many such gatherings as this, there is not co-ordination and co-operation on the scale required b the demands of the situation;—certainly not when compared with that which is applied to the problems of our city material resources.

I say to you, friends, that to take the boys and girls in this city of great business and of great opportunities and to teach them how to do business and how to make money is not enough. It may be a very dangerous thing to teach young people how to do business and how to make money, and to neglect the inculcation of ethical ideals especially. We cannot teach religion in our public scvhools. The Sunday-schools are supposed to do that; but they are not as efficient as they ought to be; they have hard work to maintain efficiency against the irreligious and money-making tendency of our time. We cannot teach religion in our schools as they do in Germany where spiritual educators are provided by large religious bodies and children are expected to make their choice as to religious instructions and to receive religious instruction. We don't want that, but we lose a great deal of the idealistic teaching that comes through religion and a way to supply it must be found.

For a number of years, during a period now past by, the cheap amusements of the city were vicious, demoralizing, indecent. Some of us predicted that the city would reap a bad harvest,—and it did.

Many young people going into the five and ten cent,—and even the penny—shows that were popular during that time, saw demoralizing and degrading pictures, and they naturally developed vitiated ideas. The city has reaped a miserable harvest of miserable things as the result of the condition in that period. I do not know of a more inspiring event that ever happened in this city than that which occurred in the latter part of Mayor McClellan's administration. A number of good people knowing what was going on and what it meant in the lives of the young people of the city, came together and the result of their deliberation and co-operation was a gathering of citizens in the Aldermanic chamber at the City Hall. Mayor McClellan sat on the high seat, and there were representatives of every sort of decent organization in the City of New York. The Cardinal was represented, the Jewish people were represented, the, Protestants in all the various denominations were represented as were the Youn Men's Christian Association, the Young Men's Hebrew Association, the Society for the Prevention of Cruelty to Children and other societies. They said to the Mayor, "We stand here for the children and youth of our city; we stand on a common platform; we are here regardless of religious and political differences which have separated us in the past; we make one common appeal to you: That something be done with these cheap amusements which shall not wipe them out but shall cut out the demoralizing features, that our young people may be spared that kind of education." The Mayor responded magnificently, and acted promptly.

The measure which he adopted was the measure of the time. It was the only one which he could take at that moment. These people retained their combination and they put before the legislature two bills which were enacted in obedience to the combined demand of that sound public spirit in this city. The result of those laws has been the removal from the picture boards and theatre boards advertising of demoralizing pictures, certain shows and entertainments. I speak of that as an illustration of what ought to be and can be accomplished when people combine in that way, and the resulting improvement in young life. May I illustrate again. For two or three years in our city the demoralizing of young life has been going on in another way. You will understnd that I don't come here to criticize any official or department of the city government; but you, as educators, want to see things in a broad way, so I speak of it. The re-arrangement of the Police Department has left in a large degree the growing youth of our city without police oversight or control. There has been a great increase in gang life, and I suppose you know it. There is an increase in the tendency for boys to run together in large numbers in the city and to perpetrate small offences and small crimes, growing in their character and in their extent until they become very serious. Officially I have had to investigate that condition in the county of New York. I have had information from hundreds of people. I have examined records of the Police Department. I say that many districts in our city in the last two or three years have been terrorized by gangs of young criminals who have committed robberies, burglaries, and sometimes murders. It would make your heart bleed to see how young are many of the hardened criminals we have to deal with in the major criminal courts of this county. The gravest crimes known to our law, are being committed by mere boys. The young criminals who have been most in the public eye of late, those who have done the hardest, the wickedest things in the city, in popular estimation, are products of our city life. Some of them are graduates of our schools, born here, educated here and they should have been saved to good citizenship. Several of them I know came from good families and I smypathize with them in their sorrow.

The stories that have been told me by parents of the way their boys, and their girls too, even while attending public schools,—even, while in high schools,—and shortly after going out,—have been sucked in by the whirlpool of vice so that parental restraint was of no use, so that good influences were useless and powerless, so that young people were drawn away from the arms of parents and out of their homes, out of the schools and out of the Sunday-schools and dragged into the ranks of that system of crime which is being maintained and which fattens on young life. I know a clergyman, a very practical man who lives in a densely populated locality. His church work was much impeded by the actions of a lot of young loafers in the neighborhood. He found there was two crowds of them.. He determined to reach them, and began by showing a kindly interest in their leaders. He found the leaders of these two gangs and approached them.

To the first young captain he said, "Well, you are the leader of your crowd. What is the name of it?"

"We are the Young Toughs," was his answer.

He asked the other leader, "What is the name of your crowd?" and he said, "We are the Young Crooks."

Those titles represented the ideals of the young men of those streets. I mentioned that to a friend of mine, a man of some importance in the city and he said, "I know that locality. I used to live down there. My father had his business right there. I like to go down there. One Sunday I saw some carriages pass, a youth was standing on the curb. I asked him, 'What does this mean?'. He looked at me and snarled, 'Ah, you do not belong in this part of the town. Go uptown where you belong!'" There was down there a feeling that they were entitled to their sort of life, to their notions of prosperity, to their notion of success, and they didn't want to be disturbed by good manners. The supremacy of our city as a business center, the wonderful power and influence that men feel here in politics, in business, and all sorts of life, appeal powerfully to young people, and they discover that nothing suceeds like success. They discover that men may amass fortunes and nobody will question very strongly as to how they got them. No man is foolish eoough to ask another how he "got it." A teacher told me that she received aletter from the father of one of her children enclosing three dollars. The letter read: "Enclosed please find $3. Promote Johnny. (Laughter.) Why not Why not? Do you suppose that the only graft in the city of New York is in the Police Department? (More laughter.) If you think it is, just ask the boys and girls, they will tell you you are wrong.

One of the greatest lessons I ever received was in a conversation with a police captain. The point he made was so evident in its connction with the Police Department, that I speak of it now. I said to him, "Captain, you belong to the 'Old Guard.' You seem to have a life tenure of your position. Police commissioners come and go frequently, but men like you stay on forever. Please tell me what kind of a police commissioner you like best." He answered, "We like a nice respectable gentleman who doesn't know that he is alive." "Explain that to me," I said. "Well, you see people will say that he is all right and everything must be right. While he stands there in front, we police do the business behind his back." Then I said, "Captain, why do you fellows take this dirty money?" He answered, "Wouldn't we be fools if we didn't? Everybody in New York works his job, even the ministers." "Do you believe that?" said I. "I know it," he answered. "But the money is so dirty," I responded. "That makes no difference, we fumigate it," was his cynical answer.

Just think of that. He was right in a very large sense. The graft disease is a general disease, and the police know it. Police graft is a symptom of that general disease. The police have more opportunities, more temptations and their system is worked out more carefully than others. A great many of them really think that they would be fools if they didn't take it. If they get dirty money it may be fumigated; all they fear is being caught in the meshes of the criminal law.

There was a rather rough story told me yesterday about some money that was offered to a clergyman. At least, a man had the money and the clergyman said, "You might as well give that money to me for the church." The fellow who had it rather tauntingly said, "If you knew where this money came from you wouldn't want it;" to which the clergman responded, "I would bless it." That may have been true or it may not; but if men and women have those notions don't you believe boys and girls have them? Don't you believe those notions of the path of success are well understood and well followed?

This city of ours is the heart of the country. The impulses of its heartbeats go out through the arteries not only of commerce but also of thought and action and are felt in the remotest quarters of the naion. When New York goes wrong other cities go wrong.

In the past the crooked combinations in other cities wanting to know what is being done in New York have sent their agents here to study and report. I am thankful to say that when we have succeeded in smashing dishonest systems here, good men in other cities have studied our plan, the New York, and used it. Courage and civic patriotism "are catching" too.

I said that for two or three years boys have not been properly supervised by the police. There is no police guard for the boys. Detective powers have been taken away from the uniformed police, and they are only little more than watchmen. They are not supposed to do detective work, and are not allowed to do duty in "plain clothes."

Detective work is confined to five or six hundred men scattered over the city in various precincts. When we come to the duty of controlling street boys and breaking up gangs, the police who are in uniform have no effective powers. When the boys see a uniformed policeman a block away they disappear. The detectives who work in plain clothes haven't the time to do it. So we have had boys committing crimes and terrorizing neighborhoods, unrestrained and uncontrolled by the police. I know localities, precincts and people involved. I am not speaking at random.

The public schools, the main body of public schools and especially the high schools are the principal places where we come in touch with the young life in this city at its crucial and critical period. It devolves upon you and your institutions to supply the young with the proper sort of moral training, so far as it can be done. You cannot wait for city fathers to take up the problem; you have got to take it up where you are, as best you can. But if you see the large problem and if you become filled with a vision as you ought to be, with the great power and influence which are in your body, you will push out for co-ordination and co-operation in the great work of idealizing the lives of our young people. The Ten Commandments reveal the moral principles of life. They are fundamental to human nature, not because they are written in any religious book, but because they are in the structure of human life. Teach them as the chart of successful life. Explode that infernal doctrine which we hear everywhere, that nothing succeeds like success and that a man's position is to be measured by what he has. Put into young life, the ideals, and the ethical principles which will make them see that real success is in being upright and true and in being able to keep company with one's self unashamed through life. Less and less have parents the ability to cope with the difficulties of young life in the city. Their children get oway from them. Environment is more potent than parental influence. So the schools must increase as moral factors.

What is very greatly needed in our city is the touch between teacher and scholar that used to be. It is now a matter of great difficulty. I speak my wish that it might come again. Here and there I find a teacher who says he has it in his class; but I find generally that a teacher has to work very hard for it or perhaps has some extraordinarv fire of enthusiasm that finds a way or makes it.

With the great crowding that you have, the immense number of pupils that have to be taken care of, the inadequacy of the system to handle the large numbers that come, the constant rolling up of the number of pupils with the inadequacy of the provision for them, the short time that you have with them, the large numbers you have to handle so that often you don't know their first names; the persoal connection grows weaker and weaker. When I was a boy I went to school in "old 49" and my teacher was James R. Pettigrew, dear old Jimmie Pettigrew. I had the good fortune to be a member of his class before he became principal; we had a year with him. One day he suddenlv jumped up from his chair and said: "Boys, I want to say something to you. Don't ever say anything that you wouldn't like your mother to hear. Don't ever go where you wouldn't take your mother. Don't ever do anything that you wouldn't like your mother to know." Here I am fifty-three years old; I was about thirteen at that time, and that is one of the sharpest points in my memory. Another day he said: "Boys, if I was a business man and one of you come to me for a position what do you think I would do. I'd look at your feet. What for? To see if your shoes were blacked. Do you think I would look at the front of your shoes? No! I would make you turn around and I would see whether you blacked the backs of them, also."

That is just an illustration of the way a teacher may get next to his boys if he has time and knows them well.

Recently I had the occasion to speak to the principal of a school about a small annoyance and I said: "Suppose you just put that matter before the boys and put them on their honor, wouldn't that be enough?" He answered: "Not in these days with these scholars; they have no honor." Why, when Jimmie Pettigrew put us on our honor, if one of the boys broke that pledge the others would jump on him. That was because of the bond that existed between the teacher and the scholars. We felt responsible for the honor of that class. Our teacher managed to get it into us and we learned honor in that way. I don't mean to say that it isn't done now. I don't mean to say that the case I mentioned is a typical one; I don't know whether is it or not. But we have got to find some way to put honor into the lives and hearts of our young people, and it seems to me that if they take the pledge for civic honor as they do for the glory of the nation, it will be easy to put in their minds the thought of the honor of our city; and to bring it will be easy to bring the power of national patriotism down upon our city life; as we concentrate the rays of the sun with a burning glass till we set fire to things. It ought to be possible to do it. I am sure it is.

I don't know of anything that has happened since that meeting with Mayor McClellan that has given me more joy than the recent exercises in the College of the City of New York. There they graduated seventy-seven young men and every one of these young men took a pledge to stand by the city of New York, in the form of the Athenian oath of old. As each young man took the oath, the arms of the city were pinned upon his coat sleeve, and he went out as though he were an oath-bound knight, having sworn that he would uphold the city and he would look upon all other citizens as brothers, that he would do no act which would bring shame upon the city.

We do not need to discuss religion with our young people. We don't need to get on any danger line, but when we discuss unselfish devoted patriotism we are pretty near the heavenly city, we are getting pretty close to religion, and we are getting to a religion that holds us all. No danger of prejudice and hatred on that line. I am longing for the day when opposed to the criminal system in this city will be a system of goodness established and developed by strong and brave men and women loving their city. As they go to other cities in this country they will not need to be ashamed of New York, and when New York is named they will stand just so much taller. They will believe in the city and stand for the city because it is the greatest aggregation of human units in the world, because the battles of civilization are being fought out in this city as nowhere else, and because it is good to be in such a struggle. We must reach the point in our city when all these great matters which affeact the conditions of men must be attended to by all good people, whether they be Christians or Jews, Catholics or Protestants, religious or non-religious, Democrats or Republicans, or Progressives; whether they originated in Germany, Italy, or Ireland, or any other country. We must stand together and work out our common interests and fight this battle for civilization in which the whole world is interested. The one thing that will enable this mighty combination to exist and to endure will be our common interest in our boys and girls. That common interest brings us together and holds us to gether and enables us to reach a common brotherhood in our cosmopolitan city—a common citizenship in which we put our pride and our love.

The thought that I want to leave with you is that the development of the great resources of our city, the development of heart and soul in our young people, the forming out of it all of a new and glorious citizenship, the development of a great pride in our city and a deep love for it. It will be glorious to be called a New Yorker.

I have a vision of a New York that is to be glorious—opulent, patriotic—meeting its duties, rising to its privileges, where the battle between Right and Wrong will ever be manfully waged by a puissant host of good citizens knit together by the bond of citizenship in the great city which they love and to which they give their best powers. The standards of human life will be elevated and the nation will be blessed because the noble life developed out of the well-fought struggle ever and ever will raise the standard of moral living, and will send forth through the arteries of all the nation the impulses and the warm life current of a noble living up to noble ideals.

SUPERINTENDENT STEVENS ON THE STATUS OF THE FIRST ASSISTANT.

Hon. Arthur S. Somers, Chairman Committee on High Schools and Training Schools, Board of Education.

Dear Mr. Somers:—

The status of First Assistants in High Schools and the opportunities offered to persons on eligible lists came to the attention of your committee on Thursday last. In order that this whole matter may be considered with full knowledge, may I submit to you and members of the committee the following statement.

Soon after the organization of the Bovs' High School in Brooklyn, it was decided to officer the several departments of instruction. The position of "Head of Department" was constituted and suitable persons were nominated as heads of the departments of Mathematics, History, Ancient Languages, etc. These nominees were duly licensed, but were not required to take a **competitive** examination; nor were any high school teachers of any grade in any Borough of Greater New York required to pass or take a **competitive** exmination until 1902. After consolidation, 1898, to 1902, high school teachers took only a pass examination.

In 1897 upon the organization of high schools in Manhattan (old New York) three grades of service were provided for in the by-laws and in the salary schedules,—1st assistant, 2nd assistant, 3rd assistant. A large number of 2nd assistants were appointed; about half as many 3rd assistants; and several 1st assistants. While the by-laws and the salary schedules seem to indicate that the position of 1st assistant was a salary grade, it is a fact that only **one** person in each department in each school was appointed to such position. The examination being a **pass** examination, no one was examined who was not an expectant nominee, and I presume that no one was proposed for nomination who was not proposed in the first instance by the principal of the school.

All this time there were several schools in which there were Vice-Principals or Assistant Principals. These were in Brooklyn, Queens and Richmond. The schools which I have in mind and in which these positions existed were the Girls, Erasmus Hall, Jamaica and Stapleton. There may have been others.

March 3rd, 1913.

In 1900, the Davis Law "bunched" all these positions in one schedule, hence Heads of Department, First Assistants, Vice Principals and Assistant High School Principals come under one classification and have since then been placed in the same salary schedule. In 1902, the Revised Charter made all the examinations for High School positions, except Principal, competitive. The **pass** examination went out. It therefore happened that in any one school there might be, as there have been, two or three or even more, eligibles on the list, holding the same license and all applicants for promotion.

The question was at once raised—shall this position be considered a salary grade or as a definite administrative position.

The matter has been before the Board of Superintendents and before your Committee in various ways for **nine years.** Your Committee during this long period has steadily held in practice to the policy of regarding it as a definite administrative position and has been averse to approving nominations of more than one person to the position named in any department in any one school. However, I call your attention to the very definite policy to the contrary, formulated in the resolutions adopted in 1907, a policy which has not been made effective.

In connection with this statement may I ask your consideration of the following from reports made by me to the City Superintendent during the past six years.

I am, your respectfully,

EDWARD L. STEVENS,
Associate City Superintendent.

EXCERPT FROM THE 8th ANNUAL REPORT OF THE CITY SUPERINTENDENT OF SCHOOLS.

"Considerable dissatisfaction has arisen because of our policy of confining the number of first assistants in each school to one in each subject. The result of this policy has been that if two or three persons in a particular school secure a license as first assistant in a subject, such as mathematics, there is opportunity for the promotion or assignment of but one. If the annual appropriations available for the General School Fund permit, I believe it would be well to regard the position of first assistant as a salary grade to which any assistant teacher may aspire for promotion after a sufficient amount of successful service and the passing of an examination."

EXCERPT FROM THE 9th ANNUAL REPORT OF THE CITY SUPERINTENDENT OF SCHOOLS.

"The status of first assistants and of persons securing that license is still undetermined.

The Committee on High Schools and Training Schools of the Board of Education has adopted the following report and recommendations:

RESOLVED, That it is the sense of the Committee that whenever it is practicable and desirable persons holding licenses as First Assistants should be advanced within the schools in which they are employed, and that they should not be appointed to vacancies in other High Schools without their full and free consent.

RESOLVED, That it is the sense of the Committee that persons holding licenses as First Assistants in the High Schools, who shall not have received appointments as First Assistants before the maximum salary of assistant teachers shall be entitled, subject to approval as to fitness and merit, to receive an annual increment in each year after serving a year at said maximum equivalent to the amount which they would have received if duly appointed to positions as First Assistants, such increments to continue until the maximum salary of a First Assistant is reached; and, that the Board of Superintendants may be requested to give this matter consideration and to report to this Committee such amendments to the By-Laws as may be necessary to carry it into effect.

RESOLVED, That it is the sense of this Committee that the provision of the statute in regard to appointments from eligible lists should be amended in such a manner as to permit the nomination from the eligible list of First Assistants of the persons best fitted in the judgment of the Board of Superintendants to fill the particular vacancy which exists in each instance, and that the Board of Superintendants be requested to take this matter under consideration and report to this Committee thereon, submitting the form of such amendment to the statute as would be necessary to carry this resolution into effect.

RESOLVED, That it is the sense of this Committee that opportunities should be given at frequent intervals to all persons who are eligible for license as First Assistant to obtain that license before attaining the maximum salary as assistant teacher and that the Board of Superintendents be informed that this Committee does not deem it advisable to exhaust the eligible list for First Assistants at any time.

RESOLVED, That in replenishing an eligible list for First Assistants this Committee is of the opoinion that standing in an examination alone is not a sufficient reason for placing those who qualify at a later examination above those who are already upon the list, unless a superior mark and a greater length of service as assistant teacher or in an equivalent rank are combined. In other words, this Committee is of the opinion that where it appears that a person qualifying at a new examination has a higher mark and has served longer in the position of assistant teacher or one of equal rank than persons elready upon the eligible list, the person so newly qualifying may be and should be placed above the said persons already upon the eligible list."

EXCERPT FROM THE 9th ANNUAL REPORT OF THE CITY SUPERINTENDENT OF SCHOOLS.

"The number of persons appointed to the position of first assistant in High Schools being small, few of our assistants could aspire to any advancement in the High Schools. Many have, therefore, made preparation and passed the examination for license as principal in the elementary schools. While this has not been a bad thing for the elementary schools, it has resulted in the loss to the High Schools of many strong and desirable men. Under the present schedule of salaries and requirements for license, if two young men graduate from the High School at the same time, and one prepares to teach in elementary schools, the other in High Schools, the first will have a considerable financial advantage over the second during a period of twenty-five years, if they both move in regular course to the higher positions open to competitive examination. Two points in particular may be commented upon: first, the annual increment paid to men is absolutely and relatively small; second, the first assistant receives a salary of $500 per annum less than that paid to an elementary school principal.

Certain readjustments should be made whether the proposed general increase in teachers' salaris is made or not."

EXCERPT FROM THE 10th ANNUAL REPORT OF THE CITY SUPERINTENDENT OF SCHOOLS.

"The status of persons holding a first assistant's license is still very unsatisfactory. In the corps of our High Schools, a considerable number of teachers have obtained, or are about to obtain licenses as first assistant in certain subjects, modern languages for example. It is evident that many years will pass before they all will receive appointment. There is no hope of advancement in the particular schools in which they are teaching under our present policy and there are already incumbents of first assistantships in most of the other High Schools.

The operation of our present policy results as follows: In some one school there is a sufficient number of teachers of biology, perhaps, but no first assistant in that subject. Yet there is an eligible list of persons holding that license. The principal of the school does not desire appointment from that eligible list because one or more of his teachers in that subject hope to acquire at some subsequent examination, such a license, and thereupon will expect promotion in that school. At the same time the appointment of a first assistant would make an excess of teachers in that subject in that school and one would be transferred out. Such a summary transfer, perhaps undesirable and unfair to the teacher himself, may be exceedingly difficult to bring about because of the statutory provision concerning transfers from one borough to another.

I regard it as exceedingly unfortunate that a state of facts exists such that in most cases a school must be deprived of the service of its best teachers when they seek promotion, because such promotion is only possible when they are sent to some other school.

Under our present policy, therefore, only those persons who are serving in schools in which there is no first assistant in the subjects taught by them, have the greatest inducements to enter an examination for this license. Even in such cases the place upon an eligible list occupied by a person who passes, may be such that a long period may elapse before the name can be reached.

I do not believe that this state of affairs was ever contemplated in the enactments of the statute or the By-Laws."

THE CITY OF NEW YORK
Office of the
PRESIDENT OF THE BOARD OF ALDERMEN
John Purroy Mitchel, President
51 Chambers Street

New York, March 8th, 1913.

MR. WILLIAM T. MORREY,
President High School Teachers Association,
535 West 111th Street, New York City.

MY DEAR MR. MORREY:—I have your letter of February 25th, 1913, in which you ask that I arrange with the printer for you to secure 1,000 copies of the interim report of Dr. Ballou at 11¾c per copy, and 1,000 copies of the interim report of Dr. Davis at 8c per copy. These were the prices that the printer quoted to me over the telephone the day that you called to discuss the matter with me for 2,000 copies of each report.

I have taken up the matter with the printer, and he states that the price quoted over the telephone was really the price made for as high as 50,000 copies of some of the reports, and not less than 10,000 copies of any of the reports, and that, upon consultation with the binding and folding department heads and the officers of the company, he finds that he is unable to make the price quoted for 1,000 copies. On March 4th, he sent me the following letter indicating prices contained therein:

> "We shall be pleased to furnish you with 1,000 copies of the BALLOU REPORT for $170.00. This price includes the charts printed, but without the machine ruling, and 1,000 copies of the DAVIS REPORT for $114.00.
>
> Trusting that these prices will meet with your approval, we remain,
>
> Very truly yours,
> J. J. LITTLE & IVES CO."

I am very sorry that the printer finds himself unable to furnish these copies at the prices quoted, for it is very embarrassing to me after having stated the prices at which the work could be done. I will, however, see that each High School and annex is supplied with five copies of the report of Dr. Ballou and Dr. Davis as soon as the Davis' report is released for publication.

Trusting this will be satisfactory under all the circumstances, and stating that when the next edition of 1,000 copies of the final report is printed we will furnish the High Schools with as many copies as possible, I remain,

Respectfully yours,
BURDETTE G. LEWIS,
Examiner, Executive Staff,
President, Board of Aldermen.

NOVEMBER 27, 1913, MEETING OF BOARD OF REPRESENTATIVES.

The Board of Representatives met November 27, in the Washington Irving High School, on East 12th Street. The minutes of the October meeting were read and adopted.

On the motion of Mr. White, of Morris, it was decided to adjourn from the conclusion of this meeting to the January meeting, omitting the meeting of December.

The President announced that committees are being filled slowly, but he would be glad of suggestions for still vacant places.

President Morrey then gave a brief account of the ways in which various committees have conducted the work undertaken by them. Much disapproval was expressed by the members of the Board present of that form of committee work by which reports have been submitted to the public press purporting to come through the H. S. T. Association, when they have not been presented to the Board of Representatives, or even obtained a majority approval in the committees themselves.

As a line of work for the year, the study of High Schools by departments, was suggested. Assuming that a new High School is to be built, what would be ideal equipment in each department? Discussion followed as to possible methods of obtaining the information desired.

Mr. Overholzer suggested that it would be of great value if a definite plan for work in summer schools might be outlined, particularly in modern language, that certain standard books might not be read below a certain grade.

Another problem presented to the Board was in regard to the disposition of unused books and apparatus with which schools are charged year after year. No satisfactory solution had been reached when the meeting adjourned at 5:30.

(Signed) AGNES CARR, Secretary.

JANUARY 29, 1913, MEETING OF REPRESENTATIVES.

The January meeting of the Board of Representatives was held at Washington Irving High School, January 29. In the absence of the secretary, Miss Eleanor Baker was appointed Secretary pro tem.

The treasurer reported 322 members. Balance in treasury, $293.29.

Discussion followed of a a proposed questionnaire regarding the various reports on the school system.

(Signed) ELEANOR R. BAKER,
Secretary pro tem.

FEBRUARY 25, 1913, MEETING OF REPRESENTATIVES.

The Board of Representatives met on February 25 at Washington Irving High School. The minutes of the January meeting were read and adopted. The treasurer reported 431 members; balance in treasury, $401.29; seven schools not yet reported.

The Board was fortunate in having present at this meeting Mr. Clarence D. Kingsley, chairman of the Committee on Articulation of Schools and Colleges, who had been called from New York to serve the State Board of the Department of Education of Massachusetts.

Mr. Kingsley gave an interesting account of his work of visiting the small schools of the State, which, though not under state control, receive state appropriation under certain conditions. One part of the work of the Board is to inspect the schools and see if such appropriation is warranted. In the larger schools, the conditions are such that a pupil must make up his mind on entering high school whether he intends going to college. In an ideal course the first two years in high school would help a student make this decision, and would be equally valuable whether the last of the course were spent in preparation for an academic or a business career.

Mr. Oberholser, chairman of the Committee on the Status of Librarians, reported that Mr. Sullivan was to bring the matter before the Committee on High Schools, but in view of the fact that a new régime was about to be inaugurated, thought better to do nothing at present.

Mr. Perrine, chairman of the Committee on Grammar Nomenclature, reported that the pamphlet sent out by the Board of Education to teachers of English was not received by teachers of foreign languages. An effort is being made to have names of constructions used in the teaching of foreign languages incorporated in this report, and copies sent to all language teachers.

Mr. Falion, chairman of the Committee on Teachers' Ratings, presented a preliminary report signed by all the members of his committee, stating that this seems an inopportune time for an extensive report, since the matter is being considered by State legislations, and by legislation of the Board of Education.

A point of policy was raised by Mr. Dotey, who asked if it would not be better to help matters on by acting now, than to wait until a decision has been rendered and then present a protest.

President Morrey then spoke of the investigation of the Hanus report carried on in committee made up of members of the various associations.

It was moved and carried that this association authorize the president to supply to its members copies of the Ballou and Davis reports.

Mr. Doty presented the following resolution which was carried:

Resolved, That the Board of Representatives of the New York High School Teachers' Association most heartily endorse the following amendments to the By-Laws, proposed by the New York High School Principals' Association:

(a) Amend Section 52, paragraph 3, by striking out words "First Assistant."

Insert:

(b) Every assistant teacher in high schools who has been granted a license as first assistant teacher shall be entitled to the rank and pay of a first assistant teacher without further examination or appointment, and said rank shall become effective, and said salary shall be paid from the first day of January of the year next following that in which the license as first assistant teacher is granted, provided, that no first assistant shall receive on becoming a first assistant teacher a salary less than he would have received if he had remained an assistant teacher.

(c) Examinations for the license as first assistant teacher in high schools shall be held at least biennially in all subjects for which the license as first assistant teacher is provided in the By-Laws.

(Signed) AGNES CARR,
Secretary.

MARCH 25, 1913, MEETING.

The March meeting of the Board of Representatives was held on the twenty-fifth, in the Washington Irving High School. The report of the secretary was read and adopted.

The treasurer reported 554 members to date (No reports as yet from Clinton, Commerce, Erasmus, Flushing and Wadleigh):

Receipts to date	$950.22
Expenditures	439.68
Balance on hand	$510.54

President Morrey announced that the price finally quoted for printing the Hanus reports for the Association exceeded the first estimate by a considerable sum (about $92.50). He thought it inadvisable, therefore, to expend the money of the association in providing copies for every member, as he had been assured that copies of the reports on High Schools had been or would be forwarded to the schools, thus making the reports available to all members.

The senior representatives, to whom Hanus reports were to be sent, were asked to furnish them as far as advisable to such new members as had joined the association for the purpose of receiving the reports, and to write the President for more copies to meet such demands. If such members were not supplied, their dues may be returned, on written request of senior representative.

Mr. Mann, of Morris, made a motion: "That such measures be taken as to insure the placing of one or more sets of copies of the Hanus reports in the libraries of the High Schools, to be consulted by the teachers." Carried.

The business of the next meeting of the Board will probably be the consideration of Dr. Linville's report on "High School Mortality," and "Why Students Leave the High School."

A motion was offered by Mr. White, of Morris: "That the officers of this association be requested to petition the Board of Education to close the schools on Friday, June 27, instead of Monday, June 30, and to petition other teachers' associations to take similar action." Carried.

The President asked Mr. White to draw up such a petition.

Mr. Kingsbury, of Newtown High School, introduced the subject of discontinuing credit for note book work. Some discussion followed, the point being made that much inspiration would be taken from the pupil if he felt that such work would not be recognized by the State.

Mr. Kingsbury was appointed chairman of a committee on "Use of Science Laboratory Note Books."

The remainder of the meeting was spent in reading and discussing the Ballou report. Adjourned at 5:50. (Signed) AGNES CARR, Secretary.

EXTRACTS FROM CONSTITUTION

Article III.—Membership.

Section 2.—Any teacher in a public high school in New York City may become a member of this association by signing the constitution and paying the annual dues to the Treasurer (Adopted May 10, 1902).

Article IV.—Officers.

Section 1.—The officers of this association shall be: a president, a vice-president, a secretary and a treasurer.

Section 3.—Officers shall be elected at the last regular meeting of the school year. Election shall be by ballot, and a majority of the votes cast shall be necessary for an election.

Article V.—Board of Representatives.

Section 1.—There shall be a board of representatives, consisting of the members of the executive committee and of the representatives chosen from the several high schools; each school is to be entitled to one representative for every ten members of the association, provided, however, that each school shall be entitled to at least one representative.

Section 2.—After 1905, representatives shall be elected by ballot during the week preceding th regular meeting in May, and shall hold office for one year; in 1905, the time of election shall be fixed by the executive committee. Due notice of such election shall be given to each school by the president. Vacancies may be filled by the board of representatives at any meeting.

.....

Section 3.—The board of representatives shall meet on the last school Tuesday of each month, excepting September and June, and shall have the power to act upon all matters affecting the association.

Section 4.—The president of the association shall be ex-officio chairman of the board of representatives.

Article VI.—Committees.

Section 1.—There shall be an executive committee, consisting of the four officers and three other members chosen by ballot at the same time and in the same manner as the officers.

Article VII.—Meetings.

Section 1.—Four regular meetings shall be held every year.

Section 2.—The meetings shall be held on the first Saturdays of October, December, March and May of each year, unless otherwise ordered by the executive committee, and at a time and place to be designated by the executive committee (Adopted May 4, 1901).

This Bulletin has been made sixteen pages instead of larger on account of the moving of the printer.

The next Bulletin, to appear soon, will contain Analyses and Recommendations of the Ballou, Davis and Thompson Reports to the Hanns Committee, High School Stattistics, and Dr. Hervey's address on "How to Attain Moral Efficiency."

WILLIAM T. MORREY.

OFFICIAL BULLETIN

of the High School Teachers' Association of New York City

No. 39. FRIDAY, JUNE 20, 1913

The Board of Representatives, on May 23, 1911, empowered the Executive Committee to issue a Bulletin monthly, instead of four times a year.

CONTENTS.

MEETING OF HIGH SCHOOL TEACHERS' ASSOCIATION.

The last general meeting of the High School Teachers' Association, for the year 1912-1913, was held on May 3d, at the High School of Commerce. Section meetings began at 10 o'clock and the general meeting at 11:15.

The secretary's report was read and accepted. The treasurer reported 744 paid up members to dat; 827 mmbers in sight—the largest enrolment in the history of the association, and a balance in the treasury of $605.27 on April 29, 1913, as per the printed report of the treasurer that was distributed at the meeting.

President Morrey announced that his report of the year's work would be published in the bulletin. He asked for names of any members of the association who would like to make study of the conditions in their communities, with a view to providing data on which to base the choice of high school best suited to their needs.

The next business in order was the election of officers, which resulted as follows:

President, Wm. T. Morrey, Bushwick High School; Vice-President, Jessie H. Bingham, DeWitt Clinton High School; Secretary, Mary J. Bourne, Morris High School; Treasurer, Loring B. Mullen, Girls' High School. Executive Board: Aaron I. Doty, DeWitt Clinton High School; H. Elizabeth Seelman, Girls' High School; Alexander L. Pugh, High School of Commerce.

Mr. Fred Payne, of Eastern District High School, opened the discussion on the Size and Kind of High School to be Established, speaking against the cosmopolitan high school, as recommended by the Hanus Committee.

There was no discussion on the first proposition that schools be limited in numbers to 1,500, but many arguments were presented for, both the cosmopolitan high school and the type high school. A motion was made that: "The president of this association be authorized to take a referendum vote among principals and teachers of the high schools in regard to the size and type of high schools to be established."

As there was a strong feeling that those not hearing the discussion might not be prepared to vote on this question, a motion was carried that this proposition be tabled.

The following motion was then carried: "Resolved that it is the sense of this meeting that we favor the establishment of the type high school as a policy."

A motion, that the number of voters on each side be reported, was lost.

A resolution was presented by Dr. Sullivan, of Boys' High School, and amended to stand:

"Resolved that the president of the High School Teachers' Association notify the President of the Board of Education, the Mayor of the City of New York, the Governor of the State of New York, the president of the Senate, and the Speaker of the Assembly, that the High School Teachers' Association has taken no action on the McKee Bills, either for them or against them." Carried.

The meeting was adjourned at 1:40 o'clock.

(Signed) AGNES CARR, Secretary.

WILLIAM T. MORREY, President.

CONSTITUTION.
Adopted March 2, 1900.

ARTICLE I.—Name.

Section 1.—This organization shall be known as the High School Teachers' Association of New York City. (Adopted May 10, 1902.)

ARTICLE II.—Object.

Section 1.—The object of this association shall be the advancement of secondary education and the promotion of teachers' interests.

ARTICLE III.—Membership.

Section 1.—Any teacher of the public high schools of the Boroughs of Manhattan and the Bronx who shall sign the constitution and pay the annual dues, within the month of March, 1900, shall be a charter member of the association.

Section 2.—Any teacher in a public high school in New York City may become a member of this association by signing the constitution and paying the annual dues to the Treasurer. (Adopted May 10, 1902.)

ARTICLE IV.—Officers.

Section 1.—The officers of this association shall be: a president, a vice-president, a secretary and a treasurer.

Section 2.—The duties of these officers shall be such as usually devolve upon the officers named.

Section 3.—Officers shall be elected at the last regular meeting of the school year. Election shall be by ballot, and a majority of the votes cast shall be necessary for an election.

ARTICLE V.—Board of Representatives.

Section 1.—There shall be a board of representatives consisting of the members of the executive committee and of the representatives chosen from the sevral high schools; each school is to be entitled to one representative for every ten members of the association; provided, however, that each school shall be entitled to at least one representative.

Section 2.—After 1905, representatives shall be elected by ballot during the week preceding the regular meeting in May, and shall hold office for one year; in 1905, the time of election shall be fixed by the executive committee. Due notice of such election shall be given to each school by the president. Vacancies may be filled by the board of representatives at any meeting.

Section 3.—The board of representatives shall meet on the last school

Tuesday of each month, excepting September and June, and shall have the power to act upon all matters affecting the association.

Section 4.—The president of the association shall be ex-officio chairman of the board of representatives.

ARTICLE VI.—Committees.

Section 1.—There shall be an executive committee, consisting of the four officers and three other members chosen by ballot at the same time and in the same manner as the officers. The executive committee shall approve all appropriations of funds and shall audit and direct the payment of all bills.

Section 2.—There shall be a committee on teachers' interests, consisting of nine members, including the president. This committee shall be appointed by the president to serve for one year and shall report monthly to the board of representatives.

Section 3.—There shall be a committee on secondary education, consisting of nine members, including the president. This committee shall be appointed by the president, and shall serve for one year. It shall prepare programs for the four regular meetings of the association and shall report from time to time on matters of educational interest.

ARTICLE VII.—Meetings.

Section 1.—Four regular meetings shall be held every year.

Section 2.—The meetings shall be held on the first Saturdays of October, December, March and May of each year, unless otherwise ordered by the executive committee, and at a time and place to be designated by the executive committee. (Adopted May 4, 1901.)

Section 3.—A special meeting of the association may be called by the executive committee whenever the interests of the association seem to demand it. The president of the association shall be required to call a special meeting upon the demand of ten members of the association. Due notice of such meetings must be given to all members of the association.

Section 4.—Thirty members of the association shall constitute a quorum for the transaction of all business.

ARTICLE VIII.—Dues.

Section 1.—The annual dues shall be one dollar, payable at the first regular meeting of the school year.

ARTICLE IX.—Amendments.

Section 1.—This constitution may be amended at any regular meeting by a three-fourths vote of the members present, provided due notice of the proposed amendment shall have been made at a preceding regular meeting. (Adopted May 4, 1901.)

ARTICLE X.—Ratification.

Section 1.—This constitution shall go into effect immediately upon its adoption.

ELOCUTION TEACHERS.

The second meeting of the elocution teachers of the high schools of Greater New York was held in Room 201, High School of Commerce, at 10 o'clock A. M., Saturday, March 1, 1913. Sixteen teachers, representing thirteen different schools, were present. Mr. Raymond N. Kellogg, chairman of the organization, presided. After the reading and approval of the minutes of the last meeting, Mr. Kellogg gave an interesting summary of the responses to the "questionnaire" recently sent out. Of fourteen schools that responded, two have three teachers of elocution, three have two teachers, six have one teacher, and three have no teacher of the subject.

A discussion of the "questionnaire" and of means of carrying out the present requirements in Oral English folowed.

It was regularly moved secoded and carried that our chairman appoint a committee of five to draw up a tentative course of study in elocution for our city high schools. W. PALMER SMITH, Secretary.

High School Register by Terms, February 28, 1913.

	Terms	1	2	3	4	5	6	7	8	Totals
1.	Washington Irving	1499	1077	905	739	512	496	120	109	5457
2.	Morris	1178	715	577	460	234	294	221	357	4136
3.	Manual Training	1203	777	602	400	239	173	81	185	3660
4.	DeWitt Clinton	904	704	530	'452	302	266	138	285	3581
5.	Wadleigh	813	619	490	382	317	232	216	302	3371
6.	Erasmus Hall	734	610	427	297	316	251	220	258	3113
7.	Commercial	1064	708	461	335	186	146	...	...	2900
8.	Eastern District	747	538	413	361	252	262	177	141	2891
9.	Commerce	955	586	414	344	191	125	84	58	2757
10.	Stuyvesant	905	489	406	265	200	142	162	88	2657
11.	Girls	558	464	363	262	235	247	269	188	2586
12.	Bushwick	843	490	409	257	172	80	12	12	2275
13.	Boys	674	372	311	263	162	139	116	76	2113
14.	Curtis	434	206	166	117	87	66	49	75	1200
15.	Bryant	367	254	176	146	100	73	39	44	1199
16.	Bay Ridge	406	244	191	117	42	31	34	..	1065
17.	Newtown	266	195	157	106	94	99	57	52	1026
	Totals	14431	9629	7394	5659	3968	3318	2134	2351	48884
	Percentages	100%	66.7	51.2	39.2	27.4	22.9	14.7	16.2	338.3
	Approximate	30%	20	15	12	8	7	4	5	100
	Fraction Preceeding Term	1-1	2-3	3-4	4-5	5-7	5-6	2-3	11-10	

RELATIVE PERCENTAGES OF HIGH SCHOOL PUPILS BY GRADES, BASED ON NUMBER OF FIRST TERM PUPILS, FEBRUARY, 1913.

			1	2	3	4	5	6	7	8
1.	Washington Irving		100	71	60	49	34	33	8	7
21.	Far Rockaway	86	55	45	60	20	19	11	6	297
19.	Jamaica	226	203	136	141	85	63	35	47	936
20.	Flushing	204	117	95	58	44	47	52	32	649
2.	Morris		100	60	48	38	28	25	10	30
3.	Manual Training		100	60	50	33	20	15	7	2
4.	DeWitt Clinton		100	78	58	50	33	29	15	31
5.	Wadleigh		100	76	60	47	39	29	26	37
6.	Erasmus		100	83	58	40	43	35	30	35
7.	Commercial		100	67	43	31	17	14	—	—
8.	Eastern District		100	72	55	48	33	35	23	19
9.	Commerce		100	59	43	36	20	13	9	6
10.	Stuyvesant		100	54	45	29	22	16	18	10
11	Girls'		100	83	65	56	51	55	58	33
12.	Bushwick		100	58	49	30	20	10	(2)	(2)
13.	Boys'		100	55	46	39	24	20	17	11
14.	Curtis		100	47	38	26	20	15	11	17
15.	Bryant		100	68	48	40	27	20	11	12
16	Bay Ridge		100	61	(48)	(29)	(11)	(8)	(9)	—
17	Newtown		100	73	59	40	35	37	21	10
18.	Richmond Hill		100	57	34	27	21	18	11	10
19.	Jamaica		100	90	60	62	38	28	15	21
20.	Flushing		100	57	47	28	22	23	25	16
18.	Richmond Hill	365	206	125	97	78	67	41	36	101[illegible]
21.	Far Rockaway		100	64	47	70	23	22	13	[illegible]
	Totals		100	66.7	51.2	39.2	27.4	22.9	14.7	16.[illegible]

HIGH SCHOOL TEACHERS' ASS'N OF NEW YORK CITY.

Treasurer's Report—May 16, 1912, to April 29, 1913.

RECEIPTS.		
Balance May 16, 1912	$296 62	
Dues from 1911-1912	99 00	
Dues to date, 1912-1913	744 00	
Sale of publications	2 45	
Total		$1142 07
EXPENSES.		
Sections—		
Ancient Languages	$4 10	
Modern Languages	1 00	
Mathematics	1 59	
Committees—		
Student Aid	30 60	
Secondary Education	12 20	
Teachers' Absences	12 50	
School Efficiency	3 00	
Meetings—		
Reporting Addresses	30 00	
Board of Representatives	7 00	
Janitor Service	28 00	
Coat Room	4 00	
Elevator Service	4 00	
Printing—		
Official Bulletins	330 86	
Membership Cards	2 50	
Official Stationery	1 75	
Postage and Expressage—		
Official Bulletins	43 57	
Secretary	10 98	
Treasurer for 1911-1912	5 12	
Treasurer for 1912-1913	4 03	
Total		$536 80
To Balance		605 27
		$1142 07

Respectfully submitted,

LORING B. MULLEN, Treasurer,

April 29, 1913. Girls' High School, Brooklyn.

This is to certify that we have examined the above account of Loring B. Mullen, Treasurer of the High School Teachers' Association of New York City, and found the same to be correct.

GRACE HELENE MILLER,

ANNE ELIZABETH STANTON,

Bushwick High School,

Auditing Committee.

Total Enrollment for 1912-1913, up to June 17, 1913....................856

THE HIGH SCHOOLS AND MORAL EFFICIENCY.

An Address Before the High School Teachers' Association of New York City by Dr. Walter L. Hervey of the Board of Examiners.

In order to deal intelligently with the problem of Moral Efficiency in the schools, we must first take account of the moral situation in the community. For while the general problem of moral education is set by human nature, the special problems for any group of schools are set by the community itself.

In the City of New York there exists a situation that is peculiarly complex and difficult. What are the elements in this situation?

First numbers: The impersonality and the irresponsibility of the crowd. Then, the fact that so large a proportion of those with whom we have to deal are alien—in customs, in standards of living, in views of life: having few if any instincts and traditions of self-government, and responding more readily to measures of repression than to opportunities for responsible self-direction.

Again there is a distinct breaking up of moral traditions, seen in the weakening of a certain type of authority, both in the home and in the church; in certain ways of dressing, dancing and behaving that are not seemly; in the spread of a debased and debasing attitude toward work; in the prevalence of a perverted notion of group loyalty and of civic and social responsibility.

And back of all these things, and partly causing them, there is a tremendous world-wide economic pressure, industrial revolt, commercial unsettlement, social unrest, all of which must be reckoned with by teachers as vital elements in the moral situation.

But there is, of course, another side to the picture,—hopeful elements in the situation that must be kept steadily in view: these great members only enlarge our opportunity: those whom I have called aliens have extraordinary possibilities of development: these is a strong impulse for democracy, even among the school teachers, and for social justice. There is the steady dawning of an era of publicity in all matters affecting the public good; and there are definite advances toward the single standard of morals as between rich and poor and as between men and women, all of which must be entered on the credit side of our moral ledger.

In the midst of this situation, the high school stands, with its objective of attaining, as nearly as may be, the ideal of Moral Efficiency. What is that ideal? It is, I take it, that the pupils shall individually and in their various groups develop the power and the habit of reacting to moral situations in appropriate moral ways: that, for example, in a situation calling for obedience they shall obey; in a situation calling for faithful performance of duty they shall be faithful; for fair play, they shall play fair; for loyalty, they shall be loyal; and that all these reactions shall not be blind and merely habitual but progressively enlightened and reasonable. Or, to state the problem in another way, the task of the high school is, to take these great masses of young men and young women—in whom at the beginning of the high school course a knowledge of the good is but rudimentary, in whom social imagination is largely deficient, in whom loyalty is misdirected, who—many of them apparently without compunction, will lie, cheat and steal, and so to direct their impulses, form their habits, enlighten their minds and organize their lives, that before they have gone out from the high school, they will have transferred the seat of authority from without to within themselves, will have formed habits of social behavior, will have developed an interest in moral progress and a loyalty to moral ideals and will have become so pre-occupied with the good that evil will have largely lost its power.

Such being the problem, what is the attitude of the high schools—of principals and teachers toward it? And in order that I may not seem to be evading my own responsibility in the premises I will preface that inquiry with another: What is the attitude of the Board of Examiners toward the question of morality in the schools? Our tests, it must be confessed, are not primarily moral tests, and yet we are, I think I may say, keenly alive to the presence, or the lack, in candidates, of those qualities that fit a prospective teacher to become a rallying point and a distributing center of moral force in a school. We do consider such matters and we debar outright, as a matter of course, anyone on whom rests any taint or suspicion of moral deficiency.

But moral qualities are less examinable—less formally examinable—than the others, and moreover such qualities may be developed—have been developed under pressure of need in our high schools, sometimes in apparently poor material. And it is too true that under the urgent demand for teachers we have been constrained to admit to the schools, on temporary license, of course, persons who have not demonstrated their powers in this regard, and who even seem a bit unpromising. Of course, if such persons do not make good, their licenses may be cancelled at the end of one year. It may be noted, however, that the hopeful attitude of the Board of Examiners seems often to be shared by those who have to do with the renewal of license, and teachers who at the start were a trifle unpromising in this regard, yet not demonstrately unfit, and who, after a trial, have not demonstrated their fitness, have been continued in the system, often with change of environment, generally, it is to be hoped, to the advantage of all concerned.

Now, for the attitude and practice of the high schools in the matter of moral efficiency, I have not been able to make a complete survey of the field, but so far as I have gone, I have found not one that is not attacking the problem vigorously. I know of no two that are attacking it in the same way. Several there are that are making distinct, original contributions to the subject, and not one, so far as I can ascertain, is saying very much about what is being attempted or being done.

All of which indicates to my mind a healthy and hopeful condition.

After this preliminary survey let us come to closer grips with the subject. How is Moral Efficiency in the High School to be attained? I answer, in three ways: by Practice, by Precept and by Personality.

I. First and foremost among the means whereby Moral Efficiency is to be attained I place **the practice of morality in the ordinary routine of the school.** If, as Professor James holds, "to think is the moral act," if the effort of attention by which we hold fast to an idea is the elemental form of morality, then the center of the moral life of the school is to be sought in the classroom and in the study hall—in the simple business of getting and reciting lessons, and of maintaining the conditions that render such activities possible. It is in the arrangements—of which there are many in every large well-ordered school—for seeing to it that pupils come to time, obey the rules, take their turns and expect no favors, and **get their lessons,**—or suffer penalties that are as sure as the operation of natural law,—that the ground-work of moral efficiency in any school is to be found.

And yet, it must be at once added, in these very arrangements there must be definite provision for helping pupils to control and govern themselves, else the ideal of complete moral efficiency will fail of realization. In other words, the practice of morality in the ordinary routine of the school as a school must be reinforced and completed by **the practice of moral conduct in the organized life of the school as a community.**

The importance of organization, with its committees, its delegated responsibilities, its varied opportunities for team work and for bringing out the instinct and the power of leadership, can in my judgment scarcely be over-estimated.

This was brought home to me—literally brought home—by my own son, many years ago. He went out from home one morning an individual, he came back at noon a committee—charged with the duty of clearing the blackboard every morning. He had visibly grown, enlarged the borders of his personality between breakfast and lunch time.

The cruder system under which many of us grew up, in which there were no organized, but merely personal relations, is not only ineffective in itself but is a poor preparation for life—especially the life of a city like our own. As a mere individual a pupil in one of our high schools is comparatively nothing. As a member of a group he is everything,—everything that the group is and everything that the group stands for. Moreover, his responsibility—and his sense of it—is greatly enlarged and intensified. To be responsible as a mere individual, if such a thing were conceivable, is far less potent for moral efficiency than to be responsible as a member of—perhaps as an officer in—a social group.

From group activity and group responsibility we may trace the development further. First, a recognition of group authority,—an authority exercised not by individuals but by the community, the seat of authority being gradually transferred from without to within the person under authority. For, when a person conforms to the law of the group of which he is a member, he is obeying himself in the group. Then the replacing of arbitrariness by rationality; for when one looks into matters—as one must when one assumes responsibility for their proper conduct—one sees the reason. It is then not a rule of the school that one obeys so much as a law of the universe. Finally, as the fruitage of all the rest, loyalty—to the group, to the school, to the law, to the right.

The forms which these principles assume in their working out are various. The following are typical of what may be found in our schools; they are by no means exhaustive.

I have to leave out those things that go without saying, but I must say here that athletics is one of the most fundamental and effective means of training in the practice of moral conduct; since its activities are so objective, its opportunities for team work so numerous, its penalties so palpable, so inevitable, and its appeal to normal instincts so real. The main trouble with athletics is that those forms in which team-play is best are for the comparatively few, at least under existing conditions.

It has come to me quite direct from a high authority on such matters that "saloons are on the bum—largely because of the interest in athletics." It may be well believed—if they are on the bum—that athletics should come in for a considerable share of the blame.

Next in importance to athletics I place the various student organizations, all of which involve self-government to a greater or less degree.

In one school there is reported a system of self-government in the classes of the entire school, the pupils keeping order in the absence of the teacher, holding debates on matters of discipline, and working out schemes for pupil self-government.

In another school there is a Student Self-Government Association, the purpose of which is "to enact and to enforce laws of school government in accordance with the charter granted to the Association by the principal of the school, and to exercise its power and influence to further the interests of the school."

A most interesting and original experiment which is being worked out in one school is the Honorable Order of School Chivalry with its grades of page, esquire, knight, gentleman, based on scholarship and on other activities. Its aim is to cultivate honor, industry, self-reliance, helpfulness and loyalty in its members.

A system of Courts has been in operation in another school for more than a year. There are class courts, day courts, the supreme court, 83 in all. Before these courts come cases of discipline. There is a trial before a jury of peers. Sentence is pronounced and executed. Minutes are kept, and an examination of a whole year's minutes of one court shows good judgment in imposing penalties, and authority in enforcing them. It is reported that delinquents have a wholesome fear of being haled into court.

A new plan for still another school is to bring social pressure and social sanctions to bear on pupils through the Employment Bureau. A refractory pupil is taken off the list of those to be recommended for employment. But she may be restored to the same for cause.

The Housekeepers' Union, in the same school, is an organization emanating from the girls themselves, whose business it is to keep the floors clean. There are ninety-four members. If there is something on the floor one of the union persuades someone else nearby to help pick it up. She is not to pick it up herself alone. The motive is common ownership. This is a type of organization that might be indefinitely multiplied. There is room, I should think, for unions in every school.

The members of the two highest classes in a certain school are ipso facto charged with the preservation of order in the halls, and are designated by a uniform, the wearing of which is obligatory.

In another school the teacher in charge of disciplinary cases is assisted by a squad of twenty-seven boys, chosen from the better sort, who give their study time to patrol duty and similar service. The honor is a coveted one, and the assistance rendered is valuable, both to the school and the squad.

I have reserved for the last one form of student organization which seems to me to be of peculiar significance and value. This organization has for its conscious aim "to create, maintain and extend throughout the school high standards of Christian character, to raise the general moral standard and to promote a greater spirit of sociability among the students of the ——High School and also between the students of this high school and —— High School." There is a corresponding club in the neighboring high school, and also five alumni associations whose purpose is, severally, "(1) to maintain and extend a spirit of friendship and sociability among its members, to have those members be of some definite service to society, (2) to be of assistance and to give permanency to the —— club (the undergraduate club of the same school) to foster a love for the school and to assist in raising the general moral standard of the school to the highest possible degree."

The members of these clubs dine together, study together, plan together, hold meetings before or after athletic contests, arrange speakers for the Assembly in their respective schools.

All is done under the guidance and with the co-operation of an outside agency, expert, disinterested, efficient. I have observed the workings of this plan with the greatest interest. I know of no reason why it should not be widely extended. I believe in it most thoroughly. thoroughly.

So much for a hasty survey of these various organizations, which to a greater or less degree engage in deliberation, investigation, legislation, administration, in connection with assembly, social functions, athletics, lunches, water supply, social service and special problems. Let us now consider briefly certain conditions of their successful operation:

1. There should be enough of these organized groups to go around—enough to exert an efficient pull on every individual.

The limit to the number of groups is on the one hand the number of things to be done by them, and on the other the power within the school to vitalize them.

The opportunities for service and distinction, in athletics, in scholarship, in social activities should be open to all and should be within reasonable reach of all.

It is a bad thing for any individual to be an inert member—a mere tailender—in any group; but especially so when he might be an effective member if he were not submerged. One trouble with the fraternity system is that there are some who are left out. No high school is completely efficient morally if boys and girls are left out. Herein lies the great merit of the signal contribution made by Dr. Crampton in his plan for drawing the maximum number into athletic contests, everyone of them feeling that it is a real contest and yet that everyone may win. Herein lies the advantage, also, of the organization of the school under section officers, each officer having a group of about thirty, all of whom he teaches daily.

2. There should be a progressive development—an increasing burden of social responsibility, self-direction and self-government, from term to term, so that, for example, boys and girls who, when they enter school, are disorderly, whether under the teacher's eye or not, will reach the point when they will not take advantage of his absence to be disorderly, and finally, will attain the height of being as orderly when he is there as when he is away.

A boy I knew once came home, saying, "I got a thrashing this morning." . . "The boys thrashed me. I cut up when the teacher was out of the room. They said: 'You may cut up all you please when she is there, but we won't stand for anything dishonorable!' " This marked an intermediate stage between cutting up under any and all circumstances and cutting up under no circumstances.

The application of this principle to the honor system is obvious. There is absolutely no inherent reason why a spirit should not be developed in time that should be intolerant of cheating, devoid of all moral sense in that regard as many seem to be now.

3. It is evident that what will work in one school would not work in another; and that what one principal would prize another would not consider for a moment. The conditions are so essentially different in various schools that this is precisely as it should be. The main thing is that each school should be on the alert to develop, adopt or adapt such measures as will tend to increase its own moral efficiency. But I am inclined to think that if each school knew what every other school is doing, it might tend to the enrichment of all of them.

4. Finally, most of what is found in our schools has been a gradual growth, an evolution from within rather than a sudden imposition from without. Nothing could be more wholesome than this. The same principle applies to other matters besides moral efficiency.

II. The very mention of group loyalty, which we see in this city in a debased form in "The System," suggests that moral conduct is not merely the result of organized activity. Moral conduct is activity called forth and directed by ideas of value or worth—activity that involves an intelligent choosing between that which is less and that which is more worthy. There can be no morality without a reverent, enduring wholehearted interest in righteousness, and no interest can persist save as it is reasonable. (John Dewey). My second topic is, therefore, **Moral Instruction As a Factor in Moral Efficiency.**

Should there be formal teaching of Ethics in high schools? If a poll were taken in this or in any other audience of teachers. I am quite sure that the vote would be overwhelmingly adverse. There are reasons for this attitude. We believe that it is better to have practice without theory than to have theory wihout practice. We do not want to take the resopnsibility of having helped to make moral prigs. We think talking and thinking about being good is often a cheap substitute for being good.

We know the rather discouraged—at least very conservative—position Felix Adler has taken after thirty years of continuous and devoted experimentation in this field. **Corruptio optimi pessima.** We know what George Herbert Palmer has said about the purpose of his work as teacher of ethics—that it was not to make his students better men.

We believe moreover in the side door theory of moral influence and instruction. We know too well that that which comes pompously and formally up to the front door is shown into the parlor—where no one comes, except in an unnatural garb and in an unnatural frame of mind; while that which enters informally by the side door finds itself in the living room where the family gather familiarly around and hear and heed even when they seem least to be listening.

And yet——.

It is inconceivable that with definite problems out in the world that are to be wisely solved by these young people only by their being wise, by having knowledge and a right view of the world; and with certain kinds of knowledge that the high school is better able to give than any other of the moral agencies in the community; and with high school teachers—some of them—in possession of this wisdom—it is inconceivable, I say, that some way should not be found to impart it effectively.

And such a way is being sought in our high schools and is being found.

In the first place it should be said that every subject taught in high schools has its peculiar contribution to make to morality, and no teacher of any subject can be called entirely successful if he does not help to secure this contribution. Many of our teachers are making it their business to do this.

In the second place there are problems peculiar to adolescent boys and girls, and these are being attacked in a very quiet and a very wise way by our teachers of biology, of hygiene and of physical training. There is necessary here the utmost wisdom: a rare combination of frankness and reserve, of scientific information and personal influence, and a motivation that shall be a vitalizing complex of prudence and principle, fear and reverence, care for one's self and care for one's fellow-men and fellow-women.

One may envy the teachers in these departments their opportunity—and at the same time be relieved not to have the burden of their responsibility.

It is interesting to know that some of our high school boys feel that such teaching may well be amplified. But the danger involved in so doing is obvious.

There is, thirdly, another set of problems arising out of the general moral conditions in the community which were referred to at the outset. In view of these conditions it should not be surprising that the moral notions of many of our high school boys and girls are crude, selfish, materialistic, distorted. The cubists and futurists are not confined to art. The same apparently wrong-end-to ideas in the realm of morals, expressed with the same frankness and naïveté, are met with in the high schools.

This need may be met, in part, by the teachers of literature, history, civics, economics, and I have the testimony of a group of high school boys to the effect that is is so being met. It may be that there is room and need for a new course in Social Efficiency, with provision for field work, such as visiting milk stations and employment bureaus of the better sort, and making a social survey of a block and noting the agencies for social service there. The more concrete and objective and the less bookish and theoretical such work, the better. Such a course has been projected. A course along somewhat similar lines, entitled "The Modern City of God," has to my personal knowledge met with the greatest success in a certain Sunday School.

The help derived from personal talks with teachers is prized by the students, who wish that there were more opportunities for such relationships in our big schools. It is certainly a misfortune if it ever happens that the organization of a school is such that the opportunities for a sufficiently prolonged personal acquaintance and influence are decreased.

Again the students find that ethical talks in Assembly are very effective if the speaker is good and an authority in his subject. I know how large the if is. I have spoken in Assembly.

I must leave this part of the subject with a single further comment. Granting that moral practice should greatly exceed theory, and that practice should both precede and follow theory, and that theory should grow out of practice, and that all ethical systemizing should be shunned, and that none should touch this subject but those who are morally and mentally competent to do so,—I believe that just as some intellectual illumination is necessary to efficiency in every line, so the need of such illumination can not be neglected here. I have had experience enough in trying to do this thing myself to know how excessively difficult it is to do it well, and how repaying when well done. But some insight and interpretation and illumination there must be. And such things do not come of themselves. In some way the boys and girls in our high schools must not only be trained in moral habits, but be given moral insight—insight of the sort (to take two or three simple examples) that, with James, draws the fundamental distinction between inhibition by substitution and inhibition by repression; that shows that "to think is the moral act;" that interprets a case of being a "pig" in manners as Dewey interprets it—not as selfishness, necessarily, but as blindness to certain elements in the situation,—"seeing simply the seat and not the seat and the lady."

But this is a problem that must be worked out in each school in each school's own way. The most one outside the school can or should try to do is to define the problem and suggest lines of solution.

III. But at this point some objector can restrain himself no longer and demands to be heard. "Moral Efficiency," says he, "does not come from organization, still less from theoretical instruction. It comes from inspiration. It is not a question of mechanism but of Spirit. What we need in the high school is personal influence and an atmosphere that emanates from persons of power, of devotion, sincerity, singlemindedness; who love their work, who believe in boys and girls and understand and like them, and whose highest pleasure and real reward come from working with them and for them."

I agree with this outburst, if you will allow me one modification: Inspiration is the great thing—it does the work of a thousand uninspired devices, and what the inspired teacher is speaks louder than any number of uninspired teachers can say. But inspiration comes from organization of social units into a working whole, and it comes from knowledge of the truth, as well as from persons. Having made this point clear, I am prepared to admit—nay even, to claim—that the moral efficiency of any school depends chiefly upon the **persons** who administer the organization, and who give the instruction, and who are what they are in the presence of the young people who feel and know what they are, and who respond to that influence in vital ways that they themselves do not know or feel.

There are in every large school some who are positive forces for good, others at the other extreme who are found wanting, and those between who follow as best they can but who never lead, or who are inert or ineffectual, so far as strong, positive influence on character is concerned.

In one school it is estimated that one-third of the teachers are strong, positive, either organizing centres or emanating centres of light and power; that one-tenth are sneerers and non-co-operative, unsocializing; while the remainder follow the lead of the better sort and do fairly well.

I know how many influences there are in this great system that tend to make the teacher forget the real things of his work. I realize, too, how certain tendencies of our time are against placing the emphasis on personal influence, and are for placing it instead on a certain scientific detachment and impersonality. But I must still maintain that personality after all—in spite of all I may have seemed to say to the contrary—is at the centre of the moral problem—that it is indeed the kingpin of moral efficiency.

If that be true, one further question is in order. I have said nothing thus far about religion, which is at the very centre of personality, and which no one can deny has a very vital part to play in the development of moral efficiency.

What is the relation of religion to moral efficiency? **My own** answer to this question is very brief and positive. The place of religion in the teaching of morality is not (so far as I can see at present) in the curriculum but in the heart and life of the teacher. And there the form it will take is reverence and faith—the reverence that dignifies every human activity and relationship by viewing it **sub specie aeternitatis**; the faith that, without losing hold of the things that are seen, has a firm grasp of the things that are unseen and eternal. It is the teacher of such reverence and such faith whose personality will be most potent for moral efficiency.

PENSION BOARD REQUIREMENTS—VERIFICATION OF OUTSIDE EXPERIENCE.

The Board of Education requires the following form of statement concerning teaching experience outside of the New York City schools, if such experience is to receive credit when applying for a pension:

This is to certify that M.................................taught

in....................School, in (town or city)...................

for..............years (1890-1894) date.

Signed.

The above should be signed either by the principal or by a member of the Board of Trustees. If on the stationery of the school the signature need be attested by a Notary Public. Otherwise, the signature must be attested by a Notary Public.

If the school is defunct and the signature of the principal of a trustee cannot be obtained, a similar statement from a patron of the school, or from a pupil whom you taught, will be accepted, provided the signature is attested before a Notary Public.

Since the requirements for retirement will probably become more stringent as the pension fund becomes depleted, it would be advisable to have all signatures, whether made on school stationery or not, attested before a Notary Public.

GROWTH OF THE H. S. T. A. OF NEW YORK CITY.

Year	President	Members
1900-1901	Frank Rollins (Manhattan and Bronx only)	174
1901-1902	" " (Manhattan and Bronx only)	246
1902-1903	James J. Sheppard	Unknown
1903-1904	" " "	Unknown
1904-1905	Charles H. J. Douglas	456
1905-1906	James F. Wilson	494
1906-1907	" " "	734
1907-1908	John L. Tildsley	577
1908-1909	" " "	555
1909-1910	Arthur L. Janes	579
1910-1911	" " "	685
1911-1912	William T. Morrey	731
1912-1913	" " "	856
1913-1914	" " "	—

HANUS REPORTS.
SECTION C.
PROBLEMS IN ORGANIZATION AND ADMINISTRATION OF HIGH SCHOOLS.

BY FRANK W. BALLOU, Ph. D.

Director of School Affiliation and Assistant Professor of Education, University of Cincinnati.

ANALYSIS OF CONTENTS

(I) THE SIZE OF SECTIONS (CLASSES)

Introduction
1. A committee of the board of superintendents.
2. The principals as executive heads.
3. The first assistants.

(I) The Size of Sections (Classes)
1. What constitutes effective high school organizations?
2. The size of sections in German and mathematics in the city as as a whole. (Tables I. and II.).
   (1) Small sections in every high school.
   (2) Large sections in every high school.
   (3) Great variation in size of sections among high schools.
   (4) The size of sections for the city as a whole does not sufficiently approximate a standard.
   (5) The size of sections in individual schools does not sufficiently approximate the established standards.
      a. Sections in first term.
      b. Sections in the second to eighth terms, inclusive.
3. Size of sections in German in selected schools.
   (1) Important facts which Table I. does not show, and which can be shown only by further detailed study.
      a. Whether the small or large sections are inevitable and hence defensible, or whether they could be avoided by a different distribution of pupils.
      b. The actual size of sections in each term.
      c. The range of size of sections in each term.
      d. The desirability of increasing the number of sections to reduce large sections.
      e. The possible combination of sections to reduce the number of small sections.
   (2) Detailed study of sections in selected schools.
      a. Morris High School.
      b. Boys' High School.
      c. Richmond Hill High School.
         (a) The school as a whole.
         (b) Each term within the school.
4. Proposed standard size of sections.
   (1) What is the proper size of section?
   (2) Provisional standard of thirty pupils recommended.
   (3) How far is the present practice from that standard?
5. Summary of findings and recommendations.

Our findings concerning the size of sections may be summarized as follows:

1. Large sections are due to
   (1) The present official standard size—which is too large.
   (2) The lack of the necessary teachers.
   (3) In a few cases, a bad distribution of pupils by the principal.
2. Small sections are due to

(1) The inevitably small number of pupils in the upper terms of work.

(2) In a few cases, a bad distribution of pupils by the principal.

Hence, we recommend:

1. The adoption of a standard size of section of thirty pupils for all terms as a provisional standard to be tested in practice. (1)
2. The employment of enough teachers to make it possible for principals to keep the size of sections reasonably within the limits of the standard—twenty-eight to thirty-five pupils. (2)
3. A careful study by the principals of the subject of program-making, to the end that unnecessary over-size sections may be reduced, and unnecessary under-size sections may be avoided. (3)

(II) THE WORK OF CHAIRMEN OF DEPARTMENTS (31-53)

Classification of teachers—

(a) First assistants.
(b) Teachers.

Provisions in the By-Laws—

1. Work as a teacher (Periods of teaching).
- **(1) In the larger high schools.**
- **(2) In the smaller high schools.**
- **(3) Amount of time left for "other assigned duties".**
  - **(a) In the larger high schools.**
  - **(b) In the smaller high schools.**
- **(4) Teaching and study hall supervision.**
  - **(a) In the larger high schools.**
  - **(b) In the smaller high schools.**
- **(5) Summary.**
- **(6) Standard teaching assignments for chairmen of departments.**

2. Work as assistant to principal—
- **(1) Scope and character.**

3. Work as chairman of department—
- **(1) Responsibilities of the chairman of a department.**
- **(2) Bad results from lack of supervision.**
- **(3) Amount of time needed for supervision.**

4. Recommendations—

The following recommendations are made:

1. The chairmen of a department should, as in the case of other teachers, be allowed one free period each day. (4)

2. The chairman of a department should be ollowed two periods each month for the class room visits and supervision of each teacher in his department. (5)

3. If the chairman of a department is assigned administrative duties (as first assistant), his number of teaching periods should be correspondingly reduced, in order that he may still have the required amount of time for the satisfactory supervision of his department. (6)

4. The chairman of a department should be relieved, as far as possible, from all purely clerical work, which work should be performed by additional clerks. (7)

5. First assistants should be relieved, as far as possible, from supervising study halls, and, except occasionally, also from an official class, in order that their time may be devoted to a higher grade of professional work. (8)

(III) THE WORK OF OTHER TEACHERS (57-76)

TABLE OF CONTENTS

a. **Teachers of English, German, Mathematics, Biology and History.**
b. **Teachers of English.**
c. **Teachers of German, Mathematics, Biology and History**

2. **Other assigned duties (in addition to teaching and study hall supervision).**
(1) **Scope and character.**
(2) **Classification of these duties.**
(3) **Should these functions be assigned to teachers or to special administrative officers?**
(4) **How much of the teaching staff should the principal have at his disposal for administrative purposes?**

3. **Summary, Conclusions and Recommendations.**

---

1. Of the 671 teachers under consideration, 15.50 per cent. are teaching less than twenty periods; 82.11 per cent. are teaching from twenty to twenty-five periods, and 2.39 per cent. are teaching more than twenty-five periods.

2. Of the 226 teachers of English, 25.66 per cent. are teaching less than twenty periods per week; 32.3 per cent. are teaching more than twenty-one periods, and only 42 per cent. are taching twenty or twenty-one periods—the standard fixed by the Department of Education.

3. Of the teachers of German, mathematics, biology and history, 10.3 per cent. are teaching less than twenty periods; 2.7 per cent. are teaching more than twenty-five priods, and 86.96 pr cent. are teaching from twenty to twenty-five periods—the standard fixed by the Department of Education.

If study hall supervision is added to teaching, the following results are obtained:

1. Of the 671 teachers, 2.4 per cent. are doing less than twenty periods of work; 41.4 per cent. are doing more than twenty-five periods of work, and 56.2 per cent. are doing from twenty to twenty-five periods of work.

2. Over 50 per cent. of all the teachers have administrative duties to perform in addition to teaching and study hall supervision.

3. Of the teachers of English, none are doing less than twenty periods of teaching and study hall supervision; 3.09 per cent. are doing twenty or twenty-one periods of work; 96.90 per cent. are doing over twenty-one periods of work; 26.5 per cent. are doing over twnty-five periods, and 33.6 per cent. are doing twenty-five periods.

4. Of the teachers in other departments under consideration, 3.6 per cent. are doing less than twenty periods of work; 48.98 per cent. are doing more than twenty-five periods of work, and 47.41 per cent. are doing from twenty to twenty-five periods.

Our analysis of the work done by teachers has led us to the following conclusions and recommendations:

1. Over 15 per cent. of the teachers under consideration are teaching less than the minimum standard—twenty periods—because they are doing work other than teaching. Are not some of these teachers doing too little teaching? **We recommend that the Committee on High Schools of the Board of Superintendents investigate the qustion and report to the Board of Superintendents.** (9)

2. If to teaching we add study hall supervision, we find that only a trifle over 2 per cent. of the teachers are doing less than twenty periods; and that over 41 per cent. are doing more than twenty-five periods of work (i. e., they do not have a free period each day). Are not some of these teachers doing too much work? We recommend, as before, that the Committee on High Schools of the Board of Superintendents investigate the question and report to the Board of Superintendents. (10)

3. In addition to teaching and study hall supervision, over 50 per cent. of the teachers have other assigned duties.

4. We find, on examination, that some of these other assigned duties are purely clerical, and that a large part of them are administrative.

We recommend that the principals and the Board of Superintendents differentiate very definitely between what is clerical and what is administrative work. (11)

6. We recommend (a) that the principal of each high school be furnished a sucient number of competent clerks to perform the clerical work, and (b)

also, that the principal of each high school be definitely allowed a certain portion of the time of his teaching staff for the discharge of such administrative functions as he finds it necessary to assign to them. (12).

(IV). ADMINISTRATIVE CONTROL OF THE HIGH SCHOOLS, AS IT AFFECTS INTERNAL ORGANIZATION.

TABLE OF CONTENTS

C. Summary of Findings and Recommendations.

Summary of our findings and recommendations by topics:

A. The Principal's Responsibility for the Daily Program. We find:

1. That the principals are responsible for the organization of recitation sections in their respective schools.
2. That some of the principals have organized large and small sections in the same term of work, each of which could have been avoided by a different distribution of pupils.
3. That the effective organization of the schools, as to number and

size of sections, by the principals is directly affected by factors controlled by the Department of Education.

4. That these factors are the program ("course") of studies, the size of school, the size and number of class rooms, and the number of teachers employed.

We recommend:

That a thorough-going investigation be undertaken of program-making by the principals. This investigation should be made by a committee of high school principals and a committee of the Board of Superintendents working together. (13)

B. The Department of Education's Responsibility for

1. **The Program of Studies.** We raise these questions:

(1) Has the Board of Superintendents considered the extent to which which the larger number of curricula ("general," "commercial," "manuel training," " . . . .") in a school increases the number of small sections, and, hence, increases the amount of teaching to be done to care for a given number of pupils?

(2) Has the Board of Superintendents considered to what extent, if any, the number of electives in a curriculum increases the cost of instruction, and whether the increased cost, if any, produces commensurate educational returns?

(3) Has the Board of Superintendents followed any well conceived plan in determining the time allotments for high school subjects? Has it considered the daily program of the school in determining time allotments?

We recommend:

(1) That each question raised above be the subject of an investigation by the Board of Superintendents in order to determine—

a. Whether, educationally and economicallly, there should be a single curriculum or several curricula in one high school. (14)

b. Whether the number of "electives" increases the cost of instruction and, if so, whether the educational results are commensurate with the increased cost. (15)

c. A plan for assigning time allotments to subjects which shall take into consideration not only the educational value of each subject, but also whether it admits of making a satisfactory daily program. (16)

(2) That the courses of study and curricula be subjected to continual but gradual revision and modification by committees of high school principals and teachers, and corresponding committeesc of the Board of Superintendents working together. (17)

2. **The Size of the High Schools.** We find:

(1) That the high schools in New York City, in most cases, are so large that (a) it is doubtful whether the principal can discharge satisfactorily his responsibility to pupils, parents and teachers; (b) that their very size interferes with their effective administration, and (c) that an assembly of all students at one time is impossible, and general facilities, such as lunch rooms, lockers, etc., cannot be adequately provided.

(2) That the system of annexes is unsatisfactory, because, among other reasons,

a. The opinion prevails that the teachers are inferior to those in the main building.

b. The teachers change often.

c. The teachers do relatively more teaching than in the main building, and often teach subjects other than those which they are licensed to teach.

d. The sections are too large, being considerably larger than sections in the main building.

e. The students drop out faster than in the main building.

f. The educational offering is not equivalent to the offering in the main building.

g. School spirit is lacking; teachers and pupils both prefer the main school.

h. The organization of the school as a whole cannot be as effective with annexes as it could be if all pupils were in one building.

We recommend:

(1) That high schools hereafter established be limited to 1,500 pupils (18)

(2) That a definite policy be adopted of establishing high schools in various parts of the city to take the place of annexes, and that additional high schools be established in accordance with that policy. (19)

(3) That a plan be adopted of establishing the different types (specialized and cosmopolitan, particularly the former) of high schools throughout the city, and that a careful study of their comparative effectiveness be made from year to year. (20)

3. The Size and Number of Class Rooms. We find:

(1) That some small sections are the result of the principals being forced to use small rooms in the main building.

(2) That some large sections are the result of the principals being forced to use large rooms, particularly in annexes; some are also the result of filling class rooms in the main building to overflowing on account of congested conditions.

(3) That small sections mean expensive instruction, because the teaching reaches a comparatively small number of students.

(4) That large sections often mean ineffective instruction, because the number of pupils a teacher can satisfactorily teach is limited.

We recommend:

(1) That the seating capacity of class rooms be limited to the maximum standard size of section to make over-size sections impossible. (21)

(2) That in the new buildings constructed, and, as far as practicable in the building now in use, special study halls, seating 125 to 150 pupils, be provided, so that less time of teachers would be required in study hall supervision, and regular class rooms could be used more largely for recitation purposes. (22)

(3) That more class rooms be provided through the building of more high schools. (23)

4. The Number of Teachers Employed. We find:

(1) That the method of increasing or decreasing the number of teachers in a department of study does not insure the appointment of teachers where they are needed.

(2) Nor does it insure the declaring of teachers "in excess" where they are not nedd.

(3) That, in many schools, there is not a sufficient number of teachers to maintain the standard size of section and the standard week's work for a teacher fixed by the Board of Superintendents.

(4) That, in some schools, there are more teachers than would have necessary had the size of section not been abnormally small.

(5) That the blank now used in the organization above noted is inadequate for its purpose.

We recommend:

(1) That a reorganization blank be adopted which shall furnish the following essential facts, on which the need of changing the number of teachers in a department is based. (24)

A. Concerning the size of sections:

a. How many pupils are there in the department, and how are they distributed by terms of work pursued? (25)

b. What is the number and size of sections by terms of work, as organized at the time of the application? (26)

c. Is the size of sections, as organized, in accordance with the standards fixed by the Board of Superintendents? (27)

B. Concerning the amount of teaching:

a. How many periods of teaching and other work are teachers already employed in the department doing? (28)
b. How much teaching and other work is there for the additional teacher or teachers to do. (29)
c. Is the number of periods of teaching now being done by teachers in the department in accord with the standard fixed by the Board of Superintendents? (30)

(V) ESTIMATING THE NEED OF HIGH SCHOOL TEACHERS

TABLE OF CONTENTS

Our conferences with the high school principals on the new blank have revealed no little fear on their part, that the data might be misinterpreted by those who have to approve of budget estimates. Nevertheless, the principals have expressed themselves as satisfied with the blank. It is obviously important that there should be a clear understanding of the purpose of the blank, and the method of using it. (32)

The blank is the result of careful deliberation by us, and by the high school principals, in view of the needs of the high schools, and of the information required by the school authorities, and the Board of Estimate and Apportionment.

We suggest that a representative of the high school principals be invited to be present at all confernces of the school authorities and the Board of Estimate and Apportionment, in which the high school estimates are under consideration. (33)

Summary

To sum up:
1. The principals, the Board of Education, and the Board of Estimate and Apportionment should have a clear understanding of the purpose and method of using this blank. (34)
2. The purpose of this blank is to provide a means of putting the estimated need of teachers by the high school principals on a basis of recorded facts. (35)

3. After the principal has furnished the necessary data on which he makes his estimate, the responsibility for approving these estimates rests on the Board of Superintendents, and the responsibility for granting the required funds on the Board of Estimate and Apportionment.
4. The data and estimates must be interpreted in the light of high school conditions and needs, and not according to elementary school conditions and needs. (37)
5. The school authorities and the Board of Estimate and Apportionment should exercise the same care in passing on the data and the estimates, that has been devoted to the preparation of the data and estimates by the principals. (38)
6. The blank should be used for a reasonable period of time; and it should be revised by the principals as experience suggests the need of revision—always, however, with a view to providing more adequately the information needed by the school authorities and the Board of Estimate and Apportionment. (39)

PART II. SUBDIVISION III.

High Schools. Section A.—"Courses" (Programs) of Study, Except Commercial Courses.

By

CALVIN O. DAVIS, Ph. D.

Assistant Professor of Education, Inspector of High Schools, University of Michigan, Ann Arbor, Mich.

TABLE OF CONTENTS

VI. **Criticisms and Recommendations Respecting the General Organization and Administration of the High School Programs (Courses) of Study in New York City.**

Introductory—

1. **The "General Course" and general school considered.**
   (1) **As to availability.**
   (2) **As to adaptability.**
   (3) **As to scope.**
   (4) **As to intensiveness.**
   (5) **As to flexibility.**
      (a) **Total prescriptions for graduation.**
      (b) **Prescriptions for graduation by subject.**
      (c) **Prescription by years.**
2. **The "Special Courses" and the Special Schools.**
   (1) **Availability.**

VII. **Summary of Recommendations (pp. 72-76).**

VII—Summary of Recommendations

The following is a complete summary of the recommendations made in this report:

A. Respecting the General Course of Study.

I. It should be rendered more available to all young people of the city by means of— (41)

1. Several additional high schools of different types and so distributed throughout the several districts of the city as to meet the needs of the pupils for whom they are intended. (42
2. Giving serious consideration to the possible plan of defraying the expenses of transportation of those pupils who reside beyond walking distance, and for whom the cost of transportation is a barrier to obtaining a high school education. (43)

II. It should be better adapted to the varied needs of pupils by— (44)

1. Extending the scope of studies to include— (45)
   (a) Manual training.
   (b) Domestic science and art in every school.
   (c) Applied art for girls.
   (d) Additional commercial subjects.
   (e) Advanced courses in mathematics, including the "Principles of Statistics," "Principles of Actuarial Science," and kindred subjects.
   (f) Intensified specialized courses in natural science.
   (g) "Appreciation" or general information courses in the departments of the older academic subjects.
   (h) Specialized courses in Music and Fine Arts.
   (i) Courses in musical appreciation and art appreciation.
   (j) Mechanical drawing.
   (k) A course in introductory social science, including local government, local industries, study of vocations, history of the recent past, and current topics.
   (l) Household economics, including household accounts, purchasing, dietetics, home decoration, home architecture, household sanitation and household chemistry. (46)
2. Giving a greater intensiveness and continuity to some of the instruction by providing— (47)
   (a) That the work in English be allotted four or five periods throughout the entire course.
   (b) That plane geometry be assigned five periods per week in the second year, to conform to the standards set by the state.
   (c) That algebra and geometry of the third years be or-

ganized into two half courses of four periods each for one term.

(d) That as speedily as possible the recently issued syllabi in history be adopted by all schools.

(e) That all science courses after the first year be accompanied by individual laboratory work on the part of the pupils, and that to facilitate this work such science courses be assigned not fewer than five periods per week.

(f) That courses in music, art and drawing be multiplied and be assigned three or four periods per week.

(g) That oral expression be given much attention in every class exercise, particularly in class exercises in English, and that a three-period course be made available in the third or fourth year.

(h) That physical training provide a minimum of theory and a maximum of practice, exercise and games.

3. Making the administration more flexible by— (48)

(a) Prescribing for graduation a much smaller amount of rigidly specified work than at present, such prescriptions to include only— (49)

1. Three years' work in English (including oral expression), aggregating fifteen periods.
2. One year's work in introductory natural science, aggregating four periods.
3. One year's work in introductory social science, aggregating four periods.
4. One year's work in United States history and civics, aggregating five periods.
5. One year's work in manual training for boys or domestic science and art for girls, aggregating four periods.
6. Two years' work in drawing, aggregating two periods.
7. Two years' work in music, aggregating two periods.
8. Four years' work in physical training, aggregating eight periods.
9. Assembly throughout the course, aggregating four periods.

Or a total of forty-eight periods.

(b) Prescribing by specific subjects, for the respective years, not to exceed the following: (50)

1. First year—

	Periods
English, including oral expression	5
Introductory natural science	4
Introductory social science	4
Physical training	2
Drawing	1
Music	1
Assembly	1
Total	18

2. Second year—

English	5
Manual training or domestic science and art	4
Physical training	2
Drawing	1
Music	1
Assembly	1
Total	14

3. Third year—

English	5
Physical training	2
Assembly	1
Total	8

4. Fourth year—

United States history and civics	5
Physical training	2
Assembly	1
Total	8

(c) Making foreign language study alternative with mathematics (51), and, upon the advice and approval of the principal of the school, waiving the alternative entirely for such individuals as can profit more by taking some other subject (52).

(d) Encouraging principals, in conjunction and co-operation with their respective corps of teachers, to study needs (53) and to modify their courses of study and programs of study in accordance with their findings (54).

(e) Organizing the program of studies into a series of suggestive parallel curricula, each containing the prescribed subjects, and, in addition, elective subjects, arranged so as to give an intensive training in some one or at most two fields of knowledge (55).

(f) Issuing more than one type of diploma—for example, the Regents' high school diploma (56) and the New York City high school diploma.

B. Respecting the Special Courses or the Special Schools.

I. They should be made more available to all young people of the city by means of— (57)

1. Several additional high schools distributed throughout the several districts of the city (58).
2. The incorporation of additional special or technical courses parallel to the general course in the general high schools (59).
3. The incorporation, as electives in the general course, of elementary courses in semitechnical work (60).

II. The high schools should be made more adaptable to the varied needs of pupils by— (61)

1. Extending the scope of work in each type of school (62).
2. Differentiating the subject matter and instruction of the included academic subjects so as to give them a decided technical bent (63).
3. Giving a somewhat greater intensiveness than at present to the prescribed academic courses (64).
4. Permitting, during the third and fourth years, individual specialization in aspects of the work that have aroused peculiar interest (65).
5. Encouraging principals of high schools freely to organize special courses and special curricula to meet the needs of pupils whose stay in school must be short, and whose interests are best served by giving them "appreciation courses" and much practical knowledge and training (66).

PART II. SUBDIVISION III.

Section B.—Commercial High Schools and Commercial Courses in High Schools.

By
FRANK V. THOMPSON, Ph. D.
Assistant Superintendent of Schools, Boston, Mass.

TABLE OF CONTENTS

Summary and Recommendations.

1. The contemporary conception of commercial education in New York City should be largely expanded and should emphasize the larger and more important aspects of commercial activities (67), such as merchandising (68), salesmanship (69), business organization (70), and advertising (71).

2. A temporary special commission should be created to consist of commercial teachers temporarily detached from teaching service, who should cooperate with business experts, and xamine into business conditions in relation to commercial education. A commission of this kind will discover a more adequate basis for commercial instruction, whether in day, evening, or in continuation schools, than the city now has. The partial studies presented in this report regarding business conditions affecting commercial education can with profit be carried on until clearer and more positive conclusions can be reached (72).

3. There should be a council of chairmen of commercial departments in high schools to study, weigh and recommend to the Department of Education (Board of Superintendents and Board of Education), improvements in courses and methods pertaining to commercial education (73); in other words, there should be a definite agency, officially recognized, for the organization and unification of educational experience in the field of commercial education (74).

4. The sexes in commercial courses should, wherever possible, be separated (75). The training for each sex should be differentiated in accordance with the differing tastes and apitudes of boys and girls, and the different vocational demands which each will meet (76).

5. The regents' tests for commercial subjects and related academic subjects should be abandoned to give larger scope for objective standards drawn from the business world (77).

6. Teachers of academic subjects in commercial courses and in special commercial schools should possess, either through actual business experience or through theoretical study, or both, a knowledge of and a sympathy with the proper ideals of commercial education (78). To this end there should be separate eligible lists for all teachers giving instruction in commercial schools and courses (79).

7. There should be a supervisor of commercial work for all grades, whether in intermediate schools, evening and continuation schools, or in day schools (80). There should be a unified policy throughout the whole range of the work. The divided attention of a number of general supervisors, some concerned with day schools and others concerned with evening schools, can yield neither unified policy nor comprehensive treatment (81).

8. Special teachers should be appointed to act as field agents for commercial schools and courses. These teachers may be calld vocational assistants and should perform duties in connection with commercial education similar to those of "coordinators" in connection with industrial education. See Dean Schneider's report (82).

9. Cooperative relations between commercial schools and commercial houses should be sought and established. Teachers and business men must unite upon a common plan (83). That New York City business men realize the importance of such cooperation is shown by the Chamber of Commerce in appointing a special committee on commercial education. Other commercial bodies should adopt a similar policy (84). Business men must share the burden of education with the state, and must share this burden in a direct way by giving opportunity for participation in practice during the period of school training (85). Advisory committees of business men (with advisory functions only) should be established to guide and counsel commercial schools on the one hand (86), and, on the other, to awaken business men generally to a sense of their responsibilities with respect to commercial education (87). It is only by an equal partnership of the schoolmaster and the business man that the problem can be solved in a comprehensive and effective way. Up to the present time the schoolmaster has borne more than his share in the attempted solution of the problem.

EAST NEWYORK AND BROWNSVILLE HIGH SCHOOL.

Study No. 1.

Those Intending to Enter High School January 22, 1912.

FROM PUBLIC SCHOOLS.

No.	Boys	Girls	Totals	
64	23	21	44	
72	29	28	57	
73	34	21	55	
76	19	12	31	
84	78	65	143	
108	63	45	108	
109	76	74	150	
144	8	6	14	(½ of 28)
149	44	41	85	
155	35	22	57	
158	25	23	48	
165	40?	41?	81?	(Estimated)
12	474	399	873	

TO HIGH SCHOOLS.

Names	Boys	Girls	Totals
Commercial High School	160	—	160
Boys' High School	126	—	126
Bushwick High School	45	28	123
Eastern District High School	20	98	118
Girls' High School	—	94	94
Jamaica High School	16	60	76
Manual Training High School	47	16	63
Erasmus Hall High School	14	16	30
Scattered and Estimated (Uncertain)			
Richmond Hill	3		
Flushing	1		
Stuyvesant	2		
Washington Irving	3		
Morris	1		
City College	1		
Vocational School	2		
Manhattan Trade	1		
Total to Competing High Schools	428	362	790
Percentages	54%	46%	100%

BY COURSES OF STUDY (ESTIMATED)

	Boys	Girls	Totals	
Latin	170	172	342	(8) Classes
German	40	40	80	(2) "
Commercial	175	160	335	(8) "
Manual Training	43	—	43	(1) "
	428	362	790	(19) Classes of 40

The feeding schools to proposed High School would fill a school ranking about fourteenth among those then existing. January 1, 1912, when the totals were as follows for the smallest seven, in order of size:

No. 13, Bushwick	1074
No. 14, Bryant	885
No. 15, Jamaica	797
No. 16, Curtis	797
No. 18, Richmond Hill	694
No. 19, Flushing	501
No. 20, Far Rockaway	233
No. 21, Bay Ridge Annex	567

EAST NEW YORK AND BROWNSVILLE CONDITION, FEBRUARY, 1913.

A careful study of the Applications for Admission to High Schools for February, 1913, from the eleven public schools in the Brownsville neighborhood of Brooklyn (P. S. 64, 72, 73, 76, 84 Boys, and Girls, 108, 109 B. & G., 149, 155, 158 and 165) show that:

In round numbers there were 1,300 pupils to graduate, of whom about 850 expected to enter High Schools.

The High Schools preferred were: Boys', 144; Bushwick, 127; Commercial, 170; Eastern District, 100; Erasmus, 39; Girls', 92; Jamaica, 46; Manual Training, 49; Richmond Hill, 52; Stuyvesant, 4; Vocational, 4; Washington Irving, 5; rest scattering.

An analysis by courses would result in approximately:

General Latin,	360	pupils in, say,	6 classes;
General German,	140	" " "	3 "
Commercial,	400	" " "	10 "
Manual Training,	50	" " "	2 "
Totals	850	" " "	21 "

Probably at least 700 of them entered High Schools by the end of February.

There were in the various years of various High Schools from 1,800 to 2,000 pupils who would be properly in a Brownsville High School if it were then running. Twice that number would be ready before a building for them could be erected. Two buildings should be started.

CONDITION JUNE, 1913.

From the preceding two studies and from the tables on page 92 of this Bulletin, we estimate that after the June promotions this district will have in various high schools:

Pupils of First Term,	800	to	900	100%
" " Second "	530	"	600	67%
" " Third "	400	"	450	51%
" " Fourth "	320	"	350	39%
" " Fifth "	200	"	240	27%
" " Sixth "	180	"	200	23%
" " Seventh "	120	"	130	15%
" " Eighth "	130	"	140	16%
Pupils of all Terms,	2680	to	3010	338%

DIRECTORY OF HIGH SCHOOLS OF NEW YORK CITY

School	Telephone	Location	Principal or Teacher in Charge of Annex
Bay Ridge	711 Bath Beach	86th st., near 18th av. (P. S. 101)	Harry A. Potter.
Annex	1273 Bay Ridge	92d st. and Gelston av. (P. S. 104).	
Boys'	690 Bedford	Marcy and Putnam avs. and Madison st.	James Sullivan.
*New Bronx	643 Westchester	Randolph, St. Lawrence and Hammond aves. (P. S. 47)	Gilbert S. Blakely
Annex	5634 Tremont	196th st., Bainbridge and Driggs avs. (P. S. 46)	
Bryant	40 Astoria	Wilbur av., Academy and Radde sts., L. I. City	Peter E. Demarest.
Annex	1146-W Astoria	Van Alst av., near Flushing av., L. I. City (P. S. 7)	
Bushwick	13 Bushwick	Evergreen av., Ralph and Grove sts. (P. S. 75)	Frank Rollins.
Annex	5055 Wmsburg	St. Nicholas and Willoughby avs. and Suydam st. (P. S. 162)	William T. Morrey
Annex	7411 Prospect	Ryerson st., near Myrtle av. (P. S. 69)	Julius M. Johnson
Annex	3514 Bushwick	Quincy st., near Stuyvesant av. (P. S. 129)	Lewis B. Semple.
Commercial	3[illegible]32 Bedford	Albany av., Bergen and Dean sts.	William Fairley.
Annex	7736 Bedford	Bedford and Jefferson sts	W. E. Doggett.
Curtis	851-J. Tompkinsville	Hamilton av. and St. Mark's pl., New Brighton	
Annex	922-J Tottenville	Academy pl., Tottenville (P. S. 1)	D. L. Feldman.
De Witt Clinton	4175 Columbus	10th av., 58th and 59th sts	John L. Tildsley.
Eastern District	4565 Wmsburg	Marcy av., Rodney and Keap sts	W. T. Vlymen.
Annex	1[illegible]15 Greenpoint	Havemeyer, N. 6th and 7th sts (P. S. 143)	Anna L. Phillips.
Erasmus Hall	288 Flatbush	Flatbush av., near Church av	W. B. Gunnison.
Far Rockaway	95 Far Rockaway	Far Rockaway	S. J. Ellsworth.
Flushing	321 Flushing	Sanford av., Flushing	J. H. Clark.
Girls'	[illegible]72 Bedford	Nostrand av., Halsey and Macon sts.	W. L. Felter.
Annex	5926 Prospect	St. Mark's and Classon avs. (P. S. 42)	M. Ellen Barker.
H. S. of Commerce	2658 Columbus	65th and 66th sts., west of Broadway	J. J. Sheppard.
Annex	8114 Bryant	120 West 46th st. (P. S. 67)	Alfred C. Bryan.
Jamaica	165 Jamaica	Hillside av., Jamaica	T. C. Mitchill.
Manual Training	1380 South	7th av., 4th and 5th sts	C. D. Larkins.
Annex	24 South	Prospect av., opp. Reeve pl	Charles Perrine.
Annex	2627 Main	Duffield, Johnson and Gold sts	Arthur L. Baker.
Morris	605 Melrose	166th st., Boston rd. and Jackson av.	John H. Denbigh.
Annex	2360 Melrose	Mott av. and 144th st. (P. S. 31)	Irving A. Heikes.
Newtown	40 Newtown	Elmhurst	J. D. Dillingham.
Annex	122 Newtown	Elmhurst (P. S. 89)	
Richmond Hill	26 Richmond Hill	Elm st., Richmond Hill	Isaac N. Failor.
Stuyvesant	8739 Stuyvesant	15th and 16th sts., west of 1st ave.	E. R. von Nardroff
Wadleigh	1892 Morningside	114th and 115th sts., west of 7th av.	Stuart H. Rowe.
Annex	4865 Harlem	138th st., west of 5th av. (P. S. 100)	Kath. A. Speir.
Washington Irving	8292 Stuyvesant	Irving pl., 16th ard 17th sts	W. McAndrew.
*New Manhattan	2446 Stuyvesant	34½ East 12th st	A. M. Wolfson.
Annex	4061 Chelsea	60 West 13th st	
Annex	1612 Chelsea	140 West 20th st. (P. S. 55)	

*New Bronx and New Manhattan High Schools not yet officially named, etc.

FIRST ASSISTANTS IN HIGH SCHOOLS OF NEW YORK CITY, APRIL, 1913. (101 Men, 21 Women. Total, 123).

HIGH SCHOOL	BIOLOGY	ENGLISH	FRENCH AND GERMAN	HISTORY	LATIN	MATHEMATICS	PHYSICAL SCIENCE	COMMERCIAL Vice-Principals
BAY RIDGE	Bruckman, Louise			Proper, Emberson E		Schuyler, Elmer		(Art)
BOYS'	Lewis, F. Z.	Fisher, William W.	)verholser, Charles E.	Jackson, Warwick P.	Riess, Ernest	Parsons, Edw. B.		
BRYANT		Munroe, Harry K.					Bement, Frederic	
BUSHWICK	Johnson, Julius M.	Semple, Lewis B.	Keener, Robt. H.	Morrey, William T.		Humason, Thomas A.		
COMMERCE	Eddy, Walter H.	Heydrick, Benjamin A	Roessler, Erwin W.	Bryan, Alfred C.			Mills, Jos. E. Cheston, H. C.	Pugh, A. L. Greene, R.
COMMERCIAL	Gruenberg, Benj. C.	St. John, Robt. P.	Marvin, Robt. M. Harrison, Earl S.	Trask, Thomas C.		Teeter, Charles H.	Clark, John A.	Doggett, Wm. E. Kip, Arthur R.
CURTIS	Grout, Abel J.	Abbott, Frances	Shepherd, Florence D.			Dean, Philip R.		Welsh, John C. Crane, Wm. A. (V.P.)
DEWITT CLTN.	Hunter, George W.	Garrigues, Ellen E.	Monteser, F'd'k. Frank, Colman D.	*Wolfson, Arthur M.	Bice, Hiram H.	Anthony, Oscar W.	Whitsit, Jesse E. Timmermann, C. E.	
EAST'N DIST.	Hazen, Anna P.	Hartwell, Charles S.	Bole, John A.	Paine, Frederick H	Dixon, Charles E.	Mayo, Marion J.		Baltz, Frank P.
ERASM. HALL	King, Cyrus A.	Farrar, Preston C.	Holmes, Mary H.	Boynton, George E.	Harter, Eugene W.			Turner, Kate (V. P.)
FAR ROCK'W'Y								Belding, Albert G.
FLUSHING		Read, Warren W.	Baumeister, John	Miller, Frank H.	Jenks, Paul R.	Barnwell, Walter		
GIRLS'	Leeuente, Margaret T.	Wendt, Cordelia	Higgins, Alice	Cahill, Rose H.	Ford, Celia	Mullen, Loring B.	Arey, Albert L.	Pyles, (VP) Marion
JAMAICA	Linville, Henry R.	Fairley, Edwin	Krause, Carl A.	Lawrence, Antoinette	Chickering, Edward C.		Vosburgh, Chas. H.	Starkey, Warren L.
MAN. TRAIN.	Hunt, Arthur E.	Bates, Herbert	Lamb, Wm. W.	Low, J. Herbert	Shumway, Edgar S.	Baker, Arthur L. Colston, Albert L.	Weed, Henry T.	Shinn, (Art) Victor I.
MORRIS	Peabody, James E.	*Blakely, Gilbert S.	Althaus, Edward	Bates, Abby B.	Davis, Josephine A	Heikes, Irving A.	Pyle, Willard R.	
NEWTOWN					Radin, Max			
RICHM'D HILL	Valentine, Morris	Gaston Chas. Robt.				Landers, Leland L.		
STUYVESANT		Law, Frederick H.	Elmer, Clement G.	Wilson, James F.	Foster, Walter E.	Breckenridge, Wm. E.	Fuller, Robert W.	Howe, (Art) Chas. B.
WADLEIGH	Kupfer, Elsie M.	Smith, Jessie F. (Now Mrs. Ford)	Zick, Henry	Wood, Elizabeth C.	Hodges, Archibald L	Bruce, Grace A.	Cornish, Robt. H.	
WASH. IRV'G	Sage, Lillian B.	Lowd, Emma F. Douglas, C. H. J.	Blackwell, Nannie G.	Galloway, Ida G.		Arnold, David L.		Hayward, William R.

*Principals Elect

SLACK, EARL B.—Assistant Physical Science, Washington Irving H. S.; 600 Academy St., Manhattan. Tel. 2305 Audubon.
SLATER, FLORENCE W.—Assistant Biology, Washington Irving H. S.; Women's University Club, 106 E. 52d St., Manhattan. Tel. 7800 Plaza.
SLATER, HENRY B.—Commercial Branches, Newtown H. S.; 127 4th St., Elmhurst, L. I.
SMALLHEISER, ALBERT LEE—Substitute License History, Physical Training, Bushwick H. S.; 259 Hart St., Brooklyn. Tel. 3912 Williamsburg.
SMITH, ANNA H.—Assistant English, De Witt Clinton H. S.; 121 N. Maple Ave., East Orange, N. J.
SMITH, CHARLOTTE—Assistant Mathematics, Girls' H. S.; 92 Gates Ave., Brooklyn.
SMITH, CHAS. M.—Commercial Branches, Newtown H. S.; 24 De Koven St., Forest Hills, L. I. Tel. 6238-R Forest Hills.
SMITH, ERNEST E.—Assistant History, Boys' H. S.; 186 Maple St., Brooklyn. Tel. 2935-R. Flatbush.
SMITH, JOSEPH—Assistant Spanish, Commercial H. S.; 75 McDonough St., Brooklyn. Tel. 2285 Bedford.
SMITH, J. CLARENCE—Assistant Latin, Manual Training H. S.; 430 4th St., Brooklyn. Tel. 3315-W South.
SMITH, DONALD E.—Assistant History, Morris H. S.; 1161 Amsterdam Ave., Manhattan. Tel. 4619 Morningside.
SMITH, EDITH IVES—Assistant Physical Training, Julia Richman H. S.; 225 W. 14th St., Manhattan. Tel. 2055 Chelsea.
SMITH, FRANCES A.—Assistant English, Washington Irving H. S.; 197 Gates Ave., Brooklyn. Tel. 4933 Prospect.
SMITH, FRANKLIN H.—Assistant Mathematics, Wadleigh H. S.; 414 W. 120th St. Tel. 3895 Morningside.
SMITH, GRACE L.—Assistant Music, Manual Training H. S.; 48 Sterling Pl., Brooklyn. Tel. 3067-J Prospect.
SMITH, G. MONTGOMERY—Assistant French, Washington Irving H. S.; 75 McDonough St., Brooklyn. Tel. 2285 Bedford.
SMITH, HARRIET K.—Assistant Stenography and Typewriting, Evander Childs H. S.; 2674 Valentine Ave., The Bronx, N. Y. C. Tel. 1430 Fordham.
SMITH, HELEN—Assistant Biology, Manual Training H. S.; 620 E. 17th St., Brooklyn. Tel. 6231-R Flatbush.
SMITH, HERBERT O.—Assistant Chemistry, De Witt Clinton H. S.; 146 Fenimore St., Brooklyn.
SMITH, JAMES V.—Clerical Assistant, Stuyvesant H. S.; 84 Grove St.
SMITH, LOUISE—Assistant English, Bushwick H. S.; 59 Downing St., Brooklyn.
SMITH, L. BREWSTER—Assistant Mathematics, H. S. of Commerce; 97 Vista Pl., Mt. Vernon, N. Y.
SMITH, MARGUERITE—Assistant Biology, Bushwick H. S.; Hotel San Remo, Manhattan. Tel. 6700 Columbus.
SMITH, MAUD—Domestic Science, Newtown H. S.; 106 Morningside Drive, Manhattan.
SMITH NATALIE A.—Assistant English, Erasmus Hall H. S.; 2181 Bedford Ave., Brooklyn.
SMITH, SEYMOUR L.—Assistant Machine Shop, Stuyvesant H. S.; 70 Morningside Drive, Manhattan.
SMITH, THOMAS P.—Assistant English, De Witt Clinton H. S.; 302 Barclay St., Flushing, L. I. Tel. 918-J Flushing.
SMITH, WALTER M.—Assistant Manual Arts (Machine Shop), Stuyvesant H. S.; 2342 Aqueduct Ave., The Bronx, N. Y. C.
MITH, W. PALMER—Assistant Oral English, Stuyvesant H. S.; 330 E. 19th St., Brooklyn. Tel. 1318-W Flatbush.
MITHERS, HERLINDA G.—Assistant Spanish, Bay Ridge H. S.; 425 W. 144th St., New York.
NIDER, ANNIE MAUDE—Assistant English, Washington Irving H. S.; 113 E. 18th St., Manhattan. Tel. 1134 Gramercy.
NOW, ELLA M.—Assistant French, Bryant H. S.; 500 W. 121st St., Manhattan. Tel. 4590 Morningside.
NOW, MINNIE R.—Assistant Mathematics, Manual Training H. S.; 386 4th St., Brooklyn. Tel. 784-R South.
NYDER, B. LOUIS—Assistant Physical Science, Manual Training H. S.; 474 3d St., Brooklyn. Tel. 2638 South.
OHON MICHAEL D.—First Assistant Physical Science, Morris H. S.; 1344 Chilholm St., The Bronx, N. Y. C.
OLOMON, CHARLES—Assistant Mathematics, Manual Training H. S.; 144 Sterling St., Brooklyn. Tel. 5069-W Flatbush.
OLOMON, MICHAEL—Assistant Latin, De Witt Clinton H. S.; 982 Aldus St., Bronx. Tel. 5911 Melrose.
OMMERFIELD, ALFRED—Assistant Commercial Branches, Washington Irving H. S.; 536 W. 143d St., Manhattan. Tel. 2898 Audubon.
OULE, BERTHA LOUISE—Assistant Latin, Manual Training H. S.; 204 Columbia Heights, Brooklyn. Tel. 3590 Main.
OUTHWELL, ETTA ESTELLE—Assistant Biology, Bushwick H. S.; 161 Emerson Pl., Brooklyn. Tel. 5274 Prospect.
ARKMAN, C. F.—Substitute French, De Witt Clinton H. S.; 54 W. 10th St., Manhattan.
ARKS, MINNIE E.—Assistant German, Erasmus Hall H. S.; 2173 Bedford Ave., Brooklyn.
AULDING, FRANK B.—Assistant Physics and Chemistry, Boys' H. S.; 324 Decatur St., Brooklyn. Tel. 2220-W. Bedford.
ERLING, HARRY—Assistant Physical Training, Eastern District H. S.; 391 Marlborough Rd., Flatbush.
EAR, AUSTIN E.—Assistant Modern Languages, H. S. of Commerce; 419 S. Columbus Ave., Mt. Vernon, N. Y.
ENCER, MARY—Assistant Drawing, Girls' H. S.; 61 Livingston St., Brooklyn.
ENCER, ESTELLA—Assistant Drawing, Morris H. S.; 1051 Tinton Ave., The Bronx, N. Y. C.
ERLING, HARRY E.—Physical Training, Eastern District H. S.; 391 Marlborough Rd., Flatbush.
IER, KATHERINE A.—Assistant Teacher in Charge of Annex, Wadleigh H. S. Annex; 127 Lincoln St., Montclair, N. J.

SPILLER, SUSAN M.—Substitute French, Washington Irving H. S.; 2465 Broadway, Manhattan. Tel 4848 Riverside.
SPRAGUE, ALMEDA—Assistant English, Girls' H. S.; 1764 Bedford Ave., Brooklyn.
SPRAGUE, HAYES C.—Assistant Drawing, H. S. of Commerce; 97 W. 163d St., The Bronx, N. Y. C Tel. 5666 Melrose.
SPRAGUE, LAURA E.—Assistant History and English, Erasmus Hall H. S.; 580 E. 21st St., Brooklyn
SQUIRES, MARTHA U.—Assistant German, Bushwick H. S.; 25 McDonough St., Brooklyn.
STACEY, SIDNEY G.—Assistant Latin, Erasmus Hall H. S.; 177 Woodruff Ave., Brooklyn.
STAEHLIN, LEONIE E.—Assistant German, Morris H. S.; 461 Ft. Washington Ave., Manhattan. Tel. 409 Audubon.
STAHL, GEORGE F.—Assistant Manual Arts (Joinery), Stuyvesant H. S.; 2804 Pond Pl., The Bronx, N. Y. C.
STAMM, CAROLINE L.—Assistant German, Evander Childs H. S.; 25 N. 7th Ave., Mt. Vernon, N. Y. Tel. 2791-R Mt. Vernon.
STANNARD, J. E.—Assistant Chemistry, Boys' H. S.; 51 Quincy St., Brooklyn. Tel. 1772 Prospect.
STANTON, ANNA ELIZABETH—Biology, Bushwick H. S.; 419 Ocean Ave., Brooklyn. Tel. 3936 Flatbush.
STAPFF, HETTA—Assistant German, Curtis H. S. (Rosebank Annex); 445 Richmond Rd., Richmond, N. Y. Tel. 176-R New Dorp.
STAPLETON, CHRISTOPHER ROBERT—Assistant English, Stuyvesant H. S.; 6 Caryl Ave., Yonkers, N. Y.
STARKEY, WARREN L.—First Assistant Commercial Branches, Jamaica H. S.; 464 E. 26th St., Brooklyn. Tel. 966 Flatbush.
STEBBINS, CHARLES M.—Assistant English, Boys' H. S.; 1427 Union St., Brooklyn. Tel. 7111 Prospect.
STEERS, EDNA L.—Assistant Biology, Girls' H. S.; 1251 Pacific St., Brooklyn.
STIEG, FERN—Asst. Physical Training, Bushwick H. S.; 1321 Bedford Ave. Tel. Bedford 3381-J.
STEIGMAN, BENJAMIN M.—Assistant English, Stuyvesant H. S.; 1538 Minford Pl., New York.
STEINBERG, PAULINE—Assistant Stenography and Typewriting, Bryant H. S.; 530 Manhattan Ave., Manhattan. Tel. 3927 Morningside.
STEINECKE, JEANNETTE A.—Substitute Stenography and Typewriting, Annex 129, Bushwick H. S.; 55a Lynch St., Brooklyn. Tel. 1150 Williamsburg.
STEINERT, JOHN BERNHARDT—Assistant Joinery, Stuyvesant H. S.; Hastings-on-Hudson, N. Y. Tel. 749 Hastings.
STEPANEK, BEATRICE—Latin, Eastern District H. S.; 601 W. 115th St., Manhattan. Tel. 8704 Morningside.
STERN, REGINE—Assistant German, Manual Training H. S.; 434 7th St., Brooklyn.
STERNBERG, GEORGE—Assistant German, Commercial H. S.; 173 W. 140th St., Manhattan.
STEVENS, ALICE A.—Assistant History, Girls' H. S.; 427 Nostrand Ave., Brooklyn.
STEVENS, HENRY J.—Assistant Latin, De Witt Clinton H. S.; 525 W. 150th St., Manhattan.
STEVENS, WILLIAM S.—Assistant Mathematics, De Witt Clinton H. S.; 33 Greystone Park, Yonkers. Tel. 1705 Yonkers.
STEVENSON, BEULAH E.—Assistant Drawing, Girls' H. S.; 1098 E. 38th St., Brooklyn.
STEWART, CHARLES A.—Assistant Commercial Branches, Richmond Hill H. S.; 739 Hamilton Ave., Richmond Hill, L. I.
STILSON, WILLIAM E.—Assistant Mathematics, Richmond Hill H. S.; 508 Chestnut St., Richmond Hill, L. I.
ST. JOHN, EMILY P.—Assistant English, Girls' H. S.; 294 Argyle Rd., Brooklyn. Tel. 4831-J Flatbush.
ST. JOHN, ROBERT P.—First Assistant English, Commercial H. S.; 815 E. 14th St., Brooklyn.
STOCKES, JOHN H.—Assistant Physics, Erasmus Hall H. S.; 197 E. 17th St., Brooklyn. Tel. 4576-W Flatbush.
STONE, BERTHA R.—Assistant Phonography, Washington Irving H. S.; 202 W. 74th St., Manhattan. Tel. 3948 Columbus.
STONE, LIMOND C.—Assistant Mathematics, Boys' H. S.; 148 Putnam Ave., Brooklyn. Tel. 4430-R. Bedford.
STONE, KATHARINE W.—Assistant Latin, Erasmus Hall H. S.; 365 Monroe St., Brooklyn.
STONE, LULU M.—Assistant English, Girls' H. S.; 1433 Union St., Brooklyn.
STONE, MARY M.—Assistant Mathematics, Erasmus Hall H. S.; 1234 Pacific St., Brooklyn.
STONE, MABEL—First Assistant Girls' Shop, Manual Training H. S.; 566 7th St., Brooklyn. Tel. 2191-M South.
STONE, MAUDIE L.—Assistant Biology, Manual Training H. S.; 525 5th St., Brooklyn. Tel. 1384-W South.
STONE, M. GRACE—Assistant Latin, Wadleigh H. S.; 609 W. 177th St. Tel. 5568 Audubon.
STONER, PRISCILLA G. (Mrs. T. W.)—Assistant English, Wadleigh H. S.; 537 W. 121st St. Tel. 5120 Morningside.
STORY, HELEN M.—Assistant Domestic Science, Morris H. S.; 1018 E. 163d St., The Bronx, N. Y. C. Tel. 4600 Melrose.
STOTLER, ALBERT—Assistant Manual Arts (Woodturning), Stuyvesant H. S.; 98 Bechknoll Rd., Forest Hills, L. I.
STRATFORD, ALINE C.—Assistant English, Eastern District H. S.; 163 Clinton Ave., Brooklyn. Tel 5368-W Prospect.
STRATFORD, ALINE C.—English, Eastern District H. S.; 163 Clinton Ave., Brooklyn. Tel. 5368-W Prospect.
STRASBURGER, BERTHA—Assistant Mathematics, Wadleigh H. S.; 55 W. 95th St. Tel. 6621 Riverside.
STRAUSS, JULIUS—Assistant Physical Training, De Witt Clinton H. S.; 971 E. 179th St., Manhattan. Tel. 3412 Tremont.
STRAYER, FRANKLIN R.—Assistant Physics, Morris H. S.; 11 Primrose Ave., Mt. Vernon, N. Y. Tel. 262-W Mt. Vernon.
STROM, CARL A. W.—Assistant Mathematics, Erasmus Hall H. S.; 446 74th St., Brooklyn. Tel. 798-W Bay Ridge.

OFFICIAL BULLETIN

of the High School Teachers' Association of New York City

No. 40 OCTOBER 1913

The Board of Representatives, on May 23, 1911, empowered the Executive Committee to issue a Bulletin monthly, instead of four times a year.

THE FIRST GENERAL MEETING FOR 1913-1914 will be held Saturday, November 1, 1913, at the High School of Commerce.

DEPARTMENT MEETINGS begin at 10 A. M. Besides the programs as given below, there will be in some Sections elections of Chairmen for 1913-1914.

For more detailed announcements see papers.

GENERAL MEETING begins at 11.15 A. M. in Auditorium.

ORDER OF BUSINESS:

REPORTS OF OFFICERS.

REPORTS OF CHAIRMEN OF COMMITTEES.

ELECTION OF DELEGATES to choose members of Teachers' Advisory Council. The Association is to choose two High School Principals, two First Assistants, two Men High School Teachers, and two Women High School Teachers to represent the Association in the Conference, to be held November 13, 1913.

NEW BUSINESS.

WILLIAM T. MORREY, President.

MARY J. BOURNE, Secretary.

DEPARTMENT MEETINGS, 10 A. M.

ANCIENT LANGUAGES—Room 534, Dr. Walter E. Foster, Stuyvesant High School, Chairman. Discussion of question:

What Latin should be taught in the New York City High Schools by Dr. Walter E. Foster, Chairman of Committee to study Hanus High School Course of Study. Recommendations.

What should be the work of this department for 1913-1914?

Election of Chairman for 1913-1914.

BIOLOGY—Room 301, Mr. Harvey B. Clough, H. S. of Commerce, Chairman; Frank Merrill Wheat, DeWitt Clinton H. S., Secretary.

Topic: "The Chemistry of Photosynthesis," by Dr. Walter H. Eddy, Chairman of the Department of Biology, High School of Commerce, and Assistant in Biological Chemistry, Columbia University.

BOOKKEEPING SECTION—Room 303, William R. Hayward, Head of Commercial Department, Washington Irving High School, Chairman.

"Topic: "Vocational Guidance" with a Discussion of what has been done in the Commercial High School, by Gilbert S. Raynor, Commercial High School.

On the Revision of Courses of Study in Commercial High Schools, by the Chairman.

DRAWING—Room 302, Eunice F. Faulkner, Eastern District High School, Chairman.

An important business meeting and a discussion of Plans for the Department of Drawing for the year.

ELOCUTION—Room 201, Mr. Raymond W. Kellogg, Chairman; W. Palmer Smith, Stuyvesant High School, Secretary.

"The Teaching of Phonetics," by Miss Margaret Klein, Flushing High School.

Discussion of the Tentative Syllabus for Elocution in New York City High Schools.

All teachers of Elocution, Voice Culture and Oral Expression are cordially invited.

HISTORY AND ECONOMICS—Room 205, Mr. Alfred C. Bryan, Head of Department of History, High School of Commerce, Chairman.

Topic: ""Geography and History in High Schools;" some concrete suggestions presented for discussion by Mr. Augustus S. Beatman, High School of Commerce.

EXHIBIT—"A New Use for an Old Wall Map," by William T. Morrey, Head of Department of History, Bushwick High School.

MODERN LANGUAGES—Room 401, Co'man Dudley Frank, DeWitt Clinton, High School, Chairman.

Election of Chairman and Officers of the Department for 1913-1914.

MATHEMATICS—Room 304, Mr. Edward A. Hook, Commercial High School.

"Efficiency in Teaching Mathematics With Special Regard to Methods of Saving Time," by Mr. Ralph P. Bliss, Commercial High School.

Preliminary Report from the Committee on Reference Books for Mathematical Libraries, by Mr. Elmer Schuyler, Head of Department of Mathematics, Bay Ridge High School, Chanrman of Committee.

PHYSIOGRAPHY—Room 506, Mr. Earl B. Slack, Washington Irving High School, Chairman.

"Field Observation and its Advantages to Teachers of Geography," by Prof. Raymond B. Earle, Normal College.

Illustrated by Stereopticon.

SHORTHAND—Room 216, Mr. William P. O'Ryan, Commercial High School, Chairman.

Exhibit and Demonstration of the Stenotype.

TEACHERS OF ENGLISH.

Dr. William H. Maxwell will give an address on "The Essentials of English" at 10:30 A. M. on Saturday, November 15, 1913, at the Washington Irving High School, Room 601, before the New York City Association of High School Teachers of English. Mr. Charles S. Hartwell, Head of Department of English, Eastern District High School, President..

All elementary school teachers of English above the sixth year are invited to be present.

ANNOUNCEMENT.

The Board of Representatives meets the last school Tuesday of every school month, except September and June. The first meeting will be Oct. 28th.

Dues for the year should be paid to your Senior Representatives and by him forwarded before the first General Meeting to the Treasurer, Dr. Loring B. Mullen, Girs' High School, Brooklyn.

The November Bulletin of the Association is nearly all in type. Its 40 or more pages will contain first Biennial Report of the President, Dr. Linville's Committee's Report on High School Mortality, Mr. Kingsbury's Committee's Report on Credit for Laboratory Note Books, a Report from Mr. Weaver on Vocational Guidance, High School Directory and Statistics.

WILLIAM T. MORREY,
President.

October 18, 1913.

FIRST ASSISTANTS IN HIGH SCHOOLS OF NEW YORK CITY, 101 Men, 21 Women.

HIGH SCHOOL	BIOLOGY	ENGLISH	FRENCH AND GERMAN	HISTORY	LATIN	MATHEMATICS	PHYSICAL SCIENCE	COMMERCIAL Vice-Principals (Art)
BAY RIDGE	Bruckman, Louise			Proper, Emberson E		Schuyler, Elmer		
BOYS'	Lewis, F. Z.	Fisher, William W.	Overholser, Charles E.	Jackson, W. P. Wilson, Jas. F.	Riess, Ernest	Parsons, Edw. B.		
BRYANT		Munroe, Harry K.					Bement, Frederic	
BUSHWICK	Johnson, Julius M.	Semple, Lewis B.	Keener, Robt. H.	Morrey, William T.		Humason, Thomas A.		
COMMERCE	Eddy, Walter H.	Heydrick, Benjamin A	Roessler, Erwin W.	Bryan, Alfred C.			Mills, Jos. E. Cheston, H. C.	Pugh, A. L. Greene, R.
COMMERCIAL	Gruenberg, Benj. C.	St. John, Robt. P.	Marvin, Robt. M. Harrison, Earl S.	Trask, Thomas C.		Teeter, Charles H.	Clark, John A.	Doggett, Wm. E Kip, Arthur R.
CURTIS	Grout, Abel J.	Abbott, Frances	Shepherd, Florence D.			Dean, Philip R.		Welsh, John C. Crane, Wm. A. (V.P.)
DEWITT CLTN.	Hunter, George W.	Garrigues, Ellen E.	Monteser, F'd'k. Frank, Colman D.		Bice, Hiram H.	Anthony, Oscar W.	Whitsit, Jesse E. Timmermann, C. E.	
EAST'N DIST.	Hazen, Anna P.	Hartwell, Charles S.	Bole, John A.	Paine, Frederick H	Dixon, Charles E.	Mayo, Marion J.		Baltz, Frank P.
ERASM. HALL	King, Cyrus A.	Farrar, Preston C.	Holmes, Mary H.	Boynton, George E.	Harter, Eugene W.			Turner, Kate (V. P.)
EVANDER CHILDS								
FAR ROCK'W'Y								Belding, Albert G.
FLUSHING		Read, Warren W.	Baumeister, John	Miller, Frank H.	Jenks, Paul R.	Barnwell, Walter		
GIRLS'	Leeuente, Margaret T.	Wendt, Cordelia	Higgins, Alice	Cahill, Rose H.	Ford, Celia	Mullen, Loring B.	Arey, Albert L.	Pyles, (VP) Marion
JAMAICA	Linville, Henry R.	Fairley, Edwin	Krause, Carl A.	Lawrence, Antoinette	Chickering, Edward C.		Vosburgh, Chas. H.	Starkey, Warren L.
JULIA RICHMAN						Arnold, David L.		
MAN. TRAIN.	Hunt, Arthur E.	Bates, Herbert	Lamb, Wm. W.	Low, J. Herbert	Shumway, Edgar S.	Baker, Arthur L. Colston, Albert L.	Weed, Henry T.	Shinn, (Art) Victor I.
MORRIS	Peabody, James E.		Althaus, Edward	Bates, Abby B.	Davis, Josephine A	Heikes, Irving A.	Pyle, Willard R.	
NEWTOWN					Radin, Max			
RICHM'D HILL	Valentine, Morris	Gaston Chas. Robt.				Landers, Leland L.		
STUYVESANT		Law, Frederick H.	Elmer, Clement G.		Foster, Walter E.	Breckenridge, Wm. E.	Fuller, Robert W.	Howe, (Art) Chas. B.
WADLEIGH	Kupfer, Elsie M.	Smith, Jessie F. (Now Mrs. Ford)	Zick, Henry	Wood, Elizabeth C.	Hodges, Archibald L	Bruce, Grace A.	Cornish, Robt. H.	
WASH. IRV'G	Sage, Lillian B.	Lowd, Emma F. Douglas, C. H. J.	Blackwell, Nannie G.	Galloway, Ida G.				Hayward, William R.

DIRECTORY OF HIGH SCHOOLS OF NEW YORK CITY

School	Telephone	Location	Principal or Teacher in Charge of Annex
Bay Ridge	711 Bath Beach	86th st., near 18th av. (P. S. 101)	HARRY A. POTTER.
Annex	1273 Bay Ridge	92d st. and Gelston av. (P. S. 104).	
Boys'	690 Bedford	Marcy and Putnam avs. and Madison st.	JAMES SULLIVAN.
Bryant	40 Astoria	Wilbur av., Academy and Radde sts., L. I. City	PETER E. DEMAREST.
Annex	1146-W Astoria	Van Alst av., near Flushing av., L. I. City (P. S. 7)	
Bushwick	3403 Bushwick	400 Irving Ave	FRANK ROLLINS.
Annex	13 Bushwick	Evergreen av., Ralph and Grove sts (P. S. 75)	WILLIAM T. MORREY
Annex	3514 Bushwick	Quincy st., near Stuyvesant av. (P. S. 129)	LEWIS B. SEMPLE.
Commercial	3732 Bedford	Albany av., Bergen and Dean sts.	WILLIAM FAIRLEY.
Annex	7736 Bedford	Bedford and Jefferson sts	W. E. DOGGETT.
Curtis	351-J Tompkinsville	Hamilton av. and St. Mark's pl., New Brighton	D. L. FELDMAN.
Annex	922-J Tottenville	Academy pl., Tottenville (P. S. 1)	
De Witt Clinton	4175 Columbus	10th av., 58th and 59th sts	JOHN L. TILDSLEY.
Eastern District	4565 Wmsburg	Marcy av., Rodney and Keap sts	W. T. VLYMEN.
Annex	1715 Greenpoint	Havemeyer, N. 6th and 7th sts (P. S. 143)	ANNA L. PHILLIPS.
Erasmus Hall	288 Flatbush	Flatbush av., near Church av	W. B. GUNNISON.
Evander Childs	643 Westchester	Randolph, St. Lawrence and Hammond aves. (P. S. 47)	GILBERT S. BLAKELY
Annex	5634 Tremont	196th st., Bainbridge and Driggs avs. (P. S. 46)	
Far Rockaway	95 Far Rockaway	Far Rockaway	S. J. ELLSWORTH.
Flushing	321 Flushing	Sanford av., Flushing	J. H. CLARK.
Girls'	372 Bedford	Nostrand av., Halsey and Macon sts.	W. L. FELTER.
Annex	5926 Prospect	St. Mark's and Classon avs. (P. S. 42)	M. ELLEN BARKER.
H. S. of Commerce	2658 Columbus	65th and 66th sts., west of Broadway	J. J. SHEPPARD.
Annex	8114 Bryant	120 West 46th st. (P. S. 67)	ALFRED C. BRYAN.
Jamaica	165 Jamaica	Hillside av., Jamaica	T. C. MITCHILL.
Julia Richman	2446 Stuyvesant	34½ East 12th st	A. M. WOLFSON.
Annex	4061 Chelsea	60 West 13th st	
Annex	1612 Chelsea	140 West 20th st. (P. S. 55)	
Manual Training	1380 South	7th av., 4th and 5th sts	C. D. LARKINS.
Annex	24 South	Prospect av., opp. Reeve pl	CHARLES PERRINE.
Annex	2627 Main	Duffield, Johnson and Gold sts	ARTHUR L. BAKER.
Morris	605 Melrose	166th st., Boston rd. and Jackson av.	JOHN H. DENBIGH.
Annex	2360 Melrose	Mott av. and 144th st. (P. S. 31)	IRVING A. HEIKES.
Newtown	40 Newtown	Elmhurst	J. D. DILLINGHAM.
Annex	122 Newtown	Elmhurst (P. S. 89)	
Richmond Hill	26 Richmond Hill	Elm st., Richmond Hill	ISAAC N. FAILOR.
Stuyvesant	3739 Stuyvesant	15th and 16th sts., west of 1st ave.	E. R. VON NARDROFF
Wadleigh	1892 Morningside	114th and 115th sts., west of 7th av.	STUART H. ROWE.
Annex	4865 Harlem	138th st., west of 5th av. (P. S. 100)	KATH. A. SPEIR.
Washington Irving	3292 Stuyvesant	Irving pl., 16th and 17th sts	W. McANDREW.

OFFICIAL BULLETIN

of the High School Teachers' Association of New York City

No. 41 NOVEMBER 1913

The Board of Representatives, on May 23, 1911, empowered the Executive Committee to issue a Bulletin monthly, instead of four times a year.

THE SECOND GENERAL MEETING FOR 1913-1914 will be held Saturday, Dec. 6, 1913, at the High School of Commerce. Details in the next Bulletin. Chairmen of Sections should send in programs of their sections at once.

NEXT MEETING OF THE BOARD OF REPRESENTATIVES will be held Tuesday, Nov. 25, 1913, at the High School of Commerce.

Chairmen of Sections and Chairmen of Committees are expected to be present to outline their plans of work for the year.

Senior Representatives are expected to report on the membership of their schools. Dues for 1913-1914 should be paid.

Each Senior Representative should bring with him, as of Oct. 31, 1913, or later:

(1) A Library Card for every teacher, showing: (1) Name (last name first); (2) position; (3) subject; (4) high school; (5) home address; (6) telephone.

(2) Two complete lists of teachers by departments, each department on separate sheets of paper.

(3) An alphabetical list of all teachers in school, ready to go to printer.

Discussion of the question: What subjects should be brought to the attention of the Teachers' Council?

WILLIAM T. MORREY, President.

MARY J. BOURNE, Secretary.

PRESIDENT'S BIENNIAL REPORT.

The President thanks his friends in the Association for honoring him with a third term.

This will enable him, he hopes, to have completed and published studies on: (1) The Ideal Courses of Studies for High Schools; (2) The Ideal Equipment of the Various Departments in the Ideal High School; and (3) A Directory of the High School Teachers. He will continue in 1913-1914 the lines of work planned when he was first elected in May, 1911.

Purpose.

He then had in mind the Application of the Principles of Scientific Management to High School Problems, that is, the Study of Efficiency. This purpose has for two years been carried out along three lines—in the general meetings, in the department meetings, and in the work of the various committees of this Association. This purpose has influenced other associations also, for Mr. Feldman told the Schoolmaster's' Association of New York City and Vicinity in January, 1913: "As far as I know, every gathering of secondary teachers in New York City, this school year, has had for its topic of discussion "Efficiency" in some form or other."

The Organization.

The 850 members are represented by about seventy-seven representatives in the **Board of Representatives**, which meets on the last school Tuesday of every school month, excepting September and June, with "power to act upon all matters affecting the association."

All schools are advised to **send** all their representatives or substitutes duly accredited to every meeting, bringing some idea as a contribution.

The **Executive Committee** consists of the President, Vice-President, Secretary, Treasurer, and three other elected members. It has the power to "approve all appropriations of funds and shall audit and direct the payment of all bills."

Standing Committees—Teachers' Interests and Secondary Education, each with nine members, including the President.

Such other Committee as may be ordered or as may be appointed by the President, who may also remove chairmen and members.

Finances.

The finances of the Association for many years have been carefully attended to by the Treasurer, Dr. Loring B. Mullen, Head of the Department of Mathematics, Girls High School. He reports the following facts:

Deducting from the amount in the Treasury when this administration began, the secretary paid out for Year Book, Postage, Room Rent, etc., chargeable to the preceeding administration of President Janes there was a net balance of $13.39.

The first year the receipts were $740.78, the expenses $531.06, the balance during the year was increased $209.72.

The second year the receipts were $858.85, the expenses $568.69, the balance was increased $290.16.

The balance in the Treasury Oct. 28, 1913, $600.37 (with this Bulletin to be paid for.)

Bulletins.

The policy of issuing Bulletins instead of Year Books has been continued. It is more expensive, but it publishes addresses and reports in a comparatively short time after they are ready.

The President has enjoyed the little time he has spent in the printing office for it has brought back his boyhood experience as a printers' devil.

President's Appointing Power.

He was empowered by Board of Representatives on Oct. 31, 1911, to appoint a Committee on Efficiency and such other committees as he sees fit to call. [Bulletin No. 3, p. 3.] May 28, 1912, power to appoint was renewed and power to remove was added. [Bulletin No. 35, p. 3.] These powers were again renewed by the Board of Representatives on October 28, 1913.

Policy

The President has tried:

First. To bring about as friendly relations as possible between the men and women in the high schools and among their various organizations.

Jan. 7, 1911, the Board of Representatives passed a resolution, that this Association pledges itself to take no part in any salary proposition! [See Bulletin No. 29, p. 3.]

Second. To devote the two years' work to a practical examination of the Principles of Scientific Management and their use in increasing High School Efficiency.

Third. To find out who wanted to do some valuable piece of work, to help form their committees, to support them financially.

Fourth. To give full credit to whom credit is due.

Relations With Other Associations.

The President has tried to bring about friendly relations with the other associations. This association has been addressed by representatives of the Association of High School Principals, the President of the Association of High School First Assistants, Mr. Alfred C. Bryan, and by the President of the Male High School Teachers' Association, Mr. Robert H. Keener. The President of the Women's High School Teachers Association, Miss Lina E. Gano, was invited to address the Association; she said she was unable to do so, but suggested a substitute.

These various associations have, everyone, its own legitimate field, but there are many questions in which all are interested. It was planned to take up in this association the study of the relations between High Schools and Elementary Schools, a vital topic, but this was abandoned out of courtesy to the Women's High School Teachers' Association.

In a similar way this association did not prosecute its studies in Programs and Program Making, out of deference to the High School Principals' Association.

The President will be glad to be informed of fields into which others desire to enter. The harvest is plenty, the laborers are few. If several associations desire to enter the same field let them co-operate, or defer one to another.

This Association has a convenient means, in its Bulletin, for the publication of such work as may be of general interest to high school teachers—whether this work is done by an individual, by a school, or by a committee.

Relations to the N. E. A.

The work of Mr. Clarence D. Kingsley for this association and his work along similar lines for the National Educational Association have brought the two associations into close relations.

The President does not know whether his plan, to have the Ideal Course of Study worked out by Departments in New York City, is in any way responsible for Mr. Kingsley's Commission of the N. E. A. on the Reorganization of Secondary Education.

The General Meetings.

The general meetings have served as a forum for the discussion of school problems and as a source of inspiration.

If the reports of these meetings should be published as a book with the title "Efficiency Studies of New York City High Schools," the various chapters would be:

I. The Principles of Scientific Management and How they would affect School Efficiency, by Mr. Harrington Emerson, Consulting Engineer.

II. What is this School System for? A Re-Examination of Educational Commonplaces, by Prof. Paul H. Hanus of Harvard University.

III. Efficiency in Administration, by Associate Superintendent Edward L. Stevens, Principal James Sullivan of Boys' High School; First Assistant Alfred C. Bryan, High School of Commerce and President of Male High School First Assistants' Association; Grade Adviser Miss H. Elizabeth Seelman of Girls' High School, and (Class Teacher Miss Maud E. Manfred of Richmond Hill High School.)

IV. Efficiency in Type of High School—Large vs. Small, and Specialized vs. Cosmopolitan, by Mr. Frederick H. Paine of Eastern District High School, and Mr. Clarence D. Kingsley formerly of Manual Training High School.

V. Efficiency in the Recitation, by District Superintendent Darwin L. Bardwell, in Charge of High Schools.

VI. Efficiency in the Various Departments—Address by Alfred C. Bryan, on Duties of First Assistants. This work is to be carried on during 1913-1914 in the various section meetings of the association. High standards have been set for these studies, by two already made in the Department Meetings:

(a) Efficiency in the Mathematics Recitation, by Daniel D. Feldman, formerly First Assistant in Erasmus Hall High School, now Principal Curtis High School.

(b) Efficiency in the History Recitation, by Arthur M. Wolfson, formerly First Assistant in History DeWitt Clinton High School, now Principal Julia Richman High School.

VII. How to Test Pupils—A means of Judging Efficiency of Teaching, by Prof. Charles H. Judd of University of Chicago.

VIII. The Efficient Teacher: "What Constitutes the Teacher of Superior Merit?" A Discussion by Examiner George H. Smith, Superintendent Edward L. Stevens, and Principals Clark, Denbigh, Fairley, Felter, Larkins, McAndrew, and Tildsley.

IX. High Schools and Moral Efficiency—Addresses by Hon. Frank Moss, Assistant District Attorney of New York City, and Examiner Walter L. Hervey.

Superior Merit.

The largest meeting in the history of the High School Teachers' Association was that of March 16, 1912, devoted to a discussion of this question. The addresses of Examiner George J. Smith, Associate City Superintendent Edward L. Stevens and Principals Clark of Flushing, Denbigh of Morris, Fairley of Commercial, Felter of

Girls', Larkins of Manual Training, McAndrew of Washington Irving, and Tildsley of DeWitt Clinton are in Bulletin 34, pp. 4-27.

The Association on March 24, 1912, took formal action through its Executive Committee, ratified also by the Board of Representatives at the March 28, 1912, meeting, asking the Committee on High Schools of the Board of Education:

(1) To rate as of Superior Merit all teachers whose marke are B+ or higher; **superior** being a comparative term and not a superlative, not equivalent to supreme.

(2) To rate as of Superior Merit those receiving the maximum salaries of their grade, prior to Jan. 1, 1912.

(3) To rate as approved for twelve years, such as have been approved for nine years and have in addition received credit for three additional years in the adjustment of the Junior Teacher Question.

First Assistants.

This position, at first a salary grade, is the most available avenue to increase salary for the efficient teacher. It is his Door of Hope.

The Association has taken an active interest in restoring it to a salary grade. May 23, 1911, the Board of Representatives recommended:

1. That first assistants be appointed on the grounds of efficiency in teaching and administrative work without regard to chairmanship of a department.

2. That it be desirable that one first assistant be appointed in high schools for every 150 pupils registered. [Bulletin No. 29, p. 2.]

The Board of Representatives endorsed, Feb. 25, 1913, the following amendments to the By-Laws, proposed by the New York High School Principals' Association: (a) Amend Section 52, paragraph 3, by striking out words "First Assistant." Insert:

(b) Every assistant teacher in high schools who has been granted a license as first assistant teacher shall be entitled to the rank and pay of a first assistant teacher without further examination or appointment, and said rank shall become effective, and said salary shall be paid from the first day of January of the year next following that in which the license as first assistant teacher is granted, provided, that no first assistant shall receive on becoming a first assistant teacher a salary less than he would have received if he had remained an assistant teacher.

(c) Examinations for the license as first assistant teacher in high schools shall be held at least biennially in all subjects for which the license as first assistant teacher is provided in the By-Laws.

Committees on Principles of Scientific Management as Applied to High School Problems.

This committee was organized with Dr. Edward H. Fitzpatrick as Chairman. It was under certain conditions to become the Committee on Efficiency. The Chairman gave an excellent preliminary address to the Board of Representatives and later prepared a report. The President regrets that the Chairman did not prepare, as requested, a systematic report as to the best methods to be adopted. Dr. Fitzpatrick's suggestive Annual Report before he left to take part in Wisconsin State School Inquiry may be found in Bulletin No. 36, pp. 43-46.

The report on Teaching of Stenography by Mr. Edward J. McNamara, of Jamaica High School, was set up and galley proof copies were used as a basis of a Section Meeting. It was the basis of very strenous discussion. By the time it was to be published, many of the criticisms no longer held, and at Mr. McNamara's request publication was held up. A report on Typewriting by Mr. David H. O'Keefe of the Jamaica High School has been promised.

Dr. Henry R. Linville's Committee.

Dr. Linville's painstaking and valuable report on the Mortality in High Schools is published in this Bulletin.

It represents much hard work, careful investigation, and temperance in statement. It well deserves most careful consideration.

Laboratory Note Books.

Mr. George H. Kingsbury, of Newtown High School, organized a committee and made a careful study of this question. The valuable report of the committee appears in this Bulletin.

Uniform Grammatical Terminology.

The President had hoped soon to be able to report progress by Mr. Charles Perrine's Committee. This Committee should co-ordinate the excellent work done by the High School English Teachers' Association with work done along similar lines in England, and should work out, if possible, a terminology that will hold when the pupil takes up his German, his French, his Latin, or his other foreign language.

Last Day of School.

March 25, 1913, the Board on initiation of Mr. Frederick C. White, of Morris, started a movement that he carried into other associations and that finally led to closing the schools Friday, June 27, instead of Monday, June 30. (Bulletin 38, p. 88.)

Similar action should be taken to have the schools opened after the Christmas Holidays Monday, January 5, instead of Friday, January 2, 1914.

New High Schools.

Studies were made of high school conditions in Brownsville and East New York partions of Brooklyn for three terms for graduates of Public Schools in January 1912' and for January and for February 1913. (See Bulletin No. 39, pp. 117 and 118.)

Studies of many other local conditions should be made this year. Materials for such studies will be issued in the Bulletin.

Committee on Students Aid and Employment.

During the last two years the committee has co-operated with other associations in the movement for systematic efforts in vocational guidance and as all the high schools have had committees in operation, this committee has confined its activities to the extension of its list of vocational bulletins. The sale of the bulletins has paid for their printing so that no demands have been made upon the treasury of the association. The Chairman is preparing a financial statement. Bulletins and circulars of information have been furnished free to all applicants who were members of the association.

In September the various subcommittees on particular industries resumed their weekly meetings. These are held on Monday evenings at 25 Jefferson avenue, Brooklyn. The new bulletins, which are in course of preparation, will be printed as funds become available.

Vocational Instruction.

The Board of Representatives, May 28, 1912, directed the Secretary to urge that the New York City members of Congress consider the Page Bill in support of an appropriation of $14,000,000 for Vocational Education.

Committee on Conference with Colleges.

The Report of the Committee of Nine, was favored by five out of six members of the Committee. Dr. Sullivan believed that both mathematics and a foreign language should be required for entrance to college.—Meeting of Representatives, Oct. 31, 1911. - [See Bulletin No. 31, p. 3.]

Teachers' Absences

Mr. Charles R. Fay, of Erasmus Hall, formed a committee whose report was approved by the Board of Representatives on April 30, 1912, and by the Board recommended to the Board of Education. The report is printed in full, Bulletin 34, pp. 31-46.

Sabbatical Year.

The most important of Mr. Fay's recommendations is that a sabbatical year for study or travel be allowed on half pay.

These recommendations were taken up by Mr. Fay and his committee with a Committee of the Board of Education; but no action has been taken by the Board.

The subject is growing in interest and will undoubtedly be taken up by other Teachers' Associations and by the Teachers' Advisory Council and again laid before the Board of Education.

All interested in this vital question owe a vote of thanks to Mr. Fay.

We believe that if a sabbatical year is granted there will be fewer break downs in the service and a diminished demand on the Pension Fund.

Pension Legislation.

Frederick H. Paine of Eastern District High School has been chairman of Committee on Pensions and has ably represented the Association in the various conferences.

The logic of events is showing the soundness of Mr. Paine's contention that the City should pay an increasingly larger share into the fund.

The pension of a retired teacher plus the salary of a beginning teacher, may amount to less than the full salary received by the pensioner just before he was pensioned.

In addition to thus saving money there is also an increased efficiency from younger and more enthusiastic teachers.

It is good business policy to retire the weak.

Pensions are looked upon by some as simply deferred payments on inadequate salaries.

Hanus Committee.

At the Jan. 30, 1912, meeting it was moved that a committee be formed at the discretion of the President, to represent the High School Teachers' Association before the Hanus Committee. [Bulletin No. 33, p. 2.]

At Feb. 27, 1912, meeting Mr. Kingsley reported that 16 were present at the first meeting of this Conference Committee on Course of Study, and that there was entire agreement on the need of greater flexibility in the high school course.

The committee was enlarged to 57, of whom 40 were present at the second meeting. At this meeting a sub-committee was appointed to put its recommendations into shape.

This preliminary draft of the report of the sub-committee was read to the Board of Representatives and discussed—especially the five subject and four subject plans and the requirements.

The report was finally amended and adopted by the committee March 5, 1912, and published in full with list of members of committee on pages 10-12 of Bulletin No. 33.

It recommends that the Course of Study in New York High Schools have (1) greater flexibilty: (2) the introduction into the general course "under proper restrictions, such subjects as may be demanded by a reasonable number of students, and for which there are qualified teachers in the school; (3) greater concentration upon fewer subjects; (4) the five-subject plan per week, each subject allotted four hours per week of prepared work, enabling those desiring to specialize to take two-fifths of their work vocational and three-fifths academic.

The Central Council to Study Hanus Reports.

The President planned to devote much of the energy of the association to the study of the Hanus Reports during 1912-1913; but the reports were slow in appearing, and when they did appear, those relating to High Schools showed so much evidence of consultation and conference with high school principals, first assistants, and teachers that it seemed better that these reports should be studied by high school people not by themselves but in conjunction with others.

Accordingly the President thought it best to assist in the coordinating and co-operating efforts of all interested in studying the Hanus Reports.

The President of the Association served on several sub-committees of the Central Council and his suggestions as to the most suitable high school men and women to be appointed upon the various committees were generously and graciously acted upon.

Men and women that had been antagonistic on salary questions found that they could work harmoniously on purely professional questions.

The weekly conferences participated in by both elementary and high school teachers and principals have done much to promote a better understanding and mutual respect.

It is the belief of the President that those Hanus Reports on High Schools on which there was hearty co-operation and consultation with high school superintendents, principals, first assistants, and teachers, were the reports that were most suggestive and most valuable, although not most sensational—Prof. Ballou's for example.

Teachers' Advisory Council.

The President was asked by President Churchill to give his suggestions with reference to the formation of an Advisory Council. He has served on various committees of organization.

The personal opinion of the President is that, for years all school authorities could have had for the asking the hearty co-operation of the various teachers' organizations.

Election of Teachers' Council.

The preliminary arrangements for the meeting for the election of members of the Teachers' Council were referred by the Central Council to a Committee of Organization or Steering Committee, of which your President was a member. There arose the following questions which it seemed to him should be settled by the Delegates themselves, their Committee on Credentials, or their Chairman:

(1)—A formal complaint against the admission of delegates from the Schoolmasters' Association of New York City and Vicinity on the ground that of their 111 members but 37 were in New York City public schools.

(2)—The High School Association of German Teachers reported that its delegates had been elected BY THE EXECUTIVE COMMITTEE on October 30.

The Plan of Organization, Art. VI. Section 7 provides that "In the election of delegates EVERY MEMBER OF AN ASSOCIATION shall be entitled to a vote."

A resolution of the Board of Education also provides that "The delegates representing the voluntary organizations in the election of the Teachers' Council shall be elected annually by their respective associations IN THE SAME MANNER AS OFFICERS and shall serve one year."

Question—Did the election by the Executive Committee give every member of the association a vote OR Were the delegates elected in the same manner as officers?

(3)—The Chairman of the Association of First Assistants in High Schools stated in answer to a letter from Mr. Morrison that the association was AN INFORMAL ORGANIZATION, that it was organized February 18, 1913, and that ITS ONLY OFFICER WAS A CHAIRMAN.

Question—Does an INFORMAL organization SO officered constitute such an ORGANIZATION as was intended in the Plan?

There was a meeting of the Committee on Organization just before the meeting of the delegates. Your President heard no suggestion, while he was in the room, of a plurality vote instead of a majority vote deciding. It was understood that the Chairman would nominate members of the Committee on Organization and the President of the Central Council, Mr. Magnus Gross, as a Committee on Credentials. The function of such a committee is to determine who have the right to vote. They should report as soon as possible and always before there is any voting. The committee was so named by the Chairman, and, inasmuch as its members had already heard the points at issue, it could have reported in a few moments, and most of the committee expected to do so, as was shown by its presence on the platform. But instead the Committee was asked to report AT THE NEXT MEETING.

Such an arrangement was not made by the Committee, and until announced to the delegates, was unknown to your President. He does not know who is responsible for either the Plurality Idea or the Postponement Idea.

If he had anticipated such decisions, he would have opposed both, for he believed in neither.

In the Group of High School First Assistants, where he was a candidate for the Council, the effect of the postponement was to disfranchise six delegates—five of whom he believed would vote against him. Whatever he thought of their eligiblity* your President felt and feels that they had a right to have their Status settled before voting began.* Postponement was an injustice to them.

Because he was not then in a position to say that the Committee had not decided on such actions, he could explain his attitude and proposition in part only. This he did, refused to vote on either the nominating or the final ballot, and at the proper time asked his supporters to vote for another person.

He has felt that if he had remained a candidate he could have been elected a member of the Teachers' Council, a great honor and a fine opportunity for service. But he did not feel that he wanted to gain it by an injustice, even if not committed by him, and if planned without his knowledge or the knowledge of the committee.

Recommendations.

This Association has not waited to be called upon but has submitted several recommendations to our school authorities. Some of these are: a sabbatical year; first assistant, a salary grade; that Teachers' Records be consolidated and kept in one place in the Hall of the Board of Education; that all adverse ratings and reports be made in writing and that the teacher be furnished with a copy of such ratings and reports.

McKee Bills.

Though the association has ventured to make certain suggestions along purely professional lines it has carefully refrained from entering, as an association, into the field of school politics.

An adroit effort to place it on record on the McKee Bills resulted merely in passing a resolution that the President notify the President of the Board of Education, the Mayor, the Governor, the President of the Senate, and the Speaker of the Assembly that "The High School Teachers' Association has taken no action on the McKee Bills, either for them or against them."

Acknowledgments.

The President wishes to thank publicly those who have so generously helped him. He believes that members of the Association have felt free to give him advice and counsel. He has felt just as free about accepting, modifying, or rejecting it.

The President owes particular mention, in addition to those already mentioned, to Mr. Alexander L. Pugh of the High School of Commerce for valuable suggestions and help along the lines of Scientific Management; to Clarence D. Kingsley, now of Massachusetts Board of Education, for work on High School Relations with Colleges and in our relations with the National Educational Association, and to Mr. Aaron I. Dotey, of De Witt Clinton High School, for efficient, generous service and for his obtaining one of our most inspiring speakers, the Hon. Frank Moss.

*The Credentials Committee later disqualified all six.

The President believes that the success of this Association, as of all organizations, depends upon the spirit of mutual helpfulness, between members and officers. If you have any good ideas, pass them along; if they are used full credit will be given you. A good executive needs (1) a few good ideas of his own, with the ability to recognize good ideas of others; (2) the ideas of many others, and (3) the help of others in carrying out these ideas.

The President has thoroughly enjoyed his work. He has done much of his thinking and planning during the two hours per day he spends in traveling to and from his school work. He believes that it is restful to change work.

November 21, 1913. WILLIAM T. MORREY.

REPORT OF THE COMMITTEE ON SECONDARY EDUCATION OF THE HIGH SCHOOL TEACHERS' ASSOCIATION, NEW YORK CITY.

To the President of the High School Teachers' Association:

In the year, February, 1910-January, 1911, three thousand pupils were lost to the high school system of the City of New York from three of its large, but not its largest, high schools. The schools were the Morris High School (enrolling boys and girls), the Boys' High School of Brooklyn and the Girls' High School also of Brooklyn. The percentage of pupils lost varied from 30 per cent. in one school to 37 per cent. in another.

These three high schools were selected for study because of their being good representatives of schools giving the "general" course, which covers the subjects of language, mathematics, history, science, etc. These schools are also well established in their respective communities, and enjoy exceptional reputations for the excellence of their scholarship.

The largest of the schools is the Morris High School. It is located in the Borough of the Bronx. This school draws its boys and girls from localities of extremely varied character. Some come from crowded tenements, others from homes in the better appointed apartment houses, and still others from houses in the suburban districts. The pupils belong to practically all the races composing the cosmopolitan population of the city.

The Boys' High School and the Girls' High School are much older schools than Morris. They are located near one another, and draw pupils from much the same area, as well as from families of similar economic and social position. The range of wealth represented, however, is probably as great as in Morris, and the variety of races in attendance is similarly numerous.

The Boys' High School and the Girls' High School are surrounded with high schools giving similar courses, as well as with high schools of other kinds. The fact that Brooklyn has a Commercial High School and a Manual Training High School, beside technical (crafts) and semi-technical private schools of high standing, while Bronx possesses none of these, doubtless bears important relation to certain facts indicated in the findings of the committee.

A great deal has been said and written about the extent and the causes of "mortality" or losses in registration in the high schools. It is a very simple matter to determine the extent of the loss in any school for any given time, or for the several terms in the course, or even for any month in any term in the course. This the committee has done and indicated by graphs in terms of percentage in certain of the charts published herewith. (See p. 17 and following.)

But when one approaches the study of the **causes** for pupils leaving the high schools, the difficulties in the way of obtaining an accurate solution of the problem are very great. Many interrelated individual, family and social factors enter into the situation and play their parts with varying emphasis. A category of "causes of leaving" can only approximate completeness. That fact coupled with the fact that parents may say pupils are leaving for certain reasons when quite different ones are the real ones, makes it continually impossible to learn the exact truth. If it were possible to visit and become acquainted with the families of all the pupils leaving the high schools, a closer approximation to ascertaining the real causes for pupils leaving would of course be possible. But the expenditure of time and energy involved in a work of that kind would hardly yield commensurate results.

In the State of New York the law requires that before a child can be excused from attendance at school, he must pass through the fifth grade and must be at least fourteen years of age. One hundred and thirty days of attendance in school must also stand to his credit within the first twelve months after his thirteenth birthday. If the pupil's parents or guardian desire him to leave school at any time between the ages of fourteen and sixteen, the Board of Health must issue so-called "working papers." Working papers are required by law for a child, even though he is to remain at home while engaged in a gainful occupation. Theoretically, employers (even parents) of children under sixteen are liable to prosecution and fine if papers have not been taken out, but in practice the "truancy" bureau of the Department of Education is without the power to enforce the law.

For the purposes of this investigation, the reasons for leaving are grouped under six heads: (1) on account of going to a private school; (2) on account of personal illness; (3) on account of home conditions; (4) on account of going to work; (5) on account of removal from the city, and (6) for unknown reasons. It is obvious that the reasons given for leaving may not be genuine. Pupils may be tired of school. They may have entered at first because it was easy and little was expected of them. They may yearn for wider activity, with its promise of money return and personal independence. Their parents may be unable to forego their economic assistance. The pupils may be mentally unadapted to book work, and willing to take any risk to sever relations with an intolerable environment. Lack of sympathy from parents or teachers, sharp criticism and complaint may discourage some.

In the light of what has been said, it would be profitable to examine the character of the causes of leaving as given by pupils. Some of the apparent causes may really be results. This might be especially true of "going to a private school," because of the lack of adaptation of a four-year course to the economic urgency of the pupil's needs. Illness is often obviously a result rather than a cause in origin. This is especially true of girls. Teachers are probably too cynical about trusting the statements of pupils who give that reason for leaving. It would be strange if the strenuous character of high school duties did not work havoc with pupils in unstable physical condition. "Home conditions" is often a genuine first cause, although it is doubtless sometimes a subterfuge of the unadaptive girls. "Going to work" is ofttimes a result, especially in the case of boys, many of whom are taken out of school and sent to work as a punishment for their being unadapted to the school course (or for the school course being unadapted to them). Thus, it is difficult to estimate the extent to which the ultimate causes operate in bringing about the loss of pupils to the high schools. The first part of this study is based upon the acceptance of the statements of parents and children as to why the children left. The second part is based upon the statements of pupils taken under other circumstances.

I

Your committee examined the record of discharges of pupils that was made during the year from February 1, 1910, to January 31, 1911. In examining the discharge books of the Boys' High School and the Morris High School, the following categories of facts were established for each pupil. The books of Girls' High were studied less fully.

Boy or Girl	Month of Discharge	Term of Discharge	Age	Age and Cause	Age and No. of Failures on Leaving

With these data the committee could command all the facts singly or in correlation. After the history of each case was recorded in this fashion, numberless calculations were made to express the facts in the necessary relations.

During the year the Morris High School had an average monthly registration of 3,780 pupils. The Boys' High School had 1,787, and the Girls' High School, 3,146. Of these the Morris High School lost 1,410 or 37.3 per cent., the Boys' High School 539 or 30.2 per cent., and the Girls' High School, 1,044 or 33.2 per cent. Every one of these pupils was lost to the New York public high school system. Transfers to other New York City public high schools were, of course, not included in the count.

Chart A shows the percentage of loss in registration in each term of the course in each half of the year. The percentage is high in the first, second, third and fourth terms (I, II, III, IV), but decreases gradually to a small percentage at the end of the course. The high percentage shown in the graph of the Boys' High School in the eighth term, September to January term, is due to the fact that many boys, having received the requisite number of "Regents" points, leave without graduation, and even without giving notice to the school. They enter professional schools where graduation from a high school is not required.

The higher percentage of discharge shown in the September to January term is analyzed in Charts B, C^1 and C^2. No doubt the intervening summer vacation creates the opportunity for many pupils to sever their connection with the high school, and that without giving any reason for going. As a rule, inquiries sent from the school bring no reply.

Chart B shows the percentage of loss by months throughout the terms in the course for the entire year. This percentage is based on the registration for each month of the number of pupils taking the work of each term in the course. The months are indicated under the Roman numerals standing for each term by the initial capital letters of the months from February to June in the upper portion of the chart, and of the months from September to January in the lower portion. With few exceptions the highest percentage of loss occurs in the first month of the terms, especially in September. In that month all who were drawn away by some other interest in the summer vacation were discharged, except in those cases of discharge that were recorded in October for the same cause.

In Charts C^1 and C^2 the graphs indicate in the totals of the percentages the total discharge of each term in the course. That is to say, the number of discharges for each term in the course stands as 100 per cent. The loss of each month for each term of work is represented in the graph as the per cent. of the total loss of the term of the course. These charts show in a striking way that the great losses in either half year are in the first month of the term, that is, in February and in September.

Charts D^1 and D^2 exhibit the correlation of the cause of leaving and the age at the time of leaving. The interval of age are indicated in half-years, because it was thought that the event of leaving school might have some important connection with the attainment of the fourteenth birthday. The age as put down for each pupil was calculated to the nearest year or half-year. The six columns for causes are repeated under each age division. The graph in each column stands for a percentage of the total number leaving at that age.

The large percentage of discharges from the Boys' High School for which no cause was assigned interferes with deductions from the graphs of these charts. It appears from the examination of the graphs of the Morris boys of the several ages that a rather high percentage varying from about ten to forty leave the high school to go to some private school. At practically every age interval a much higher percentage of girls than boys leave that school for this reason. Possibly some pupils go to private schools having a similar course of study. However, there seem to be few of these in the Borough of the Bronx, while there are many private commercial schools in that part of the city.

The percentage of those who leave on account of personal illness varies from 0 to 22. Beginning at fifteen years the percentage of girls who leave for reason of personal illness predominates continuously over the percentage of boys leaving for the same cause.

At every age interval the percentage of girls leaving because they are "needed at home" is greatly in excess of the percentage of boys leaving for the same cause. This is what would be expected. Except at the extremes of thirteen and one-half years and seventeen, the percentage of girls needed at home is less than the percentage of girls leaving to go to private schools. The percentage of boys of the Morris High School needed at home does not exceed five, and is usually close to zero, while the percentage of Morris girls leaving because they are needed at home approaches or exceeds thirty.

At practically every age interval there are very many more boys than girls leaving for the reason of "going to work." The high percentages of boys leaving for that reason are at fourteen, fifteen, fifteen and one-half and sixteen. The highest percentages are at fifteen and fifteen and one-half, when 55 per cent. go from Morris High School and 31 per cent. from Boys' High School. The percentage of boys leaving at sixteen and one-half is also very high, 30 to 35 per cent., indicating that the need or the desire to enter a gainful occupation is not restricted by the legal requirement of taking out working-papers. Indeed, the coming of the opportunity to leave at fourteen years of age with working-papers is not attended by an exodus as great as occurs in later years. The significance of these points is that certain factors are operating without reference to the law. The probabilities are that these factors are the economic need of parents, the greater economic availability of the boy older than fourteen, the desire for economic independence, the mal-adjustment of school and pupil, and the vagueness of the connection of the school with life as the pupil sees life opening out before **him**. Certain evidence for this interpretation is presented in a later section of this report.

The percentage of pupils leaving the city has no special significance in this study. It is included for the sake of completeness.

The large percentages of pupils who succeed in severing their connection with the school system without giving any reason whatsoever indicate that the official hold of the system on the children is far from being effective. Moreover, the signs are very clear that the thousands of pupils who leave the New York high schools every year for "unknown" reasons include those boys and girls who have the least respect of any of the pupils for academic ideals. The state of mind of these future citizens should be a matter of great concern to all who are engaged in practical education.

Charts E^1 and E^2 show the correlation between the term of the course in which the pupils left and the number of failures in their scholarship standing as estimated at the marking period just preceding the date of leaving. The charts indicate the percentages leaving with the clear record of no failures, and with one, two, three, four failures at the preceding marking period, and with no record (x).

The factors shown under I, the first term in the course, exhibit a strong contrast with those of the later terms. In the first term great numbers leave within the first ten weeks or before they have received a record of scholarship standing. Many leave with two, three and four failures in their record. Few leave with no failures. Without doubt the meaning of these facts is mal-adjustment. The difference in methods and ideals in the elementary and high schools is too great, and thousands drop by the wayside.

Beginning with the second term a striking change becomes manifest. In the last seven terms the greatest percentages leave with a clear record of no failures or with one or two failures. This means that complete or partial adjustment has been attained—for the ones that are left. Furthermore, it indicates that pupils do not leave in those terms primarily because they cannot do the work.

II

The committee presents here the study of about eleven hundred letters written on request by pupils in several high schools in the city. It will be observed that the letters give a great deal of valuable information bearing in one way or another on the problem of why pupils leave the high schools. The co-operation of the Departments of English made it possible to obtain so large a body of pupil opinion.

In the DeWitt Clinton High School seventy-two boys wrote letters describing the cases of other boys who had left school. The analysis of these letters has been prepared by Mr. Colman D. Frank of this committee:

Reasons for Leaving DeWitt Clinton High School.

1. Desire for financial independence because brothers, sisters or friends make money 12
2. Mental incapacity, especially for Algebra 26
3. Need of helping financially at home 25
4. Forced to help in the store at home; have no time to study.... 2
5. Parents unsympatheic with school ideals 3
6. Took courses not fitted to ability........................... 6
7. Sickness 0
8. Left because school does not fit for business...............11
9. Too large for his class mates................................ 2
10. Discouraged by teachers 9
11. Forced to stay for a time by parents; win them over and quit, eager for business 2
12. Wanted to get into business more quickly; went to business school 2
13. Did not like it,—too tame 13
14. Got jobs in summer, and stayed out 5
15. Could not afford carfare 3
16. Too much home-work 4
17. Too great interest in the opposite sex; no mind for study..... 4

NOTE.—In some cases more than one reason is given as applying to a particular boy.

Comments Taken From Letters.

1. "Henry ——'s father runs a dance hall. Henry has to tend it every night from 8 to 12. That means that he must study afternoons, but Henry loves baseball and prefers to play ball in the afternoon. Hence, failed in school, and quit."

2. "James ——'s father has a saloon under a boxing club's quarters. James tends bar and helps at the door on boxing bout nights. School is a very tame, childish place in comparison. He gets disgusted and quits.

3. "James ——'s father runs a cafe and cabaret-restaurant on the East Side. James tends bar, oversees the waiters and otherwise helps every night. He is out of all sympathy with his history, mathematics and French in the morning; soon leaves."

4. "Herman ——'s father never had an education, but he struck it rich in the ladies' underwear business. He was determined that his boy should have an education. At home Herman heard nothing but "dollars," how many his father made, how many his mother spent."

5. "James ——, a particularly promising Italian boy of high ideals had to leave school because his father ran away, leaving a wife and a large family penniless. James was their only hope of support. He gave up his chances of a career to help them."

6. "Hyman —— was an orphan. After his parents died, Hyman had to do the housework, while his older sister and brother went to work to earn money for the family. In the morning Hyman had to cook the breakfast, wash the dishes, dust and clean. He had to wash the faces and hands of his little brother and sister, and start them off to school. He came to school late very often, and had to stay in the tardy room. At last it got too hard for him to do all the housework, and have to take punishment for being tardy, so he quit school."

7. "Israel —— left school because he could not get sympathy. He supported himself and his little brother by selling papers at Columbus Circle. He worked hard, but he was too tired to study hard, and often did not have his lessons. He thought that the teachers who knew how hard he worked were cruel not to let him off from the lessons assigned to the other boys. They expected the same from him as from the Riverside Drive boys. So in disgust he left school."

8. "Louis ——left school because he could not afford to pay carfare. He also stopped school because he said the teachers gave him too much home-work. He had no time to get fresh air. Now he is helping father in the business."

9. "—— wanted to go to school. He was good in his lessons, but it was on account of his older sisters. They were working, and they brought money into the house. When night came he did his lessons, but his sisters picked up arguments with him. They said that they did not want to support him, that he was man enough to look after himself. They refused to give their wages in the house until he would go to work. Their parents being old, had to do as they were told, and he left school."

10. "J. D. was in the fifth term of the High School of Commerce. His parents were well off. When he started in that school he decided to remain until he graduated. After staying there a year he grew sick of school life, because after finishing his home-work, he had five hours each day in which he had nothing to do. His father forbade him to go out for athletic teams, and kept him as a baby.

"When he was promoted to the fifth term, a teacher in the school told him he had a very fine vacancy in a wholesale silk house. J. D. inquired about the position, and found it to be as good as any boy of his age could get. He accepted the position, and now continues his studies at the Evening School. The idea he had in accepting this position was that by the time he would have graduated from Commerce, he will be advanced in his position, thereby having a better start in business than if he had started work after graduation from Commerce."

11. "About three years ago when I was in the second term in the DeWitt Clinton High School, I was greatly astonished to find that a personal friend of mine in the same class was intending to leave at the end of the term. As he had been doing very good work, passing in all his subjects with honor, this came as a great surprise. Naturally, being his friend, I inquired from him his reasons for doing it.

"It seemed that he was tired of going to school, and wanted to make money for himself. His older brother was on the vaudeville stage, and he intended to go there himself, in conjunction with his brother and a friend. This may seem absurd for a second term high school boy, but this lad could dance, sing and perform as well as his brother who was receiving $35.00 a week for his salary, that was without travelling expenses. The result was that my friend joined his brother, with whom he now is, and became a vaudeville actor at the age of fifteen."

Wadleigh High School 120 girls wrote about friends who had left the high school. This analysis was made by Miss Louise Thompson of this committee:

Reasons for Leaving Wadleigh High School.

1.	Course did not appeal	11
2.	Personal illness	7
3.	Worked too hard in school	25
4.	Wanted to go to work	8
5.	Real poverty	43
6.	Too old	1
7.	Too tall	1
8.	To study art	2
9.	Trouble with teacher	1
10.	To be married	1
11.	Too lazy	10

Comments Taken From Letters.

1. "My friend, Elsie ——, said that the reasons she left high school were because the lessons were too hard, and she thought four years was too long to go to school after she had been in the elementary school eight years. She also said she always felt sick riding in the cars."

2. "Mary —— left high school because she could not afford the expense of dressing like the other girls. This made her feel very bad, because the wealthier girls snubbed her."

3. "Mary —— left while in the first term of the high school

because she was not going to be a teacher, and her parents agreed with her that the high school work was unnecessary. She now goes to work. The family is well-to-do.

4. "Dora —— left in the first term of high school, because she had too much housework to do at home. She was a delicate girl."

5. "Julia —— was a kind of dumb girl, that is, she could not grasp the meaning of things quickly. Near the middle of the term she told me that she was not going to stay in high school, because she had too much home-work. She said she knew that she would not be promoted, so sooner than be left back she would leave school and go to some business school."

6. "My friend, Sally, and I had been going to high school for six months when one day I noticed that she seemed rather sad and depressed. I asked her what was the trouble, and she told me that she had to leave school the following week and go to work. She then said that her father had not been working for several months, and now that her mother was ill and was not able to work, she would have to try to earn some money to help keep the house."

7. "Mary —— left high school because she could not afford to get a gymnasium suit."

8. "Amy —— left school because she was a child of poverty, and her parents needed her assistance in the care of the family."

9. "Ella —— became discouraged because she wanted to have a nice time, but she could not study and have as nice a time as she wished to have."

In the Jamaica High School 475 letters were written on the subject, "Why I Am In School." These letters were credited as theme work in English. Incidentally, they gave the Department of English much useful information about the pupils. Like all the letters examined by the committee they ring true.

The analysis of the Jamaica letters shows forty-one factors that are tending to keep the pupils in school, or tending to cause their separation from it. In the order of their frequency in being mentioned, the first nine are as follows:

1. Desire to obtain an education for social and intellectual reasons.
2. Decision to take high school course made by parents.
3. Held in high school by the good times they have, and by having friends there (mentioned especially by girls).
4. Discouraged at times, but stimulated by parents.
5. Ambitious to become teachers.
6. Ambitious to prepare for business (mentioned usually by pupils taking the Commercial course).
7. Desire to enter college.
8. Discouraged at times, but encouraged by teachers.
9. Staying in high school, not knowing what else to do.

In the Boys' High School, of Brooklyn, the pupils wrote on the topic, "Why I Find It Difficult (or Easy) to Remain in High School." The analysis of the 472 letters was made by Mr. John A. Swenson of this committee. Of the 472 boys who wrote, 328 found it easy to remain in the high school, 144 found it difficult.

Reasons Why It Is Difficult to Remain in High School.

1.	Financial difficulties	52
2.	Because of having outside work	40
3.	Too much home-work	30
4.	Poor facilities for study at home	30
5.	No time for recreation	12
6.	Sickness of parents	5
7.	Absence through illness	5
8.	Poor eye-sight	7
9.	Deafness	2
10.	Greater interest in outside activities	8
11.	Difficulty in special subjects	14
12.	Lack of sympathy on the part of parents	5
13.	Lack of sympathy on the part of teachers	18
14.	Absences due to observance of religious holidays	2
15.	Too many periods of work	3
16.	Transferred from another school	1

The Stress of Economic Conditions.

Financial difficulties are by far the greatest hindrance to completing a high school course. Comments from essays written by the boys on "Why I Find It Difficult (or Easy) to Remain in High School" will illustrate how great these difficulties are. One boy writes: "There are many things that make it difficult for me to attend high school, but the first and fore most reason is poor financial circumstances. We are a family of eight souls. Now, there are two persons working to support the family. My father who works in a shop earns eleven dollars per week, and my brother makes about sixteen. My father has stopped working for the last eight weeks. If we should average up his earnings for the whole year we should find that he earns about eight dollars a week."

Another says: "There are eight in our family, and the sole supporter is an older brother. My father being an old man is now unable to work."

Still another writes: "It is indeed hard for me to stay in school. My father is weak in body, sick, tired out and in financial straits. He cannot afford to have me in school. I realize this, and it worries me. I want to get out and help him."

Another boy has no support other than what he himself earns. He tells of it thus: "I certainly do find it hard to stay in high school. With no parents or relatives to support me, I have to do the best I can. Some cold winter mornings I have to work from three to six o'clock, and from four to seven in the evening selling newspapers to different stands."

To School Work Is Added Other Work.

Out of the financial stringency in the home arises the second difficulty in continuing in high school—the boy is engaged in outside work, with the exception of a few cases where the boy is saving his money for a college education, or where the parents think that a little knowledge of business along with his school's work will do him good, the boy earns money to help support himself or help in the support of the rest of the family. That their lives are by no means along paths of roses can be seen from the following extracts from essays.: "Every afternoon when I come from school, I have to go to work to make our living, and I do not get home till seven o'clock. If I am detained in school and do not get to work till after 3:30 I have to stay as long after seven o'clock as I am late. Every Friday evening I work until ten o'clock, and all day Saturday until twelve at night."

Here is a story with a different side to it: "I find it hard to stay in high school for the reason that I have to work outside of school. My parents are well able to send me to school, but they say that I should get some real practice in outside life that will prepare me for the future. They say that if I gain a little knowledge of the business world while going to school, it will be so much to my benefit when I graduate." Cases of this kind are rare. In almost every case the boy has to work because of poor financial circumstances in the home. Another boy tells of getting up early to study his lessons and goes on to say: "I must not stay in for any teacher at two-thirty. I go home and practice music till four o'clock. I then begin to give lessons in algebra, geometry, English, violin and piano. The reason why I give these various lessons is a simple one. It is this—when I graduate from high school I want to go to college, and in order to do this I must make the necessary money." We find these boys engaged in a variety of occupations. There are newsboys and errand boys. Some work in stores, others drive wagons. One plays a musical instrument at a recreation center in the evening, another plays at a moving picture show.

It is generally characteristic of those cases where the boy has to do outside work that there is no complaint of too much home-work. Many say that they find their time limited for doing the daily home-work, but few grumble about the amount. Of course, an occasional one who is slow but also a good student finds the home-work heavy. Let us select from the information given by the boys. One says, "I simply cannot do home-work, and home-work is everything in Boys' High School. I keep putting it off, and the end is that I go to school next morning without any home-work." Another writes, "Though I have most of the advantages that a boy could wish for, I find it hard to stay in high school. The main reason is that I find the work too hard for me. I cannot seem to concentrate my mind on my work when I try to study. When I recite in classroom I cannot remember what I have studied." This from another: "The most important reason why I find it hard to stay in high school is the required home-work. The Latin and the physics take me about two and one-half hours. When the two hours for English, German and history are added, most of my free time is gone."

Here is the view of an optimist: "I have to work after school. Therefore, I have no time whatever to go out for any recreation on any day in the week except Sunday. As to my studies, I get along finely and pass with high per cents because I devote all my spare time to my home-work."

Lack of Privacy for Studying.

There is another difficulty in the way of preparing home-work. The rooms in the homes of the poor are small and few in number. It is impossible to find in most of them a place quiet enough for concentration of mind. Then, too, the added expense of heating and lighting a room other than that used by the rest of the family is often a prohibitive burden. One boy writes, "I have to study in a room which is noisy, for it is natural for children to laugh and play. This prevents me from concentrating my thoughts on what I am reading." Another writes, "Lack of space in my home makes it impossible for me to have a separate room, and so I must study in the midst of noise. Although I appreciate the fact that the members of my family try to diminish the noise as much as possible, still the conditions are not as I would like to have them." Still another says, "I find it is very hard to prepare my lessons at home, as I am constantly being disturbed by visitors. I have found out by experience that I can do twice as much in school as at home." One other, "The facilities for study at home are not what they should be. It is true I may shut myself up in some room, and devote myself to learning my lessons. But it is not very comfortable to peruse Virgil or Moliere with the thermometer at two below zero. Therefore, I must hearken to a veritable babel of voices—such torture to undergo—though the entire infernal racket is created by two of the gentler sex."

Although many boys are employed out of school as errand boys, etc., getting fresh air and exercise enough, still they have very little relaxation. One boy states his case thus: "I work after school and do not get enough time for play, though I do get plenty of fresh air." A boy, who works for his father, says that very often he does not begin to study till after ten o'clock. Even then he is disturbed at times. He works on his studies till one o'clock. He says, "It is not unusual for me to remain awake till three o'clock. Sleeping so little and working so hard, I find it difficult to get up in the morning on time. As a result I never have a minute for recreation or exercise."

Family and Personal Ill-Health.

Another difficulty in the way of some boys in the high school is the ill-health of the parents. In these cases the boys have many added duties in helping with the housework or with the parents' work. In one family the mother is an invalid, and the father and the boy have to do the housework and prepare the meals. Some parents are old. The father of one boy is blind; the father of another is lame.

Some of the pupils are always in poor health. Others have had protracted illnesses, which have kept them out of school. These conditions cause them to lose work and thus fail in one or more subjects. In order to make up their deficiencies, they "double" in those subjects; that is, they take a subject in the grade in which they have failed, and also in the next higher grade.

A boy writes of all the advantages he has, a fine home, every facility for study, numerous reference books, well educated relatives and friends; and absolutely no domestic duties. Despite all these apparent aids," he says, "I have one drawback—ill-health. After being absent several days, it becomes necessary to make up lost work. The process of making up the work, much careful planning and considerable patience, in order that from overwork I may not fall back into the same sort of sickness." Another boy writes, "One reason why I find it difficult to remain in high school is that in November I was sick for three weeks before the mid-terms. As a result I did not pass English or history that term. Last term I doubled in history, and this term I am doubling in English."

Poor eyesight makes high school difficult. For anyone so afflicted, board work, night study and the constant focusing of the eyes in reading from books aggravate the trouble. Many pupils suffer from this misfortune to a greater or less degree, but only seven mention it in their list of difficulties. "The chief cause of my difficulty is my poor eyesight. My eyes 'water' so that I am compelled to put aside my book for several minutes at a time or else keep looking up from the book." Another boy says he must finish all his work by daylight, as he cannot use his eyes in artificial light.

Deafness is a great drawback. One boy says, "In those subjects which do not depend so much on hearing as on reading I am very proficient. But those like chemistry and physics are very hard for me to master. I learn all that is contained in the books but not what the instructors explain to the class." Another deaf boy says, "As I do not hear well enough to understand discussions, I am forced to depend almost entirely on books."

Outside Interests.

Outside interests make the high school course difficult for some. Many boys would like to leave and go into business. One boy says that on account of time spent in athletics he has little time for study. Another blames the track team for taking a great deal of his time. One has social aspirations which interfere with his more serious work. He has a love for entertaining his friends and being entertained by them. **A great many are restless to be out in the world making their own living.**

Difficulties with the Curriculum.

Of course few boys have the same aptitude for all subjects, and some have very little aptitude for two or even for one subject. There is hardly a subject in the curriculum (physical training and music are not mentioned) that some boys do not have trouble with. The rule that a pupil must complete one year of work in two years, or two years' work in three years, causes trouble for some. Language and mathematics are subjects found difficult by most. More find the classics harder than the modern languages.

The Need of Sympathy and Understanding.

It is rare that we find a lack of sympathy on the part of parents. Only five complain of this. One boy tells of his poor marks and of the warnings sent by his grade adviser, "but they only served the purpose of bringing on civil discord." He says with much glee that although his failure in several subjects was foretold, he passed in everything." In another instance a boy works hard, and still receives no encouragement at home. "The thing which is discouraging me most is the inclination of my folks to tell me that a high school education is a waste of time."

Although few complain of lack of sympathy at home, there is much complaint of lack of sympathy in school. It is often true that teachers give adverse criticism where a little help and encouragement would set the pupil straight, and give him an incentive for greater effort in the future. However, to a certain degree the lack of sympathy exists only in the imagination of the pupil. The teacher in a moment of impatience speaks sharply, forgetting soon what has occurred. But the boy does not forget. He takes the reproof to mean that the teacher has a special grudge against him.

On reading of the troubles of school boys one would think that lack of harmony between pupils and teachers must interfere seriously with work. The methods, the manners and even the personal appearance of the teachers are criticised in the letters received by us. Here is a frankly stated view that strongly suggests the intellectual tragedy of school life: "I feel out of place in high school. The curriculum is bad enough. Such dry subjects as Latin are more than I can bear. The teachers are to blame for this. Instead of teaching us Latin as an art, telling us of Cicero's oratory, the condition of Rome, they will speak ten minutes on whether a clause is conditional, substantive or what not. It bores my mind. I feel that reading a good book is better than such trash. The teachers only give us their rules and grammar, not the beauties and benefits that can be derived from their respective subjects. They make the boys memorize books, nothing more. The —— teacher uses such slang and colloquial phrases that I really blush and feel like reporting him to the principal. The history teachers do not keep in touch with the political and economic topics of the times. They only want the facts that are given in the book."

Such an arraignment of educational practice made by a pupil can not be ignored. We that are members of the profession know that the boy speaks the truth, although we may not hold ourselves primarily responsible for conditions thus pointed out.

Summary.

1. In one year three public high schools in New York City registering in all nearly 9,000 pupils lost 3,000, one-third the total number enrolled.

2. The solution of the problem of why pupils leave school is attended with considerable difficulties, because of the complexity of the human factors involved.

3. The reasons for leaving school as recorded for the 3,000 pupils are grouped in this study under six heads: (1) to go to a private school; (2) personal illness; (3) on account of home conditions; (4) to go to work; (5) removal from the city; (6) unknown.

4. Some of the causes given by pupils when leaving are upon analysis found to be effects or results, rather than causes.

5. The greates losses in registration occur in the early terms of the course.

6. In each term of the year and for each term of the course the largest percentage are discharged in the first month, indicating that many leave at the end of the preceding term, or (in the case of the September discharges) during the summer vacation.

7. A greater percentage of girls than boys leave school to enter private schools, probably because most private schools are commercial or business schools. And more girls than boys are employed as secretaries.

8. The percentage of girls who leave for reasons of personal illness is sometimes high; the percentage of boys who leave for that reason is low.

9. Many more girls than boys give the reason, "needed at home."

10. The greatest loss of registration among boys for a known or assigned reason takes place at the age of fifteen and one-half years, for the reason of going to work.

11. The coming of the fourteenth birthday for boys is not found to be attended by the great exodus to go to work that has been presumed to occur.

12. The large number who succeed in severing their relation with the high school without giving any reason indicates in part, inefficient business methods on the part of the school, but chiefly widespread indifference to the school as an institution.

13. Of those who leave the high schools in their first term few leave with a good record in scholarship, while large numbers leave with two, three and four failures, indicating mal-adjustment. Irregular attendance is very apt to accompany these failures.

14. Of those who leave in the second and later terms the greater number leave with no failures or with one or at most two failures, indicating also that other factors than failure to pass are operating.

15. The letters from pupils indicate that economic necessity is a potent factor is causing pupils to leave the high school to go to work, although it is not the only factor operating to the same end.

16. Other conspicuous causes for pupils leaving are the desire for economic independence, the lack of apparent connection of school life with after-school life, and the absence of taste for purely book information..

17. The current educational ideal that as many boys and girls as possible should start to obtain a classical education is evidently engaged in a losing struggle with the stern economic and social facts of human existence. The obvious way to stop the struggle is to discover a flexible system of education that will meet the varying needs of our civilization as we find it to-day.

Committee on Secondary Education, H. S. T. A.:

HENRY R. LINVILLE, Chairman, Jamaica High School.
L. LOUISE ARTHUR, Bryant High School.
M. ELLEN BARKER, Girls' High School.
COLMAN D. FRANK, DeWitt Clinton High School.
A. EVERETT PETERSON, Morris High School.
JOHN A. SWENSON, Boys' High School.
LOUISE THOMPSON, Wadleigh High School.

CHART A

Percentage of Loss by Terms in the Course.

Graph for Morris High School, Boys and Girls, ——·——·——·——

Graph for Boys' High School ————————————————

Graph for Girls' High School..................................

The percentages represented in this chart are based on the average register of each term in the course, I to VIII. For example, the average register for the first term of the course in the Boys' High School (February to June, 1910) was 504. During the term February to June, 1910, 104 pupils were discharged. The per cent. of the loss on the average register was thus 20.6.

The percentages of loss for the several terms in the three schools are as follows:

	I	II	III	IV	V	VI	VII	VIII
Morris H. S.								
Feb.-June, '10	24.5	13.6	15.0	9.8	12.7	9.3	5.0	3.9
Sept., '10-Jan., '11..........	25.2	21.8	25.7	25.0	22.3	12.1	12.0	8.4
Boys' H. S.								
Feb.-June, '10	20.6	10.4	10.6	10.1	8.7	9.9	9.5	5.4
Sept., '10-Jan., '11.........	22.9	14.4	12.8	12.7	15.7	8.3	17.5	39.6
Girls' H. S.								
Feb.-June, '10	23.5	18.4	13.2	12.9	11.9	6.0	2.1	1.3
Sept., '10-Jan., '11.........	19.5	26.2	23.5	16.5	17.0	14.6	4.6	4.9

In the February-June term for all three schools the percentage of loss is very similar from the first to the last term in the course.

In the September, '10-January, '11, term there are wide divergences in Terms II, III and IV, the Boys' High School, being comparatively fortunate in holding its pupils in those terms. The high percentage of loss in the last term in the Boys' High School is due to many leaving to go to professional schools, as explained in text.

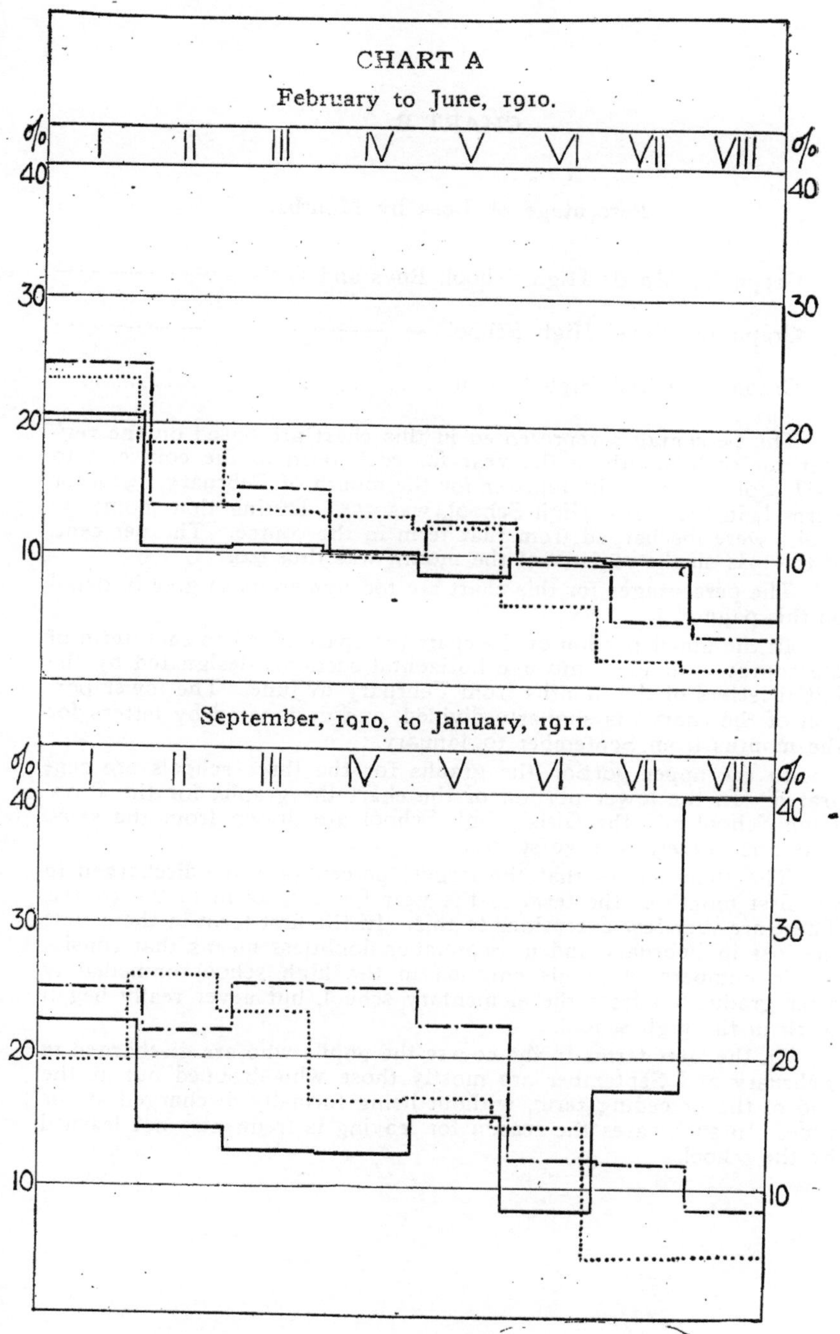
CHART A
February to June, 1910.
%
I II III IV V VI VII VIII
%
40
30
20
10
September, 1910, to January, 1911.
%
I II III IV V VI VII VIII
%
40
30
20
10

CHART B

Percentage of Loss by Months.

Graph for Morris High School, Boys and Girls, ——————

Graph for Boys' High School, ————————————

Graph for Girls' High School, ...

The percentages represented in this chart are based on the register for each month in the year for each term in the course, I to VIII. For example, the register for the month of February, 1910, for Term I, in the Boys' High School, was 555. During that month 50 pupils were discharged from that term in the course. The per cent. of the loss on the register of the month was thus 9.0.

The percentages for this chart are too numerous to give in detail on this page.

In the upper portion of the chart the space given to each term of the course is divided into five horizontal sections, designated by the initial letters of the months from February to June. The lower portion of the chartis is similarly divided, and designated by letters for the months from September to January.

In the upper portion the graphs for the three schools are separated. In the lower portion of the chart the graphs for the Boys' High School and the Girls' High School are drawn from the same base line, merely to save space.

The chart shows that the largest percentages are discharged in the first month of the term in the year for each term in the course. There are very few exceptions to this. In the first term in the course the loss in February and in September doubtless means that considerable numbers of pupils enrolled in the high school immediately after graduation from the elementary school, but never really began work in the high school.

In the later terms in the course the pupils who are discharged in February and September are mostly those who dropped out at the end of the preceding term, without being formally discharged at the time. In such cases the reason for leaving is frequently not learned by the school.

CHART B

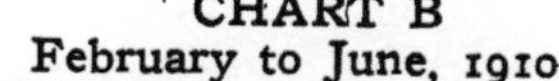

February to June, 1910.

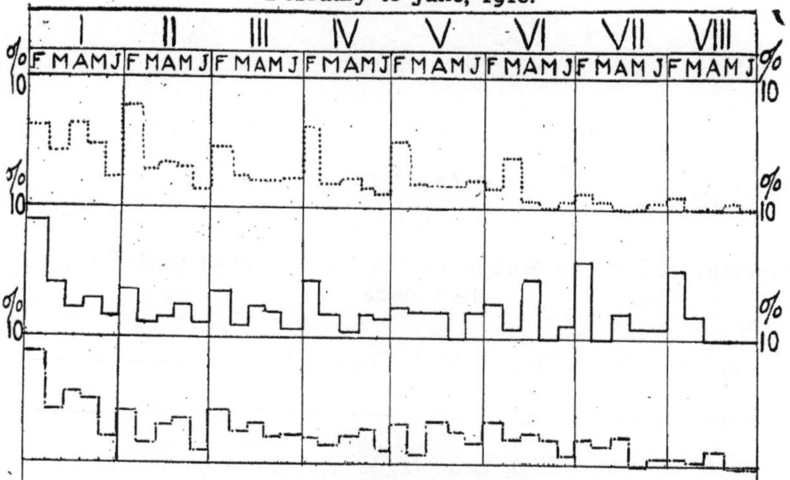

I II III IV V VI VII VIII

F M A M J F M A M J F M A M J F M A M J F M A M J F M A M J F M A M J F M A M J

September, 1910, to January, 1911.

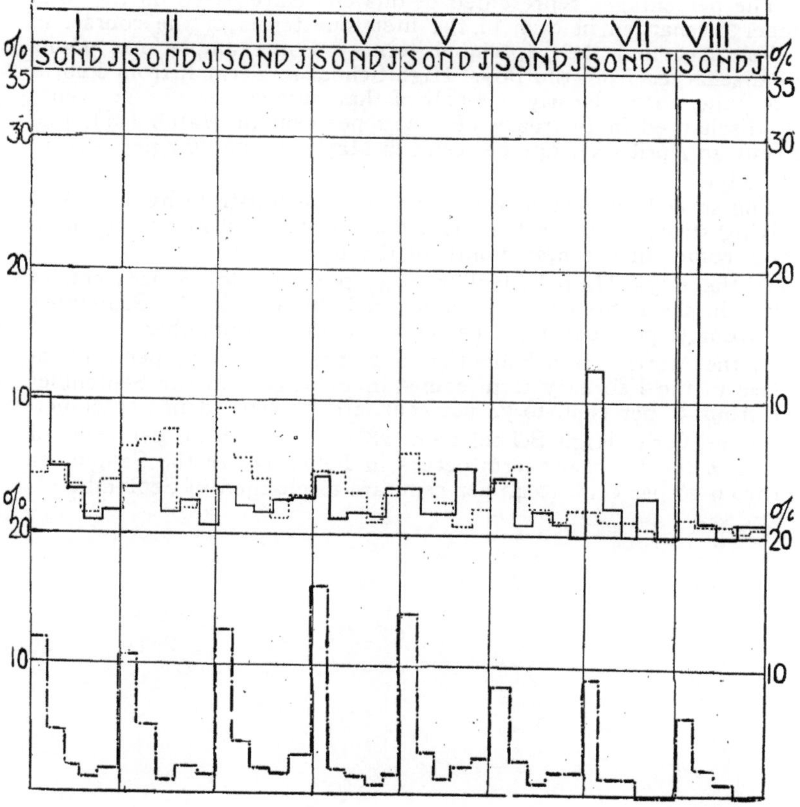

I II III IV V VI VII VIII

S O N D J S O N D J S O N D J S O N D J S O N D J S O N D J S O N D J S O N D J

CHART C[1]

Percentage of Loss by Months on the Total Loss of Each Term in the Course.

Graph for Morris High School, Boys and Girls, —·—·—·—·

Graph for Boys' High School, ————————————

Graph for Girls' High School, ...

The percentages represented in this chart are based on the total number discharged in each of the first four terms of the course, in the February and the September terms. For example, 104 pupils were discharged from the Boys' High School in Term I, from February to June, 1910. Nearly one-half of that number, or 48.1 per cent., were discharged in February (F), 20.2 per cent in March (M), 10.6 per cent. in April (A), 14.4 per cent. in May (M), and 6.7 per cent. in June (J).

The special purpose of this chart is to demonstrate by a method involving stronger contrast the fact that the greatest loss to the high schools comes in the first month of the term.

In the Boys' High School from 35 per cent. to 48 per cent. of the loss in the February term comes in February; in the September term, from 30 per cent. to 50 per cent. comes in September.

In the Morris High School from 20 per cent. to 35 per cent. of the loss in the February term comes in February; in the September term, from 51 per cent. to 74 per cent. are discharged in September.

In the Girls' High School from 28 per cent. to 49 per cent. of the loss in the February term occurs in February; in the September term from 26 per cent. to 42 per cent. are discharged in September.

CHART C[1]

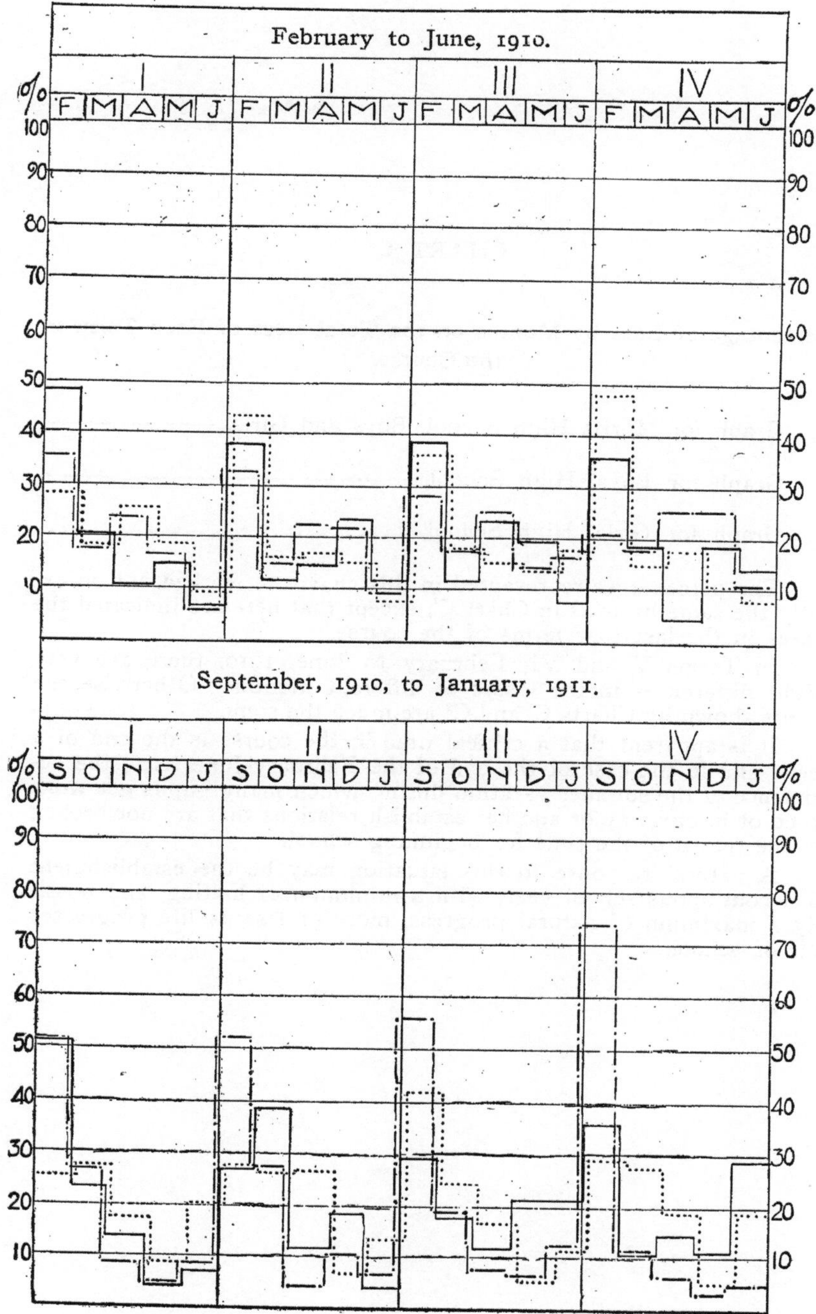
February to June, 1910.
I
II
III
IV
%
F M A M J F M A M J F M A M J F M A M J
100
90
80
70
60
50
40
30
20
10
September, 1910, to January, 1911.
S O N D J S O N D J S O N D J S O N D J

CHART C^2

Percentage of Loss by Months on the Total Loss of Each Term in the Course.

Graph for Morris High School, Boys and Girls, ——·——·——·

Graph for Boys' High School, ————————————

Graph for Girls' High School, ...

The percentages represented in this chart are worked out on exactly the same basis as in Chart C^1, except that here are indicated the losses in the last four terms of the course.

In Terms V and VI, February to June, 1910, there are very slight differences in the losses of different months. Otherwise the points shown by Charts C^1 and C^2 are much the some.

It is apparent that a critical time in the course is the end of a term, and in the case of the end of the February-June term, the occurrence of the summer vacation during which many pupils get work to do or in one way or another establish relations that are not broken by the return of the time for beginning school.

A natural response to this situation may be the establishment of a continuous school year, with a minimum of halting, and possibly a maximum of natural progress, more or less as life progresses out of school.

CHART C²

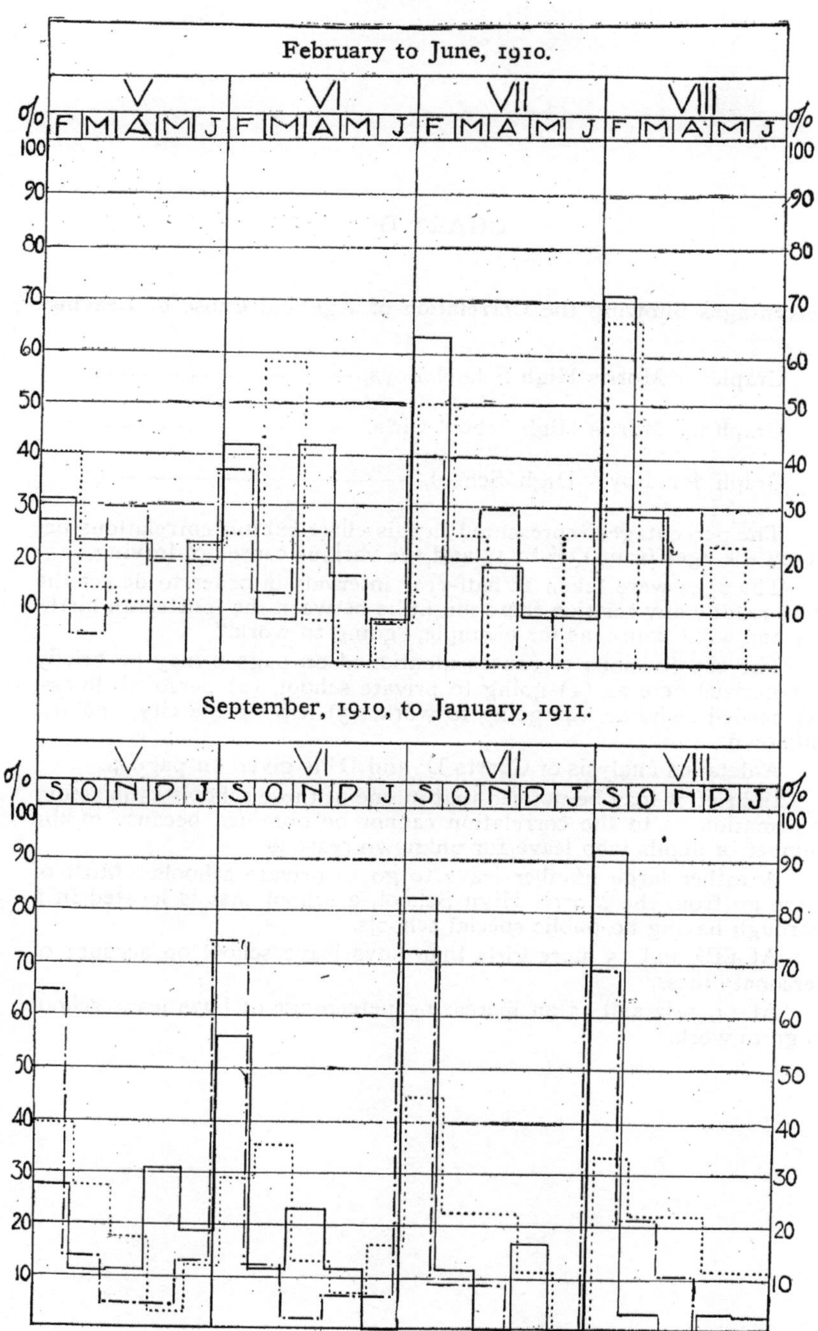
February to June, 1910.
V
VI
VII
VIII
%
F M A M J F M A M J F M A M J F M A M J
100
90
80
70
60
50
40
30
20
10
September, 1910, to January, 1911.
S O N D J S O N D J S O N D J S O N D J

CHART D¹

Percentages Showing the Correlation of Age and Cause of Leaving.

Graph for Morris High School Boys, — — — — — — — —

Graph for Morris High School Girls, - - - - - - - - - - - - - - -

Graph for Boys' High School, ————————————

The percentages represented in this chart exhibit correlations between the ages from 13½ to 15 and the various causes of leaving.

The ages were taken at half-year intervals in order to detect the more readily any relation there might be between the fourteenth birthday and some cause, as for example, "going to work."

The six divisions of causes mentioned on page 2 may be briefly summarized here as (1) going to private school, (2) personal illness, (3) needed at home, (4) going to work, (5) leaving the city, and (6) unknown.

A detailed analysis of Charts D¹ and D² is given on page 4.

In brief, it may be noticed that in one of these schools satisfactory information as to the correlation cannot be obtained because of the number of pupils who leave for unknown reasons.

A rather large number leave to go to private schools. Most of these go from the Morris High School, a school that is located in a Borough having no public special schools.

At 14½ and 15 more girls than boys leave school on account of personal illness.

At 14, 14½ and 15 an increasing percentage of boys leave school to go to work.

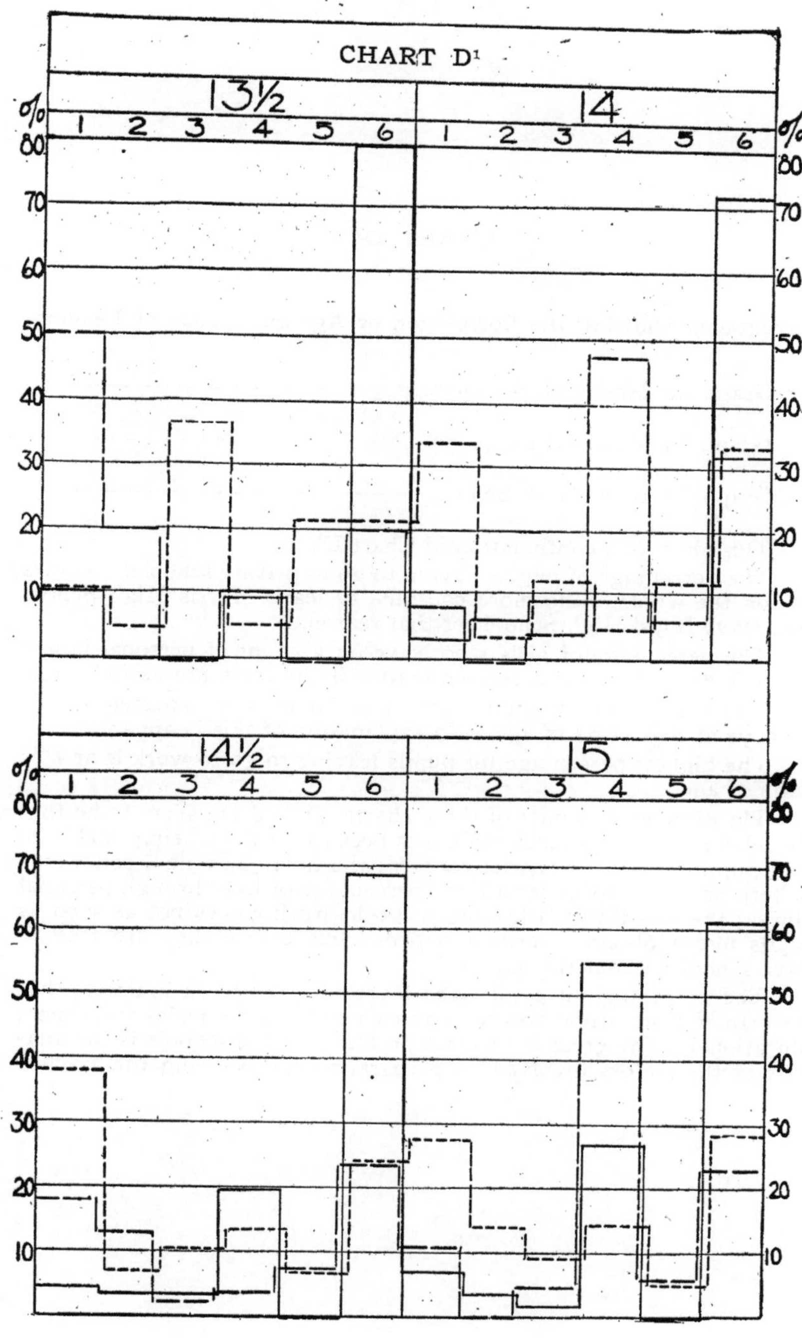
CHART D[1]
13½
14
14½
15
%
1
2
3
4
5
6
80
70
60
50
40
30
20
10

CHART D[2]

Percentages Showing the Correlation of Age and Cause of Leaving.

Graph for Morris High School Boys, — — — — — — — — —

Graph for Morris High School Girls, - - - - - - - - - - - - - - - -

Graph for Boys' High School, ————————————

This chart is a continuation of Chart D[1].

The percentage of pupils leaving to go to private schools, becomes less on the whole, altho more continue to leave Morris High School than leave Boys' High School for that reason.

The percentage of girls who leave on account of personal illness becomes as high as 22, a serious matter if the facts are as indicated.

The percentage of pupils needed at home is unexpectedly high for boys at 16½ years of age. No explanation of this is apparent.

The highest percentage for pupils leaving to go to work is at 15½ years of age.

The significant points of these charts, D[1] and D[2], seem to be that the schools suffer a considerable loss because of their being unable to hold pupils who want special courses; the home or school conditions or both are responsible for a large percentage of loss through personal illness; the loss through leaving to go to work comes not as soon as pupils might obtain "working papers," but before they are free to leave school without the papers.

The percentage of pupils who leave to go to work indicates that powerful factors are at work, some economic, some social and others educational. The great immediate problem for the schools is the analysis of the factors involved, in preparation for stopping the exodus.

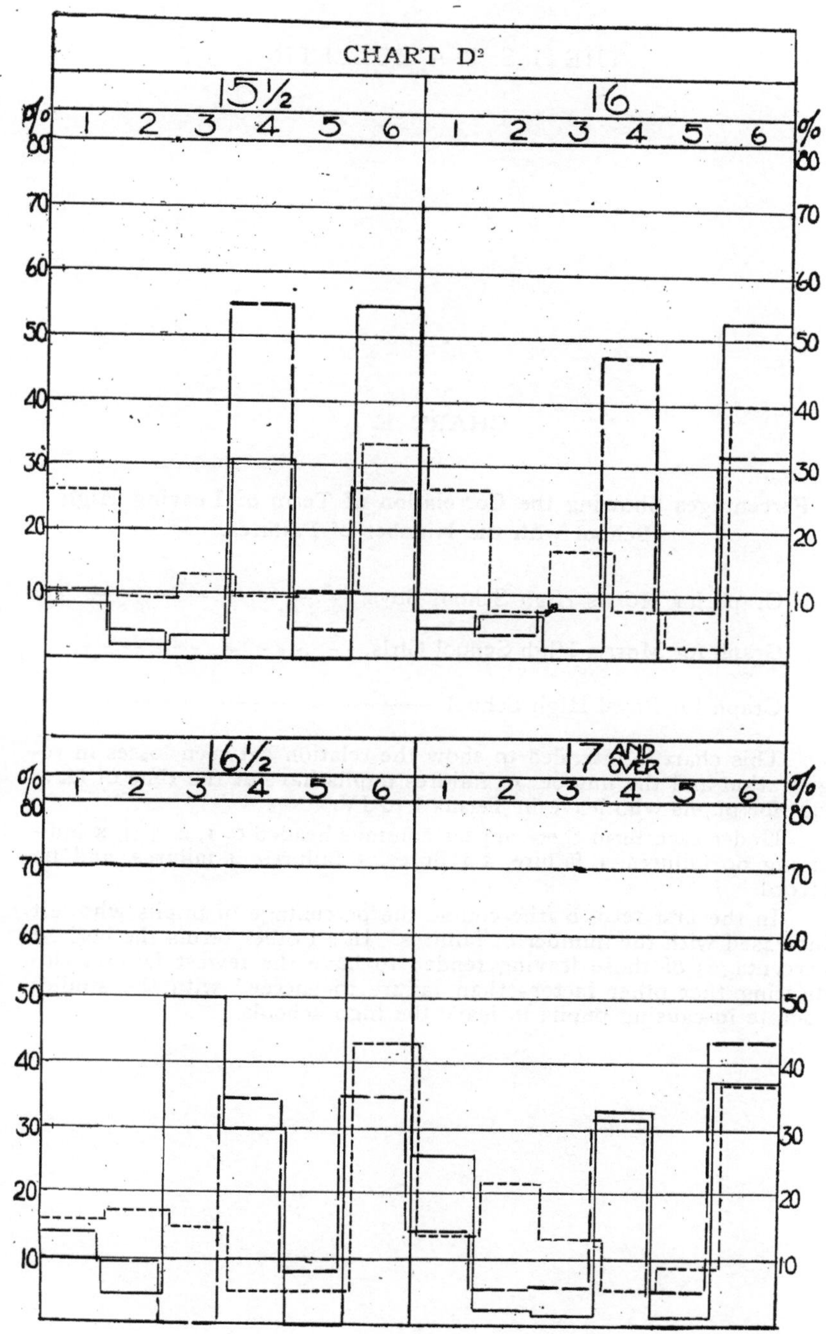
CHART D2
15½
16
16½
17 AND OVER
%
1
2
3
4
5
6
80
70
60
50
40
30
20
10

CHART E[1]

Percentages Showing the Correlation of Term of Leaving High School with the Number of Failures.

Graph for Morris High School Boys, — — — — — — — —

Graph for Morris High School Girls, - - - - - - - - - - - - - - - -

Graph for Boys' High School, ————————————

This chart is intended to show the relation between losses in registration and the number of failures pupils have at the time of leaving, for pupils who leave in Terms I to IV.

Under each term there appear columns headed 0, 1, 2, 3, 4, x indicating no failures, 1 failure, 2 failures, 3 failures, 4 failures, and no record.

In the first term o fthe course the percentage of pupils who left increased with the number of failures. In all other terms the highest percentages of those leaving tended to have the fewest failures, indicating that other factors than failure to succeed with the studies operate in causing pupils to leave the high schools.

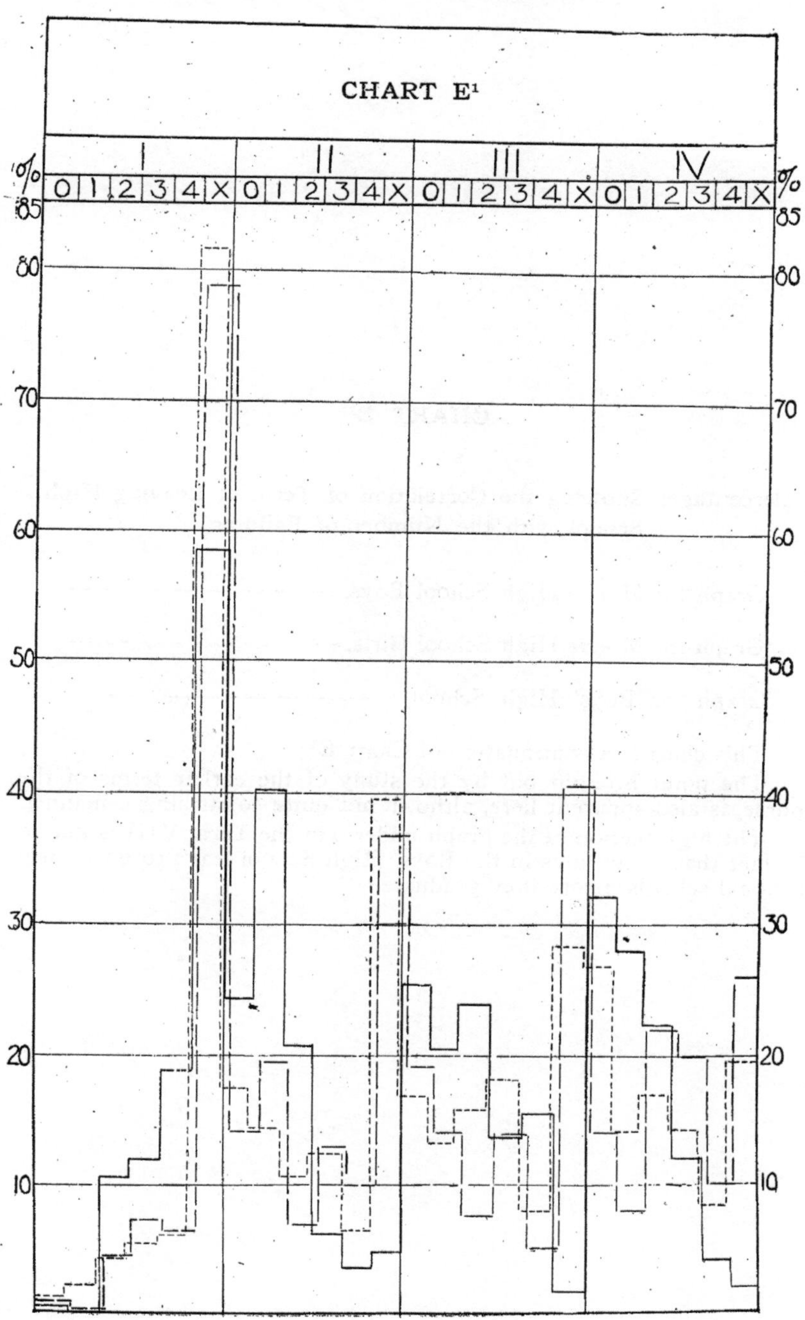
CHART E[1]
I
II
III
IV
%
0 1 2 3 4 X 0 1 2 3 4 X 0 1 2 3 4 X 0 1 2 3 4 X
%
85
80
70
60
50
40
30
20
10

CHART E^2

Percentages Showing the Correlation of Term of Leaving High School with the Number of Failures.

Graph for Morris High School Boys, — — — — — — — —

Graph for Morris High School Girls, - - - - - - - - - - - - - - - -

Graph for Boys' High School, ————————————

This chart is a continuation of Chart E^1.

The point brought out by the study of the earlier terms of the course, is also apparent here, altho in not quite so striking a manner.

The high section of the graph under o in the Term VIII is due to the fact that many boys in the Boys' High School leave to go to professional schools before they graduate.

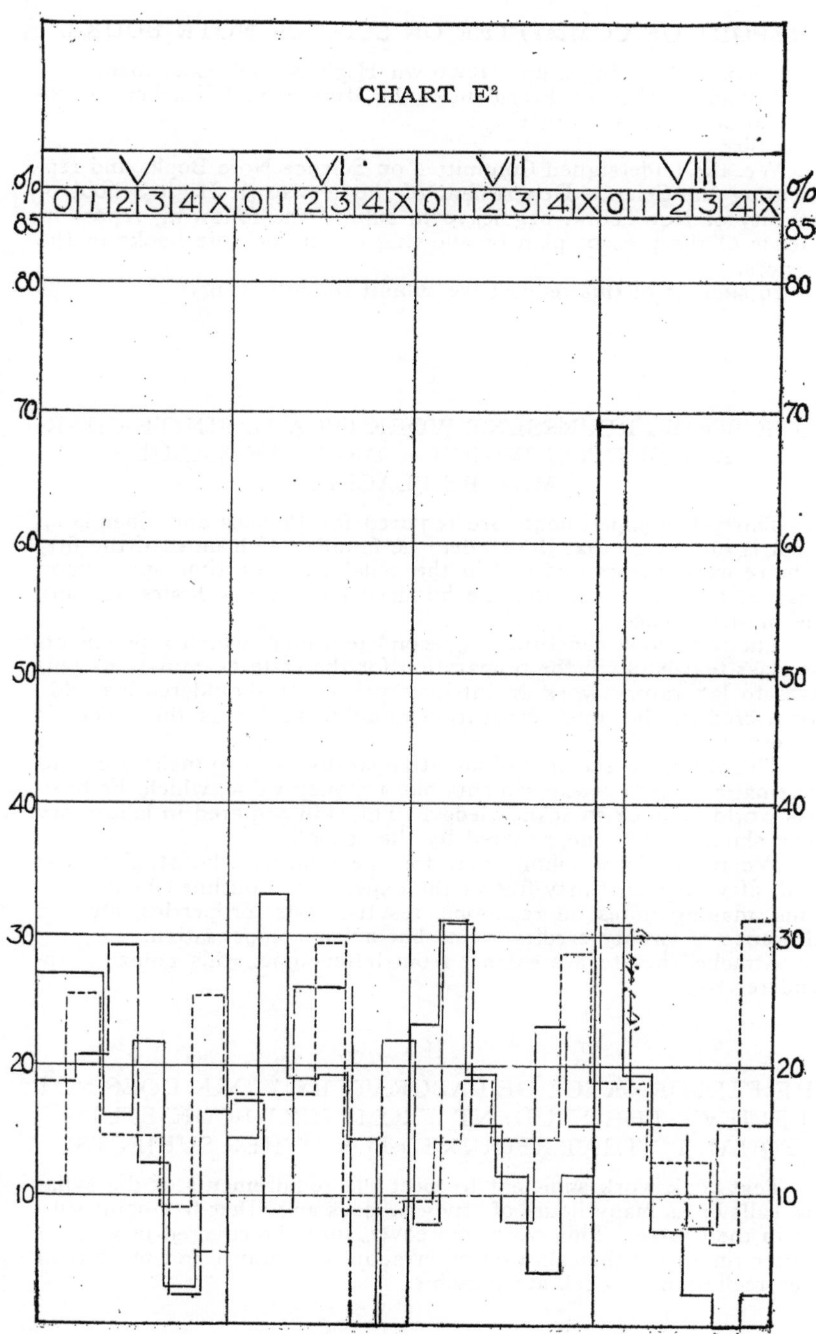
CHART E²
V
VI
VII
VIII
%
0 1 2 3 4 X 0 1 2 3 4 X 0 1 2 3 4 X 0 1 2 3 4 X
85
80
70
60
50
40
30
20
10

REPORT OF COMMITTEE ON SCIENCE NOTE BOOKS.

George H. Kingsbury, Newtown High School, Chairman.

To William T. Morrey, President of the High School Teachers' Association of New York City:

Dear Sir:

We, the undersigned Committee on Science Note Books and representing the Science Department of the Newtown High School in the City of New York, beg leave to submit the following report in defense of the present plan of allowing credit for note books in the sciences.

In support of this request we submit the following:

I

NOTE BOOKS REPRESENT WORK OF A DEFINITE CHARACTER UPON WHICH A DEFINITE VALUE MAY BE PLACED.

Thirty-five experiments are required for Physics and Chemistry, but it is important that the student be familiar with most of the fifty or more experiments outlined in the syllabus. The time spent upon these is, at a low estimate, one hundred and twenty hours, for any one of the sciences.

The note book constitutes a second text-book which supplements the class text-book, in the preparation for the state examination. This gives to laboratory work an intrinsic value. It should receive additional credits, the only recognition possible so far as the school is concerned.

The ability to set up and adapt apparatus, and to make accurate, systematic records of experiments has a money value, which the business world is quick to acknowledge. The skill acquired in laboratory work should not be depreciated by the school.

We respectfully submit that for the student who studies, first hand, fifty or even thirty-five of the experiments outlined in the syllabus, making notes on reactions, results, tests, properties, etc., an allowance of twenty credits seems but a fair compensation.

Attached hereto are extract from letters upon this point. (Appendixes 1-5.)

II

THE PERFORMANCE OF LABORATORY WORK DOES NOT RELIEVE THE STUDENT FROM TEXT-BOOK STUDY EQUAL TO THAT REQUIRED FOR OTHER SUBJECTS.

Text-book work sufficient to meet the requirements of the syllabus, calls or as many hours of study as does any other five-point subject in the course. This work, moreover, must be covered in a much shorter time than that allowed other subjects, because not more than three recitations a week are possible.

III

SO RADICAL A CHANGE AS THAT INVOLVED IN THE WITHDRAWAL OF NOTE-BOOK CREDITS, SEEMS NOT QUITE CONSISTENT WITH THE ESTABLISHED POLICY OF THE STATE.

For years our students of science have had before them the prospect of a special credit for laboratory work, and this has proved a powerful incentive in the preparation of note-books. Students were ambitious to excel in individual laboratory work. They felt, besides, a certain security and confidence under the present system, for each experiment performed and recorded was credited directly toward the state examination. The announcement, now, that credit for note-books has been withdrawn, means deep disappointment to the students, a feeling o insecurity, and a deplorable lack of interest in science note-books.

The announcement, will, moreover, carry with it the impression that the policy of twelve years or more has been a mistaken one. We submit that the Department of Education has never adopted a plan which was afterwards found impracticable. It has been the policy of the state to extend, not to withdraw privileges, and we urge that this custom of twelve years' standing be continued.

IV

THE WITHDRAWAL OF CREDIT FOR LABORATORY NOTE-BOOKS, DEPRIVES SCIENCE STUDENTS OF PRIVILEGES GRANTED BY THE STATE TO STUDENTS OF HISTORY, AND TO STUDENTS OF A MODERN LANGUAGE.

It will be admitted that a science note-book represents as much time and energy and skill on the part of the student and as much attention on the part of the teacher, as do note-books in history, or the dictation in a foreign language.

Attention is called to the fact that the value of science note-books depends largely upon the accuracy of observation, that many experiments must be repeated if details are to be complete; that notes must be written up under the supervision of the teacher; and that skill in using and adapting apparatus and materials is also considered in estimating science note-book credits.

There is no state inspection, moreover, of the history notes, or the dictation in a modern language. The estimate made by the teacher is accepted. The same is true of certain features of the examination in drawing, in music, and in some commercial subjects.

We respectfully call attention to the fact that at the same time that he order granting science note-books was recalled, an order extending note-book credits in history was issued.

We respectfully urge that students in science departments be given equal opportunities with those of other departments in our high schools.

COMMITTEE ON SCIENCE NOTE-BOOKS.

Geo. H. Kingsbury, Chairman.
Anna E. McAuliffe,
Mary F. Morris,
Nellie P. Hewins.

AUTHORITIES ON POINT I—OF BRIEF ATTACHED.

Extracts of letters received by Mr. George H. Kingsbury, Instructor in Physics, in reply to his request for an opinion on note-book credits.

Mr. Glenn M. Hobbs, for sixteen years instructor in Physics in the UNIVERSITY OF CHICAGO, now with the AMERICAN SCHOOL OF CORRESPONDENCE of the same place, replies as follows:

"I would divide the 100% for the final grade in the science considered, into three parts; 33 1-3% for the **final examination**; 33 1-3% to be the **average** of the **written tests** given throughout the term; and 33 1-3% for laboratory work and note-book.

POPULAR ELECTRICITY MAGAZINE.

From Mr. B. E. Blanchard, Associate Editor of the Popular Electricity Magazine, and formerly employed in the laboratories of the Commonwealth Edison Co.

"There is also one other reason why I think the pupil should be encouraged in note-book work, by knowing that this will be given credit at the close of the course and that is that a great deal of this work is done outside or not dirctly under the eye of the teacher, and while this is being done the pupil is helping himself and deciding one question after another, just as he would have to do in actual life."

POPULAR MECHANICS MAGAZINE.

Mr. N. N. Windson, Editor.

"It would seem to me that a note-book record of experiments correctly performed under proper supervision should be given at least EQUAL CREDIT IN FINAL EXAMINATIONS with the record of book knowledge which the pupil may have acquired. In fact, I can conceive of a laboratory course being so carefully planned that the pupil who completed it creditably should be entitled to graduate upon his laboratory record alone."

Dear Sir:—

My judgment is rather against laboratory work in the preparatory schools, unless conducted in an elementary and simple way.

Yours very truly,

CHARLES WHITING BAKER,
Editor Electrical World.

SCIENTIFIC AMERICAN.

Dear Sir:—

Certainly we favor laboratory work wherever science is studied. There is no other way in which a science can be learned than by the practiced application of the principles in real work with the appliances suited to the subject. No one can learn to be a carpenter, except by using the tools to do the work of a carpenter. So no one can learn to be a chemist without working with the chemist's tools.

In a school a student is entitled to credit for all that he does, for any kind of useful work.

The percentage to be credited for a special part of the work depends wholly upon the system of the school, and cannot be decided in an editorial sanctum.

Faithfully yours,

MUNN CO.

GENERAL MEETING, NOVEMBER 1, 1913.

The first general meeting of the High School Teachers' Association for the year 1913-1914 was called to order by the President, November 1, in the High School of Commerce at 11:30.

The minutes of the last meeting were accepted with corrections. The treasurer reported a balance of $600.37 in the treasury. President Morrey announced that his report would appear in the November Bulletin.

Mr. Frederick H. Paine, of Eastern District High School, reported for the Committee on Pensions. The results of the actuarial examination were briefly summarized, showing the present unsatisfactory condition of the fund and also the incomplete examination of those conditions by the actuaries. The committee reported that there were many statistics which should have been compiled in order to rectify the mistakes of the present system.

Mr. E. W. Weaver, of the Boys' High School, Brooklyn, reported for the Committee on Vocational Guidance. He showed the work that had been accomplished by the committee, especially through the publications issued.

Mr. Benjamin C. Gruenberg, of Commercial High School, spoke on the Grand Rapids Conference on Vocational Guidance.

The next business of the association was the election of delegates to the Advisory Council. It was voted to elect no representatives from the Training Schools to the Council.

The results of the election were as follows:

HIGH SCHOOL PRINCIPALS—Daniel D. Feldman, of Curtis, and James Sullivan, of Boys', with James J. Sheppard, of Commerce, as alternate.

FIRST ASSISTANTS IN HIGH SCHOOLS—Wiliam T. Morrey, of Bushwick, and Alexander L. Pugh, of Commerce, with Frederick H. Paine, of Eastern District, and George E. Boynton, of Erasmus, as alternates.

MEN HIGH SCHOOL TEACHERS—Sanford L. Cutler, of Morris, and Clayton G. Durfee, of Evander Childs, with Harry B. Penhollow, of De Witt Clinton, as alternate.

WOMEN HIGH SCHOOL TEACHERS—Harriet E. Wyckof, of Eastern District, and Helen E. Bacon, of Wadleigh, with Violette E. Scharff, of Morris, and Nellie A. Strum, of Washington Irving, as alternates.

EVENING HIGH SCHOOL TEACHERS—Milo F. McDonald, of Bushwick, and Claude T. Benjamin, of Curtis, with Roscoe A. Grant, of Jamaica, and Grace H. Miller, of Bushwick as alternates.

The meeting was adjourned at 1:40.

WILLIAM T. MORREY, President.

MARY J. BOURNE, Secretary

COMMITTEE ON VOCATIONAL GUIDANCE.

The Vocational Guidance Committee* has just completed a new handbook, Vocation for Girls, which is published for the committee by A. S. Barnes Co. It is a book of 200 pages, neatly and attractively bound. It covers all the fields open to women and contains information about local conditions and a complete index of vocational training opportunities in New York City.

The book is arranged for class use in connection with the English work of the high schools or as a reading book for the upper grades of the elementary schools. Each chapter contains suggestions for investigations, subjects for compositions and statistical studies.

Interspersed in the chapters of information will be found selections from the foremost writers bearing on the problems connected with efficient work.

A leading employer to whom the manuscript was submitted immediately placed orders for enough copies to present to each of his working girls. The Buffalo Chamber of Commerce ordered a special editin to be prepared at the expense of that body for use in the schools of the city.

The price is 75 cents, and copies can be ordered from the publishers or from the committee.

The other publications of the committee which are available for distribution this time are:

Choosing a Career for Boys, 10 cents.
The Printing Trades, 10 cents.
The Graphic Arts, 10 cents.
Accountancy and the Business Professions, 10 cents.
The Household Arts, 5 cents.
The Civil Service, 5 cents.

Manilla Employment blanks suitable for any school can be secured at $1.00 per 100.

E. W. WEAVER, 25 Jefferson Ave., Brooklyn.

* Strange to say the book has nothing to indicate that it is the work of a Vocational Guidance Committee of the High School Teachers' Association of New York City, or that the Association had anything to do with it—W. T. Morrey.

OFFICERS, 1912-1913.

PRESIDENT—William T. Morrey, Bushwick High School.

VICE-PRESIDENT—Mrs. Henrietta Rodman de Fremery, Wadleigh High School.

SECRETARY—Miss Agnes Carr, of Morris High School.

TREASURER—Dr. Loring B. Mullen, Girls' High School.

ADDITIONAL MEMBERS OF EXECUTIVE COMMITTEE—
Mr. Aaron L. Dotey, De Witt Clinton High School.
Miss H. Elizabeth Seelman, Girls' High School.
Mr. Clarence D. Kingsley, Manual Training (resigned).

REPRESENTATIVES IN HIGH SCHOOL TEACHERS' ASSOCIATION 1912-1913

*Senior Representatives.

BAY RIDGE—*Emberson E. Proper
Mabel R. Benway
Emil Gluck

BOYS'—*Charles E. Overholser
Francis T. Hughes
Frederick B. Jones
S. Ridley Parker
Alfred A. Tansk

BRYANT—*Mary E. Reid
Harry K. Munro

BUSHWICK—*George M. Falion
Mary E. Green
Carolyn L. Francis
Grace Helene Miller
Etta E. Southwell

COMMERCIAL—*Edwin A. Bolger
Geoge W. Harman
Robert O. St. John
Benjamin C. Gruenberg

COMMERCE—*Julius Blume
Horace G. Healey
Alfred H. Lewis
Alexander L. Pugh
George H. Van Tuyl

CURTIS—*William R. Hayward
Mabel G. Burdick

DE WITT CLINTON—*Aaron I. Dotey
Oscar W. Anthony
Ellen E. Garrigues
Fayette E. Moyer
Charles E. Timmerman
Jesse E. Whitsit

EASTERN DISTRICT—*Eloise B. Santee
Harold G. Campbell
Gertrude S. Burslingham
Nina Bowman
Marion J. Mayo
Florence E. Meyer

EVANDER CHILDS—(Not organized)

ERASMUS HALL—*Preston C. Farrar
George E. Boynton
Edith M. Everett
William F. Tibbetts
Kate E. Turner
Mary H. Holmes

FAR ROCKAWAY—*Elmer M. Van Dusen

FLUSHING—*Frank H. Miler

GIRLS'—*Loring B. Mullen
H. Elizabeth Seelman

JAMAICA—*Edward J. McNamara
Benjamin H. Thorp
Lydia Root

JULIA RICHMAN—(Not organized

MANUAL TRAINING—*A. Latham Baker (Johnson St. Annex)
Eleanor R. Baker (Main Bldg., 7th Ave.)
Marion Hackedorn
Mary A. Hall
Clarence D. Kingsley
Charles Perrine (Prospect Ave. Annex)
M. Helen Smith

MORRIS—*Paul B. Mann
Agnes Carr
Harriet L. Constantine
Fred C. White

NEWTOWN—*George H. Kingsbury
Alexander H. Zerban

RICHMOND HILL—*William E. Stilson
Gertrude M. Leete

STUYVESANT—*T. Harry Knox
Clayton G. Durfee
Joseph L. Beha
Stanley A. Gage
Charles F. Moors
Ernest S. Quimby
(These are as of 1911-1912)

WADLEIGH—*William W. Clendenin
Helen E. Bacon

WASHINGTON IRVING—*Elizabeth A. Roche
Mary C. Craig
Idelette Carpenter

List of Members of the High School Teachers' Association for the Year 1912-1913.

BAY RIDGE HIGH SCHOOL
86th Street, Near 18th Avenue
Annex
92d Street and Gelston Avenue (P. S. 104)

Allen, Winifred S.
Bai ???
Benway, Mabel R.
Gilliland, Alice M.
Gluck, Emil
Natelson, Rachel
Schuyler, Elmer
Schmidt, Clara

BOYS' HIGH SCHOOL
Marcy and Putnam Avenues and Madison Street
Annexes
Bedford and Jefferson Avenues
Schenectady Avenue, Bergen and Dean Streets (P. S. 83)
JAMES SULLIVAN, Principal, Plandome, L. I.

Alden, Henry T.
Andrews, William H.
Bates, Clifton W.
Bergstresser, C. A.
Bishop, Merle L.
Brummer, Sidney D.
Buttrick, Harold E.
Clark, Clinton
Cohen, A. Broderick
Diller, James G.
Downing, Georg B.
Edwards, William H.
Esselstyn, Henry H.
Fairchild, Ralph P.
Fisher, William W.
Fontaine, Andre C.
France, Sanford D.
Freeborn, Frank W.
Gemson, Irving
Hanson, G. C.
Hobson, George P. F.
Hopkins, Walter D.
Hughes, Charles E.
Hughes, Frances T.
Janes, Arthur L.
Jeffords, Clyde R.
Jenner, William A.
Jones, Frederick B.
Levine, Herman B.
Lewis, Frederick Z.
Mattes, Max H.
McCartney, Hoge
Munson, Daniel G.
Overholser, Charles E.
Parker, S. Ridley
Parsons, Edward B.
Parsons, Herbert H.
Pasternak Nathaniel
Raiman, Robert I.
Reynolds, James I.
Richardson, Roy S.
Riess, Ernst
Smith, Ernest E.
Spaulding, Frank B.
Swenson, John A.
Tausk, Alfred A.
Tressler, Jacob C.
Weaver, Eli W.
Wilson, Henry E.
Wood, George C.
Yoder, Arthur L.

BRYANT HIGH SCHOOL
Wilbur Avenue, Academy and Radde Streets, Long Island City
Van Alst Avenue, near Flushing Avenue, Long Island City (P. S. 7)

Arthur, L. Louise
Byrne, Margaret C.
Carter, Bertha A.
Courtney, Bertha F.
Dickson, Tenny V.
Garrity, Julia F.
Grubman, Adolph J.
Heermance, Emma W.
Jones, Frances E.
Joseph, Myrtle J.
Lewis, Edward F.
Loewy, George J.
McIntyre, Edith A.
Munroe, Harry K.
Noble, Helen G.
Price, Anna G.
Reid, Mary E.
Riblet, Mary V.
Snow, Ella M.
Swett, Carolyn Patten
Vincent, Charlotte M.
Welch, Alberta M.

BUSHWICK HIGH SCHOOL
Evergreen Avenue, Ralph and Grove Streets (P. S. 75)
Annexes
Reyerson Street, near Myrtle Avenue (P. S. 69)
Gates Avenue, near Stuyvesant Avenue (P. S. 129)
St. Nicholas Avenue and Suydam Street (P. S. 162)
FRANK ROLLINS, Principal, 175 Amity Street

Barlow, Margaret M.
Barrows Tessie
Bonotaux, Henriette
Bertschey, Maud
Berkowitz, Leo
Briggs, Era E.
Batchelder, Margaret
Canning, Etta M.
Cohen, Bertha
Cohen, Morris
Collier, Katharine B.
Dempsey, Josephine A.
Crossley, Arthur L.
Conant, M. Sybil
Dewitt, Louis L.
Durand, William B.
Falion, George M.
Fleischer, Edward
Foley, Henry J.
Francis, Carolyn L.
Gilbert, Clara M.
Goldsmith, Elizabeth
Goodman, Arthur
Green, John C.
Green, Mary P.
Hall, Henrietta
Handrich, Paul
Houley, Elizabeth
Humason, Thomas A.
Humphries, George F.
Johnson, Julius M.
Keener, Robert H.
Leyenberger, Harry W.
Leibovitz, Nathan
Levine, Manuel
Lebowitz, Leo.
Lingg, Amalie S.
Littig, M. Josephine
Manfred, Maud E.
McConville, Lillian M.
McDonald, Milo F.
Merington, Ruth
Miller, Charles
Miller, Grace H.
Mohan, Lucy F.
Morrey, William T.
Nanes, Philip
Norton, George W.
Newcomer, Harvey
Nevins, Nannie R.
O'Donnell, Agnes T.
O'Donnell, Margaret M. A.
Otten, Henry L.
Seaman, Mary
Semple, Lewis B.
Smith, Louise
Smith, Marguerite
Southwell, Etta E.
Staelin, Leonie E.
Stanton, Anna E.
Taylor, Arthur M.
Townsend Charles W.
Townsend, May E.
Tufts, Anna B.
Umbrecht, Martha (Mrs. Squires)
Zorn, Freda

HIGH SCHOOL OF COMMERCE

65th and 66th Streets, West of Broadway
Annex
120 West 46th Street (P. S. 67)
JAMES J. SHEPPARD, Principal, 308 West 97th Street

Aldinger, Harry E.
Barbour, William C.
Beatman, Augustus S.
Blume, Julius
Brennan, Alfred T. V.
Bryan, Alfred C.
Carter, Raymond
Cheston, Henry C.
Clough, Harvey B.
Eddy, Walter H.
Flatow, Jacob
Flynn, Oscar R.
Foster, Wilfred L.
Grant, Forest
Grant, Willis H.
Greene, Russell T., Jr.
Hahn, Clarence W.
Hall, Gamble
Hance, William
Hartung, Ernest W.
Hartwell, Frank W.
Healey, Horace G.
Heydrick, Benjamin A.
Kahn, Joseph
Berkowitch, Louis B.
Beygran, Frederick R.
Guldner, Chas. M.
Henin, Benjamin H.
Knickerbocker, Edwin Van B.
Koopman, Sietse B.
Lagerwall, C. J.
Lewis, E. D.
Lewis, Alfred H.
Lindsey, Frederick B.
Long, Reuben L.
McGrath, William J.
Mills, Joseph S.
May, Alfred A.
Minnick, John D.
Montrose, Chas. G.
O'Neil, William R.
Opdycke, John B.
Porter, George H.
Pugh, Alexander L.
Remy, Alfred
Rochow, John P.
Roberts, Albert
Roessler, Erwin W.
Rosenblum, Abraham
Rotherham, Philip J. E.
Skinner, Herbert C.
Schlauch, William S.
Sinagnan, Leon
Skipp, Henry J.
Smith, L. B.
Sprague, C. Hayes
Van Tuyl, George H.
Walsh, Daniel O'C.
Wharton, William P.
Whiffen, Edwin
Weinberger, George G.
Woodman, Irving L.

COMMERCIAL HIGH SCHOOL

Albany Avenue, Bergen and Dean Streets
Annex
Conover, Sullivan and Wolcott Streets (P. S. 30)
WILLIAM FAIRLEY, Principal, 195 Kingston Avenue

Austin, Harry W.
Bagenstose, Harvey L.
Bliss, Ralph P.
Bolger, Edwin A.
Chestnut, D. Howard
Dann, Matthew L.
Denenholz, Alexander
Donovan, Herbert D. A.
Eels, Burr G.
Finnegan, William E.
Goate, William B.
Greenberg, Morris
Gross, Henry I.
Gruenberg, Benjamin C.
Harman, George W.
Harrison, Earl S.
Hoffman, Alfred L.
Hook, Edward A.
Joseph, Samuel
Loftus, John J.
Loughran, John
McNally, Edward
Newman Joseph
O'Ryan, William P.
Proctor, Robert H.
Raynor, Gilbert J.
Ross, William A.
Sawyer, George A.
Scarborough, Andrew J.
Shea, John J.
Shearer, Robert J.
Sternberg, George
St. John, Robert P.
Teeter, Charles H.
Van Buskirk, Edgar H.

CURTIS HIGH SCHOOL

St. Mark's Place and Hamilton Avenue, New Brighton
Annex
Academy Place, Tottenville (P. S. 1)

Abbot, Frances H.
Austin, Mary E.
Benjamin, Claude T.
Blanpied, Ethel O.
Brewer, Francis E.
Burdick, Mabel
Close, Maud M.
Crane, William A.
Dean, Philip R.
Dowell, Philip
Fleuring, Carrie O.
French, Linda M.
Gallagher, Ellen M.
Goode, Elizabeth
Goodwin, W. Grant
Grout, Abel J.
Harkness, Alma deB.
Hayward, William R.
Hopkins, Rupert H.
Kerr, Frank E.
McMillan, Harlon
Powers, Florence
Shepherd, Florence
Shipley, James H.
Welsh, John C.
Whitmore, Clara H.

DeWITT CLINTON HIGH SCHOOL

10th Avenue, 58th and 59th Streets
JOHN L. TILDSLEY, Principal, Spuyten Duyvil

Abbott, Royal A.
Adams, Milly E.
Anthony, Oscar W.
Armand, Louis H.
Barber, Harry G.
Baylis, Sara
Bedford, Edgar A.
Berry, James F.
Bierman, Henry
Bingham, Jesse H.
Boylan, Arthur A.
Broadhurst, Philip H.
Bryant, Arthur A.
Call, R. Ellsworth
Campbell, Ralph
Carpentier, Marius
Chamberlain, Raymond
Clark, Randolph F.
Connelly, Douglas L.
Grow, Frederick S.
Haas, Arthur
Ham, Geo.
Heller, Henry
Haug, Emanuel
Hewitt, George E.
Herzog, Charles
Hirsch, James A.
Hooks, David M.
Hunter, George W.
Jackson, Eugene
Jonas, J. B. Edward
Johnson, Walter R.
Keller, Franklin J.
Kelley, Frank B.
Klein, Morris G.
Knox, Jaxon
Krause, Arthur K.
Landsman, Charles M.
Mufson, Thom.
Newman, Charles
Osborn, Ralph
Parelhoff, Bernard M.
Parmelee, William J.
Patterson, Samuel W.
Penhollow, Harry B.
Perry, Edward O.
Pickelsky, Frank
Pokorney, Rudolph
Raubicheck, Charles
Rosenthal, Daniel C.
Schmalhausen, Sam.
Salzano, Francis
Scheneer, A. Henry
Sharpe, Richard W.
Sherman, Frederick D.
Smith, Thomas P.
Solomon, Michael

Covello, Leonard
Currie, Thomas H.
Davidson, Henry
Decker, Nicholas P.
Delaney, Edward C.
Donnelly, Joseph P.
Dotey, Aaron I.
Donaldson, George
Erwin, Edward J.
Foote, Carlton A.
Foote, Edmund W.
Fox, Alice E.
Frank, Colman D.
Frank, Maude
Garrigues, Ellen E.
Goldberg, Israel
Gomberts, George K.
Laden, Jos. E
Levene, Harry
Loew, Joseph
Loewinthan, Albert
Lyon, Lorenzo G.
Lucey Michael H.
MacLaren, Donald C.
Mason, Lucius J.
McCarthy, John D.
McTiernan, Thomas
Miles, Dudley H.
Michaels, Norris H.
Mirsky, Israel
Monteser, Frederick
Marquard, Edw.
Morse, Charles F.
Moyer, Fayette E.
Stevens, William S.
Strauss, Julius
Taylor, Albert S.
Tobin, Jas. L.
Tildsley, John L.
Timmerman, Charles E.
Wait, Horace C.
Wheat, Frank M.
Whitsit, Jesse E.
Wilford, Herbert E.
Wilkins, Lawrence A.
Wolfson, Arthur M.
Works, Austin M.
Wright, Herman H.
Wright, Kenneth W., Jr.
Yokel, Arthur
Zacharie, Jean B.

EASTERN DISTRICT HIGH SCHOOL

Marcy Avenue, Rodney and Keap Streets
Annex
Havemeyer, North 6th and North 7th Streets (P. S. 143)
WILLIAM T. VLYMEN, Principal, 379 Front Street, Hempstead, L. I.

Adler, David
Baltz, Frank P.
Beeckman, Florence L.
Beitel, Helen S.
Blumenberg, Frieda
Bole, John A.
Bowman, Nina
Brace, Edith M.
Burlingham, Gertrude S.
Campbell, Harold G.
Carey, Margaret E.
Chater, Ellen D.
Dithridge, Rachel L.
Faulkner, Eunice F.
Genung, Ina E.
Griffiths, Anna B.
Gurnee, Blandina H.
Hartwell, Charles S.
Hazen, Anna P.
Helmuth, Lou
Higbee, Anna M.
Heouch ?
Hoy, Elizabeth R.
Ikelheiemr, Minnie
Jacobsen, Walter
Kauffman, William A.
Kelly, William H.
King, Helen L.
Klock, Claude W.
Kuhn, Adelina
Lanz, Jeanne M.
Lemowitz, Nathan H.
Loughran, Agnes M.
Maynard, Ernest A.
Mayo, Marion J.
Meigs, Katherine H.
Meyer, Florence E.
Meyers, Willard L.
Osborne, Mabel E.
Paine, Frederick H.
Phillips, Anna L.
Pinch, Minnie A.
Pond, Pearl F.
Reed, Mary A.
Ribber, Emma
Rittenhouse, Hawley O.
Russum, Ruth E.
Santee, Eloise B.
Schradieck, Helen E.
Hutschmar ?
Smith, Franklin H.
Stepanek, Beatrice
Stratford, Aline C.
Sullivan, Mary
Tomlin, Stella M.
Trowbridge, Cornelia B.
Warren, James P.
Wyckoff, Harriet E.

ERASMUS HALL HIGH SCHOOL

Flatbush Avenue, near Church Avenue
Walter B. Gunnison, Principal, 77 Wilson Street

Boynton, Geo. E.
Brickelmaier, Alice G.
Bryant Frank L.
Campbell, Joseph A.
Cashman, Joseph F.
Chesley, Mabel L.
Connell, Wesley J.
Crane, Ella E.
Crockett, Esther M.
Doggett, Allen B.
Edgell, Frank D.
Estes, Chas. S.
Everett, Edith M.
Farrar, Preston C.
Fay, Chas. R.
Feldman, Daniel D.
Foster, Sarah P.
Gordon, John J.
Habermeyer, ouise C. M.
Hancock, Wm. J.
Harley, Walter S.
Hewitt, Helen F.
Hodgdon, Katherine I.
Holmes, Mary H.
Howe, Alice C.
Huntington, Fred'k W.
King, Cyrus A.
Lasher, Wm. R.
Lauder, Mary A.
Merchant, Manton E.
Neiswender, Ada B. C.
Peabody, Susan P.
Raynor, Geo. C.
Scovill, Florence M.
Sparks, Minnie E.
Sprague, Laura E.
Stocker, John H.
Strong, Wm. M.
Talbot, A. May
Tibbetts, Wm. F.
Valentine, Henry D.
Vedder, Estella M.
Volentine, Mary F. (Mrs.)
Whitney, N. Belle
Wight, Walter A.
Wilder, Geo. F.
Williams, Lewis C.

FAR ROCKAWAY HIGH SCHOOL

State Street and Roanoke Avenue, Far Rockaway

Barnes, Edwin A.
Belding, Albert G.
Booth, Frederick M.
Broomall, Laura B.
Jennison, Emily M.
Kennedy, Anna J.
Prescott, Lucy M.
Roberts, May
Van Dusen, Eldon M.

GIRLS' HIGH SCHOOL

Nostrand Avenue, Halsey and Macon Streets
Annex
St. Mark's and Classon Avenues (P. S. 42)
WILLIAM L. FELTER, Principal, 996 Sterling Place

Cochran, Mary
Cushman, Earl P.
Ellis, Sophia
Ford, Celia
Higgins, Alice
Hyde, Isabella
Ingalls, Margaret L.
Jenness, Jennie M.
Joannes, Jules S.
Lee, Marguerite T.
Mullen, Loring B.
Schumer, Jacob H.
Seelman, H. Elizabeth
Smith, Charlotte
Sullivan, Bessie
White, Bessie R.
Willard, Gladys
Winslow, Julia E.
Wright, Mabel

FLUSHING HIGH SCHOOL

Sanford Avenue and Union Street, Flushing

Baumeister, John
Jenks, Paul R.
Miller, Frank H.

JAMAICA HIGH SCHOOL

Hillside and Union Avenues, Jamaica

THEODORE C. MITCHILL, Principal, 325 West 56th Street, Manhattan

Bradley, Susan M.
Brown, Adelaide W.
Busbee, Christiana
Chickering, Edward C.
Dilger, Marie
Edgerton, Myra T.
Fairley, Edwin
Epler, Alice
Fennebresque, Louis
Ferris, Mary D.
Gay, Laura S.
Grant, Roscoe A.
Hoadley, Harwood
Hochderffer, Mary J.
Kibby, Warren J.
Krause, Carl A.
Lawrence, Antoinette
Linville, Henry R.
Luetscher, George D.
MacConnell, Marie F.
McNamara, Edward J.
O'Keefe, David H.
Quick Oscar
Root, Lydia F.
Silverman, Henry J.
Starkey, Warren L.
Thompson, Kirk W.
Thorp, Benjamin H.
Vosburgh, Charles H.
Ward, Ada Webster
Wilkin, Josephine D.

MANUAL TRAINING HIGH SCHOOL

7th Avenue, 4th and 5th Streets

Annexes

Duffield, Johnson and Gold Streets

Prospect Avenue, opposite Reeve Place

CHARLES D. LARKINS, Principal, 225 Argyle Road, Flatbush.

Abbott, Frederick B.
Aldridge, Vincent
Allen, J. Trevette
Baker, Arthur Latham
Baker, Eleanor R.
Barasch, Morris
Bawden, Sarah E.
Boecker, Alexander
Boole, Emily R.
Braman, Mary L.
Bryant, Elizabeth E.
Cambern, J. Raymond
Coan, Charles
Colony, M. Elizabeth
Colsten, Albert L.
Daris, Eunice M.
Dickinson, Henry N.
Dickman, Mary B.
Dithridge, Caroline M.
Elting, Mabel
Fanning, Grace M. W.
Geiss, M. Paula
Green, Florence (Mrs.)
Hackedorn, Marion
Hall, Mary A.
Harris, Lena
Heyer, Ella G.
Holzmann, Abraham
Hunt, Arthur E.
Kingsley, Clarence D.
Lenfest, Bertram A.
Leonard, Howard C.
Low, J. Herbert
Luther, Edith M.
Mageworth, J. Otis
McArdle, John P.
McCall, Carleton C.
McDonald, John J.
Meneely, John H.
Mueller, Ernest G.
Murphy, Margaret L.
Nevins, Dora R.
Oswald, Frederick W., Jr.
Odell, Louis S.
O'Donnell, J. Emmett
Perrine, Charles
Peters, Frederick A.
Puig, Louise M.
Richardson, William C.
Robinson, Alfred T.
Robinson, Franklin D.
Russell, Warren L.
Schutze, Elizabeth
Shimberg, Jeannette
Shinn, Victor I.
Smith, J. Clarence
Smith, M. Helen
Snow, Minnie R.
Stern, Regine
St. John, Emily P.
Stone, Mabel
Taylor, Nettie
Terrel, Lillian A.
Vall, Clarence W.
Walker, Alice J.
Weed, Henry T.
Wolcott, Henry G.
Wright, Helen S. (Mrs.)

MORRIS HIGH SCHOOL

166th Street, Boston Road and Jackson Avenue

Annexes

Matilda Street, Wakefield (P. S. 16)

Mott Avenue and 144th Street (P. S. 31)

JOHN H. DENBIGH, Principal, 2676 Creston Avenue

Althaus, Amalie L.
Avent, John M.
Baer, Dena
Bates Abby B.
Bates, Thomas S.
Bergman, Morris L.
Bourne, Mary J.
Bridgman, Anne T.
Burt, Clara M.
Carey, Alice
Carleton, Bessie G.
Carr, Agnes
Constantine, Harriet L.
Cutler, Sanford L.
Davis, Josie A.
Denbigh
Diedrich, Marie M.
Evans, Austin H.
Falk, Anna A. (Mrs.)
Fraser, Effie
Hazen, Louise C.
Hixon, Kate B.
Horwitz, Lillian
Howell, Logan D.
Kellogg, Raymond N.
Knowlton, Mary E.
Landau, Laura
Lewis, Arthur C.
Look, Samuel M.
Mann, Paul B.
Matthews, Archibald J.
Mendum, Georgiana
Miller, Charles A.
Morse, Elizabeth E.
Normile, Mary
Palmer, Anna M.
Parker, Margaret M.
Peabody, James E.
Read, Edith
Scharff, Victor
Scott, Cora A.
Scudder, John O.
Shannahan, Willard D.
Skeele, Otis C.
Sohon, Michael D.
Story, Helen M.
Surrey, Frank M.
Theobald, Jacob, Jr.
Thompson, Annie S.
Tracy, Edwin S.
Vanderbilt, Grace W.
White, Fred C.
Williams, Joseph S.
Winslow, Isabel G.
Young-High, Caroline (Mrs.)

NEWTOWN HIGH SCHOOL

Chicago Avenue and Grove Street, Elmhurst

JAMES D. DILLINGHAM, Principal, 189 9th Street, Elmhurst

Book Arthur E.
Kingsbury, George H.
Larsh, Charles H.
Meras, Albert A.
Radin, Max
Schmidt, Carl G.
Slater, Henry B.
Smith, Charles M.

RICHMOND HILL HIGH SCHOOL

Elm Street and Stewart Avenue, Richmond Hill.
ISAAC N. FAILOR, Principal, 5 Maple Street, Richmond Hill

Allen, Ralph W.
Atwater, John C.
Barber, Sara M.
Beard, Stella S.
Beers, Florence M.
Burrage, M. A.
Chapin, Jennie E.
Chapin, H. E.
Emery, Stephen
Fent, S. B.
Flint, A H.
Finnigan, James J.
Forbes, Abby B.
Gammon, Montague
Gaston, Charles Robert
Golde, Margaret D.
Greene, Lillian L.
Henderson, Royal L.
Hubbard, Ruth E.
Johnson, Estella M.
Kilburn, Florence M.
Knapp, Annie M.
Landers, Leland L.
Leete, Gertrude M.
Loomis, J. D.
Relph, Marion F.
Root, Eva R.
Stilson, Wm. E.
Trowbridge, Cornelia R.
Valentine, Morris C.
Voorhees, Sophia
Richardson, Morris G.
Wortmann Johanna C.

STUYVESANT HIGH SCHOOL

15th and 16th Streets, West of 1st Avenue
ERNEST R. Von NARDROFF, Principal, 397 Madison Street, Brooklyn

Andrews, Richard M.
Brandau, George J.
Breckenridge, Wm. E.
Brownlee, Raymond B.
Bruce, Murray
Cheney, Thomas C.
Clark, John P.
Clark, John P.
Cooley, George E.
Cornell, Charles F.
Dorfman, Waldemar L.
Ellard, Charles H.
Elmer, Clement G.
Fink, Frederick W.
Fuller, Robert W.
Foster, Walter E.
Fritz, Henry E.
Gage, Stanley A.
Gardner, Frank A.
Goldberger, Henry H.
Goodrich, Moses F.
Greenberg, Abraham B.
Griswold, Clifford B.
Griswold, Edward D.
Hein, Henry E.
Henriques, Maurice C.
Hoffman, Mark
Hopkins, William C.
Hoew, Charles B.
Jacobs, Olin M.
Klafter, Simeon H.
Knox, T. Harry
Lavers, Earl R.
Law, Frederick H.
Leavitt, William M.
Leonhard, Theodore S.
Maulitt, Hower E.
Mattock, Jacob A.
Marks, Lazarus
Maier, Augustus
Marston, Charles W.
Mehrtens, Henry E.
Mersereau, Samuel F.
Messenger, John, Jr.
Norris, John S.
Pax, Donald J.
Parrot, Alfred F.
Quimby, Ernest S.
Reynolds, Frank
Ross, A. Franklin
Sackman, Gilbert R.
Silberstein, Nathan
Sindelar, Charles
Smith, Walter M.
Smith, W. Palmer
Stahl, George
Way, Abner P.
Wilson, James F.
Worth, William A.
Wyman, William T.
Rodman, Bayard B.

WADLEIGH HIGH SCHOOL

114th and 115th Streets, West of 7th Avenue
Annex
138th and 139th Streets, West of 5th Avenue (P. S. 100)
STUART H. ROWE, Principal, 104 Hillcrest Avenue, Park Hill, Yonkers, N. Y.

Bacon, Helen E.
Blumenstock, M.
Beach, Mary R., A.L.H.
Beare, Cornelia, A.E.
Bruce, Grace A.
Cameron, Morton T.
Clendenin, Wm. W.
Colburn, Mary P., A.E.
Coman, Caroline
Cornish, Robert H.
Davis, Genevieve
Dike, Cornelia D.
Drake, Rutm W., A.D.
Ford, Jessie Frances
Gavin, Helen, H.B.
Gelbach, Marie, A.G.
George, Auguste
Goodrich, Martha, A.F.
Griffith, Priscilla
Harris, Mary E.
Harris, Sadie
Heermans, Florence
Heller, Louie R., A.E.
Herrmann, Hattie, A.M.
Hobbs, Mrs., A.E.
Hodges, Archibald L.
Hovey, W. H. M.
Houston, Jessie F., A. M.
Howard, Charlotte B., A.L.
Judge, Anna G.
Judd, S. M.
Jackson, Alice, A.E.
Kupfer, Elsie M.
Marsh, Bessie K.
Meserve, Elizabeth
Middleton, Florence, A.B.
Moss, Olive, A.M.
Norwood, Claretta, A.M.
Robinson, Alice M., A.M.
Ross, Helen, A.D. Jr.
Saltzberg, Florence
Saniel, Marie, A.D.B.
Speir, Katharine A., Inch.
Syms, Louis C.
Taylor, Jane I.
Taylor, Miriam L.
Tefft, Mary Bickmore
Thompson, ouise, A.G.L.
Underwood, Elizabeth, A.M.
Zick, Henry

WASHINGTON IRVING HIGH SCHOOL

34 1-2 E. 12th St., and 5 Annexes.
WILLIAM McANDREW, Principal, 2758 Kingsbridge Terrace, Kingsbridge.

Ammerman, S. Lewis
Arndt, Emma
Arnold, David L.
Alley, M. I.
Beach, Jessie A.
Belcher, Frances S.
Carpenter, Idelette
Catren, Ida M.
Cohen, Helen L.
Craig, Mary C.
Douglas, Charles H. J.
Donnelly, W.
Falk, Louis J.
Freeman, Mary L.
Galloway, Ida G.
Merdes, Adrienne
Goller, Gratia
Goodman, Annie E.
Greenstein, Max
Goertner, Rose
Guthrie, Kenneth
Hodgkins, Georgina
Holran, Rose A.
Lancaster, Bertha
Leonard, Nina V.
Langdon, Amanda
Marshall, J. Adelaide
Mattfeld William
Klees, C. Mathilde
Roche, Elizabeth A.
Sage, Lillian B.
Skinner, E. Mabel
Slack, Earl B.
Sommerfield, Alfred
Stone, Bertha R.
Thompson, Christina M.
Trautvetter, Ida
Truckenbrodt, Lewis
Willard, Florence M.

FIRST ASSISTANTS IN HIGH SCHOOLS OF NEW YORK CITY, 101 Men, 21 Women.

HIGH SCHOOL	BIOLOGY	ENGLISH	FRENCH AND GERMAN	HISTORY	LATIN	MATHEMATICS	PHYSICAL SCIENCE	COMMERCIAL Vice-Principals (Art)
BAY RIDGE	Bruckman, Louise			Proper, Emberson E		Schuyler, Elmer		
BOYS'	Lewis, F. Z.	Fisher, William W.	Overholser, Charles E.	Jackson, W. P. Wilson, Jas. F.	Riess, Ernest	Parsons, Edw. B.		
BRYANT		Munroe, Harry K.					Bement, Frederic	
BUSHWICK	Johnson, Julius M.	Semple, Lewis B.	Keener, Robt. H.	Morrey, William T.		Humason, Thomas A.		
COMMERCE	Eddy, Walter H.	Heydrick, Benjamin A	Roessler, Erwin W.	Bryan, Alfred C.			Mills, Jos. E. Cheston, H. C.	Pugh, A. L. Greene, R.
COMMERCIAL	Gruenberg, Benj. C.	St. John, Robt. P.	Marvin, Robt. M. Harrison, Earl S.	Trask, Thomas C.		Teeter, Charles H.	Clark, John A.	Doggett, Wm. E Kip, Arthur R.
CURTIS	Grout, Abel J.	Abbott, Frances	Shepherd, Florence D.			Dean, Philip R.		Welsh, John C. Crane, Wm. A. (V.P.)
DEWITT CLTN.	Hunter, George W.	Garrigues, Ellen E.	Monteser, F'd'k. Frank, Colman D.		Bice, Hiram H.	Anthony, Oscar W.	Whitsit, Jesse E. Timmermann, C. E.	
EAST'N DIST.	Hazen, Anna P.	Hartwell, Charles S.	Bole, John A.	Paine, Frederick H	Dixon, Charles E.	Mayo, Marion J.		Baltz, Frank P.
ERASM. HALL	King, Cyrus A.	Farrar, Preston C.	Holmes, Mary H.	Boynton, George E.	Harter, Eugene W.			Turner, Kate (V. P.)
EVANDER CHILDS								
FAR ROCK'W'Y								Belding, Albert G.
FLUSHING		Read, Warren W.	Baumeister, John	Miller, Frank H.	Jenks, Paul R.	Barnwell, Walter		
GIRLS'	Leeuente, Margaret T.	Wendt, Cordelia	Higgins, Alice	Cahill, Rose H.	Ford, Celia	Mullen, Loring B.	Arey, Albert L.	Pyles, (VP) Marion
JAMAICA	Linville, Henry R.	Fairley, Edwin	Krause, Carl A.	Lawrence, Antoinette	Chickering, Edward C.		Vosburgh, Chas. H.	Starkey, Warren L.
JULIA RICHMAN						Arnold, David L.		
MAN. TRAIN.	Hunt, Arthur E.	Bates, Herbert	Lamb, Wm. W.	Low, J. Herbert	Shumway, Edgar S.	Baker, Arthur L. Colston, Albert L.	Weed, Henry T.	Shinn, (Art) Victor I.
MORRIS	Peabody, James E.		Althaus, Edward	Bates, Abby B.	Davis, Josephine A	Heikes, Irving A.	Pyle, Willard R.	
NEWTOWN					Radin, Max			
RICHM'D HILL	Valentine, Morris	Gaston Chas. Robt.				Landers, Leland L.		
STUYVESANT		Law, Frederick H.	Elmer, Clement G.		Foster, Walter E.	Breckenridge, Wm. E.	Fuller, Robert W.	Howe, (Art) Chas. B.
WADLEIGH	Kupfer, Elsie M.	Smith, Jessie F. (Now Mrs. Ford)	Zick, Henry	Wood, Elizabeth C.	Hodges, Archibald L	Bruce, Grace A.	Cornish, Robt. H.	
WASH. IRV'G	Sage, Lillian B.	Lowd, Emma F. Douglas, C. H. J.	Blackwell, Nannie G.	Galloway, Ida G.				Hayward, William R.

DIRECTORY OF HIGH SCHOOLS OF NEW YORK CITY

NOTICE—Many of the telephones are on the desk of the Principals and Teachers in Charge. They should be used for school business only and then only when there is need of haste.

School	Telephone	Location	Principal or Teacher in Charge of Annex
Bay Ridge	711 Bath Beach	86th st., near 18th av. (P. S. 101)	Harry A. Potter.
Annex	1273 Bay Ridge	92d st. and Gelston av. (P. S. 104)	
Boys'	690 Bedford	Marcy and Putnam avs. and Madison st.	James Sullivan.
Bryant	40 Astoria	Wilbur av., Academy and Radde sts., L. I. City	Peter E. Demarest.
Annex	1146-W Astoria	Van Alst av., near Flushing av., L. I. City (P. S. 7)	
Bushwick	3403 Bushwick	400 Irving Ave.	Frank Rollins.
Annex	13 Bushwick	Evergreen av., Ralph and Grove sts. (P. S. 75)	William T. Morrey
Annex	3514 Bushwick	Quincy st., near Stuyvesant av. (P. S. 129)	Lewis B. Semple.
Commercial	8732 Bedford	Albany av., Bergen and Dean sts.	William Fairley.
Annex	7736 Bedford	Bedford and Jefferson sts	W. E. Doggett.
Curtis	351-J Tompkinsville	Hamilton av. and St. Mark's pl., New Brighton	D. L. Feldman.
Annex	922-J Tottenville	Academy pl., Tottenville (P. S. 1)	
De Witt Clinton	4175 Columbus	10th av., 58th and 59th sts	John L. Tildsley.
Eastern District	4565 Wmsburg	Marcy av., Rodney and Keap sts.	W. T. Vlymen.
Annex	1715 Greenpoint	Havemeyer, N. 6th and 7th sts (P. S. 143)	Anna L. Phillips.
Erasmus Hall	288 Flatbush	Flatbush av., near Church av	W. B. Gunnison.
Evander Childs	643 Westchester	Randolph, St. Lawrence and Hammond aves. (P. S. 47)	Gilbert S. Blakely
Annex	5634 Tremont	196th st., Bainbridge and Driggs avs. (P. S. 46)	
Far Rockaway	95 Far Rockaway	Far Rockaway	S. J. Ellsworth.
Flushing	321 Flushing	Sanford av., Flushing	J. H. Clark.
Girls'	372 Bedford	Nostrand av., Halsey and Macon sts.	W. L. Felter.
Annex	5926 Prospect	St. Mark's and Classon avs. (P. S. 42)	M. Ellen Barker.
H. S. of Commerce	2658 Columbus	65th and 66th sts., west of Broadway	J. J. Sheppard.
Annex	8114 Bryant	120 West 46th st. (P. S. 67)	Alfred C. Bryan.
Jamaica	165 Jamaica	Hillside av., Jamaica	T. C. Mitchill.
Julia Richman	4557 Chelsea	60 West 13th st	A. M. Wolfson.
Annex	482 Chelsea	140 West 20th st. (P. S. 55)	
Annex	8437 Schuyler	82nd st. and West End av	
Annex	5748 Lenox	88th st., east of 1st av	
Manual Training	1380 South	7th av., 4th and 5th sts	C. D. Larkins.
Annex	24 South	Prospect av., opp. Reeve pl	Charles Perrine.
Annex	2627 Main	Duffield, Johnson and Gold sts	Arthur L. Baker.
Morris	605 Melrose	166th st., Boston rd. and Jackson av.	John H. Denbigh.
Annex	2360 Melrose	Mott av. and 144th st. (P. S. 31)	Irving A. Heikes.
Newtown	40 Newtown	Elmhurst	J. D. Dillingham.
Annex	122 Newtown	Elmhurst (P. S. 89)	
Richmond Hill	26 Richmond Hill	Elm st., Richmond Hill	Isaac N. Failor.
Stuyvesant	3739 Stuyvesant	15th and 16th sts., west of 1st ave.	E. R. von Nardroff
Wadleigh	1892 Morningside	114th and 115th sts., west of 7th av.	Stuart H. Rowe.
Annex	4865 Harlem	138th st., west of 5th av. (P. S. 100)	Kath. A. Speir.
Washington Irving	3292 Stuyvesant	Irving pl., 16th and 17th sts	W. McAndrew.

YEAR BOOK 1908-1909, JOHN L. TILDSLEY, PRESIDENT.

YEAR BOOK 1909-1910, ARTHUR L. JANES, PRESIDENT.

YEAR BOOK 1910-1911, ARTHUR L. JANES, PRESIDENT.

BULLETINS ISSUED BY WILLIAM T. MORREY, PRESIDENT.

BULLETIN NO. 34.

BULLETIN 35.

BULLETIN NO. 36.

BULLETIN 37.

BULLETIN 38.

BULLETIN 39.

BULLETIN 40.

CONTENTS OF THIS BULLETIN 41.

[Year-Books 20c. each, Bulletins 10c. each—Miss Mary J. Bourne, Secsetary Morris High School.]

HIGH SCHOOL STATISTICS FOR OCTOBER, 1913.

Name	First Asst.		Teachers			First Term Pupils		Pupils		
	M.	W.	M.	W.	Ttl.	Boys	Girls	Boys	Girls	Total
Wash. Irving	2	4	26	142	168	1150			4412	4412
De Witt Clinton.	7	1	115	14	129	954		3434		3434
Man. Train.	9	0	82	60	142	581	566	1709	1707	3416
Morris	4	2	47	69	116	289	400	1138	2017	3155
Erasmus Hall ...	4	2	49	68	117	281	532	1062	1978	3040
Wadleigh	3	4	15	124	139		676		2985	2985
Commerce	8	0	94		94	850		2719		2719
Commercial	9	0	104		104	948		2700		2700
Eastern Dist. ...	6	1	32	67	99	178	410	859	1831	2690
Girls	2	5	10	96	106		686		2576	2576
Stuyvesant	6	0	97	0	97	107		2565		2565
Bushwick	5	0	33	46	79	195	587	618	1621	2239
Boys	6	0	76		76	689		2173		2173
Julia Richman ..	2	0	5	37	42		674		1568	1568
Bryant	2	0	10	37	47	180	184	543	639	1182
Curtis	4	2	21	27	48	167	204	475	647	1122
Bay Ridge......	2	1	19	37	56	51	251	238	848	1086
Rich. Hill	5	0	16	24	40	156	259	371	713	1084
Newtown	1	0	15	27	42	136	157	429	573	1002
Evander Childs .	0	0	22	14	36	164	363	289	633	922
Jamaica	6	1	21	22	43	88	134	317	600	917
Flushing	5	0	13	18	31	82	145	231	432	663
Far Rockaway .	1	0	6	11	17	39	58	120	177	297

OFFICIAL BULLETIN

of the High School Teachers' Association of New York City

No. 42. DECEMBER 6 1913

THE SECOND GENERAL MEETING FOR 1913-1914 will be held Saturday, December 6, 1913, at the High School of Commerce.

DEPARTMENT MEETINGS begin at 10 A. M.

Programs of sections given below.

For more detailed announcements see papers.

GENERAL MEETING begins at 11.15 A. M. in Auditorium.

ORDER OF BUSINESS:

REPORTS OF OFFICERS.

REPORTS OF CHAIRMEN OF COMMITTEES.

ADDRESS: **"An Outline of the Proposed Activities of the New Division of Reference and Research of the Board of Education."**

By Albert Shiels, Director.

DISCUSSION.

NEW BUSINESS.

WILLIAM T. MORREY, President.

MARY J. BOURNE, Secretary.

DEPARTMENT MEETINGS, 10 A. M.

ANCIENT LANGUAGES—Room 534, Dr. Walter E. Foster, Stuyvesant High School, Chairman of question.

No meeting December 6, 1913, but instead there will be a Dinner at 5:30 P. M., Friday, December 12, 1913, at the Fifth Ave. Restaurant, 24th St. and Broadway—One Dollar.

Preliminary Report by Dr. W. E. Foster, Chairman of Committee on Ancient Languages, of the National Educational Association's Commission on the Re-organization of Secondary Education.

Discussion of the Policy of the Latin Teacher of New York City.

Election of Chairman for 1913-1914.

BIOLOGY—Room 301. Mr. Edgar Bedford, DeWitt Clinton High School, Chairman; Frank Merrill Wheat, DeWitt Clinton H. S., Secretary.

On the Use of Note Books in High School Biology, Teachers from various high schools will discuss the kind and use of note-books in their respective schools.

Representative note-books will be exhibited.

BOOKKEEPING SECTION—Room 303, William R. Hayward, Head of Commercial Department, Washington Irving High School, Chairman.

A Round Table Conference on what should be in the proposed new courses of study in Commercial Branches, by the Chairman of Superintendent Meleney's Committee and the Committee of the Male High School Teachers' Association.

DRAWING—Room 302, Eunice F. Faulkner, Eastern District High School, Chairman.

(The regular monthly conference of High School Teachers of Drawing will be held Thursday, December 4, 1913, at 4 P. M. in the Auditorium of School No. 59, Manhattan, 228 East 57th St. A conference exhibit of current School work at 3:40. Attendance at these conferences is required, pursuant to the direction of the City Superintendent James P. Haney, Director of Art in High Schools.)

ELOCUTION—Room 201. Mr Raymond W. Kellogg, Chairman; W. Palmer Smith, Stuyvesant High School, Secretary.

No meeting of Elocution Section December 6, but there will be a special, called meeting in January, 1914. of which due notice will be given.

HISTORY AND ECONOMICS—Room 205. Mr. Alfred C. Bryan, Head of Department of History, High School of Commerce, Chairman.

An address on the "Correlation of History and Civics," by Prof. Charles E Beard of Columbia University—a **live** man **wired** for service.

MODERN LANGUAGES—Room 401, Colman Dudley Frank, DeWitt Clinton High School, Chairman.

An address on the Fusion of Geometry and Algebra, by Mr. Merle L. Bishop, Boys' High School.

What shall be put in the first year of modern language work to make it valuable for the pupils who leave High School as well as for the pupils who contine?

Discussion led by the candidate for First Assistant license.

MATHEMATICS—Room 304, Mr. Edward A. Hook, Commercial High School.

PHYSIOGRAPHY—Room 506, Mr. Earl B. Slack, Washington Irving High School, Chairman.

The new Regent's Ruling, abolishing the 20 credits for Laboratory Work in Sciences.

How will it affect us and how can we best prepare for it?

Discussion opened by Frank L. Bryant, Erasmus Hall High School.

EXHIBIT—"A New Use for an Old Wall Map," by William T. Morrey, Head of Department of History, Bushwick High School.

SHORTHAND—Room 216, Mr. William P. O'Ryan, Commercial High School, Chairman.

Changes in the Isaac Pitman System for 1914. General Discussion opened by Professor Beygrau, of High School of Commerce.

Minutes of November 25, 1913 Meeting of Representatives.

What are the Best Courses of Study for our New York City High Schools?

The Commission of the N. E. A. on the Reorganization of Secondary Education, with the Clarence D. Kingsley, Chairman, has already organized 11 Committees. This association is well represented. Dr. Walter Eugene Foster, of the Stuyvesant High School, is Chairman of Committee on Ancient Languages, and Alexander L. Pugh, of High School of Commerce, Chairman of Committee on Business. Benjamin A. Heydrick, High School of Commerce, is on Committee on English, J. Herbert Low, of Manual Training High School and William T. Morrey, of Bushwick High School, on Committee on Social Studies, including History, Dr. Carl F. Krause, Jamaica High School, on Committee on Modern Languages, Miss Florence Willard of Washington Irving High School, on Committee on Household Arts, Charles B. Howe, of Stuyvesant High School, on Committee on Manual Arts, and Sieste B. Koopman, of High School of Commerce on Committee on Business.

The gentlemen mentioned above are invited to form New York City Committees and to use this Bulletin for the publication of their Announcements and Preliminary Reports, if not too extensive.

The Association and its members stand ready to assist all working for the Revision of our High School Courses of Study.

The best equipment of the various High School Departments is a subject always changing, and one in which there should be a constant interchange of opinion and of information.

Mr. Bedford, Chairman of the Biology Section reported that his section during the year would take up and discuss Note Books, course of first year Biology. Efficiency in Biology Teaching.

Mr. Hunter, Head of Department of Biology, DeWitt Clinton, said report on Standard Equipment has been pigeon-holed at 59th St. A committee has been appointed by the Board of Superintendents to investigate the course in Biology.

Miss Skinner, of the Commercial Section reported that a talk was to be given by representative of the State Department of Education on Commercial Branches in High Schools.

Members for 1913-1914. Most high schools have not reported to date. Bay Ridge 30, Bushwick 70, and Morris 5.

Moved by Mr. Dotey of DeWitt Clinton, that it is the sense of the Board of Representatives that eligibility to the High School Teachers' Association is limited to teachers and supervisers in the public day high schools of New York City and in the high school departments of Normal College and City College. Carried.

Moved by Mr. Dotey: The Secretary be instructed to direct the senior representatives to take a vote of the represntativs concerning a change in time of meeting from Tuesday to Friday afternoon and report to the President. Carried.

Moved by Mr. Goodman: That when we adjourn we adjourn till Jan. 13, 1914. Carried.

Moved by Miss Carr: That a commitee be appointed to request the Board of Education, and to suggest to other associations that they request the Board, to re-open the schools on Jan. 5, 1914, rather than on Jan. 2, 1914. Carried.

Mr. Dotey was appointed as a committee of one to see Mr. Shiels, to request him to address the next general meeting of Dec. 6.

Adjourned, 5:25.

F. M. SURREY, Secretary Pro. Tem.

Materials for Directory.

Senior Representatives will kindly send at once to the President the following information revised to Nov. 30, 1913, or later.

(1) A Library Card for every teacher, showing: (1) Name (last Name first); (2) position; (3) subject; (4) high school; (5) home address; (6) telephone.

(2) Two complete lists of teachers by departments, each department on separate sheets of paper.

(3) An alphabetical list of all teachers in school, ready to go to printer.

Suggestions from all interested will be gladly received on What should the High School Directory contain to make it most valuable as a Hand Book?

Please send samples of High School Manuals and Directories to the President.

Discussion of the question: What subjects should be brought to the attention of the Teachers' Council?

Corrections of Lists.

The Preliminary Lists of H. S. T. A. members to the various High Schools were submitted in Galley Proof to the Senior Representatives, and the Proofs as revised were inserted in Bulletin 41.

Flushing High School should have Principal John Holley Clark, John Baumeister, WalterBarnwell, Edward C. Wood, Paul T. Jenks, Frank H. Miller, Elena P. Nearing, Warren W. Read and Annie Ross as members for 1912-1913, a total of 9 instead of 3.

Bushwick High School's List should have the name of Miss Anna E. Stanton as Member of Board of Representatives.

Other corrections should be sent to the President.

NEXT MEETING OF THE BOARD OF REPRESENTATIVES will be held Tuesday, Jan. 13, 1914, at the High School of Commerce.

Chairmen of Sections and Chairmen of Committees are expected to be presen to outline their plans of work for the year.

Senior Representatives are expected to report on the membership of their schools. Dues for 1913-1914 should be paid.

OFFICERS, 1913-1914.

PRESIDENT—William T. Morrey, Bushwick High School.
VICE-PRESIDENT—Miss Jessie H. Bingham, DeWitt Clinton High School.
SECRETARY—Miss Mary J. Bourne, of Morris High School.
TREASURER—Dr. Loring B. Mullen, Girls' High School.

ADDITIONAL MEMBERS OF EXECUTIVE COMMITTEE—

Mr. Aaron L. Dotey, De Witt Clinton High School.
Miss H. Elizabeth Seelman, Girls' High School.
Mr. Alexander L. Pugh, High School of Commerce.

REPRESENTATIVES IN HIGH SCHOOL TEACHERS' ASSOCIATION 1913-1914.

* Senior Representatives

BAY RIDGE—*Emberson E. Proper
Mabel R. Benway
Emil Gluck

BOYS'—*Charles E. Overholser
Francis T. Hughes
Frederick B. Jones
S. Ridley Parker
Alfred A. Tansk

BRYANT—*Harry K. Munro
Margaret C. Byrne

BUSHWICK—*George M. Falion
Mary E. Green
Anna A. Stanton
Grace Helene Miller (Annex 129)
Nathan Leibowitz
Louise Smith (Annex 75)
Arthur Goodman

COMMERCIAL—*Harry M. Love
Edwin A. Bolger
George W. Harman
Benjamin C. Gruenberg

COMMERCE—*Julius Blume
Horace G. Healey
Alfred H. Lewis
Alexander L. Pugh
George H. Van Tuyl
William S. Schlauch

CURTIS—*Mabel G. Burdick
Philip R. Dean

DE WITT CLINTON—*Aaron I. Dotey
Edgar A. Bedford
Edmund W. Foote
George W. Hunter
Oscar W. Anthony
Ellen E. Garrigues
Fayette E. Moyer
Charles E. Timmerman
Jesse E. Whitsit
Harry B. Penhollow

EASERN DISTRICT—*Elizabeth R. Hoy
Edith M. Brace
Agnes M. Houghron
Frederick H Paine
Charles Dixon
Frank P. Baltz

EVANDER CHILDS—

ERASMUS HALL—*Preston C. Farrar
George E. Boynton
Alice C. Howe
Edith M. Everett

FAR ROCKAWAY—*Elmer M. Van Dusen
Emily M. Jennison

FLUSHING—*Annie Ross

GIRLS'—*Loring B. Mullen
H. Elizabeth Seelman

JAMAICA—*Edwin J. McNamara
Christine Busher
Roscoe A. Grant

JULIA RICHMAN—(Not organized

MANUAL TRAINING—*A. Latham Baker (Johnson St. Annex)
Eleanor R. Baker (Main Bldg., 7th Ave.)
Marion Hackedorn
Mary A. Hall
Charles Perrine (Prospect Ave. Annex)
M. Helen Smith

MORRIS—*Agnes Carr
Harriet L. Constantine
Fred C. White
Clara M. Burt
Sonford L. Cutler
Frank M. Surrey

NEWTOWN—*George H. Kingsbury
Alexander H. Zerban

RICHMOND HILL—*William E. Stilson
Gertrude M. Leete

STUYVESANT—*John Messenger, Jr.
T. Harry Knox
Joseph L. Beha
Stanley A. Gage
Charles F. Moors
(List uncertain)

WADLEIGH—*William W. Clendenin
Helen E. Bacon

WASHINGTON IRVING—*Elizabeth A. Roche
Mary C. Craig
E. Mabel Skinner

OFFICIAL BULLETIN

of the High School Teacher's Association of New York City

No. 43 MARCH 7 1914

THE THIRD GENERAL MEETING FOR 1913-1914 will be held SATURDAY, March 7, at the High School of Commerce.

DEPARTMENT MEETINGS begin at 10 A. M.

Programs of sections given below.

For more detailed announcements see papers.

GENERAL MEETING begins at 11.15 A. M. in Auditorium.

ORDER OF BUSINESS:

REPORT OF OFFICERS.

REPORTS OF CHAIRMEN OF COMMITTEES.

DISCUSSION: The Efficiency of **FACTORY METHODS IN EDUCATION** as exemplified in the **DOUBLE AND TRIPLE SESSIONS OF OUR LARGE HIGH SCHOOLS.**

DISCUSSION to be opened by Principals, who feel strongly and who can express themselves vigorously.

This topic comes very naturally after our nine previous studies in the Application, to High School Problems, of the Principles of Scientific Management, first enunciated in the industrial world:

1) Statement of the Principles by Harrington Emerson, Efficiency Engineer.
2) Purpose of the School System by Prof. Hanus of Harvard.
3) Efficiency in Administration by representatives of the superintendents, principals, first assistants and grade advisers.
4) Efficiency in Type of High School by Mr. Frederick H. Paine and Mr. Clarence D. Kingsley.
5) Efficiency in Recitation by Superintendent Bardwell.
6) Department Efficiency by Messrs. Alfred C. Bryan, Daniel D. Feldman and Arthur M. Wolfson.
7) How to Test Pupils by Prof. Judd, of Chicago University.
8) The Efficient Teacher—"Superior Merit" from the point ot view of the Examiners and Principals.
9) Moral Efficiency by Hon. Frank Moss.

Those desiring to speak should send the President a very brief outline of points, they desire to make, so that the order of speaking will best bring out both the advantages and the disadvantages of the system.

WLLIAM T. MORREY, President.

MARY J. BOURNE, Secretary.

DEPARTMENT MEETINGS, 10 A. M.

ANCIENT LANGUAGES—Room 534, Dr. Walter E. Foster, Stuyvesant High School, Chairman.

"How to Acquire a Latin Vocabulary."

BIOLOGY—Room 301. Mr. Edgar Bedford, DeWitt Clinton High School, Chairman; Frank Merrill Wheat, DeWitt Clinton H. S., Secretary.

The proposed changes in the Biology Syllables for New York City High Schools. Quesion of sex education.

Discussion opened by Dr. George W. Hunter, Head of Department of Biology, De Witt Clinton High School.

BOOKKEEPING SECTION—Room 303, William R. Hayward, Head of Commercial Department, Washington Irving High School, Chairman.

New York State Inspector of Commercial Branches, W. E. Bartholomew, will address the Section on: "Recent Criticisms of Commercial Education in the High Schools." General discussion.

DOMESTIC SCIENCE AND ART—Room 302, Miss Margaret Loring Dike, Chairman, **Pro Tem.**

Topic for Discussion: "The Course of Study in Domestic Science and Art."

ELOCUTION—Room 201, Mr. Raymond W. Kellogg, Chairman; W. Palmer Smith, Stuyvesant High School, Secretary.

An Address by Miss Lucy Allen, Head of the Department of English, New York Training School. Topic:

"Oral Deficiencies of Training School Candidates."

HISTORY AND ECONOMICS—Room 203, Mr. Alfred C. Bryan, Head of Department of History, High School of Commerce, Chairman.

Constructive Discussion of the New York State Modern History Course (Terms III and IV in particular).

Discussion opened by Miss Antoinette Lawrence, Head of Department of History in Jamaica High School; followed by Mr. Wm. W. Rogers of Boys'

NOTE.—A revision has been decided upon. Every teacher doubtlss has suggestions of value. Bring your History Syllables and come prepared to discuss.

How can we inspire honesty and patriotism while teaching Recent History of the Treaty Obligations of the United States?

Question stated by Mr. William T. Morrey, Head of Department of History, Bushwick High School.

MATHEMATICS—Room 304, Mr. Edward A. Hook, Commercial High

The New Course of Commercial Algebra in the High School of Commerce.

A brief introductory talk by Mr. John D. Minnick of the High School of Commerce.

Discussion opened by Mr. Wm. S. Schlauch of the High School of Commerce.

A large attendance is urged, because the paper will be of unusual interest, espcially to those who would like to see mathematics made more practical.

MODERN LANGUAGES—Room 401, Colman Dudley Frank, DeWitt Clinton High School, Chairman. Mary C. Hall, Evander Childs, Secretary.

The Chairman considers himself rarely privileged in being able to present to the Modern Language teachers Mary Stone Bruce, recently of Boston, author of the Grammaire Raisonnée, Lectures Faciles and other books, who will talk on "The Yersin Method." Miss Bruce is one of the foremost teachers of French in America to-day and the Yersin Method one of the livest methods in use in Modern Language teaching. Miss Clio M. Chilcott of the Washington Irving High School, will lead the discussion.

PHYSIOGRAPHY—Room 506, Mr. Earl B. Slack, Washington Irving High School, Chairman.

"Suggestions for Laboratory Work in the Physiography of the Lands."

Lecture, with Lantern, by Prof. Douglas W. Johnson, of Columbia University.

SHORTHAND—Room 216, Mr. William P. O'Ryan, Commercial High School, Chairman.

Round Table Discussions:

Efficiency Problems and Devices,

Proposed Commercial Course for General High Schools.

Minutes of October 28, 1913, Meeting of Representatives.

The meeting of the Board of Representatives of the High Shoolc Teachers' Association was held October 28 at the High School of Commerce. Mr. Morrey called the meeting to order at 4:10. The reading of the minutes was omitted. The treasurer reported as follows: balance (1912-1913) $605.27, dues (1912-1913) $113.00, dues (1913-1914) $89.00, expenses $206.90, leaving a balance to date of $600.37.

The President reported that he had been engaged in issuing the November Bulletin and in planning a H. S. T. A. Directory which should be of great service to all interested in New York City High Schools. He expressed his indebtedness to various members of the Association who had assisted him by helpful suggestions in regard to the general meetings; he also stated that reports of committees would appear in the next bulletin.

The election of delegates to the Teachers' Advisory Council was fully discussed, especially the question of the method of nomination. It was voted that nominations be made from the floor.

On motion of Mr. White of Morris, the board voted that the President be empowered to appoint such committees as he sees fit and also to remove from committees such members as may seem inefficient.

The meeting was adjourned. MARY J. BOURNE, Secretary.

What are the Best Courses of Study?

The Commission of the N. E. A. on the Reorganization of Secondary Education, with the Clarence D. Kingsley, Chairman, has already organized 11 Committees. This association is well represented. Dr. Walter Eugene Foster, of the Stuyvesant High School, is Chairman of Committee on Ancient Languages, and Alexander L. Pugh, of High School of Commerce, Chairman of Committee on Business. Benjamin A. Heydrick, High School of Commerce, is on Committee on English, J. Herbert Low, of Manual Training High School and William T. Morrey, of Bushwick High School, on Committee on Social Studies, including History, Dr. Carl F. Kraus, Jamaica High School, on Committee on Modern Languages, Miss Florence Willard of Washington Irving High School, on Committee on Household Arts, Charles B. Howe, of Stuyvesant High School, on Committee on Manual Arts, and Sieste B. Koopman, of High School of Commerce on Committee on Business.

The gentlemen mentioned above are invited to form New York City Committees and to use this Bulletin for the publication of their Announcements and Preliminary Reports, if not too extensive.

Materials for Directory.

Senior Representatives will kindly send at once to the President

(1) A Library Card for every teacher, showing: (1) Name (last Name first). (2) position; (3) subject; (4) high school; (5) home address; (6) telephone.

(2) Two complete lists of teachers by departments, each department on separate sheets of paper.

(3) An alphabetical list of all teachers in school.

Suggestions from all interested will be gladly received on What should the High School Directory contain to make it most valuable as a Hand book? Please send samples of High School Manuals and Directories to the President.

For Teachers of English.

The Association of High School Teachers of English, of New York City, Charles S. Hartwell, President, will hold an adjourned meeting on Saturday, March 14, 1914, at 10.30 A. M., in Room 601, Washington Irving High School, to consider the following committee reports:

1. On the Articulation of High School and Training School English;
2. Ethics in Recitation;
3. Oral English;

and to discuss them and the two reports of the last meeting on:

4. The Articulation of Elementary and High School English;
5. Department Pedagogy.

OFFICERS, 1913-1914.

PRESIDENT—William T. Morrey, Bushwick High School.
VICE-PRESIDENT—Miss Jessie H. Bingham, DeWitt Clinton High School.
SECRETARY—Miss Mary J. Bourne, of Morris High School.
TREASURER—Dr. Loring B. Mullen, Girls' High School.
ADDITIONAL MEMBERS OF EXECUTIVE COMMITTEE—
Mr. Aaron I. Dorey, DeWitt Clinton High School.
Miss H. Elizabeth Seelman, Girls' High School.
Mr. Alexander L. Pugh, High School of Commerce.

REPRESENTATIVES IN HIGH SCHOOL TEACHERS' ASSOCIATION 1913-1914.

* Senior Representatives

BAY RIDGE—*Emberson E. Proper
Mabel R. Benway
Emil Gluck

BOYS'—*Charles E. Overholser
Francis T. Hughes
Frederick B. Jones
S. Ridley Parker
Alfred A. Tansk

BRYANT—*Harry K. Munro
Margaret C. Byrne

BUSHWICK—*George M. Falion
Mary E. Green
Anna E. Stanton
Grace Helene Miller (Annex 129)
Nathan Leibowitz
Louise Smith (Annex 75)
Arthur Goodman

COMMERCIAL—*Harry M. Love
Edwin A. Bolger
George W. Harman
Benjamin C. Gruenberg

COMMERCE—*Julius Blume
Horace G. Healey
Alfred H. Lewis
Alexander L. Pugh
George H. Van Tuyl
William S. Schlauch

CURTIS—*Mabel G. Burdick
Philip R. Dean

DE WITT CLINTON—*Aaron I. Dotey
Edgar A. Bedford
Edmund W. Foote
George W. Hunter
Oscar W. Anthony
Ellen E. Garrigues
Fayette E. Moyer
Charles E. Timmerman
Jesse E. Whitsit
Harry B. Penhollow

EASTERN DISTRICT—*Elizabeth R. Hoy
Edith M. Brace
Agnes M. Loughran
Frederick H. Paine
Charles Dixon
Frank P. Baltz

EVANDER CHILDS—*M. W. Greditser
Clayton G. Durfee
Louis B. Cohn

ERASMUS HALL—*Preston C. Farrar
George E. Boynton
Alice C. Howe
Edith M. Everett

FAR ROCKAWAY—*Elmé M. Van Dusen
Emily M. Jennison

FLUSHING—*Annie Ross

GIRLS'—*Loring B. Mullen
H. Elizabeth Seelman

JAMAICA—*Edward McNamara
Christiana Busbee
Josephine D. Wilkin
Roscoe A. Grant

JULIA RICHMAN—David L. Arnold

MANUAL TRAINING—*A. Latham Baker (Johnson St. Annex)
Eleanor R. Baker (Main Bldg., 7th Ave.)
Marion Hackedorn
Mary A. Hall
Charles Perrine (Prospect Ave. Annex)
M. Helen Smith

MORRIS—*Agnes Carr
Harriet L. Constantine
Fred C. White
Clara M. Burt
Sanford L. Cutler
Frank M. Surrey

NEWTOWN—*George H. Kingsbury
Alexander H. Zerban

RICHMOND HILL—*William E. Stilson
Gertrude M. Leete

STUYVESANT—*John Messenger, Jr.
Beha, Joseph L.
Bruce, Murray
Gage, Stanley A.
Hein, Henry E.
Goldberger, Henry H.
Knox, T. Harry
Wyman, Wm. T.

WADLEIGH—*William W. Clendenin
Helen E. Bacon

WASHINGTON IRVING—*Elizabeth A. Roche
Mary C. Craig
E. Mabel Skinner

OFFICIAL BULLETIN

of the High School Teacher's Association of New York City

No. 44. MAY 2. 1914.

THE FOURTH GENERAL MEETING FOR 1913-1914 will be held SATURDAY, May 2, at the High School of Commerce.

DEPARTMENT MEETINGS begin at 10 A. M.

Program of sections.

ELECTION OF OFFICERS FOR 1914-1915.

For more detailed announcements see papers.

GENERAL MEETING begins at 11.15 A. M. in Auditorium.

ORDER OF BUSINESS:

REPORT OF OFFICERS.

REPORTS OF CHAIRMEN OF COMMITTEES

ELECTION OF OFFICERS FOR 1914-1915.

NEXT MEETING OF THE BOARD OF REPRESENTATIVES will be held Tuesday, April 28; at the High School of Commerce.

WLLIAM T. MORREY, President.

MARY J. BOURNE, Secretary.

DEPARTMENT MEETINGS, 10 A. M.

ANCIENT LANGUAGES—Room 534, Dr. Walter E. Foster, Stuyvesant High School, Chairman.

BIOLOGY—Room 301. Mr. Edgar Bedford, Stuyvesant High School, Chairman; Frank Merrill Wheat, DeWitt Clinton H. S., Secretary.

Civic Biology—In a Girls' High School, Dr. Elsie M. Kupfer Wadleigh High School.

Civic Biology in a Boys' High School, Dr. George W. Hunter, De Witt Clinton High School.

BOOKKEEPING SECTION—Room 303. William R. Hayward, Head of Commercial Department. Washington Irving High School, Chairman.

DOMESTIC SCIENCE AND ART—Room 302, Miss Margaret Loring Dike, Chairman, **Pro Tem.**

Topic for Discussion: "The Course of Study in Domestic Science and Art."

ELOCUTION—Room 201. Mr. Raymond W. Kellogg, Chairman; W. Palmer Smith, Stuyvesant High School, Secretary.

Election of officers and Brief Reports.

HISTORY AND ECONOMICS—Room 203, Mr. Alfred C. Bryan, Head of Department of History, High School of Commerce. Chairman.

MATHEMATICS—Room 304. Mr. Edward A. Hook, Commercial High

"The Report of the Committee on High School Mathematics Libraries." Mr. Elmer Schuyler. Bay Ridge High School, chairman of the committee will be the principle speaker. The other members of the committee, Miss Jessie Beach, of Curtis; Mr. Merle Bishop of Boy's; Miss Louise Hazen, of Morris; Mr. D. C. Mac Lane, of Erasmus; will speak on the special phases of the work which they have followed up.

A large attendance is urged, because the paper will be of unusual interest,

MODERN LANGUAGES—Room 401, Colman Dudley Frank, DeWitt Clinton

High School, Chairman. Mary C. Hall, Evander Childs, Secretary.
PHYSIOGRAPHY—Room 506, Mr. Earl B. Slack, Washington Irving High School, Chairman.
SHORTHAND—Room 216, Mr. William P. O'Ryan, Commercial High School, Chairman.

CONTENTS OF THIS BULLETIN NO. 44.

GENERAL MEETING, MARCH 7, 1914.

The meeting was called to order at 11.30 with the President in the chair. The minute of the last meeting were read and approved. The treasurer reported as follows: Total receipts $1423.06, expenses $488.72, balance $934.34.

Mr. Frederick H. Payne, Eastern District High School, reported for the pensios committee.

Dr. Tildsley, for the special cammittee, reported tsat he had presented at the hearing on pensions the desires of the Association as previously expressed.

The President briefly outlined the topic for the general meeting which was: The Efficiency of Factory Methods in Education as exemplified in the Double and Triple Sessions of our large High Schools.

Dr. Larkins, Manual Training High School, stated his experience in trying to adjust the enlarged school to the double and triple sessions plan. He said that is was like a game of checkers: "You can put more checkers on the board but it spoils the game." He showed the various methods which had been employed to dispose of the additional school population but especially dwelt on the results of the double or triple session plan, on the child, the teacher and the school plant. He summarized the results under two heads of confussion and irresponsibility—there is confusion inattention, lost time and inefficiency. The school plant suffers—partically the laboratories. Pupils are deprived of study periods and teachers of the opportunity to teach how to study. After-school activities must be suspended.

Dr. Tildsley, De Witt Clinton High School, submitted a report compiled by Mr. Deubigh of Morris High School, which was published in the Brooklyn Eagle under date of March 5, 1914 and which Dr. Tildsley considered the ablest ever published on this subject.

Dr. Fildsley then reviewed the financial aspest of the question, illustrating his conclusions by statistics compiled in his own school. His conclusions were: That there is no actual saving of money by the double session plan; that the life of the high school is demoralized; that the actual "mortality" is higher in a double session high school; that boys need more hours with a teacher rather than less, for purposes of character formation; that a larger provision at his school for contactt with the teacher has resulted in a marked decrease in the percentage of failures.

Dr. Sullivan Boys' High School, emphasized the fact that part time solution of over-crowded conditions only deceives the public into thinking that there is a financial gain thereby.

Dr. Rollins, Bushwick High School, emphasized the following points: The deterioration of the plant under the double session plan is more than doubled; the checking of truancy is almost impossible; the establishment of many continuation schools would reduce the number entering high schools, thus leaving place for those who have proved their capacity for such work, and at the same time providing satisfactorily for those who do not really care for High School.

Dr. Greenberg showed graphically the changing efficiency of the individual at certain times of the day especially at night.

On motion of Mr. B. A. Heydrick, High School of Commerce, the following resolution was adopted (two dissenting votes):

RESOLVED, That the H. S. T. A. after full discussion of the matter, places itself upon record as strongly opposed to the plan of double and triple sessions for high schools.

RESOLVED, Further, that a committee consisting of Dr. Tildsley, Mr. Denbigh and Dr. Larkin, be appointed to represent this association before the Board of Education and the Board of Estimate in presenting our views in opposition to this plan.

On motion the meeting was adjourned at 1.30.

MARY J. BOURNE, Secretary.

DISCUSSION BY PRINCIPAL ROLLINS OF BUSHWICK HIGH SCHOOL.

Principal Tildsley has concluded that the City would save only five hundred dollars per year by holding double sessions in the De Witt Clinton High School over and above the cost of maintaining another plant of equal value; but in his estimates he has neglected the extra wear and tear of a plant used by double shifts of teachers and students with the accompanying difficulty in fixing responsibility for damage to building and equipment and the difficulty and extra expense involved in cleaning, renovating and repairing a building used on double time. These items of expense and loss would alone offset his small balance left in favor o fdouble sessions.

The advocates of double sessions seem wholly to ignore the effect of double sessions on the enforcement of the compulsory education law and the great problem of truancy. When all children are required to attend school from nine in the morning till half past two or three o'clock in the afternoon. It is easy enough for alert and industrious attendance officers to keep the streets and vacant lots clear of children who ought to be in school; but under the double or triple session plan, any child in the streets at any hour may baffle the attendance officer with the statement that he is on part time and is due in school only at a later or an earlier hour.

The main argument for double sessions is based on the inability of the City to raise funds to build new schools; but if some way can be found to check the wanton squandering of the people's money on useless and inefficient commissions and on the tribute levied by modern robber barons of politics on the construction of highways, canals and other public works, there will be money enough for all the schools that are needed in the entire State.

So far as high schools are concerned, the demand will be materially reduced when the city provides for each gaduate of the elementary schools the means of education suited to his ability and his prospective work. At present almost the only opportunity for education beyond the elementary grades must be sought in the high schools. Other opportunities for genuine continuation work should be provided near the homes of the children for those whose limitations of mental capacity for book-learning or of financial ability render the completion of a four years high school course impracticable. If the present method of throwing the entire output of the elementary schools into the high schools without much regard to ability, attainments, or plans for the future, could be replaced by a more rational and discriminating provision for continued education; the problem of congestion in high schools would disappear.

Thus far in the discussion to-day I have heard no mention of the extra cost involved in repeating studies and grades in part-time high schools. An experience of several years with part-time classes has proved to me that the number of students who fail and have to be taught over again in the same grade is much larger in part-time classes than in regular classes. Every additional failure means an extra expense to he City for instruction, books, supplies, fuel, and service. If the extra cost to the City for these items of expense were the worst result of part-time instruction, the people might endure it patiently; but when part-time involves the waste of the life and time of large numbers of children, the taxpaying parents of these children will sooner or later detect and resent any attempt to substitute for normal, full-time education some other device however conspicuously labeled "JUST-AS-GOOD."

Great credit is due to the Board of Education and to Superintendents for restricting the part-time evil to a minimum and for the ingenious plans that have been devised for mitigating the serious and deplorable consequences of part-time. Surely it goes without saying that every high school in the City will do its utmost to make the best of part-time sessions so long as they must be endured; but from the duscussion of the morning it also seems evident that the high schools will throw their undivided influence on the side of full time for every student where full time is possible.

FACTORY METHODS IN THE HIGH SCHOOL.

Dr. Denbigh Points Out Some of the Evils of Part-Time System.

Brooklyn Daily Eagle of March 5, 1914

All the high school principals of the City of New York, save one, are opposed to what is well-styled as "Factory Education." This is the subject which is to be discussed by the High School Teachers Association on Saturday morning at the High School of Commerce. Not only are the principals opposed to "Factory Education," but the teachers are as much opposed to it as are they. Two-part time or three-part time is an abomination, whether in high school or elementary school; whether it is called "part-time" or by any other name. It is bad in an elementary school after the first two or three years; it is much worse in a high school by whomsoever conducted.

Dr. John H. Denbigh, principal of the Morris High School, who has had experience with part-time, in a report on Professor Ballou's report, which has never been published, said of part-time (and "part-time" means factory methods of schoolkeeping):

"In actual practice the course offered to students in these extended sessions or 'part-time' has not been curtailed in the number of subjects taken or in the number of recitations required in each subject, but the students have been deprived of study periods in school, and so have lost an opportunity to acquire the habit of concentrated study, the most valuable habit the school might under other more favorable conditions, develop. Students in these extended sessions either begin work earlier than 9 a. m., and are dismissed before the hour of 2:30 p. m., or else they assemble later than 9 a. m., and are dismissed correspondingly later than 2:30 p. m.—sometimes as late as 4:45 p. m., or even 5:15 p. m.

"Any comment on this subject would be incomplete if it did not touch briefly upon the evils of 'part-time' for adolescent students. Your committee is unanimously of the opinion that these evils militate so seriously against real efficiency in education, that they consider that the perpetuance of 'part-time' far from being an economical method of administration by which school buildings may be made to yield a larger return upon their original cost, is in reality most extravagant and wasteful since it is a most serious detriment both to work and character of students at the most critical period of habit formation.

How Part-Time Affects the Students.

"To prove this point your committee invites attention to the following disadvantages under which students of 'part-time' sessions labor:

"1. They miss the best hours—the morning hours—for school recitation.

"2. They are deprived of study periods in school and so lose the most valuable opportunity to form right habits of study.

"3. They lose the additional help that weak students should receive after the close of the day.

"4. Detention for disciplinary reasons is not possible.

"5. They must return to their homes on crowded cars.

"6. They are deprived of all natural playtime, excluded from all social life of the school and cannot take part in or witness school games.

"7. They are disinclined to begin preparation for the next day's work in the evening, and but few of them have sufficient determination to make proper use of the morning hours for this purpose. Even if they do prepare in the morning, the day is broken only by their trip to school and is too long for young students.

"8. Those who waste the morning hours acquire indolent habits, lose in power of concentration and fail in their work.

"9. Many of the more ambitious students take up outside work which distracts them from their school work; e. g., the girls take music lessons or the boys run errands for storekeepers and very often drop out of school when a position for the whole day is offered to them.

"10. Instead of meeting an official class teacher twice a day—at the beginning and close of school—they meet him but once and then only for recitation. This induces a lack of a feeling of responsibility to some one person and is most harmful.

How Part-Time Affects the School.

"In addition to the many disadvantages under which the individual 'part-time' student works, there are disadvantages just as serious to the school as a whole. Some of these are:

"1. The coming and going of large groups of students at different times.

"2. The overcrowding of music and physical training classes to provide empty classrooms for other subjects.

"3. The provision of double lunch periods and the consequent necessity for keeping silence in one part of the building while another has recess.

"4. In the case of early sessions, keeping one portion of the building quiet while students of the 9 o'clock group are arriving.

"5. When there are more classes than classrooms, some classes must be dismissed from different rooms from those in which they assemble; e. g., to permit of recitations going on after 2:30 p. m., the classes usually assembling in the morning, at 9 o'clock, in those recitation rooms, must be dismissed at 2:30 p. m. from some other place, probably the auditorium.

"6. Afternoon teachers cannot attend the regular faculty or departmental meetings.

"7. The fact that after a certain hour the students of the early session, and before a certain hour the students of the afternoon session, are not in school, frequently complicates the issue of orders that should reach the whole school at the end or at the beginning of a day.'

ONE PROPOSED REMEDY.
HIGH SCHOOLS FOR FIRST YEAR PUPILS.

School Editor of The Globe: Thursday, March 19, 1914.

Sir—Is not the time opportune for The Globe to emphasize again, as it has so often in years past, the importance of the precademic or intermediate school, or what I prefer to call the junior high school?

This is a vastly better solution than placing high schools on double sessions. I do not agree with The Globe in its strictures on five prominent principals who had the courage of their convictions in stating plainly their protest against part time and double sessions. Factory education is an evil of tremendous proportions, and you will find the overwhelming sentiment of those in the system who do the work is with those principals and not against them.

While I venture to offend The Globe and prevent the publication of this letter by the above, I wish to express my admiration for the principal who has these double sessions and manages them so well. He has taken the task given him and shown masterly skill in meeting its problems, but he is killing himself in the effort and his teachers are wearing out very fast. Only the strongest teachers can endure the strain of his system and follow his example. It is one thing to acknowledge his courage and ability. It is another to advocate placing the other high schools in the same predicament.

I believe the Board of Education and the Board of Superintendents both are doing grand work in meeting the crisis before us. But the great help needed is to come from the Board of Estimate, which should without delay furnish money to place plain, ample junior high school buildings in every crowded section on sites already acquired, and I am willing that no more high school organs should be put in until the junior high school is a fact.

CHARLES S. HARTWELL. Brooklyn, N. Y., March 18.

MINUTES OF DECEMBER 6, 1913, GENERAL MEETING.

A regular meeting of the Association was held in the H. S. of Commerce, Saturday, December 6, 1913.

147 members present.

The meeting was called to order at 11.15 A. M. by the President, William T. Morrey.

In the absence of the Secretary, Miss Lowd, of Washington, Irving H. S. was appointed Secretary pro tem.

Minutes of the last meeting were read and approved.

VOTED, on motion of Mr. Dotey, to suspend order of business, as designated, in order that discussion of pension legislation might precede other business.

VOTED, that a committee of three, to represent the Association at the hearing on pension legislation, be elected by the Association.

Informal discussion was permitted on:

a. Conditions of retirement.
b. Per cent. of tax.
c. Per cent. of tax.
d. Permanent fund.
e. Guaranty of funds.
f. State responsibility.

Opinion expressed that the present 1 per cent. tax remain, if necessary, and that the City make good any deficit by a mandatory appropriation by the Board of Esimate.

Mr. Dotey felt that the fund should **not** be increased by a tax on sick teachers.

MR. MONTE'S pension was not primarily mutual benefit association, not support of teachers in old age, in interest of the system based on principle of terms of office. Business of City to get rid of inefficient. May do it by pensioning teachers.

MR. TILDSLEY: Pensions for benefit of the system, not of the individual. Purpose of pension should be:

1. To get rid of the inficient.
2. To improve the system.

Unsound to create fund by contributions. Same per cent. and half pay for all. Submit to 1 per cent. because it is established, and let the Board of Estimate do the rest.

MR. HARTWELL: Fire and Police budget 10 per cent. of excise tax to 5 per cent. allowed teachers' pension fund.

VOTED, on motion, to suspend business under discussions to listen to the speaker of the day, Supt. Albert Shiels.

The subject of Mr. Shiels' address was the new Bureau of Reference and Research recently established by the Board of Education, with Mr. Shiels as Director.

As Mr. Shiels left immediately it was voted to waive "discussion" of the address. The Association moved a vote of thanks to Mr. Shiels for his interesting address.

Nominations for delegates to hearing: Messrs. Sanford L. Cutter, of Morris; Schlanch, of H. S. Commerce; Dotey, of Clinton (withdrew); Charles R. Tracy, of Erasmus; F. Z. Lewis, of Boys' High.

The business of nominating delegates was continued. Name of Dr. John L. Tildsley, De Witt Clinton, and Dr. Linville, of Jamaica, were added. Nominations closed.

Tellers appointed, Mr. O'Kee, Mr. White.

Decided that the three receiving the highest number of votes should be declared elected. In case of tie, lots to be drawn.

Ballot resulted in election of Dr. Tildsley, Dr. Witt Clinton, Charles R. Fray, Erasmus, Sanford L. Cutter, Morris.

For the instruction of delegates the following resolutions, presented by Mr. Bryan, were **passed:**

1. City to provide such portion of pension as needed above 1 per cent. contributed.
2. After 30 years of service, 15 of which shall have been in City of New York, a teacher shall have the right to retire.
3. Half salary for pension; no pension to be less than $600.00 (9 opsed.)
4. No sex discrimination in age of retirement. (Withdrawn.)
4. Provision for refund of contributions if one withdraws voluntarily.

MR. ANTHONY proposed, as a constructive recommendation, that "accruals" should be used for the pension fund. Carried.

VOTED on motion of Mr. Fay that the Association go on record about 15 or 20 years service in the City.

VOTED, that 15 years, as at present, be required.

VOTED, on motion of Mr. Gruenberg, that it be the sense of the Association that no pension legislation be adopted until after referendum to all teachers in the City.

Meeting adjourned at 1.25 P. M.

EMMA F. LOWD,
Secretary pro tem.

The Bureau of Reference and Research

Outline of Address by Director Albert Shiels.

[Outline made by Miss Emma F. Lowd of Washington Irving High School, Secretary **Pro Tem.**, H. S. T. A.

The speaker made the following divisions of the material of his address:

1. Origion of Division or Department.
2. Purpose and spirit.

3. Work it can do.
4. Limitations.

A recommendation made in the recent school inquiry was read: "The establishment of a Bureau of investigators or appraisers under the direction of a superintendent to gather statistics, data, etc."

Absence of a reference library, a notable deficiency, at the outset. It is intended that the

A. **Department** should
   1. Collect literature.
   2. Answer inquiries about data irrespective of Departments.
   3. Keep the Board informed of school progress outside the city.
B. **Spirit and Aim** to
   1. Give Coöperation.
   2. Perform service at this end.
   3. Work objectively.
   4. Deal with **facts.**
   5. Welcome all suggestions and requests.
   6. Have professional spirit.
   7. Represent no party or faction.
   8. Present facts as they exist in the minds of each member of the system.
C. The Bureau should be a competent bureau of routine information, to where people may obtain this information.
   1. Continuously.
   2. Clearly.
   3. Promptly, or receive an honest confession of why it can not be given.
   4. Definitely.
D. Supplementary purpose or work as Bureau of Complaints or Appeal for
   a. Any body concerned.
   b. To follow up the case.
   c. Notify person concerned of the result.
   No pigeon-holing.
E. Serve the Board of Education.
   1. By reports of matters referred to the Bureau.
   2. By reading and summarizing of report for practical use.
   3. By original investigations.

Every activity should be measured by financial value, and have a business basis. Money should be used not to reduce costs but to increase efficiency.

Investigators will be needed with an impersonal attitude, a spirit of enthusiasm and faith. Much aid will be needed involving great labor and little skill.

Officers of the Bureau:

2. Assistant Director.
3. Numerous clerks and stenographers.

Standard of opinion about teachers should be raised so that they will be considered as a great democracy of men and women interested in the educational system.

The division will be:

1. A storehouse.
2. A clearing-house.
3. A work-shop.

Bureau will aim first to establish a place for information, but must have **facts first**. It may not satisfy all remands, but it will be honest, courteous. **Its measure of value will be the confidence inspired in the teaching force.**

Facts as they are found will be given, without implicttions or conclusions, **facts not opinions.** It must succeed, because the teachers will help.

Minutes of October 28, 1913, Meeting of Representatives.

The meeting of the Board of Representatives of the High Shoolc Teachers' Association was held October 28 at the High School of Commerce. Mr. Morey called the meeting to order at 4:10. The reading of the minutes was omitted. The treasurer reported as follows: balance (1912-1913) $605.27, dues (1912-1913) $113.00, dues (1913-1914) $89.00, expenses $206.90, leaving a balance to date of $600.37.

The President reported that he had been engaged in issuing the November Bulletin and in planning a H. S. T. A. Directory which should be of great service to all interested in New York City High Schools. He expressed his indebtedness to various members of the Association who had assisted him by helpful suggestions in regard to the general meetings; he also stated that reports of committees would appear in the next bulletin.

The election of delegates to the Teachers' Advisory Council was fully discussed, especially the question of the method of nomination. It was voted that nominations be made from the floor.

On motion of Mr. White of Morris, the board voted that the President be empowered to appoint such committees as he sees fit and also to remove from committees such members as may seem inefficient.

The meeting was adjourned. MARY J. BOURNE, Secretary.

Minutes of November 25, 1913, Meeting of Representatives.

Mr. Bedford, Chairman of the Biology Section reported that his section during the year would take up and discuss Note Books, course of first year Biology, Efficiency and Biology Teaching.

Mr. Hunter, Head of Department of Biology, DeWitt Clinton, said report on Standard Equipment has been pigeon-holed at 59th St. A committee has been appointed by the Board of Superintendents to investigate the course in Biology.

Miss Skinner, of the Commercial Section reported that a talk was to be given by representative of the State Department of Education, on Commercial Branches in High Schools.

Members for 1913-1914. Most high schools have not reported. To date, Bay Ridge 30, Bushwick 70, and Morris 5.

Moved by Mr. Dotey of DeWitt Clinton, that it is the sense of the Board of Representatives that eligibility to the High School Teachers' Association is limited to teachers and supervisers in the public day high schools of New York City and in the high school departments of Normal College and City College. Carried.

Moved by Mr. Dotey: The Secretary be instructed to direct the senior rpresentatives to take a vote of the representatives concerning a change in time of meeting from Tuesday to Friday afternoon and report to the President. Carried.

Moved by Mr. Goodman: That when we adjourn we adjourn till Jan. 13, 1914. Carried.

Moved by Miss Carr: That a committee be appointed to request the Board of Education, and to suggest to other associations that they request the Board, to re-open the schools on Jan. 5, 1914, rather than on Jan. 2, 1914. Carried.

Mr. Dotey was appointed as a committee of one to see Mr. Shiels, to request him to address the next general meeting of Dec. 6.

Adjourned, 5:25. F. M. SURREY, Secretary Pro. Tem.

MEETING OF THE REPRESENTATIVES JANUARY 13, 1914.

The meeting was called to order at 4.10 by the president. Reports of committees were called for.

Th report of the Treasurer showed a balance of $742.35 in the treasury.

Mr. White, Morris High School, spoke on the question of noise in the vicinity of schools, asking that this subject be referred to the Teachers' Council for further consideration. The following resolution were offered.

RESOLVED, That we request the Board of Education to take such action as they deem wise and expedient to secure:

First—A better enforcement of the city ordinance (copy attached) in relation to the erection of warning signs to promote quietude of pupils and teachers in the schools, especially Section 2, authorizing the Commissioner of Police in his discretion, to divert all heavy, noisy vehicular traffic from the immediate block or blocks upon which schools are located between 8.45 and 3.15 P. M.

Second—The co-operation of the Street Cleaning Department to the end that the scraping of pawments adjacent to school buildings be performed, as far as practicable, outside of school hours.

Third—The unloading of coal for schools outside of school hours.

The resolutions were adopted.

Mr. Blume of Commerce asked to request the Board to require workmen in the school to desist from work during school hours.

Miss Seelman spoke of the antiquated methods of sweeping in schools, asking some relief.

Mr. Gruenberg moved the adoption of Mr. White's resolution which should be forwarded to the Board of Education. Motion was carried.

Miss Roche. Washington Irving. spoke on the question of the enlarging of membership in the Association.

Mr. Pugh reported on the work of the new Teachers' Council.

The Secretary asked for a ruling on the mailing of bulletins to public libraries etc. The Secretary was empowered to send sample copies to the chief libraries with a request that a desire to continue the same must be forwarded to the secretary.

Mr. Pugh reported that a local committee of the National Education Association on commercial branches has been organized. The first meeting was held ind Christmas vacation. He also stated that the National Bureau of Education is to conduct a clearing house on Civic Questions.

The meeting adjourned to Tuesday, February 24.

REPRESENTATIVES MEETING, FEBRUARY 24 1914.

The meeting of the representatives was called to order at 4:10 by the President. The minuts of the last meeting were read and approved. The treasurer's report showed a balance of $904.55 in the treasury. The President outlined the plans for the next general meeting which is to deal with the "Efficiency of Factory Methods in Education" as exemplefied in Double and Triple Sessions of our large High Schools.

Reports on the school directory were called for.

Mr. Gruenberg. for the Biology Section. reported that a new course in biology of the third or fourth year was being prepared with special reference to the needs of city children.

Mr. Munro of Bryant High School reported that the English Teachers' Association had now a total membership of about 290. The special work of the Association now is to secure better teaching conditions for English teachers; the principal object is to give "the pupil more teacher."

Mr. Dotey spoke on the method employed at De Witt Clinton to use study periods to assist in giving additional time for the study of languages and mathematics.

Mr. White reported that the present evening high school course in history and civics was so inadequate that it is now under revision in order to secure greater freedom in developing eiics, economics and modern history.

At the request of the President, Mr. Gruenberg spoke of the trip to Grand Rapids taken by him last October to attend the conference on vocational guidance.

Mr. Pugh reported for the Commercial Committee that various sub committees have held meetings in regard to revision of parts of the syllabus. He also stated that the work of organizing the Teachers' Council was not yet completed.

MEETING OF REPRESENTATIVES, MARCH 31, 1914.

The meeting was called to order by ihe President at 4.20. The minutes of the last meeting wtre approved as read. The Treasurer reported a balance of $933 in the treasury.

Reports on the Directory were called for. There was a spirited discussion of the advisability of changing tht present commercial course.

Miss Carr suggested that the Board of Representatives make two or more nominations for each office to be filled at the annual meeting, these nominations to be announced in the Bulletin as suggestions. Mr. Morrey, Mr. Dotey and others thought this unwise, but the opinion seemed general that the election is of such importance that it ought not to be held near the end of a long general meeting.

Mr. Dotey of De Witt Clinton moved that a committee be appointed to prepare a brief in favor of allowing principals of large high schools to select assistants-to-pricipals from the eligible list of first assistants. It was shown that some teachers art acting at the same time as heads of departments and as office assistants and that either position needs the entire attention of one teacher. The following committee was then appointed: Mr. Dotey De Witt Clinton, Mr. Cutler, Morris, Mr. White, Morris.

On motion the meeting adjourned.

MARY J. BOURNE,
Secretary.

MINUTES OF MEETING OF ELOCUTION TEACHERS JANUARY 10, 1914.

A special meeting of the Elocution teachers of the High Schools of Greater New York was caled by the president for Saturday, January tenth, 1914. Thirteen teacheds representing eleven different different High Schools were in attendance. Mr. Raymond N. Kellok, the president, openet the meeting and called for the secretary's report of the last meeting. Regular business was then taken up.

As copies of the tentative syllabus were in the hands of those present, it was deemed unnceessary for the chairman of the committee on the tentative syllabue to read th items contained in it. After a brief discussion a motion was made, seconded an carried to adopt the syllabus for the first year of the High School course. This was followed by a motion which was seconded and carried to adopt the syllabus for the second year of the High School course. Then the syllabus for the fourth year was adopted in a similar manner.

It was moved by Miss Murray and seconded by Mr. Smith that our chairman, Mr. Kellogg be authorized to present this syllabus to the authorities at Fifty-ninth Stree. The motion was unamimously carried.

By a regular motion, seconded and carried, our chairman was authorized to recommend that regular teachers of English be required to assist teachers of oral English in working for higher standards of spoken English.

The chairman was authorized, also, to ask for an interpretation of what is expected in the examination of candidates for graduation from High Schools, and that all pupils in the first and fourth years of the High School course be required to take class work in Oral English.

The meeting adjourned at 11.30 o'clock.

Respectfully submitted,

W. PALMER SMITH,

RECENT CRITICISM OF COMMERCIAL EDUCATION. HIGH SCHOOLS.

By W. E. BARTHOLOMEW

New York State Inspector of Commercial Education.

These are times of uncertainty in all matters pertaining to education. Everybody seems to feel that something is wrong with our present scheme of education; a great many have volunteered to criticise certain phases; a few have been given the task of making surveys of the field for the purpose of fixing the points of weakness: nobody has yet fully satisfied himself as to the remedies that must be applied to make up the existing deficiencies.

In the last few years the educational problem has been receiving much consideration on all sides. Forces have been set to work in different directions in the effort to find some basis for re-establishing the whole system of education and to formulate principles for the guidance of those charged with the responsibility of administration.

It is only natural that commercial education should receive its share of consideration. Here in New York City the Committee on Commercial Education of the Chamber of Commerce and the Committee on School Inquiry have directed their attention to a study of the problem of commercial education. You are already familiar with the results of the investigations. I shall not endeavor to analyze to any extent the criticisms made in these reports; I hope to show, however, that the criticisms have not been directed to things that are of vital importance and that they have not been so constructive as we had reason to expect.

I cannot help referring to an interesting parallel that this period of unrest and of readjustment in education has in the commercial and industrial world. Anyone who has studied the economic conditions of the country for the past few years realizes that a readjustment is taking place. A new era in the economic history of our country is ahead of us. In the past the development of commerce and industry has been largely extensive; that is, it has been what might be called "a covering of the field." Expansion has been the keynote. Commercial and industrial development in the coming era will be largely intensive; that is, it will be a "conquering of the world in hand," rather than a "seeking of more worlds to conquer." Efficiency will be the keynote. Instead of forcing long lines of railways into unsettled regions, the railway systems already established will develop a greater operating efficiency; instead of increasing the acreage of our wheat fields, the farmer will direct his efforts toward securing a larger yield per acre; instead of enlarging his plant, the manufacturer will be first concerned about getting a maximum output at a minimum cost per unit.

In many respects the United States stands today where Germany stood at the close of the Franco-Prussian War. The marvellous development of Germany in the past forty years is an indication of what this country will witness in the next few decades. Incidentally the demand will be not for men capable of projecting huge enterprises, men of bold spirit, but for men capable of securing a high degree of efficiency in a single enterprise, men of keen and scientific spirit. Until the new order has been established and until the adjustment to the changed conditions has been made, there will be an unsettled season in the economic world.

It is apparent that there is a similar readjustment in process in the educational field. The season is unsettled and we are casting about to find a way to establish a new order in education. A charge has been made against the whole educational scheme that it is not furnishing the vast army of children the preparation for life,—the ultimate purpose of education. In our successful efforts to expand the territory of education, we have failed to get efficiency in the territory we have laid out. The getting of adequate returns has been neglected as an element of consideration. In our own field of commercial education we find that its development has been almost wholly confined to the last fifty years; that as a phase of high school education its development belongs almost entirely to the last ten or fifteen years. I suppose I am safe in saying that three-fourths of the high schools now maintaining commercial courses have introduced them within the last ten years. It has been pretty largely a "covering of the field." Policies have been established as to the form which commercial education should take, courses of study have been outlined, and, to some extent, the character of the subject material has been determined upon. The time has arrived, however, when we must turn our attention in another direction. We must now concern ourselves chiefly with finding ways and means by which results in commercial education may be more adequately obtained.

It is in making the diagnosis of the situation and in suggesting the remedies that investigators and committees of inquiry have almost wholly failed. There is a notable exception to which I shall refer a little later. Most reports on school systems and educational systems usually conclude with the statements that the curriculum of studies is all wrong and that certain standard results are not being obtained. The course of study must, therefore, be revised and various remedies, such as lengthening the school day, abolishing home study, offering free election of studies, asking pupils to take only the subjects they like, and so on, are suggested. Dr. Leonard P. Ayres, of the Russell Sage Foundation, says that progress in education has come from shifting the form of inquiry from asking, "What results can or might we get?" to "What results are we getting?" Dr. F. V. Thompson, in his report on commercial education in the New York city schools, says that "the crux of the shortcomings pointed out lies in the failure to conceive commercial education as vocational education." They are as far from the real issue as the Dakota farmer would be if, in his efforts to get a larger yield of wheat per facre, he stopped with informing himself of what the average yield of his farm should be or with a re-plotting of his fields, or with a mere selecting of seed wheat. The farmer must direct his attention to a study of methods of cultivation and to the tilling of the soil before we can expect any great increase in his wheat crop. In like manner, until we shift our inquiry to the question, "How can we get the results we should get?" and to the teaching and the teaching methods, we shall make little progress in getting effective results in education. The fundamental weakness in education is found in the class room. The educational problem is a class room problem. The report, recently published, of a survey made of the Vermont school system emphasizes this point and is different in this respect from similar reports that have been made heretofore. It states the situation so clearly that I ask your permission to make some quotations from it:

"What the secondary school needs is not primarily a curriculum, but good teaching. This is not to say that the curriculum be done away with, but that it must be controlled and improved by the schoolmen themselves—skilled teachers in direct contact with the problems. The present subordination of the teacher to the curriculum must be reversed, and the curriculum be subordinated to the teacher, if therre is to be real progress...

"The important thing is the skill with which the teacher selects and applies the tools; success is due to his insight and technique; failure indicates poor judgment on his part much oftener than poor stuff in the pupil...

"A majority of the teachers are teaching subjects in which they are ill-prepared; their range of information is therefore limited and their application of it is likely to be timid and forceless, or else incorrect. There results, therefore, to an extreme degree, the great American pedagogical vice—slavish dependence upon a text-book...

"The conditions indicated are reflected in the class work. Instead of striding forward with the confidence of sure knowledge and trusted power, as every group of youth loves to do if expertly led, the classes creep; response is slow and furtive; answers have to be 'pumped' or suggested, and spontaneous reaction to the content of the lesson is unusual.

"The effect of this on the pupil is depressing or hardening. In so far as instruction fails to arouse a genuine interest and develop a pleasurable sense of power, it is not only negatively useless, it is a positive discouragement to a child's education, however loyal he may be to the teacher personally."

Further the report says. "Few of the teachers have ever had the opportunity of observing skillful secondary instruction with a view to studying it as such, and practically none has ever practiced teaching under skilled criticism. A system is defective that permits them to teach what they have not studied thoroughly, and, providing no critical leader, loads them with an excessive number of classes.

"The remedy for these conditions seems axiomatic—the same remedy that has been efficacious in all successful school systems: First, require that the teachers know thoroughly the subjects they propose to teach. Second, require them to teach only those subjects."

Now, I do not think that these criticisms characterize the teaching of commercial subjects any more than they do the teaching of other groups of subjects. But this is true: The development of commercial education has been so rapid that the supply of adequately prepared teachers has not met with the demand, and commercial subjects are therefore too commonly taught by teachers of very little training and by teachers who have not caught the spirit of what commercial education means. It is also true that the teaching methods have not been so thoroughly formulated in commercial subjects, and consequently new and inexperienced teachers frequently have nothing to guide them except what their own intelligence suggests to them as the correct method of procedure. Furthermore, there has been lacking in commercial teaching the skilled direction and criticism referred to in the report from which I have just quoted. There are other reasons, of course, why better results ae not always obtained in commercial work. Lack of proper facilities, overcrowded conditions, heavy teaching schedules, uncontrolled election of subjects, may make even the work of a good teacher ineffective.

I do not mean to imply that courses of study must be left out of consideration or that any effort to adapt the instruction in commercial subjects to business conditions should be abandoned,—attention must constantly be given to these things; but I do wish to emphasize the fact that **efficient work in the class room with its consequent efficient results is the chief justification for the presence of commercial education in the high school curriculum.**

The problem of making commercial education efficient lies then primarily with the teacher, not with the investigator. The details by which the desired improvement can be brought about must be worked out by persons who are competent to undertake the task, the persons who are out on the firing line.

Whatever progress commercial education will make in New York city must be effected by the commercial teachers themselves. Whatever development there will be must come through your own efforts. In the past, commercial teachers have not been consulted enough when plans for commercial teaching were being outlined. The matter has rested too entirely with persons who were perhaps well meaning enough, but who were not sufficiently familiar with commercial subjects to say what should be done with them in the high school courses. Indications are that a change in policy has taken place and that hereafter you will be generally consulted on matters pertaining to your special field. It seems to me, however, that if you are going to make the most of your opportunity you must first of all organize yourselves into one effective organization. There should be a single association including all the commercial teachers of New York City. There must be unity of purpose in commercial education in this city and every teacher must be enlisted to bring this about. With such an association well established, the various problems concerning commercial education in your high schools can be attacked and mastered with some degree of success.

It was to be expected that Dr. Thomson would direct some of his criticism to Regents examinations. Among other things he says that the present purpose of the examinations is too limited and that they do not really serve as tests of vocational efficiency. I agree with him that no Regents examination can be made to test vocational efficiency, and I also agree with him when he says that the true test of vocational efficiency is the success of the individual in business. But is this not true in every other phase of specialized education? The engineering student receives his real test of vocational efficiency in the field; the medical student in his practice; the theological student in the pulpit; so the commercial student must receive his real test of efficiency in the business office. There is no reason, therefore, why Regents examinations in commercial subjects should be singled out for his criticism; and, moreover, nobody has ever made the claim that he assumes is made, namely, that these examinations do test vocational efficiency. If his criticism applies at all, it must be applied to the general scheme of examinations.

The question of whether or not examinations serve a useful purpose has been the concern of educators for a long time. I think the accepted opinion is that examinations, properly administered, are a valuable part of an educational system. At any rate, we find that examinations are in more general use than ever. We find not only that educational institutions condition promotion and graduation partly on examinations, but that entrance to the various professions, to the public service positions and even to some lines of business activity is controlled by an examination in some form or other. As I understand the purpose of an examination, it is not so much a testing as a selecting process. It cannot test all the knowledge the applicant possesses on a subject or his full measure of ability; it should test his knowledge of certain fundamental principles in the subject in which the examination is set and his ability to make some application of these principles. This testing should serve as a means of selection. The examination should bring forward those persons who are properly qualified and who can give reasonable assurance that they can do the work ahead of them, whether it is the work of the next higher grade in school, the work in a profession, the work of the business office, or whatever it may be. Now, if Regents examinations fail to serve this purpose, they should be modified to do so more adequately.

There is danger, however, in any state wide examination system that it may sometimes prevent high schools from serving fully the needs of their communities. Unless a provision is made,—and this applies especially to commercial subjects,—whereby the work in any high school can be adapted to suit the community in which it is given, a uniform course of study with uniform examinations might become detrimental to the welfare of education in the state.

Dr. Thompson says that the Regents examinations have fettered the commercial work in New York city; that the full development of commercial education has not been possible because of the requirements laid down by the State Department. He has absolutely no warrant for any such conclusion and he shows that he is not at all familiar with the policy of the Department. If I have the correct idea, the State Syllabus as prescribed by the Department sets forfth what is considered fundamental in the various high school subjects. There is nothing to prevent high schools after they have reached the general standard set by the Syllabbus to extend their work to a higher level if they have the means and facilities to do so and if the communities demand it. More than that, **the Department stands ready to approve courses that are not named in the Syllabus and will give credit toward a high school diploma on the certification of the principal.** If the uniform State Syllabus operates to reduce all schools to a dead level, it must be admitted that the operation is self-inflicted. The policy of the Department is a "pulling up" policy, not a "holding back" policy.

Now so far as the courses outlined in the syllabus in commercial subjects are concerned, I maintain that they are fundamental in character and as such can be prescribed for the whole State and the examinations can safely be given in all the high schools of the State. If these courses are not fundamental, they schould be revised. When it is desired to differentiate the instruction in commercial subjects to fit the conditions of the community, the differentiation should be made only after the fundamental principles in the various subjects have been established. There is little use in specializing the courses until proper foundations have been laid. **The first concern of the Department is to see that the high schools of the State are giving sound instruction in the fundamental subjects.**

There is full opportunity to adapt commercial education in New York city to the conditions peculiar to the city, and the State Department will encourage any effort in this direction. Some time ago I submitted to Dr. Wheelock, Assistant Commissioner for Secondary Education, a plan by which high schools might receive the approval of the Department for certain commercial subjects of an advanced or of a special nature not now prescribed in the Syllabus. I proposed the following:

High schools may hereafter obtain the approval of commercial subjects not prescribed in the Syllabus and credit will be given by the Department without examination for the satisfactory completion of the work in the subjects to approved. For the pr sent, the Department will consider the approval of any of the following subjects: Elementary Accounting, Business Organization, Business Mathematics and Secretarial Practice.

Because of the different treatment each of these subjects must receive in different parts of the State, no general Syllabus can be prescribed. The planning of the courses is left to the high schools. It is expected, however, that each subject will be outlined to give the proper emphasis to topics important because of local business conditions and that each subject will be treated in conformity with local practice. The value of the work done in these subjects will depend upon how well this relation to the business community has been established. The following outlines are merely suggestive:

ELEMENTARY ACCOUNTING. This subject should include a study of the principles of accounting as applied in the organization of systems of accounts and in the preparation of business and financial statements; it should also include the interpretation and analysis of statements such as may be obtained from published reports of business corporations; and some attention should be given to the elements of cost accounting. The subject should be outlined primarily to give pupils the knowledge of the elementary principles of accounting, with their applications, that the man of business should possess.

BUSINESS ORGANIZATION. This subject should include a study of the institutions that have been established in the development of commerce, with special attention to the local exchanges, markets, banking facilities etc. It should also include a study of the organization of some of the larger business concerns for the application made of the principles of organization and efficiency.

BUSINESS MATHEMATICS. This subject should include a

thorough study of applied mathematics to corporation and municipal finance under the various heads of stocks and bonds, taxes, sinking funds and annuities. Exchange, customs, insurance, partnership settlements and other topics should also be given proper consideration.

SECRETARIAL PRACTICE. The course in this subject should be planned to prepare high school graduates for the higher positions in stenographic and secretarial work. The study of shorthand should be continued until a speed of 125 words a minute is attained. Special attention should be given to the methods adopted for handling and filing office records. The course should provide for some practice in operating the office appliances in common use.

Courses in the special subjects will be considered for approval provided, (1) that the high school making application prescribes as a part of the curriculum a four years' commercial course sufficiently well organized to justify the addition of the special subjects, (2) that the special subjects are offered in the last two years of the course, each subject to be given at least two recitation periods a week for a school year, (3) that the instruction in these subjects is given by teachers duly qualified by education and experience, and (4) that detailed outlines of the courses to be approved accompany the application for approval.

Upon evidence furnished to the Department that a candidate has completed satisfactorily the course of study outlined in an approved subject and has passed the school examination, he will be entitled to two academic counts for the subject. Credit will not be given, however, for Elementary Accounting unless the candidate has previously passed the Regents examination in Advanced Bookkeeping and Office Practice, or for Business Mathematics unless he has passed the Regents examinations in Commercial Arithmetic and hplementary Algebra, or for Secretarial Practice unless he has passed the Regents examinations in Shorthand II and Typewriting.

Dr. Wheelock is in accord with my proposition and I am quite sure that he will consider favorably any application for approval and credit in these special subjects and others not here mentioned, if there is merit in the application.

In view of what I have said relative to the purpose of Regents examinations and to the latitude that high schools have in adapting the work in commercial subjects, I fail to see any real basis for the objections Dr. Thompson has made.

I should like to stop just long enough to show how criticisms of the examinations often vanish into thin air when they are followed out to the end.

Just about so often, a critic appears who says that Regents examinations are not based on business practice and that when a teacher prepares his pupils for the examinations he unfits them for the business office. Not long ago, the Department had some correspondence with one of these critics. His letter contained this paragraph:

"It would appear that many of the Regents Bookkeeping examination questions are founded upon some textbook or other. I do not mean by this, one particular textbook, but these questions seem to be largely taken from textbooks rather than from business conditions. The questions seem to be mostly textbook questi ons, not business or real bookkeeping questions...... why not test the student's knowledgge of the actual work and conditions rather than his knowledge of a particular text."

The person who made this sweeping criticism was asked to be good enough to examine some of the recent question papers in bookkeeping and was urged to criticise specifically the questions given on the papers and to suggest others that would be in accord with business conditions as he understood them to be. He was asked to submit sample question papers that would be suitable tests in the subject.

When his criticisms were finally received, they were: first, that a three party draft remitted in settlement of account in a transaction which formed the basis for a question, was not used in business, but that a two party draft would be used almost exclusively in such a transaction (which is true to a certain extent); second, that a transaction in which furniture was sold to a second hand dealer called for entries that were too difficult for the class of pupils taking the examination; third, that a statement of a transaction in whch freight was paid for goods received was faulty because it did not state whether the goods were merchandise purchased for the purpose of selling or for other purposes, or for machinery, or for raw material, etc.; fourth, that furniture and fixtures should not be inventoried because a loss in value should be provided for in a depreciation account.

These were the criticisms offered, partly justified, perhaps, but very incidental in character; they certainly did not furnish sufficient ground for the condemnation made in the first place. What there was in the papers which showed that they were not based on business conditions the writer failed to point out. My good critic did not suggest any change in the makeup of the examination papers and he submitted no specimen questions that he considered as more in accord with his ideas on the subject. In fact, he prefaced his criticisms with the statement that "the examination papers were, in the main, admirable." He reached the climax of inconsistency, however, when he closed his letter with the following paragraph:

"Possibly it will appear that in our opinion any young bookkeeper who learned the subject in a business office attempting your state examination would probably fail; and if he kept books in a business office in the way he would be required to keep them in order to pass this state examination, he would probably be discharged."

The unfortunate part of such criticisms is that they serve only to discredit. They are harmful because persons who do not stop to inquire into the basis for the criticism will accept them at face value and will reach the conclusion that things are all wrong.

I am glad to say that this is an extreme case and not at all typical. I should not like to have you get the opinion that we resent criticism; instead, we invite criticism at all times and some of you here know that suggestions for the improvement of question papers have been freely accepted. The examinations are your examinations and the question committees are made up of teachers from your own number. It is your duty and privilege by your honest criticism and

helpful suggestions to assist us in making the examinations as nearly ideal as it is possible to make them. I think we have a right, however, to protest against the sort of baseless criticism that I have just cited.

Dr. Thompson made the subject of business education a matter of inquiry among business men in Boston, his own city, and later in this city. The same letter of inquiry was also used in a similar investigation in Pittsburgh. Among other things, the replies received indicated that the business man in the selection of his employees attaches first importance to training in fundamental suibjects and general education and gives little or no consideration to training in clerical subjects. With this fact in mind Dr. Thompson expresses himself thus: "It is significant that business men do not point out any superiority of the commercial school product over the general school product. We cannot escape the conclusion that the non-commercial schools have a larger influence in the sum total upon business than do the special schools, and it is an open question whether or not the general school is not giving at present more appropriate training for the major business needs. The pupil in the general high school does not get false impressions concerning business demands; he is not led to believe that clerical ability is the one essential, and in applying for a position he does not seek office work as the only business opportunity."

Is there any significance in the fact that business men do not point out any superiority of the commercial school product over the general school product? Does the pupil from the general high school get consideration because he is not handicapped by the "false impressions" his brother in the commercial high school is receiving? Professor Paul Klapper, of the College of the City of New York, in the Educational Review for November, 1913, states the attitude that the business man takes in the selection of his employees. He says. **"The practical business man would prefer the product which the school sends him to be capable of doing accurate work, to be trained in the capacity for sustained effort, to possess powers of concentration, and to be able to think quickly in the emergencies inevitable in the day's work."** Although the business man does not express himself so clearly, he means the same thing when he says: "The more education, the better"; "We wants **'brains', not 'diplomas'**;" or as one man expressed it, "We want **traits, not accomplishments."**

The complaints that the business world makes of the schools are in the last analysis based on the failure of the schools to give their pupils the qualities that Prof. Klapper indicated as desirable. The business world takes the boy who has these qualities regardless of whether he comes from the general school, commercial school or the school at the country cross roads. **It is, therefore, relatively unimportant what subjects the boy has studied so long as he has acquired the mental habits requisite to bring about his business success.** The point I want to make is this: that even after we have established our commercial courses with the subject material and the instruction fully related to the needs of business life, our efforts will be largely futile if we do not consider the curriculum of studies as a vehicle by which our pupils may receive the training that Prof. Klapper so well points out. Quoting once more from the Vermont report: "No study or group of studies has any importance for its own sake; its value consists altogether in the extent to which it assists the teacher in bringing a pupil into those relations with his environment that are agreeable, stimulating, and promising for him personally and profitable to society...... Its potency consists not in itself, but in the intelligence with which it is applied."

It sems to me that this points out the real problem in commercial education. Whatever else may have to be done, success must come ultimately from the way in which the two most important elements, teacher and pupil, will work out the full purpose of their particular field of education.

AN INVESTIGATION OF SCHOLARSHIP RECORDS OF HIGH SCHOOL PUPILS.

AARON I. DOTEY,

Department of Latin, DeWitt Clinton High School, New York City.

The data used in this investigation were the term grades received by pupils in the DeWitt Clinton High School (for boys), New York City, on prepared work for their first and second terms (one year). Five periods per week in English, in mathematics, and in biology were required of all pupils. One group had five periods per week in Latin, one five periods per week in German, and one five periods per week in French. As pupils enter semi-annually, two sets of grades were used:

1. Febr., 1911, to Febr., 1912.

708 pupils: Latin, 271; German, 222; French, 215

2. Sep., 1911, to June, 1912.

689 pupils: Latin, 265; German, 222; French, 202

Total in both classes:

1397 pupils: Latin, 536; German, 444; French, 417

The purpose of the investigation is three-fold. 1. To determine the place in scholarship held respectively by the Latin, German and French groups. 2. To discover some facts concerning elimination and retardation. 3. To discover, if possible, the policy to be pursued in making programs for repeaters.

PART ONE

The Place in Scholarship Held by Each of the Foreign Language Groups.

In order to throw some light on the question as to the kind of pupils who elect the different languages, the reports from the elementary schools upon the pupils entering in February were examined and the results tabulated. Unfortunately the reports upon the pupils entering in September, were not available. Of the February reports, a random selection of two-fifths of the whole number was made; giving for the Latin group, 108 samples; for the German, 88; and for the French, 86. Each report contains three kinds of grades: 1. A "general estimate" grade on the work in each of eleven subjects. These grades are given by the principal, and are based upon the more detailed estimate made by the class teacher, in consultation with the principal, upon the various phases of the work in any given subject. 2. A "class standing" grade. This is the estimate placed by the class teacher upon the pupil's work as a whole. 3. The "principal's estimate" grade. This is identical in nature with the preceding, except that it is given by the principal instead of the class teacher.

As all these grades are expressed by the letters A, B+, B, C, and D, it was necessary for purposes of comparison, to assign arbitrary values to the letters. After consultation with Dr. Albert Shiels, Director of the Division of Reference and Research of the Department of Education, the following values were assigned to them: A = 90 to 100; B = 75 to 89.99×; B = 60 to 74.99+; C = 45 to 59.99+; D = 0 to 44.99+. Medians* were then obtained for each language group in each of the three kinds of grades with the following results:

*Note. A **median** is that point above which and below which 50 per cent. of the cases lie.

TABLE I.

Median of each Language Group in the Elementary School.

	General Estimate	Class Standing	Principal's Estimate
Latin Group..........	72.46	72.46	72.09
German Group........	70.05	70.42	69.85
French Group	71.31	71.31	71.12

From this comparison it appears that the pupils who, on entering high school, elect Latin are slightly better in scholarship than those who elect French; and that those who elect French are slightly better than those who elect German. From the table it is seen that, in each case, the difference is approximately one per cent.

Tables II., III., and IV. give the results of the first term's work in high school. As Table I. was based wholly upon the elementary school reports of the February class, while this investigation is based upon the grades of the February and September classes combined, the medians of each class are given seperately and then are followed by the medians of the two classes combined, in order to show that the combined results differ but very little from those of the February class when considered alone, in so far as the relative standings of the language groups are concerned.

In these tables the medians in the columns headed "Three" were found by taking the grades in English, mathematics, and biology and finding their median **as grades**, regardless of the subject or of the pupil who made them. The same process was employed to obtain the medians in the columns headed "Four," which includes, however, the grades obtained in the languages.

TABLE II.

Medians of the February Class.

Groups	Eng.	Math.	Biol.	Three	Lang.	Four.
Latin	69.51	65.18	65.37	67.56	65.33	66.79
German	64.33	60.47	63.16	63.21	60.21	62.46
French	65.15	64.54	62.08	64.51	59.89	62.12

TABLE III.

Medians of the September Class.

Groups	Eng.	Math.	Biol.	Three	Lang	Four.
Latin	69.76	64.88	69.75	68.18	67.95	68.13
German	65.44	64.81	65.28	65.19	62.83	64.90
French	69.62	63.10	60.43	64.98	63.25	64.78

TABLE IV.

Medians of the two Classes Combined.

Groups	Eng.	Math.	Biol.	Three	Lang.	Four.
Latin	69.63	65.00	67.88	67.91	67.10	67.77
German	64.77	62.83	64.78	64.69	60.45	64.51
French	67.59	63.80	61.71	64.76.	60.32	63.50

According to Table I., the Latin group entered high school with a lead of one per cent. over the French group and two per cent. over the German group. According to Table IV., the Latin group has not only maintained this lead, but has greatly increased it in every subject except mathematics. Here it now leads the French group by 1.2 per cent. and the German group by 2.17 per cent. A comparison between the French and German groups shows that the French group has increased its lead in English, has maintained it in mathematics, but has fallen behind the German group in both language and biology. This reduces its lead in the three subjects other than language to .07 per cent. In all four subjects combined, the French group has fallen 1.01 per cent. behind the German group.

As all three groups have three subjects in common, a more accurate basis of comparison is established when the language grades are eliminated. This gives added value to any comparisons based on columns "Three." The next table possesses this value. Column "Three" of Table IV. shows that the median of the Latin group in the three subjects common to all the groups was 67.91; of the German group, 64.69; and of the French group, 64.76. Table V. shows what per cent. of each group attained the medians of the other groups in the three subjects common to all the groups.

TABLE V.

Percentage of each Group above Medians of the other Groups.

	Latin Group	German Group	French Group
Latin median of 67.91 attained by	50.	39.	41.
German median of 64.69 attained by	59.+	50.	50.+
French median of 64.76 attained by	58.+	49.+	50.

This table substantiates the points brought out in Table IV. It also throws new light upon the situation. For example, it shows that in exactly the same subjects only 39 per cent. of the German group reached the median of the Latin group, while 59 per cent. of the Latin group reached that of the German group; that only 41 per cent. of the French group reached the median of the Latin group, while 58 per cent. of the Latin group reached that of the French group.

The medians in column "Three" may also be used as a standard for measuring the relative efficiency of the groups in language work. As these three medians are based on similar data, viz., the grades in subjects common to all three groups, the percentage of Latin, of German, and of French pupils attaining these medians in language, will be a measure of their efficiency in language relative to their work not only in the three other subjects, but also to the language work of the two other groups. This may be seen by an examination of the following table.

TABLE VI.

Percentage of Language Grades in Each Group, above Median of Each Group in the Three other Subjects.

	Latin Group	Germ. Group	Fre. Group
Latin Median of 67.91 attained in Language by..	47.9	31.3	32.7
German Median of 64.69 attained in Language by	55.3	43.2	37.7
French Median of 64.76 attained in Language by	55.0	42.4	37.4

This table reveals the fact that no group did so well in language work as in the combined work of the three other subjects, but that their respective medians were attained in language work as follows: By the Latin group, 47.9 per cent.; German, 43.2 per cent.; French, 37.4 per cent. It is also seen by what per cent. of each group the various medians were attained, thus showing the relative efficiency of each group in language work. For example, the first line of the table shows that the median of the Latin group, 67.91, was attained in language by 47.9 per cent. of the Latin group; 31.3 per cent. of the German group; 32.7 per cent. of the French group.

In view of the method of measuring results, employed in most schools, no paper such as this would be complete unless it contained a table showing the per cent. of pupils promoted. Therefore, the next table will give this information. The passing grade is 60. per cent. In columns "Three" and "Four" the figures do not mean that such percentages of the pupils passed in all three or in all four subjects, but that of all the grades recorded in the three or in the four subjects such percentages were equal to or above the passing mark. Grades only were considered without regard to the subject or to the pupil who made them.

TABLE VII.

Percentage of Passing Grades.

Groups	Eng.	Math.	Biol.	Three	Lang.	Four.
Latin	88.6	72.5	87.3	82.8	73.1	80.4
German	76.6	68.0	78.8	74.5	66.4	72.5
French	82.9	69.8	74.8	75.8	64.2	72.9

This table in no way modifies the points brought out by the previous tables, viz., that the Latin group has not only maintained, but has actually increased the lead that it had on entering high school; that the French and German groups are, in general, drawing together—in that one group is ahead in two subjects, while the other is ahead in the other two, and in all four subjects combined they are separated by only .4 per cent.

From the superior work of the Latin group, some may infer that the best teachers in English, in mathematics, and in biology were assigned to pupils who elected Latin. Such, however, was not the case, as the following table proves.

TABLE VIII.

Number of Teachers, Other Than of Language, Who Teach in More Than One Group.

Groups	English	Mathematics	Biology
Latin	7 out of 10	14 out of 15	7 out of 7
German	5 out of 9	8 out of 11	6 out of 7
French	8 out of 11	9 out of 10	6 out of 7

The gain made by the Latin group cannot be ascribed to the study of Latin; for, it must be remembered, the above grades were made the first term the pupils were in high school. And, however much one would like to claim that this result was brought about by the study of Latin, it would be difficult to convince anyone that this study could accomplish such results in so short a time. The true explanation, perhaps, can be found in the fact previously established, viz., that the best pupils from the elementary schools elect Latin on entering high school.

Generally speaking, this means that the Latin group is composed of pupils who possess ambition and determination in a high degree; who have learned how to cope with difficulties and to face responsibilities. Such boys do not require so long a time to adjust themselves to a new environment as do their less gifted mates in the French and the German groups. If such gain is made later in the high school course, after all the pupils have become adjusted to their new environment, then the position that the gain was due to the study of Latin will be more tenable. This point will properly come up again when the grades for the second term are under discussion.

Of the 1,397 pupils who took the first term's work, 345 failed to return the second term.

TABLE IX.

Showing Numbers Eliminated, by Groups.

	First Term	Eliminates	Second Term
Latin	536	83	453
German	444	143	301
French	417	119	298
Total	1397	345	1052

The grades of the eliminates were, of course, included in the Tables II. to VII. inclusive. In all subsequent tables they will be omitted unless it is specifically stated that they are included. Table X. shows the effect produced by casting out these grades.

TABLE X.

Showing Increase in Medians of Table IV. by Omitting Grades of Eliminates.

Groups	Eng.	Math.	Biol.	Three	Lang.	Four.
Latin	.31	.08	1.68	.80	.96	.65
German	3.35	2.28	.58	.95	4.38	.79
French	.75	1.16	2.87	.62	1.22	1.46

Upon the whole the standing of the French group was raised most by elimination, while that of the Latin group was affected least. In other words, the Latin group was not improved by the elimination of its inferior members to the extent that the two other groups were. On the other hand, the percentage of work to be repeated the second term is, in the Latin group, 16.12 per cent.; in the German group, 18.50 per cent.; in the French group, 20.72 per cent. This gives an advantage to the groups having the fewer repeaters; for, as will appear later, the ratio of failures to number of chances is, in repeated work, 1 to 3.56; in new work, 1 to 6.19. In dealing with the grades of the second term, however, no distinction will be made between new and repeated work.

The next step toward determining the place held in scholarship by each of the three language groups, will be a series of comparisons between the results of the first and second term's work in each group, and also among the groups themselves. In these comparisons, both the upper and lower quartiles*, as well as the medians will be compared.

---

*Note. The upper quartile is that point above which 25 per cent. of the cases lie. The lower quartile is that point below which 25 per cent. of the cases lie.

TABLE XI.

Upper Quartiles—First Term.

Groups	Eng.	Math.	Biol.	Three	Lang.	Four.
Latin	79.19	75.27	78.18	77.57	79.64	78.14
German	74.90	74.74	74.56	74.75	72.44	74.68
French	74.79	75.38	74.71	74.93	73.00	74.83

TABLE XII.

Upper Quartiles—Second Term.

Groups	Eng.	Math.	Biol.	Three	Lang.	Four.
Latin	78.11	79.69	78.35	78.97	79.66	79.00
German	72.83	77.39	72.44	74.63	71.69	74.25
French	73.80	75.12	75.40	74.92	70.39	74.66

TABLE XIII.

Found by subtracting Table XI. from Table XII.

Groups	Eng.	Math.	Biol.	Three	Lang.	Four.
Latin	—1.08	+4.42	+ .17	+1.40	+ .02	+ .86
German	—2.18	+2.65	—2.12	— .12	— .75	— .43
French	— .99	— .26	+ .69	— .01	—2.61	— .17

Tables XI. and XII. show that in every case (except Math. First Term) the upper quartile of the Latin group is much higher than that of either the German or the French group. Columns "Three" and "Four" of Table XIII. show that, in general, the upper quartiles of the Latin group were higher the second term than they were the first, while those of the two other groups were lower.

TABLE XIV.

Medians—First Term.

Groups	Eng.	Math.	Biol.	Three	Lang.	Four.
Latin	69.94	65.08	69.56	68.71	68.06	68.42
German	68.12	65.11	65.37	65.64	64.83	65.30
French	68.34	64.96	64.58	65.38	61.54	64.96

TABLE XV.

Medians—Second Term.

Groups	Eng.	Math.	Biol.	Three	Lang.	Four.
Latin	69.97	69.76	69.95	69.95	69.70	69.87
German	67.62	64.97	65.34	65.60	63.44	65.26
French	67.14	64.67	68.83	66.40	63.25	65.30

TABLE XVI.

Found by Subtracting Table XIV. from Table XV.

Groups	Eng.	Math.	Biol.	Three	Lang.	Four.
Latin	+ .03	+4.68	+ .39	+1.24	+1.64	+1.45
German	— .50	— .14	— .03	— .04	— .39	— .04
French	—1.20	— .29	+4.25	+1.02	+1.71	+ .34

Tables XIV. and XV. show that in every case (except Math. First Term) the median of the Latin Group is higher than that of either the French or the German group. Table XVI. shows that in every case the median of the Latin group was higher the second term than it was the first, while in every case that of the German group was lower. The French group gained in biology and in language, but fell back in English and in mathematics. There was a general gain as shown by columns "Three" and "Four" of the same table, but not so great as that made by the Latin group.

TABLE XVII.

Lower Quartiles—First Term.

Groups	Eng.	Math.	Biol.	Three	Lang.	Four.
Latin	64.36	59.51	60.37	60.23	59.63	60.11
German	59.17	59.58	60.08	59.87	59.64	59.86
French	60.40	59.58	59.71	59.85	52.00	59.72

TABLE XVIII.

Lower Quartiles—Second Term.

Groups	Eng.	Math.	Biol.	Three	Lang.	Four.
Latin	62.82	60.10	60.34	60.42	59.67	60.25
German	60.26	52.25	59.90	59.82	59.55	59.74
French	60.37	59.60	60.61	60.07	55.07	59.87

TABLE XIX.

Found by Subtracting Table XVII. from Table XVIII.

Groups	Eng.	Math.	Biol.	Three	Lang.	Four.
Latin	—1.54	+ .59	— .03	+ .19	+ .04	+ .14
German	+1.09	—6.23	— .18	— .05	— .09	— .12
French	— .03	+ .02	+ .90	+ .22	+3.07	+ .15

Tables XVII. and XVIII. show that, with the exception of three cases, the lower quartile of the Latin group is higher than that of either the French or the German group. The three cases are,—Math. First Term, lower than that of either group; Lang. First Term, lower than that of the German group; and Biol. Second Term, lower than that of the French group. Table XIX. shows a gain for the French group in every case except English and a loss for the German group in every case except English. The Latin group gains in mathematics and language, but falls back in English and in biology. Columns "Three" and "Four" show a slight loss for the German group, and a slight gain for each of the two other groups. The gains for the French group are respectively .03 per cent. and .01 per cent. greater than for the Latin group.

TABLE XX.

Percentage of Passing Grades, First Term.

Groups	Eng.	Math.	Biol.	Three	Lang.	Four.
Latin	92.7	75.2	90.7	86.2	76.6	83.8
German	85.4	76.4	86.4	82.7	76.7	81.5
French	88.9	76.5	80.5	82.0	71.1	76.7

TABLE XXI.

Percentage of Passing Grades, Second Term.

Groups	Eng.	Math.	Biol.	Three	Lang.	Four.
Latin	90.5	81.9	87.8	86.7	77.0	84.3
German	85.4	72.1	83.0	80.2	76.1	79.1
French	85.6	76.8	87.0	83.2	72.5	80.5

TABLE XXII.

Found by Subtracting Table XX. from Table XXI.

Groups	Eng.	Math.	Biol.	Three	Lang.	Four.
Latin	—2.2	+6.7	—2.9	+ .5	+ .4	+ .5
German	0.0	—4.3	—3.4	—2.5	—1.6	—2.4
French	—3.3	+ .3	+6.5	+1.2	+1.4	+3.8

Tables XX. and XXI. show that in every case except two the Latin group has a higher percentage of passing grades than either the French or the German group. The two cases are,—Math. First Term, lower than that of either group; Lang. First Term, lower than that of the German group.

Nothing shows more clearly the fallacy of judging quality of work by percentage of promotions than a comparison of columns "Three" and "Four" of Table XXII. with the corresponding columns of Table XVI. The median under "Three" of the Latin group shows .22 per cent. more of increase than that of the French group. Yet the French group shows .7 per cent. more of increase in promotions. Again, the median under "Four" of the Latin group shows 1.11 per cent. more of increase than that of the French group. Yet the French group shows 3.3 per cent. more of increase in promotions. Evidently, an increase in the **number of promotions** is not necessarily attended by a corresponding increase in the quality of the work.

In the next table, the median attained by the Latin group the first term in any subject (or combination of subjects) is used as the basis of comparison of work done in that subject (or combination of subjects) both by terms and by language groups.

TABLE XXIII.

Percentage of Each Group, in Each Term and in Each Subject (or Combination of Subjects) above Median Attained by Latin Group, the First Term in that Subject (or Combination of Subjects).

Subject	Median		Latin Group	German Group	French Group
Eng.	69.94	attained first term by	50.0	41.5	40.9
Eng.	69.94	" second " "	50.4	36.2	36.9
Mat.	65.08	attained first term by	50.0	50.1	49.0
Mat.	65.08	" second " "	61.4	49.2	45.9
Bio.	69.56	attained first term by	50.0	41.2	37.6
Bio.	69.56	" second " "	53.9	42.2	48.6
Three	68.71	attained first term by	50.0	43.8	42.7
Three	68.71	" second " "	55.4	43.1	45.0
Lang.	68.06	attained first term by	50.0	48.1	42.9
Lang.	68.06	" second " "	53.6	38.5	36.2
Four	68.42	attained first term by	50.0	42.7	42.2
Four	68.42	" second " "	54.9	41.9	42.1

As the basis of comparison employed in each subject, is the grade attained by 50 per cent. of the Latin group in that subject the first term, variations can be more easily seen if 50 per cent. be deducted from each per cent. in the above table.

In reading the following table it should be borne in mind that per cents are based upon the entire group in each case, and not upon the half that is expected to attain the median. For example, in English the first term, 8.5 per cent. of the German group failed to attain the standard set for them as a group, because 50 per cent. of the group, instead of 41.5 per cent. of it, should have attained the median 69.94.

TABLE XXIV.

Variations in Each Subject by Terms and by Groups.

	Latin Group	German Group	French Group
Var. from English standard, first term	0.0	— 8.5	— 9.1
Var. from English standard, second term,	+ .4	—13.8	—13.1
Var. from Math. standard, first term,	0.0	+ .1	— 1.0
Var. from Math. standard, second term,	+11.4	— .8	— 4.1
Var. from Biol. standard, first term,	0.0	— 8.8	—12.4
Var. from Biol. standard, second term,	+ 3.9	— 7.8	— 1.4
Var. from Three standard, first term,	0.0	— 6.2	— 7.3
Var. from Three standard, second term,	+ 5.4	— 6.9	— 5.0
Var. from Lang. standard, first term,	0.0	— 1.9	— 7.1
Var. from Lang. standard, second term,	+ 3.6	—11.5	—13.8
Var. from Four standard, first term,	0.0	— 7.3	— 7.8
Var. from Four standard, second term,	+ 4.9	— 8.1	— 7.9

This table shows that in the second term the Latin group in every case rose above the standard set the first term; that the German group fell below the standard in every case both terms except in first term mathematics and that its second term's work was poorer than that of the first term except in biology; that the French group fell below the standard in every case both terms and that its second term's work was poorer than that of the first term except in biology. Here, however, the gain was so great that it brought column "Three" above the work of the first term.

If the per cent. of variation for the first term in each subject and group be subtracted from the corresponding per cent. for the second term, we get the following table which shows the per cent. of gain or loss of the second term over the first.

TABLE XXV.

Found by Subtracting Variations of First Term from those of Second Term.

	Latin Group	German Group	French Group
Difference in variations in English	+ .4	—5.3	— 4.0
Difference in variations in Mathematics	+11.4	— .9	— 3.1
Difference in variations in Biology	+ 3.9	+1.0	+11.0
Difference in variations in Three	+ 5.4	— .7	+ 2.3
Difference in variations in Language	+ 3.6	—9.6	— 6.7
Difference in variations in Four	+ 4.9	— .8	— .1

The assumption is valid that the above per cents will hold true of such groups even though they be somewhat larger or smaller. They may be made commensurable in terms of pupils, therefore, if the groups are regarded as of the same size. In the following table, it is assumed, therefore, that the German and French groups each contain the same number of pupils as the Latin group, viz., 453.

TABLE XXVI.

Showing Gain or Loss in Number of Pupils Who Reached the Standard the Second Term in Comparison with the First Term.

	Latin Group	German Group	French Group
Difference in variations in English	+ 2.	—24.	—18.
Difference in variations in Mathematics	+52.	— 4.	—14.
Difference in variations in Biology	+18.	+ 5.	+50.
Difference in variations in Three	+24.	— 3.	+10.
Difference in variations in Language	+16.	—43.	—30.
Difference in variations in Four	+22.	— 4.	0.

In order to show the gain or loss of one group over another during the second term, it will be necessary to compare the columns in the above table, two at a time. For example, the gain of the Latin group over the German will be found by subtracting the figures in the German column from the corresponding figures in the Latin column. The following table was obtained by this process.

TABLE XXVII.

Showing Gain or Loss in Number of Pupils who Reached the Standard in one Group, in Comparison with the Number Who Reached the Standard in Another.

	Latin above Ger.	Latin above Fre.	German above Fre.
Comparative gain in English	+26.	+20.	— 6.

Comparative gain in Mathematics	+56.	+66.	+10.
Comparative gain in Biology	+13.	—32.	—45.
Comparative gain in Three	+27.	+14.	—13.
Comparative gain in Language	+59.	+46.	—13.
Comparative gain in Four	+26.	+22.	— 4.

It would seem that no more evidence is needed to prove that during the second term the Latin group made great gains over each of the other groups. The superiority of this group the first term was ascribed to the fact they were a superior group when they entered high school and, therefore, could more easily adjust themselves to their new environment. During the second term, however, were not the French and German groups sufficiently adjusted to their environment, at least, to hold their own? But this investigation has shown that while the Latin group was rising above the standard of the first term's work, both the French and German groups were falling below it, in whole or in part. Is it not possible, then, that after all there is some truth in the theory that disciplinary power is derived from the study of Latin? Or, are these changes due to the fact that the "Direct Method" was extensively employed in German, to a limited extent in French, and not at all in Latin? Or, are they due to a combination of these causes?

PART TWO.

Some Facts Bearing upon Elimination and Retardation.

As stated elsewhere, out of the 1,397 pupils who completed one term, 345 left at the end of the first term. These were drawn from the February and September classes and from the three language groups as follows:

TABLE XXVIII.

Showing Distribution of Eliminates by Classes and Groups.

	February Class			September Class			Combined Classes		
Groups	Base	Elim	Per Ct.	Base	Elim	Per Ct.	Base	Elim	Per Ct.
Latin	271	56	20.66	265	27	10.18	536	83	15.48
German	222	92	41.44	222	51	22.97	444	143	32.21
French	215	74	34.41	202	45	22.27	417	119	28.53
Total	708	222	31.35	689	123	17.62	1397	345	24.69

The above table reveals two facts: 1. That the class which completed its first term in June, lost more pupils than the class that completed its first term in January. 2. That the per cent. of loss from the Latin group was much less than that from either the French or the German group, and that that of the French group was a little less than that of the German group.

TABLE XXIX.

Showing Percentage of Eliminates with No Failure, One Failure, etc., on Total Number with No Failure, One Failure, etc.

Groups	No Failure	One Failure	Two Failures	Three Failures	Four Failures
Latin	9.18	11.96	33.33	32.50	52.94
German	15.42	36.03	35.18	59.52	77.77
French	18.28	24.24	30.00	60.00	70.37
Totals	13.43	23.85	36.64	50.42	70.00

From Table XXIX. one can readily see that the percentage of eliminates tends to increase as the number of failures per pupils increase. This fact might lead some to infer that failure in studies is one of the chief causes of elimination. Such, however, is not the case to the extent that it is generally supposed to be.

TABLE XXX.

Showing Percentage of Eliminates with No Failure, One Failure, etc., on Total Number of Eliminates.

Groups	No Failure	One Failure	Two Failures	Three Failures	Four Failures
Latin	33.73	16.86	22.89	15.66	10.84
German	20.97	27.97	13.28	17.48	19.58
French	28.57	20.16	17.64	17.64	15.96
Totals	26.95	22.60	17.10	17.10	16.23

From Table XXX. it appears that of the 345 eliminates, more than one-fourth of them failed in no subject, while practically one-half of them failed in only one subject or less. Certainly, failure in subjects was not the cause of their elimination, nor does the table furnish much proof that it is even an important factor in elimination at all.

The claim is often made that certain subjects, because of their inherent difficulties, cause pupils who fail in them to leave school. The next two tables bear on this point.

TABLE XXXI.

Showing Percentage of Eliminates Who Failed in Any Subject on Total Number of Failures in That Subject.

Groups	Eng.	Lang.	Math.	Biol.
Latin	49.50	26.38	23.97	38.23
German	57.69	55.03	50.00	55.31
French	53.52	42.28	44.44	45.28
Totals	53.38	41.40	39.13	47.01

This table shows that a greater per cent. of those who failed in English and in biology left school than of those who failed in language and in mathematics.

TABLE XXXII.

Showing Percentage of Failures of Eliminates in Each Subject on Total Number of Eliminates.

Groups	Eng.	Lang.	Math.	Biol.
Latin	33.73	45.78	42.16	31.32
German	41.95	57.34	49.65	36.36
French	31.93	52.94	47.03	40.33
Totals	36.52	53.04	46.95	36.52

This table shows that a greater per cent. of eliminates failed in language and in mathematics than in English and in biology.

The explanation of this seeming contradiction between the two tables is this: The number of failures in English and in biology was much smaller than that in language and in mathematics. Therefore, while the actual number of eliminates in the former two subjects is smaller than in the latter two, yet the per cent. on number of failures is larger, owing to the relative smallness of the base on which the per cent. is calculated. The safer rule (as in the case of Tables XXIX. and XXX.). is to employ as the base, the total number of eliminates rather than the total number of something not under discussion. It is safer, therefore, to conclude that failure in mathematics and in language contributed more to elimination than failure in English and in biology.

The term in which the pupil is in school seems to have some effect upon retardation as well as upon elimination (see Table XXVIII.). The fall term seems to be less productive of failures than the spring term. The data upon which this conclusion is based are as follows:

TABLE XXXIII.

Showing Number of Failures by Terms in Each Class and Group (after Deducting Eliminates).

	February Class		September Class	
Groups	Spring Term	Fall Term	Fall Term	Spring Term
Latin	141	106	151	178
German	109	105	115	147
French	126	93	121	142
Totals	376	304	387	467

Summary: Spring Term—843; Fall Term—691

This investigation has revealed the following facts regarding elimination and retardation:

1. Elimination is greater at the end of June than of January.
2. Elimination is least in the Latin group and greatest in the German group.
3. Failure in subjects is not so fruitful a cause of elimination as it is generally supposed to be.
4. More eliminates failed in mathematics and in language than in English and in biology.
5. More failures occur in the spring term than in the fall term.

PART THREE.

Policy to be Pursued in Making Programs for Repeaters.

One of the most important questions that confronts the program maker is, What shall be done with the repeaters? Shall they be placed in a class by themselves, or, with those who are new to the subject? Growing out of this question is the related one, What are the chances of passing in repeated work as compared with new work?

TABLE XXXIV.

Comparison of Failures in Old and New Work.

Groups	Number Pupils	Chances Total	Chances Old	Chances New	Failed Old	Failed New
Latin	453	1812	292	1520	71	213
German	301	1204	224	980	79	173
French	298	1192	247	945	64	170
Totals	1052	4208	763	3445	214	556

The chance of failure in repeated work is 1 to 3.56; in new work, 1 to 6.19. Then shall the repeater be robbed of all spurs to his ambition by being placed among those who are as dull as he? or shall he become a clog to a bright class by being placed among them?

One solution often proposed is, to reduce the number of his studies. This is based on the assumption that he who fails does so because he has more work than he can do. Conversely, he who passes in every subject does not have more work than he can do, and therefore can carry a full program the following term. How baseless these assumptions are, is shown by the following table.

TABLE XXXV.

Showing Results Attained the Second Term by Pupils Who Failed in No Subject, One Subject, etc., the First Term.

			Number of Pupils Who Failed First Term				
		Total	None	One	Two	Three	Four
		1052	599	249	122	58	24
Number of Pupils Who Failed Second Term	None	567	382	111	44	23	7
	One	287	155	76	37	13	6
	Two	131	44	44	25	15	3
	Three	47	15	12	11	5	4
	Four	20	3	6	5	2	4

The horizontal line above the rectangle reads that in the first term 599 pupils failed in no subject, 249 in one subject, etc. The vertical line to the left of the rectangle reads that in the second term 567 pupils failed in no subject, 287 in one subject, etc. The first horizontal line within the rectangle reads that of the 567 pupils who failed in no subject the second term, 382 had failed in no subject the first term, 111 had failed in one subject, etc. The first vertical line at the left within the rectangle reads that of the 599 pupils who failed in no subject the first term, 382 failed in no subject the second term, 155 failed in one subject, etc.

The program of the repeater can not be based on the policy of the omission of subjects. For 185 repeaters carried full programs and came out with no failures the second term; whereas 217 who made no failures the first term came out the second term with 300 failures charged against them.

In the light of such conditions what mind short of one gifted with supernatural insight can foresee what should be done in any given case?

We offer no solution of the problem, because we have none. We simply present it as a problem met with during this investigation of the scholarship records of high school pupils.

SUMMARY OF MR. DOTEY'S PAPER.

DATA USED—Term-grades received by pupils on prepared work in English mathematics, biology, and foreign language for first and second terms in high school.

Total number pupils 1379: Latin, 536; German, 444; French, 417.

PART ONE—Place in scholarship held respectively by the Latin, German, and French groups.

1. Order of excellence based as shown by elementary school records: Latin group one per cent better than the French and two per cent better than the German.

2. During first term, Latin group not only maintained its lead in every subject, but greatly increased it in every subject except mathematics. (See Tables II to VII inclusive.)

3. Superiority not due to difference in teachers. (See Table VIII.)

4. At end of first term, German group lost greatest number of pupils; Latin group, the least. (See Table IX.)

5. Standing of French group raised most by elimination; that of Latin group, least. (See Table X.)

6. During second term, Latin group did better work in every subject that it did the first term; German group did poorer work in every subject except biology; French group did poorer work in every subject except biology. (See Tables XI to XXVI inclusive; and especially Tables XXV and XXVI.)

7. The relative gain of the Latin group was greater than that of the German in every subject, and than that of the French group in every subject except biology. The relative gain of the French group was greater than that of the German in every subject except mathematics. (See Table XXVIII.)

PART TWO—Facts concerning elimination and retardation.

1. More pupils are eliminated in June than in January.

2. Per cent of loss from Latin group was far less than from either of the other groups; that of French group was a little less than that of German group. (See Table XXVIII.)

3. Elimination not due to failure in subjects. (See Tables XXIX and XXX.)

4. Greater per cent o f eliminates failed in mathematics and foreign language than in English and biology. (See Tables XXXI and XXXII.)

5. More failures occur in spring term than in fall term. (See Table XXXIII.)

PART THREE—Programs for repeaters.

1. Chances of failure are greater in repeated work than in new work. (See Table XXXIV.)

2. Failure on the part of a given pupil the first term, however, does not necessarily imply failure on his part the second term; nor vice versa. (See Table XXXV.)

3. What to do with the repeater, is yet an unsolved problem.

IN MEMORIAN—Superintendent Edward L. Stevens.

The overwhelming truth that "in the midst of life we are in death" is again illustrated in the passing away of Dr. Edward L. Stevens in New York. Only a couple of weeks ago he visited his parents, Mr. and Mrs. Clinton Stevens, in Malone, and was hailing his boyhood friends on the street who were always delighted to see him. He had been seriosly ill and under treatment in a New York hospital, but considered himself much better and was cheerful and encouraged, though he showed marked effects of his illness. He remained here and in Chateaugay only a few days and returned to the city to attend to duties which he deemed to be urgent, never to return again alive.

A few years ago Dr. Stevens passed through a very critical illness, from which he nver quite recovered his former health and strength. Last summer, on the verge of breaking down, he obtained a leave of absence from his educational duties in New York and passed several months in Malone and vicinity, returning to the city in the fall greatly improved, but the improvement was not permanent.

As assistant superintendent of schools of the city of New York he held a most honerous posisition of great responsibility and continued to battl with its problems far beyond his physical ability to bear up under them. He was keen, original and progressive, introducing many innovations into the schools of that city and adapting them to the practical needs of a great cosmopolitan population. Possessed of a high idea of the value of country training he found places for many graduates of the rural normal schools in the city's teaching force.

Dr. Stevens was a man of fine personal presence and a deightful speaker. He was called upon often to lecture on educational subjects before conventions and assemblages of educators, and a number of his lectures had been published by teh action of thes ebodies and widely circulated in phamplet form. With truth it can be said that as an ducator Northern N. Y. never produced his superior. Many of his old acquaintances here still recall the magnificent address which he gave before the alumni of Franklin Academy at the last biennial meeting of the association in Malone.

Though his condition on his last rturn to New Yark was far from satisfactory, his death was entirely unexpected and its announcement Saturday morning proved a serious shock to his aged parents and many relatives and friends in Malone. The cause of death was pneumonia. In his weakend condition he was unable to withstand the ravages of the disease.

Dr. Stevens was born in Malone in May, 1867, and was not quite 47 years of age. The foundation of his broad culture was laid at Franklin Academy from which he graduated with honors in the class of 1885, and had long been one of its most favored sons. Later on he completed a full course at Hamilton College, which, with a year or two of law in the office of M. E. McClary, prepared him thorougly for the educational and executive duties which he was destined by natural aptitute to undertake. The practice of the law he decided early to forego, but his knowledge of it furnished ever afterward a vantage ground in his educational conquests.

His first school was at Dickinson Center, and he performed his task so well that he was soon called to the principalship of the Chateaugay high school. There his superior work soon raised the attention of educators all over the state. He won the hearts of the people of that commnuity so that they never ceased to admire and honor him as he advanced to the topmost round of his profession.

From there he was called to Catskill to fill the position of superintendent of schools of that city, and it was not long before there was the call from New York for his services and abilities. To the work there he gave conscientious attention. The field was wide and all his energies were thrown into the cauldron of the city's needs. His broad culture and ability as an educator brought him instant recognition and rapid advancement until he stood almost at the head of the department, a position which he had held for a number of years.

His death in the very prime of life is sad indeed, and has brought to an end all too soon a career of the greatest usefulness; but he imprint of his splendid work upon the schools of New York and the men and women of the future whose early life has been sheltered within that city's walls, will never pass away.

Personally, Dr. Stevens was one of the most charming and persuasive of men. He was dignified, yet democratic and approachable; poised, yet full of the warmth of human attributes. He delighted in his acquaintances and experiences and had a keen appreciation of the humorous as well as the serious side of life. With his scintillating mind and ready wit he was always the central figure of any assemblage so fortunate as to enjoy his presence. And in addition to all this he was patient, gracious, courteous and kind. His heart was big and warm and fullblooded, and his loss to his friends is acutely felt. To his venerable parents he was their joy and pride, and in their deep distress there is universal sympathy.

While principal of Chateaugay Academy he met and woed Miss Carrie Hatch, a brilliant young woman connected with the school which he taught. She and one son, Robert, survive to cherish the memory of a fond and indulgent husband and father. One brother. Robert, a prominent mechanical engineer of Erie, Pa., also survives, and accompanied the remains to Malone, arriving Sunday afternoon. The brothers were united in the closest bonds of fraternal fellowship.

As Mrs. Stevens was ill at Chateaugay and unable to attend the funeral in Malone the body was taken there on the evening of its arrival here and funeral services were held from her old home Saturday evening. On account of the feebleness of the mother of deceased, who was unable to attend the funeral in Chateaugay, and to enable Dr. Steven's relatives and multitude of friends in Malone to pay their last tribute of respect to one of the town's most brillant sons, funeral services were also held from the home of his parents here on Tuesday afternoon, interment beside the remains of his sister, Carrie, at Morningside.

IN MEMORIAM.

Principal James J. Sheppard.

Whereas, the recent death of Principal Sheppard of the High School of Commerce has removed from our organization one of the most active members, be it resolved that the following note be entered upon the minutes of the Association.

Principal James J. Sheppard, whose death occurred on March 13, 1914, was identified with this organization almost from the beginning. Even before he became a principal, he was one of the most energetic and useful members of the Association. In 1902-3 he served with distinction as president of the Association, and was re-elected the following year. His interest in the organization did not cease afterwards. He was always present at the meetings, and his voice was often heard in wise counsel.

It is fitting to recall in this connection that when the Teachers' Council was organized in 1913, the twenty-three high school principals unanimously chose Mr. Sheppard as the one fittest to represent them in this most important body. By this choice they recognized, as our Association had done, the fact that Mr. Sheppard united in a rare degree the quality of executive ability with the spirit of social service.

In his death the teachers of the whole city lost a friend, and the high school teachers lost a leader and comrade, one who spent himself freely in every good cause.

James Joseph Sheppard was born at Panola, Woodford County, Illinois, January 1, 1868. His early education was obtained in the public schools of Panola. In 1891 he graduated from the academic and normal departments of the Illinois State Normal University. While in the normal school he became the founder and editor-in-chief of the school paper "The Vidette," and the winner in one of the annual inter-society debates. He then went to Harvard University and was graduated in 1894. Subsequently he did post-graduate work at Columbia University in the years from 1897 to 1900, and at New York University in 1901 and 1902.

During the years from 1884 to 1886, Mr. Sheppard taught in the public schools of Minnesota, Iowa and Illinois. After his graduation from Harvard University he was for three years principal of the Decatur, Illinois, High School. In 1897 he was President of the High School Section of the Illinois State Teachers' Association.

As the result of a competitive examination, in 1897 he was appointed as a second assistant teacher of history in the DeWitt Clinton High School of New York, being promoted later to the position of first assistant; and in this school he had charge of the annex from 1900 to 1902. In 1902 he was promoted to the principalship of the High School of Commerce, which he organized, and which was the first institution of its kind in the United States.

Mr. Sheppard was President of the High School Teachers' Association of New York from 1902 to 1904, a member of the board of directors of the New York Teachers' Association since 1900; and a member of the Interborough Council of New York since 1904. He was also Secretary of the Committee on Instruction in Municipal Government in American Educational Institutions of the National Municipal League. Mr. Sheppard was a contributor of papers to the National Education Association and to other educational organizations; and was the editor of Appleton's Series of Texts for Commercial Schools. He was a member of the Harvard, Graduates, Schoolmasters and Rolandson Clubs. On July 12, 1905, Mr. Sheppard married Rena French Masters.

After an illness of several weeks duration he diedof anaemia at his home in Morsemere, New Jersey, March 13, 1914, loved throughout the school system of the great city of New York, whose teachers and students had learned to admire the man and appreciate his work.

To Mr. Sheppard more than to any other one person the high school teachers owe a debt of gratitude for his indefatigable work and excellent judgment in securing for them through the passage of the "Davis Law" uniform salary schedules.

He was a keen observer of men and instinctively understood their purposes and the measure of their usefulness. In the organization of the teaching corps of the High School of Commerce he selected an unusual number of able men who have since risen to higher positions, notably as elementary and high school principals.

Only a small number of his close friends knew of his extensive and intimate acquaintance with many of the most prominent educators throughout the country. He made friends slowly. Once, however, men saw through his reserve, the simplicity and the true sincerity of the man, the purity of his thought and purposes, he won their lasting affection and allegiance. To only a few were known his great fondness for little children, his extreme generosity in helping acquaintances or strangers in financial distress, his acts of kindness and thoughtfulness in times of sorrow or trouble.

Among his associates he was known as an excellent organizer and administrator. He was a man of few words, fine judgment, and once his decision was formed he possessed great courage and pertinacity in carrying out his ideas. He would not go with the crowd unless convinced that the crowd was right.

"He was, taking him all in all, what the world most needs today and what the world mourns when such a one is gone—a man, a nobleman."

The words of his favorite poem were:

Sunset and Evening Star,
And one clear call for me!
And may there be no moaning bar,
When I put out to sea.

But moving tide asleep,
Too full for sound or foam,
When that which drew from out the deep
Turns to its earliest home.

James F. Wilson.
Benjamin A. Heydrick.

ON THE WASTE OF TRIPLE SESSIONS.

By John M. Avent, Morris High School.

That the using the school plant idea manifested in the "double-session" or "triple session" does accommodate more pupils than the one session scheme, nó one denies. If you are skeptical, you are invited to count 'em.

To "count 'em," whether pupils or instruction or personal influence, is indeed the only test of educational practice that makes an impression on the guardians of the budget. Therefore, the following is a modest attempt to count the waste of the program that provides for three over-lapping blocks of students, an 8:15 to 1:40 group, a 9:00 to 2:30 group and a 10:00 to 3:15 group. The principles are not modified if the plan calls for two groups, not overlapping.

The element of waste—the leakage—occurs in what may be called "extra-classroom" instruction. No teacher, or principal, but knows that the value of a teacher is not encompassed by the bell that starts the period and the bell that ends it. Those bells include a large fraction, but still only a fraction of a teacher's instruction and influence. The other fraction is variable, but sufficiently determinable for reckoning.

To determine this fraction which we have called "extra-classroom" instruction, let us assume that the average number of teaching periods per week under any plan is 25. Let us assume that, under the single session plan, a teacher reports not a minute before the by-law requirement of 8:40. Assume also that she stays not more than 15 minutes with pupils after the by-law requirement of 2:30. Note that we have omitted all coaching of clubs and teams (of which there are over thirty-five in Morris High School) and surely this is not too large an estimate. Yet between 8:40 and the first period there are 28 minutes, which, added to the 15 minutes of after-school instruction, make 1 period per day or 5 periods per week of extra-classroom instruction. It is rather clear, therefore, that the "horse power" of a teacher is about 30 periods per week, of which 1-6 is expended outside of the regular periods. Here every tachr will say that this fraction approachs 1-3 rather than 1-6.

Now, is this one-sixth of a teacher's value lost in the three group or triple session? Count again.

The essential factor here is that a pupil in any group may have teachers in all three groups. When 1-3 of the pupils report at 8:15, only 1-3 of the teachers are available. Therefore, there is a loss of 2-3 of the maximum morning extra instruction for this group. When the 9 o'clock group reports, similarly there are only 1-3 of the teachers available (the first group are teaching and again there is a loss of 2-3 of the maximum morning extra instruction for this group. Furthermore, when the 10 o'clock group reports, there are no teachers available for there is no place to meet the pupils, all the rooms being in use. Consequently, we sustain here 3-3 of the extra morning instruction. Averaging, we find a loss of 7-9 of the maximum "extra" morning instruction.

These figures are hopelessly feeble as an estimate of a condition where it is an impracticability to meet backward or indolent pupils out of the formal periods. They are merely as consciously inadequate attempt to do what can not be done—to count 'em when you are dealing with the most subtle of all increase, the growth of mind and of character.

Nevertheless, turn to the afternoon "extra" instruction. When the 8:15 group leaves there are no teachers available for the rooms are in use. Here again we have a loss of 3-3 of th extra instruction. When the 9 o'clock group leaves at 2:30 1-3 of the teachers are available with a loss of 2-3 of the extra instruction. When the 10 o'clock group leaves at 3:15 there are no teachers available for pupils dislike to stay after that hour, many of them having long distances to travel. Here we may charge a 3-3 loss of instruction. Averaging, we have a loss of 8-9 of the extra afternoon instruction. This extra afternoon instruction is 1-3 of the total extra instruction. Therefore we have noticed a loss of 7-9 of 2-3 and 8-9 of 1-3 of the extra instruction. This indicates that we have lost 22-27 of all the extra instruction.

FACTORY EFFICIENCY IN EDUCATION*

Benjamin C. Gruenberg, of Commercial High School.

*Read before High School Teachers Association, 7 March, 1914.

Among the forces that have brought us to seek the establishment of the maximum use of the school plant, was the idea of "100% efficiency." In this the assumption has been that one hour is like every other. But this assumption is dangerously similar to the obsolescent doctrine that each child is like every other.

So far as the facts have been determined by experimental studies, we are to believe that the periods of maximum available energy are between nine and ten or eleven in the morning, and a short period after one in the afternoon. As Meumann says in his "Psychology of Learning,"

> The first hour of the day should be used for exercises in which the formal purpose of memory development is most emphasized....because in the first place, the school children possess the greatest amount of psycho-physical energy during the first and second hours, and they are then still free from the influence of fatigue; and in the second place, their memorial efficiency fluctuates between wide limits at different hours of the day.

After fatigue sets in, greater stimulus is required to produce the desired results. "Effort increases with fatigue, and output falls off." Most children cannot be held to their work after fatigue sets in; this is fortunate, because it is the only means of protection that the child has against the danger of physiological exhaustion.

Scientific studies in industrial establishments, as well as those in school, show that all hours are not alike. Some evidence from the study of accidents is interesting in this connection. These show that the number of accidents increase steadily to about the fourth hour, and then diminish. This is true in both half-days. The decrease is apparently due to the reduction in the number of workers in the various shifts. In some cases, however, it means a lowered intensity of work, which in turn results from increasing fatigue. In part, however, this is counteracted by the "warming up" process (Anregung, or incitement of the psychologists). In some industries the maximum output actually occurs later than the maximum accidents.

Aside from these fluctuations, the studies in the industries have shown a generally lower level of efficiency on the part of the night workers, as compared to the day workers. This holds even where the workers alternate periodically. The explanation for this is that the night workers do not have as good rest in the day-time, and that they are tempted to spend more of their off hours in recreation, etc. We may well ask ourselves whether the same forces do not operate among children sent to school in different shifts.

If our schooling is to be more than school-keeping, we must consider something more than units and hours We must make no concessions to the economic fallacy.

Factory methods apply where there is to be uniformity of product. The success and the efficiency of factory method depend upon the multiplication of units of standardized and identical types—wherever the same processes and the same materials can be brought together over and over again. This is not true in education. Certainly money can be saved by enlarging classes; money can also be saved by accelerating the elimination of pupils from school. But we no longer look to enlarged classes as a legitimate means of saving money Yet we do seriously consider the closer congestion of the school as a sound solution of the problem.

There are certain specific dangers that need to be considered. The efficiency of a room, for school purposes, depends to a large extent upon those small touches that reveal the personality of the teacher, or the special uses to which the room is to be put. Laboratories and shops may be standardized, perhaps; as for recitation rooms, no standardization seems possible beyond the matters of furniture, blackboards, charts and the other routine fixtures and equipments. Where two or more teachers use the same room successively, individualization of the room—which is much more important than standardization—is impossible. This is more striking when we consider the desirability of making the room serve as the home for a group of children. (Even now most of the rooms do not provide places for pupils' books, so that there is an excessive amount of carrying necessary.)

Closely related is the fact that where there are continuous sessions of new groups, it is impossible for the teacher to come into close personal relations with the pupils. It is touch and go, in the most literal sense.

The time of the pupils spend outside of school does not usually concern us. If, however, this outside time precedes the school work, I should expect it to have a decided influence on the latter. If the child works before coming to school, I should expect merely fatigue—and I am disposed to demand the best, the freshest energies for the use of the school. If, however, the pupil does not work, I should expect in a large number of cases, not necessarily fatigue, but certainly demoralization.

Superintendent Brubacher of Schenectady showed that the absences are more than twice as frequent among part-time pupils as among full time pupils (in the ratio 8.5 : 3.5) notwithstanding the fact that the latter had twice as many chances to be absent—forenoons and afternoons.

Our experience in this city with the compulsory education law that required evening school attendance of young people who are working, is in complete accord with the experience of England: it showed that it is impossible to extend the hours of activity indefinitely. And we changed our compulsory education law in recognition of the fact that the only suitable "night school" for young people to attend is a day school. The young people in our high schools are even younger than those who come within the provisions of the compulsory education law referred to; their hours of effort must be still shorter. And it does not seem to make much difference whether the fatigue is accumulated within school or outside.

The Schenectady experience shows that the effects of part-time organization are cumulative. The children that had been exposed to it one year, showed the effects, but with each succeeding year of the practise the results were worse and worse.

As for the teachers, if they use their mornings for work, they do not give the school their best energies; and if they use them for sleep and loafing, they do not give the school their best spirits.

The conclusions of Superintendent Brubacher's report are:

1. Part time schools fatigue the children and the teachers unduly. Sustained attention is hard to get.

2. The health of children in part time classes is not as good as that of children in full time classes. Attendance is 2.42 times better in full time classes.

3. Full time classes promote about 5 more children in every hundred; and

4. Full time classes are better prepared to do the work of the next higher grade since they are fortified by 50 per cent. more training as indicated by the work accomplished in reading.

5. The evils of part time are

cumulative. They are bad in the first grade, but where a child has come up through successive grades on part time, the accumulated defects become disheartening in the grammar grades and high schools. Our city has more than once seen a school under part time conditions for from five to eight years, and the pupils from such schools on reaching the eight grade or high school have been decidedly inferior to their fellows from other grammar schools where full time prevailed.

6. Part time is therefore to be condemned as an educational monstrosity. It is an unsound pedagogical device and is a sheer waste of public funds. It would be sound economy, I believe, to borrow money to provide ample facilities for all the children of our city at once.

It is true, as President McLaurin of the Massachusetts Institute of Technology points out, that a life belt is in actual use only a small part of the time; and yet we do not consider it inefficient to have large numbers of life belts lie idly about on the boats. It has been estimated that in this country there is invested in tooth-brushes the sum of $1,432,678.15; yet these articles are used only a few minutes each per day. No one advocates an increase in the use-efficiency of tooth-brushes. The best example of high use-efficiency of an article of common use was that furnished by certain southern cotton mills that shocked us all a few years ago, when we read that the beds in which the child workers slept never got cold. One shift of workers turned in as soon as the sleepers were turned out. There was no time lost. And yet we were shocked.

There is nevertheless a legitimate demand for a fuller use of the school plant. This increase in use-efficiency is not to be brought about, however, by following the method of the steel-trust, running in successive shifts of occupants for continuous use of the equipment. The city is to get its return upon the investment in school buildings by extending the use of the plant to ever new sections of the population, to ever new kinds of activities. Some of the possibilities suggested by the studies of the Russel Sage Foundation (Perry) are these: Continuation schools, Evening schools, Social centers, Public lectures and entertainments, Athletics, games, dancing, meetings, study hours, pupils' clubs, etc., reading rooms, concerts, museum extension, and others.

The present situation in the housing of high school activities presents an acute emergency. In attempting to meet this, we may properly enough resort to "part-time" schemes, or to overcrowded classes, or to double sessions, or triple sessions. But we must not forget that these are emergency measures, and we must not let others forget that they are emergency measures. We must not let anyone suppose for an instant that these schemes solve the fundamental problems of adequate housing, and we must not ourselves accept them as such solutions.

As to the inability of the city to meet the financial problem presented by the high school situation, we need not take the taxpayer's word for that In Chicago the city could not possibly find enough money to pay its teachers what the latter considered a fair wage a few years ago. The teachers' association appointed a committee of doubters and skeptics to nose into city affairs; this committee discovered that certain corporations had been systematically and efficiently evading their taxes. The teachers forced the city authorities to collect—and there was plenty of money for school needs. Now we know that the Department of Education of this city has not received enough money to build all the schools it should like to build. But perhaps if we convince the "city" that more money is really needed for school business, the money will be forthcoming.

ON SOME TREATY OBLIGATIONS OF THE UNITED STATES TO COLOMBIA PANAMA AND GREAT BRITAIN. WITH REPRINT OF SOURCES.

WILLIAM T. MORREY,

Head of Department of History, Bushwick High School.

The History Section of the High School Teachers' Association, of New York City, had too much on its regular program for me to do much more than to state my question and ask them to print in the Bulletin. Since 1892, when I first came to Brooklyn, I have been in close touch with Spanish-American thought, in history, politics, and commerce. I spent a summer in Washington among the archives of the Department of State, reading the reports of our South American ministers and consuls.

The great trouble with the Spanish-Americans is their idea of the Monroe Doctrine. We sometimes sum it up as: "America for the Americans." This is a perfectly proper interpretation if by Americans we mean the inhabitants of North, Central and South America. But my Spanish-American friends say that we mean by the Monroe Doctrine, "America for the Yankees."

They remember our acquisition of Texas, California, and Arizona from Mexico and Porto Rico from Spain.

But more important than all of these for an understanding of their distrust, is the attitude of the United States towards Colombia.

COLOMBIA.

The statesmen and newspaper men of Spanish-America and the world sometimes know what the "average American" may not know, or may have forgotten, for example, he may have heard ex-President Roosevelt say: "I took Panama," but he may not know our treaty obligations at the time

Soon after this taking of Panama I asked Prof. Albert Bushnell Hart in Cooper Union, after a long speech of praise of Roosevelt "Did President Roosevelt break our Treaty of 1846 with New Granada." Professor Hart dared not answer to that great audience.

He was still unwilling to answer after he became President of the American Historical Association.

The nation must now answer.

President Roosevelt in his Autobiography, Macmillan Company, New York City, page 554 says:

"Ever since 1846 we had had a treaty with the power then in control of the Isthmus, the Republic of New Granada, the predecessor of the Republic of Colombia and of the present Republic of Panama, by which treaty the United States was guaranteed free and open right of way across theIsthmus of Panama by any mode of communication that might be constructed, while in return our Government guaranteed the perfect neutrality of the Isthmus with a view to the preservation of free transit.

"For nearly fifty years we had asserted the right to prevent the closing of this highway of commerce."

This is true enough as far as it goes. But it is eloquent for what it omits. It fails to explain the deepseated distrust of American Diplomacy. found in Spanish-America. Light is thrown on the question by this Bidlack-Mallerino Treaty of 1846, printed as still in force in 1910, the official Senate Document 357 of the 61st Congress — 2nd Session — "Malloy's Treaties of the United States, 1776-1909," Washington Printing Office, 1910, volume I, pages 302-314.

After guaranteeing to New Granada, the perfect neutrality of the isthmus that free transit might not be interrupted or embarrassed, it continues on page 312:

"And in consequence the United States also guarantee in the same manner, the rights of sovereignty and property which New Granada has and possesses over the said territory."

It is not my purpose to discuss what some might call the unseemly haste to prevent the French Panama Canal Company's forfeiture of rights and property to Colombia.

Nor is it my purpose to discuss the failure of Colombia to sell us Panama Canal rights on our own terms.

I am interested in the attitude of Spanish-America towards the United States. It seems to me that even if it were a "hold up," as charged, $40,000,000 for Colombia's rights would not have been too much, provided that therewith we had been able to retain the confidence of Latin America in our honesty of purpose, in our desire to keep our word to our own financial disadvantage, and in our desire to give even the weakest a square deal.

Those who think that the taking of Panama from Colombia was a violation of our solemn treaty word, are divided into two classes:

Some may believe that the breaking of the treaty was justifiable under the circumstances.

Others who have read the whole of the Treaty of 1846 may feel that it was not worth while to break our word as a nation, merely to save a few million dollars or to have the canal built a year or so sooner or begun by some one man.

Forbearance on our part, courtesy without unseemly haste, and a quiet firmness would probably have won for us all that we wanted, at a less price and without raising the question of our national honor.

I believe that the Colombian people care more for their honor than they do for the $25,000,000 offered them—more for an apology than for pay.

Do we owe them an apology?

On the decision of this question may rest the fate of the president, the ex-president, and all political parties.

WHAT OF TOLLS?

In Bidlack-Mallerino Treaty of 1846, "no other tolls . . . levied on citizens of United States than is, under like circumstances levied upon, and collected from Granadian citizens." — Malloy's Treaties, Vol. I, page 312.

In the Clayton-Bulwer Treaty of 1850, in Article VIII, referred to in Preamble to the Hay-Pauncefote Treaty of 1901, "the same canals or railways, being open to the citizens and subjects of the United States and Great Britain on equal terms"—Malloy's Treaties, Vol. I, page 663, lines 4 and 5.

In the Hay-Pauncefote Treaty of 1901, Article III, Rule I. The canal shall be free and open to the vessels of commerce and of war of all nations observing these Rules, on terms of entire equality. Malloy's Treaties, Vol. I, page 783, lines 3, 4, and 5.

WHAT ARE OUR DUTIES AS SHOWN BY THE TREATIES?

SOURCES MENTIONED IN MR. MORREY'S PAPER.

(Colombia)
New Granada.
1846
Treaty of Peace, Amity, Navigation and Commerce.

Concluded Dec. 12, 1846,—ratifications, exchanged June 10, 1848; preclaimed Jan. 12, 1848.

See 61 Cong. 2d Session. Senate Doc. 357. Treaties, Conventions, International Acts, Protocols and Agreements between the United States of America and other Powers 1776-1909.
Compiled by Wm. M. Malloy in 2 Vols.
Wash. Gov't Printing Office, 1910.

Colombia, 1846
New Granada
Article XXXV, Malloy, Vol. 1, pp. 312-313

The United States of America and the Republic of New Granada, desiring to make as durable as possible the relations which are to be established between the two parties, by virtue of this treaty, have declared solemnly, and do agree to the following points:

1st. For the better understanding of the preceding articles, it is and has been stipulated between the high contracting parties, that the citizens, vessels and merchandise of the United States shall enjoy in the ports of New Granada, including those of the part of the Granadian territory generally denominated Isthmus of Panama, from its southernmost extremity until the boundary of Costa Rica.
all the exemptions, privileges and immunities concerning commerce and navigation, which are now or may hereafter be enjoyed by Granadian citizens, their vessels and merchandise; and that this equality of favors shall be made to extend to the passengers, correspondence and merchandise of the United States, in their transit across the said terriory, from one sea to the other.

The Government of New Granada guarantees to the Government of the United States that the right of way or transit across the Isthmus of Panama upon any modes of communication that now exist, or that may be hereafter constructed, shall be open and free to the Government and citizens of the United States, to any other foreign country, shall not be liable to any import duties whatever;

and for the transportation of any articles of produce, manufactures or merchandise of lawful commerce, belonging to the citizens of the United States;
that no other tolls or charges shall be levied or collected upon the citizens of the United States, or their said merchandise thus passing over any road or canal that may be made by the Government of New Granada, or by the authority of the same, than is under like circumstances, levied upon or collected from the Granadian citizens;

that any lawful produce, manufactures or merchandise, belonging to citizens of the United States, thus passing from one sea to the other, in either direction for the purpose of exportation to any other foreign country, shall not be liable to any import duties whatever;

or; having paid such duties they shall be entitled to drawback upon their exportation;

nor shall the citizens of the United States be liable to any duties, tolls or charges of any kind, to which native citizens are not subjected for thus passing the said Isthmus.

And, in order to secure to themselves the tranquil and constant enjoyment of these advantages,

and as an especial compensation for the said advantages, and for the favors they have acquired by the 4th, 5th and 6th articles of this treaty,

the United States guarantee, positively and efficaciously, to New Granada, by the present stipulation, the perfect neutrality of the before-mentioned isthmus, with the view that the free transit from the one to the other sea may not be interrupted or embarrassed in any future time while this treaty exists;

and, in consequence, the United States also guarantee, in the same manner, the rights of sovereignty and property which New Granada has and possesses over the said territory.

2d. The present treaty shall remain in full force and vigor for the term of twenty years from the day of the exchange of the ratifications;

and from the same day the treaty that was concluded between the United States and Colombia, on the thirteenth of October, 1824, shall cease to have effect, notwithstanding what was disposed in the first point of its 31st article.

3d. Notwithstanding the foregoing if neither party notifies to the other its intention of reforming any of, or all, the articles of this treaty twelve months before the expiration of the twenty years stipulated above, the said treaty sha'l continue binding on both parties **beyond the said twenty years, until twelve months from the time that one of the parties notifies its intention of proceeding to a reform.**

4th. If any one or more of the citizens of either party shall infringe, any of the articles of this treaty, such citizens shall be held personally responsible for the same, and the harmony and good correspondence between the nations sha'l not be interrupted thereby;

each party engaging in no way to protect the offender, or sanction such violation.

5th. If unfortunately any of the articles contained in this treaty should be violated or infringed in any way whatever,

it is expressly stipulated that neither of the two contracting parties shall ordain or authorize any acts of reprisal, nor shall dec'are war against the other on complaints of injuries or damages,

until the said party considering itself offended shall have laid before the other a statement of such injuries or damages, verified by competent proofs, demanding justice and satisfaction,

and the same shall have been denied, in violation of the laws and of international right.

6th. Any special or remarkable advantage that one or the other power may enjoy from the foregoing stipulation, are and ought to be always understood in virtue and as in compensation of the obligations they have just contracted, and which have been specified in the first number of this article.

ARTICLE VIII.

Clayton-Bulwer Treaty of 1850. Quoed in Preamble to Hay-Pancefote Treaty of 1901.

(Malloy's Treaties, Vol. I. pp. 662-663.)

The Governments of the United States and Great Britain having not only desired, in entering into this convention, to accomp'ish a particular object, but also to establish a general principle, they hereby agree to extend their protection, by treaty, stipulations, to any other practicable communications, whether by canal or railway, across the isthmus, which connects North and South America, and especially to the interoceanic communications, should the same prove to be practicable, whether by canal or railway, which are now proposed to be established by the way of Tehuantepec or Panama. In granting, however, their joint protection to any such canals or railways as are by this article specified, it is always understood by the United States and Great Britain that the parties constructing or owning the same shall impose no other charges or conditions of traffic thereon than the aforesaid Governments shall approve of as just and equitabe; and that the same canals or railways, being open to the citizens and subjects of the United tSates and Great Britain on equal terms, shall also be open on like terms to the citizens and subjects of every other State which is willing to grant thereto such protection as the United States and Great Britain engage to afford.

TREATY

to Facilitate the Construction of a Ship Canal.

Concluded November 18, 1901; Ratification Advised by Senate, December 16, 1901; Ratified by President, December 26, 1901; Ratifications Exchanged February 21, 1902; Proclaimed February 22, 1902.

(Malloy I, 782-4.)

ARTICLES.

I. Convention of April 19th, 1850.
II. Construction of Canal.
III. Rules of Neutralization.
IV. Change of Sovereignty.
V. Ratification.

The United States of America and His Majesty Edward the Seventh, of the United Kingdom of Great Britain and Ireland, and of the British Dominions beyond the Seas, King and Emperor of India,

being desirous to facilitate the construction of a ship canal to connect th At'antic and Pacifis Oceans, by whatever route may be considered expedient,

and to that end to remove any objection which may arise out of the Convtion o fthe 19th April, 1850, commonly called the Clayton-Bulwer Treaty, to the construction of such canal under the auspices of the Government of the United States,

without impairing the "general principle" of neutralization established in Article VIII. of that Convention.

have for that purpose appointed as their P'enipotentaries:

The President of the United States, John Hay, Secretary of State of the

United States of America;

And His Majesty Edward the Seventh, of the United Kingdom of Great Britain and Ireland, and of the British Dominions beyond the Seas, King and Emperor of India, the Right Honourable Lord Pauncefote, G.C.B., G.C.M.G, His Majesty's Ambassador Extraordinary and Plenipotentiary to the United States;

While having communicated to each after their full powers which were found to be in due and proper form, have agreed upon the followingg Articles:—

ARTICLE I.

The High Contracting Parties agree that the present Treaty shall supersede the afore-mentioned Convention of the 19th April, 1850.

ARTICLE II.

It is agreed that the canal may be constructed under the auspices of the Government of the United States, either directly at its own cost, or by gift or loan of money, to individuals or Corporations, or through subscription to or purchase of stock or shares, and that, subject to the provisions of the present Treaty, the said Government shall have and enjoy all the rights incident to such construction, as well as the exclusive right of providing for the regulation and management of the canal.

ARTICLE III.

The United States adopts, as the basis for the neutralization of such ship canal, the following Rules, substantially as embodied in the Convention of Constantinople, signed the 28th October, 1888, for the free navigation of the Suez Canal, that is to say:

1. The canal shall be free and open to the vessels of commerce and of war of all nations observing these Rules, on terms of entire equality, so that there shall be no discrimination against any such nation, or its citizens or subjects in respect of the conditions or charges of traffic, or otherwise. Such conditions and charges of traffic shall be just and equitable.

2. The canal shall never be blockaded, nor shall any right of war be exercised nor any act of hostility be committed within it. The United States, however, shall be at liberty to maintain such military police along the canal as may be necessary to protecet it against lawlesness and disorder.

3. Vessels of war of a belligerent shall not revictual nor take any stores in the canal except as far as may be strictly necessary; and the transit of such vessels through the canal shall be effected with the least possible deday in accordance with the Regulations in force, and with only such intermission as may result from the necessities of the service.

Prizes shall be in all respects subject to the same Rule as vessels of war of the belligerents.

4. No belligerent shall embark or disembark troops, munitions of war, or warlike materials in the canal, except in case of accidental hindrance of the transit, and in such case the transit shall be resumed with all possible dispatch.

5. The provisions of this Article shall apply to waters adjacent to the canal, within 3 marine miles of either end. Vesels of war of a belligerent shall not remain in such waters longer than twenty-four hours at any one time, except in case of distress, and in such case, shall depart as soon as possible; but a vessel of war of one belligerent shall not depart within twenty-four hours from the departure of a vessel of war of the other belligerent.

6. The plant, establishments, buildings and all work necessary to the construction, maintenance, and operation of the canal shall be deemed to be part thereof, for the purposes of this Treaty, and in time of war, as in time of peace, shall enjoy complete immunity from attack or injury by belligerents, and from acts calculated to impair their usefulness as part of the canal

ARTRICLE IV.

It is agreed that no change of territorial sovereignty or of the international relations of the country or countries traversed by the before-mentioned canal shall affect the general principle of neutralization or the obligation of the High Contracting Parties under the present Treaty

ARTICLE V.

The present Treaty shall be ratified by the President of the United States by and with the advice and consent of the Senate thereof, and by His Britannic Majesty; and the ratifications shall be exchanged at Washington or at London at the earliest possible time within six months from the date hereof.

In faith whereof the respective Plenipotentiaries have signed this Treaty and thereunto affixed their seals.

Done in duplicate at Washington, the 18th day of November, in the year of Our Lord one thousand nine hundred and one.

JOHN HAY (SEAL)

PAUNCEFOTE (SEAL)

[H. S. T. A. BULLETIN No. 45]

Directory of High Schools of New York City

MAY, 1914

Prepared for the

High School Teachers' Association
of
New York City

Under the Direction of
WILLIAM T. MORREY, President
1911-1914

Printed by Brown Bros., 225 W. 39th St., New York City

PREFACE

This Directory is the product of the following notice in the November, 1913, Bulletin No. 41, in the December 7th Bulletin, and in the March 7, 1914, Bulletin:

MATERIALS FOR DIRECTORY

Senior Representatives will kindly send at once to the President the following information revised to November 30, 1913, or later:

(1) A Library Card for every teacher, showing: (1) Name (last Name first); (2) position; (3) subject; (4) high school; (5) home address; **(6) telephone.**
(2) Two complete lists of teachers by departments, each department on separate sheets of paper.
(3) An alphabetical list of all teachers in school, ready to go to printer.

The responses of some of the High Schools were very prompt, showing that their Senior Representatives read the Bulletins, and carry out instructions immediately and exactly. Aside from planning the Directory I have had little to do except where Senior Representatives have been careless.

Director Albert Shields of the Division of Reference and Research has been very prompt and very obliging in furnishing the lists of those holding First Assistant Licenses, Assistant Licenses, and Substitutes' Licenses.

The paid-up membership for the year 1913-1914 was on May 21, 1914, 1,117, as compared with 857 for 1912-1913 and 731 for 1911-1912.

In case of doubt about a given teacher compare his name in long alphabetical list, and also both under his High School and under his department headings.

Those seeking substitutes should examine the long alphabetical list, because many with substitute licenses are regularly employed in some High Schools. Substitutes who have not done so are advised to report their telephone numbers, etc., on a postal to every principal and to every teacher in charge of annex.

Those interested in knowing when a given teacher entered the system, and what his salary is, may consult the City Record Supplementary Number of City Employes for January 31st or July 31st. Price, $2.50.

The lists are printed as sent in. The alphabetical lists and department lists were sent back to schools for revision.

Corrections and changes in this Directory may be sent to me for Bulletin No. 46. I had planned to issue this in June, but with the consent of President-elect Pugh I shall defer issuing it until after my return from South America. Only the most loyal co-operation of Brown Brothers has enabled me to issue this Directory before leaving.

The Directory has grown beyond the size as originally planned. I have tried to make it up to date, but infallibility is not claimed. Those desiring more and later information should address Associate Superintendent Clarence E. Meleney, 500 Park Avenue. There have been some changes in some of the Courses of Study as well as new Courses.

During the last three years I have had much hard work, but a thoroughly enjoyable time. Thanking my fellow teachers for their loyal support and many kindnesses, I am,

Sincerely,

WILLIAM T. MORREY.

535 West 111th Street, New York City, May 30, 1914.

CONTENTS.

CONSTITUTION

Adopted March 2, 1900

ARTICLE I

Name

Section 1. This organization shall be known as the High School Teachers' Association of New York City. (Adopted May 10, 1902.)

ARTICLE II

Object

Section 1. The object of this Association shall be the advancement of secondary education and the promotion of teacher's interests.

ARTICLE III

Membership

Section 1. Any teacher of the public high schools of the Boroughs of Manhattan and The Bronx, who shall sign the Constitution and pay the annual dues, within the month of March, 1900, shall be a Charter Member of the Association.

Sec. 2. Any teacher in a public high school in New York City may become a member of this Association by signing the Constitution and paying the annual dues to the Treasurer. (Adopted May 10, 1902.)

ARTICLE IV

Officers

Section 1. The officers of this Association shall be a President, a Vice-President, a Secretary and a Treasurer.

Sec. 2. The duties of these officers shall be such as usually devolve upon the officers named.

Sec. 3. Officers shall be elected at the last regular meeting of the school year. Election shall be by ballot, and a majority of the votes cast shall be necessary for an election.

ARTICLE V.

Board of Representatives

Section 1. There shall be a Board of Representatives, consisting of the members of the Executive Committee and of the representatives chosen from the several high schools; each school is to be entitled to one Representative for every ten members of the Association; provided, however, that each school shall be entitled to at least one representative.

Sec. 2. After 1905, Representatives shall be elected by ballot during the week preceding the regular meeting in May, and shall hold office for one year; in 1905 the time of election shall be fixed by the Executive Committee. Due notice of such election shall be given to each school by the President. Vacancies may be filled by the Board of Representatives at any meeting.

Sec. 3. The Board of Representatives shall meet on the last school Tuesday of each month, excepting September and June, and shall have the power to act upon all matters affecting the Association.

Sec. 4. The President of the Association shall be ex-officio Chairman of the Board of Representatives.

ARTICLE VI

Committees

Section 1. There shall be an Executive Committee, consisting of the four officers and three other members chosen by ballot at the same time and in the same manner as the officers. The Executive Committee shall approve all appropriations of funds and shall audit and direct the payment of all bills.

Sec. 2. There shall be a Committee on Teachers' Interests, consisting of nine members, including the President. This Committee shall be appointed by the President to serve for one year, and shall report monthly to the Board of Representatives.

Sec. 3. There shall be a Committee on Secondary Education, consisting of nine members, including the President. This committee shall be appointed by the President, and shall serve for one year. It shall prepare programs for the four regular meetings of the Association, and shall report from time to time on matters of educational interest.

ARTICLE VII

Meetings

Section 1. Four regular meetings shall be held every year.

Sec. 2. The meetings shall be held on the first Saturdays of October, December, March and May of each year, unless otherwise ordered by the Executive Committee, and at a time and place to be designated by the Executive Committee. (Adopted May 4, 1901.)

Sec. 3. A special meeting of the Association may be called by the Executive Committee whenever the interests of the Association seem to demand it. The President of the Association shall be required to call a special meeting upon the demand of ten members of the Association. Due notice of such meetings must be given to all members of the Association.

Sec. 4. Thirty members of the Association shall constitute a quorum for the transaction of all business.

ARTICLE VIII

Dues

Section 1. The annual dues shall be One Dollar, payable at the first regular meeting of the school year.

ARTICLE IX
Amendments

Section 1. This Constitution may be amended at any regular meeting by a three-fourths vote of the members present, provided due notice of the proposed amendment shall have been made at a preceding regular meeting. (Adopted May 4, 1901.)

ARTICLE X
Ratification

Section 1. This Constitution shall go into effect immediately upon its adoption.

OFFICERS, 1913-1914

PRESIDENT.......William T. Morrey, Bushwick High School
VICE-PRESIDENT.......Miss Jessie H. Bingham, De Witt Clinton High School
SECRETARY.......Miss Mary J. Bourne, Morris High School
TREASURER.......Dr. Loring B. Mullen, Girls' High School

Additional Members of Executive Committee

Mr. Aaron I. Dotey, De Witt Clinton High School   Miss H. Elizabeth Seelman, Girls' High School
Mr. Alexander L. Pugh, High School of Commerce

Representatives in High School Teachers' Association 1913-1914

BAY RIDGE—*Emberson E. Proper
Mabel R. Benway
Emil Gluck
BOYS'—Charles E. Ovelholser
Francis T. Hughes
Frederick B. Jones
S. Ridley Parker
Alfred A. Tansk
BRYANT—*Harry K. Munroe
Margaret C. Byrne
BUSHWICK—*George M. Falion
Mary E. Green
Anna E. Stanton
Grace Helene Miller (Annex 129)
Nathan Liebowitz
Louise Smith (Annex 75)
Arthur Goodman
COMMERCIAL—*Harry M. Love
Edwin A. Bolger
George W. Harman
Benjamin C. Gruenberg
COMMERCE—*Julius Blume
Horace G. Healey
Alfred H. Lewis
Alexander L. Pugh
George H. Van Tuyl
William S. Schlauch
CURTIS—*Mabel G. Burdick
Philip R. Dean
Claude T. Benjamin
DE WITT CLINTON—*Aaron I. Dotey.
Edgard A. Bedford
Edmund W. Foote
George W. Hunter
Oscar W. Anthony
Ellen E. Garrigues
Fayette E. Moyer
Charles E. Timmerman
Jesse E. Whitsit
Harry B. Penhollow
EASTERN DISTRICT—*Elizabeth R. Hoy
Edith M. Brace
Agnes M. Loughran
Frederick H. Paine
Charles Dixon
Frank P. Baltz

EVANDER CHILDS—*M. W. Greditser
Clayton G. Durfee
Louis B. Cohn
ERASMUS HALL—*Preston C. Farrar
George E. Boynton
Alice C. Howe
Edith M. Everett
FAR ROCKAWAY—*Elme M. Van Dusen
Emily M. Jennison
FLUSHING—*Annie Ross
GIRLS'—*Loring B. Mullen
H. Elizabeth Seelman
JAMAICA—*Edward McNamara
Christiana Busbee
Josephine D. Wilkin
Roscoe A. Grant
JULIA RICHMAN—David L. Arnold
MANUAL TRAINING—*A Latham Baker (Johnson Street Annex)
Eleanor R. Baker (Main Building, 7th Ave.)
Marion Hackedorn
Mary A. Hall
Charles Perrine (Prospect Avenue Annex)
M. Helen Smith
MORRIS—*Agnes Carr
Harriet L. Constantine
Fred C. White
Clara M. Burt
Sanford L. Cutler
Frank M. Surrey
NEWTOWN—*George H. Kingsbury
Alexander H. Zerban
RICHMOND HILL—*William E. Stilson
Gertrude M. Leete
STUYVESANT—*John Messenger, Jr.
Joseph L. Beha
Murray Bruce
Stanley A. Gage
Henry E. Hein
Henry H. Goldberger
T. Harry Knox
Wm. T. Wyman
WADLEIGH—*William W. Clendenin
Helen E. Bacon
WASHINGTON IRVING—*Elizabeth A. Roche
Mary C. Craig
E. Mabel Skinner

*Senior Representatives

OFFICERS-ELECT, 1914-1915

PRESIDENT.......Alexander L. Pugh, High School of Commerce
VICE-PRESIDENT.......Miss Jessie H. Bingham, De Witt Clinton High School
SECRETARY.......Anna E. Stanton, Bushwick High School
TREASURER.......Dr. Loring B. Mullen, Girls' High School

Additional Members of Executive Committee

Mr. Aaron L. Dorey, De Witt Clinton High School   Mr. Frederick C. White, Morris High School
Mr. Wm. T. Morrey, Bushwick High School

COURSES OF STUDY IN NEW YORK CITY HIGH SCHOOLS, AS OUTLINED FOR THE HANUS COMMITTEE

N. Y. City High School Program of Studies Prescribed Studies....black Alternatives..........bracketed Electives..........bold face See Explanatory Notes	General				Training Schools Preparatory				Girls'[3] Technical, 3 Yrs.			Girls' Library			
	I	II	III	IV	I	II	III	IV	I	II	III	I	II	III	IV
English:															
Literature, Composition, Rhetoric	5	3	3	{3 {3	5	3	3	3	5	5	5	5	5	5	5
Elocution, Oral Expression	1	1	1	1	1	1	1	1	1	[1]	[1]	1	1		
Logic															
Foreign Language:[2]															
Latin	[5]	[5]	[5]	{4 3 4 3	[5]	[5]	[5]						[5]	[4]	[4]
Greek		5	4												
French	[5]	[5]	[5]	4	[5]	[5]	[5]		[5]	[5]	[5]	[5]	[5]	[4]	[4]
German	[5]	[5]	[5]	4	[5]	[5]	[5]		[5]	[5]	[5]	[5]	[5]	[4]	[4]
Italian		5	4	4											
Spanish		5	4	4					[5]	[5]	[5]	[5]	[5]	[4]	[4]
Any 2nd or 3rd Language												2 languages			
History, Civics, and Economics:															
History, Greece and Rome		[3]′				3							3		
History, England			[2]				3							3	
History, "Modern I" (to 1066)		[3]′				3									
History, "Modern II" (from 1066)			[2]				2								
History, Mediæval and Modern				3				3							[3]
History, U. S., with Civics				4				4							4
History, 19th Century															
Economics, El. and Adv.			3				3								
Banking, Finance, Transportation															
Administrative and International Law															
Mathematics:															
Algebra	5		2—2		5										
Plane Geometry		4	2—2			4	2—2						4		
Adv. Mathematics				4											
Shop Mathematics															
Natural Science:															
Biology, Elem.	5				5										
Botany, Adv.			4—4												
Zoölogy, Adv.			4—4												
Chemistry, Elem. and Adv.		5——5													
Industrial Chemistry															
Physics, Elem. and Adv.			5				5								
Appl. Mechanics, Steam, Electr.															
Physiography		4——4				4——4									

N. Y. City High School Program of Studies	Boys' Manual Training, Industrial and Technical[3]				Girls' Manual Training[3]				Commercial,[3] 3 Yrs.			Commercial,[3] 4 Yrs. (5th Yr. Post-Graduate)				
	I	II	III	IV	I	II	III	IV	I	II	III	I	II	III	IV	Gr. V
English:																
Literature, Composition, Rhetoric	5	3	3	3	5	3	3	3	4	3	3	4	3	3	3	3
Elocution, Oral Expression	1				1	1	1	1	1			1				
Logic																3
Foreign Language:[2]																
Latin	[5]	[5]	[5]	[4]	[5]	[5]	[5]	{4 3 4 3								4
Greek						5	4									
French	[5]	[5]	[5]	[4]	[5]	[5]	[5]	4								4
German	[5]	[5]	[5]	[4]	[5]	[5]	[5]	4				[5]	[5]	[5]	[4]	4
Italian						5	4	4								
Spanish						5	4	4				[5]	[5]	[5]	[4]	4
Any 2nd or 3rd Language		[5]	[4]	[4]												
History, Civics, and Economics:																
History, Greece and Rome						3										
History, England							2									
History, "Modern I" (to 1066)						3										
History, "Modern II" (from 1066)							2			3			3			
History, Mediæval and Modern								3								
History, U. S., with Civics				4				4			4			4		
History, 19th Century																4
Economics, El. and Adv.							3								3	3
Banking, Finance, Transportation																4
Administrative and International Law																4
Mathematics:																
Algebra	5				5		2—2					[4]				
Plane Geometry		4				4	2—2								[4]	
Adv. Mathematics			3	[4]				4								4
Shop Mathematics																
Natural Science:																
Biology, Elem.					5				3			3				
Botany, Adv.							4—4									
Zoölogy, Adv.							4—4									
Chemistry, Elem. and Adv.		[5]	[4]	[4]		5——5				[4]			[4]		[4]	4
Industrial Chemistry																
Physics, Elem. and Adv.			5	[4]			5			[4]			[4]		[4]	4
Appl. Mechanics, Steam, Electr.																
Physiography						4——4										

ing																					0												
Machine Shop																																	
Building Construction																						6′												
INDUSTRIAL, GIRLS:																																	
Cooking		4	——	3					5				5										4	4									
Sewing, Dressmaking									[5]	19	21	..	[5]									4		4									
Millinery									[5]	19	21	..	[5]										3										
Library Economy															15	{[3] 12																	
COMMERCIAL:																																	
Business Practice, Penmanship, Arithmetic, etc.					5 }				5												5				5				
Stenography, El. and Adv.	}		4	3																						5	5				3	5		
Typewriting, El. and Adv.										19	21†	..															5					5	
Bookkeeping, Business Forms, Office Practice, Correspondence			3																						4					4			
Accounts, Acc'ting and Auditing																										5	2				5		4
Commercial Geography	}			3																					2				2				4
Commercial Law																											[3]′					[3]′	
Business Organization																																	4
MUSIC	1	1	1	1	1	1	1	1	1	[1]	[1]	..	1	1	1	..	1	1	..	..	1	1	1	1	1	1	1		1	1	1	1	
DRAWING:																																	
Elem. Design and Representation	2	2			2	2	1	1	2	[2]			2								2	2	1	1	2	2			2				4
Design			1	1						19	21																						
Representation			1	1																													
Free Hand																																	
Mechanical																	}4	}4	2	2							[3]′					[3]′	
Architectural																																	
PHYSICAL TRAINING, HYGIENE	2	2	2	2	2	2	2	2	2	2	2	..	2	2	2	2	2	2	2	2	2	2	2	2	2	2	2	..	2	2	2	2	2
ASSEMBLY																									1	1	1	..	1	1	1	1	..
TOTAL REQUIRED, Each Student									26	30	30	..	26	26	30	30	29	30	30	29	26	21	14	..	25	26	26	..	26	26	26	26	..

EXPLANATORY NOTES

1. *Black figures* indicate periods of recitation per week in required subjects.
   Bracketed figures indicate periods of recitation per week in alternative subjects, one of which must be chosen (e. g., in the General Course, one of three languages).
   Bracketed figures [ ]′ indicate a second group of alternative subjects, one of which must be chosen (e. g., in the General Course either History, Greece and Rome or Modern I)
   Boldface figures indicate electives, from among which enough must be chosen to make up the required number of points.
   Figures connected by a dash indicate that a subject may be taken in an upper and a lower year; not that there is an advanced course in the subject.
2. *Requirements for graduation.*
   In the General Course, and in the Training School Preparatory Course, 150 points; studies requiring no home preparation counting one point and those requiring preparation two points, per period of recitation. 20 points are regarded as a full term's work.
   In other courses, as indicated in the footings of each column.
3. *Languages*—[2] Pupils beginning a Foreign Language must continue it for two years, and are advised to continue it longer, rather than to begin another.
4. *Differentiation*—[3] In Commercial and Technical Courses, general subjects like English, History, Mathematics, and Science are somewhat modified in accordance with the main interest of the course.
   ¶ With principal's approval a boy preparing for college may substitute an academic subject for machine shop practice in the fourth year.
   † With Commercial Law and Civics.

DIRECTORY OF HIGH SCHOOLS OF NEW YORK CITY.

School	Telephone	Location	Principal or Teacher in Charge of Annex
Bay Ridge	711 Bath Beach	86th St., near 18th Ave. (P. S. 101)	Harry A. Potter.
Annex	1273 Bay Ridge	92d St. and Gelston Ave. (P. S. 104)	
Boys'	690 Bedford	Marcy and Putnam Aves. and Madison St.	James Sullivan.
Bryant	40 Astoria	Wilbur Ave., Academy and Radde Sts., L. I. City	Peter E. Demarest.
Annex	1146-W Astoria	Van Alst Ave., near Flushing Ave., L. I. City (P. S. 7)	
Bushwick	3403 Bushwick	400 Irving Ave	Frank Rollins.
Annex	13 Bushwick	Evergreen Ave., Ralph and Grove Sts. (P. S. 75)	William T. Morrey.
Annex	3514 Bushwick	Quincy St., near Stuyvesant Ave. (P. S. 129)	Lewis B. Semple.
Commercial	3732 Bedford	Albany Ave., Bergen and Dean Sts	William Fairley.
Annex	7736 Bedford	Bedford and Jefferson Sts	W. E. Doggett.
Curtis	351-J Tompkinsville	Hamilton Ave. and St. Marks Pl., New Brighton	D. L. Feldman.
Annex	922-J Tottenville	Academy Pl., Tottenville (P. S. 1)	
De Witt Clinton	4175 Columbus	10th Ave., 58th and 59th Sts	John L. Tildsley.
Eastern District	4565 Williamsburgh	Marcy Ave., Rodney and Keap Sts	W. T. Vlymen.
Annex	1715 Greenpoint	Havemeyer, N. 6th and 7th Sts. (P. S. 143)	Anna L. Phillips.
Erasmus Hall	288 Flatbush	Flatbush Ave., near Church Ave	W. B. Gunnison.
Evander Childs	643 Westchester	Randolph, St. Lawrence and Hammond Aves. (P. S. 47)	Gilbert S. Blakely.
Annex	5634 Tremont	196th St., Bainbridge and Driggs Aves. (P. S. 46)	
Far Rockaway	95 Far Rockaway	Far Rockaway	S. J. Ellsworth.
Flushing	321 Flushing	Sanford Ave., Flushing	J. H. Clark.
Girls'	372 Bedford	Nostrand Ave., Halsey and Macon Sts	W. L. Felter.
Annex	5926 Prospect	St. Marks and Classon Aves. (P. S. 42)	M. Ellen Barker.
H. S. of Commerce	2658 Columbus	65th and 66th Sts., west of Broadway	*Walter G. Eddy.
Annex	8114 Bryant	120 W. 46th St. (P. S. 67)	Alfred C. Bryan.
Jamaica	165 Jamaica	Hillside Ave., Jamaica	T. C. Mitchill.
Julia Richman	4557 Chelsea	60 West 13th St	A. M. Wolfson.
Annex	8437 Schuyler	82d St. and West End Ave. (P. S. 9)	David L. Arnold.
Annex	5748 Lenox	434 E. 88th St. (P. S. 66)	Idelette Carpenter.
Manual Training	1380 South	7th Ave., 4th and 5th Sts	C. D. Larkins.
Annex	24 South	Prospect Ave., opposite Reeve Pl	Charles Perrine.
Annex	2627 Main	Duffield, Johnson and Gold Sts	Arthur L. Baker.
Morris	605 Melrose	166th St., Boston Rd. and Jackson Ave	John H. Denbigh.
Annex	2360 Melrose	Mott Ave. and 144th St. (P. S. 31)	Irving A. Heikes.
Newtown	40 Newtown	Elmhurst	J. D. Dillingham.
Annex	122 Newtown	Elmhurst (P. S. 89)	
Richmond Hill	26 Richmond Hill	Elm St., Richmond Hill	Isaac N. Failor.
Stuyvesant	3739 Stuyvesant	15th and 16th Sts., west of 1st Ave	E. R. von Nardroff.
Wadleigh	1892 Morningside	114th and 115th Sts., west of 7th Ave	Stuart H. Rowe.
Annex	4865 Harlem	138th St., west of 5th Ave. (P. S. 100)	Katharine A. Speir.
Washington Irving	3292 Stuyvesant	Irving Pl., 16th and 17th Sts	W. McAndrew.

*Acting.

LIST OF TEACHERS

BAY RIDGE HIGH SCHOOL.

pal

Ward, Mercedes
Weeks, Marion I.
Wicks, Helen D.
Williams, Margaret
*Zinman, Meyer

BY DEPARTMENTS.

Biology Department.

Bruckman, Louisa
Baggs, Martha
Barclay, Margaret
Thompson, Martha

Commercial Branches.

Cahill, John P.
Edelson, Emanuel M.
Gluck, Emil
Mackey, Arthur J.
Putz, Edward H.

Drawing Department.

Combes, Adelaide M. W.
Hamilton, Alma L.

Domestic Science Department. (Cooking)

Gaynor, Carrie
Williams, Margaret

English Department.

Bessey, Mabel A.
Coffin, Isabelle P.
Goldstein, Alexander
Harding, Helen E.
Natelson, Rachel
Phillips, Sarah J.
Trench, Ruth
Wicks, Helen D.

Elocution.

Weeks, Marion I.

French Department

Covello, Leonard
Morrill, Frances U.
Quirk, Cecile

German Department.

Avirett, Mrs. May G.
Faust, Miss Charlotte C.
Lippner, Simon L.
Grossman, Mrs. Lena
Robinson, Eva A.
Schmidt, Clara E.

History Department.

Proper, Emberson E.
Rubenstein, Jacob

Latin Department

Allen, Winifred S.
Lawton, Maxwell F.
Medalie, Mrs. Carrie K.
Grant, Alice C.

Mathematics Department

Back, Elizabeth M.
Benway, Mabel R.
Barlow, Margaret M.
Eddy, Elise S.
Gilliland, Alice M.
Mackey, Arthur J.
Schuyler, Elmer

Music Department

Morris, Eugene C.

Physical Training Department

Ward, Mercedes

Physics and Chemistry

Kearney, Maurice W.
Robinson, L. A.

Physiography Department

Robinson, L. Archibald

Stenography and Typewriting

Rosmarin, Michael
Saphier, Conrad J.
Sugarman, Arthur M.
Zinman, Meyer E.

Spanish Department

Smithers, Herlinda G.

Clerical Assistants

Sheils, Frances B.

BOYS' HIGH SCHOOL.

Campbell, Joseph A.
*Clark, Clinton
*Cohen, A. Broderick
Cook, Charles G.
Curtis, Henry S.
Daniels, Ernest D.
*Diller, James G.
Dinsmore, Ernest L.
Downing, George B.
*Doyle, Thomas L.
*Edwards, William H.
Esselstyn, Henry H.
*Fairchild, Ralph P.
*Fisher, William W.
Flint, G. C.
*Flint, Thomas
*Fontaine, Andre C.
*France, Sanford D.
Freeborn, Frank W.
*Gemson, Irving
Gray, James E.
*Hamilton, Charles A.
Hanna, Albert S.
*Hanson, George C.

ip in H. S. T. A. for 1913-1914.

*Hobson, George P. F.
*Hopkins, Walter D.
*Hughes, Charles E.
*Hughes, Francis T.
*Jacobs, Leo
Jaffe, Isidore
*Janes, Arthur L.
*Jeffords, C. R.
*Jenner, William A.
Johnston, Henry
*Jones, F. B.
*Kaine, Joseph M.
*Levine, Herman B.
*Lewis, Frederick Z.
Mattes, Max H.
*McCartney, Hoge
McDowell, John D.
*Munson, Daniel G.
*Overholser, Charles E.
*Parker, S. Ridley
*Parsons, Edward B.
*Parsons, Herbert H.
Pasternak, Nathaniel
Pasternak, Jesse
*Raiman, Robert I.
*Reynolds, James I.
*Reynolds, Lewis G.
*Richardson, Roy S.
*Riess, Ernst
*Rogers, William W.
*Smith, Ernest E.
*Spaulding, Frank B.
Stannard, J. E.
Stebbins, Charles M.
Stone, Limond C.
Sullivan, James
*Swenson, John A.
*Tausk, Alfred A.
*Tressler, Jacob C.
*Weaver, Eli W.
*White, Walter C. L.
*Wilson, Henry E.
*Wilson, James F.
*Wood, George C.
*Yoder, Arthur L.

BY DEPARTMENTS

Department of Biology

Lewis, Mr., Chairman
Hanna, Mr.
Hughes, C. E.
Hughes, F. T.
Kaine, Mr.
Richardson, Mr.
Wood, Mr.
Pasternak Mr. (Sub.)

Department of Classics.

Riess, Dr., Chairman.
Daniels, Mr.
Edwards, Mr.
Flint, Thomas
Freeborn, Mr.
Hobson, Mr.
Hopkins, Mr.
Janes, Mr.
Jenner, Mr.
Jones, Mr.
Jeffords, Mr.
Reynolds, J.
Wilson, H.

Drawing Department

Pasternak, N., Chairman.
Boyd, Mr.
Diller, Mr.
White, Mr.

Department of English.

Fisher, Mr., Chairman.
Brill, Mr.
Buttrick, Mr.
Courtney, Mr.
Doyle, Mr.
Edelstyn, Mr.
Johnston, Mr.
Levine, Mr.
McCartney, Mr.
Munson, Mr.
Raiman, Mr.
Stebbins, Mr.
Tressler, Mr.
Hanson, Mr., Substitute

History Department

J. F. Wilson, Chairman.
Becker, Mr.
Brummer, Mr.
Parsons, H. H.
Rogers, Mr.
Smith, Mr.
Jacobs, Mr.

Mathematics Department

Parsons, E. B., Chairman
Bishop, Mr.
Bergstresser, Mr.
Blanchard, Mr.
Clark, Mr.
Downing, Mr.
France, Mr.
Hamilton, Mr.
McDowell, Mr.
Stone, Mr.
Swenson, Mr.
Weaver, Mr.
Gray, Mr. (Sub.)

Modern Languages Department

Overholser, Mr., Chairman.
Bates, Mr.
Bechert, Mr.
Cohen, Mr.
Fontaine, Mr.
Reynolds, L.
Tausk, Mr.

Music Department

Flint, G. C., Chairman
Campbell, Mr.

Physical Science Departmentt

Spaulding, Mr., Chairman.
Cook, Dr.
Curtis, Mr.
Dinsmore, Mr.
Stannard, Mr.
Yoder, Mr.

Physical Training Department.

Andrews, Mr., Chairman.
Fairchild, Mr.
Gemson, Mr.

BRYANT HIGH SCHOOL.

Demarest, Peter E., **Principal.**
Abraham, Nathan
Acker, Margaret K.
*Arthur, L. Louise
Banghart, Elizabeth
Becker, Nathaniel
Bement, Frederic
*Byrne, Margaret C.
Carll, Lydia A.
*Carter, Bertha
*Courtney, Bertha F.
*Darrin, Mrs. Mary R.
Dickson, Tenny V.
Ellert, John F.
Erhardt, Helen
*Finch, Mrs. Anna O.
Gambier, Louise M.
*Garrity, Julia F.
Grubman, Adolph J.
*Heermance, Emma W.
*Jones, Frances E.
*Joseph, Myrtle J.
*Lewis, Edward F.
*Loewy, George J.
*McIntyre, Edith A.
*McKinney, May.
McMahon, M. Mabel
*Munroe, Harry K.
*Noble, Helen G.
Perry, Mabel L.
*Price, Anna G.
*Riblet, Mary V.
Rosenbluth, Henry
Rothholz, Meta
Schachtel, Elsie
Schroeder, Mrs. Anita
Shaw, M. Edna
*Snow, Ella M.
Steinberg, Pauline
Sunderland, Florence
*Swett, Carolyn P.
Thayer, Annie M.
Thorne, Frederick
Van Leeuwen, Mary
*Vincent, Charlotte M.
Vogt, Charles A.
Waldman, Mark
*Welch, Alberta
*Wilmot, Mabel
Wilson, George W.
White, Cornelia F.

BY DEPARTMENTS

Substitutes

Thorburn-Artz, Lucretia M.
Froendt, A. H.

Clerical Assistants

Perry, Mabel L.
Van Leeuwen, Mary

Commercial Department

Abraham, Nathan
Courtney, Bertha
Lewis, Edward F. (Chairman)
Rosenbluth, Henry
Steinberg, Pauline

Domestic Art Department

Noble, Helen G.

Domestic Science Department

McIntyre, Edith

Drawing Department

Price, Anna G.

Thorburn-Artz, L. M. (Substitute)

English Department

Acker, Margaret K.
Carll, Lydia A. (Elocution)
Erhardt, Helen
Heermance, Emma W.
Jones, Frances E.
Munroe, H. K. (Chairman)
Riblet, Mary V.
Sunderland, Florence (Leave of absence)
Wilmot, Mabel

History Department

Arthur, L. Louise
Dickson, Tenny V.

Latin Department

McKinney, May
McMahon, M. Mabel (Chairman)

Manual Training Department

Grubman, Adolph J.
Thorne, Frederick
Vogt, Charles A.

Librarian

Thayer, Annie M.

Mathematical Department

Byrne, Margaret C.
Garrity, Julia F.
Rothholz, Meta
Shaw, M. Edna
Welch, Alberta M. (Chairman)

Modern Language Department (German)

Joseph, Myrtle J.
Schachtel, Elsie
Vincent, Charlotte (Chairman)
Waldman, Mark

Lopez, Anita (also Spanish) (French)
Gambier, Louise M.
Snow, Ella M. (Chairman)

Music Department

Banghart, Elizabeth

Natural Science Department

Becker, Nathaniel (Lab. Asst.)
Bement, Frederic (Chemistry), Chairman
Carter, Bertha F. (Botany)
Darrin, Mary R. (Physiography)
Finch, Anna O. (Physics)
Swett, Carolyn P. (Biology)
Wilson, George W. (Chemistry)

Physical Training Department

Ellert, John F.
White, Cornelia M.

BUSHWICK HIGH SCHOOL.

Main Building

*Frank Rollins, Principal
*Batchelder, Margaret C.
Benjamin, Edith S.
*Canning, Eta M.
*Cohen, Morris
*Conant, M. Sybil
*Conley, William E.
*Crossley, Arthur L.
*DeWitt, Louise L.
*Durand, William B.
*Falion, George M.
*Foley, Henry J.
*Fleisher, Edward
Francis, Carolyn L.
*Goldsmith, Elizabeth
*Green, John C.
*Green, Mary P.
*Houley, Elizabeth C.
*Humason, Thomas A.
*Hutchinson, Helen S.
*Johnson, Julius M.
Connor, Edith H.
*Keener, Robert H.
*Leyenberger, Harry W.
*Lieberman, Elias
*Maloubier, Henrietta B.
*Merington, Ruth
*Mohan Lucy F.
Mulholland, M. Estelle
*Nanes, Philip
*Newcomer, Harvey
*Norton, George W.
*Otten, Henry L.
*Riegger, Elizabeth
*Squires, Mrs. Martha U.
*Staelin, Leonie E.
*Stanton, Anna E.
*Taylor, Arthur M.
*Townsend, Charles W.
*Townsend, May E.
*Zorn, Freda
Brady John W.

Annex No. 75

*Morrey, William T., Teacher in Charge
*Barrows, Tessie
*Bertschy, Maude
*Briggs, Eva E.
*Cohen, Bertha
*Collier, Katherine B.
*Gilbert, Clara M.
*Goodman, Arthur
*Hendrich, Paul
*Humphries, George F.
*Kilby, J. Albert
*Lingg, Amalie S.
*Littig, M. Josephine
*Conville, Lillian M.
*Salmowitz, Rose L.
*Seaman, Mary E.
*Smith, Louise
*Smith, Marguerite
*Southwell, Etta E.
*Tufts, Anne B.
*Woodbury, Ella A.
*Reinhold, Alida B.

Annex No. 129

*Semple, Lewis B., Teacher in Charge
Auslander, Armin
*Berkowitz, Louise
*Goldberger, Louis
*Hall, Henrietta
Hannah, Florence
*Lundy, Edwin S.
*Liebowitz, Nathan
*Lieberman, Max
*Mayers, Lena
*McDonald, Milo F.
*Miller, Charles
*Miller, Grace H.
*O'Donnell, Agnes T.
*O'Donnell, Margaret M.
*Nevins, Nannie R.
*Sherman, Rose E.
*Stieg, Fern

New Teachers

Bogle, Miss
Taylor, Marion L.
Dewning, Edward A.
Brower, Miss Jane
Hoeg, Mrs. Gertrude S.
Howe, Charles B.
Maynard, Ernest A.
Osgood, Mr.
Thompson, Lucy F.
Henderson, Hazel
Rosenhaus, Maximilian

BY DEPARTMENTS

Algebra and Exp.

Green, John P.

Biology Department

Johnson, Julius M., Chairman
Conley, William. E.
Stanton, Anna E.
Southwell, Etta E.

Clerical Assistants

Brady, John W.
Connor, Edith B.
Reinhold, Alida B.

Commercial Branches

Leyenberger, Harry W., Chairman
Canning, Etta M.
Conant, M. Sybil
Foley, Henry J.
Houley, Elizabeth C.
Townsend, Charles W.
Humphries, George F.
Salmowitz, Rose L.
Auslander, Armin
Osgood, C. A.
Goldberg, Louise
Hall, Henrietta
Lundy, Edwin S.
Leibowitz, Nathan
Mayers, Lena
Miller, Charles
Nevins, Nannie R.
Rosenhaus, Maximilian

Drawing Department

Merington, Ruth, Chairman
Hutchinson, Helen S.
Bertschy, Maude
Littig, M. Josephine

Domestic Science Department

Hoeg, Mrs.

English Department

Semple, Dr. Lewis B., Chairman
Batchelder, Margaret C.
Benjamin, Edith S.
Crossley, Arthur L.

DeWitt, Louise L.
Lieberman, Elias
Mohan, Lucy F.
Townsend, May E.
Sherman, Rose E.
Collier, Katherine B.
Gilbert, Clara M.
Tufts, Anne B.
Woodbury, Ella A.
Hannah, Florence
Lieberman, Max
McDonald, Milo F.
Henderson, Hazel

History Department

Morrey, William T., Chairman
Nanes, Philip
Thompson, Lucy F.

Latin Department

Falion, George M., Chairman
Mulholland, M. Estelle
Smith, Louise

Librarian

Brower, Jan

Manual Training Department

Norton, George W.
Howe, Charles B.

Mathematics Department

Humason, Dr. Thomas A., Chairman
Cohen, Morris
Conley, William E.
Fleischer, Edward
Francis, Carolyn L.
Briggs, Eva E.
Goodman, Arthur

Department of Modern Languages

Keener, Robert H., Chairman
Goldsmith, Elizabeth
Maloubier, Henrietta M.
Otten, Henry L.
Riegger, Elizabeth
Squires, Martha U.
Staelin, Leonie E.
Zorn, Freda
Bogle, Miss
Barrows, Tessie
Hendrich, Paul
Lingg, Amalie S.
Seaman, Mary E.
Berkowitz, Louise
O'Donnell, Agnes T.
O'Donnell, Margaret M.
Taylor, Marion L.
Dewning, Edward

Music Department

Taylor, Arthur M., Chairman

Physical Training Department

Durand, William B.
Green, Mary P.
McConville, Lillian M.
Stieg, Fern

Science Department

Newcomer, Harvey
Maynard, Ernest A.

HIGH SCHOOL OF COMMERCE.

*Sheppard, James J. (died Mar. 12 1914.
*Aldinger, Harry E.
*Appell, Israel
*Baldwin, Edwin P.
*Barbour, William C.
*Beatman, Augustus S.
Benedict, Ralph C.
*Bennett, R. Grant
*Berkowitch, Louis B.
*Beygrau, Frederick B.
*Blume, Julius
*Bowles, Frank C.
*Breckstone, W.
*Brennan, Alfred T. V.
*Bryan, Alfred C.
Buck, Frederick C.
Byron, Thomas W.
Carleton, Guy M.
Carter, Raymond
Chadwick, David
*Cheston, Henry
*Clough, Harvey B.
*Cohen, Harry
Coleman, D. F., Lab. Asst.
Collins, John A., Sec.
Craver, Edwin H.
Dunham, Franklin W., Clerical Assistant
Duschatko, Alfred, Lab. Asst.
*Eddy, Walter H. (Act. Prin.)
*Fallon, George P.
Fedter, Bruno
*Firman, Arthur
*Flatow, Jacob
*Flynn, Oscar R.
*Foster, Wilfred L.
Goldstein, Samuel, Sub. Eng.
*Grant, Forest
*Grant, Willis H.
*Greene, Russel T.
*Guldner, C. M.
*Hahn, Clarence
*Hall, Gamble
Hall, Henry M.
*Hance, William
*Hartung, Ernest W.
Hartwell, F. W.
*Healy, Horace G.
Hendrian, August W.
*Henin, Benj. A.
*Heydrick, Benj. A.
Hughes, Carl C.
Hyman, Jos. C.
*Jonas, Louis
*Kahn, Joseph
*Kendzur, S.
King, Melville S.
*Knickerbocker, Edwin Van B.
*Koch, Ernest H.
*Koopman, S. Bernard
*Lagerwell, Chas J.
*Lewis, Alfred H.
*Lewis, E. D.
*Lindsey, Frederick B.
*Long, R. L.
*May, Alfred A.
*McCormick, Thomas H.
McDonald, James
*McGrath, Wm. J.
*Mills, Joseph S.
*Minnick, John D.
*Montrose, N. Lindsay
O'Neil, William
Payne, Frank O.
Peacock, Daniel L.
Polly, Britton
Pope, Seth R.
Porter, Geo. H.
*Pugh, Alexander L.
*Remy, Alfred
*Rice, Winfield
Ritt, Harold L.
*Roberts, Alfred S.
*Rochow, John P.
*Roessler, Edwin R.
Rogers, Chas. E.
*Rosenblum, Abraham
Rosenblum, Jacques C.
*Rotherham, Phillip J. E.
*Schlauch, William S.
*Siriagnan, Leon
*Skinner, Herbert C.
*Skipp, Henry J.
*Smith, L. Brewster
*Spear, Austin E.
*Sprague, C. Hayes
Swanton, Richard L., Sub. Math.
*Van Dusen, Edwin H.
*Van Tuyl, G. H.
*Walker, Claude E.
*Walsh, Daniel O. C.
*Weinberger, Geo. G.
*Warton, William
*Whiffen, Edwin T.
Williamson, George B., Sub. Eng.
*Woodman, Irving L.

BY DEPARTMENTS

Biology Department

Eddy, Walter H., Chairman & First Assistant
Barbour, William C.
Benedict, Ralph C.
Clough, Harvey B.
Firman, Arthur B.
Grant, Willis H.
Hahn, Clarence W.
Hartwell, F. W.
Payne, Frank O.
Duschatko, Alfred (Lab. Asst.)

Chemistry Department

Mills, Joseph S. Chairman First Assistant
Bennet, R. Grant
Breckstone, W.
Flynn, Oscar R.
Walker, Claude F.
Coleman, D. F. (Lab. Asst.)

Clerical Assistants

Byron, Thos. W.
Collins, John A. C.
Dunham, Franklin W.

Commercial Branches Department

Greene, Russel T., Chairman First Assistant
Baldwin, Edwin P.
Cohen, Harry
Guldner, C. M.
Hughes, Charles C.
Kendzur, S.

Jonas, Louis
King, Melville S.
Koopman, S. Bernard
Long, R. L.
MacDonald, James (Sub.)
Rogers, Chas. E.
Van Deusen, Edwin H.
Van Tuyl, G. H.
Woodman, Irving L.

Drawing Department
Grant, Forest, Chairman
Carter, Raymond
Sprague, C. Hayes
O'Neil, Wm. R.
Remy, Alfred
Rochow, John P.
Skipp, Henry J.
Singagnan, Leon
Skinner, Herbert C.
Spear, Austin E.

English Department
Heydrick, Benj. A., Chairman and First Assistant
Berkowitch, Louis B.
Carleton, Guy M.
Goldstein, Samuel, Substitute
Hall, Henry M.
Hyman, Jas. C., Substitute
Knickerbocker, Edwin V.
Lindsey, Frederick B.
McGrath, Wm. J.
May, Alfred A.
Polly, Britton, Sub.
Ritt, Harold, Sub.
Weinberger, Geo. G.
Wharton, William P.
Williamson, George B., Substitute

Economics Department
Pugh, Alexander, Chairman & First Assistant
Brennen, Alfred T. C.
Hall, Gamble
Peacock, Daniel L. (Sub.)

History Department
Bryan, Alfred C., Chairman & First Assistant
Beatman, Augustus S.
Lewis, Ernest D.
Porter, Geo. H.
Rice, Winfield S.
Roberts, Alfred S.
Whiffen, Edwin T.

Laboratory Assistants
Coleman, D. F.
Duschatko, Alfred

Librarian.
Pope, Seth E.

Mathematics Department
Minnick, John D., Chairman
Appell, Israel
Bowles, Frank C.
Fallon, George
Kook, Ernest H.
Lagerwall, Chas J.
Lewis, Alfred H.
McCormick, Thos. H.
Schlauch, William S.
Smith, L. Brewster
Swanton, Richard S.

Modern Lanugages Department
Roessler, Edwin W., Chairman and First Assistant
Blume, Julius
Chadwick, David., Sub.
Fedter, Bruno
Flatow, Jacob
Hartung, Ernest W.
Henin, Benj. L.
Montross, Chas. G.

Music Department
Norden, N. Lindsay

Physics Department
Cheston, Henry C., Chairman & First Assistant
Hance, William

Stenography and Typewriting Department
Healy, Horace G., Chairman
Beygrau, Frederick R.
Craver, Edwin H.
Rosenblum, Abraham
Walsh, Daniel O'C.

Department of Physical Training.
Aldinger, Harry E., Chairman
Foster, Wilfred L.
Hendrian Agust W.
Rotherham, Phillip J. E.

HIGH SCHOOL OF COMMERCE (Annex).

Biology Department
Benedict, Ralph C.
Barbour, William C.
Clough, Harvey B.
Hartwell (Sub.)

Department of Commercial Branches.
Cohen, Harry
Guldner, M.
Van Deusen, Edwin H.
Kendzur

Economics Department
Peacock, Daniel L. (Sub.)
Whalen, Edwin A. (Sub.)

English Department
Berkowitch, Louis B.
Weinberger, Geo. G.
Ritt (Sub.)
Polly (Sub.)

Mathematics Department
Lewis, Alfred H.
Appell
Swanton (Sub.)

Modern Languages Department
Skipp
Hartung
Spear
Fedter (Sub.)

Music Department
Norden, Lindsay N.

Physical Training Department
Hendrian, Agust W.

COMMERCIAL HIGH SCHOOL.

*Anderson, Woodford D.
*Austin, Harry W.
*Bagenstose, Harvey L.
*Barlow, W. M.
Behnken, H. Emile
Bickmore, Frank L.
*Bliss, Ralph P.
*Bolger, Edwin F.
Brace, Charles T.
*Braunstein, Wm.
Browne, Thomas J.
Buskin, Nathan E.
Callahan, Thos. J.
*Campbell, Calvin Victor
*Caplan, Elias Nathan
Carey, Charles H.
*Chestnut, D. Howard
*Clark, John F.
Coester, Alfred
Cohen, Theodore
*Coon, Clifford H.
Conant, Fred L.
*Corliss, Charles E.
*Cowles, Clarence E.
*Dann, Matthew L.
*Denonholz, Alexander
Doggett, William E.
*Donovan, Herbert D. A.
*Donvan, Walter J.
*Duncan, William H., Jr.
*Eells, Burr Gould
Failing, Wilson R.
*Fairley, Dr. Wm. (Prin.)
*Finnegan, Wm. E.
*Finney, Arthur E.
*Goate, Wm. B.
*Greenberg, Morris
Greene, Hugh G.
*Gruenberg, Benjamin C.
Hall, James A.
*Hagens, Fritz.
*Harmon, George W.
*Harrison, Earl Stanley
*Hoffman, Alfred L.
*Hook, Edward A.
Hopper, Herman T.
Jaffe, Jacob
*Joseph, Samuel
Kip, Arthur Ralph
*Konheim, Jerome A.
Kerwin, Eugene F.
*Lee, Joseph
*Loftus, John J.
*Loughran, John
*Love, Harry Melville
Loveland, Alfred E.
Levine, Michael
MacGregory, Charles C.
*McNally, Edward
MacNamara, Sylvester J.
Manheimer, Wallace A.
Male, Roy R.
*Marvin, Robt. B.
*Meehan, William
*Melson, George W.
*Melvin, Floyd J.
*Mercado, J.
Morrell, Heenry B.
*Nathan, Arthur
*Newman, Joseph
O'Ryan, William P.
*Polk, Ellery Channing

*Proctor, Robert H.
*Puorro, Michael.
*Ratner, Hyman
*Raynor, Gilbert J.
Reser, Edward N.
Rider, Lloyd A.
*Roche, Michael P.
Ross, William A.
*St, John, Robert P.
*Sawyer, George A.
*Scarborough, Andrew J.
Schoenlank, S. C.
*Shea, John J.
Svchean, C. C.
*Shearar, Joseph H.
Smith, Jos. H.
Souers, J. Marion
*Sternberg, George
Stock, Wallace T.
*Taylor, Edward F.
*Teeter, Charles H.
Trask, Thomas C.
Trostler, Emil A.
Van Buskirk, Edward P.
*Urdang, Harry
Van Houten, Charles N.
Van Name, Warren M.
Waltz, G. Edward
Watson, Elba
Wayave, Leon J.
*Zeiner, Edward J. A.

BY DEPARTMENTS

Accounts Department
Anderson, Woodford D.
Corliss, Charles E.
Harman, George W.
Meehan, William
Nathan, Arthur,
Raynor, Gilbert J.
Scarborough, Andrew J.
Kouheim, Jerome
Cowles, Clarence

Biology Department
Donvan, Walter J.
Gruenberg, Benjamin C. (First Asst.)
Puorro, Michael
Ratner, C. Hyman

Chemistry and Physics Department
Clark, John A., First Asst.
Coon, Clifford H.
Newman, Joseph

Drawing Department
Greenberg, Morris
Roche, Michael P.

English Department
Bagenstose, Harvey L.
Campbell, Calvin Victor
Caplan, Elias Nathan
Loftus, John J.
Loughran, John
Love, Harry M.
McNally, Edward
Melvin, Floyd J.
Proctor, Robert H.
Sawyer, George A.
St. John, Robert P., First Asst.
Urdang, Harry
Braunstein, William

German Department
Barlow, William M.
Eells, Burr Gould
Hagens, Fritz
Hoffman, Alfred
Marvin, Robert B., First Asst.
Sternberg, George

History Department
Dann, Matthew L.
Donovan, Herbert D. A.
Polk, Ellery Channing
Taylor, Edward F.
Fairley, William, Principal

Library.
Duncan, William H., Jr.

Mathematics Department
Bliss, Raplh P.
Hook, Edward A.
Lee, Joseph B.
Teeter, Charles H., First Asst.

Music Department
Zeiner, Edward J. A.
Goate, William B.

Shop Work Department
Austin, Harry W.

Spanish Department
Harrison, Earl Stanley, First Asst.
Finney, Arthur E.
Smith, Joseph
Mercado, Julian

Stenography and Typewriting Department
Bolger, Edwin A., Chairman
Duenholz, Alexander
Finnegan, William E.
Melson, George W.
O'Ryan, William P.
Shea, John J.
Shearer, Robert J.
Chestnut, D. Howard

CURTIS HIGH SCHOOL.

*Abbott, Frances H.
*Austin, Mrs. Mary E.
Bell, Anna
*Benjamin, Claude T.
*Blanpied, Ethel O.
*Brewer, Francis E.
*Burdick, Mabel G.
Clark, Henry F.
*Close, Maude M.
Conroy, Mary S.
Corcilius, Inez
*Crane, William A.
*Crennan, Margaret A.
Curtis, Osborn M.
*Dean, Philip R.
*Dowell, Phllip
*Feldman, Daniel D. (Prin.)
*Fisher, Ruth B.
*Flanagan, William
*French, Linda M.
*Gallagher, Ellen M.
*Goode, Elizabeth.
*Goodwin, W. Grant
*Grant, Mrs. Eva M.
Griswold, Mrs. Carolyn
*Grout, Abel J.
*Halloran, William M.
*Harkness, Mme. Alma de B.
*Hillyer, J. Blake
*Hopkins, Rupert H.
*Hummel, F. M.
*Kane, Thomas F.
*Kerr, Frank E.
Kuhn, Mina D.
*Leonard, Howard C.
*McMillan, H.
Nichols, Eda L.
*O'Brien, Charlotte E.
*Ostrander, Agnes
Peck, Elizabeth du Bois
Phillips, Julia Tracy
*Pratt, Marion
Robins, Florence F.
Ryan, Anna
*Shepard, Florence D.
*Shipley, James H.
Shapff, Hetta
*Tracy, Howard M.
Tucker, Chas. R.
Wagner, Lora M.
*Welsh, John C.
*Whitmore, Clara H.

BY DEPARTMENTS

Biology Department
Grout, Abel J., First Asst.
Conroy, Mary S.
Dowell, Philip
Fisher, Ruth B.

Chemistry Department.
McMillen, H.

Commercial Department
Welsh, John C., First Asst.
Crennan, Margaret A.
Flanagan, William
Halloran, William M.
Kerr, Frank E.
Tracy, Howard M.

Drawing Department.
Ostrander, Agnes

English Department.
Abbot, Frances H. (First Asst.)
Bell, Anna
Benjamin, Claude T.
Close, Maude M.
Nichols, Eda L.
Pratt, Marion
Robins, Florence F.
Ryan, Anna
Whitmore, Clara H.

French Department.
Harkness, Mme. Alma de B.

German Department.
Shepherd, Florence D., First Asst.
Blanpied, Ethel O.
French, Linda M.
Harkness, Mme. A. de B.
Hummel, F. M.
Leonard, Howard

Gallagher, Ellen M.
Goode, Elizabeth
Peck, Mrs. Elizabeth du Bois
Pratt, Marion

Mathematics Department.
Dean, Philip R., First Asst.
Burdick, Mabel G.
Clark, Henry F.
Grant, Mrs. Eva M.
Kane, Thomas F.

O'Brien, Charlotte E.
Shipley, James H.

Music Department.
Kuhn, Mina D.

Physics Department.
Hopkins, Rupert H.
Tucker, Charles R.

Physical Training Department.
Austin, Mary E.
Hillyer, J. Blake

WITT CLINTON HIGH SCHOOL.

*Johnson, Walter R.
*Jonas, J. B. Edward
Kaphan, Ludwig
Kaveny, Martin
*Keller, Franklin J.
Kelly, David F.
*Kelley, Frank B.
*Klein, Morris
*Knox, Jaxon
*Krause, Arthur K.
*Landsman, Charles M.
*Lapolla, Garibaldi M.
Lehrer, I. D.
*Levene, Harry S.
Loew, Joseph
*Loewinthan, Albert A.
*Long, Leslie O.
*Lucey, Michael H.
MacLaren, Donald C.
*McCarthy, John D.
*McCrae, Annie.
*McTiernan, Thomas
*Manguse, William P.
Margolies, Fred B..
*Mason, Lucius J.
*Michaels, Morris G.
*Miles, Dudley H.
*Mirsky, Israel
*Monteser, Frederick
Morgan, Gwilym S.
*Morse, Charles F.
*Moyer, Fayette E.
*Mufson, Thomas
Nachemov, Morris
*Newman, Charles
O'Connor, John P.
Orliansky, Joseph B.
*Osborn, Ralph
*Parelhoff, Bernard M.
Parmelee, William J.
*Patterson, Samuel W.
*Penhollow, Harry B.
*Perry, Edward O.
*Philbrick, Max P.
*Pickelsky, Frank
*Pickens, Rose K.
*Pike, Katherine G.
Pokorney, Rudolph C.
*Raubichek, Charles F.
Rosenthal, Daniel C.
*Salzano, Francis
*Schmalhausen, Samuel D.
*Schneer, A. Henry
*Schwarzenbach, Peter A.
*Sharpe, Richard W.
Smith, Anna H.
*Smith, Herbert O.
*Smith, Thomas P.
*Solomon, Michael
*Stevens, Henry J.
Stevens, William S.
*Strauss, Julius

*Taylor, Albert S.
*Thomas, Harrison C.
Tietz, John W.
*Timmerman, Charles E.
*Tildsley, John L.
*Tobin, James L.
Tortora, Albert
*Wait, Horace C.
Watson, Mary H.
*Wheat, Frank H.
White, Arthur E.
*White, Emory F.
Whitsit, Jesse H.
*Wilford, Herbert E.
Wilson, Randolph C.
*Wilkins, Lawrence A.
*Works, Austin M.
*Wright, Herman H.
*Wright, Kenneth W.
*Yokel, Arthur
*Zacharie, Jean B.

BY DEPARTMENTS

Biology Department.
Hunter, George W.
Barber, Harry C.
Hastings, George F.
Donaldson, George P.
McCarthy, John D.
Mason, Lucius J.
Hewitt, George E.
Morse, Charles F.
Osborne, Ralph
Sharpe, Richard W.
Tietz, John W.
Wheat, Frank

Chemistry Department.
‡Whitsit, Jesse E.
Barmeyer, George H.
Broadhurst, Phillip H.
Call, R. Ellsworth
Connelly, Douglas L.
Fleissner, Gustav L.
Mayforth, Valentine
Parmelee, William J.
Smith, Herbert O.
White, Arthur E.

Clerical Assistants.
Greenberg, Michael
Kaveny, Martin
O'Connor, John P.

Drawing Department.
Bingham, Jesse H.
Adams, Milly E.
Fox, Alice E.
Gombarts, George X.

Green, Bernard
Klein, Morris
McCrae, Annie
Schwartzenbach, Peter A.

English Department.
Garrigues, Ellen E.
Abbott, Royal A.
Boylan, Arthur A.
Erwin, Edward J.
Frank, Maude
Hill, Grosvenor B.
Horwitz, Benj.
Johnson, Walter R.
Keller, Franklin J.
Knox, Jaxon
Lapolla, Garibaldi M.
Loew, Joseph
Loewinthan, Albert
McTiernan, Thomas
Michaels, Norris H.
†Miles, Dudley H.
†Mufson, Thomas
Nye, Berthold H.
Patterson, Samuel W.
Raubicheck, Charles
Schmaulhausen, Samuel D.
Smith, Anna H.
Smith Thomas P.
Taylor, Albert S.
Watson, Mary H.
Wilson, Rudolph C.
Wright, Kenneth W.

French Department.
Frank, Coleman D.
Armand, Louis J.
Bierman, Henry
Donner, H. Montagu
Carpentier, Marius
Goldberg, Isreal
Hyde, C. W.
Perry, Edward O.
Philbrick, Max P.
Rosenthal, Daniel C.
Wilkins, Lawrence A.
Zacharie, Jean B.

German Department.
Monteser, Frederick
Campbell, Ralph
Davidson, Henry
Giovanoly, Max F.
Herrmann, Adolf
Herzog, Charles
Hirsch, James A.
Jackson, Eugene
Jonas, J. B. Edward
Works, Austin M.

History Department.
Moyer, Fayette E.
Delaney, Edward C.
Foote, Edmund W.
Ham, Charles
Kaphan, Ludwig
Kelley, Frank B.
Long, Leslie D.
Lucey, Michael H.
Newman, Charles
Thomas, Harrison C.
Tobin, James L.

Latin Department.
Bryant, Arthur A.
Deixel, Abraham
Dotey, Aaron I.
Foote, Carlton A.
Hardy, Anna L.
Pike, Katherine G.
Solomon, Michael
Stevens, Henry J.
Wait, Horace C.
Wilford, Herbert E.
Yokel, Arthur

Librarian.
Arden, Harriette

Mathematics Department
Anthony, Oscar W.
Berry, James F.
Clark, Randolph F.
Deshel, M. C.
Decken, Nicholas P.
Grow, Frederick S.
Haas, Arthur
Heller, Harry
Kelly, David F.
Krause, Arthur K.
Landsman, Charles M.
Levene, Harry
MacLaren, Donald C. (on leave of absence)
Manguse, Wm. P.
Mirsky, Israel
Morgan, Gwilym S.
Orliansky, Joseph B.
Parellhoff, Bernard M.
Penhollow, Harry B.
Pickelsky, Frank
Pokorney, Rudolph C.
Salzano, Francis
Schneer, A. Henry
Stevens, William S.
Wright, Herman H.

Music Department.
Donnelly, Joseph P.
White, Emory F.

Physical Training Department
Haug, Emanuel
Cairns, Alexander
Gorsch, Rudolph V.
Hooks, David M.
Leher, I. D.
Strauss, Julius

Physics Department.
Timmerman, Charles E.
Chamberlain, Raymond
Currie, Thomas H.
Tortora, Albert A.

Secretary.
Margolies, Fred. B.

Stenography Department
Pickens, Rose K.

Study Hall.
Baylis, Sara

†Continuous leave of absence.
‡On leave of absence.

EASTERN DISTRICT HIGH SCHOOL.

*Adler, David
*Anderson, Mary E.
*Ayres, Mary S.
Balter, Bella S.
*Baltz, Frank P.
Bannon, Agnes R.
*Beeckman, Florence
*Beitel, Helen S.
Blumenberg, Frieda
Boggs, Dora A.
*Bole, John A.
*Bowman, Nina
*Brace, Edith M.
Branower, Soloman
*Bruce, Walter A.
*Burlingham, Gertrude S.
Burn, Alice M.
*Campbell Harold G.
*Chater, Ellen McR. D.
Clarke, Madge S.
Cohn, Albert
*Colligan, Eugene A.
Davenport, Florence
Delano, Grace
*Dithridge, Rachel L.
*Dixon, Charles E.
Dreyfus, Jeanne
*Ennis, Mary G.
*Faulkner, Eunice F.
Fergeuson, Ethel
*Genung, Ina E.
Goldenberg, Irving
Greenberg, Henry
Griffiths, Anna B.
Gross, Henry I.
Gurnee, Blandina H.
Harmon, Esther
*Hartwell, Chas. S.
*Hazen, Annah P.
Helmuth, Lore
*Henoch, Stella S.
*Higbee, Mrs. Anna M.
Hincken, Elsie O.
Hirschberg, Arthur
Holmes, David H.
*Hoy, Elizabeth R.
*Hughan, Jessie W.
*Ikelhumer, Minnie
Illich, Louis L.
*Jacobson, Walter
Katz, Sidney F.
*Kauffman, William A.
*Kelly, William H.
*King, Helen L.
Kiso, Freda
*Klock, Claude W.
Kramer, Benjamin J.
Krellenstein, Ray
*Kretschamer, Magda
*Kuhn, Adelina
*Lanz, Jeanne M.
*Lemowitz, Nathan
*Loughran, Agnes
*Manahan, Mary G.
*Martin, Paul
Mayo, Marion
*McDermott, Annie
McKee, Louise
*Meigs, Katherine H.
*Meyer, Florence E.
Meyers, Willard L.
*Model, Charles
Osborne, Mabel S.
*Paine, Frederick H.
Philip, Mary I.

Domestic Science Department
Ikelheimer, Minnie

English Department
Ayres, Mary S.
Charter, Ellen
Clarke, Madge S.
Delano, Grace
Dithridge, Rachel
Griffiths, Anna B.
Hartwell, Chas.
Helmuth, Lore
Hincken, Elsie B.
Hughan, Jessie W.
Myers, Willard L.
Philip, Mary I.
Stratford, Aline C.
Warren, James R.
Wellwood, Elizabeth
Zollinhoffer, Sophie

French Department
Anderson, Mary E.
Dreyfus, Jeanne
Kuhn, Adelina
Lanz, J. M.

German Department
Adler, David
Bole, J. A.
Goldenberg, Irving
Greenberg, Henry
Harmon, Esther
Kiso, Freda
Kretschmar, Magda
Meyer, Florence E.
Russum, Edith E.
Santee, E. B.
Wagenschutz, Anna

History Department
Paine, Frederick H.
Beeckman, Florence
Campbell, Harold G.
Colligan, Eugene A.
Watson, Alice D.
Wyckoff, Harriet E.

Latin Department
Bowman, Nina
Davenport, Florence
Dixon, Charles E.
Genung, Ina E.
Holmes, David H.
Hoy, Elizabeth
King, Helen Louise
Klock, Claude W.
Pinch, Minnie E.
Stepanek, Beatrice

Mathematics Department
Blumenberg, Frieda
Gross, H. I.
Gurnee, Blaudina
Kelly, Wm. H.
Mayo, M. J.
Rittenhouse, Hawley D.
Sullivan, Mary.
Tomlin, Stella M.
Wilson, Stuart

Music Department
Ennis, Mary G.
Martin, Paul

Physical Training Department
Higbee, Anna M.
Krellenstein, Ray
Model, Chas.
Reed, Mary
Sperling, Harry

Science Department
Brace, Edith M.
Branower, Solomon
Burlingham, Gertrude
Hazen, Annah P.
Illich, Louis L.
Kaufman, Wm. A.
Meigs, Katherine H.
Osborne, Mabel
Trowbridge, Cornelia
Wilkes, Eana M.

RASMUS HALL HIGH SCHOOL.

Dwyer, Eleanor A.
*Earle, Willis
*Edgell, Frank D.
Edgell, Mrs. Frank D.
*Estes, Charles S.
*Everett, Edith M.
*Farrar, Preston C.
*Fay, Charles R.
Ferry, Orlando E.
Forcier, M. Ethel
Foster, Sarah P.
Frost, Madeleine A.
*Gordon, John J.
*Gunnison, Walter B., **Principal**
*Habermeyer, Louise C. M.
*Hancock, William J.
*Harley, Walter S.
Harter, Eugene W.
Harton, Amy M.
Herrington, Agnes M.
*Hewitt, Helen F.
*Hodgdon, Katherine I.
*Holmes, Mary H.
*Howe, Alice C.
*Huntington, Frederick W.
Hurty, Kathleen
Jaquish, Ben M.
Jeffs, Eva E.
Johnson, Marion
Johnston, Wm. H.
*Keck, Frederick R.
*King, Cyrus A.
Kingsbury, Mary A.
Knowlson, Walter S.
*Laden, James E.
*Lasher, Wm. R.
Lauder, Mary A.
*Leggett, Blanche C.

Music Department
Schmidt, Carl G., **Chairman**
Mulligan, Mary C.

Physical Science Department
Holmes, Mary H., **Head of Department.**
Stocker, John H., **Head of Department**
Bryant, Frank L.
Burnham, R. Wesley
Busch, Ella A.
Dennis, Julia B.
Habermeyer, Louise C. M.
Hancock, William J.

Huntington, Frederick W.
Jaquish, Ben M.
Levy, Harry A.
Perkins, Helen L.
Sparks, Minnie E.
Williams, Lewis C.
*Leman, George W.
Levy, Harry A.
Lovell, Katherine A.
McGill, Franklin C.
McGill, Mrs. Beatrice Shaw
McKechnie, Madeleine
MacColl, Grace B.
*MacLean, Donald C.
Marsden, Mrs. Nellie S.
Mastin, Florence J.
*Merchant, Manton E.
Moore, Sabra M.
Mulligan, Mary C.
*Neiswender, Ada C.
*Peabody, Susan P.
*Peace, Lillian B.
Perkins, Helen L.
*Raynor, George C.
Rexford, Frank A.
Schmidt, Carl G.
Scott, Izora
*Scoville, Florence M.
Sheehan, Mary J.
Simmons, Isabel
Smith, Natalie
*Sparks, Minnie
*Sprague, Laura E.
Stacey, Sidney G.
*Stocker, John H.
Stone, Katherine W.
Stone, Mary M.
*Strom, Carl A. M.
*Strong, William M.
Strout, George M.
*Talbot, A. May
Tompkins, Elizabeth
*Townsend, Arthur M.
*Tredick, Helen F.
Turner, Kate E.
*Valentine, Henry D.
*Vedder, Estella M.
Vidaud, Nathalie L.
*Volentine, Mrs. Mary F.
Warner, Elma L.
Welsh, W. Wallace
Wendell, Carrie E.
White, Elizabeth M.
Whitney, N. Belle
*Wight, Walter A.
*Wilder, George F.
*Williams, Lewis L.
Young, Charlotte S.
*Young, Louise A.
*Young, Mabel A.

BY DEPARTMENTS

Art Department
Doggett, Allen B., Chairman
Cameron, Alix S.
Currier, Clara L.
Herrington, Agnes M.
Lovell, Katherine
Merchant, Manton E.

Biology Department
King, Cyrus A., Head of Department
Hurty, Kathleen
Marsden, N. S.
Peace, Lillian B.
Rexford, Frank A.
Tompkins, Elizabeth M.
Tredick, Helen F.
Vedder, Estella M.
Young, Charlotte S.
Young, Mabel A.

Classics Department
Lasher, William R., Chairman
Harter, Eugene W., Head of Department
Beardsley, Frank J.
Branson, Roswell H.
Connell, J. Wesley
Dox, Elmer A.
Estes, Charles S.
Harley, Walter S.
Howe, Alice C.
Leggett, Blanche C.
McGill, Franklin C.
Neiswender, Ada B. C.
Peabody, Susan P.
Scott, Izora
Stacey, Sidney G.
Stone, Katharine W.
Strong, William M.
Townsend, Arthur M.
Vidaud, Nathalie L.
Volentine, Mary F.
Welsh, W. Wallace
Wendell, Carrie E.

Clerical Department
Harton, Amy M.
Johnson, Marion
McKechnie, Elizabeth M.

Elocution Department
Chinnock, Florence B.
Frost, Madeline A.

English Department
Farrar, Preston C., Head of Department
Barber, Cora L.
Battel, J. M.
Boughton, W.
Cashman, Joseph F.
Chesley, Mabel L.
Crockett, Esther M.
Dwyer, Eleanor A.
Earle, Willis
Everett, Edith M.
Ferry, Orlando E.
Forcier, L. Ethel
Foster, Sarah P.
Hewitt, Helen F.
Lauder, Mary A.
Mastin, Florence
Moore, S. Maude
Scopill, Florence M.
Simmons, Isabel
Smith, Natalie A.
Strout, George M.
Valentine, Henry D.

French Department
Wight, Walter A., Chairman
Brown, Frances E.
Douglas, Clara M.
Shaw-McGill, Beatrice
White, Elizabeth M.

Gymnastics Department
Austin, Mrs. Mary
Batchelor, Chas. B.
Edgell, Mrs. Frank D., Chairman
Sheehan, Mary
Warner, Emma L.

History Department
Boynton, George E., Head of Department
Crane, Ella E.
Cunningham, Maude M.
Davis, Jennie M.
Fay, Charles R.
Knowlson, Walter S.
MacColl, Grace B.
Sprague, Laura E.

Librarian
Kingsbury, Mary A.

Mathematics Department
Brickelmaier, Alice G.
Edgell, Frank D.
Gordon, John J.
Hodgdon, Katherine I.
Jeffs, Eva
Johnston, William H.
Keck, Fred R.
Laden, James
Lasher, William R.
Leman, George W.
MacLean, Donald C.
Raynor, George C.
Stone, Mary M.
Strom, Carl A. W.
Talbot, A. May
Whitney, N. Belle
Wilder, George F.
Young, Louise A.

EVANDER CHILDS HIGH SCHOOL.

*Ackerle, Ida V.
*Altholz, Nathaniel
*Arenwald, Mesmin
*Blakeley, Gilbert S., Principal
*Cohn, Louis B.
*Coster, Silvie de G.
*Durfee, Clayton G.
*Edmunds, Maude A.
*Greditzer, M. Moritz
*Haley, Jesse H.
*Hall, Margaret W.
Hannan, Walter S.
Healy, Mrs. Margaret E. G.
Heller, Maxwell L.
*Herrmann, Anna L.
Heuermann, Helena F.
Hubbard, Marion L.
*Hughes, Thomas H.
Keigwin, Henry W.
*Klein, Anthony W.
*Levine, Maurice
*Lippe, Adolph A.
*Lipschutz, Berthold
Low, Clara L.
McDonald, H. Rosabel
Mann, Paul B.
*Merchant, Isabel L.
*Norr, Henry I.
*Peterson, A. Everett
*Pingrey, (Mrs.) Cora E.

*Quimby, Ernest S.
*Reynolds, Gerald
*Rosenthal Terese R.
*Schamus, John B.
Schapiro, Barnet
Schonberg, Max
Siedler, Charles W.
Smith, Harriet K.
Stamm, Caroline L.
*Tracy, Mary L.
*Williams, Joseph S.
*Wirth, Charles A.
*Withers, Samuel C.
Woodman, Sophie P.
Wylie, Stella M.
*Young-High, (Mrs.) Caroline

BY DEPARTMENTS

Biology Department
Mann, Paul B., Chairman
Merchant, Isabel L.
Pingrey, Cora E.
With, Charles A.
Young-High, Caroline

Commercial Subjects.
Altholz, Nathaniel
Klein, Anthony W.
Lipschutz, Berthold, Chairman
Smith, Harriet K.

Domestic Science Department
Low, Clara L.

Drawing Department
Coster, Silvie de G., Chairman
Heller, Maxwell L.
McDonald, H. Rosabell

English Department
Cohn, Louis B.
Durfee, Clayton G.
Haley, Jesse H.
Hughes, Thomas H.
Quimby, Ernest S., Chairman
Schamus, John B.
Tracy, Mary L.
Wylie, Stella M.

French Department
Hall, Margaret W.
Hubbard, Marion L.

German Department.
Ackerle, Ida V.
Greditzer, M. Moritz, Chairman
Herrmann, Anna L.
Heuermann, Helena F.
Schonberg, Max
Stamm, Caroline L.

History Department.
Peterson, A. Everett, Chairman
Woodman, Sophie P.

Latin Department
Siedler, Charles W.
Williams, Joseph S., Chairman

Mathematics Department
Arenwald, Mesmin
Keigwin, Henry W., Chairman
Levine, Maurice
Lippe, Adolph A.
Norr, Henry I.
Rosenthal, Terese R.
Withers, Samuel C.

Music Department
Reynolds, Gerald

Physical Training Department
Edmunds, Maude A.
Schapiro, Barnet

Physics Department
Hannan, Walter S.

FAR ROCKAWAY HIGH SCHOOL.

Barbanell, A. Irving
Barnes, Edwin A.
Belding, Albert G., First Assistant
Bonfoey, Emma C.
Broomall, Laura B.
Crim, Adelaide
Ellsworth, Sanford J., Principal
Fish, Alanson L.
Flanders, Addie E.
Greenburg, Sophia
*Jennison, Emily M.
Jeschke, Martha L.
Kennedy, Anna J.
Lanz, Lea B.
Livermore, H. Louise
Marquard, Edwin G.
*Prescott, Lucy M.
*Van Dusen, Eldon M.
Wright, Grace L.

BY DEPARTMENTS

Cooking Department
Vacancy

Clerical Assistant
Greenburg, Sophia

Commercial Branches Department
Belding, Albert G.
Vacancy

Drawing Department
Wright, Grace L.

Elocution Department
Crim, Adelaide

English Department
Bonfoey, Emma C.
Vacancy

French Department
Lanz, Lea B.

German Department
Jeschke, Martha L.

History Department
Kennedy, Anna J.

Latin Department
Flanders, Addie E.
Prescott, Lucy M.

Mathematics Department
Barbanell, A. Irving
Jennison, Emily M.

Music Department
Marquard, Edward G.

Physical Training Department
Fish, Alanson L.
Livermore, H. Louise

Science Department
Barnes, Edwin A.
Broomall, Laura B.

Stenography and Typewriting Department
Van Dusen, Eldon M.

FLUSHING HIGH SCHOOL.

Avery, Elizabeth
Bardenheuer, Clara E.
*Barnwell, Walter
*Baumeister, John
Boynton, Carolyn A.
*Carey, Margaret E.
Chapman, Frances E.
*Clark, John Hally, Principal
Deihl, Frank S.
Ely, Jean
Ferry, Alice M.
Fish, Alanson L.
Fountain, Emma A.
*Green, Helen
*Hood, Edward C.
*Jenks, Paul R.
Jones, Blanche
Killen, Arthur H.
Klein, Margaret A.
Lane, Mary C.
Lay, Wilfrid
Livermore, Harriet L.
*Marquard, Edward G.
*Miller, Frank H.
*Nearing, Elena P.
Palmer, May T.
Pulvermacher, Wm. Dean
*Read, Warren W.
*Ross, Annie
Sands, Mary E.
Swick, Mary S.
Wood, Howell R.

BY DEPARTMENTS

Biology Department
Hood, Edward C.
Pulvermacher, Wm. Dean

Clerk
Sands, Mary E.

HIGH SCHOOL DIRECTORY

Commercial Branches
Carey, Margaret E.
Deihl, Frank E.

Drawing Department
Swick, Mary S.

Elocution Department
Klein, Margaret A.

English Department
Avery, Elizabeth
Boynton, Carolyn A.
Fountain, Emma A.
Jones, Blanche
Read, Warren W.

History Department
Chapman, Frances E.
Miller, Frank H.

Latin Department
Jenks, Paul R.
Lane, Mary C.
Lay, Wilfrid

Librarian
Ely, Jean

Mathematics Department
Barnwell, Walter
Nearing, Elena P.
Palmer, May T.

Modern Languages Department
Bardenheuer, Clara E.
Baumeister, John
Ferry, Alice M.
Green, Helen
Ross, Annie

Music Department
Marquard, Edward G.

Physical Training Department
Fish, Alanson L.
Livermore, Harriet L.

Science (Physics and Chemistry)
Killen, Arthur H.
Wood, Howell R.

GIRLS' HIGH SCHOOL.

*Felter, Dr. William L., Principal
Abbott, Marguerite W.
Adair, Edith
Arey, Albert L.
*Babcock, Maude R.
*Barker, M. Ellen
Beckley, Clara M.
Briggs, Emily E.
Briley, Beatrice A.
Bunting, Mildred B.
Byrnes, Esther F.
Cahill, Rose
Cann, Bertha
Carter, Effiie A.
Chase, Charlotte G.
Chatterton, Minnie E.
Childs, Lelia M.
Clark, Cora B.
*Clark, Emma K.
Clarke, Teresa A.
Clinton, Mrs. Fanny L.
Cochran, Thomas
Couch, Anne M.
*Cushman, Earl L.
Dame, Lydia M.
Davies, Rebecca H.
Davis, (Miss) Frank L.
Denfield, Charlotte S.
Dietrich, Bertha K.
Duurloo, Wilhelmine H.
*Ellis, Sophia
Evans, William F.
Farrant, Louise G.
*Ford, Celia
Gardner, Maude
Germann, Susan M.
Goodrich, Charlotte
Hale, Agnes L.
Hall, Mary E.
Hanks, Lenda T.
Hardy, Ruth G.
Harris, Mary O.
Hayes, Helen M.
*Higgins, Alice
Hoffman, Margie E.
Holman, Mabel L.
Holmes, Abby B.
Holt, Henry L.
Hughes, Annie R.
Huntington, Belle
*Ingalls, Margaret L.
Jenkins, Anna S.
Jenkins, Manford M.
*Jenness, Jennie M.
Jewell, Edith
Joannes, Jules S.
Johnston, Ina W.
Jones, Emma A.
Junge, Antonie
Keller, Anna T.
Ketchum, Daisy T.
Keyes, Rowena K.
*Lee, Marguerite T.
Leland, Genevieve M.
Lepere, Bertha B.
Liscombe, (Mrs.) Esther A.
Lumley, Eleanor P.
*Lyle, Edith K.
Mattes, Max H.
McCarty, Maria C.
Merriam, Betsey G.
*Miller, Grace H.
Miller, Mabel
Miller, Maud
*Mullen, Loring B.
Patterson, Mabel L.
Perkins, Fannie D.
Pichel, Margaret
Pyles, Marian
*Rae, Anne M.
Romaine, S. Helen
Rowe, (Mrs.) Emma L. H.
Schumer, Jacob H.
*Seelman, H. Elizabeth
Seymour, Macy I.
Simmons, Kate C.
*Smith, Charlotte
Spencer, Mary
Sprague, Almeda
Steers, Edna L.
Stevens, Alice A.
Stevenson, Beulah E.
St. John, Emily P.
Stone, Lulu M.
*Sullivan, Bessie
Taylor, Jeannette S.
Treadwell, Flora G.
Wakeman, Susan E.
Wales, Alma E.
Watrous, Louise E.
Way, Mary J.
Wendt, Cordelia
*White, Bessie R.
*Willard, Gladys
Wilson, Bessie D.
Wilson, Zada J.
*Winslow, Julia E.
Wisthaler, Johanna S.
Witherbee, Reta
Wollaston, Caroline M.
*Wright, Mabel

BY DEPARTMENTS

Biology Department
Lee, Marguerite T., Head Teacher
Bunting, Mildred B.
Byrnes, Esther F.
Dietrich, Bertha K.
Goodrich, Charlotte
Hanks, Lena T.
Hoffman, Margie E.
Rae, Anne M.
Steers, Edna L.

Cooking Department
Perkins, Fannie D.

Drawing Department
Gardner, Maude, Chairman
Jones, Emma A.
Johnston, Ina W.
Ketchum, Daisy T.
Simmons Kate C.
Spencer, Mary
Stevenson, Beulah E.

English Department
Adair, Edith
Cann, Bertha
Chase, Charlotte G.
Clinton, Mrs. Fanny L.
Davis, Miss Frank L.
Holman, Mabel L.
Holmes, Abby B.
Keyes, Rowena K.
Miller, Mabel
Romaine, S. Helen
Seelman, H. Elizabeth
Seymour, Macy I.
Sprague, Almeda
St. John, Emily P.
Stone, Lulu M.
Taylor, Jeannette S.
Wendt, Cordelia, Head Teacher
White, Bessie R.
Witherbee, Reta

French Department
Higgins, Alice, Head Teacher
Abbot, Marguerite W.
Harris, Mary O.
Lepere, Bertha B.
Wilson, Bessie D.

German Department.
Cushman, Earl L., Chairman
Babcock, Maude R.
Denfeld, Charlotte S.
Duurloo, Wilhelmine H.
Hayes, Helen M.
Junge, Antonie
Kellner, Anna T.
Wisthaler, Johanna S.

History Department
Cahill, Rose, Head Teacher
Couch, Anne M.

Davies, Rebecca H.
Hardy, Ruth G.
Lyle, Edith K.
Merriam, Betsey G.
Stevens, Alice A.
Way, Mary J.

Latin Department
Briggs, Emily E.
Clark, Emma K.
Dame, Lydia M.
Ellis, Sophia
Farrant, Louise G.
Ford, Celia, Head Teacher
Jenkins, Anna S.
Lumley, Eleanor P.
McCarty, Maria C.
Willard, Gladys
Winslow, Julia E.

Mathematics Department
Mullen, Loring B., Head Teacher
Chatterton, Minnie E.
Childs, Lelia M.
Germann, Susan M.
Hale, Agnes L.
Ingalls, Margaret L.
Jewell, Edith
Miller, Maud
Pichel, Margaret
Smith, Charlotte
Sullivan, Bessie
Wales, Alma E.
Watrous, Louise E.
Wilson, Zada J.
Wright, Mabel

Music Department
Joannes, Jules S., Chairman
Liscombe, (Mrs.) Esther A.
Mattes, Max H.

Physical Training Department
Wollaston, Caroline M., Chairman
Clark, Cora B.
Hughes, Annie R.
Huntington, Belle
Treadwell, Flora G.

Physics Department
Arey, Albert L., Head Teacher
Briley, Beatrice A.
Carter, Effie A.
Evans, William F.
Holt, Henry L.
Jenkins, Manford M.
Jenness, Jennie M.
Schumer, Jacob H.

Physiography Department
Arey, Albert L., Head Teacher
Cochran, Thomas

JAMAICA HIGH SCHOOL.

Bradley, S. M.
Brown, A. W.
Brown, C. G.
Buechner, Alice E.
*Busbee, C.
*Chickering, E. C.
Corcilius, J.
*Dilger, M.
*Edgerton, M.
Epler, Alice
*Fairley, Edwin
*Fennebresque, L.
*Ferris, M. D.
*Gay, Laura S.
*Grant, R. A.
*Hoadley, H.
*Hochderffer, Mrs. M.
Holmes, E. A.
Hook, M. A. (Clerk)
Jacob, A. G.
Joselyn, R. (Librarian)
Kessel, T. (Clerk)
*Kibby, W. J.
*Krause, Carl A.
*Lawrence, A.
*Linville, Henry R.
*Luetscher, G. D.
McConnell, M.
*McNamara, Edward J.
Mann, J.
Mannhardt, E. G.
*Mitchell, Theodore C., Principal.
Morrissey, Fannie A.
*O'Keefe, David H.
Parker, G. A.
*Quick, Oscar
Root, Minnie
Root, Lydia
Rosenstadt, B.
*Silvermann, Henry
Starkey, W. A.
*Thompson, K. W.
*Thorp, Benjamin H.
*Vosburgh, Charles H.
*Ward, A. W.
*Wilkin, J. D.
*Wilson, George F.

BY DEPARTMENTS

Biological Science Department
Linville, Henry R., Chairman.
Holmes, Ella A.

Classical Languages Department
Chickering, E. C., Chairman.
Grant, R. A.
Hoadley, H.
Root, Lydia F.

Commercial Branches Department
Starkey, Warren L., Chairman
Kibby, Warren J.
McNamara, Edward J.
Morrissey, Fannie A.
O'Keefe, David H.
Parker, George A.

Drawing Department
Epler, Alice, Chairman.
Ferris, Mary D.

Elocution Department
Ward, A. W.

English Department
Fairley, Edwin, Chairman.
Bradley, Susan M.
Brown, Adelaide W.
Hochderffer, Mary
Root, Minnie R.
Thorp, Benjamin H.

History Department
Edgerton, Myra T.
Lawrence, Antoinette, Chairman.
Luetscher, George

Mathematics Department
Wilkin, Josephine D., Chairman.
Brown, Charles G.
Busbee, Christina

Modern Languages Department
Krause, Carl A., Chairman.
Corcilius, Josephine
Dilger, Marie
Fennebresque, L.
Mannhardt, E. G.
Rosenstadt, Bertha

Music Department
McConnell, Marie

Physical Science Deepartment
Vosburgh, Charles H., Chairman.
Quick, Oscar
Thompson, K. W.

Physical Training Department
Jacob, A. Gertrude
Silverman, Henry

JULIA RICHMAN HIGH SCHOOL.

*Wolfson, Arthur, Principal
Ake, Virginia A.
*Arnold, David L.
Ashcroft, Carrie Van R.
Beck, Florence
Brand, Louis
*Brockman, May E.
*Brooks, Mabel Frances
Cahill, Mary F.
*Carpenter, Idelette
Clark, Eleanor P.
*Cole, Beulah V.
Crocker, Nellie J.
Filfus, Nathaniel
*Goller, Gratia
Hastings, Ada L.
Hazen, Charlotte
Herendeen, Jane E.
Hodgetts, Abbie S.
Howes, Emily
Hyde, Isabella
Jumnefsky, Simon J.
*Kahn, Jeannette
*Kennedy, Agnes

*Knopfmacher, Ida
*Lancaster, Bertha
*Leonard, Mrs. Nina V.
Levy, Rose Adelaide
Lewenthal, Rebecca
Linker, John
Lupton, Olive Moore
*McLane, Fannie Moulton
Maeder, Emily L.
Maloney, Katherine E.
Mitchell, Marguerite F.
*Moscovitz, Bertha J.
Mulcahy, Mary A., Cler. Asst.
Nahon, Zarita
*Opdycke, John B.
Ruggeri, Agnes C.
*Salgman, Anna
Saxton, Margaret D.
Shwitzer, Myrtle, Cler. Asst.
Smith, Edith Ives
Thomas, Lulu E.
*Topp, Emily
*Topper, Mrs. Anna
Trautvetter, Ida
Underhill, Mary
Vermilya, Mabel
*Waite, Charlotte Augusta
Walter, M. Louise
Wehle, Hanna
Wendell, May Godfrey
White, Isabelle D.
White, Mabel M.

BY DEPARTMENTS

Biology Department
Carpenter, Idelette
McLane, Fannie Moulton
Topp, Emily

Commercial Branches Department
Filfus, Nathaniel
Goller, Gratia
Jumnefsky, Simon J.
Linker, John
Salzman, Anna

Cooking Department
Brockman, May E.
Moeder, Emily L.

Drawing Department
Hastings, Ada L.
Lewenthal, Rebecca
Maloney, Katherine E.

Elocution Department
Herendeen, Jane E.
Leonard, Nina V.

English Department
Beck, Florence
Brooks, Mabel Frances
Herendeen, Jane E.
Hodgetts, Abbe S.
Howes, Emily
Lancaster, Bertha
Lupton, Olive Moore
Opdycke, John B.
Thomas, Lulu E.

French Department
Hyde, Isabella
Moscovitz, Bertha J.
Nahon, Zarita
White, Isabelle D.

German Department
Crocker, Nellie J.
Knopfmacher, Ida
Saxton, Margaret D.
Trautvetter, Ida
Wehle, Hanna
Wendell, May Godfrey

Latin Department
Clarke, Eleanor P.

Mathematics Department
Arnold, David L.
Underhill, Mary
Vermilya, Mabel

Physical Training Department
Ashcroft, Carrie Van R.
Hazen, Charlotte
Smith, Edith Ives

Physiography Department
Cole, Beulah V.

Sewing Department
Waite, Charlotte Augusta
Walter, M. Louise

Stenography Department
Ake, Virginia A.
Brand, Louis
Cahill, Mary F.
Kahn, Jeanette
Kennedy, Agnes
Levy, Rose Adelaide
Mitchell, Marguerite F.
Ruggeri, Agnes C.
Topper, Anna
White, Mabel M.

MANUAL TRAINING HIGH SCHOOL.

Abbott, Frederick B.
*Aldridge, Vincent
*Allen, J. Trevette
Baker, H. Latham
*Baker, Eleanor R.
Bachelder, Mary A.
Baldwin, Walter J.
Barasch, Morris
Bates, Herbert
*Bawden, Sarah E.
Beebe, Dee
Bergoffen, Herman
Besarick, Caroline B.
Bloom, Ira I.
Boecker, Alexander
*Boole, Emily
Boole, Florence A.
*Braman, Mary L.
Brown, Merton A.
*Brundage, Howard D.
*Bryant, Elizabeth E.
Bushong, Alice M.
Cambern, J. Raymond
*Coan, Charles W.
Colony, M. Elizabeth
Colsten, Albert L.
Cotter, Julia J.
Davis, Eunuice M.
Dickler, Nathan N.
*Dickinson, Henry N.
*Dickman, Mary B.
Dithridge, Caroline
Edwards, Sidney
*Elting, Mabel
Everson, Anna
Fanning, Grace M. W.
Foster, Edwin W.
Foster, Oscar R.
*Freeberg, Sigrid C.
Frerichs, Harrison
Gauvran, Ethel H.
*Geiss, M. Paula
Germann, Charles C.
Gilson, Channing W.
Glassberg, Benjamin
Gnade, Agnes
Gray, J. Newton
*Green, Florence
*Hackedorn, Marion
*Hall, Mary A.
Hampshire, John W.
*Harris, Lena
Hazen, Ella M.
Hertzfield, Leonore H.
Heyer, Ella G.
Hierholzer, Carlo O.
Hoffman, Mark
Holly, Harold A.
Holzman, Abraham
Hunt, Arthur E.
Jacobson, Harry
Jones, W. R.
Katz, Samuel
Kern, Albert J. W.
*Lamb, William W.
Larkins, Charles D.
Lasswell, Arthur C.
*Lenfest, Bertram A.
LeRoy, Walter I.
Lindlar, William
*Low, J. Herbert
Ludwig, Augustus
*Luther, E. M.
McArdle, John Philip
*McCall, Carleton C.
McCreary, Herbert J.
McDonald, John J.
*McDowell, Mary S.
MacColl, Robert J.
*MacKay, Alfred
Mackby, Julius C.
*Mageworth, J. Otis
Maginn, Elizabeth M.
*Marquardt, Florence
Massoneau, Robt. J., Jr.
Mattuck, J. A.
*Meneely, John H.
*Meserve, Martha C.
Mueller, Ernest G.
Murphy, Margaret L.
Nelson, Willard B.
Nevins, Dora R.
*Odell, Louis S.
O'Donnell, Emmett
Oliver, Jos. W.
*Oswald, Frederick W., Jr.
Peck, Emily S.
*Perrine, Charles
Perry, Oroli R.
Peters, Frederick A.
Pignol, Gertrude A. M.
Prentis, Hally M.
*Puig, Louise M.
*Richardson, William C.
Robinson, Alfred I.

*Robinson, F. D.
Robinson, John T.
Roeth, Natalie
*Russell, Warren L.
San Giovanni, Eduardo
Saymon, Ignatz
*Schaible, G. C.
Schradieck, H. E.
Schryver, George Orin
*Schultz, Elizabeth
*Schwartz, Edward E.
*Shimberg, Jeannette
*Shinn, Victor I.
Shumway, Edgar S.
*Smith, Mrs. Grace L.
*Smith, J. Clarence
*Smith, M. Helen
Snow, Minnie R.
*Snyder, B. Louis
Solomon, Charles
*Soule, Bertha L.
*Stern, Regine
Stone, Mabel
Stone, Maudie L.
*Taylor, Nettie
*Terrel, Lillian A.
*Vail, Clarence W.
Van Olinda, James E.
Volkaerts, Marie
*Walker, Alice J.
Walker, Ruth N.
Walton, Georgiana C.
Weed, Henry T.
Wikel, Henry H.
Wilson, Agnes W.
*Wolcott, Henry
*Wright, Helen L.
*Yarrington, Adrian
Yerbury, Chas. S.
Zaslaw, Myer

BY DEPARTMENTS

Biology Department

Braman, Mary L.
Everson, Anna E.
Hunt, Arthur E.
Lasswell, Arthur C.
Roeth, Natalie S.
Stone, Maudie L.
Walker, Ruth N.
Wolcott, Henry G.

Boys' Shop Department

Billingham, F. L.
Boecker, Dr. Alexander
Brundage, Howard D.
Edwards, Sidney
Foster, Edwin
Gilson, Channing W.
Lenfest, Dr. Bertram A.
Leroy, Walter A.
McCall, Carleton
Mackay, Alfred
Oliver, Joseph W.
Robinson, Alfred T.
Robinson, John T.

Clerical Assistants

Hertzfield, Leonore H.
Massoneau, Robert L., Jr.
Weinberger, George, Substitute

English Department

Bates, Herbert
Bawden, Sarah E.
Bergoffen, Herman
Boole, Emily R.
Boole, Florence A.
Cambern, J. Raymond
Cotter, Julia T.
Elting, Mabel
Gauvran, Ethel H.
Gnade, Agnes
Hampshire, John W.
Hoffman, Mark
Ludwig, Augustus
Luther, Edith M.
Meneely, Dr. John H.
Meserve, Martha C.
O'Donnell, James Emmett
Peck, Emily S.
Prentis, Hally M.
Saymon, Ignatz
Taylor, Nettie
Vail, Clarence W.
Walker, Alice J.

French Department

Allen, John Trevette
Bachelder, Mary A.
Klein, Leopold, Substitute
Lamb, Dr. William W.
Maginn, Eliza M.

Free Hand Drawing Department

Beebe, Dee
Buck, Fredk., Substitute
Frerichs, Harrison, M. D.
Menzel, Eda, Substitute
Murphy, Margaret I.
Shinn, Victor
Wright, Mrs. Helen S.

German Department

Bushong, Alice
Fleischer, Emanuel M., Substitute
Geiss, M. Paula
Hackedorn, Marion
Kern, Dr. Albert J. W.
Lamb, Dr. William W.
Levy, Gretchen R., Substitute
Mageworth, J. Otis
Mueller, Ernest G.
Oswald, Dr. Frederick Wm., Jr.
Peters, Frederick A.
Pignol, Gertrude A. M.
Schaible, Godfrey C.
Schutze, Eliza
Schwartz, Edward E.
Stern, Regine

Girls' Shop Department

Brockman, Mary E.
Dickman, Mary B.
Green, Mrs. Florence
Stone, Mabel
Terrell, Lillian

History Department

Fanning, Grace M. W.
Glassberg, Mr.
Hall, Mary A.
Low, J. Herbert
Marquardt, Florence
Puig, Florence M.
Yarrington, Adrian M.

Latin Department

Bryant, Elizabeth E.
Dickinson, Hy. N.
Dithridge, Caroline
Heyer, Ella G.
McDonald, John J.
McDowell, Mary S.
Perrine, Charles
Richardson, William C.
Russell, Warren L.
San Giovanni, Dr. Eduardo
Schryver, George Orin
Shumway, Dr. Edgar S.
Smith, J. Clarence
Soule, Bertha L.

Librarian.

Hazen, Ella H.

Mathematics Department

Aldridge, Dr. Vincent
Baker, Dr. Arthur L.
Baker, Eleanor R.
Baldwin, Walter J.
Banta, Mary
Barasch, Morris
Colsten, Albert L.
Davis, Eunice M.
Dickler, Nathan N.
Freeberg, Sigrid C.
Harris, Lena
Hopkins, Francis L., Substitute
Jones, Walter R.
McArdle, John Philip
McCreary, Herbert J.
MacColl, R. J.
Nevins, Dora R.
Odell, Louis S.
Robinson, Franklin D.
Shimberg, Jeanette
Snow, Minnie R.
Solomon, Charles
Walton, Georgiana C.

Mechanical Drawing Department

Abbot, Fredk. B.
Coan, Charles W.
Jacobson, Harry
Mackby, Julius C.

Music Department

Smith, Grace L.
Van Olinda, James E.
Yerbury, Charles S.

Physical Science Department

Brown, Merton A.
Foster, Oscar R.
Germann, Charles C.
Gray, J. Newton
Holly, Harold A.
Holzman, Abr.
Mackay, Alfred
Mattuck, Jacob A.
Nelson, Willard B.
Snyder, B. Louis
Weed, Henry T.

Physical Training Department

Besarick, Caroline B.
Bloom, Isador
Colony, Elizabeth
Hierholzer, Carl O.
Wikel, Henry H.
Wilson, Agnes W.

Teachers-in-Training

Duntze, Catherine, English
Hennelly, Mary F., History
Kemlo, Elizabeth W., English
Scudder, Sara, Biology

MORRIS HIGH SCHOOL.

*Denbigh, John H., Principal.
Ackerly, Jennie
Althaus, Amalie
Althaus, Edward
*Ames, Jessie T.
Andrews, Grace
Appel, Frank J.
Armand, Emma C.
*Avent, John M.
Baer, Dena
Ballard, Charles C.
Barnum, Grace E.
*Bates, Abby B.
*Bates, Thomas S.
Bergman, Morris L.
*Bogart, Elmer E.
*Bogart, Sarah H.
*Bourne, Mary J.
Brackett, Mary M.
*Brand, Josephine
*Bridgman, Anne T.
*Bryant, Mrs. Emma B.
Burt, Clara M.
Butler, Evelyn M.
*Carey, Alice M.
Carleton, Bessie G.
*Carr, Agnes
*Clarke, Helen MacG.
Cohen, Samuel
*Constantine, Harriet L.
*Cutler, Sanford L.
*Davis, Josie A.
*Diedrich, Marie M.
*Ernst, Frederic
*Evans, Austin H.
*Falk, Mrs. Anna A.
Foster, Harold E.
Franke, Clara E.
*Fraser, Effie
Freestone, Mary C.
Gaylord, Harriet E.
Gilmour, Emily J.
Hagar, Etta M.
Hathaway, Bertha F.
*Hazen, Louise C.
Heikes, Irving A.
*Hixon, Kate B.
*Horwitz, Lillian
*Howell, Logan D.
Jablonower, Benjamin
Joslin, Jennie M.
*Kellogg, Raymond N.
*Knox, Charlotte G.
*Knowlton, Mary E.
Konerman, Helene V.
*Kroeber, Elsbeth
*Landau, Laura
*Leighton, Margarette M.
*Leuchs, Fritz A. H.
*Lewis, Arthur C.
Lippert, Marie
Look, Samuel M.
*Mann, Paul B.
*Matthews, Archibald J.
Elkau, Herman M.
Emmons, Fred E.
*Lanz, Ida B.
*Mendum, Georgiana
*Miller, Charles A.
Miller, Myrtle H.
*Morse, Elizabeth E.
Muller, Ada H.
*Munro, Kate M.
*Mussey, Dela P.
*Normile, Mary
*O'Rourke, Annie F.
*Palmer, Anna M.
*Parker, Jacob
*Parker, Margaret B.
*Peabody, James E.
*Pulvermacher, Dolores
Pyle, Willard R.
*Pyne, Henry R.
*Read, Edith
*Scharff, Violette E.
Schaumloeffel, John H.
Schieb, Richard
Schoedde, Emma J.
Schlosber, Samuel
*Schoenrock, Hedwig
Schmidt, Mabel Pearson
*Scott, Cora A.
Scudder, John O.
Scully, Teresa M.
Staelin, Leonie E.
*Shannahan, Willard D.
*Shultz, Birl E.
*Skeele, Otis C.
Smith, Donald E.
Sohon, Michael D.
*Spencer, Estella
*Story, Helen M.
Strayer, Franklin R.
*Surrey, Frank M.
Swartout, Caroline H.
*Theobald, Jacob, Jr.
*Thompson, Annie S.
Tilley, Lydia L.
*Tracey, Edwin S.
Trimble, Louise M.
Van Allen, Katherine C.
Vanderbilt, Grace W.
Van Santvoord, Mrs. Alice G.
Volkhausen, William
Wahl, Emanuel M.
*White, Fred C.
Willams, Edward M.
Williams, Sarah P.
*Winslow, Isabel G.
Wohlfarth, Amelia

First Assistants
Althaus, Edward
Bates, Abby B.
Davis, Josie A.
Heikes, Irving A.
Peabody, James E.
Pyle, Willard R.
Sohon, Michael D.

BY DEPARTMENTS

Ancient Languages Department
Davis, Josie A., Head of Department.
Bogart, Elmer E.
Bogart, Sarah H.
Carr, Agnes
Constantine, Harriet L.
Cutler, Sanford L.
Evans, Austin H.
Fraser, Effie
Pyne, Henry R.
Shannahan, Willard R.

Biology Department
Peabody, James E., Head of Department.
Hixon, Kate B.
Kroeber, Elsbeth
Read, Edith
Vanderbilt, Grace W.

Chemistry Department
Sohon, Michael D., Head Teacher

Clerical Assistants
Brackett, Mary M.
Scully, Theresa
Van Santvoord, Alice G.
O'Rourke, Anne F.

Commercial Branches Department
Williams, Edward M., Head of Department.
Cohn, Samuel
Jacobia, Spencer P.
Volkhausen, William

Domestic Science Department
Story, Helen M.

Drawing Department.
Mussey, Dela P.
Ames, Jessie T.
Morse, Elizabeth
Parker, Margaret B.
Spencer, Estella
VanAllen, Katherine C.

English Department
Foster, Harold E., Head of Department.
Avent, John M.
Ballard, Charles C.
Ernst, Frederic
Falk, Anna A.
Gaylord, Harriet E.
Howell, Logan D.
Knox, Charlotte G.
Knowlton, Mary E.
Look, Samuel M.
Matthews, Archibald J.
Mendum, Georgiana
Muller, Ada H.
Normile, Mary
Schlosberg, Samuel
Trimble, Louise M.
Williams, Sarah B.
Munro, Kate M.
Schmidt, Mabel Pearson

Elocution Department
Bates, Thomas S.
Kellogg, Raymond N.

French Department
Diedrich, Marie M., Head of Department.
Armand, Emma C.
Carlton, Bessie G.
Bryant, Emma B.
Konerman, Helen V.
Lanz, Ida B.
Schoedde, Emma J.
Scharff, Violette

German Department
Althaus, Edward, Head of Department.
Althaus, Amelie
Appel, Frank J.
Franke, Clara E.
Leuchs, Fritz A. H.
Lippert, Marie P.
Scheib, Richard
Schoenrock, Hedwig
Swartout, Caroline H.
Tilley, Lydia L.
Wahl, Emanuel M.
Wohlfarth, Amelia
Staehlin, Leonie E.

History Department
Bates, Abby B., Head of Department.

Andrews, Grace
Baer, Dena M.
Bourne, Mary J.
Bridgeman, Anna T.
Carey, Alice M.
Thompson, Annie S.
White, Fred C.

Laboratory Assistants
Jablonower, Benjamin
Schaumloeffel, John

Librarian
Hathaway, Bertha F.

Mathematics Department
Heikes, Irving A., Head of Department.
Ackerly, Jennie.
Bergman, Morris L.
Clarke, Helen MacG.
Gilmour, Emily
Hazen, Louise C.
Joslin, Jennie M.
Landau, Laura
Leighton, Margarette
Lewis, Arthur C.
Miller, Myrtle H.
Scott, Cora A.
Theobald, Jacob
Winslow, Isabel G.
*Brand, Josephine
Elkar, Herman M.

Music Department
Tracy, Edwin S., Head of Department.
Palmer, Anna M.
Reynolds, Gerald

Physical Training Department
Skeele, Otic C., Head Teacher
Barnum, Grace E.
Butler, Evelyn M.
Freeston, Mary C.
Parker, Jacob
Pulvermacher, Dolores

Physics Department
Pyle, Willard R.
Burt, Clara M.
Scudder, John C.
Strayer, Franklin R.
Emmons, Fred E.

Physiography Department
Miller, Charles A., Head of Department.
Surrey, Frank M.

Stenography Department.
Hagar, Etta M.
Horwitz, Lillian

NEWTOWN HIGH SCHOOL.

Baldwin, Jessie M.
Bedell, Julia I.
Book, Arthur E.
Briggs, Larry
Bryant, Grace
Clinton, Emma A.
Collins, Catherine
Craft, Anna W.
Crooche, Maxwell A.
Eggleston, Charlotte
Gomph, Anna M.
Grant, Alma M.
Gross, Irene
Hewins, Nellie P.
Hills, Caroline M.
Kingsbury, George H.
Larsh, Charles H.
McAuliffe, Anna M.
McMahon, Kathryn
Marshall, Agnes M.
Meras, Albert A.
Messenger, Leslie
Miller, Maude E.
Morris, Mary F.
Nicholas, Clyde B.
Peck, Fannie C.
Powers, Minnie M.
Preston, Helen N.
Putney, Edith N.
Radin, Max
Rogers, Cora M.
Seeber, Elizabeth
Schmidt, Carl G.
Shanley, Mary E.
Shaw, Adele M.
Slater, Henry B.
Smith, Charles M.
Swenson, Celeste C.
Wells, Nellie E.
White, Cornelia B.
White, Ruth E.
Woodruff, Frank E.
*Zerban, Alex. H. W.
Valentine, C. I.
Machay, Catherine

BY DEPARTMENTS

Commercial Department
Book, Arthur E.
Hills, Caroline M., Chairman
Larsh, Chas. H.
Nichols, Clyde B.
Peck, Fannie C.
Slater, Henry B.
Smith, Chas. M.

Domestic Art Department
Grant, M. Alma

Domestic Science Department
Smith, Maud

Drawing Department
Crafft, Anna W.
Gardner, Gertrude

English Department
Baldwin, Jessie M.
Gross, Irene
Marshall, Agnes M.
Rogers, Cora M.
Shanley, Mary E.
Shaw, Adele M., Chairman
White, Ruth E.

French and Spanish Department
Clinton, Emma A.
Meras, Albert A., Chairman

German Department
Miller, Maude E.
Seeber, Elizabeth
Wells, Nellie P.
White, Cornelia B.
Zerban, Alex H., Chairman

History Department
Briggs, Larry
Gomph, Anna M.
Preston, Helen C., Chairman

Joinery and Mechanical Drawing Department
Messenger, Leslie

Latin Department
Radin, Max, First Assistant
Swenson, Celeste C.

Library
Bedell, Julia I.

Mathematics Department
Eggleston, Charlotte
Powers, Minnie M., Chairman
Putney, Edith M.
Woodruff, Frank E.

Music Department
Valentine, Chas. I.

Office Assistant
Bryant, Grace
Mackay, Catherine

Oratory Department
Collins, Catherine

Physical Training Department
Croohe, Maxwell A.
McMahon, Kathryn

Science Department
Hewins, Nellie P.
Kingsbury, Geo. H., Sr. Rep.
McAuliffe, Anna E.
Morris, Mary F.

RICHMOND HILL HIGH SCHOOL.

Allen, Ralph W.
Atwater, John C.
Barber, Sara M.
Beard, Stella S.
Beers, Florence E.
Burrage, Myra Allen
Chapin, Henry E.
*Chapin, Jennie E.
Clough, Jessie L.
*Emery, Stephen
Failor, I. N.
*Finnigan, James J.
*Flint, Arthur H.
*Forbes, Abby Beal
*Gammon, Montague
*Gaston, Charles Robert
*Golde, Margaret D.
Greene, Lillian L.
*Henderson, Royal L.
*Hubbard, Ruth E.
*Johnson, Estelle M.

*Kulburn, Florence M.
*Klein, Joseph J.
*Knapp, Annie M.
Lambert, Marcus B.
*Landers, Leland L.
*Leete, Gertrude M.
*Lent, Suzanne B.
Manfred, Maud E.
Relph, Marion F.
*Richardson, Marion G.
*Root, Eva R.
Stewart, Charles A.
*Stilson, William E.
*Trowbridge, Cornelia R.
*Valentine, Morris C.
*Voorhees, Sophia
Wortmann, Johanna C.

BY DEPARTMENTS.

Ancient Languages Department
Beers, Florence E.
Johnson, Estella M.
Voorhees, Sophia

Biology Department.
Henderson, Royal L.
Valentine, Morris C.

Commercial Branches Department
Hubbard, Ruth E.
Kilburn, Florence M.
Klein, Joseph J.
Stewart, Charles A.

Drawing Department
Allen, Ralph W.
Clough, Jessie L.
Flint, Arthur H.

Elocution Department
Barber, Sara M.

English Department.
Beard, Stella S.
Forbes, Abby Beal
Gaston, Charles Robert
Lent, Suzanne B.
Root, Eva R.
Trowbridge, Cornelia R.

French Department
Finnigan, James J.

German Department
Burrage, Myra Allen
Golde, Margaret D.
Lambert, Marcus B.
Manfred, Maude E.
Wortmann, Johanna C.

History and Economics Department
Knapp, Annie M.
Leete, Gertrude M.

Mathematics Department
Landers, Leland L.
Emery, Stephen
Relph, Marion F.
Stilson, William E.

Music Department
Greene, Lillian L.

Physical Science and Chemistry Department
Atwater, John C.

Physical Training Department
Chapin, Jennie E.
Gammon, Montague

Physiography Department
Chapin, Henry E.

Shorthand and Typewriting Department
Richardson, Marion G.

STUYVESANT HIGH SCHOOL.

*Von Nardroff, Ernest R., Principal.
*Andrews, Richard M.
*Augsbury, Earl S.
*Baier, Joseph G.
Batt, David
Battey, Lewis B.
Bedford, Edgar A.
Beha, Joseph L.
*Brandau, George G.
*Breckenridge, William E.
*Bright, Robert A.
*Brownlee, Raymond B.
*Bruce, Murray
*Brundage, Milton B.
Chatfield, William A.
*Cheney, Thomas C.
Chrystall, Maurice M.
Clark, John P.
*Cooley, George E.
Corbett, Joseph S.
*Cornell, Charles E.
*Davidoff, Henry
Dorfman, Waldemar K.
Downey, Frank
Dunbar, William F.
*Durkee, Ernest S.
*Ellard, Charles H.
*Elmer, Clement G.
*Fink, Frederick W.
*Fisher, Philip
*Foster, Walter E.
*Fritz, Henry E.
*Fuller, Robert W.
*Gage, Stanley A.
*Gardner, Frank A.
Germann, Aaron
*Goldberger, Henry H.
*Goodrich, Foster
*Greenberg, Abraham B.
*Greenberg, Jacob
*Griswold, Clifford B.
*Griswold, Edward B.
*Hanford, Clarence D.
*Hein, Henry E.
*Henriques, Maurice C.
*Hingsberg, Thomas
Hollander, Edward
*Hopkins, William C.
*Jacobs, Olin M.
Johnson, Leslie A.
*Klafter, Simeon H.
*Knox, T. Harry
Korey, Abraham J.
*Law, Freederick H.
*Leavitt, William W.
*Leonard, Theodore S.
*Leventhal, Murray J.
Lipsky, Abram
Lockwood, Cornelius
*Maier, Augustus
Mankiewicz, Frank
*Mantel, Herman E.
*Marks, Lazarus E.
*Marston, James P.
Mehrtens, Henry E.
*Mersereau, Samuel F.
*Messenger, John
Mott, Howard W.
*Neumarker, John G.
Nochkes, Adolph
*Norris, John S.
O'Brien, William J.
*Page, Donald T.
Parrott, Alfred F.
*Reynolds, Frank A.
*Rodman, Bayard B.
*Ross, A. Franklin
*Sackman, Gilbert R.
San, Louis J.
Sanford, Clarence H.
*Schwarzkopf, Ernst
*Silberstein, Nathan
*Sindelar, Charles
Smith, James V.
*Smith, Seymour L.
*Smith, Walter M.
Smith, W. Palmer
*Stahl, George F.
Stapleton, Christopher E.
*Steigman, Benjamin M.
*Steinert, John B.
Stotler, Albert
*Tennant, George B.
*Uhlig, William C.
*Wallace, Minot L.
*Way, Abner P.
*Wedge, Alfred H.
*Weiser, Samuel
Whitehall, Frank M.
*Worth, William A.
*Wyman, William T.

BY DEPARTMENTS

Biology Department
Bedford, Edgar A.

Mechanical Drawing Department
Battey, Lewis B.
Gardner, Frank A.
Greenberg, Abraham B.
Knox, T. Harry
Leonard, Theodore S.
Sackman, Gilbert R.

Chemistry Department
Bright, Robert A.
Brundage, Milton B.
Ellard, Charles H.
Fuller, Robert W.
Rodman, Bayard B.
San, Louis James
Uhlig, William C.

Clerical Assistant
Batt, David (Librarian)
Chrystall, Maurice M.
Germann, Aaron
Smith, James V.

English Department
Bruce, Murray
Davidoff, Henry
Dore, Edward S.
Goldberger, Henry H.
Hein, Henry Emmo.
Korey, Abraham J.
Law, Frederick H.
Marks, Lazarus E.
Marston, James P.
Smith, W. Palmer
Stapleton, Christopher R.
Steigman, Benjamin M.
Tennant, George B.
Whitehall, Frank M.

Freehand Drawing
Chatfield, William A.
Fisher, Philip
Fritz, Henry E.

French Department
Dorfman, Waldemar K.
Greenberg, Jacob
Parrott, Alfred F.

German Department
Beha, Joseph L.
Brandau, George J.
Elmer, Clement G.
Fink, Frederick W.
Klafter, Simeon H.
Lipsky, Abram
Mankiewicz, Frank
Mantel, Herman E.
Neumarker, John
Nochkes, Adolph
Norris, John S.
Weiser, Samuel

History Department
Dunbar, William F.
Ross, A. Franklin

Latin Department
Foster, Walter E.
Leavitt, William M.
Reynolds, Frank H.
Wallace, Minot L.
Wedge, Alfred H.

Manual Arts Department
(Metal Working)
Gage, Stanley A.
Griswold, Clifford B.
Schwarzkopf, Ernst
Smith, Seymour L.
Smith, Walter M.
Wyman, William T.
(Wood Working)
Goodrich, M. Foster
Griswold, Edward D.
Hanford, Clarence D.
Hingsberg, Thomas
Mehrtens, Henry E.
Mersereau, Samuel F.
Messenger, John
Stahl, George F.
Steinert, John B.
Stotler, Albert
Worth, William A.

Mathematics Department
Andrews, Richard M.
Augsbury, Earl
Breckenridge, William E.
Cheney, Thomas Clyde
Clark, John P.
Corbett, Joseph S.
Cornell, Charles F.
Durkes, Ernest S.
Henriques, Maurice C.
Hollander, Edward
Leventhal, Murray J.
Marston, Charles W.
O'Brien, William J.
Page, Donald T.
Silberstein, Nathan
Sindelar, Charles

Music Department
Downey, Frank

Physical Training Department
Cooley, George E.
Maier, Augustus
Way, Abner P.

Physics Department
Baier, Joseph G.
Brownlee, Raymond B.
Jacobs, Olin M.
Johnson, Leslie A.
Lockwood, Cornelius W.
Mott, Howard M.
Sanford, Clarence H.

WADLEIGH HIGH SCHOOL.

*Bacon, Helen E.
*Barrett, Martha
Barrett, Miss M. B.
Barton, Rose M.
Bass, Bertha
Beach, Mary R.
Beare, Cornelia
Beckwith, Frances A.
*Bennett, Ray
*Blair, Elizabeth E.
Blenker, Anna C.
*Blumenstock, J. Lewis
*Bowman, Cora M.
*Bruce, Grace A.
*Bruere, Alice H.
Bugbee, Harriet C.
Burchard, Anna S.
Cahill, Margaret
*Cameron, Walter S.
Carter, Mary K.
Case, Florence L.
Cassett, Edith
Cavallier, Emilie
Churchill, Martha B.
Clark, Martha M.
*Clendenin, William W.
Colburn, Mary P.
*Coman, Caroline
*Cornish, Robert H.
Crane, Elizabeth
Cremins, Julia C.
Davenport, Margery
*Davis, Alice
*Davis, Genevieve C.
Delano, Sally N.
Denis, Bertha
Dike, Crnelia A.
*Dike, Margaret L.
Dobbin, Christine M.
*Doty, Eleanor S.
*Dowden, Florence A.
Drake, R. W.
Eastman, Marjorie M.
Elliot, Lilian M.
*Ford, Jessie F.
*Fry, Rose L.
Gano, Lina E.
*Gavin, Helen
*George, Auguste
Gibson, J. Stewart
Goodrich, Martha N.
*Greiff, Lottie
*Haefelin, Fanny J.
Haney, Jennie Prudence
*Harris, Gertrude B.
*Harris, Mary E.
Harris, Sadie
Hart, Clara Orvis
Hermann, Hattie
*Hermans, Florence
*Henry, Margaret Y.
Hervey, Mary B.
Hicks, Clara K.
Hilker, Heding W. D.
*Hobbs, Alice E.
*Hodges, Archibald L.
Horner, Charlesanna
Houston, Jessie
*Hovey, Horace M.
Howard, Charlotte B.
Hugmeier, Charles
Jackson, Alice R.
*Judd, Samuel E.
*Judge, Anna G.
Keen, J. R.
*Kelsey, Louise H.
Kelsey, Lucile F.
King, Elizabeth E.
*Kupfer, Elsie M.
Lapatinkof, Paula
*Lenz, George J.
Loekee-Henry, Anna W.
*McVay, Anna Pearl
Marsh, Bessie K.
Martin, Harriet
Mayer, Anne S.
McBride, Elinor
McDowell, Florence
*McMiller, Florence
Meserve, Elizabeth
Middleton, Florence
Minor, Marie L.
*Morrow, Julia M.
Moulton, Frances
*Murray, Jennie E.
Nammock, Elizabeth F.
Norwood, Claretta
Osborn, L. N.
Petrie, Jean DeE.
Potter, Mary G.
Reynolds, Ione A.
Robinson, Alice M.
*Rodman, Henrietta
Roessler, Nellie Lloyd
Ross, Helen
*Rowe, Dr. Stuart H.
Royce, S. Grace
*Russell, Helen G.
Saltzberg, Florence B.
Sanial, Marie L.
Schulz, Bertha
Seidensticker, Clara
Sesso, Pauline
*Sheely, Jan Van D.
*Smith, Franklin H.
Spier, Katherine A.
Stone, M. Grace

*Stoner, Priscilla G.
*Strasburger, Bertha
Sweeney, Helen M.
*Syrus, Louis Charles
*Taylor, Jane I.
*Taylor, Miriam L.
*Tefft, Mary B.
Thompson, Louise
Thomson, Myrtle E.
Tweedy, Grace B.
Underwood, E. S.
Van Vliet, Jessie L.
Vincent, Blanche E.
Watt, Helen S.
White, Emma W.
*Womack, Mary D.
*Wood, Elizabeth C.
Woodward, Adele M.
*Zick, Dr. Henry

BY DEPARTMENTS

Biology Department

Gavin, Miss
Hicks, Miss
Kupfer, Miss
Loeke-Henry, Dr.
Meserve, Miss
Middleton, Miss
Minor, Miss
Sanial, Miss
Tweedy, Miss, Laboratory Asst.
Watt, Miss
Womack, Miss
Woodhull, Miss, Tchr. in Training

Clerical Assistants

Beaton, Miss
Grove, Miss
Scheibe, Miss

Domestic Art and Science Department

Dike, Miss M.
Foy, Miss

Drawing Department

Blenker, Miss
Carter, Miss
Crane, Miss
Cremins, Miss
Davis, Miss G. V.
Drake, Miss
Hobbs, Miss
Ross, Miss

English Department

Bacon, Miss
Barton, Miss
Beare, Miss
Cahill, Miss
Colburn, Miss
Fremery, Mrs. de
Dike, Miss C. A.
Doty, Miss
Eastman, Miss
Eaton, Miss
Elliot, Miss
Ford, Mrs.
Jackson, Miss
Keen, Mrs.
Kelsey, Miss
King, Miss
McDowell, Miss
Martin, Miss
Morrow, Miss
Murray, Miss
Osborn, Miss
Saltzberg, Miss
Stoner, Miss
Sweeny, Miss
White, Miss

French Department

Cavallier, Mme.
George, Mr.
Goodrich, Miss
Hilborn, Miss, Tchr. in Training
Horner, Miss
Hugnenin, Mr.
Schulz, Miss
Syrus, Mr.
Tweedy, Miss
Vincent, Miss
Woodward, Miss

German Department

Haefelin, Miss
Harris, Miss G. B.
Hilke, Miss
Lapatinkof, Miss
Leidensticker, Miss
Lenz, Mr.
Sesso, Miss
Schreiber, Miss, Tchr. in Training
Thompson, Miss L.

History Department

Barrett, Miss M. E.
Bass, Miss
Beckwith, Miss
Bennett, Mr.
Blumenstock, Mr.
Davis, Miss A.
Gano, Miss
Haney, Mrs.
Sheely, Miss
Taylor, Miss
Thomson, Miss
Wood, Miss
Youngham, Miss, Tchr. in Training

Latin Department

Beach, Miss
Case, Miss
Churchill, Miss
Clark, Miss
Delano, Miss
Fox, Miss, Tchr. in Training
Henry, Miss
Hodges, Mr.
Howard, Miss
Judd, Mr.
McBride, Miss
Mac Voy, Miss
Nammock, Miss
Roessler, Mrs.
Royce, Miss
Stone, Miss
Van Vliet, Miss

Mathematics Department

Bowman, Miss
Bruce, Miss
Bugbee, Miss
Burchard, Miss
Coman, Miss
Deenis, Miss
Gerschauck, Miss (Teacher i Training)
Goertz, Miss (Teacher in Train ing)
Harris, Miss M. E.
Harris, Miss S.
Hart, Miss
Hermann, Miss
Houston, Miss
Hovey, Mr.
Kelsey, Miss L. H.
McMillen, Miss
Mayer, Miss
Norwood, Miss
Reynolds, Miss
Robinson, Miss
Smith, Miss
Strasburyer, Miss
Underwood, Miss

Music Department

Barrett, Miss M.
Blair, Miss
Judge, Miss

Physics and Chemistry Departmen (Physics)

Bruere, Miss
Cameron, Mr.
Cassett, Miss, Laboratory Assistant
Cornish, Mr.
Greiff, Miss, Laboratory Assistan

(Chemistry)

Gibson, Mr.
Hermans, Miss
Russell, Miss

Physiography Department

Clendenin, Mr.
Taylor, Miss M. S.
Tefft, Mrs.

Physical Training Department

Dobbins, Miss
Hervey, Miss
Marsh, Miss
Moulton, Miss
Petrie, Miss
Potter, Dr.

Teachers in Training

Fox, Etta B.
Gerschauck, Celia
Goertz, Matilda
Hilborn, Rita
Schreiber, Emma F.
Woodhull, Mildred

WASHINGTON IRVING HIGH SCHOOL.

Adams, A. Isabelle
Alexander, Elizabeth W.
*Alley, M. Ida
Allyn, Louise
Ammerman, S. Lewis
Annett, Sarah E.
*Arndt, Emma
Arnowitz, M. Leon
Averill, Ethel H.
Barberis, Eligo G.
Barnard, Julia E.
Barnett, Sarah E.
Barron, Honora
Barry, Loretta
Bassett, Elizabeth W.
*Beach, Jessie A.
Beck, Alga M.
*Belcher, Frances S.

Katz, Henry D.
Keller, Hermina
Kemna, Charlotte
Kinnan, Madeline
Kivlen, Maude D.
Klees, C. Mathilde
Kraker, Goldie
Lacey, Bertha J.
Lambert, Sophie W.
Langdon, Amanda
Langdon, Ruth J.
Lawton, Mary A.
LeBel, Emilie M.
Levins, Julia M.
Levy, Henry
Linden, Mary V.
Logue, Annie E.
Longnecker, Anna B.
Loos, Richard F.
*Lowd, Emma F.
Loring, Jacob M.
Marshall, J. Adelaide
*Mattfeld, Wilhelm
*McAndrew, William
McCain, Blanche
McCain, Maude
*McCutcheon, H. Louise
McGowin, Margaret O.
McIntire, Ruby C.
McKenna, Mary
McQuade, Rose M.
*Meyenberg, Amelia
Mills, Emily W.
*Molwitz, Ernestine J.
Mooney, Lawrence
Morrissey, Alice
Muhleman, Harriet
Mullen, Rosemary
Neidlinger, William
Newcomb, Florence A.
Nightingale, Eleanor M.
*Nightingale, Ida E.
Nolan, Grace E.
Northrop, Cora E.
Oller, Marie
*O'Neill, Alice M.
*O'Neill, Edith F.
Orr, Ella J.
Pierce, Alice M.
Pinkham, Martha
Pintler, Harriet
Pond, Harriet
Pownall, Edythe M.
Pratt, Winifred
Quigg, Helen T.
Ray, Medora L.
Reynolds, Alice R.
Richards, Ellen M.
Riordan, Elizabeth
Robinson, Deborah P.
*Roche, Elizabeth A.
Rochester, M. Muriel
Roe, Ada
Roll, Rose
Rostetter, Alice
Ryan, Elizabeth G.
*Sage, Lillian B.
Sandman, Ida
Scales, Carrie L.
Shulman, Morris
*Skinner, E. Mabel
*Slack, Earl B.
Slater, Florence
Smith, Frances A.
Smith, Georgina M.
Snider, Annie M.
*Sommerfield, Alfred
Stone, Bertha R.
*Strum, Nellie A.
Tamboise, Madeleine
Thompson, Christina M.
Thompson, Dora R.
Thorndike, Mildred L.
*Truckenbrodt, Lewis
Tuthill, Mary
Tuttle, Edith M.
Waller, Phoebe M.
Warr, F. Louise
Watters, Dorothy
Weisner, Harry L.
Weiss, Alma
Welt, Ida
Wessa, Ida
*Willard, Florence
Willard, Meriel W.
Williams, S. Elizabeth
Winward, Leonora
Wood, Mary M.
Zagat, Lillie
Zaisser, Matilda

By Departments

Biology Department

Cohen, Lena, Lab. Assistant.
Dithridge, Louise M.
Hamilton, Mary S.
Lambert, Sophia W.
Mullen, Rosemary
Pintler, Harriet
Sage, Lillian B., **Chairman**
Slater, Florence

Bookbinding Department

Holran, Rose A., **Chairman**

Clerical Assistants

Bush, Mary F.
Gulliver, Barbara A.
Kraker, Goldie
LeBel, Emilie M.
Longenecker, Anna B.
Nolan, Grace E.

Commercial Department

Arnowitt, M. Leon
Berger, William H.
Falk, Louis J.
Fox, S. Wordsworth
Freeman, Benjamin
Freeman, Mary L.
Gallagher, Margaret F.
Goldsmith, Morgan J.
Goodman, Annie E.
Greenstein, Max
Hamilton, Mary S.
Hinds, George K.
Hayward, William R., **Chairman**
Katz, Henry D.
Langdon, Amanda
Levy, Henry
McCain, Blanche
McCain, Maude
O'Neil, Alice M.
O'Neill, Edith F.
Shulman, Morris
Skinner, E. Mabel
Sommerfield, Alfred

Declamation Department

Copeland, Lillian S.
*Nightingale, Ida E.
Nightingale, Eleanor M., **Chairman**
Pinkham, Martha G.
Ryan, Elizabeth G.

Domestic Art Department

Barron, Honora
Consalus, Frances
Dunford, Honora A.
Fueslin, Irma
Johnson, Harriet M. B.
Kemna, Charlotte

Levins, Julia M.
Logue, Annie E.
McGowin, Margaret O.
Reynolds, Alice R.
Richards, Ellen M.
Thompson, Christina M.
Willard, Meriel W., Chairman

Domestic Science Department
Crane, Emma H.
Dean, Nellie
Dowd, Mary T.
Jameson, Jennie D.
Pond, Harriet
Roe, Ada
Willard, Florence, Chairman

Drawing Department
Adams, A. Isabelle
Averill, Ethel H.
Barnard, Julie E.
Booth, Mary S.
Cheney, Janet D., Chairman
Cowan, Georgia C.
Daley, Helen S.
Ferris, Laura C.
Gurnee, Marie E.
Hillman, Mercy A.
Hurlbut, Martha A.
Lacey, Bertha J.
Newcomb, Florence A.
Pratt, Winifred M.
Tuthill, Mary

English Department
Lowd, Emma F., Chairman
Barry, Loretta
Bergamini, Rachel
Bressler, Helen B.
Bussard, Gertrude E.
Cohen, Helen L.
Davis, Martha M.
Doherty, Helen F.
Douglas, Charles H. J.
Edge, Florence M.
Ferro, Helene
Gere, Lovisa B.
Hastings, Elinor
Hodgkins, Georgiana
Hubert, Marie R.
Johnson, Mary H.
Keller, Hermina H.
Kivlen, Maude D.
Lawton, Mary A.
Marshall, J. Adelaide
Mills, Emily W.
McIntire, Ruby C.
Muhleman, Harriet
Northrop, Cora E.
Oller, Marie
Pierce, Alice R.
Pownall, Edythe M.
Quigg, Helen T.
Rostetter, Alice
Rochester, M. Muriel
Smith, Frances A.
Snider, Annie M.
Strum, Nellie A.
Thorndike, Mildred L.
Thompson, Dora R.
Tuttle, Edith M.
Waller, Phoebe M.
Wood, Mary M.

French and Italian Department
Blackwell, Nannie G., Chairman
Boyd, Olive A.
Barberis, Eligio G.
Bouvard, Germaine
Chilcott, Clio M.
Goudal, Emilie
Guthrie, Kenneth S.
McCutcheon, H. Louise
Ray, Medora L.
Smith, Georgina M.
Tamboise, Madeleine
Willams, S. Elizabeth

German Department
Arndt, Emma
Buttner, Frieda
Crandall, Ernest L., Chairman
Edwards, Minna H.
Eltzner, Dorothea
Fette, Elizabeth W.
Hellin, Lilian
Hochheimer, Rita
Loos, Richard F.
Molwitz, Ernestine J.
Warr, F. Louise
Weiss, Alma
Weisner, Harry L.

History Department
Galloway, Ida G., Chairman
Bassett, Elizabeth W.
Belcher, Frances S.
Chapman, Lena M.
Goertner, Rose
Hall, Caroline D.

Latin Department
Guthrie, Grace
Hopkins, Frances S.
Wessa, Ida, Chairman

Library Assistants
Alexander, Elizabeth W.
Annett, Sarah E., Chairman

Library Practice
Dodd, Helen W.
Fritz, Louise P., Chairman

Mathematics Department
Beach, Jessie A., Chairman
Dolgenas, Jacob A.
Eaton, Clara C.
McKenna, Mary
McQuade, Rose H.
Roll, Rose
Zagat, Lillie

Music Department
Mattfeld, William, Chairman
Caron, Emma C.,
Mooney, Lawrence
Neidlinger, William

Physical Training Department
Barnett, Sarah E., Chairman
Beck, Alga M.
Garlock, LuNette M.
Gill, Lulu G.
Morrissey, Alice
Sandman, Ida
Scales, Carrie L.
Watters, Dorothy

Physics, Chemistry and Physiography Department
Alley, M. Ida
Ammerman, S. Lewis
Hayner, Burton A.
Slack, Earl B., Chairman
Welt, Ida.

Placement and Investigation Assistant.
Gittoe, Ethel T.

Stenography Department
Allyn, Louise
Boothby, Nellie M.
Catren, Ida M.
deMers, Adrienne V.
Ennis, Agnes A.
Frank, Charles L.
Kinnan, Madeline
Klees, C. Mathilde
Langdon, Ruth J.
Linden, Mary V.
Loring, Jacob M.
Meyenberg, Amelia
Orr, Ella J.
Riordan, Elizabeth
Robinson, Deborah P.
Roche, Elizabeth A., Chairman
Stone, Bertha R.
Truckenbrodt, Lewis

TEACHERS CLASSIFIED BY DEPARTMENTS

DEPARTMENT OF ACCOUNTS

Commercial High School
Cowles, Clarence E.
Corliss, Charles E.
Anderson, Woodford D.
Harman, George W.
Konheim, Jerome
Mechan, William.
Nathan, Arthur
Raynor, Gilbert J.
Scarborough, Andrew J.

BIOLOGY DEPARTMENTS

Bay Ridge High School
Bruckman, Louis
Baggs, Martha
Thompson, Martha

Bryant High School
Carter, Bertha F. (Botany)
Swett, Carolyn P. (Biology)
Lewis, Mr., Chairman.
Hanna, Mr.
Hughes, C. E.
Kaine, Mr.
Richardson, Mr.
Wood, Mr.
Pasternak, Mr., (Sub.)

Bushwick
Johnson, Julius M., Chairman.
Conley, William E.
Southwell, Etta E.
Stanton, Anna E.

High School of Commerce
Eddy, Walter H., Chairman and First Assistant.
Barbour, William C.
Benedict, Ralph C.
Clough, Harvey B.
Firman, Arthur B.
Grant, Willis H.
Hahn, Clarence W.

Commercial High School
Donovan, Walter. J.
Greenberg, Benjamin C., First Assistant.
Puoero, Michael
Ratner, C. Hyman

Curtis High School
Grout, Abel J., First Assistant.
Conroy, Mary S.
Dowell, Philip
Fisher, Ruth B.

De Witt Clinton High School
Hunter, George W.
Barber, Harry C.
Bedford, Edgar A.
Hastings, George F.
Donaldson, George P.
McCarthy, John D.
Hewitt, George E.
Morse, Charles F.
Osborne, Ralph
Sharpe, Richard W.
Wheat, Frank

Erasmus Hall High School
King, Cyrus A., Head of Department
Hurty, Kathleen
Marsden, N. S.
Peace, Lillian B.
Rexford, Frank A.
Tompkins, Elizabeth M.
Tredick, Helen F.
Vedder, Estella M.
Young, Charlotte S.
Young, Mabel A.

Evander Childs High School
Mann, Paul B., Chairman.
Merchant, Isabel L.
Pingrey, Cora E.
Young, Caroline

Flushing High School
Hood, Edward C.
Pulvermacher, William Dean

Girls' High School
Lee, Margueritee T., Head Teacher.
Bunting, Mildred B.
Byrnes, Esther F.
Dietrich, Bertha K.
Goodrich, Charlotte
Hanks, Lena T.
Hoffman, Margie E.
Rae, Anne M.
Steers, Edna L.

Jamaica High School
Linville, Henry R., Chairman.
Holmes, Ella A.

Julia Richman High School
Carpenter, Idelette
McLane, Fannie Moulton
Topp, Emily

M. T. High School
Braman, Mary L.
Everson, Anna E.
Hunt, Arthur E.
Lasswell, Arthur C.
Roeth, Natalie S.
Scudder, Sara (Teacher in Training)
Stone, Maudie L.
Walker, Ruth N.
Wolcott, Henry G.

Morris High School
Peabody, James E., Head of Department.
Hixon, Kate B.
Kroeber, Elsbeth
Read, Edith
Vanderbilt, Grace W.

R. H. High School
Henderson, Royal L.
Valentine, Morris C.

Stuyvesant High School
Bedford, Edgar A.

Wadleigh High School
Kupfer, Miss
Gavin, Miss
Hicks, Miss
Loeke-Henry, Dr.
Meserve, Miss
Middleton, Miss
Minor, Miss
Sanial, Miss
Watt, Miss
Womack, Miss
Tweedy, Miss, Laboratory Asst.
Woodhull, Miss., Tchr. in Training.

Washington Irving High School
Cannon, Gerturde L.
Cohen, Lena (Laboratory Assistant)
Dithridge, Louise M.
Hamilton, Mary S.
Lambert, Sophia W.
Mullen, Rosemary
Pintler, Harriet
Sage, Lillian B. (Chairman)
Slater, Florence

BOOKBINDING

Washington Irving High School
Holran, Rose A., Chairman.
Freeman, Sarah J. (Sub.)

CLERICAL ASSISTANTS

Bay Ridge High School
Gee, Carol C.
Sheils, Frances B.

Bryant High School
Perry, Mabel L.
Van Leuwen, Mary

Bushwick High School
Brady, John W.
Connor, Edith B.
Hooker, Theodora H.
Green John P. (Algebra & Exp.)

De Witt Clinton High School
Margolies, Fred B., Secretary.
Greenberg, Michael
Kaveny, Martin
O'Connor, John P.

Far Rockaway High School
Greenburg, Sophia

Flushing High School
Sands, Mary E.

High School of Commerce
Byron, Thomas W.
Collins, John A. C.
Dunham, Franklin W.

Manual Training High School
Massonneau, Robert L., Jr.
Hertzfield, Leonore H.
Weinberger, George (Sub.)

Morris High School
Brackett, Mary M.
Scully, Theresa
Van Santvoord, Alice G.
O'Rourke, Anne F.

Newtown High School
Bryant, Grace (Chairman and Head)
Mackay, Catherine

Stuyvesant High School
Batt, David (Librarian)
Chrystall, Maurice M.
Germann, Aaron
Smith, James V.

Wadleigh High School
Benton, Miss
Grove, Miss
Scheibe, Miss

Washington Irving High School
Bush, Mary F.
Crowley, Isabelle (Sub.)
Gulliver, Barbara A.
Kraker, Goldie
LeBel, Emilie M.
Longenecker, Anna B.
Nolan, Grace E.
Gittoe, Ethel T. (Civil Service)

CHEMISTRY DEPARTMENTS

Bryant High School
Bement, Frederic

High School of Commerce
Mills, Joseph S., Chairman and First Assistant.
Bennet, R. Grant
Breakstone, W.
Flynn, Oscar R.
Walker, Claude F.
Coleman, D. F., Laboratory Assistant.

Commercial High School
Clark, John A., First Assistant
Coon, Clifford H.
Newman, Joseph

Curtis High School
McMillen, H.

De Witt Clinton High School
Whitsit, Jesse E.
Barmeyer, George H.
Broadhurst, Philip H.
Call, R. Ellsworth
Connelly, Douglas L.
Fleissner, Gustav L.
Parmelee, William J.
White, Arthur E.

Morris High School
Sohon, Michael D., Head of Department.

Richmond Hill High School
Atwater, John C.

Stuyvesant High School
Bright, Robert A.
Brundage, Milton B.
Ellard, Charles H.
Fuller, Robert W.
Rodman, Bayard B.
San, Louis James
Uhlig, William C. (Physics)
Baier, Joseph G.
Brownlee, Raymond B.
Jacobs, Olin M.
Johnson, Leslie A.
Lockwood, Cornelius W.
Mott, Howard M.
Sanford, Clarence H.

COMMERCIAL DEPARTMENTS

Bay Ridge High School
Cahill, John P.
Edelson, Emanuel M.
Gluck, Emil
Mackey, Arthur J.
Putz, Edward H.
Courtney, Bertha F.
Lewis, Edward F., Chairman.
Steinberg, Pauline

Substitutes.
Berall, Louis J.
Kaplan, A. D.
Froendt, A. H.
Greenee, Russel T., Chairman & First Assistant.
Baldwin, Edwin P.
Cohen, Harry
Guldner, C. M.
Hughes, Charles C.
Kenzier S.
Jonas, Louis
King, Melville S.
Koopman, S. Bernard
Long, R. L.
Macdonald, James (Sub)
Rogers, Charles E.
Van Deusen, Edwin H.
Van Tuyl, G. H.
Woodman, Irving L.

Bushwick
Leyenberger, H. W., Chairman
Canning, Etta M.
Conant, M. Sybil
Foley, Henry J.
Houley, Elizabeth C.
Townsend, Chas. W.
Humphries, George F.
Salmowitz, Rose L.
Auslander, Armin
Osgood, C. A.
Goldberg, Louise
Hall, Henrietta
Lundy, Edwin S.
Leibowitz, Nathan
Mayers, Lena
Miller, Charles
Nevins, Nannie R.
Rosenhaus, Maximilian

Eastern District High School
Baltz, Frank B.
Beitel, Helen S.
Bruce, W. A.
Jacobson, Walter
Lemowitz, Nathan
Loughran, Agnes
McKee, Louise
Ribber, Emma
Seamans, Mary
Unger, Gertrude

Curtis High School
Miller, Grace H.
Welsh, John C., First Assistant.
Crennan, Margaret A.
Flanagan, William
Halloran, William M.
Kerr, Frank E.
Tracy, Howard M.

Evander Childs High School
Lipschutz, Berthold, Chairman.
Altholz, Nathaniel
Klein, Anthony W.
Smith, Harriet K.

Far Rockaway High School
Belding, Albert G.
Vacancy

Flushing High School
Deihl, Frank E.
Carey, Margaret E.

Jamaica High School
Starkey, Warren L., Chairman.
Kibby, Warren J.
McNamara, Edward J.
Morrissey, Fannie A.
O'Keefe, David H.
Parker, George A.

Julia Richman High School
Filfus, Nathaniel
Goller, Gratia
Jumnefsky, Simon J.
Linker, John
Salzman, Anna

Morris High School
Williams, Edward M., Head of Department.
Cohn, Samuel
Jacobia, Spencer P.
Volkhausen, William

Newtown High School
Book, Arthur
Hills, Caroline M., Chairman.
Larsh, Charles
Nichols, Clyde B.
Slater, Henry B.
Smith, Charles M.

Richmond Hill High School
Hubbard, Ruth E.
Kilburn, Florence M.
Klein, Joseph J.
Stewart, Charles A.

Washington Irving High School
Arnowitt, M. Leon
Berger, William H.
Falk, Louis J.
Fox, S. Wordsworth
Freeman, Benjamin
Freeman, Mary L.
Gallagher, Margaret F.
Goldsmith, Morgan J.
Goodman, Annie E.
Greenstein, Max
Hamilton, Mary S.
Hinds, George K.
Hayward, William R., Chairman.

Isaacson, Gertrude (Sub.)
Katz, Henry D.
Langdon, Amanda
Levy, Henry
McCain, Blanche
McCain, Maude
O'Neil, Alice M.
O'Neill, Edith F.
Schwager, Harry (Sub.)
Shulman, Morris
Skinner, E. Mabel
Sommerfield, Alfred

DOMESTIC ART DEPARTMENTS

Bryant High School
Noble, Helen G.

Erasmus Hall High School
Doggett, Allen B., Chairman
Cameron, Alix S.
Currier, Clara L.
Herrington, Agnes M.
Merchant, Manton E.
Lovell, Katherine

Julia Richman High School
Waite, Charlotte Augusta
Walter, M. Louise

Newtown High School
Grant, Alma M.

Washington Irving High School
Barron, Honora
Consalus, Frances
Dunford, Honora A.
Fueslein, Irma
Johnson, Harriet M. B.
Kemna, Charlotte
Levins, Julia M.
Logue, Annie E.
McGowin, Margaret O.
Reynolds, Alice R.
Richards, Ellen M.
Thompson, Christina M.
Willard, Muriel W., Chairman.

DOMESTIC SCIENCE AND COOKING DEPARTMENTS

Bay Ridge High School
Perry, Maybelle P., Cooking.
Gaynor, Carrie, Cooking.

Bryant High School
McIntyre, Edith
Perkins, Fannie D.

Bushwick High School
Hoeg, Mrs.

Evander Childs High School
Low, Clara L.

Eastern District High School
Ikelheimer, Minnie

Far Rockaway High School
Vacancy

Julia Richman High School
Brockman, May E.
Maeder, Emily L

Morris High School
Story, Helen M.

M. T. High School
Girls' Shop
Brockman, Mary E.
Dickman, Mary B.
Green, Mrs. Florence
Stone, Mabel
Terrell, Lillian

Newtown High School
Smith, Maud

Washington Irving High School
Crane, Emma H.
Dean, Nellie
Dowd, Mary T.
Jameson, Jennie D.
Pond, Harriet
Roe, Ada
Willard, Florence, Chairman.

Wadleigh High School
Foy, Miss
Dike, Miss M.

DRAWING DEPARTMENTS

Bay Ridge High School
Combes, Adelaide M. W.
Hamilton, Alma L.
Radell, O'Delia

High School of Commerce
Grant, Forest, Chairman.
Carter, Raymond
Sprague, C. Hayes

Bushwick High School
Merington, Ruth, Chairman
Hutchinson, Helen S.
Bertschy, Maude
Littig, M. Josephine

Bryant High School
Price, Anna G.
Thorburn, Arty L. M. (Sub.)

Boys
Pasternak, N., Chairman.
Boyd, Mr.
Diller, Mr.
White, Mr.

Commercial High School
Greenberg, Morris
Roche, Michael P.

Curtis High School
Ostrander, Agnes

De Witt Clinton High School
Bingham, Jessie H.
Adams, Milly E.
Fox, Alice E.
Gombarts, George K.
Green, Bernard
Klein, Morris
Schwartzenbach, Peter A.
Woolley, Alice E.

Eastern District High School
Burn, Alice M.
Faulkner, Eunice F.
Henoch, S. Stella
Manahan, Mary G.
Pond, Pearl F.

Evander Childs High School
Coster, Silvie de G.
Heller, Maxwell L.
McDonald, H. Rosabel

Far Rockaway High School
Kennedy, Anna J.
Wright, Grace L.

Flushing High School
Swick, Mary S.

Jamaica High School
Epler, Alice, Chairman.
Ferris, Mary D.
Gardner, Maude, Chairman.
Jones, Emma A.
Johnston, Ina W.
Ketchum, Daisy T.
Simmons, Kate C.
Spencer, Mary
Stevenson, Beulah E.

Julia Richmand High School
Hastings, Ada L.
Lewenthal, Rebecca
Maloney, Katherine E.

Morris High School
Ames, Jessie T.
Morse, Elizabeth
Mussey, Dela P.
Parker, Margaret B.
Spencer, Estella
VanAllen, Katherine C.

Newtown High School
Craft, Anna W., Chairman.
Gardner, Gertrude

Wadleigh High School
Carter, Miss
Blenker, Miss
Crane, Miss
Cremins, Miss
Davis, Miss G. V.
Drake, Miss
Hobbs, Miss
Ross, Miss

MECHANICAL DRAWING DEPARTMENTS

M. T. High School
Abbot, Frederick B.
Coan, Charles W.
Jacobson, Harry
Mackby, Julius C.

Stuyvesant High School
Battey, Lewis B.
Gardner, Frank A.
Greenberg, Abraham B.
Howe, Charles B.
Knox, T. Harry
Leonard, Theodore S.
Sackman, Gilbert R.

FREE HAND DRAWING

M. T. High School
Beebe, Dee
Buck, Frederick (Sub.)
Frerichs, Harrison, M.D.
Menzel, Eda (Sub.)
Murphy, Margaret L.
Shinn, Victor
Wright, Mrs. Helen S.

Richmond Hill High School
Allen, Ralph W.
Clough, Jessie L.
Flint, Arthur H.

Stuyvesant High School
Chatfield, William A.
Fisher, Philip
Fritz, Henry E.

Washington Irving High School
Adams, A. Isabelle
Averill, Ethel H.
Barnard, Julia E.
Booth, Mary S.
Cheney, Janet D., Chairman
Cowan, Georgia C.
Daley, Helen S.
Dodd, Minerva K. (Sub.)
Ferris, Laura C.
Gurnee, Marie E.
Hillman, Mercy A.
Hurlbut, Martha A.
Lacey, Bertha J.
Newcomb, Florence A.
Pratt, Winifred M.
Tuthill, Mary
Whitney, Clara (Sub.)
Winward, Leonora (Sub.)

ELOCUTION DEPARTMENTS

Bay Ridge High School
Weeks, Miss Marion I.

Erasmus Hall High School
Chinnock, Florence B.
Frost, Madeline A.

Far Rockaway High School
Crim, Adelaide

Flushing High School
Klein, Margaret A.

Jamaica High School
Ward, A. W.

Julia Richman High School
Herendeen, Jane E.
Leonard, Nina V.

Morris High School
Bates, Thomas S.
Kellogg, Raymond N.

Newtown High School
Collins, Catherine

Richmond Hill High School
Barber, Sara M.

Washington Irving High School
Copeland, Lillian S.
Frame, Rachel (Sub.)
Nightingale, Eleanor M., Chairman.
Nightingale, Ida E. (Sub.)
Pinkham, Martha G.
Ryan, Elizabeth G.

DEPARTMENT OF ECONOMICS

High School of Commerce
Pugh, Alexander, Chairman and First Assistant.
Brennen, Alfred T. C.
Hall, Gamble
Peacock, Daniel L. (Sub.)

ENGLISH DEPARTMENTS

Bay Ridge High School
Bessey, Mabel A.
Coffin, Isabelle P.
Goldstein, Alexander
Harding, Helen E.
Natelson, Rachel
Phillips, Sara J.
Trench, Ruth
Wicks, Helen D.

Bryant High School
Acker, Margaret K.
Carll, Lydia A. (Elocution)
Erhardt, Helen
Heermance, Emma W.
Jones, Frances E.
Munroe, H. K., Chairman
Riblet, Mary V.
*Sunderland, Florence (on leave of absence).
Wilmot, Mabel
*Brenner, Charlotte M. (Sub.)

Boys
Fisher, Mr., Chairman.
Brill, Mr.
Buttrick, Mr.
Courtney, Mr.
Doyle, Mr.
Esselstyn, Mr.
Johnston, Mr.
Levine, Mr.
McCartney, Mr.
Munson, Mr.
Raiman, Mr.
Stebbins, Mr.
Tressler, Mr.
Hanson, Mr. (Sub.)

Bushwick High School
Semple, Dr. Lewis B., Chairman.
Batchelder, Margaret C.
Benjamin, Edith S.
Crossley, Arthur L.
Collier, Katherine B.
DeWitt, Louise L.
Gilbert, Clara M.
Hannah, Florence
Lieberman, Elias
McDonald, Milo F.
Mohan, Lucy F.
Sherman, Rose E.
Townsend, May E.
Tufts, Anne B.
Woodbury, Ella A.
Lieberman, Max
Henderson, Hazel

High School of Commerce
Heydrick, Benjamin A., Chairman and First Assistant.
Berkowitch, Louis B.
Carleton, Guy M.
Goldstein, Samuel (Sub.)
Hall, Henry M.
Lindsey, Frederick B.
McGrath, William J.
May, Alfred A.
Polly, Brirron (Sub.)
Ritt, Harold A. (Sub.)
Weinberger, George G.
Wharton, William P.
Williamson, George B. (Sub.)
Hyman, James C. (Sub.)
Knickerbocker, Edwin V.

Commercial High School
Bagenstose, Harvey L.
Braunstein, William

Lauder, Mary A.
Mastin, Florence
Moore, S. Maude
Scovill, Florence M.
Simmons, Isabel
Smith, Natalie A.
Strout, George M.
Valentine, Henry D.

Evander Childs High School
Quimby, Ernest S., Chairman.
Cohn, Louis B.
Durfee, Clayton G.
Haley, Jesse H.
Hughes, Thomas H.
Schamus, John B.
Tracy, Mary L.
Wylie, Stella M.

Far Rockaway High School
Bonfoey, Emma C.
Vacancy

Flushing High School
Read, Warren W.
Boynton, Carolyn A.
Carey, Elizabeth
Fountain, Luna A.

Girls' High School
Wendt, Cordelia, Head Teacher
Adair, Edith
Cann, Bertha
Chase, Charlotte G.
Clinton, Mrs. Fanny L.
Davis, Miss Frank L.
Holman, Mabel L.
Holmes, Abby B.
Keyes, Rowena K.
Miller, Mabel
Romaine, S. Helen
Seelman, H. Elizabeth
Seymour, Macey I.
Sprague, Almeda
St. John, Emily P.
Stone, Lulu M.
Taylor, Jeannette S.
White, Bessie R.
Witherbee, Reta

Jamaica High School
Fairley, Edwin, Chairman
Bradley, Susan M.
Brown, Adelaide W.
Hochderffer, Mary
Root, Minnie R.
Thorp, Benjamin H.

Julia Richman High School
Beck, Florence
Brooks, Mabel Frances
Herendeen, Jane E.
Hodgetts, Abbe S.
Howes, Emily
Lancaster, Bertha
Lupton, Olive Moore
Opdycke, John B.
Thomas, Lulu E.

Manual Training High School
Bates, Herbert
Bawden, Sarah E.
Bergoffen, Herman
Boole, Emily R.
Boole, Florence A.
Cambern, J. Raymond
Cotter, Julia T.
Duntze, Catherine, Teacher in Training
Elting, Mabel
Gauvran, Ethel H.
Gnade, Agnes
Hampshire, John W.
Hoffman, Mark
Kemlo, Elizabeth W., Teacher in Training
Ludwig, Augustus
Luther, Edith M.
Meneely, Dr. John H.
Meserve, Martha C.
O'Donnell, James Emmett
Peck, Emily S.
Prentis, Hally M.
Saymon, Ignatz
Taylor, Nettie
Vail, Clarence W.
Walker, Alice J.

Morris High School
Foster, Harold E., Head of Department
Avent, John M.
Ballard, Charles C.
Ernst, Frederic
Falk, Anna A.
Gaylord, Harriet E.
Howell, Logan D.
Knox, Charlotte G.
Knowlton, Mary E.
Look, Samuel M.
Matthews, Archibald J.
Mendum, Georgiana
Muller, Ada H.
Normile, Mary
Schlosberg, Samuel
Trimble, Louise M.
Williams, Sarah P.
Munro, Kate M.
Schmidt, Mabel Pearson

Newtown High School
Baldwin, Jessie M.
Gross, Irene
Marshall, Agnes
Rogers, Cora
Shanley, Mary E.
Shaw, Adele M., Chairman
White, Ruth E.

Richmond Hill High School
Beard, Stella S.
Forbes, Abby Beel
Gaston, Charles Robert
Lent, Suzanne B.
Root, Eva R.
Trowbridge, Cornelia R.

Stuyvesant High School
Bruce, Murray
Davidhoff, Henry
Dore, Edward S.
Goldberg, Henry H.
Hein, Henry Emmo.
Korey, Abraham J.
Law, Frederick H.
Marks, Lazarus E.
Marston, James P.
Smith, W. Palmer
Stapleton, Christopher R.
Steigman, Benjamin M.
Tennant, George B.
Whitehall, Frank M.

Wadleigh High School
Ford, Miss
Bacon, Miss
Barton, Miss
Beare, Miss
Cahill, Miss
Colburn, Miss
De Fremery, Mrs.
Dike, Miss C. A.
Doty, Miss C. A.
Eastman, Miss C. A.
Eaton, Miss
Elliot, Miss
Jackson, Miss
Keen, Mrs.
Kelsey, Miss
King, Miss
McDowell, Miss
Martin, Miss
Morrow, Miss
Murray, Miss
Osborn, Miss
Saltzberg, Miss
Stoner, Miss
Sweeny, Miss
White, Miss

Washington Irving High School
Lowd, Emma F., Chairman
Barry, Loretta
Bergamini, Rachel
Bressler, Helen B.
Bussard, Gertrude E.
Cohen, Helen L.
Davis, Martha M.
Doherty, Helen F.
Douglas, Charles H. J.
Edge, Florence M.
Ferro, Helene
Gere, Lovisa B.
Hastings, Elinor
Hodgkins, Georgiana
Hubert, Marie R.
Johnson, Mary H.
Keller, Hermina H.
Kivlen, Maude D.
Lawton, Mary A.
Marshall, J. Adelaide
Mills, Emily W.
McIntire, Ruby C.
Muhleman, Harriet
Northrop, Cora E.
Olle, Marie
Pierce, Alice R.
Pownall, Edythe M.
Quigg, Helen T.
Rostetter, Alice
Rochester, M. Muriel
Smith, Frances A.
Snider, Annie M.
Strum, Nellie A.
Thorndike, Mildred L.
Thompson, Dora R.
Tuttle, Edith M.
Waller, Phoebe M.
Wood, Mary M.

FRENCH DEPARTMENTS

Bay Ridge High School
Covello, Leonard
Morrill, Frances U.
Quirk, Cecile

Curtis High School
Harkness, Mme. Alma de B.

De Witt Clinton High School
Frank, Colman D.
Armand, Louis J.
Bierman, Henry
Donner, H. Montagu
Carpentier, Marius
Goldberg, Israel
Perry, Edward O.
Rosenthal, Daniel C.
Zacharie, Jean B.
Wilkins, Lawrence A.

Eastern District High School
Anderson, Mary E.
Dreyfus, Jeanne
Kuhn, Adelina
Lanz, J. M.

Erasmus Hall High School
Wight, Walter A., Chairman
Browne, Frances E.
Douglas, Clara M.
Shaw-McGill, Beatrice

Evander Childs High School
Hall, Margaret W.
Hubbard, Marion L.

Far Rockaway High School
Lanz, Lea B.

Girls' High School
Higgins, Alice, Head Teacher
Abbot, Marguerite W.
Harris, Mary O.
Lepere, Bertha B.
Wilson, Bessie D.

Julia Richman High School
Hyde, Isabella
Moscovitz, Bertha J.
Nahón, Zarita
White, Isabelle D.

Manual Training High School
Allen, John Trevette
Bachelder, Mary A.
Lamb, Dr. William W.
Maginn, Eliza M.
Klein, Leopold, Substitute

Morris Heights High School
Diedrich, Marie M., Head of Department
Armand, Emma C.
Carlton, Bessie G.
Bryant, Emma B.
Konerman, Helen V.
Lanz, Ida B.
Schoedde, Emma J.
Scharff, Violette

Newtown High School
(French and Spanish)
Clinton, Emma
Meras, Albert A., Chairman.
Roth, S.

Richmond Hill High School
Finnigan, James J.

Wadleigh High School
George, Mr.
Cavallier, Mme.
Goodrich, Miss
Horner, Miss
Huguenin, Mr.
Schulz, Miss
Syrus, Miss
Tweedy, Miss
Vincent, Miss
Woodward, Miss
Hilborn, Miss, Tchr. in Training

Washington Irving High School
(French and Italian)
Blackwell, Nannie G., Chairman
Boyd, Olive A.
Bouvard, Germaine
Chilcott, Clio M.
Goudal, Emilie
Guthrie, Kenneeth S.
McCutcheon, H. Louise
Ray, Medora L.
Smith, Georgina M.
Spiller, Susan M., Substitute
Tamboise, Madeleine
Williams, S. Elizabeth

GERMAN DEPARTMENTS

Bay Ridge High School
Avirett, Mrs. May G.
Faust, Charlotte C.
Lippner, Simon L.
Mandell, Lena
Robinson, Eva A.
Schmidt, Clare E.

Bryant High School
(Modern Languages Department)
(German)
Joseph, Myrtle J.
Schachtel, Elsie
Vincent, Charlotte, Chairman
Waldman, Mark
Lopez, Anita (also Spanish)
(French)
Gambier, Louise M.
Snow, Ella M., Chairman

Boys' High School
(Modern Languages Department)
Overholser, Mr., Chairman
Bates, Mr.
Bechert, Mr.
Cohen, Mr.
Fontaine, Mr.
Reynolds, L.
Tausk, Mr.

Bushwick High School
(Modern Languages Department)
Keener, Robert H., Chairman
Goldsmith, Elizabeth
Maloubier, Henrietta M.
Otten, Henry L.
Riegger, Elizabeth
Squires, Martha U.
Steelin, Leonie E.
Zorn, Freda
Bogle, Miss
Barrows, Tessie
Hendrich, Paul
Lingg, Amalie S.
Seaman, Mary E.
Berkowitz, Louise
O'Donnell, Agnes T.
O'Donnell, Margaret M.
Taylor, Marion L.
Dewning, Edward

High School of Commerce
(Modern Languages Department)
Roessler, Edwin W., Chairman and First Assistant
Blume, Julius
Chadwick, David, Substitute
Fedter, Bruno
Flatow, Jacob
Hartung, Ernest W.
Henin, Benj. L.
Montross, Chas. G.
O'Neil, Wm. R.
Remy, Alfred
Rochow, John P.
Skipp, Henry J.
Singanan, Leon
Skinner, Herbert C.

Commercial High School.
Barlow, William M.
Eells, Burr Gould
Hagens, Fritz
Hoffman, Alfred
Marvin, Robert B., First Asst.
Sternberg, George

Curtis High School
Shepherd, Florence D., First Assistant
Blanpied, Ethel O.
French, Linda M.
Harkness, Mme. A. de B.
Hummel, F. M.
Leonard, Howard
Stapff, Etta
Wagner, Lora M.

DeWitt Clinton High School
Montesser, Frederick
Campbell, Ralph
Davidson, Henry
Giovanoly, Max F.
Herrmann, Adolf
Herzog, Charles
Hirsch, James A.
Jackson, Eugene
Jonas, J. B. Edward
Works, Austin M.

Bole, J. A.

Eastern District High School
Adler, David
Goldenberg, Irving
Harmon, Esther
Kiso, Freda
Kretschmar, Magda
Wagenschutz, Anna
Santee, E. B.
Greenberg, Henry
Meyer, Florence E.
Russum, Edith E.

Erasmus Hall High School
Holmes, Mary H., Head of Department
Busch, Ella A.
Dennis, Julia B.
Habermeyer, Louise C. M.
Perkins, Helen L.
Sparks, Minnie E.

Evander Childs High School
Greditzer, M. Moritz, Chairman
Ackerle, Ida V.
Herrmann, Anna L.
Heuermann, Helena F.
Schonberg, Max
Stamm, Caroline L.

Far Rockaway High School
Jeschke, Martha L.

Flushing High School
(Modern Languages Department)
Baumeister, John
Bardenheuer, Clara E.
Green, Helen
Ferry, Alice M.
Ross, Annie

Girls' High School
Cushman, Earl L., Chairman
Babcock, Maude R.
Deufeld, Charlotte S.
Duurloo, Wilhelmine H.
Hayes, Helen M.
Junge, Antonie
Kellner, Anna T.
Wisthaler, Johanna S.

Jamaica High School
Krause, Carl A., Chairman
Corcilius, Josephine
Fennebresque, L.
Dilger, Marie
Mannhardt, E. G.
Rosenstadt, Bertha

Julia Richman High School
Crocker, Nellie J.
Knopfmacher, Ida
Saxton, Margaret D.
Trautvetter, Ida

Wehle, Hanna
Wendell, May Godfrey

Manual Training High School
Bushong, Alice
Fleischer, Emanuel M., Substitute
Geiss, M. Paula
Hackedorn, Marion
Kern, Dr. Albert J. W.
Lamb, Dr. William W.
Levy, Gretchen R., Substitute
Mageworth, J. Otis
Mueller, Ernest G.
Oswald, Dr. Frederick M., Jr.
Peters, Frederick A.
Pignol, Gertrude A. M.
Schaible, Godfrey C.
Schutze, Eliza
Schwartz, Edward E.
Stern, Regine

Morris High School
Althaus, Edward, Head of Department
Althaus, Amalie
Appel, Frank J.
Franke, Clara E.
Leuchs, Fritz A. H.
Lippert, Marie P.
Scheib, Richard
Schoenrock, Hedwig
Swartout, Caroline H.
Tilley, Lydia L.
Wahl, Emanuel M.
Wohlfarth, Amelia
Staehlin, Leonie E.

Newtown High School
Miller, Maud E.
Seeber, Elizabeth
Wells, Nellie P.
White, Cornelia B.
Zerban, Alex. H., Chairman

Richmond Hill High School
Burrage, Myra Allen
Golde, Margaret D.
Lambert, Marcus B.
Manfred, Maude E.
Wortmann, Johanna C.

Stuyvesant High School
Beha. Joseph L.
Brandau. George J.
Elmer, Clement G.
Fink, Frederick W.
Klafter, Simeon H.
Lipsky, Abram
Mantel, Herman E.
Mankiewicz, Frank
Neumarker, John
Nochkes, Adolph
Norris, John S.
Weiser, Samuel
(French)
Dorfman, Waldemar K.
Greenberg, Jacob
Parrott, Alfred F.

Wadleigh High School
Zick, Dr.
Haefelein, Miss
Harris, Miss G. B.
Hilke, Miss
Lapatinkopf, Miss
Lenz, Mr.
Leidensticker, Miss
Sesso, Miss
Thompson, Miss L.
Schreiber, Miss, Tchr. in Training

Washington Irving High School
Arndt, Emma
Baron, Lucille, Substitute
Buttner, Frieda
Crandall, Ernest L., Chairman
Edwards, Minna H.
Eltzner, Dorothea
Fette, Elizabeth W.
Hellin, Lillian
Hochheimer, Rita
Loos, Richard F.
McGivney, Mabel, Substitute
Molwitz, Ernestine J.
Schoenfeldt, Eugenia, Substitute
Wagner, Julia
Warr, F. Louise
Weiss, Alma
Weisner, Harry L.
Zaisser, Matilda

GREEK DEPARTMENT

Curtis High School
Pratt, Marion

HISTORY DEPARTMENTS

Bay Ridge High School
Proper, Emberson E.
Rubenstein, Jacob

Bryant High School
Arthur, L. Louise
Dickson, Tenny V.

Boys' High School
Wilson, J. F., Chairman
Brummer, Mr.
Parsons, H. H.
Rogers, Mr.
Smith, Mr.
Jacobs, Mr.

Bushwick High School
Morrey, William T., Chairman
Nanes, Philip
Smith, Louise
Thompson, Lucy F.

High School of Commerce
Bryan, Alfred C., Chairman and First Assistant
Beatman, Augustus S.
Lewis, Ernest D.
Porter, Geo. H.
Rice, Winfield S.
Roberts, Alfred S.
Whiffen, Edwin T.

Commercial High School
Dann, Matthew L.
Donovan, Herbert D. A.
Polk, Ellery Channing
Taylor, Edward F.

Curtis High School
Curtis, Osborn M.
Goodwin, W. Grant

DeWitt Clinton High School
Moyer, Fayette E.
Delaney, Edward C.
Foote, Edmund W.
Ham, Charles
Raphan, Ludwig
Kelley, Frank B.
Lucey, Michael H.
Newman, Charles
Thomas, Harrison C.
Tobin, James L.

Eastern District High School
Paine, Frederick H.
Beeckman, Florence
Campbell, Harold G.
Colligan, Eugeni A.
Watson, Alice D.
Wyckoff, Harriet E.

Erasmus Hall High School
Boynton, George E., Head of Department
Crane, Ella E.
Cunningham, Maude M.
Davis, Jennie M.
Fay, Charles R.
Knowlson, Walter S.
MacColl, Grace B.
Sprague, Laura E.

Evander Childs High School
Peterson, A. Everett, Chairman
Woodman, Sophie P.

Far Rockaway High School
Kennedy, Anna J.

Flushing High School
Miller, Frank H.
Chapman, Frances E.

Girls' High School
Cahill, Rose, Head Teacher
Couch, Anne M.
Davies, Rebecca H.
Hardy, Ruth G.
Lyle, Edith K.
Merriam, Betsey G.
Stevens, Alice A.
Way, Mary J.

Jamaica High School
Lawrence, Antoinette, Chairman
Edgerton, Myra T.
Leutscher, George

Manual Training High School
Fanning, Grace M. W.
Glassberg, Mr.
Hall, Mary A.
Hennelly, Mary F., Teacher in Training
Low, J. Herbert, Head Teacher
Marquardt, Florence
Puig, Florence M.
Yarrington, Adrian M.

Morris High School
Bates, Abby B., Head Teacher
Andrews, Grace
Baer, Dena M.
Bourne, Mary J.
Bridgman, Anna T.
Carey, Alice M.
Thompson, Annie S.
White, Fred C.

Newtown High School
Briggs, Larry
Gomph, Anna M.
Preston, Helen C., Chairman

Richmond Hill High School
Knapp, Annie M.
Leete, Gertrude M.

Stuyvesant High School
Dunbar, William F.
Fay, Harrison G.
Ross, A. Franklin

Wadleigh High School
Wood, Miss
Barrett, Miss M. B.
Bass, Miss

Beckwith, Miss
Bennett, Mr.
Blumenstock, Mr.
Davis, Miss A.
Gano, Miss
Haney, Mrs.
Sheely, Miss
Taylor, Miss
Thomson, Miss
Youngham, Miss, Tchr. in Training

Washington Irving High School
Galloway, Ida G., Chairman
Bassett, Elizabeth W.
Belcher, Frances S.
Chapman, Lena M.
Goertner, Rose
Hall, Caroline D.

LABORATORY ASSISTANTS

Bryant High School
Becker, Nathaniel

High School of Commerce
Coleman, D. F.
Duschatko, Alfred

Morris High School
Jablonower, Benjamin
Schaumoeffel, John

LATIN DEPARTMENTS

Bay Ridge High School
Allen, Winifred S.
Lawton, Maxwell F.
Medalie, Mrs. Carrie K.
Grant, Alice C.

Boys' High School
Riess, Dr., Chairman
Daniels, Mr.
Edwards, Mr.
Flint, Thos.
Freeborn, Mr.
Hobson, Mr.
Hopkins, Mr.
Janes, Mr.
Jenner, Mr.
Jones, Mr.
Jeffords, Mr.
Reynolds, J.
Wilson, H.

Bryant High School
McKinney, May
McMahon, M. Mabel, Chairman

Bushwick High School
Falion, George M., Chairman
Mulholland, M. Estelle
Smith, Louise

Curtis High School
Brewer, Francis E., Chairman
Corcilius, Inez
Gallagher, Ellen M.
Goode, Elizabeth
Peck, Mrs. Elizabeth du Bois
Pratt, Marion

DeWitt Clinton High School
Bice, Hiram H.
Bryant, Arthur A.
Dotey, Aaron L.
Hardy, Anna L.
Solomon, Michael
Wait, Horace C.
Wilford, Herbert E.
Yokel, Arthur
Foote, Carlton A.

Eastern District High School
Dixon, Charles E.
Bowman, Nina
Davenport, Florence
Genung, Ina E.
Holmes, David H.
Hoy, Elizabeth
King, Helen Louise
Klock, Claude W.
Pinch, Minnie E.
Stepanek, Beatrice

Erasmus Hall High School
Harter, Eugene W., Head of Department
Beardsley, Frank J.
Branson, Roswell H.
Connell, J. Wesley
Dox, Elmer A.
Estes, Charles S.
Harley, Walter S.
Howe, Alice C.
Leggett, Blanche C.
McGill, Franklin C.
Neiswender, Ada B. C.
Peabody, Susan P.
Scott, Izora
Stacey, Sidney G.
Stone, Katherine W.
Strong, William M.
Townsend, Arthur M.
Vidaud, Nathalie L.
Volentine, Mary F.
Welsh, W. Wallace
Wendell, Carrie E.

Evander Childs High School
Williams, Joseph S., Chairman
Siedler, Charles W.

Far Rockaway High School
Prescott, Lucy M.
Flanders, Addie E.

Flushing High School
Jenks, Paul R.
Lane, Mary C.
Lay, Wilfrid

Girls' High School
Ford, Celia, Head Teacher
Briggs, Emily E.
Clark, Emma K.
Dame, Lydia M.
Ellis, Sophia
Farrant, Louise G.
Jenkins, Anna S.
Lumley, Eleanor P.
McCarty, Maria C.
Willard, Gladys
Winslow, Julia E.

Jamaica High School
Chickering, F. C., Chairman
Grant, R. A.
Hoadley, H.
Root, Lydia F.

Julia Richman High School
Clarke, Eleanor P.

Manual Training High School
Bryant, Elizabeth E.
Dickinson, Hy. N.
Dithridge, Caroline
Heyer, Ella G.
McDonald, John J.
McDowell, Mary S.
Perrine, Charles
Richardson, William C.
Russell, Warren L.
San Giovanni, Dr. Edoardo
Schryver, George Orin
Smith, J. Clarence
Soule, Bertha L.
Shumway, Dr. Edgar S.

Morris High School
Davis, Josie A., Head of Department
Bogart, Elmer E.
Bogart, Sarah H.
Carr, Agnes
Constantine, Harriet L.
Cutter, L. Sanford
Evans, Austin H.
Fraser, Effie
Pyne, Henry R.
Shannahan, Willard R.

Newtown High School
Radin, Man, Head of Department
Swenson, Celeste C.

Richmond Hill High School
Beers, Florence E.
Johnson, Estelle M.
Voorhees, Sophia

Stuyvesant High School
Foster, Walter E.
Leavitt, William M.
Reynolds, Frank H.
Wallace, Minot L.
Wedge, Alfred H.

Washington Irving High School
Guthrie, Grace
Hopkins, Frances S.
Wessa, Ida, Chairman

Wadleigh High School
Hodges, Mr.
Beach, Miss
Case, Miss
Churchill, Miss
Clark, Miss
Delano, Miss
Henry, Miss
Howard, Miss
Judd, Mr.
McBride, Miss
MacVay, Miss
Nammack, Miss
Roessler, Mrs.
Royce, Miss
Stone, Miss
Van Vliet, Miss
Fox, Miss, Tchr. in Training

LIBRARIANS

Bryant High School
Thayer, Annie M.

Bushwick High School
Brower, Miss Jan

High School of Commerce
Pope, Seth E.

Commercial High School
Duncan, William H., Jr.

DeWitt Clinton High School
Arden, Harriette (Music Department)
Donnelly, Joseph P.
White, Emory F.

Flushing High School
Ely, Jean

Morris High School
Hathaway, Bertha F.

Newtown High School
Bedell, Julia I.

Morris High School
Hazen, Ella H.

Washington Irving High School
Alexander, Elizabeth W.
Annette, Sarah E., Chairman
O'Donnell, Marjorie, Substitute

LIBRARY PRACTICE

Washington Irving High School
Dodd, Helen W.
Fritz, Louise P., Chairman

MANUAL TRAINING DEPARTMENTS

Bryant High School
Grubneau, Adolph J.
Loewy, George J.
Vogt, Charles A.

Bushwick High School
Norton, George W.
Howe, Charing B.

Morris High School
Heikes, Irving A., Head of Department
Ackerly, Jennie
Bergman, Morris L.
Brand, Josephine
Clarke, Helen MacG.
Elkan, Herman M.
Gilmour, Emily
Hazen, Louise C.
Joslin, Jennie M.
Landau, Laura
Leighton, Margarette
Lewis, Arthur C.
Miller, Myrtle H.
Scott, Cora H.
Theobald, Jacob
Winslow, Isabel G.

Commercial High School
(Department of Shop Work)
Austin, Harry W.

Manual Training High School
(Boys' Shop)
Billingham, F. L.
Boecker, Dr. Alexander
Brundage, Howard D.
Edwards, Sidney
Foster, Edwin W.
Gilson, Channing W.
Lenfest, Dr. Bertram A.
Leroy, Walter A.
McCall, Carleton C.
Mackay, Alfred
Oliver, Joseph W.
Robinson, Alfred T.
Robinson, John T.

Newtown High School
(Joinery and Mechanical Drawing)
Messenger, Leslie, Chairman

Stuyvesant High School
(Wood Working)
Goodrich, M. Foster
Griswold, Edward D.
Hanford, Clarence D.
Hingsberg, Thomas
Mehrtens, Henry E.
Mersereau, Samuel F.
Messenger, John, Jr.
Stahl, George F.
Stotler, Albert
Steinert, John B.
Worth, William A.
(Metal Working)
Gage, Stanley A.
Griswold, Clifford B.
Schwarzkopf, Ernst.
Smith, Seymour L.
Smith, Walter M.
Wyman, William T.

MATHEMATICS DEPARTMENTS

Bay Ridge High School
Back, Elizabeth M.
Benway, Mabel R.
Barlow, Margaret M.
Eddy, Elise S.
Gilliland, Alice M.
Mackey, Arthur J.
Schuyler, Elmer

Boys' High School
Parsons, E. B., Chairman
Bishop, Mr.
Bergstresser, Mr.
Blanchard, Mr.
Clark, Mr.
Downing, Mr.
France, Mr.
Hamilton, Mr.
McDowell, Mr.
Stone, Mr.
Swenson, Mr.
Weaver, Mr.
Gray, Mr., Substitute

Bryant High School
Byrne, Margaret C.
Garrity, Julia F.
Rothholz, Meta
Shaw, M. Edna
Welch, Albert M., Chairman

Bushwick High School
Humason, Dr. Thomas A., Chairman
Cohen, Morris
Conley, William E.
Fleischer, Edward
Green, John P. (Alg. and Exp.)
Francis, Carolyn L.
Briggs, Eva E.
Goodman, Arthur

High School of Commerce
Minnick, John D., Chairman
Appel, Israel
Bowles, Frank C.
Fallon, George
Kock, Ernest H.
Lagerwall, Chas. J.
Lewis, Alfred H.
McCormick, Thos. H.
Schlauch, William S.
Smith, L. Brewster
Swanton, Richard S.

Commercial High School.
Bliss, Ralph P.
Hook, Edward A.
Lee, Joseph B.
Teeter, Charles H., First Asst.

Curtis High School
Dean, Philip R., First Asst.
Burdick, Mabel
Clark, Henry F.
Grant, Mrs. Eva M.
Kane, Thomas F.
O'Brien, Charlotte E.
Shipley, James H.

DeWitt Clinton High School
Anthony, Oscar W.
Berry, James F.
Clark, Randolph F.
Deshel, M. C.
Grow, Frederick S.
Haas, Arthur
Heller, Harry
Kelly, David F.
Krause, Arthur K.
Landsman, Charles M.
Levene, Harry
MacLaren, Donald C. (on leave of absence)
Mirsky, Israel
Morgan, Gwilym S.
Parellhoff, Bernard H.
Penhollow, Harry B.
Pickelsky, Frank
Pokorney, Rudolf C.
Salzano, Francis
Wright, Herman H.
Schneer, A. Henry
Stevens, Willliam S.

Evander Childs High School
Keigwin, Henry W., Chairman
Arenwald, Mesmin
Levine, Maurice
Lippe, Adolph A.
Norr, Henry I.
Rosenthal, Terese R.
Withers, Samuel C.

Eastern District High School
Mayo, M. J.
Gross, H. I.
Gurnee, Blaudina
Kelly, Wm. H.
Rittenhouse, Hawley D.
Sullivan, Mary
Tomlin, Stella M.
Wilson, Stuart
Blumenberg, Freda

Music Department
Ennis, Mary G.
Martin, Paul

Erasmus Hall High School
Lasher, William R., Head of Department
Brickelmaier, Alice G.
Edgell, Frank D.
Gordon, John J.
Hodgdon, Katherine I.
Jeffs, Eva
Johnston, William H.
Keck, Fred R.
Laden, James
Leman, George W.
MacLean, Donald C.
Raynor, George C.
Stone, Mary M.
Strom, Carl A. W.
Talbot, A. May
Whitney, N. Belle
Wilder, George F.
Young, Louise A.

Far Rockaway High School
Jennison, Emily M.
Barbanell, A. Irving

Flushing High School
Barnwell, Walter
Nearing, Slena P.
Palmer, May T.

Girls' High School
Mullen, Loring B., Head Teacher
Chatterton, Minnie E.
Childs, Lelia M.
Germann, Susan M.
Hale, Agnes L.
Ingalls, Margaret L.
Jewell, Edith
Miller, Maud
Smith, Charlotte
Sullivan, Bessie
Wales, Alma E.
Wilson, Jada J.
Wright, Mabel

Jamaica High School
Wilkin, Josephine D., Chairman
Brown, Charles G.
Busbee, Christiana

Manual Training High School
Aldridge, Dr. Vincent
Baker, Dr. Arthur L.
Baker, Eleanor R.
Baldwin, Walter J.
Banta, Mary
Barasch, Morris
Colsten, Albert L.
Dickler, Nathan N.
Davis, Eunice M.
Freeberg, Sigrid C.
Harris, Lena
Hopkins, Francis L., Substitute
Jones, Walter R.
MacCool, R. J.
McArdle, John Philip
McCreary, Herbert J.
Nevins, Dora R.
Odell, Louis S.
Robinson, Franklin D.
Shimberg, Jeannette
Snow, Minnie R.
Solomon, Charles
Walton, Georgiana C.

Julia Richman High School
Arnold, David L.
Underhill, Mary
Vermilya, Mabel

Newtown High School
Eggleston, Charlotte
Powers, Minnie, Chairman
Putney, Edith
Woodruff, Frank

Richmond Hill High School
Landers, Leland L.
Emery, Stephen
Ralph, Marion F.
Stilson, William E.

Stuyvesant High School
Andrews, Richard M.
Augsbury, Earl
Breckenridge, William E.
Cheney, Thomas Clyde
Clark, John P.
Corbettt, Joseph S.
Cornell, Charles F.
Durkee, Ernest S.
Henriques, Maurice C.
Hollander, Edward
Leventhal, Murray J.
Marston, Charles W.
O'Brien, William J.
Page, Donald T.
Silberstein, Nathan
Sindelar, Charles

Wadleigh High School
Bruce, Miss
Bowman, Miss
Bugbee, Miss
Burchard, Miss
Coman, Miss
Denis, Miss
Harris, Miss M. E.
Harris, Miss S.
Hart, Miss
Hermann, Miss
Houston, Miss
Hovey, Mr.
Kelsey, Miss L. H.
Mayer, Miss
McMillen, Miss
Norwood, Miss
Reynolds, Miss
Robinson, Miss
Smith, Miss
Strassburger, Miss
Underwood, Miss
Gerschauek, Miss, Tchr. in Training
Goertz, Miss, Tchr. in Training

Washington Irving High School
Beach, Jessie A., Chairman
Dolgenas, Jacob A.
Eaton, Clara C.
McKenna, Mary
McQuade, Rose M.
Roll, Rose
Zagat, Lillie

MUSIC DEPARTMENTS

Bay Ridge High School
Morris, Eugene C.

Boys' High School
Flint, G. C., Chairman
Mattes, Mr.

Bushwick High School
Taylor, Arthur M., Chairman
Wilson, George E.

Bryant High School
Bankhart, Elizabeth

High School of Commerce
Norden, N. Lindsay

Commercial High School
Zeiner, Edward J. A.
Goate, William B.

Curtis High School
Kuhn, Mina D.

Erasmus Hall High School
Schmidt, Carl G., Chairman
Mulligan, Mary C.

Evander Childs High School
Reynolds, Gerald

Far Rockaway High School
Marquard, Edward G.

Flushing High School
Marquard, Edmond G.

Girls' High School
Joannes, Jules S., Chairman
Barrett, Mary C.
Liscombe, Mrs. Esther A.

Jamaica High School
McConnell, Marie

Manual Training High School
Smith, Grace L.
Yerbury, Charles S.
Van Olinda, James E.

Morris High School
Tracy, Edwin S., Head of Department
Palmer, Anna M.
Reynolds, Gerald

Newtown High School
Valentine, Chas. I.

Richmond Hill High School
Greene, Lillian L.

Stuyvesant High School
Downey, Frank

Wadleigh High School
Judge, Miss
Barrett, Miss M.
Blair, Miss

Washington Irving High School
Matttfeld, William, Chairman
Caron, Emma C., Substitute
Mooney, Lawrence
Neidlinger, William

PHYSICAL TRAINING DEPARTMENTS

Bay Ridge High School
Barnett, Sadie R.
Beck, Alga May
Ward, Mercedes

Boys' High Schcool
Andrews, Mr., Chairman
Fairchild, Mr.
Gemson, Mr.

Bryant High School
Ellert, John F.
White, Cornelia M.

Bushwick High School
Durand, William B.
Green, Mary P.
McConville, Lillian M.
Stieg, Fern

Commerce High School
Aldinger, Harry E., Chairman
Foster, Wilfred L.
Hendrian, August W.
Rotherham, Philip J. E.

Curtis High School
Austin, Mary E.
Hillyer, J. Blake

Evander Childs High School
Edmunds, Maude A.
Schapira, Barnet

Eastern District High School
Higbee, Anna M.
Krellenstein, Ray
Model, Charles
Sperling, Harry
Reed, Mary

Erasmus Hall High School
Edgell, Mrs. Frank D., Chairman
Austin, Mrs. Mary
Batchelor, Chas. B.

Sheehan, Mary
Warner, Elma L.

Far Rockaway High School
Fish, Alanson L.
Livermore, H. Louise

Flushing High School
Fish, Alanson L.
Livermore, Harriet L.

Girls' High School
Clark, Cora B., Chairman
Hughes, Annie R.
Huntington, Belle
Treadwell, Flora G.
Wollaston, Caroline M.

Julia Richman High School
Ashcroft, Carrie Van R.
Hazen, Charlotte
Smith, Edith Ives

Jamaica High School
Jacob, A. Gertrude
Silverman, Henry

Manual Training High School
Brown, Merton A.
Foster, Oscar R.
Germann, Charles C.
Gray, J. Newton
Holly, Harold A.
Holzman, Abr.
Lindlar, Willliam
Mackay, Alfred
Mattuck, Jacob A.
Nelson, Willard B.
Snyder, B. Louis
Weed, Henry T.

Morris High School
Skeele, Otis C., Head of Department
Barnum, Grace E.
Butler, Evelyn M.
Freeston, Mary C.
Parker, Jacob
Pulvermacher, Dolores

Newtown High School
Crooke, Maxwell A.
McMahon, Kathryn, Chairman

Richmond Hill High School
Chapin, Jennie E.
Gammon, Montague

Stuyvesant High School
Cooley, George E.
Maier, Augustus
Way, Abner P.

Wadleigh High School
Moulton, Miss
Dobbins, Miss
Hervey, Miss
Marsh, Miss
Petrie, Miss
Potter, Dr.

Washington Irving High School
Barnett, Sarah E., Chairman
Beck, Alga M.
Garlock, LuNette M.
Gill, Lulu G.
Morrissey, Alice
Sandman, Ida
Scales, Carrie L.
Watters, Dorothy

PHYSICAL SCIENCE AND BIOLOGY

Eastern District High School
Brace, Edith M.
Branower, Solomon
Burlingham, Gertrude
Hazen, Annah P.
Illich, Louis L.
Kaufman, Wm. A.
Meigs, Katherine H.
Trowbridge, Cornelia
Wilkes, Eana M.
Osborne, Mabel

Erasmus Hall High School
Stocker, John H., Chairman
Bryant, Frank L.
Burnham, R. Wesley
Hancock, William J.
Huntington, Frederick W.
Jaquish, Ben M.
Levy, Harry A.
Williams, Lewis C.

Far Rockaway High School
Barnes, Edwin A.
Broomall, Laura B.

Wadleigh High School
(Physics)
Cornish, Mr.
Bruere, Miss
Cameron, Mr.
Hermans, Miss
Grieff, Miss, Laboratory Asst.
(Chemistry)
Gibson, Mr.
Russel, Miss
Cassett, Miss, Laboratory Asst.
(Physiography)
Clendenin, Mr.
Taylor, Miss M. L.
Tefft, Miss

PHYSICS AND CHEMISTRY DEPARTMENTS

Bay Ridge High School
Kearney, Maurice W.

Boys' High School
Spaulding, Mr., Chairman
Cook, Dr.
Curtis, Mr.
Stannard, Mr.
Yoder, Mr.

Bryant High School
Finch, Anna O.

Bushwick High School
Newcomer, Harvey
Maynard, Ernest A.

High School of Commerce
Creston, Henry C., Chairman and First Assistant
Hance, William

Curtis High School
Hopkins, Rupert H.
Tucker, Charles R.

DeWitt Clinton High School
Timmerman, Charles E.
Chamberlain, Raymond
Currie, Thomas H.
Tortora, Albert A.

Evander Childs High School
Hannan, Walter S.

Flushing High School
Word, Howell T.
Killen, Arthur H.

Girls' High School
Arey, Albert L., Head Teacher
Briley, Beatrice A.
Carter, Effie A.
Evans, William F.
Holt, Henry L.
Jenkins, Manford M.
Jenness, Jennie M.
Schumer, Jacob H.

Jamaica High School
Vosburgh, Charles H., Chairman
Quick, Oscar
Thompson, K. W.

Manual Training High School
Besarick, Caroline B.
Bloom, Isador
Colony, Elizabeth
Hierholzer, Carl O.
Wikel, Henry H.
Wilson, Agnes W.

Morris High School
Pyle, Willard R.
Burt, Clara M.
Scudder, John C.
Strayer, Franklin R.
Emmons, Fred E.

Newtown High School
Hewins, Nellie P.
Kingsbury, Geo. H., Chairman
McAuliffe, Anna E.
Morris, Mary F.

Washington Irving High School
Alley, M. Ida
Ammerman, S. Lewis
Hayner, Burton A.
Slack, Earl B., Chairman
Welt, Ida

PHYSIOGRAPHY DEPARTMENTS.

Bryant High School
Darrin, Mary R.

Girls' High School
Arey, Albert L., Head. Teacher
Cochran, Thomas

Julia Richman High School
Cole, Beulah V.

Morris High School
Miller, Charles A., Head of Department
Surrey, Frank M.

Richmond Hill High School
Chapin, Henry E.

Washington Irving High School
Slack, Earl B.
Hayner, Burton A.

SPANISH DEPARTMENTS

Bay Ridge High School

Smithers, Herlinda G.

Commercial High School.
Harrison, Earl Stanley, First Assistant

Finney, Arthur E.
Mercado, Julian
Smith, Joseph

STENOGRAPHY AND TYPEWRITING DEPARTMENTS

Bay Ridge High School
Rosmarin, Michael
Saphier, Conrad J.
Sugarman, Arthur M.
Zinman, Meyer E.

High School of Commerce
Healy, Horace G., Chairman
Beygrau, Frederick R.
Craver, Edwin H.
Rosenblum, Abraham
Walsh, Daniel O'C.

Commercial High School
Bolger, Edwin A., Chairman
Chestnut, D. Howard
Deuenholz, Alexander
Finnegan, William E.
Melson, George W.
Shea, John J. A.
O'Ryan, William P.
Shearer, Robert J.

Far Rockaway High School
Van Dusen, Eldon M.

Julia Richman High School
Ake, Virginia A.
Brand, Louis
Cahill, Mary F.
Kahn, Jeannette
Kennedy, Agnes
Levy, Rose Adelaide
Mitchell, Marguerite F.
Ruggeri, Agnes C.
Topper, Anna
White, Mabel M.

Morris High School
Hagar, Etta M.
Horwitz, Lilian

Richmond Hill High School
Richcardson, Marion G.

Washington Irving High School
Allyn, Louise
Boothby, Nellie M.
Catren, Ida M.
de Mers, Adrienne V.
Ennis, Agnes A.
Frank, Charles L.
Kinnan, Madeline
Klees, C. Mathilde
Langdon, Ruth J.
Linden, Mary V.
Loring, Jacob M.
Meyenberg, Amelia
Orr, Ella J.
Riordan, Elizabeth
Robinson, Deborah P.
Roche, Elizabeth A., Chairman
Stone, Bertha R.
Truckenbrodt, Lewis

STUDY HALL

DeWitt Clinton High School
Baylis, Sara

FIRST ASSISTANTS IN HIGH SCHOOLS OF NEW YORK CITY, 101 Men, 21 Women.

HIGH SCHOOL	BIOLOGY	ENGLISH	FRENCH AND GERMAN	HISTORY	LATIN	MATHEMATICS	PHYSICAL SCIENCE	COMMERCIAL Vice-Principals (Art)
BAY RIDGE	Bruckman, Louise	....	....	Proper, Emberson E	....	Schuyler, Elmer	....	....
BOYS'	Lewis, F. Z.	Fisher, William W.	Overholser, Charles E.	Jackson, W. P. Wilson, Jas. F.	Riess, Ernest	Parsons, Edw. B.	....	....
BRYANT	....	Munroe, Harry K.	....	....	....	....	Bement, Frederic	....
BUSHWICK	Johnson, Julius M.	Semple, [illegible]is B.	Keener, Robt. H.	Morrey, William T.	....	Humason, Thomas A.	....	....
COMMERCE	Eddy, Walter H.	Heydrick, Benjamin A	Roessler, Erwin W.	Bryan, Alfred C.	....	....	Mills, Jos. E. Cheston, H. C.	Pugh, A. L. Greene, R.
COMMERCIAL	Gruenberg, Benj. C.	St. John, Robt. P.	Marvin, Robt. M. Harrison, Earl S	Trask, Thomas C.	....	Teeter, Charles H.	Clark, John A.	Doggett, W. E Kip, Arthur R.
[illegible]IS	[illegible]t, Abel J.	Abbott, Frances	Shepherd, Florence D.	....	....	Dean, Philip R.	....	Welsh, John C. Crane, Wm. A. (V.P.)
DEWITT CLTN.	Hunter, George W.	Garrigues, Ellen E.	Monteser, F'd'k. Frank, Colman D.	....	Bice, Hiram H	Anthony, Oscar W.	Whitsit, Jesse E. Timmermann, C. E.	....
EAST'N DIST.	Hazen, [illegible]a P.	Hartwell, Charles S.	Bole, John A.	Paine, Frederick H	Dixon, Charles E	Mayo, Marion J	....	Baltz, Frank P.
ERASM. HALL	King, Cyrus A.	Farrar, Preston C.	Hol[illegible]es, Mary H.	Boynton, George E.	Harter, Eugene W.	....	....	[illegible]r, Kate (V. P.)
EVANDER CHILDS	....	....	....	....	....	....	....	....
FAR ROCK'W'Y	....	....	....	....	....	....	....	Belding, Albert G.
FLUSHING	....	Read, Warren W.	Baumeister, John	Miller, Frank H.	Jenks, Paul R.	Barnwell, Walter	....	....
GIRLS'	Leeuente, Margaret T.	Wendt, Cordelia	Higgins, Alice	Cahill, Rose H.	[illegible]rd, Celia	Mullen, Loring B.	Arey, Albert L.	Pyles, (VP) a[illegible]on
JAMAICA	Linville, Henry R.	Fairley, Edwin	Krause [illegible]l A.	Lawrence, Antoinette	Chickering, Edward C.	....	Vosburgh, Chas. H.	Starkey, Warren L.
JULIA RICHMAN	....	....	....	....	....	Arnold, David L.	....	....
MAN. TRAIN.	Hunt, Arthur E.	Bates, Herbert	Lamb, Wm. W.	Low, J. Herbert	Shumway, Edgar S.	Baker, Arthur L. Colston, Albert L.	Weed, Henry T.	[illegible]hn, (Art) Victor I.
MORRIS	Peabody, James E.	....	Althaus, Edward	[illegible], Abby B.	Davis, Josephine A	Heikes, Irving A.	Pyle, W. R., Schoen, M. D.	....
NEWTOWN	....	....	....	....	Radin, Max	....	....	....
RICHM'D HILL	Valentine, Morris	Gaston Chas. Robt.	....	....	....	Landers, Leland L.	....	....
STUYVESANT	....	Law, Frederick H.	[illegible]r, Clement G	....	Foster, Walter E.	Breckenridge, Wm. E.	Fuller, Robert W.	Howe, (Art) Chas. B.
WADLEIGH	Kupfer, Elsie M.	Smith, Jessie F. (Now Mrs. Ford)	Zick, Henry	Wood, Elizabeth C.	Hodges, Archibald L	Bruce, Grace A.	Cornish, Robt. H.	....
WASH. IRV'G	Sage, Lillian B.	Lowd, Emma F. Douglas, C. H. J.	Blackwell, [illegible]le G.	Galloway, Ida G.	....	....	....	Hayward, William R.

LIST OF THOSE HOLDING FIRST ASSISTANT LICENSES, AS OF MAY 15, 1914

Accounting, Economics and Commercial Law

RAYNOR, GILBERT J., 84.665%; Commercial.

Biology (Biological Science)

VAN DENBURG, JOSEPH K., 82.25%; Prin. P. S No. 40, Manhattan.
PAYNE, FRANK O., 83.875%; Commercial.
WOOD, GEORGE C., 83.875%; Boys'.
MANN, PAUL B., 83.5%; Morris.
MATHEWSON, CHESTER A., 83.125%; B. T. S.
BEDFORD, EDGAR A., 81.5%; Stuyvesant.

Biological Science

HEWINS, NELLIE P., 76.875%; Newtown.

Classical Language

PYNE, HENRY R., 79.25%; M. R. B. S.; 81.25% Morris.
BRYANT, ARTHUR ALEXIS, 89.25%; De Witt C.
BOGART, ELMER E., 87.25%; Morris.
HOADLEY, HARWOOD, 83.875%; Jamaica.
JENNER, WILLIAM A., 82.5%; Boys'.
TIBBETTS, WILLIAM F., 81.125%; Curtis.
DOTEY, AARON I., 81%; De Witt Clinton.

English.

MILES, DUDLEY HOWE, 80.25%; De Witt C.
TRESSLER, JACOB C., 75.25%; Boys'. Eng. also Jr. and A. Eloc. W. New.
CAPLAN, ELIAS N., 74.875%; Commercial.
STOCK, WALLACE T., 73.375%; Commercial.
COHEN, HELEN L., 82.875%; W. I.
HUGHES, JESSIE WALLACE, 78.5%; E. District.

Fine Arts

FRITZ, HENRY E., 79.35%; Stuyvesant.
CARTER, J. RAYMOND, 78.15%; H. S. C.

History

MOYER, FAYETTE E., 86.125%; De Witt Clinton.
DANN, MATTHEW L., 85.25%; Commercial.
BRUMMER, SIDNEY D., 79.125%; Boys'.
WAYAVE, LEON J., 78.875%; Commercial.
SMITH, ERNEST E., 76.375%; Boys'.
ROGERS, WILLIAM W., 76.25%; Boys'.

Mathematics

EMERY, STEPHEN, 76.975%, Z. B. M. X. R.; 78.9%, R. H. H. S.
SWENSON, JOHN A., 83.333%; Boys'.
WRIGHT, HERMAN H., 80%; De Witt Clinton.
BISHOP, MERLE L., 79.165%; Boys'.
HOOK, EDWARD A., 74.875%; Commercial.
WELCH, ALBERTA, 80.25%; Bryant.

Mechanical Arts

GAGE, STANLEY A., 85%; Stuyvesant.
STAHL, GEORGE F., 80.75%; Stuyvesant.
GARDNER, FRANK A., 80.5%; Stuyvesant.

Modern Language

PRICE, WILLIAM R., 95%; D. W. C.; H. S. C. State Education Dept., Albany, N. Y.
CRANDALL, ERNEST L., 93.5%; W. I.
JONAS, J. B. EDWARD, 92.875%; D. W. Clinton.
COHEN, ABRAHAM BRODERICK, 85.375%; Boys'.
WILKINS, LAWRENCE, 82.25%; De Witt Clinton.
MERAS, ALBERT A., 82%; Newtown.
PERRY, EDWARD O., 82%; De Witt Clinton.
REMY, ALFRED, 80.75%; H. S. Commerce.

Physical Science

WALKER, CLAUDE F., 78.5%; H. S. Commerce.
NEWCOMER, HARVEY, 78.25%; Bushwick.
MILLER, CHARLES A., 77.25%; Morris.
STOCKER, JOHN H., 75.75; E. H. H. S.

Stenography and Typewriting

HEALEY, HORACE G., 81.75%; H. S. Commerce.
BOLGER, EDWIN A., 81.5%; Commercial.
McNAMARA, EDWARD J., 81.5%; Jamaica.

LISTS OF THOSE LICENSED AS ASSISTANTS BUT NOT APPOINTED, AS OF MAY 16, 1914.

Applied Mechanics—Steam and Electricity

RATHBUN, SHERRIL S., 88%; R. F. D. No. 3, Oneonta, N. Y.
JENSEN, ARTHUR R., 82%; 561 E. Seventh St., Brooklyn.

Biology

HESS, J. AMMON, 70.5%; 77 Hamilton St., Rahway, N. J.
THORBERG, MARIE BRUNDIN, 76%; 625 Jensen Ave., Fresno, Cal.
BLOOMINGDALE, GERTRUDE, 70%; Alabama, N. Y.

Biology, Junior

FINK, ALBERT, 71.75%; 550 W. 174th St., New York City.
WAGNER, ELIAZBETH D., 78.75%; 162 Jerome St., Brooklyn.
THORBERG, MARIE BRUNDIN, 76%; 625 Jensen Ave., Fresno, Cal.
5251—GALLEY L

Chemistry

GOODMAN, ARTHUR, 81.5%; 53 Seventh St., Manhattan.
EASSLEY, CHARLES W.; Orono, Me.
FRIEDMAN, ELISHA; 102 E. 96th St., Manhattan.
BRUNDAGE, MILTON B., Stuyvesant H. S.
ATWATER, JOHN C.; R. H.
SMITH, MYRTIE ANNA, 73.5%; Fairport, N. Y.
GREEN, MARY W., 67%; 613 Prospect St., West New Brighton, S. I.
SCHMIDT, CLARA HELENE, 76.5%; 31 N. Bleecker St., Mt. Vernon, N. Y.

Chemistry—Junior

FRIEDMAN, ELISHA, 74%; 317 E. 79th St., Manhattan.
BLUM, ASHER, 73%; 557 E. 169th St., Manhattan.

Clerical Assistant

TODD, JOHN F., 75%; 755 E. 168th St., The Bronx, N. Y. C.
SILVERMAN, ARTHUR, 79.5%; 1 Goerck St., Manhattan.
JACOBS, JOSEPH, 79.25%; 218 Henry St., Manhattan.
ZINNER, SIGMUND, 84%; 443 Miller Ave., Brooklyn.
FOX, HARRY R., 80.75%; 822 E. 163d St., Manhattan.
GRABSON, EMANUEL, 77.5%; 185 Seventh St., Manhattan.
HEYLMAN, EMMA ADEL, 80%; 395 Ft. Washington Ave., Manhattan.
HEARN, GERTRUDE L., 78.5%; 1430 Greenwood Road, Brooklyn.
WHITNEY, CATHERINE ELIZABETH, 77%; 3604 Broadway, Manhattan.
STENBUCK, BERTHA E., 74%; 422 DeKalb Ave., Brooklyn.

Commercial Branches

FANCELL, AUGUSTINE J., 71.875%; 1354 Beach Ave., Manhattan.
WALLACE, WILLIAM C., 80.832%; 76 Brookside Pl., New Rochelle, N. Y.
GODNICK, SAMUEL P., 73.25%; 234 W. 111th St., Manhattan.
CANDEE, BENJAMIN K., 72.25%; 891 Fox St., The Bronx, N. Y. C.
WEINSTEIN, REUBEN, 70.5%; 403 E. 52d St., Manhattan.
FOX, JESSE G., 74.7%; 772 St. Nicholas Ave., Manhattan.
ULLMAN, FELIX, 73.75%; 320 Broadway, Manhattan.
ISKOWITZ, JOSEPH H., 84.375%; 534 E. 142d St., Manhattan.
SCHOENLANK, SIDNEY C., 78.875%; 1129 Lefferts Ave., Richmond Hill, S. I.
LOBENTHAL, MICHAEL SPIRO, 78.375%; 242 W. 112th St., Manhattan.
WEINBERGER, WILLIAM, 77.832%; 825 E. 163d St., The Bronx, N. Y. C.
GARFINKEL, MAURICE A., 76.75%; 1199 Eastern Parkway, Brooklyn.
ADKINS, COSTON B., 75.875%; 34 Hendrix St., Brooklyn.
MILLER, DAVID, 75.25%; 121 W. 116th St., Manhattan.
CROUTHAMEL, WALLACE K., 74.625%; Concord, Mass.
KLEIN, EDWARD, 72.665%; 559 W. 164th St., Manhattan.
EISENMAN, MAX J., 72.5%; 1058 Southern Boulevard, The Bronx, N. Y. C.
FEUERLICHT, S. JULIUS, 72.5%; 1544 Minford Pl., The Bronx, N. Y. C.
GOLDENSOHN, JOSEPH A., 72.5%; 1 W. 112th St., Manhattan.

GOTTLIEB, MORRIS, 72.25%; 116 W. 114th St., Manhattan.
GILBERT, MAX, 72%; 944 Tiffany St., The Bronx, N. Y. C.
LANDSMAN, MORRIS J., 71.4%; 21 W. 111th St., Manhattan.
KISER, FREDERICK G., 71.25%; Bronxville, N. Y.
KAPLAN, JULIUS, 70.75%; 1533 Pacific St., Brooklyn.
MARVIN, JESSIE A., 82.75%; 132 Cottage Ave., Mt. Vernon, N. Y.
KILBURN, FLORENCE M.

Cooking

DOWNING, BESSIE (MRS. WARD), 80%; Hanover, N. H.
OBER, ALICE M., 78.5%; 238 W. 56th St., Manhattan.
SKELTON, CHRISTINE P., 77.5%—78.5%; 65 Bay 32d St., Brooklyn.
GORTON, HARRIETTE, 78%; 479 Prospect Pl., Brooklyn.
ROSE, MABEL M., 78%; 801 Ocean Ave., Brooklyn.
DORMAN, JESSIE T., 77.5%; 111 Park Pl., Brooklyn.
BOWER, SARAH E., 77%; 536 W. 143d St., Manhattan.
CLARK, ANNA, 76.5%; 500 Second Ave., Astoria, L. I.
MARTIN, MILDRED G., 76.5%; 91 Clinton Ave., Brooklyn.
GREGG, MARY J., 76%; 258-A Emerson Pl., Brooklyn.
HUGGINS, ISABEL S., 75.5%; 407 E. 6th St., Plainfield, N. J.
EILBECK, WINONA M., 75%; 524 W. 122d St., Manhattan.
WOOLSON, SARAH A., 74.5%; Hastings-on-Hudson, N. Y.
GAMGEE, EDITH C., 74%; 497 Eighth St., Brooklyn.
SINSHEIMER, ELEANOR, 72.5%; Hotel Walton, W. 70th St., Manhattan.
WESTFALL, MARTHA, 72.5%; 631 W. 142d St., Manhattan.
STANTON, JOSEPHINE, 70.5%; 378 Greene Ave., Brooklyn.
DRUMMOND, GRACE, 70%; 104 S. 10th St., Newark, N. J.
LANDRU, LOUISE, 70%; 365 Park Ave., Paterson, N. J.
ROE, WINIFRED A., 78.5%; 614 Lexington Ave., Manhattan.
HUCKEL, B. EUGENIE, 72%; 231 Ryerson St., Brooklyn.
HESS, EMMA C., 75%; 258-A Emerson Pl., Brooklyn.
COHEN, AMELIA, 75.5%; 325 Central Park West, Manhattan.
KELLY, MOLLIE SMEALLIE, 76%; 201 Hamilton St., Albany, N. Y.

Cooking—Junior

KELLY, MOLLIE S., 76%; 199 Hamilton St., Albany, N. Y.
COHEN, AMELIA, 75.5%; 325 Central Park West, Manhattan.

Drawing

BROWN, HAROLD H., 86%; 6045 Kimbark Ave., Chicago, Ill.
ISLER, MAUDE M., 75.05%; 612 First Ave., Asbury Park, N. J.

Economics

HUGHAN, JESSIE WALLACE, 84%; 61 Quincy St., Brooklyn.

Economics—Junior

BLUM, ASHER, 82%; 544 Fifth St., Manhattan.
LIPSCHUTZ, BERTHOLD A., 76.5%; 162 W. 144th St., Manhattan.

Elocution

KANE, JAMES J., 75.5%; 266 Jay St., Brooklyn.
GRISWOLD, VIRGINIA A., 72%; 787 Carroll St., Brooklyn.
NIGHTINGALE, IDA E., 79%; 202 Lefferts Pl., Brooklyn.
HARTLEY, ALICE CUSHING, 72%; 747 Warburton Ave., Yonkers, N. Y.
HASKINS, THERESA H., 71.5%; 299 Sherman St., Brooklyn.

English

BOECKER, ALEXANDER, 77.5%; 494 Third St., Brooklyn.
MEYERS, DAVID, 71%; 619 W. 127th St., Manhattan.
WESTCOTT, ALLAN F., 82.5%; Alexandria Bay, N. Y.
NORRIS, WALTER BLAKE, 77%; Annapolis, Md.
POHL, FREDERICK J., 70.5%; 1625-A Pacific St., Brooklyn; 68 W. Central Ave., Delaware, Ohio.
CORSON, LIVINGSTON, 77%; 95 Brooklyn Ave., Brooklyn.
COHEN, JOSEPH, 77%; 266 Hewes St., Brooklyn.
MASON, GABRIEL R., 76%; 1107 Forest Ave., The Bronx, N. Y. C.
ROSENBERG, JACOB M., 75%; 1325 Franklin Ave., The Bronx, N. Y. C.
BEER, MORRIS ABEL, 72%; 945 E. 163d St., The Bronx, N. Y. C.
TRAPP, FRANK G., 71.5%; 2349 Davidson Ave., The Bronx, N. Y. C.
HANSON, GEORGE C., 70.5%; 518 Jefferson Ave., Brooklyn.
SCHUMAN, SAMUEL, 70%; 949 Tiffany St., The Bronx, N. Y. C.
CENTER, STELLA S., 77%; Forsyth, Georgia.
WHITE, VIOLA C., 70.5%; 277 Decatur St., Brooklyn.
GOSS, LEONARDA, 76.5%; 38 Washington Square, Manhattan.
MURPHY, EDITH H., 78.75%; 1551 Fifty-fifth St., Brooklyn.
SPERRY, HENRIETTA, 76.5%; 18 Belmont Pl., Passaic, N. J.
GORDON, MARGERY, 76%; 128 W. 13th St., Manhattan.

MANGAM, GRACE LEWIS, 76%; 295 Monroe St., Brooklyn.
KING, MARIE B., 75.25%; 798 Valley Rd., Upper Montclair, N. J.
MANGAM, EMILY A., 74.5%; 295 Monroe St., Brooklyn.
MURPHY. FLORENCE SHILLARD, 72.5%; 126 Lincoln Pl., Brooklyn.
STAGEN, RUTH M., 72.5%; 459 Bement Ave., West New Brighton, S. I.
SPEAR, DOROTHY A., 72%; 850 Trinity Ave., The Bronx, N. Y. C.
RUSSELL. NELLIE SHIRLEY, 71%; 363 Grand Ave., Brooklyn.

English—Junior

POHL, FREDERICK J., 70.5%; Delaware, Ohio.

Forge Work

LENFEST, BERTRAM A., 94%; 1524 Seventy-sixth St., Brooklyn.
KAMHOLTZ, ALBERT, 75.5%; 142 W. 142d St., Manhattan.

French

CRAMER, JESSE G., 89.3%—98.3%; 70 Lenox Ave., Orange, N. J.
EATON, ARTHUR L., 88%; 20 State Road, Beachmont, Mass.
FITZ GERALD, EDWARD, 80.5%; Derby, Conn.
FREEMAN, THOMAS J., 72.5%; 359 W. 58th St., Manhattan.
VIDERE, JEANNE A., 73.33%; 117 W. 43d St., Manhattan.
BOYD, MARTHA J., 78.5%; 120 S. 34th St., Brooklyn.
NOYES, MRS. MARGARET W., 77.5%; care Chelsea Bank, 135th St. and Seventh Ave., Manhatt
GAYNOR, MARGARET A., 77.5%; 7 W. 129th St., Manhattan.
MUSSAENS, MARIE G., 71%; 503 W. 122d St., Manhattan.
FAGNANT, ANNE MARIE, 96%; 821 N. Charles St., Baltimore, Md.
PAGET, FRANCES, 89%; 12 Gladstone St., Rochester, N. Y.
KELLEY, EDITH A., 88%; 158 Central Ave., Dover, N. H.
WATKINS, JULIA C., 87%; 11 James St., Montclair, N. J.
DAGGETT, MABEL CORNELIA, 85.5%; 306 E. Second St., Elmira, N. Y.
ALLEN, L. MARY, 85%; 15 Whitveld Court, Newport, R. I.
ISABEL, ERNESTINE C., 81.5%; 251 W. 98th St., Manhattan.
SANDAL, CAROLINE, 81%; 303 Dean St., Brooklyn.

German—Junior

GOETZ, HERBERT, 70%; 207 E. 55th St., Manhattan.

German

ALLEN, RUSSELL H., 83%; 297 Ryerson St., Brooklyn.
BAKER, GEORGE MERRICK, 80%; 8 S. 12th St., Philadelphia, Pa.
KLEIN, LEOPOLD, 75.5%; 137 W. 119th St., Manhattan.
HEIN, HENRY E.; 2433 Southern Boulevard, The Bronx, N. Y. C.
BROWN, ETHEL E., 75%; 55 Church St., Montclair, N. J.
FREIDENRICH, EDYTH, 75.5%; 3505 Jackson St., San Francisco, Cal.
STERN, BESSIE C., 71%; 580 Broadway, Paterson, N. J.
PROCTOR, HARRIET DAVIS, 88.5%; 14 E. Kinney St., Newark, N. J.
HUNT, MABEL M., 84%; 112 S. Third St., Mt. Vernon, N. Y.
WEYMANN, LINDA E., 83%; 148 E. 16th St., Manhattan.
VICTORY, BEATRICE M., 82%; 918 W. Dauphin St., Philadelphia, Pa.
MUSSAENS, MARIE G., 81.5%; 503 W. 122d St., Manhattan.
SAUL, GERTRUDE ELIZABETH, 79%; 429 Ninth Ave., Astoria, L. I.
LITSKY, ROSE, 78%; 218 E. 11th St., Manhattan.
LAW, MARION F., 77.5%; 700 W. 178th St., Manhattan.
HILL, ALICE TAYLOR, 74%; 783 Greene Ave., Brooklyn.
NEUMAN, LIBBY, 73%; 121 W. 115th St., Manhattan.
CASSEL, THERESE, 70.5%; Hotel Brunswick, 22 E. 89th St., Manhattan.

History—Junior

WEINREB, SAMUEL, 81.5%; 43 W. 112th St., Manhattan.
NEUMANN, SEYMOUR H., 76%; 875 Gates Ave., Brooklyn.
KATZ, SIDNEY F., 74%; 76 W. 82d St., Manhattan.
KLEIN, CHARLES L., 72.5%; 3602 Third Ave., The Bronx, N. Y. C.
RAPP, PAUL L., 72%; 492 Third Ave., Manhattan.
HALEY, OWEN A., 71.5%; 305 E. 161st St., The Bronx, N. Y. C.
SWANTON, RICHARD L., 70.5; 124 St. James Pl., Brooklyn.
DICKINSON, FLORENCE, 83.5%; 196 E. 205th St., The Bronx, N. Y. C.
McGUIRE, LORETTO, 78.5%; Jamaica, L. I.
BURGER, FRANCES, 78%; 430 Saratoga Ave., Brooklyn.
HASTINGS, ELINOR ISABEL, 77.5%; 11 E. 87th St., Manhattan.
KIVLEN, MAUD D., 74.5%; 365 Edgecombe Ave., Manhattan.
WICKS, HELEN DAVIS, 74.5%; 62 Montague St., Brooklyn.
READ, FLORENCE W., 72.5%; 70 Morningside Ave., Manhattan.
GORE, ANNA W., 72%; 2 Lexington Ave., Winfield, L. I.
MURPHY, FLORENCE S., 71.5%; 126 Lincoln Place, Brooklyn.
FLEMING, CARRIE O., 70%; 450 E. 26th St., Brooklyn.

History

ORTON, JESSE F., 75%; 73 Sixth St., Elmhurst, L. I.
WEINREB, SAMUEL, 81.5%; 43 W. 112th St., Manhattan.
NEUMANN, SEYMOUR H., 76%; 875 Gates Ave., Brooklyn.
KATZ, SIDNEY F., 74%; 76 W. 82d St., Manhattan.
KLEIN, CHARLES L., 72.5%; 1128 Clay Ave., The Bronx, N. Y. C.
RAPP, PAUL LOUIS, 72%; 35 Clifton Place, Brooklyn.
HALEY, OWEN A., 71.5%; 305 E. 161st St., The Bronx, N. Y. C.
SWANTON, RICHARD L., 70.5%; 124 St. James Place, Brooklyn.
ABELSON, PAUL, 86%; 1 W. 10th St., Manhattan.
MOYER, FAYETTE E.; 2 Grove Terrace, Montclair, N. J.
FITZPATRICK, EDWARD A.; 8 W. 101st St., Manhattan.
O'RYAN, WILLIAM P.; 1051 Prospect Place, Brooklyn.
WOOD, GEORGE C.; 798 Lincoln Place, Brooklyn.
WATERS, HELEN L. (MRS. BOYD), 83.5%; 343 Senator St., Brooklyn.
BENNETT, MARTHA C., 80%; 281 Lafayette Ave., Passaic, N. J.
QUINLAN, GRACE M., 79.5%; 2007 Bedford Ave., Brooklyn.
OSGOOD, ELLEN L., 77%; 17 Myrtle Ave., Plainfield, N. J.
SCHUTZ, META E., 75%; 803 Union St., Brooklyn.
CUNNIFFE, KATHARINE, 74.5%; 340 E. 194th St., The Bronx, N. Y. C.
DIETRICH, MRS. LUCY G., 73.4%; Bay Shore, N. Y.
WELLS, MILDRED A., 71.6%; 549 Springfield Ave., East Orange, N. J.
BASSETT, ELIZABETH W., 71.2%; 116 W. 123d St., Manhattan.
DICKINSON, FLORENCE, 83.5%; 196 E. 205th St., The Bronx, N. Y. C.
WESTAWAY, LOIS BESSIE, 79%; 803 Fifty-eighth St., Brooklyn.
McGUIRE, LORETTO, 78.5%; 147 Liberty Ave., Jamaica, L. I.
READ, FLORENCE WALLACE, 72.5%; 70 Morningside Drive, Manhattan.
GORE, ANNA W., 72%; 2 Lexington Ave., Winfield, L. I.
MURPHY, FLORENCE SHILLARD, 71.5%; 126 Lincoln Place, Brooklyn.
FLEMING, CARRIE O., 70%; 450 E. 26th St., Brooklyn.
WICKS, HELEN DAVIS; Huntington, L. I.

Joinery

ARNOLD, FREDERICK C., 75.25%; 111 E. 168th St., The Bronx, N. Y. C.
LEVY, JOSEPH A., 77.5%; 36 Berwick St., Orange, N. J.

Laboratory

LOEBENBERG, ALFRED, 70.5%; 51 Bainbridge St., Brooklyn.
BIRNBAUM, SIMON, 77%; 1562 Washington Ave., The Bronx, N. Y. C.
HOROWITZ, BENJAMIN, 76%; 2 E. 111th St., Manhattan.
WEINIK, SAMUEL, 82.5%; 332 S. 7th St., Newark, N. J.
TIETZ, JOHN WINFIELD, 81%; 429 Johnson Ave., Richmond Hill, L. I.
JAYSON, ALFRED R., 80%; 356 Hunterdon St., Newark, N. J.
RITTER, CHARLES P., 75%; 466 E. 25th St., Brooklyn.
GROSS, BEATRIX H., 75.5%; 620 W. 179th St., Manhattan.
TWEEDY, MARY M., 74%; 930 West End Ave., Manhattan.

Library

KATZ, JEROME F., 82.5%; 76 W. 82d St., Manhattan.
COWING, HERBERT L., 87.5%; 201 Mansfield St., New Haven, Conn.
BLACK, ELIZABETH L., 79.5%; 1018 Park Place, Brooklyn.
COWING, AGNES, 82.5%; 52 Garden Place, Brooklyn.
McKNIGHT, ELIZABETH BELLE, 82.5%; 130 Second Ave., Newark, N. J.
JENNINGS, LOU LYON, 81.5%; 520 E. 77th St., Manhattan.
SABIN, DAISY B., 81.5%; 26 Harrison Ave., Glen Falls, N. Y.
HAMLIN, M. LOUISE, 80%; 150 Putnam Ave., Brooklyn.
ROBESON, JULIA GOODRICH, 79.5%; 69 Montague St., Brooklyn.
CHRISTOPHER, KATHARINE M., 78.5%; 72 W. 124th St., Manhattan.
WHITE, MABEL GORDON, 76%; 138 W. 111th St., Manhattan.
MUZZY, ADRIENNE FLORENCE, 75%; 421 W. 121st St., Manhattan.
KENT, DOROTHY, 73%; 253 Emerson Place, Brooklyn.
ELDER, VERZA, 72%; Irvington-on-Hudson, N. Y.
HARDY, ANNA MARIE, 72%; 158 W. 81st St., Manhattan.
LIEBMANN, ESTELLE L., 72%; 254 Jefferson Ave., Brooklyn.
TIEMANN, EDITH WINIFRED, 72%; 67 Midwood St., Brooklyn.
JOHNSTONE, URSULA K., 70%; Binghamton, N. Y.

Latin

TONSOR, CHARLES A., 84.25%; 2316 Andrews Ave., University Heights, N. Y.
STRYKER, RUSSELL F., 82.5%; 129 W. High St., Bound Brook, N. J.
SANBORNE, G. GATES, 77.5%; 906 Bloomfield St., Hoboken, N. J.
MANN, JACOB, 70%; 1302 Sixty-seventh St., Brooklyn.
STAPLETON, CHRISTOPHER R.
MELLICK, ANNA C., 83.5%; 316 W. 84th St., Manhattan.
HAZEN, MARTHA M., 77.5%; 74 Central Ave., Hackensack, N. J.
SCHUTZ, META E., 75.75%; 803 Union St., Brooklyn.
HAWTHORN, CARRIE; 247 Hawthorne St., Brooklyn.
SWENSON, MARY E., 81.25%; 5 Elm Pl., Flushing, N. Y.

PECK, ELIZABETH DU BOIS, 86%; care Miss D. Mussey, 672 St. Nicholas Ave., Manhattan.
WENDEL, CARRIE E., 82.25%; 419 Sixteenth St., Brooklyn.
FULTON, MARY ELIZABETH, 80.5%; 237 Macon St., Brooklyn.
SMITH, FLORENCE M., 80%; 72 Summit St., Nyack, N. Y.
MORRIS, MARY ALICE, 79.5%; 205 W. 88th St., Manhattan.
O'BRIEN, JOSEPHINE G., 78.5%; 211 Jefferson Ave., Brooklyn.
HUENE, AMELIA HERMINE, 76.5%; 128 Weirfield St., Brooklyn.
JAGGARD, ALICE GRANGER, 74.75%; 394 McDonough St., Brooklyn.
BUCKLEY, KATHERINE R., 87.1%; 12 W. 89th St., Manhattan.
WHITE, EDNA, 78.2%; 44 Madison St., Jersey City, N. J.
ROBERTS, MRS. MARY McCABE, 76%; care McCabe, 614 St. Marks Ave., Brooklyn.
WHITE, HELEN LANGDON, 83%; 373 Commonwealth Ave., Boston, Mass.
HALE, HARRIET FLORENCE, 78.5%; 487 Halsey St., Brooklyn.
MILLER, SERENA, 78%; 112 W. Tulpohocken St., Germantown, Pa.
HODGES, MILDRED L., 75.5%; 414 W. 120th St., Manhattan.
COYLE, MOLLY BROOKE T., 73.5%; 457 W. 123d St., Manhattan.
JAQUES, MARY VOORHEES, 72%; 44 Morningside Drive, Manhattan.

Latin—Junior

SWENSON, MARY E., 81.25%; 5 Elm Place, Flushing, L. I.
KRAMER, EDNA P., 81%; 47 E. 88th St., Manhattan.
FULTON, MARY E., 80.5%; 237 Macon St., Brooklyn.
KIPP. ETHEL M., 80%; 2189 Clarendon Road, Brooklyn.
SMITH, FLORENCE M., 80%; R. F. D. No. 33, Trumansburg, N. Y.
MORRIS, MARY A., 79.5%; 205 W. 88th St, Manhattan.
CLEAVELAND, RUTH H., 79.25%; 220 W. 59th St. Manhattan.
O'BRIEN, JOSEPHINE G., 78.5%; 247 Marcy Ave., Brooklyn.
HUENE, AMELIA H., 76.5%; 128 Weirfield St., Brooklyn.
McCABE, MARY E., 76%; 614 St. Marks Ave., Brooklyn.
SCHUTZ, META E., 75.75%; 803 Union St., Brooklyn.
JAGGARD, ALICE G., 74.75%; 417 Hancock St., Brooklyn.
RICHARDSON, ADELAIDE A., 71.75%; 839 Jennings St., Manhattan.

Machine Shop Practice

COHEN, HENRY, 72.5%; 1060 Findlay Ave., The Bronx, N. Y. C.
CADY, HENRY D., 80.5%; Brown University, Providence, R. I.
BILLINGHAM, FRANK L., 75.1%; 373 Seventh Ave., Brooklyn.
GAGE, STANLEY A.; Stuyvesant H. S.

Mathematics

EDGERTON, EDWARD I., 71.25%; 601 W. 185th St., Manhattan.
DE GRAFF, FORREST A., 76%; 5937 Carpenter Ave., Philadelphia, Pa.
McCORMACK, JOSEPH P., 93%; 15 N. Broadway, Tarrytown, N. Y.
JABLONOWER, JOSEPH, 79%; 1390 Clinton Ave., The Bronx, N. Y. C.
GLUGOSKI, ARTHUR, 78.25%; 1246 Woodycrest Ave., The Bronx, N. Y. C.
GAYLOR, WILLIAM M., 75%; Sag Harbor, N. Y.
ROBINSON, ROBERT, 74%; 239 W. 111th St., Manhattan.
WEAVER, ROBERT L., 72.75%; Hasbrouck Heights, N. J.
GOLDMAN, SAMUEL, 71%; 161 W. 140th St., Manhattan.
HIRSCH, BLANCHE, 76%; 944 Park Ave., Manhattan.
SCALES, EDNA R., 70%; 62 Garrison Ave., Jersey City, N. J.
ROSANOFF, LILLIAN, 88.75%; 364 Alexander Ave., The Bronx, N. Y. C.
EGAN, HANNAH M., 78.5%; 1848 Mayflower Ave., Westchester, N. Y.
DUNN, LILLIAN CECELIA, 75.25%; 31 Prospect St., Trenton, N. J.
HEIDEN, IRMA F., 70%; 118 E. 74th St., Manhattan.

Mathematics—Junior

SCALES, EDNA R., 70%; 62 Garrison Ave., Jersey City, N. J.

Mechanical Drawing

DRUCKER, MAX., 83.1%; 70 West 118th St., Manhattan.
STEINERT, JOHN B., 75.6%; Hastings-on-Hudson, N. Y.
EATON, JOSEPH I., 89%; 25 Overlook Terrace, Yonkers, N. Y.
MINER, ROBERT L, 79%; 1432 Kemble St., Utica, N. Y.
BALL, HAROLD H., 73.9%; 20 Jackson St., New Rochelle, N. Y.
GREEN, JOHN C., 478 W. 159th St., Manhattan.
GRISWOLD, CLIFFORD B.
SMITH, SEYMOUR L.

Mechanical Drawing—Junior

DRUCKER, MAX, 83.1%; 724 Third Avenue, Manhattan.
BALL, HAROLD H., 73.9%; 20 Jackson St., New Rochelle, N. Y.

Music

WILSON, GEORGE ARTHUR, 84.5%; 144 Garfield Place, Brooklyn.
VALENTINE, CORNELIUS I., 81.5; 1036 Bloomfield St., Hoboken, N. J.
REYNOLDS, GERALD, 78.625%; 238 West Fifty-sixth St., Manhattan.
WHITE, EMORY F., 74.75%; 504 West 131st St., Manhattan.
DANIELSON, CARL, 74.375%; Glen Ridge, N. J.

HOEXTER, HERMANN, 71.5%; 1090 St. Nicholas Ave., Manhattan.
HART, EDITH L., Brooklyn only; 484 Jamaica Ave., Brooklyn.
BENNETT, EVA LAWTON, 81.375%; 60 North Ninth St., Newark, N. J.
GOULD, FRANCES REBA, 77.375%; 858 Jewett Ave., West New Brighton, N. Y.
CARON, EMMA C., 70%; 204 West Ninety-second St., Manhattan.

Physical Training

HASTINGS, EDWIN HAMILTON, 76.75%; 38 Randolph St., Yonkers, N. Y.
KIRKPATRICK, T. BRUCE, 82.05%; 429 West 117th St., Manhattan.
GLEICH, MORRIS, 73.25%; 81 Sheriff St., Manhattan.
LEHRER, ISIDORE D., 77.225%; 1485 St. Marks Ave., Brooklyn.
CAIRNES, ALEXANDER, 71.05%; 150 Fourth St., Woodside, L. I.
O'KEEFE, EMILY ALICE, 83.25%; 100 Morningside Drive, Manhattan.
STREETER, FRANCES A., 80.5%; 73 Willow St., Brooklyn.
MARKS, E. JEANNETTE, 72.79%; 485 Sixth St., Brooklyn.
CHALLIS, ANN., 72.625%; Rye Seminary, Rye, N. Y.
MALONE, MARY AGNES, 74.1%; 448 St. Nicholas Ave., Manhattan.

Physics

BAKER, FRANK L., 77%; 9 Lawrence St., Yonkers, N. Y.
SHELLARD, WARREN P., 73%; 434 Putnam Ave., Brooklyn.
CAMERON, WALTER S., 95%; 239 W. 136th St., Manhattan.
GREEN, EDWARD A., 78%; 123 Walnut Ave., Ardmore, Pa.
SPRAGUE, HAROLD CHRISTOPHER, 77.5%; Little Valley, N. Y.
THOMAS, GUY R., 74.75%; 334 Irving Ave., Port Chester, N. Y.
LINDLAR, WILLIAM, 72%; 2725 Albemarle Rd., Brooklyn.
SURREY, FRANK M.
STRESSEMAN, ADELE EMILY, 79%; Riverdale, N. Y.
EDWARDS, SARAH CORNELIA, 77%; Metuchen, N. J.

Physics—Junior

BLUM, ASHER, 70.5%; 544 Fifth St., Manhattan.
STADIE, WM. C., 72%; 270 Willis Ave., The Bronx, N. Y. C.

Physiography

BLUMENKRANZ, ADOLPH, 74%; 802 West 181st St., Manhattan.
BUCHHOLTZ, LOUIS, 74.75%; 815 Cauldwell Ave., The Bronx, N. Y. C.
PEACOCK, DANIEL L., 74%; 469 Waverly Ave., Brooklyn.
BAKER, DANIS LEE, 81%; 65 Howe Ave., Passaic, N. J.
CLARK, JACOB EARL, 78.5%; Roslyn, N. Y.
NELSON, WILLARD B.
SLEETH, ADDIE A., 76.5%; North Syracuse, N. Y.
BRYAN, MARY N., 75.25%; Armour Villa Park, Bronxville, N. Y. Care of R. H. Gates.
FISHER, RUTH BOOTH.

Physiography—Junior

HALSEY, GEORGINA, 73%; 58 East 177th St., The Bronx, N. Y. C.

Placement and Investigation

ADLER, MILTON M., 78.75%; 593A Macon St., Brooklyn.
KEIL, MINNIE, 73.5%; 234 West 129th St., Manhattan.
GITTOE, ETHEL T., 88%; 597 Putnam Ave., Brooklyn.

Sewing and Dressmaking

JOHNSEN, HARRIET M. B., 80.166% W. I.; Hotel Grenoble, 56th St. and Seventh Ave., Manhatt
PATRICK, FLORENCE, 79.833%; 50 Edgecombe Ave., Manhattan.
FELT, CARRIE E., 84.716%; 20 Morningside Ave. E., Manhattan.
VARONA, BERTHA L., 74.544%; 805 St. Nicholas Ave., Manhattan.
CLAFFY, KATHARINE, 70.75%; 245 Carroll St., Brooklyn.
HOBRAN, ROSE A., 382A Clinton St., Brooklyn.

Spanish

FLATOW, JACOB.
MULLINS, KATHLEEN L., 82.5%; 517 West 148th St., Manhattan.
DETOVA, MARGARITA M., 78.5%; 139 West Eighteenth St., Manhattan.

Stenography and Typewriting

FINKLER, ISADORE, 87.75%; 125 Van Buren St., Brooklyn.
WEISER, SAMUEL, 83.5%; 90 Lewis St., Manhattan.
GOLD, ELIAS, 75%; 427 Logan St., Brooklyn.
PRICE, ISAAC, 73.5%; 72 East Ninety-sixth St., Manhattan.
MURPHY, GEORGE F., 84.75%; 842 East Front St., Plainfield, N. J.
JACOBS, JOSEPH, 82.75%; 218 Henry St., Manhattan.
JAFFE, ISIDORE, 78%; 214 Henry St., Manhattan.
COHEN, LOUIS R., 77.5%; 319 East Thirteenth St., Manhattan.
DUNBAR, JOHN G., 75%; 195 Halsey St., Brooklyn.
GREENLICK, LOUIS, 73.5%; 251 West 129th St., Manhattan.
McKENNA, CHARLES J., 73%; 10 Regent Place, Brooklyn.
NEUWIRTH, ISADOR, 79.75%; 568 Bedford Ave., Brooklyn.
BUNNING, EDWARD, 73.75%; 1363 Clay Ave., The Bronx, N. Y. C.
STRUMPF, HAROLD, 84.75%; 979 East 163d St., The Bronx, N. Y. C.

GERMAN, AARON, 81.5%; 974 Union Ave., The Bronx, N. Y. C.
ARNSTEIN, SIDNEY, 80.75%; 941 Intervale Ave., The Bronx, N. Y. C.
WALSH, JOHN V., 80.25%; 2930 Haskin St., Westchester, The Bronx, N. Y. C.
BROWNE, BYRON T., 80%; 518 Greenwood Ave., Richmond Hill, L. I.
LUDWIG, AUGUSTUS, 80%; 528 West 139th St., Manhattan.
BRODY, ALEXANDER, 78.5%; 61 West 115th St., Manhattan.
BERNSTEIN, DAVID R., 78%; 63 East 117th St., Manhattan.
AROND, MICHAEL, 77.75%; 233 East Tenth St., Manhattan.
CONN, CHARLES, 77.75%; 814 East 163d St., The Bronx, N. Y. C.
DONOVAN, BERNARD J., 76%; 325 Jay St., Brooklyn.
FLANAGAN, WILLIAM E., 76%; 179 Marcy Ave., Brooklyn.
KAPLAN, ABRAHAM D., 74.75%; 1486 Fifth Avenue, Manhattan.
GORDON, MASTEN, 74%; 855 Hunts Point Ave., The Bronx, N. Y. C.
SEROTA, RUTH, 75.5%; 142 West 111th St., Manhattan.
AKE, VIRGINIA A., 74.5%; 210 Walnut St., Jenkintown, Pa.
RICE, MABEL E., 73.5%; 69 West Eleventh St., Manhattan.
SHAPIRO, MRS. SARAH M.; 73%; 539 West 156th St., Manhattan.
READ, MARY E., 70.25%; 9 Adams St., Mt. Vernon, N. Y.
DUFFY, KATHARINE, 72%; 211 West 121st St., Manhattan.
CLEMENT, FANNIE M., 84%; 141 Buckman St., Everett, Mass.
FINK, ANNA H., 83%; 522 Grand St., Brooklyn.
STEINECKE, JEANETTE A., 77.75%; 55A Lynch St., Brooklyn.
DEMPSEY, JOSEPHINE A., 77%; 467 Fifty-fifth St., Brooklyn.
SCHENONE, ADELAIDE L., 77%; 1921 Howard St., Brooklyn.
CARYL, ETHEL E., 74.5%; 96 Highland St., Brockton, Mass.
MARTIN, AMY N., 72.25%; 358 Seventy-third St., Brooklyn.

Stenography and Typewriting—Junior

WEISER, SAMUEL, 79.5%; 90 Leewis St., Manhattan.
CANNOLD, LESTER, 76%; 25 East 112th St., Manhattan.
GOLD, ELIAS, 75%; 60 West 119th St., Manhattan.
BUNNING, EDWARD, 73.75%; 1363 Clay Ave., The Bronx, N. Y. C.
McKENNA, CHARLES J., 73%; 209 Nassau St., Brooklyn.
DUFFY, KATHARINE, 72%; 211 West 121st St., Manhattan.

Woodturning and Pattern Making

CARBONE, MARIO G., 70.5%; 103 West Fifty-sixth St., Manhattan.

LIST OF HIGH SCHOOL SUBSTITUTES, AS OF MAY 15, 1914

Biology

ACHENBACH, HELEN M., 396 Prospect St., Ridgewood, N. J. Tel. 526-M Ridgewood.
BARRETT, ALICE, 600 West 163d St., Manhattan.
BINKLEY, GRACE A., 310 W. 129th St., Manhattan.
BRINE, BLANCHE, 98 W. 183d St., The Bronx, N. Y. C. Tel. 2398-R Tremont.
BRUGGEMAN, JOSEPHINE, 217 W. 68th St., Manhattan. Tel. 10249 Columbus.
COMMISKEY, GRACE, 189 Sixth Ave., Brooklyn. Tel. 3760 Prospect.
DAVENPORT, MARJORY, Boston Road, N. Y. C.
FITZPATRICK, ELIZABETH T., 919 Ogden Ave., The Bronx, N. Y. C. Tel. 476 Melrose.
FRANK, JEANNETTE, 533 W. 156th St., Manhattan.
GOLDIN, FANNIE, 47 Norfolk St.
GRAHAM, MARGARET, Westchester, N. Y. C.
HALBERT, LOUISE, 204 E. 53d St., Manhattan. Tel. 1986 Plaza.
HARRIS, MABEL, 1157 E. 33d St., Flatbush, Brooklyn.
JUD, F. C., 119 Franklin St., Jersey City, N. J. Tel. 4228 Jersey City.
LINKER, ANNA, 1943 Atlantic Ave., Brooklyn.
MARTIN, FLORENCE J., 1089 E. 18th St., Brooklyn.
O'CONNELL, EUGENIE, 354 E. 79th St., Manhattan. Tel. 2155 Lenox.
SCUDDER, SARA A., Huntington, L. I. Tel. 123-M Huntington.
SOLOMON, MATILDA L., 96 E. Seventh St.

Chemistry

ABELSON, JOSEPH, 1551 Hoe Ave., The Bronx, N. Y. C. Tel. 5757 Tremont.
BRODOSKI, ALEXANDER, 2117 Dean St., Brooklyn.
GINSBERG, INNAR, 1052 Findlay Ave.
LOUGHRAN, VINCENT, 155 Second Ave., Long Island City. Tel. 1082-W Astoria.
LOWY, ALEXANDER, 1457 Bryant Ave., The Bronx, N. Y. C. Tel. 1854 Tremont.
MUNGER, VAN VECHTEN, 605 W. 142d St., Manhattan.
NEHB, FREDERICK, 506 E. 162d St., Manhattan.
SALPETER, ARNOLD S., 976 DeKalb Ave., Brooklyn.
WEIRICH, CLARENCE L., 11 E. 127th St., Manhattan.
WINSLOW, WILLIAM, 614 W. 113th St., Manhattan.

Clerical Assistant

CROWLEY, ISABEL A., 71 E. 87th St.
ELIKANN, ADELE, 791 Jackson Ave.
FINK, ANNA H., 522 Grand St., Brooklyn. Tel. 3664 Stagg.
GARINAN, SUSAN, 128 W. 117th St.
GRIFFIN, MARJORIE, Indian Orchard, Mass.
LAZARUS, ARTHUR, 293 Knickerbocker Ave., Brooklyn.
MASON, EMMA R., 624 Hancock St., Brooklyn.
MAYER, SABRINA, 71 Clark Ave., Far Rockaway. Tel. 250 Far Rockaway.
SHERMAN, IDA, Monticello, N. Y.
SHIPLEY, JOSEPH T., 508 W. 162d St. Tel. 3484 Audubon.
SMITH, MARY C., 366 Macon St., Brooklyn.
TANZER, EDITH P., care Cohman, 2626 Broadway. Tel. 2590 Riverside.
WEINBERGER, GEORGE, 377 Vernon Ave., Brooklyn.

Commercial Branches

ADLER, SAMUEL, 1022 Hopkinson Ave., Brooklyn.
BERALL, LOUIS J., 278 W. 130th St. Tel. 8576 Morningside.
BERNEY, ARTHUR A., 477 Miller Ave., Brooklyn.
CIVIC, MAXWELL, 21 W. 115th St.
GREEN, HARRY Y., Bartertown, N. J.
LOOMIS, JAMES D., 22 Barnet St., Newark, N. J.
MILLER, HERMAN, 1369 Intervale Ave., The Bronx, N. Y. C.
PALLEY, DAVID M., 1412 Pitkin Ave., Brooklyn.
PYNE, JOHN, 220 Broadway, Manhattan. Tel. 3845 Cortland.
SCHAPIRO, JACOB, 40 Wyckoff St., Brooklyn.
SEGAL, LOUIS, 648 Broadway.
SILVERMAN, ARTHUR, 1 Goerck St.
TEADORE, HERMAN, 22 E. 106th St.
WALDMAN, LOUIS, 850 E. 156th St.
ZATZ, MORRIS S., 139 E. 16th St. Tel. 2644 Stuyvesant.

Cooking

BIVINGSEN, EMILY C., 523 W. 121st St.
BURKE, ANNIE, 9208 Hough Ave., Cleveland, Ohio.
FOOTE, ALICE B., 328 Sixth Ave.
HARDING, KATHERINE A., 1298 Dean St., Brooklyn.
O'DRISCOLL, FRANCES M., 489 Jefferson Ave., Brooklyn.
SCHOENFELD, ALVINA, 438 E. 83d St. Tel. 5427 Lenox.
WHITNEY, JENNIE, 401 Washington. Ave.

Costume Designing

GORMLEY, ANNA F., 436 W. 20th St. Tel. 8253 Chelsea.

Drawing

BARKER, FLORENCE P., 516 Manhattan Ave.
BUCK, FREDERICK C., 115 E. 19th St.
FRERICHS, ALMA J., 408 W. 150th St.
FUESLEIN, LEONIE A., 888 E. 176th St. Tel. 3260 Tremont.
GARDNER, GERTRUDE A., 474 Washington Ave., Brooklyn.
LOEB, MITCHELL, 493 Alabama Ave.
McDONALD, HELEN R., 309 Dyckman St.
McDONALD, HELEN R., 209 Dyckman St.
SAX, CAROL M., 407 Central Park West.
SLACK, HELEN L., 143 E. 53d St.
SMITH, VIOLET E., 1034 Lincoln Pl., Brooklyn.
STEVENS, MRS. SALLY F., 109 St. James Pl., Brooklyn.
THORBURNART, LUCRETIA, 1744 Broadway.
WHITNEY, CLARA G., 3604 Broadway.
WINNARD, LEONOR E., Beverly Apt., Tompkins Ave., West New Brighton.

Elocution

MAXWELL, ROSE, 301 Sterling Pl., Brooklyn. Tel. 6277 Prospect.
PRYOR, SARA S., 505 W. 124th St.

English

ALEXANDER, COLVIL, 545 W. 156th St.
ARKWRIGHT, GEORGE A., 411 Halsey St., Brooklyn.
BALKAM, LEONORA A., 883 Jennings St., The Bronx, N. Y. C.
BERNSTEIN, BENJAMIN, 162 East Broadway.
BOHN, FRANK, 106 Northern Ave.
BRADY, HELEN E., 58 Clifton Pl., Brooklyn. Tel. 3648-W Prospect.
BRAND, ANNA R., 2567 Decatur Ave., The Bronx, N. Y. C. Tel. 2161 Tremont.
BURROWS, HELEN J., 82 W. 105th St.
COOKE, DOROTHY, 208 Oak St., Richmond Hill.
CRANDELL, HELEN H., 515 W. 122d St. Tel. 5540 Morningside.
CUSACK, GERTRUDE C., 611 Putnam Ave., Brooklyn.
DANHEISER, RUTH V., 63 W. 106th St. Tel. 2569 Riverside.
DEACON, EDITH M., 502 W. 143d St.
DONOHUE, JOHN J., 270 Alexander Ave., The Bronx, N. Y. C.
DARE, EDWARD S., 301 E. 63d St.
DOUGINE, GENEVIEVE, 2261 Loring Pl., The Bronx, N. Y. C.
DOWLER, VESTA M., 160 St. John's Pl., Brooklyn. Tel. 7771-J Prospect.
EMRICK, ANNA L., Ulster St., Hollis, L. I. Tel. 6319-J Hollis.
EVANS, JEAN O., 169 Macon St., Brooklyn. Tel. 4743 Bedford.
FEIGENBAUM, ESTELLE A., 174 Woodruff Ave., Brooklyn. Tel. 9277-M Flatbush.
FRISBIE, ALICE N., 1101 Lincoln Pl., Brooklyn. Tel. 6951-J Bedford.
GOLDBERG, IDA C., 916 Southern Boulevard, The Bronx, N. Y. C.
GOLLOMB, LOUIS C., 18 E. 108th St. Tel. 5800 Tremont, Ext. 13.
GRAY, KATHLEEN, 48 W. 167th St. Tel. 7875-W Melrose.
GUNNISON, ADELAIDE F., 77 Wilson St., Brooklyn.
HAMBURGER, NANNETTE F., 445 W. 153d St. Tel. 6360 Audubon.
HASBERG, GLADYS, 99 Claremont Ave.
HAYS, BESSIE R., 276 Riverside Drive. Tel. 1448 Riverside.
HEILBRUNN, STELLA, 848 Park Pl., Brooklyn. Tel. 3137-W Bedford,
HESSEY, RUTH, 15 Shepherd Ave., Brooklyn.
HICKOX, ELINORA C., 519 W. 121st St. Tel. 8790 Morningside.
HORWITZ, BENJAMIN, 446 E. 79th St.
JEWELL, MARJORIE, 126 Willoughby Ave., Brooklyn. Tel. 6069 Prospect.
KEARSING, EDWIN I., 349 E. 22d St., Brooklyn. Tel. 4812-W Flatbush.
KEMLO, ELIZABETH, 315 Macon St., Brooklyn.
KINNEY, EDITH, 152 E. 22d St. Tel. 1440 Gramercy.
LONDON, IRENE, 564 Riverside Drive. Tel. 8050 Morningside.
LONG, DORIS, 42 Lenox Road.
LOUIS, EVANGELINE I., 1381 Washington Ave., The Bronx, N. Y. C.
LYNCH, THOMAS F., 286 Windsor Pl., Brooklyn.
McCORMACK, MADELEINE, 864 Prospect Pl., Brooklyn. Tel. 1023-M Bedford.
McGINN, CATHERINE A., 220 Seventy-ninth St., Bay Ridge.
McKEE, JOSEPH V., 890 E. 176th St. Tel. 4786-W Tremont.
MACDONALD, JAMES, Hotel Ennis, 42d St.

MacFARLAND, HAZEL M., 289 Clermont Ave., Brooklyn. Tel. 5969-W Prospect.
MARKS, WM. B., 1114 Ward St., Richmond Hill. Tel. 1348-W Richmond Hill.
MARTIN, SHIRLEY L., 361 E. 25th St., Flatbush.
MOORE, WILMOT H., 216 Richmond Terrace, New Brighton.
MORRILL, GEORGIANA, 253 W. 42d St. Tel. 3195 Bryant.
MUSGRAVE, EDITH, 122 E. 66th St. Tel. 1064 Plaza.
MYERS, ALFRED S., 309 W. 70th St.
NELSON, HAZEL W., 474 Halsey St., Brooklyn. Tel. 5309-W Bedford.
NOBIS, AGNES, 251 W. 101st St.
O'BRIEN, EUGENIE M., 162 Hewes St., Brooklyn.
OTTEN, EDNA M., 34 Jefferson Ave., Brooklyn. Tel. 3300 Prospect.
PAXTON, SHELBY, 429 Convent Ave. Tel. 4236 Audubon.
PEARSE, WILLIAM, 41 Lefferts Ave., Richmond Hill. Tel. 2681 Richmond Hill.
PEASE, ROYAL S., 549 Second Ave., Long Island City.
PISTNER, BERNARD, 189 Rodney St., Brooklyn. Tel. 3236-W Williamsburgh.
PITTS, MAUDE L., 94 S. Oxford St., Brooklyn.
POLLEY, BRITTON, 1163 Washington Ave., The Bronx, N. Y. C. Tel. 1971 Melrose.
POPPER, HILDA L., 260 W. 93d St.
POWERS, FLORENCE M., **56 Macon St., Brooklyn.**
RILEY, FLORENCE M., 164 E. 89th St.
RITT, HAROLD L., 253 Liberty Ave., Brooklyn.
ROONEY, FRANK J., 33 W. 61st St.
ROWAN, JOSEPH T., 461 W. 164th St.
RUEL, GRACE M., 1818 Clinton Ave., The Bronx, N. Y. C. Tel. 143-M Tremont.
RINGON, HELEN D., 420 W. 146th St.
SABBATINO, PETER L. F., 339 E. 12th St.
SANDBERG, BERTHA, 122 E. 107th St.
SEALY, ALICE, Hempstead Ave., Lynbrook, L. I. Tel. 894-R Lynbrook.
SEGUINE, EDITH C., Rosebank, S. I.
SHANNON, LEONORE R., 324 W. 71st St.
SHAUGHNESSY, IRENE, 64 Bradford St., Brooklyn. Tel. 958 East New York.
SHIPLEY, JOSEPH T., 508 W. 162d St. Tel. 3484 Audubon.
SLOANE, MARTHA G., 469 Pacific St., Brooklyn.
SOLIS, CAROLINE, 307 W. 77th St. Tel. 8862 Schuyler.
SPEAR, DOROTHY A., 850 Tinton Ave.
STITES, KATHERINE F., 1256 Fifty-sixth St., Brooklyn.
SUTPHIN, CAROLINE M., 268 Hillside Ave., Jamaica.
THACKRAY, ETHEL M., 272 Hancock St., Brooklyn.
TWEEDY, MARY M., 371 W. 120th St.
WARNER, MARGARET B., 218 Hancock St., Brooklyn.
WECHSLER, PHILIP, 460 Grand St.
WILLIAMS, MAY, 716 Hamilton Ave., Richmond Hill.
WILLIAMSON, GEORGE F., Columbia University.

Forge Work

PASTERNAK, JESSE, 303 President St., Brooklyn. Tel. 1186 Hamilton.

Freehand Drawing

BEHAR, ELY M., 523 W. 151st St., Tels. 2813 Audubon; 4762 Beekman.
DAVIS, EDWIN A., 46 Monmouth St., Red Bank, N. J.
EVANS, GEORGE, 909 Bedford Ave., Brooklyn.
KEAN, JOHN A., JR., 1565 E. 28th St., Brooklyn.
MAY, LOTTIE, 110 Morningside Drive. Tel. 984 Morningside.
MEYER, META D., 40 Ellis Pl., Ossining, N. Y.
WAY, LAURA R., 49 W. 9th St.

French

ABRAMOVITZ, PHILIP, 35 Allen St.
CLARKE, JAMES B., 758 Monroe St., Brooklyn.
COLLA, CLARA, 3603 Broadway, Manhattan. Tel. 4266 Audubon.
CROSS, EPHRAIM, 227 Alexander Ave., The Bronx, N. Y. C. Tel. 197 Melrose.
DONOVAN, HELEN C., **501 Park Pl., Brooklyn.**
LAMBERT, PAULA C., 621 W. 135th St., Manhattan. Tel. 4538 Morningside, Apt. 14.
LIVINGSTON, ANNIE L. M., 317 W. 119th St., Manhattan. Tel. 5642 Morningside.
NATELSON, REBEKAH, 1451 Forty-sixth St., Brooklyn.
REISS, JOSEPH, 18 E. 106th St.
ROSENBERG, JOSEPH, 814 E. 163d St.
SHAPIRO, JULIA, 182 West End Ave.
SPILLER, SUSAN M., 2185 Broadway, Manhattan.
TROSTEN, SOPHIE, 304 E. 8th St.
UNTI, IRMA, 78 W. 11th St.
ZWERBEL, ABRAHAM D., 11 Ridge St.

ARONSON, META J., 1875 Madison Ave.
BARON, LUCILLE, 2098 Vyse Ave., The Bronx, N. Y. C. Tel. 4891 Tremont.
BLENDERMAN, HELEN R., 815 W. 179th St., Tel. 6510 Audubon.
BLUMGARTEN, SARA L., 1114 Madison Ave.
BOSE, HENRY P., 909 Greene Ave., Brooklyn. Tel. 2791 Williamsburgh.

BOYNTON, MARY L., 466 E. 18th St., Flatbush. Tel. 2281-M Flatbush.
BRUNING, EMILIE E. M., 317 Seventy-third St., Brooklyn. Tel. 1925 Bay Ridge.
CHADWICK, DAVID, 332 Osborn St., Brooklyn.
FIEBIG, ANNA F., 313 E. 57th St.
GENUNG, MARY L., 325 Chemung St., Waverly, N. Y.
GOLDSTEIN, REBECCA, 54 E. 108th St. Tel. 6749 Harlem.
GOTTLIEB, SARAH, 210 W. 79th St. Tel. 5033 Schuyler.
HAMBURGER, JOHANNA W., 53 W. 126th St., care of Taylor. Tel. 3464 Harlem.
HERSHKOWITZ, HARRY, 201 Avenue B. Tel. 630 Orchard.
HUBERTY, MARY A., 43 Linden St., Brooklyn. Tel. 5084 Bushwick.
KESSLER, HARRY, 247 Second St.
KOLK, LAURA A., 184 Hancock St., Brooklyn.
KUHNERT, HERBERT, George Jr. Republic, Freeville, N. Y.
KUTNER, MARGARET, 714 W. 180th St.
LANE, FRANZ, 416 W. 118th St.
LAVINE, SARA L., 350 W. 118th St.
LAW, MARION F., 700 W. 178th St.
LINDNER, CLARA A., 527½ Sixth Ave., Brooklyn.
LINGG, SOPHIE C., 303 St. Poul's Ave., Tompkinsville, S. I.. Tel. 286-R Tompkinsville.
MAHLER, ANNA B., 1970 Hughes Ave., The Bronx, N. Y. C.
MANKWURCZ, FRANK, 2785 Third Ave.
MASCHMEDT, MARIE R., 72 Hanover St., Elmhurst, L. I. Tel. 706-M Newtown.
NEWMARK, SOPHIA, 951 Sherman Ave.
NOSCHKES, ADOLPH, 420 Grand St. Tel. 6299 Orchard.
REINER, MRS. ANNA M., 1137 Park Pl., Brooklyn. Tel. 527-M Bedford.
ROBINSON, CHARLES W., 200 W. 70th St.
SAUL, GERTRUDE E., 429 Ninth Ave., Long Island City.
SCHLESINGER, ETHEL, 275 Central Park West.
SCHMIDT, META, 176 W. 87th St.
SCHOENFELDT, EUGENIA, 346 E. 20th St.
SCHACHT, HENRY, 71 St. Marks Pl., Manhattan.
SMITH, AUGUSTUS D., 148 Henry St.
TOEPLITZ, JEAN, 275 Central Park West.
VON DOENHOFF, DOROTHEA, Cedar St., Elmhurst, L. I.
VON FEST, MELAINE, 41 Burger Ave., W. Brighton. Tel. 647 W. Brighton.
WAGNER, JULIA A., 243 E. 68th St. Tel. 6930 Plaza.
WEYMANN, LINDA C., 148 E. 16th St.
WILLIAMS, ROSE, 2089 Pacific St., Brooklyn.
WUNDERLICH, ELSA P., Philipse Manor, Tarrytown. Tel. 331 Tarrytown.
ZAISSER, MATILDA, 506 W. 168th St.
ZEITLIN, IDA A., 1346 Lyman Pl., The Bronx, N. Y. C. Tel. 2646 Tremont.

History.

ABELOW, SAMUEL P., 367 Clifton Pl., Brooklyn.
ARTHE, ETHEL K., 175 Quincy St., Brooklyn. Tel. Decatur 1261-J.
BETSCH, GERTRUDE E., 11 Second St., Brooklyn.
BIRBER, ISADORE, 820 E. 14th St., Flatbush.
BREWSTER, ADELAIDE, 442 Putnam Ave., Brooklyn. Tel. 6845-W Bedford.
CONOVITZ, MICHAEL, 35 Morrell St., Brooklyn.
CONROY, MARY S., 26 Townsend Ave., Stapleton. Tel. 1648-W Tompkinsville.
DESHEL, MORRIS C., 646 E. 183d St., Manhattan.
DONEGAN, SARAH C., 5 Henderson Pl., Manhattan. Tel. 7710 Lenox.
DORNEY, HELEN R., 18 E. 80th St., Manhattan.
DRESSNER, ROBERT H., 763 Tinton Ave., The Bronx, N. Y. C.
FEELEY, VERA E., 586 City Island Ave., City Island.
FLEMING, EDITH J., 544 W. 157th St., Manhattan.
FRACKMAN, MARK, 1339 Forty-fifth St., Brooklyn.
FRAENDT, ANTONIA H., 522 E. 86th St., Manhattan.
FRANKLIN, MARJORY L., 39 Claremont Ave., Manhattan. Tel. 6480 Morningside, Apt. 82.
GIDEN, ABRAHAM, 89 Pitt St., Manhattan. Tel. 1510 Orchard.
GILBERT, GRACE R., 209 Clinton St., Brooklyn.
GITTLESON, WILLIAM, 14 E. 113th St., Manhattan.
GOLDBLOOM, SIMON, 672 E. 21st St., Brooklyn.
HALL, MARY A., 4 De Windt St., Fishkill-on-the-Hudson.
HENNELLY, MARY F., 47 St. Marks Pl., Brooklyn.
HOLLIS, IDA M., 320 W. 115th St., Manhattan.
HYMAN, JOSEPH C., 1552 Hoe Ave., The Bronx, N. Y. C.
JESSER, EDWARD A., Central Ave., Richmond Hill.
JESSER, FLORENCE M., Central Ave., Richmond Hill.
JONES, FLORENCE I., 676 Delamere Pl., Brooklyn.
KAPLAN, MICHAEL, 1708 Pitkin Ave., Brooklyn.
KAPLAN, PETER G., 119 E. 104th St., Manhattan. Tel. 5779 Harlem.
McGIVNEY, MABEL, 789 West End Ave., Manhattan.
McGUIRE, MARGUERITE E., 162 Himrod St., Brooklyn.
MARKEY, FRANCES, 436 E. 140th St., Manhattan.
MERRILL, ESTELLE W., 171 Steuben St., Brooklyn.
MONROE, ELIZABETH J., 144 W. 104th St., Manhattan. Tel. 291 Riverside.
MURPHY, MARIE E., 817 Tenth Ave., Manhattan.
NACHEMOR, MORRIS, 1764 Hoe Ave., The Bronx, N. Y. C.
PALLEY, DAVID M., 1412 Pitkin Ave., Brooklyn.
RAUTH, LILLIAN, 695 Lafayette Ave., Brooklyn. Tel. 965 Bedford.
REESE, CLARE H., 478 W. 145th St., Manhattan. Tel. 793 Audubon.

RILEY, EUGENE B., 466 Humboldt St., Brooklyn.
SALZMAN, ANNA B., 5403 Fifteenth Ave., Brooklyn.
SAMUELS, FLORENCE, 688 Putnam Ave., Brooklyn.
SAYLER, FLORENCE E., 544 Second St., Brooklyn.
SHEINHOUSE, HERMAN, 1004 Trinity Ave., Melrose 3544-M.
SIMMONS, GLADYS C., 676 Tenth St., Brooklyn.
SMALLHOUSER, 259 Hart St., Brooklyn.
SMITH, DONALD, 1161 Amsterdam Ave., Manhattan.
STEINMETZ, WILLIAM, 1111 Portland Ave., Woodhaven. Tel. 1757-W Richmond Hill.
TRACY, HELEN L., 431 Fifty-fourth St., Brooklyn.
WHALEN, EDWIN A., 1219 Taylor Ave., Manhattan.
WHALEN, FRANK D., 223 W. 105th St., Manhattan. Tel. 9061 Riverside.

Italian

TOGLIA, VETO G., 456 Main St., New Rochelle, N. Y.

Laboratory
Laboratory Assistant

DODD HELEN W., 1465 Avenue A.
VALENTINE, MAYFORTH, 856 Bushwick Ave., Brooklyn.

Latin

ARNOLD, EDITH S., 331 Greene Ave., Brooklyn. Tel. 2597 Prospect.
BELL, ANNA, 92 Elizabeth St., W. Brighton. Tel. 32 W. Brighton.
BRENNER, CHARLOTTE, 34 Woodbine St., Brooklyn. Tel. 2317-W Bushwick.
BRILEY, ELSIE N., 1893 Pacific St., Brooklyn. Tel. 415-R East New York.
CHILD, ANDREW M., JR., 906 Summit Ave., The Bronx, N. Y. C.
DEMPSEY, JOSEPHINE A., 467 Fifty-fifth St., Brooklyn. Tel. 5126-W Sunset.
EPSTEIN, BERNARD, 853 Beck St., The Bronx, N. Y. C. Tel. 9110 Melrose.
FALK, HANNAH C., 304 W. 99th St.
FAY, HARRISON A., 601 W. 164th St.
FOX, ETTA B., 581 W. 161st St. Tel. 2026 Cortland.
FRAME, RACHEL M., 27 S. Thirteenth Ave., Mt. Vernon, N. Y.
FRISCH, JANET R., 144 Schenectady Ave., Brooklyn.
FRUENBERG, BENJAMIN, 6 E. 118th St.
GALLIS, MARGARET M., 309 N. Mountain Ave., Montclair, N. J. Tel. 314-M Montclair.
GERSTEIN, ROSE, 468 Monroe St., Brooklyn.
GRAF, BERTHA, 850 Union St., Brooklyn. Tel. 1090 Prospect.
HENDERSON, MARY, 1867 Seventh Ave. Tel. 3223 Morningside.
HILLMAN, MARJORIE, 5 Delaware Pl., Flushing, L. I. Tel. 1355-W Flushing.
HINES, JAMES D., 75 Seventh Ave.
HODGES, MILDRED L., Laureate Hall, 119th St. and Amsterdam Ave., Manhattan.
KEENAN, IRENE, 70 Third Pl., Brooklyn.
KLEIN, SYDNEY, 163 South Ninth St., Brooklyn. Tel. 2324-J Williamsburgh.
LAX, HERMAN, 71 Avenue D.
LEVY, JOSEPH, 408 Douglas St., Brooklyn. Tel. 583-J Prospect.
LIND, JACOB J., 45 Floyd St., Brooklyn.
McGUFFEY, ALICE, St. James Rectory, Elmhurst, L. I.
McKENZIE, ISABEL, 67 Lenox Ave., East Orange, N. J.
McMAHON, MARY J., 201 W. 112th St.
MAHER, ADELAIDE E., 72 E. 121st St.
MANN, JACOB, 1302 Sixty-seventh St., Brooklyn.
MORRIS, GERTRUDE E., 396 E. 171st St. Tel. 5580 Tremont.
O'FARRELL, ELIZABETH, 139 W. 36th St.
ORLINSKY, JOSEPH B., 7 W. 111th St.
OSTERBERG, RUTH, 270 W. 118th St.
PAPE, CHARLES, JR., 811 Ocean Parkway, Brooklyn. Tel. 2332-J Flatbush.
RICHARDSON, MARGARET, 18 Guion St., New Rochelle, N. Y.
SANBORN, MILDRED E., 1477 Lexington Ave.
SCHUSTER, MATILDA, 1326 Webster Ave., The Bronx, N. Y. C.
SEYMOUR, IDA I., 440 E. 57th St. Tel. 5361 Plaza.
TOBIN, LAURETTA M., 108 W. 126th St. Tel. 4983 Morningside.
TOWLE, JAMES A., 13 Avalon Ave., Jamaica, L. I. Tel. 284-M or J Jamaica.
UPSON, KATHRYN I., 2287 University Ave., Fordham. Tel. 6007 Tremont.
VENTRES, ADELAIDE B., 424 W. 119th St. Tel. 3350 Morningside.
WEBER, GRACE M., 659 Eightieth St., Brooklyn.
YOUNG, ANNE W., 8807 Seventeenth Ave., Bath Beach.

Latin and Stenography

SINOPOLI, EMILIA F., 3089 Broadway. Tel. 1338 Morningside.

Library Assistant

BEHAR, ELY M., 523 W. 151st St. Tels. 2813 Audubon; 4762 Beekman.
JOSEPH, NANNINE V., 514 W. 122d St. Tel. 3632 Morningside.
KNIGHT, MARION A., 79 Beaver Hill Ave., Lynn, Mass.
O'DONNELL, MARJORIE, 2870 Briggs Ave., Bedford Park.
STAGER, FREYA, 101 E. 78th St.
WILMOT, HARRIET E., 391 Dean St., Brooklyn.

Machine Shop

DUSTIN, HAROLD M., 1062 Fifty-second St., Brooklyn.

Mathematics

BARON, JACOB, 859 Kelly St., The Bronx, N. Y. C. Tel. 1926 Melrose.
BINGHAM, NELLIE H., 432 Fourth St., Brooklyn. Tel. 3315 South.
BOMAN, JOHN S., 1113 Lexington Ave. Tel. 7398 Lenox.
BUECHNER, ELSIE E., Ozone Park (Rockaway Rd.).
BURNE, ELEANOR, Pine St., Douglaston, N. Y. Tel. 2653 Bayside.
COLVILLE, ELISE H., 102 York Ave., New Brighton.
CRESPI, ALBERT A. R., 346 Rutland Rd., Brooklyn. Tel. 1143-M Flatbush.
DENHAM, SIDONIE B., 184 S. Oxford St., Brooklyn.
DOWNS, JOSEPHINE A., 414 Pacific St., Brooklyn. Tel. 3582 Main.
EASTON, EDWARD R., 437 W. 57th St.
EHRLICH, SARA E., 2776 Eighth Ave.
ELDER, MAUREEN, 18 Pierpont St., Brooklyn.
FIEBIG, EMMA, 313 E. 57th St.
FRIEND, ETTA V., 62 W. 124th St.
GARRETSON, KATE, 73 W. 124th St.
GLASER, HENRY, Dunellen, N. J.
GOLDSTEIN, SAMUEL, 155 W. 65th St.
GRUNERT, RUBERTA, 2409 Richmond Rd., New Dorp, S. I.
HAMBURGER, MILDRED V., 445 W. 153d St.
HULNEWINCKEL, ROBERT, 437 Macon St., Brooklyn.
JOHNSON, MARGERETE, 168 Hancock St., Brooklyn. Tel. 3351-M Bedford.
KENNY, JOSEPHINE, 430 Jefferson Ave., Brooklyn.
KNOX, MARGUERITE, 243 Washington St.
LAVINE, ROSE, 352 W. 117th St.
LESKOWITZ, ALBERT, 370 Marcy Ave., Brooklyn.
MAMELOK, LOUIS, 220 East Broadway. Tels. 2981 and 6172 Orchard.
MASLEN, EDYTHE W., 2312 University Ave., The Bronx, N. Y. C. Tel. 4425 Tremont.
MORRIS, EDITH M., 396 E. 171st St.
MOSES, SOPHIA, 228 Westchester Ave., Mt. Vernon.
NEU, BLANCHE, 226 E. 71st St.
O'BRIEN, WILLIAM J., 36 Wellington Court, Brooklyn.
PAUL, MABEL L., 1346 Teller Ave.
PERO, SALLIE E., 30 Convent Ave. Tel. 6680 Morningside.
ROSENTHAL, JULIUS M., 1855 Park Pl., Brooklyn.
ROWELL, GEORGIA E., 523 Fifty-fourth St., Brooklyn.
SELIGMAN, NATHAN, 100 Avenue C.
SEVESO, ANGELINA, 43 Tillary St., Brooklyn. Tel. 3837-W Main.
SIMONS, MARION L., 231 William St., Port Chester, N. Y.
WARSCHAUER, JOSEPHINE, 166 E. 67th St.
WEINER, MEYER, 413 New Jersey Ave., Brooklyn.
WOOD, JAMES M., JR., 162 Cleveland St., Brooklyn.
YEAN, RUA L., Bay View Ave., New Rochelle, N. Y.

Millinery

FARRELL, FRANCES J., 346 Clifton Pl., Brooklyn.
HALL, LEILA F., 937 Greene Ave., Brooklyn. Tel. 2351-W Bushwick.

Mechanical Drawing

BYRNES, J. HOWELL, 50 N. 19th St., Flushing. Tel. 1805-W Flushing.
SIEGEL, SAMUEL, 107 E. 10th St.

Music

CARSON, EMMA A., 204 W. 92d St.
GOULD, FRANCES R., 858 Jewett Ave., West Brighton.
HOCHSTEIN, BEATRICE, 8 W. 116th St. Tel. 3387 Harlem.
LINDORFF, THEODORE J., 140 Barclay St., Flushing.
REYNOLDS, GERALD, 238 W. 56th St.
TRAVER, HELEN W., 242 W. 109th St.
WOOD, MINNIE S., 601 W. 156th St. Tel. 3280 Audubon.
WORTMANN, JOHANNA C.

Physical Training

CLARK, HELEN A., 80 Decatur St., Brooklyn.
DIX, GERTRUDE A., 144 Riverside Drive.
GORSCH, RUDOLPH V., 3332 Decatur Ave., The Bronx, N. Y. C.
HOLZBERG, LILIAN, 233 W. 111th St.
KRANEY, SIDNEY, 73 Ridge St.
LANGDON, DOROTHY, 610-A Third St., Brooklyn.
LEVERIDGE, ETHEL S., 277 East Broadway. Tel. 1544 Orchard.
LEVIN, IRVING, 835 Beck St., The Bronx, N. Y. C.
LIVINGSTON, GERTRUDE C., 226 Edgecomb Ave.
McMILLEN, ELEANOR, 1 W. 101st St.
MULLEN, JOHN A., 420 E. 84th St.
NEIDHART, AUGUSTA W., 332 W. 51st St., Tel. 8111 Columbus.

OBLER, DAVID M., 192 Rivington St.
OSTROFF, MAE, 879 Flatbush Ave. Tel. 640-W Flatbush.
PAUL, PHILIP, 605 E. 11th St.
RANSONE, EMMA A., 326 Audubon Ave.
REYNOLDS, PERCY L., 129 E. 10th St. Tel. 4645 Orchard.
ROSEN, DAISY E., 24 Lewis Ave., Brooklyn.
RYAN, LORETTA C., 143 W. 84th St.
SCHILING, HELEN, 38 Martense St., Flatbush.
SCHMAUSS, VERA S., 50 E. 86th St.
SCHOELLER, ELLA M., 121 Sixth St., Elmhurst, L. I.
SEELEY, ELLIE W., 158 St. Marks Ave., Brooklyn.
SILBERT, JACOB, 109 W. 114th St.
STAHL, JULIA, 332 W. 51st St.
WARREN, S. FLORENCE, 517 W. 113th St.
WESTON, CAROLINE R., 205 W. 103d St.
WICKS, HELEN E., 108 Ft. Greene Pl., Brooklyn.
WILSON, RANDOLPH C., 618 W. 138th St. Tel. 4889-M Audubon.
WUCHNER, MARY B., 652 E. 149th St.
ZENKER, HELEN, 351 E. 84th St. Tel. 2042 Lenox.
ZUCKERMAN, ROSE, 359 Bristol St., Brooklyn. Tel. 3532 East New York.

Physics

ARCHER, CATHERINE, 175 E. 74th St. Tel. 3507 Lenox.
CEROW, GEORGIA, 503 W. 175th St. Tel. 5146-J Audubon.
DEMAREST, MARY C., Manuet, N. Y.
GREENBERG, HYMAN, 1115 Westchester Ave., The Bronx, N. Y. C.
McCORMICK, GRACE M., 176 E. 71st St.

Physiography

HALLECK, PARKER S., College Point, L. I.

Sewing

CLARK, SARAH V., Junior League House.
FERRIGAN, ROSALIE, 2176 Sixty-sixth St., Brooklyn.
GEER, ELONE E., 130 Claremont Ave. Tel. 281 Morningside.
GORMAN, ANNA L., 218 Van Wyck Ave., Richmond Hill. Tel. 327-M Jamaica.
McKEON, MARY J., 564½ Clinton St., Brooklyn.
MARTIN, JANE, 208 W. 184th St.
SACKMAN, LILLIAN, 540 Manhattan Ave. Tel. 5770 Morningside.
SMITH, EDNA L., 106 Hancock St., Brooklyn. Tel. 309-J Bedford.

Spanish

BOVE, ANTHONY J., 946 Herkimer St., Brooklyn.
DE TOVA, MARGARETA M., 139 W. 16th St.
HEMINGWAY, GERTRUDE C., 218 W. 121st St. Tels. 754 Morningside and 7800 Hanover.
MATIENGO, CARLOTA, Whittier Hall.
SPARKMAN, COLLYE, 32 Waverly Place.
TOWES, ARTURO, 524 W. 123d St.

Stenography

ARNSTEIN, SIDNEY, 941 Intervale Ave., The Bronx, N. Y. C. Tel. 5771 Melrose.
CHAPMAN, WILMA C., 117 First Pl., Brooklyn.
FINK, ANNA H., 522 Grand St., Brooklyn. Tel. 2664 Stagg.
FRANKEL, RACHEL, 1057 Hoe Ave., The Bronx, N. Y. C.
GALLAGHER, ANNIE B., 328 E. 124th St.
GRAHAM, MARGARET, 163 W. 105th St.
JOHNSON, GRACE M., 1307 Clifton St., Washington, D. C.
KAPLAN, ABRAHAM, 1486 Fifth Ave.
KEENAN, IRENE, 70 Third Pl., Brooklyn.
KEUNE, EMMA, 10 Sherman Pl., Jersey City, N. J. Tel. 4118-J Jersey City.
McELLINNEY, ANDREW J., 142 W. 131st St.
MANN, ANNIS, 976 Tinton Ave., The Bronx, N. Y. C.
MINER, MILDRED, 918 Hancock St., Brooklyn.
O'CONNELL, JOHN J., 340 Dean St., Brooklyn.
SCHWAGER, HARRY, 517 W. 144th St. Tel. 2770 Audubon.
STEINECKE, JEANNETTE A., 56½ Lynch St., Brooklyn. Tel. 1150 Williamsburgh.

Stenography and Typewriting.

BERNSTEIN, DAVID, 63 E. 117th St. Tel. 4017 Cortland.
JAFFE, ISIDORE, 214 Henry St.
NEARING, FANNIE, 689 Putnam Ave., Brooklyn.
RYAN, EDWARD J., 457 Forty-eighth St., Brooklyn.

Woodworking

SOPER, ARTHUR R., 1182 Putnam Ave., Brooklyn.

ALPHABETICAL LIST OF ALL HIGH SCHOOL TEACHERS

A

ABRAHAM, NATHAN—Assistant Commercial Subjects; 20 East 97th St., Manhattan. Tel. 5563 Lexington.
ABBOT, FRANCIS H.—First Assistant English, Curtis H. S.; 12 Castleton Park, W. Brighton, N. Y. Tel. 413-J Tompkinsville.
ABBOTT, FREDERICK B.—Assistant Mechanical Drawing, Manual Training H. S.; 419 9th St., Brooklyn.
ABBOT, MARGUERITE W.—Assistant French, Girls' H. S.; 1205 Bergen St., Brooklyn.
ABBOTT, ROYAL A.—Assistant English, De Witt Clinton H. S.; 882 E. 10th St., Brooklyn.
ACKER, MARGARET K.—Assistant English, Bryant H. S;. 50 Woolsey St., Astoria, N. Y.
ACKERIE, IDA V.—Assistant German, Evander Childs H. S.; 110 E. 159th St., The Bronx, N. Y. C.
ACKERLEY, JENNIE—Assistant Mathematics, Morris H. S.; 416 W. 118th St., Manhattan. Tel. 3502 Morningside.
ADAIR, EDITH—Assistant English, Girls' H. S.; 566 Greene Ave., Brooklyn.
ADAMS, ISABEL—Assistant Art Department, Washington Irving H. S.; 128 W. 82d St., Manhattan. Tel. 8614 Schuyler.
ADAMS, MILLY E.—Assistant Drawing, De Witt Clinton H. S.; 211 W. 85th St., Manhattan.
ADLER, DAVID—Assistant German, Eastern District H. S.; 593-A Macon St., Brooklyn. Tel. 6768-J Bedford.
ADLER, DAVID—German, Eastern District H. S.; 593A Macon St.; Brooklyn. Tel. 6768-J Bedford.
AKE, VIRGINIA A.—Assistant Stenography and Typewriting, Judia Richman H. S.; 215 E. 15th St., Manhattan. Tel. 2934 Stuyvesant.
ALDEN, HENRY T.—Assistant to Principal, Boys' H. S.; 185 Quincy St., Brooklyn; Telephone, 6361-J Bedford.
ALDINGER, HARRY E.—Assistant Physical Training, H. S. of Commerce; 736 Riverside Drive. Tel. 4160 Audubon.
ALDRIDGE, VINCENT—Assistant Mathematics, Manual Training H. S.; 32 Clarkson Ave., Brooklyn. Tel. 921-J Flatbush.
ALTHAUS, AMALIE—Assistant German, Morris H. S.; 2770 Briggs Ave., The Bronx, N. Y. C.
ALTHAUS, EDWARD—First Assistant Modern Languages, Morris H. S.; 2770 Briggs Ave., The Bronx, N. Y. C.
ALLEN, J. TREVETTE—Assistant French, Manual Training H. S.; 1548 E. 46th St., Brooklyn.
ALLEN, RALPH W.—Assistant Drawing, Richmond Hill H. S.; 325 Herald Ave., Richmond Hill, L. I.
ALLEN, WINIFRED S.—Assistant Latin, Bay Ridge H. S.; 112 Prospect Pl., Brooklyn.
ALLEY, M. IDA—Assistant Physical Science, Washington Irving H. S.; 215 E. 15th St., Manhattan. Tel. 2934 Stuyvesant.
ALLYN, LOUISE—Assistant Shorthand and Typewriting, Washington Irving H. S.; 128 W. 11th St., Manhattan. Tel. 661 Chelsea.
AMES, JESSIE T.—Assistant Drawing, Morris H. S.; 1 W. 127th St., Manhattan. Tel. 5770 Harlem.
AMMERMAN, S. LEWIS—Assistant Physical Science, Washington Irving H. S.; 1305 Dorchester Rd., Brooklyn.
ANDERSON, MARY—Assistant French, Eastern District H. S.; 431 Classon Ave., Brooklyn. Tel. 2597 Prospect.
ANDERSON, MARY E.—French, Eastern District H. S.; 431 Classon Ave., Brooklyn.
ANDERSON, WOODFORD D.—Assistant Accounts, Commercial H. S.; 1535 Fifty-fourth St., Brooklyn.
ANDREWS, GRACE—Assistant History, Morris H. S.; 65 Jefferson Ave., Brooklyn. Tel. 5621 Bedford.
ANDREWS, RICHARD M.—Assistant Mathematics, Stuyvesant H. S.; 373 W. 116th St., Manhattan. Tel. 6620 Morningside.
ANDREWS, WM. H.—Assistant Physical Training, Boys' H. S.; 265 Hawthorne St., Brooklyn; Tel. 7151-W Flatbush.
ANNETT, SARAH E.—Library Assistant, Washington Irving H. S.; 609 W. 127th St., Manhattan. Tel. 6204 Morningside.
ANTHONY, OSCAR W.—First Assistant Mathematics, De Witt Clinton H. S.; Plandome, L. I. Tel. 148-J Manhasset.
APPEL, FRANK J.—Assistant German, Morris H. S.; 382 Wadsworth Ave., Manhattan. Tel. 6030 Audubon.
ARDEN, HARRIETTE—Librarian, De Witt Clinton, H. S.; 6 W. 91st St., Manhattan.
ARENWALD, MESMIN—Assistant Mathematics Evander Childs H. S.; 1145 Vyse Ave., New York.
AREY, ALBERT L.—First Assistant Physical Sciences, Girls' H. S.; Roslyn, N. Y.
ARMAND, EMMA C.—Assistant French, Marris H. S.; 550 W. 149th St., Manhattan.
ARMAND, LOUIS T.—Assistant French, De Witt Clinton H. S.; 50 W. 149th St., Manhattan.
ARNDT, EMMA—Assistant German, Washington Irving H. S.; 206 E. 17th St., Manhattan. Tel. 1580 Stuyvesant.

ARNOLD, DAVID L.—First Assistant Mathematics, Julia Richman H. S.; 128 Drake Ave., New Rochelle, N. Y. Tel. 867-W New Rochelle.
ARNOWITT, LEON—Assistant Commercial Branches, Washington Irving H. S.; 130 W. 113th St., Manhattan. Tel. 2112 Morningside.
ARTHUR, L. LOUISE—Assistant History, Bryant H. S.; 515 Lexington Ave., Manhattan. Tel. 1435 Murray Hill.
ASHCRAFT, CARARIE VAN R.—Assistant Physical Training, Julia Richman H. S.; 204 W. 136th St., Manhattan.
ATHOLZ, NATHANIEL—Assistant Commercial Branches, Evander Childs H. S.; 1543 Minford Pl., The Bronx, N. Y. C.
ATWATER, JOHN C.—Assistant Physics (Physics and Chemistry), Richmond Hill H. S.; 224 Stoothoff Ave., Richmond Hill, L. I.
AUGSBURY, EARL S.—Assistant Mathematics, Stuyvesant H. S.; 16 Arden St., Manhattan. Tel. 3212 Audubon.
AUSLANDER, ARMIN—Assistant Stenography, Typewritng and Correspondence, Bushwick H. S.; 222 W. 140th St., Manhattan. Tel. 3073 Harlem.
AUSTIN, HARRY W.—Assistant Shop Work, Commercial H. S.; Forest Hills Inn, Forest Hills, L. I.
AUSTIN, MARY—Assistant Physical Training, Erasmus Hall H. S. 228-W Fordham.
AUSTIN, MRS. MARY E.—Assistant Physical Training, Curtis H. S.; 54 Summit Ave., New Dorp, S. I.
AVENT, JOHN M.—Assistant English, Marris H. S.; 3 Woodcrest Ave., White Plains, N. Y. Tel. 44-J White Plains.
AVERILL, ETHEL H.—Assistant Art Department, Washington Irving H. S.; 217 Brooklyn Ave., Brooklyn. Tel. 1131-J Bedford.
AVIRETT, MAY G.—Assistant German, Bay Ridge H. S.; 1023 Carroll St., Brooklyn.
AYRES, MARY S.—Assistant English, Eastern District H. S.; 480 Clinton Ave., Brooklyn.
AYRES. MARY S.—English, Eastern District H. S.; 480 Clinton Ave., Brooklyn.

B

BABCOCK, MAUDE R.—Assistant German, Girls' H. S.; 204 Macon St., Brooklyn.
BACH, ELIZABETH M.—Assistant. Mathematics, Bay Ridge H. S.; 25 S. Oxford St., Brooklyn.
BACHELDER, MARY A.—Assistant French, Manual Training H. S.; 567 6th St., Brooklyn.
BACON, HELEN E.—Assistant English, Wadleigh H. S.; 537 W. 121st St. Tel. 5120 Morningside.
BAER, DENA—Assistant History, Morris H. S.; 150 St. Nicholas Ave., Manhattan.
BAGENSTOSE. HARVEY—Assistant English, Commercial H. S.; 298 Parkside Ave., Brooklyn.
BAGGS, MARTHA.—Assistant Biology, Bay Ridge H. S.; 112 25th St., Brooklyn.
BAIER, JOSEPH G.—Assistant Physics ,Stuyvesant H. S.; 310 Sanford St., New Brunswick, N. J. Tel. 539-J New Brunswick.
BAKER, A. LATHAM—First Assistant Mathematics, Manual Training H. S.; 41 Slocum Crescent. Forest Hills Gardens, L. I. Tel. 6313-W Forest Hills.
BAKER, ELEANOR R.—Assistant Mathematics, Manual Training H. S.; 430 W. 118th St., Manhattan. Tel. 3880 Morningside.
BALDWIN, EDWIN F.—Assistant Commercial Branches, H. S. of Commerce, 600 W. 178th St., Manhattan.
BALDWIN, JESSIE M.—English, Newtown H. S.; 59 Gerry Ave., Elmhurst, L. I.
BALDWIN, JULIA I.—Librarian, Newtown H. S.; 1742 Mt. Hope Ave., The Bronx, N. Y. C.
BALDWIN, WALTER J.—Assistant Mathematics, Manual Training H. S.; 253 Carlton Ave., Brooklyn.
BALTOR, MRS. BELLA M.—Clerical Assistant, Eastern District H. S.; 1636 49th St., Brooklyn. Tel. 2874-R Borough Park.
BALTY, FRANK B.—First Assistant Commercial Branches, Eastern District H. S.; 56 Morningside Ave. East, Manhattan.
BALTZ, FRANK P.—Substitute Commercial Branches, Eastern District H. S.; 56 Morningside Ave. East, Manhattan.
BALLARD, CHARLES C.—Assistant English, Morris H. S.; 200 Claremont Ave. Tel. 211 Morningside.
BANGHART, ELIZABETH—Assistant Music, Bryant H. S.; The Adlon, 54th St. and Seventh Ave., Manhattan. Tel. 9490 Columbus.
BANNON, AGNES R.—Clerical Assistant, Eastern District H. S.; 336 Park Pl., Brooklyn. Tel. 4873-M Prospect.
BARADENHEUER, CLARA E.—Assistant German, Flushing H. S.; 628 8th St., College Point, L. I.
BARASCH, MORRIS—Assistant Mathematics, Manual Training H. S.; 701 Prospect Ave., The Bronx, N. Y. C.
BARBANELL, A. IRVING—Assistant Mathematics, Far Rockaway H. S.; 144 Pennsylvania Ave., Brooklyn.
BARBER, CORA L.—Assistant English, Erasmus Hall H. S.; 191 Lefferts Pl., Brooklyn. Tel. 5478 Prospect.
BARBER, HARRY G.—Assistant Biology, De Witt Clinton H. S.; 12 Clay Ave., Roselle Park, N. J.
BARBER, SACO M.—Assistant Oral English, Richmond Hill H. S.; 191 Lefferts Pl., Brooklyn. Tel. 5478 Prospect.
BARBERIS. ELIGIO G.—Assistant French (Italian), Washington Irving H. S.; 106 44th St., Corona, L. I. Tel, 343-W Newtown.
BARBOUR, WIILLIAM C.—Assistant Biology, H. S. of Commerce; 149 Newark Ave., Bloomfield, N. J. Tel. 3314 Bloomfield.
BARCLAY, MARGARET—Assistant Biology, ay Ridge H. S.; 74 Rutland Rd., Brooklyn.
BARKER, M. ELLEN—Assistant Mathematics (in charge of Annex in P. S. 42), Girls' H. S.; 637 St. Marks Ave., Brooklyn.
BARLOW, MARGARET M.—Assistant Mathematics, Bay Ridge H. S.; 15 Glendale Pl., Brooklyn.
BARLOW, WILLIAM M.—Assistant German, Commercial H. S.; 282 Halsey St., Brooklyn.
BARMEYER, GEORGE H.—Assistant Chemistry, De Witt Clinton; First St., Bayside, L. I.
BARNARD, JULIA E.—Assistant Drawing, Washington Irving H. S.; 9 Spring St., Stamford, Conn. Tel. 298 Stamford.

BARNES, EDWIN A.—Assistant Physical Science, Far Rockaway H. S.; 155 Crescent St., Far Rockaway, N. Y. Tel. 2030 Far Rockaway.
BARNUM, GRACE E.—Assistant Physical Training, Morris H. S.; 50 Morningside Drive. Tel. 5020 Morningside.
BARNWELL, WALTER—First Assistant Mathematics, Flushing H. S.; Plandome, L. I. Tel. 357 Manhasset.
BARON, LUCILLE E.—Substitute German, Washington Irving H. S.; 2098 Vyse Ave., The Bronx, N. Y. C. Tel. 4891 Tremont.
BARRETT, MARTHA BELLE—Assistant History, Wadleigh H. S.; 435 W. 123rd St. Tel. 583 Morningside.
BARRETT, MARY C.—Assistant Music, Wadleigh H. S. Annex; 759 E. 158th St. Tel. 1718-M Melrose.
BARRETT, MARY C.—Assistant Music, Girls' H. S.; 759 E. 158th St., Manhattan.
BARRON, HONORA A.—Assistant Domestic Arts, Washington Irving H. S.; 253 W. 136th St., Manhattan. Tel. 7645 Audubon.
BARROWS, TESSIE—Assistant German, Bushwick H. S.; 203 W. 119th St., Manhattan.
BARRY, LORETTA—Assistant English, Washington Irving H. S.; 225 W. 14th St., Manhattan. Tel. 5402 Chelsea.
BARTON, ROSE M.—Assistant English, Wadleigh H. S.; 508 W. 112th St. Tel. 3830 Morningside.
BASS, BERTHA—Assistant History, Wadleigh H. S. Annex; 501 W. 120th St. Tel. 4590 Morningside.
BASSETT, ELIZABETH W.—Assistant History, Washington Irving H. S.; 400 W. 118th St., Manhattan. Tel. 4769 Morningside.
BATCHELDER, MARGARET GOLD—Assistant English, Bushwick H. S.; 54 Woolsey St., Astoria, L. I. Tel. 1710-W. Astoria.
BATCHELOR, CHARLES B.—Assistant Physical Training, Erasmus Hall H. S.; 218 Martense St.
BATES, ABBY B.—First Assistant History, Morris H. S.; 1421 University Ave., The Bronx, N. Y. C. Tel. 5656 Tremont.
BATES, CLIFTON W.—German, Boys' H. S.; 363 Grand Ave., Brooklyn; Tel. 883-M Prospect.
BATES, HERBERT—First Assistant English, Manual Training H. S.; Northport, L. I.
BATES, THOMAS S.—Assistant Elocution, Morris H. S.; 244 E. 86th St., Manhattan.
BATT, DAVID—Librarian, Stuyvesant H. S.; 1 E. 119th St., Manhattan.
BATTELL, JOHN M.—Assistant English, Erasmus Hall H. S.; 529 5th St., Brooklyn.
BATTEY, LEWIS B.—Assistant Mechanical Drawing, Stuyvesant H. S.; 189 Claremont Ave., Man-
BAUMEISTER, JOHN—First Assistant Modern Languages (German), Flushing H. S.; 402 Amity St., Flushing, L. I. Tel. 919 Flushing.
BAWDEN, SARAH E.—Assistant Eng., Manual Training H. S.; Queens, L. I. Tel. 6128-W Hollis.
BAXTER, FLORENCE—Assistant Mathematics, Washington Irving H. S.; 210 E. 17th St., Manhattan. Tel. 3770 Stuyvesant.
BAYLIS, SARA—Assistant Study Hall, De Witt Clinton H. S.; 760 N. Oak Drive, Bronxwood Park.
BEACH, MARY R.—Assistant Latin, Wadleigh H. S. Annex; 302 Convent Ave. Tel. 6890 Audubon.
BEACH, JESSIE A.—Assistant Mathematics, Washington Irving H. S.; 503-507 W. 121st St., Manhattan. Tel. 5010 Morningside.
BEARD, STELLA S.—Assistant English, Richmond Hill H. S.; 435 Greenwood Ave., Richmond Hill, L. I. Tel. 748 Richmond Hill.
BEARDSLEY, FRANK J.—Assistant Latin, Erasmus Hall H. S.; 443 E. 4th St.
BEARE, CORNELIA—Assistant English, Wadleigh H. S. Annex; 430 W. 119th St.
BEATMAN, AUGUSTUS S.—Assistant History, H. S. of Commerce; 1455 Undercliff Ave., The Bronx, N. Y. C. Tel. 4576 Tremont.
BEATON, AUGUSTA C.—Clerical Assistant, Wadleigh H. S.; 525 W. 123nd St.
BECHERT, ALEXANDER OTTO—Assistant German, Boys' H. S.; 600 Decatur St., Brooklyn.
BECK, FLORENCE—Junior English, Julia Richman H. S.; 520 W. 123d St., Manhattan. Tel. 9007 Morningside.
BECKER, CLARENCE H.—Assistant History, Boys' H. S.; 890 Putnam Ave., Brooklyn.
BECKER, NATHANIEL—Laboratory Assistant, Bryant H. S.; 334 Broome St., Manhattan. Tel. 1453 Orchard.
BECKLEY, CLARA M.—Assistant Librarian, Girls' H. S.: Box 204, Fort Lee, N. J. Tel. 193-J.
BECKMAN, FLORENCE I.—History, Eastern District H. S.; 141 W. 104th St., Manhattan.
BECKWITH, FRANCES A.—Assistant History, Wadleigh H. S.; 106 E. 52nd St. Tel. 7800 Plaza.
BEDFORD, EDGAR A.—Assistant Biology, Stuyvesant H. S.; Hollis, L. I. Tel. 6174-W Hollis.
BEEBE, DEE—Assistant Free Hand Drawing, Manual Training H. S.; 185 Berkeley Pl., Brooklyn.
BEECKMAN, FLORENCE L.—Assistant History, Eastern District H. S.; 141 W. 104th St., Manhattan.
BEERS, FLORENCE E.—Assistant Latin, Richmond Hill H. S.; 1288 Dean St., Brooklyn. Tel. 613 Bedford.
BEHA, JOSEPH L.—Assistant German, Stuyvesant H. S.; 171 W. 95th St., Manhattan. Tel. 4857 Riverside.
BEITEL, HELEN S.—Assistant Commercial Branches, Eastern District H. S.; 315 W. 94th St., Manhattan. Tel. 3700 Riverside.
BEITEL, HELEN S.—Commercial Branches, Eastern District H. S.; 315 W. 84th St., Manhattan. Tel. 3700 Riverside.
BELCHER, FRANCES S.—Assistant History, Washington Irving H. S.; 603 14th Ave., Paterson, N. J.
BELDING, ALBERT G.—First Assistant Commercial Branches, Far Rockaway H. S.; Cedarhurst, L. I. Tel. 1850-W Far Rockaway.
BELL, ANNA—Substitute Physical Training, Drawing, Music, Elocution, History, Curtis H. S. (Tottenville Annex); 92 Elizabeth St., W. Brighton, S. I. Tel. 32 W. Brighton, care Miss Bouton.
BEMENT, FREDRIC—First Assistant Chemistry (Natural Science), Bryant H. S.; Bayside, N. Y. Tel. 3083 Bayside.
BENEDICT, RALPH C.—Assistant Biology, H. S. of Commerce; 2979 Decatur Ave., The Bronx, N. Y. C. Tel. 697-W Tremont.
BENJAMIN, CLAUDE T.—Assistant English, Curtis H. S.; 410 Bard Ave., W. New Brighton, N. Y. Tel. 268-J W. Brighton.
BENJAMIN, EDITH SIBLEY—Assistant English, Bushwick H. S.; 282 McDonough St., Brooklyn. Tel. 3348-J. Bedford.

BENNETT, RAY—Assistant History, Wadleigh H. S.; 105 W. 163rd St., Bronx. Tel. 4413 Melrose.

BENNETT, R. GRANT—Assistant Chemistry, H. S. of Commerce; Hastings-on-Hudson, N. Y. Tel. 708 Hastings.

BENWAY, MABEL R.—Assistant Mathematics, Bay Ridge H. S.; 62 Pierrepont St., Brooklyn.

BERGAMINI, RACHEL—Assistant English, Washington Irving H. S.; 175 Claremont Ave., Manhattan. Tel. 5750 Morningside.

BERGER, WM. H.—Assistant Commercial Branches, Washington Irving H. S.; 339 E. 25th St., Brooklyn.

BERGHOFFEN, HERMAN—Assistant English, Manual Training H. S.; 1464 50th St., Brooklyn. Tel. 2636 Borough Park.

BERGMAN, MORRIS L.—Assistant Mathematics, Morris H. S.; 183 2d St.

BERKOWITCH, LOUIS B.—Assistant English, H. S. of Commerce; 952 Tiffany St., The Bronx, N. Y. C.

BERKOWITZ, LOUIS—Assistant German, Bushwick H. S.; 537 Willoughby Ave., Brooklyn.

BEYGRAU, FREDERICK R.—Assistant Stenography and Typewriting, H. S. of Commerce; 16 Woodcrest Ave., White Plains, N. Y. Tel. 1269-J White Plains, N. Y.

BERGSTRESSER, C. A.—Assistant Mathematics, Boys' H. S.; 216 Kingston Ave., Brooklyn; Tel. 8720-W Bedford.

BERRY, JAMES F.—Assistant Mathematics, De Witt Clinton H. S.; 601 W. 148th St., Manhattan. Tel. 4266 Audubon.

BERTSCHY, MAUDE—Assistant Drawing, Bushwick H. S.; 476 Clinton Ave., Brooklyn. Tel. 7261 Prospect.

BESARICK, CAROLINE B.—Assistant Physical Training, Manual Training H. S.; 1722 Caton Ave., Brooklyn. Tel. 9311 Flatbush.

BESSEY, MABEL A.—Assistant English, Bay Ridge H. S.; 64 Monroe St., Brooklyn.

BETSCH, GERTRUDE ELSIE—History, Erasmus Hall H. S.; 11 2d St., Brooklyn, Tel. 2243-J Hamilton.

BIERMAN, HENRY—Assistant French, De Witt Clinton H. S.; 431 E. 85th St., Manhattan.

BINGHAM, JESSIE H.—Assistant Drawing (Chairman), De Witt Clinton H. S.; 509 W. 121st St., Manhattan. Tel. 7800 Morningside.

BISHOP, M. L.—Assistant Mathematics, Boys' H. S.; 153 Halsey St., Brooklyn.

BLACKWELL, NANNIE G.—First Assistant French, Washington Irving H. S.; 8 E. 9th St., Manhattan. Tel. 5230 Stuyvesant.

BLAIR, ELIZABETH E.—Assistant Music, Wadleigh H. S.; 508 W. 122nd St. Tel. 902 Morningside.

BLAKELY, GILBERT S.—Principal Evander Childs H. S.; 2207 University Ave., New York. Tel-

BLANCHARD, D. HIRAM.—Assistant Mathematics, Boys' H. S.; 632 Eastern Parkway, Brooklyn.

BLANPIED, ETHEL O.—Assistant German, Curtis H. S.; Tompkinsville, N. Y. Tel. 339-W Tompkinsville.

BLENKER, ANNA C.—Assistant Drawing, Wadleigh H. S.; 405 W. 118th St. Tel. 1051 Morningside.

BLISS, RALPH P.—Assistant Mathematics, Commercial H. S.; 101 Hawthorne St., Brooklyn. Tel. 1141-M Flatbush.

BLOOM, IRA I.—Assistant Physical Training, Manual Training H. S.; 478 W. 158th St., Manhattan. Tel. 6047 Audubon.

BLUM, VIVIENNE H.—Assistant French, Washington Irving H. S.; 254 W. 98th St., Manhattan. Tel. 4248 Riverside.

BLUME, JULIUS—Assistant Modern Languages, H. S. of Commerce; 616 W. 137th St. Tel. 2250 Audubon.

BLUMENBERG, FRIEDA—Mathematics, Eastern District H. S.; 222 S. 9th St., Brooklyn. Morningside.

BLUMENSTOCK, J. LEWIS—Assistant History, Wadleigh H. S.; 134 Clifton Pl., Brooklyn. Tel. 7654-W Prospect.

BLUMGARTEN, SARA L.—Substitute German, Washington Irving H. S.; 958 Hoe Ave., The Bronx, N. Y. C. Tel. 2228 Melrose.

BOECKER, ALEXANDER—Assistant Shop, Manual Training H. S.; 554 7th St., Brooklyn.

BOGART, ELMER E.—Assistant Latin, Morris H. S.; 1125 Boston Rd., The Bronx, N. Y. C.

BOGART, SARAH H.—Assistant Latin, Morris H. S.; 352 E. 200th St., The Bronx, N. Y. C. Tel. 3997 Tremont.

BOGGS, DORA—Clerical Assistant, Eastern District H. S.; 1117 Waverly Pl., care Armstrong, Manhattan.

BOLE, JOHN A.—German, Eastern District H. S.; 39 Elmhurst Ave., Elmhurst, L. I. Tel. 281-R Newtown.

BOLE, JOHN A.—First Assistant Modern Languages, Eastern District H. S.; 39 Elmhurst Ave., Elmhurst, L. I. Tel. 281-R Newtown.

BOLGER, EDWIN A.—Assistant Stenography (Chairman of Dept.), Commercial H. S.; 426 Kosciuska St., Brooklyn. Tel. 1456-W Bushwick.

BONFOEY, EMMA—Assistant English, Far Rockaway H. S.; 1238 Pacific St., Brooklyn. Tel 6256 Bedford.

BOOK, ARTHUR E.—Commercial Branches, Newtown H. S.; 90 Cook Ave., Elmhurst, L. I.

BOOLE, EMILY—Assistant English, Manual Training H. S.; 1429 Avenue H, Brooklyn. Tel. 1123 Flatbush.

BOOLE, FLORENCE A.—Assistant English, Manual Training H. S.; 1429 Avenue H., Brooklyn. Tel. 1123 Flatbush.

BOOS, HERMAN J.—Assistant Physical Training, De Witt Clinton H. S.

BOOTH, S. MARY—Assistant Drawing, Washington Irving H. S.; 523 W. 121st St., Manhattan. Tel. 5271 Morningside.

BOOTHBY, NELLIE M.—Assistant Commercial Branches, Washington Irving H. S.; 19 W. 102d St., Manhattan. Tel. 2785 Riverside.

BOUGHTON, WILLIS—Assistant English, Erasmus Hall H. S.; 364 E. 21st St. Tel. 3997-J Flatbush.

BOURNE, MARY J.—Assistant History, Morris H. S.; 418 W. 118th St., Manhattan. Tel. 6656 Morningside.

BOUVARD, GERMAINE B.—Assistant French, Washington Irving H. S.; 544 W. 149th St., Manhattan. Tel. 2757 Audubon.
BOWLES, FRANK C.—Assistant Mathematics, H. S. of Commerce; 421 W. 121st St. Tel. 6769 Morningside.
BOWMAN, CORA M.—Assistant Mathematics, Wadleigh H. S.; 151 W. 105th St. Tel. 4182 Riverside.
BOWMAN, MINA—Assistant Latin, Eastern District H. S.; 527 W. 121st St., Manhattan. Tel. 5271 Morningside.
BOWMAN, NINA—Latin, Eastern District H. S.; 527 W. 121st St., Manhattan. Tel. 5271 Morningside.
BOYD, MAURICE C.—Assistant Drawing, Boys' H. S.; 30 Clarendon Pl., Bloomfield, N. J.; Tel. 2434-J Montclair.
BOYD, OLIVE A.—Assistant French, Washington Irving H. S.; 259 Decatur St., Brooklyn. Tel 1286 Bedford.
BOYLAN, ARTHUR A.—Assistant Elocution, De Wittt Clinton H. S.; 162d St. and Woodycrest Ave., Manhattan. Tel. 3052 Melrose.
BOYNTON, CAROLYN A.—Assistant English, Flushing H. S.; 102 Jagger Ave., Flushing, L. I. Tel. 322-W Flushing.
BOYNTON, GEORGE E.—First Assistant English, Erasmus Hall H. S.; 466 E. 18th St., Brooklyn.
BOYNTON, MARY LOUISE—German, Erasmus Hall H. S.; 466 E. 18th St., Brooklyn. Tel. 2281-M Flatbush.
Tel. 2281-M Flatbush.
BRACE, EDITH M.—Assistant Science, Eastern District H. S.; 1131 Bergen St., Brooklyn. Tel. 8281 Bedford.
BRACE, EDITH M.—Biology, Eastern District H. S.; 1131 Bergen St., Brooklyn. Tel 8281 Bedford.
BRACKETT, Mary M.—Clerical Assistant, Morris H. S.; 604 W. 115th St., Manhattan. Tel. 6740 Morningside.
BRADLEY, SUSAN M.—Assistant English, Jamaica H. S.; 45 Union Ave., Jamaica, N. Y.
BRADY, JOHN W.—Clerk, Bushwick H. S.; 280 Johnston Ave., Richmond Hill, L. I. Tel. Richmond Hill 204-M.
BRAMAN, MARY L.—Assistant Biology, Manual Training H. S.; 511 6th St., Brooklyn. Tel 1981 South.
BRAND, JOSEPHINE—Assistant Mathematics, Morris H. S.; 501 W. 138th St., Manhattan. Tel. 1670 Audubon.
BRAND, LOUIS—Assistant Stenography and Typewriting, Julia Richman H. S.; 954 Hoe Ave., The Bronx, N. Y. C.
BRANDAU, GEORGE J.—Assistant German, Stuyvesant H. S.; 626 E. 29th St., Brooklyn. Tel. 6712-W Flatbush.
BRANOWER, SOLOMON—Physics, Eastern District H. S.; 1815 7th Ave., Manhattan. Tel. 1214 Morningside.
BRANSON, ROSWELL HARRIS—Assistant Latin, Erasmus Hall H. S.; 239 Pennington Ave., Passaic, N. J. Tel. 2577 Passaic.
BRAUNSTEIN, WILLIAM—Assistant English, Commercial H. S.; 445 Pulaski St., Brooklyn.
BRECKENRIDGE, WM. E.—First Assistant Mathematics, Stuyvesant H. S.; 25 Park Ave., Mt. Vernon, N. Y. Tel. 2810-W Mt. Vernon.
BRENNAN, ALFRED T. W.—Assistant Economics, H. S. of Commerce; 106 E. 81st St., Manhattan.
BRESSLER, HELEN B.—Assistant English, Washington Irving H. S.; 158 2d Ave., Long Island City.
BREWER, FRANCIS E.—Assistant Latin, Curtis H. S.; 41 Hamilton Ave., New Brighton, N. Y. Tel. 337-W Tompkinsville.
BREWSTER, ADELAIDE—Substitute History, Erasmus Hall H. S.; 442 Putnam Ave, Brooklyn.
BRICKELMAIER, ALICE G.—Assistant Mathematics, Erasmus Hall H. S.; 639 Carlton Ave., Brooklyn.
BRIDGMAN, ANNE T.—Assistant History, Morris H. S.; 157 W. 123d St., Manhattan.
BRIGGS, EMILY E.—Assistant Latin, Girls' H. S.; 92 Gates Ave., Brooklyn.
BRIGGS, EVA E.—Assistant Mathematics, Bushwick H. S.; 92 Gates Ave., Brooklyn. Tel. 4280 Prospect.
BRIGGS, LARRY—History, Newtown H. S.; 160 Hanover Ave., Elmhurst, L. I.
BRIGHT, ROBERT A.—Assistant Chemistry, Stuyvesant H. S.; 6 Church St., Paterson, N. J.
BRILEY, BEATRICE A.—Assistant Physics, Girls' H. S.; 1893 Pacific St., Brooklyn. Tel. 415-R East New York.
BRILL, ABRAHAM—Assistant English, Boys' H. S.; 736 Home St., The Bronx. Tel. 8434 Melrose.
BROADHURST, PHILIP H.—Assistant Chemistry, De Witt Clinton H. S.; 119 Cortelyou Rd., Brooklyn.
BROCKMAN, MARY E.—Assistant Cooking, Julia Richman H. S.; 619 W. 127th St., Manhattan. Tel. 2920 Morningside.
BROOKS, MABEL FRANCES—Assistant English, Julia Richman H. S.; 417 W. 120th St., Manhattan. Tel. 5286 Morningside.
BROOMALL, LAURA BAKER—Assistant Biology, Far Rockaway H. S.; 32 Nostrand Ave., Far Rockaway, N. Y.
BROWER, JANE—Assistant Librarian, Girls' H. S.; 188A Emerson Pl., Brooklyn.
BROWN, CHARLES G.—Assistant Mathematics, Jamaica H. S.; 110 Hardenbrook Ave., Jamaica. Tel 1590-R Jamaica.
BROWN, MERTON A.—Assistant Physical Science, Manual Training H. S.; 202 79th St., Brooklyn.
BROWNE, FRANCES E.—Assistant French, Erasmus Hall H. S.; 354 Ocean Ave., Brooklyn.
BROWNLEE, RAYMOND B.—Assistant Physics, Stuyvesant H. S.; Woodmere, L. I. Tel. 3950-W Woodmere.
BRUCE, GRACE A.—First Assistant Mathematics, Wadleigh H. S.; 128 W. 11th St. Tel. 661 Chelsea.
BRUCE, MURRAY—Assistant English, Stuyvesant H. S.; 615 52d St., Brooklyn.
BRUCE, WALTER A.—Commercial Branches, Eastern District H. S.; 25 W. 129th St., Manhattan.
BRUCE, WALTER A.—Assistant Stenography, Eastern District H. S.; 25 W. 129th St., Manhattan. Tel. 1148-J Harlem.
BRUCKMAN, LOUISA—First Assistant Biology, Bay Ridge H. S.; 209 W. 97th St., New York City.
BRUÈRE, ALICE H.—Assistant Physics, Wadleigh H. S.; 400 Riverside Drive. Tel. 117 Morningside.
BRUMMER, SIDNEY D.—Assistant History, Boys' H. S.; 1356 Madison Ave., New York. Tel. 3875 Lenox.

BRUNDAGE, HOWARD D.—Assistant Boys' Shop, Manual Training H. S.; 618 11th St., Brooklyn. Tel. 4075 South.
BRUNDAGE, MILTON B.—Assistant Chemistry, Stuyvesant H. S.; 522 William St., East Orange, N. J. Tel. 1971-M Orange.
BRUNING, EMILIE E.—Substitute German, Annex 129 Bushwick H. S.; 317 73rd St., Brooklyn. Tel. Bay Ridge 1925.
BRYAN, ALFRED C.—First Assistant History, H. S. of Commerce; 416 Clermont Ave., Brooklyn. Tel. 1591-M Prospect.
BRYANT, ARTHUR A.—Assistant Latin, De Witt Clinton H. S.; 120 Convent Ave., Manhattan. Tel. 4576 Morningside.
BRYANT, ELIZABETH E.—Assistant Latin, Manual Training H. S.; 145 Prospect Park West, Brooklyn. Tel. 3846 South.
BRYANT, FRANK L.—Assistant Physiography, Erasmus Hall H. S.; 628 Amersfort Pl., Brooklyn. Tel. 5919-J Flatbush.
BRYANT, GRACE—Office Assistant, Newtown H. S.; Woodside Ave., Woodside, L. I.
BRYANT, MRS. EMMA B.—Assistant French, Morris H. S.; 65 W. 127th St., Manhattan.
BUECHNER, ELSIE E.—Teacher in Training, Mathematics, Jamaica H. S.; Rockaway Rd., Ozone Park, L. I. Tel. 700-W Richmond Hill.
BUGBEE, HARRIET C.—Assistant Mathematics, Wadleigh H. S.; 400 W. 118th St. Tel. 4769 Morningside.
BUNTING, MILDRED B.—Assistant Biology, Girls' H. S.; 811 Beverly Rd., Brooklyn. Tel. 2992-W Flatbush.
BURCHARD, ANNA T.—Assistant Mathematics, Wadleigh H. S.; 415 W. 118th St. Tel. 511 Morningside.
BURDICK, MABEL G.—Assistant Mathematics, Curtis H. S.; 35 Harrison St., Stapleton, N. Y. Tel. 267-R Tompkinsville.
BURLINGHAM, GERTRUDE S.—Biology, Eastern District H. S.; 556 Lafayette Ave., Brooklyn.
BURLINGHAM, GERTRUDE S.—Assistant Science, Eastern District H. S.; 556 Lafayette Ave., Bklyn.
BURN, ALICE M.—Drawing, Eastern District H. S.; 469 Washington Ave., Brooklyn. Tel. 5600 Prospect.
BURNHAM, R. WESLEY—Assistant Physics, Erasmus Hall H. S.; 1801 Dorchester Rd., Brooklyn.
BURRAGE, MYRA ALLEN—Assistant German, Richmond Hill H. S.; 26 Irving St., Spencer, Mass.; 1244 Dean St., Brooklyn. Tel. 2090 Bedford.
BURT, CLARA M.—Assistant Physics, Morris H. S.; 1 W. 127th St., Manhattan. Tel. 5770 Harlem.
BUSBEE, CHRISTINE—Assistant Mathematics, Jamaica H. S.; 413 Hillside Ave., Jamaica, L. I.
BUSCH, ELLA ADELINE—Assistant German, Erasmus Hall H. S.; 1819 Beverly Rd., Brooklyn.
BUSH, MARY F.—Clerical Assistant, Washington Irving H. S.; 342 E. 17th St., Manhattan.
BUSHONG, ALICE M.—Assistant German, Manual Training H. S.; 442 9th St., Brooklyn.
BUSSARD, E. GERTRUDE—Assistant English, Washington Irving H. S.; 419 W. 119th St., Manhattan. Tel. 7700 Morningside.
BUTLER, EVELYN M.—Assistant Physical Training, Morris H. S.; Ardsley, N. Y. Tel 290-W Dobbs Ferry.
BUTTNER, FRIEDA—Assistant German, Washington Irving H. S.; 985 Aldus St., The Bronx, N. Y. C. Tel. 3665 Melrose.
BUTTRICK, HAROLD E.—Assistant English, Boys' H. S.; 1253 Bergen St., Brooklyn. Tel. 5686-J Bedford.
BYRNE, MARGARET C.—Assistant Mathematics, Bryant H. S.; 338 Decatur St., Brooklyn. Tel. 7403-W. Bedford.
BYRNES, ESTHER F.—Assistant Biology, Girls' H. S.; 193 Jefferson Ave., Brooklyn.

C

CAHILL, JOHN P.—Assistant Commercial Branches, Bay Ridge H. S.; 28 Montgomery Pl., Brooklyn.
CAHILL, MARY F.—Assistant Stenography, Julia Richman H. S.; 2 Beekman Pl., E. 50th St., Manhattan.
CAHILL, MARGARET—Assistant English, Wadleigh H. S.; 29 Clinton Ave., Jersey City. Tel. 2645 Bergen.
CAHILL, ROSE—First Assistant History, Girls' H. S.; 427 Nostrand Ave., Brooklyn.
CAIRNS, ALEXANDER—Substitute Physical Training, De Witt Clinton H. S.; 15 W. 4th St., Woodside, L. I.
CALL, R. ELLSWORTH—Assistant Physiography and Physiology, De Witt Clinton H. S.; 200 W. 85th St., Manhattan.
CAMBERN, J. RAYMOND—Assistant English, Manual Training H. S.; 372 Jefferson Ave., Brooklyn. Tel. 3797-J Bedford.
CAMERON, ALIX S.—Assistant Drawing, Erasmus Hall H. S.; 34 Wellington Court, Flatbush.
CAMERON, SR., WALTER—Assistant Biology, Wadleigh H. S.; 239 W. 136th S. Tel. 5241-M Audubon.
CAMERON, WALTER S.—Assistant Biology, Wadleigh H. S.; 239 W. 136th St. Tel. 5241-M Audubon.
CAMPBELL, CALVIN VICTOR—Assistant English, Commercial H. S.; 302 Brooklyn Ave., Brooklyn. Tel. 7244 Bedford.
CAMPBELL, HAROLD G.—History, Eastern District H. S.; 373 E. 26th St., Brooklyn.
CAMPBELL, HAROLD G.—Assistant History, Eastern District H. S.; 373 E. 26th St, Brooklyn. Tel. 7327-J Flatbush.
CAMPBELL, JOSEPH A.—Music, Boys' H. S.; 923 Puhnam Ave., Brooklyn. Tel. 1440 Bushwick.
CAMPBELL, RALPH—Assistant German, De Witt Clinton H. S.; 700 W. 179th St., Manhattan.
CANN, BERTHA—Assistant English, Girls' H. S.; 27 Monroe St., Brooklyn.
CANNING, ETTA M.—Assistant Stenography, Bushwick H. S.; 358-A Lafayette Ave., Brooklyn.
CANNON, GERTRUDE LOUISE—Assistant Biology, Washington Irving H. S.; 1786 Clay Ave., New York City.

CAPLAN, ELIAS NATHAN—Assistant English, Commercial H. S.; 269 E. Broadway, Manhattan.
CAREY, ALICE M.—Assistant History, Morris H. S.; 196 Edgecomb Ave., Manhattan.
CAREY, MARGARET E.—Assistant Commercial Branches, Flushing H. S.; 224 Franklin Pl., Flushing, L. I.
CARLETON, BESSIE G.—Assistant French, Morris H. S.; 617 W. 143d St., Manhattan. Tel. 4286 Audubon.
CARLETON, GRAY M.—Assistant English, H. S. of Commerce; 30 W. 44th St., Manhattan.
CARLL, L. ADELE—Assistant English (Voice Culture), Bryant H. S.; The Adlon, 54th St. and 7th Ave. Tel. 9094 Columbus.
CARON, EMMA C.—Substitute Music, Washington Irving H. S.; 204 W. 92d St., Manhattan. Tel. 9830 **Riverside.**
CARPANTIER, MARIUS—Assistant French, De Witt Clinton H. S.; 602 Madison St., Brooklyn.
CARPENTER, IDELETTE—Assistant Botany, Julia Richman H. S.; Maplewood, N. J. Tel. 649-J South Orange.
CARR, AGNES—Assistant Latin, Morris H. S.; Hartsdale, N. Y. Tel. 186-M White Plains.
CARTER, BERTHA—Assistant Biology, Bryant H. S.; 287 Jamaica Ave., Astoria, N .Y.
CARTER, EFFIE A.—Assistant Physics, Girls' H. S.; 404 Westminster Rd., Brooklyn.
CARTER, MARY K.—Chairman of Dept. Drawing, Wadleigh H. S.; 435 S. 4th Ave., Mt. Vernon, N. Y. Tel. 1373-M.
CARTER, RAYMOND—Assistant Drawing, H. S. of Commerce; 609 W. 127th St. Tel. 6204 Morningside.
CARTER, RAYMOND—Assistant Drawing, H. S. of Commerce; 609 W. 127th St., Manhattan. Tel. 6204 Morningside.
CASE, FLORENCE L.—Assistant Latin, Wadleigh H. S. Annex; 382 Jefferson Ave., Brooklyn. Tel. 1499 Bedford.
CASHMAN, JOS. F.—Assistant English, Erasmus Hall M. S.; 470 Eastern Parkway, Brooklyn. Tel. 8371 Bedford.
CASSETT, EDITH—Laboratory Assistant Chemistry and Physics, Wadleigh H. S.; 435 W. 119th St. Tel. 8200 Morningside.
CATREN, IDA M.—Assistant Shorthand, Washington Irving H. S.; 156 W. 123d St., Manhattan. Tel. 1473 Morningside.
CAVALLIER, EMILIE—Assistant French, Wadleigh H. S.; 63 W. 55th St.
CEROW, GEORGIA A.—Substitute Mathematics, Erasmus Hall H. S.; 503 W. 175th St., Manhattan.
CHAMBERLAIN, RAYMOND—Assistant Physics, De Witt Clinton H. S.; 71 Currie Ave., Paterson, N. J.
CHAPIN, JENNIE E.—Physical Training, Richmond Hill H. S.; 37 Briggs Ave., Richmond Hill, L. I. Tel. 1111-J Richmond Hill.
CHAPIN, HENRY E.—Assistant Physiography, Richmond Hill, H. S.; Lefferts Ave., Richmond Hill, L. I.
CHAPMAN, FRANCES E.—Assistant History, Flushing H. S.; 13 3rd St., Woodside, L. I.
CHAPMAN, LENA M.—Assistant History, Washington Irving H. S.; 58 E. 102d St., Manhattan. Tel. 3644 Lenox.
CHAPMAN, LENA M.—Assistant English, Washington Irving H. S.; 58 E. 102d St., Manhattan. Tel. 3644 Lenox.
CHASE, CHARLOTTE G.—Assistant English, Girls' H. S.; 205 Quincy St., Brooklyn.
CHATER, ELLEN D.—Assistant English, Eastern District H. S.; Women's University Club, 106 E. 52d St., Manhattan. Tel. 7800 Plaza.
CHATER, ELLEN McR. D.—English, Eastern District H. S.; Englewood, N. J. Tel. 177-R Englewood.
CHATFIELD, WILLIAM A.—Assistant Freehand Drawing, Stuyvesant H. S.; Millington, N. J.
CHATTERTON, MINNIE E.—Assistant Mathematics, Girls' H. S.; 85 Pierrepont St., Brooklyn.
CHENEY, JANET D.—Assistant Art Department, Washington Irving H. S.; 106 W. Lincoln Ave., Mt. Vernon, N. Y.
CHENEY, THOMAS CLYDE—Assistant Mathematics, Stuyvesant H. S.; 326 West End Ave., Manhattan. Tel. 10253 River.
CHESTER, HENRY C.—First Assistant Physics, H. S. of Commerce; 564 Van Cortlandt Park Ave., Yonkers, N. Y.
CHESLEY, MABEL—Assistant English, Erasmus Hall H. S.; 2022 Beverley Rd., Brooklyn.
CHESTNUT, D. HOWARD—Assistant Stenography, Commercial H. S.; 945 E. 14th St.
CHICKERING, EDWARD C.—First Assistant Latin, Jamaica H. S.; The Franklin, Jamaica, L. I. Tel. 385 Jamaica.
CHILCOTT, CLIO M.—Assistant French, Washington Irving H. S.; 66 St. James Pl., Brooklyn. Tel. 2241 Prospect.
CHILDS, LELIA M.—Assistant Mathematics, Girls' H. S.; 1112 Dean St., Brooklyn.
CHINNOCK, FLORENCE B.—Assistant Elocution, Erasmus Hall H. S.; 157 6th Ave., Brooklyn. Tel. 5469-J Prospect.
CHRYSTALL, MAURICE M.—Clerical Assistant, Stuyvesant H. S.; 55 E. 101st St., Manhattan.
CHURCHILL, MARTHA B.—Assistant Latin, Wadleigh H. S.; 611 W. 111th St. Tel. 4740 Morningside.
CLARK, CLINTON.—Assistant Mathematics, Boys' H. S.; 195 Kingston Ave., Brooklyn.
CLARK, CORA B.—Assistant Physical Training, Girls' H. S.; 19 Arlington Pl., Brooklyn.
CLARK, EMMA K.—Assistant Latin, Girls' H. S.; 248A Monroe St., Brooklyn.
CLARK, HENRY F.—Assistant Mathematics, Curtis H. S.; Simonson Ave., Stapleton, N. Y. Tel. 185-W Tompkinsville.
CLARK, JOHN A.—First Assistant Physics, Commercial H. S.; 1411 Avenue I, Brooklyn. Tel. 6068-R Midwood.
CLARK, JOHN HOLLEY—Principal, Flushing H. S.; 231 Sanford Ave., Flushing, L. I. Tel. 493-M Flushing.
CLARK, JOHN P.—Assistant Mathematics, Stuyvesant H. S.; 15 Glenada Pl., Brooklyn. Tel. 4400 Bedford.
CLARK, MARTHA M.—Assistant Latin and Greek, Wadleigh H. S.; 44 N. Arlington Ave., East Orange, N. J. Tel. 2801 Orange.

CLARK, RANDOLPH F.—Assistant Mathematics, De Witt Clinton H. S.; 194 Christie Heights St., Leonia, N. J. Tel. 745-M Leonia.
CLARKE, ELEANOR P.—Assistant Latin, Julia Richman H. S.; 243 Sanford Ave., Flushing, L. I. Tel. 532-J Flushing.
CLARKE, HELEN MAC G.—Assistant Mathematics, Morris H. S.; 504 W. 112th St. Tel. 1095 Morningside.
CLARKE, MADGE S.—English, Eastern District H. S.; 64 Montague St., Brooklyn. Tel. 2045 Main.
CLARKE, TERESA A.—Clerical Assistant, Girls' H. S.; 281 Van Buren St., Brooklyn.
CLENDENIN, WM. W.—Second Assistant Physiography, Wadleigh H. S.; 53 W. 104th St.
CLINTON, MRS. FANNY L.—Assistant English, Girls' H. S.; 19 Arlington Pl., Brooklyn.
CLINTON, EMMA A.—French and Spanish, Newtown H. S.; 171 W. 73d St., Manhattan.
CLOSE, MAUD M.—Assistant. English, Curtis H. S.; 351 Tompkins Ave., Tompkinsville, N. Y. Tel. 348-J Tompkinsville.
CLOUGH, HARVEY B.—Assistant Biology, H. S. of Commerce; 569 E. 185th St., Manhattan. Tel.
CLOUGS, JESSIE L.—Assistant Drawing, Richmond Hill H. S.; Richmond Hill, L. I.
COAN, CHAS W.—Assistant Mechanical Drawing, Manual Training H. S.; 627 Westminster Rd. Tel. 4051-J Flatbush.
COCHRAN, THOMAS—Assistant Physiography, Girls' H. S.; 301 Clermont Ave., Brooklyn.
COFFIN, ISABELLE P.—Assistant English, Bay Ridge H. S.; 116 Garfield Pl., Brooklyn.
COHEN, A. BRODERICK.—Assistant German, Boys' H. S.; 1787 Union St., Brooklyn.
COHEN, BERTHA—Assistant Mathematics, Bushwck H. S.; 5205 Third Ave., Brooklyn.
COHEN, HARRY—Assistant Commercial Branches, H. S. of Commerce; 635 E. 169th St., The Bronx, N. Y. C.
COHEN, HELEN LOUISE—Assistant English, Washington Irving H. S.; 38 W. 93d St., Manhattan. Tel. 2688 Riverside.
COHEN, LENA—Laboratory Assistant, Biology, Washington Irving H. S.; 73 W. 30th St., Bayonne, N. J.
COHEN, MORRIS—Assistant Mathematics, Bushwick H. S.; 289 Wyona St., Brooklyn.
COHEN, SAMUEL—Assistant Commercial Branches, Morris H. S.; 982 E. 165th St., The Bronx, N. Y. C.
COHN, ALBERT—Commercial Branches, Eastern District H. S.; 2025 Madison Ave., Manhattan. Tel. 4737 Harlem.
COHN, LOUIS B.—Assistant English Evander Childs H. S.; 1182 West Farms Rd., New York. Tel. 1384-R Melrose.
COLBURN, MARY P.—Assistant English, Wadleigh H. S.; Annex; 424 W. 119th St. Tel. 3350 Morningside.
COLE, BEULAH V.—Assistant Physiography, Julia Richman H. S.; 128 W. 11th St., Manhattan. Tel. 661 Chelsea.
COLEMAN, D. F.—Laboratory Assistant Chemistry, H. S. of Commerce; 7497 Amboy Rd., Tottenville, N. Y. Tel. 970-J Tottenville.
COLLIER, KATHARINE B.—Teacher English, Bushwick H. S.; 282 DeKalb Ave., Brooklyn. Tel. 8055-W. Prospect.
COLLIGAN, EUGENE A.—History, Eastern District H. S.; 724 Benedict Ave., Woodhaven.
COLLIGAN, EUGENE A.—Assistant History, Eastern District H. S.; 724 Benedict Ave., Brooklyn.
COLLINS, CATHERINE—Oratory, Newtown H. S.; 615 W. 145th St., The Bronx, N. Y. C.
COLLINS, JOHN A.—Office Assistant, H. S. of Commerce; 228 W. 10th St., Manhattan. 7230 Audubon.
COLONY, M. ELIZABETH—Assistant Physical Training, Manual Training H. S.; 193 Park Pl. Tel. 755 Prospect.
COLSTEN, ALBERT L.—First Assistant Mathematics, Manual Training H. S.; 1556 73d St., Brooklyn. Tel. 1011-W Bath Beach.
COMAN, CAROLINE—Assistant Mathematics, Wadleigh H. S.; 356 W. 145th St. Tel. 900 Audubon.
COMBS, ADELAIDE M. W.—Assistant Drawing, Bay Ridge H. S.; 55 Bay 25th St., Brooklyn.
CONANT, M. SYBIL—Assistant Shorthand and Typewriting, Bushwick H. S.; 12 Clifton Pl., Brooklyn. Tel. 6613 Prospect.
CONLEY, WILLIAM E.—Biology, Bushwick H. S.; 1286 Jefferson Ave., Brooklyn.
CONNELL, J. WESLEY—Assistant Latin, Erasmus Hall H. S.; 33 Woodruff Ave., Brooklyn.
CONNELLY, DOUGLAS L.—Assistant Physics, De Witt Clinton H. S.; 1470 Vyse Ave., Manhattan.
CONNOR, EDITH B.—Clerical Assistant, Bushwick H. S.; 352 Carlton Ave., Brooklyn.
CONROY, MARY S.—Substitute Biology, Curtis H. S.; 26 Townsend Ave., Stapleton, N. Y. Tel. 1648-W Tompkinsville.
CONSALUS, MRS. FRANCES H.—Assistant Domestic Arts, Washington Irving H. S.; 33 Astor Pl., Jersey City, N. J. Tel. 673-W Bergen.
CONSTANTINE, HARRIET L.—Assistant Latin, Morris H. S.; 127 E. 146th St., Manhattan. Tel. 1768 Murray Hill.
COOK, CHAS. G.—Assistant Chemistry, Boys' H. S.; 227A Monroe St., Brooklyn; Tel. 4065-J Bedford.
COOLEY, GEORGE ELLIOTT—Assistant Physical Training, Stuyvesant H. S.; 609 W. 127th St., Manhattan. Tel. 6204 Morningside.
COON, CLIFFORD H.—Assistant Chemistry, Commercial H. S.; 1032 E. 24th St. Tel. 8485-W Midwood.
COPELAND, LILLIAN S.—Assistant Declamation Department, Washington Irving H. S.; 401 W. 118th St., Manhattan. Tel. 198 Morningside.
CORBETT, JOSEPH S.—Assistant Mathematics, Stuyvesant H. S.; 2549 Decatur Ave., The Bronx, N. Y. C. Tel. 6123-W Tremont.
CORCILIUS, INEZ—Assistant Latin, Curtis H. S. (Totttenville Annex); 579 Elliott Ave., Tottenville, S. I. Tel. 1095-W Tottenville.
CORCILIUS, JOSEPHINE—Assistant Modern Languages, Jamaica H. S.; 28 Hardenbrook Ave., Jamaica, L. I.
CORLISS, CHARLES E.—Assistant Accounts, Commercial H. S.; 1295 Park Pl., Brooklyn. Tel. 4369-R Bedford.
CORNELL, CHARLES F.—Assistant Mathematics, Stuyvesant H. S.; 33 Alsop St., Jamaica, L. I. Tel. 1617-J Jamaica.
CORNISH, ROBERT H.—First Assistant and Head of Department of Physics, Wadleigh H. S.; 211

COSTER, SILVIE DE G.—Assistant Drawing, Evander Childs H. S.; 600 E. 167th St., The Bronx, N. Y. C.
COTTER, JULIA J.—Assistant English, Manual Training H. S.; 384 E. 18th St., Brooklyn.
COUCH, ANNE M.—Assistant History, Girls' H. S.; 934 Sterling Pl., Brooklyn.
COURTNEY, BERTHA F.—Assistant Stenography and Typewriting, Bryant H. S.; 160 E. 91st St., Manhattan. Tel. 2430 Lenox.
COVELLO, LEONARD.—Assistant French, Bay Ridge H. S.; 445 W. 124th St., New York City.
COWAN, GEORGIA C.—Assistant Drawing, Washington Irving H. S.; 14 Saint James Pl., Brooklyn.
COWLES, CLARENCE E.—Assistant Accounts, Commercial H. S.; 421 Hart St., Brooklyn.
CRAFT, ANNA W.—Drawing, Newtown H. S.; Glen Cove, L. I.
CRANE, ELIZABETH E.—Assistant Art, Wadleigh H. S.; 478 William St., E. Orange, N. J. Tel. 4195 W. Orange.
CRANE, ELLA G.—Assistant History, Erasmus Hall H. S.; 33 Linden Ave., Brooklyn.
CRANE, EMMA H.—Assistant Domestic Science, Washington Irving H. S.; 478 William St., East Orange, N. J. Tel. 4195-W East Orange.
CRANE, WILLIAM A.—First Assistant in Charge, Vice-Principal, Curtis H. S. (Rosebank Annex); 15 Claremont Ave., Manhattan. Tel. 5136 Morningside.
CRANDALL, ERNEST L.—Assistant German, Washington Irving H. S.; 664 Lafayette Ave., Brooklyn. Tel. 1026 Bedford.
CRAVER, E. H.—Assistant Stenography and Typewriting, H. S. of Commerce; 16 Woodcrest Ave., White Plains, N. Y.
CREMINS, JULIA C.—Assistant Drawing, Wadleigh H. S.; 356 E. 57th St.
CRENNAN, MARGARET A.—Assistant Stenography, Curtis H. S.; Harbor View Court, Tompkinsville, N. Y. Tel. 365-R Tompkinsville.
CRIM, ADELAIDE—Assistant Elocution and English, Far Rockaway H. S.; 32 Nostrand Ave., Far
CROCKER, NELLIE J.—Assistant German, Julia Richman H. S.; 414 W. 121st St., Manhattan. Tel. 7830 Morningside.
CROCKETT, ESTHER M.—Assistant English, Erasmus Hall H. S.; 154 Parkside Ave., Brooklyn.
CROOKE, MAXWELL 9.—Physical Training, Newtown H. S.; 184 Georgia Ave., Brooklyn.
CROWLEY, ISABELLE A.—Clerical Assistant, Washington Irving H. S.; 71 E. 87th St., Manhattan. Tel. 8620 Lenox.
CUNNINGHAM, MAUD—Assistant History, Erasmus Hall H. S.; 815 Ocean Ave., Brooklyn.
CURRIE, THOMAS H.—Assistant Physics, De Witt Clinton H. S.; 344 Harrison Ave., Hasbrouck Heights, N. J. Tel. 136-M Hasbrouck Heights.
CURRIER, CLARA L.—Assistant Drawing, Erasmus Hall H. S.; 749 Ocean Ave., Brooklyn. Tel. 970 Flatbush.
CURTIS, HENRY S.—Assistant Physics, Boys' H. S.; Terrace Ave., Jamaica, L. I. Tel. 312-W Jamaica.
CURTIS, OSBORN M.—Assistant History, Curtis H. S.; Walden, N. Y. Tel. 530 Tompkinsville.
CUSHMAN, EARL L.—Assistant German (chairman), Girls' H. S.; 286 St. Johns Pl., Brooklyn. Tel. 2602 Prospect.
CUTLER, SANFORD L.—Assistant Latin, Morris H. S.; 103 W. Tremont Ave., The Bronx, N. Y. C. Tel. 315-W Tremont.

D

DALEY, HELEN S.—Assistant Drawing, Washington Irving H. S.; 296 Lafayette Ave., Brooklyn. 3791 Prospect.
DAME, LYDIA M.—Assistant Latin, Girls' H. S.; 92 Gates Ave., Brooklyn.
DANIELS, ERNEST DARWIN.—Assistant in Latin, Boys' H. S.; 157 Midwood St., Brooklyn. Tel. 1707-W. Flatbush.
DARRIN, MRS. M. R.—Assistant Physiography, Bryant H. S.; 523 W. 121st St., Manhattan. Tel. 5271 Morningside.
DAVIDOFF, HENRY—Assistant English, Stuyvesant H. S.; 1956 Crotona Parkway, The Bronx, N. Y. C. Tel. 2275 Tremont.
DAVIDSON, HENRY—Assistant German, De Witt Clinton H. S.; 832 E. 165th St., Manhattan. Tel. 3585-W Melrose.
DAVIES, REBECCA H.—Assistant History, Girls' H. S.; 218 St. James Pl., Brooklyn.
DAVENPORT, FLORENCE—Latin, Eastern District H. S.; 771 Lincoln Pl., Brooklyn. Tel. 7108-J Bedford.
DAVENPORT, MARGERY—Substitute Biology, Wadleigh H. S.; Bolton Road, Manhattan. Tel. 7530 Audubon.
DAVIS, ALICE—Assistant History, Wadleigh H. S. 23 Nagle Ave. Tel. 7050 Audubon.
DAVIS, EUNICE M.—Assistant Mathematics, Manual Training H. S.; 203 Underhill Ave., Brooklyn. Tel. 7116 Prospect.
DAVIS, FRANK L. (Miss)—Assistant English, Girls' H. S.; 988 Bergen St., Brooklyn. Tel. 5610 Prospect.
DAVIS, GENEVIEVE V.—Assistant Drawing, Wadleigh H. S.; 352 Manhattan Ave.
DAVIS, JENNIE M.—Assistant History, Erasmus Hall H. S.; Hotel St. George, Brooklyn.
DAVIS, JOSIE A.—First Assistant Ancient Languages, Morris H. S.; 416 W. 118th St., Manhattan. Tel. 3502 Morningside.
DAVIS, MARTHA M.—Assistant English, Washington Irving H. S.; 209 Barbey St., Brooklyn. Tel. 2269-W East New York.
DANN, MATTHEW L.—Assistant History, Commercial H. S.; 520 Greenwood Ave., Richmond Hill.
DEAN, NELLIE—Assistant Domestic Science, Washington Irving H. S.; 54 W. 82d St., Manhattan. Tel. 1018-2 Schuyler.
DEAN, PHILIP R.—First Assistant Mathematics, Curtis H. S.; 73 Sherman Ave., Tompkinsville, N. Y. Tel. 639-W Tompkinsville.
DECKER, NICHOLAS P.—Assistant Mathematics, De Witt Clinton H. S.; 930 St. Nicholas Ave., Manhattan.

DEIHL, FRANK E.—Assistant Commercial Branches, Flushing H. S.; 50 Chestnut St., Flushing, L. I. Tel. 482-W Flushing.
DEIXEL, A.—Assistant Latin, De Witt Clinton H. S.; Central Ave., cor. N. 5th St., Newark, N. J.
DELANEY, EDWARD C.—Assistant History, De Witt Clinton H. S.; 101 W. 75th St., Manhattan. Tel. 7868 Schuyler.
DELANO, GRACE—English, Eastern District H. S.; 512 Lexington Ave., Brooklyn. Tel. 1784-W Bedford.
DELANO, SALLY H.—Assistant Latin, Wadleigh H. S.; 401 W. 118th St. Tel. 198 Morningside.
DEMAREST, PETER E.—Principal, 11 E. 87th St. Tel. 2961 Lenox.
DEMPSEY, JOSEPHINE A.—Substitute Latin, Bushwick H. S.; 467 Fifty-fifth St., Brooklyn. Tel.
DENBIGH, JOHN H.—Principal, Morris H. S.; 2676 Creston Ave., The Bronx, N. Y. C. Tel. 2098-W Tremont.
DENENHOLZ, ALEXANDER—Assistant Stenography, Commercial H. S.; 473 Hancock St., Brooklyn. 5126-W. Sunset.
DENFELD, CHARLOTTE S.—Assistant German, Girls' H. S.; 1304 Dean St., Brooklyn.
DENIS, BERTHA—Assistant Mathematics, Wadleigh H. S.; 401 W. 117th St. Tel. 1100 Morningside.
DENNIS, JULIA BARCLAY, Assistant German, Erasmus Hall H. S.; Franklin Arms, 66 Orange St., Brooklyn.
DESHEL, M. C.—Substitute Mathematics, De Witt Clinton H. S.; 646 E. 183d St., Manhattan. Tel. 1163 Tremont.
DE MERS, ADRIENNE V.—Assistant Stenography, Washington Irving H. S.; 40 Gramercy Park, Manhattan. Tel. 2309 Gramercy.
DE WITT, LOUISE L.—Assistant English, Bushwick H. S.; 140 Herkimer St., Brooklyn.
DICKE, CORNELIA A.—Assistant English, Wadleigh H. S.; 648 W. 158th St. Tel. 47 Audubon.
DICKINSON, HENRY N.—Assistant Latin, Manual Training H. S.; 195 Kingston Ave., Brooklyn. Tel. 1352-J Bedford.
DICKSON, T.—Assistant History, Bryant H. S.; 401 W. 118th St., Manhattan. Tel. 198 Morningside.
DICKLER, NATHAN N.—Assistant Mathematics, Manual Training H. S.; 1271 37th St., Brooklyn.
DICKMAN, MARY B.—Assistant Girls' Shop, Manual Training H. S.; 566 Carlton Ave., Brooklyn. Tel. 3474-W Prospect.
DIEDRICH, MARIE M.—Assistant French, Morris H. S.; 2394 7th Ave., Manhattan. Tel. 1970 Audubon.
DIETRICH, BERTHA K.—Laboratory Assistant Biology, Girls' H. S.; 204 Macon St., Brooklyn.
DIKE, MARGARET LORING—Assistant Domestic Science, Wadleigh H. S.; 15 E. 38th St. Tel. 560 Murray Hill.
DILGER, MARIE—Assistant Modern Languages, Jamaica H. S.; 588 Park Pl., Brooklyn. Tel. 5734 Prospect.
DITHRIDGE, LOUISE M.—Assistant, Washington Irving H. S.; 734 Van Nest Ave., The Bronx, N. Y. C.
DITHRIDGE, RACHEL L.—Elocution, Eastern District H. S.; 1114 E. 18th St., Brooklyn.
DIXON, CHARLES E.—Latin, Eastern District H. S.; 391 E. 15th St., Flatbush.
DIXON, CHARLES E.—First Assistant Latin and Greek, Eastern District H. S.; 391 E. 15th St., Brooklyn.
DOBBINS, CHRISTINE M.—Assistant Physical Training, Wadleigh H. S.; 410 W. 115th St. Tel. 9736 Morningside.
DODD, MINERVA K.—Substitute Art Department, Washington Irving H. S.; 129 Midland Ave., East Orange, N. J.
DOGGETT, ALLEN B.—Assistant Drawing, Erasmus Hall H. S.; 466 E. 17th St., Brooklyn.
DOHERTY, HELEN FRANCES—Assistant English, Washington Irving H. S.; 72 S. 12th St., Newark, N. J.
DOLGENAS, JACOB A.—Assistant Mathematics, Washington Irving H. S.; 1771 Madison Ave., Manhattan. Tel. 7146 Harlem.
DONALDSON, GEORGE—Assistant Physiology, De Witt Clinton H. S.; 371 W. 117th St., Manhattan. Tel. 5350 Morningside.
DONNELLY, JOSEPH P.—Assistant Music (Chairman), De Witt Clinton H. S.; 409 W. 129th St., Manhattan. Tel. 8500 Morningside.
DONNER, H. MONTAGUE—Assistant French and German, De Witt Clinton H. S.; 622 W. 114th St., Manhattan. Tel. 2884 Morningside.
DONOVAN, HERBERT D. A.—Assistant History, Commercial H. S.; 1210 Sterling Pl., Brooklyn.
DOWNING, GEORGE B.—Assistant Mathematics, Boys' H. S.; 966 St. Marks Ave., Brooklyn.
DOYLE, THOMAS L.—Assistant Teacher English, Boys' H. S.; 356 Halsey St., Brooklyn.
DONVAN, WALTER J.—Assistant Biology, Commercial H. S.; 1848 Bathgate Ave., Bronx.
DORFMAN, WALDEMAR L.—Assistant French, Stuyvesant H. S.; 783 Beck St., The Bronx, N. Y. C.
DOTEY, AARON I.—Assistant Latin (Chairman Dept.), De Witt Clinton H. S.; 34 Ft. Charles Pl.,
DOTY, ELEANOR STRANAHAN—Assistant English, Wadleigh H. S.; 114 Morningside Drive. Tel. 320 Morningside.
DOWELL, PHILIP—Assistant Biology, Curtis H. S. (Rosebank Annex); 86 Bond St., Port Richmond, N. Y.
DOUGLAS, CHARLES H. J.—First Assistant English, Washington Irving H. S.; 815 Marcey Ave., Brooklyn.
DOUGLAS, CLARA M.—Assistant French, Erasmus Hall H. S.; 255 Steuben St., Brooklyn.
DOX, ELMER A.—Assistant Latin, Erasmus Hall H. S.; 316 E. 25th St.
DOWD, MARY T.—Assistant Domestic Science, Washington Irving H. S.; 22 Pierrepont St., Brooklyn. Tel. 4134 Main.
DOWDEN, FLORENCE A.—Library Assistant, Wadleigh H. S.; 547 W. 123rd St. Tel. 5280 Morningside.
DOWNEY, FRANK—Assistant Music, Stuyvesant H. S.; 42 Van Buren St., Brooklyn.
DRAKE, R. W.—Assistant Drawing, Wadleigh H. S. Annex; 547 W. 123rd St. Tel. 5280 Morningside.
DREYFUS, JEANNE—French, Eastern District H. S.; 64 W. 82d St., Manhattan.
DUNBAR, WIILLIAM F.—Assistant History, Stuyvesant H. S.; 1083 E. 40th St., Brooklyn.
DUNCAN, WILLIAM H., JR.—Librarian, Commercial H. S.; 108 Woodruff Ave., Brooklyn. Marble Hill, Manhattan. Tel. 764 Marble Hill.

DUNFORD, HONORA A.—Assistant Domestic Arts, Washington Irving H. S.; 505 W. 122d St., Manhattan. Tel. 9351-W Morningside.
DURAND, WILLIAM B.—Assistant Physical Training, Bushwick H. S.; 260 Gates Ave., Brooklyn. Tel. 7186 Prospect, Ext. 32.
DURFEE, CLAYTON G.—Assistant English (in charge of Fordham Annex) Evander Childs H. S.; 2247 Valentine Ave., The Bronx, N. Y. C. Tel. 3007-J Fordham.
DURKEE, ERNEST S.—Assistant Mathematics, Stuyvesant H. S.; 14 S. 10th Ave., Mt. Vernon, N. Y. Tel. 1384-W Mt. Vernon.
DUURLOO, WILHELMINE H.—Assistant German, Girls' H. S.; 427 Nostrand Ave., Brooklyn.
DUSCHATO, ALFRED—Laboratory Assistant Biology, H. S. of Commerce; 493 Fletcher Pl., The Bronx, N. Y. C.
DWYER, ELEANOR—Assistant English, Erasmus Hall H. S.; 531 3d St., Brookyln. Tel. 3668 South.

E

EASTMAN, MARJORIE McCLINTOCK—Assistant English, Wadleigh H. S.; 504 W. 143rd St. Tel. 1180 Audubon.
EATON, CLARA C.—Assistant Mathematics, Washington Irving H. S.; 206 W. 39th St., Manhattan.
EDDY, ELISE S.—Assistant Mathematics, Bay Ridge H. S.; 23 Prospect Pl., Brooklyn.
EDDY, WALTER H.—First Assistant Biology, H. S. of Commerce; 387 Lafayette Ave., Brooklyn. Tel. 2567-R Prospect.
EDELSON, EMANUEL M.—Assistant Commercial Branches, Bay Ridge H. S.; 1076 E. 15th St., Brooklyn.
EDGE, FLORENCE—Assistant English, Washington Irving H. S.; 340 W. 85th St., Manhattan.
EDGELL, FRANK DEXTER—Assistant Mathematics, Erasmus Hall H. S.; 1418 E. 17th St., Brooklyn.
EDGELL, GATHERINE C. (Mrs. F. D.)—Assistant Physical Training, Erasmus Hall H. S.; 1418 E. 17th St., Brooklyn.
EDGERTON, MYRA T.—Assistant History, Jamaica H. S.; 4630 Central Ave., Richmond Hill, L. I.
EDMUNDS, MAUDE A.—Assistant Physical Training, Evander Childs H. S.; Ardsley, N. Y. Tel. 171 Dobbs Ferry.
EDWARDS, MINNA H.—Assistant German, Washington Irving H. S.; 202 W. 74th St., Manhattan. Tel. 3948 Columbus.
EDWARDS. SIDNEY—Assistant Boys' Shop, Manual Training H. S.; 378 Halsey St., Brooklyn. Tel. 2134-J Bedford.
EDWARDS, WILLIAM H., Assistant Latin, Boys' H. S.; 363 Grand Ave., Brooklyn.
EELLS, BURR GOULD—Assistant German, Commercial H. S.; 1461 President St., Brooklyn. Tel. 7686-M Bedford.
EGGLESTON, CHARLOTTE—Mathematics, Newtown H. S.; 97 Cook Ave., Elmhurst, L. I.
ELLERT, J. F.—Assistant Physical Culture, Bryant H. S.; 243 W. 107th St., Manhattan. Tel. 4335 Riverside.
ELLIS, SOPHIA—Assistant Latin, Girls' H. S.; 60 Clark St., Brooklyn.
ELTING, MABEL—Assistant English, Manual Training H. S.; 187 Emerson Pl., Brooklyn.
ELLARD, CHARLES H.—Assistant Chemistry, Stuyvesant H. S.; Great Neck, L. I. Tel. 101-J Great Neck and 4446 Cortland.
ELLIOT, LILIAN M.—Assistant English, Wadleigh H. S.; The Ferncliff, 120th St. and 7th Ave. Tel. 3358 Morningside.
ELKAN, HERMAN M.—Assistant Mathematics, Morris H. S.; 948 Tiffany St., The Bronx, N. Y. C. Tel. 6081 Met.
ELLSWORTH, SANFORD J.—Principal, Far Rockaway H. S.; 78 Oak St., Far Rockaway, N. Y. Tel. 455 Far Rockaway.
ELMER, CLEMENT G.—First Assistant German, Stuyvesant H. S.; 415 Washington Ave., Brooklyn.
ELTZNER, DOROTHEA—Assistant German, Washington Irving H. S.; 114 E. 54th St., Manhattan.
ELY, JEAN—Librarian, Flushing H. S.; 18 Ash St., Flushing, L. I. Tel. 1477-J Flushing.
EMERY, STEPHEN—Assistant Mathematics, Richmond Hill H. S.; 412 Welling St., Richmond Hill, L. I. Tel. 1450-W Richmond Hill.
EMMOUS, FRED E.—Assistant Physics, Morris H. S.; 29 Maple Terrrace, East Orange, N. J.
ENNIS, AGNES A.—Assistant Stenography, Washington Irving H. S.; 400 W. 152d St., Manhattan. 716 Audubon.
ENNIS, MARY G.—Assistant Music, Eastern District H. S.; 31 First Pl., Brooklyn. Tel. 1486 Hamilton.
ENNIS, MARY G.—Music, Eastern District H. S.; 31 First Pl., Brooklyn.
ERALE, WILLIS—Assistant English, Erasmus Hall H. S.; 119 Montague St., Brooklyn.
ERNST, FREDERIC—Assistant English, Morris H. S.; 1382 Plimpton Ave., The Bronx, N. Y. C.
ERHARDT, HELEN—Assistant English, Bryant H. S.; 1062 Herkimer St., Brooklyn.
ERWIN, EDWARD J.—Assistant Engineer, De Witt Clinton H. S.; 1120 Amsterdam Ave., Manhattan.
ESSELSTYN, HENRY H.—Assistant English, Boys' H. S.; 399 Lafayette Ave., Brooklyn. Tel. 1399-M. Prospect.
ESTES, CHARLES S.—Assistant Latin, Erasmus Hall H. S.; 275 St. James Pl., Brooklyn.
EVANS, WILLIAM F.—Assistant Physics, Girls' H. S.; 11 McDonough St., Brooklyn.
EVANS, AUSTIN H.—Assistant Latin, Morris H. S.; 795 Crotona Park North, The Bronx, N. Y. C. Tel. 5614 Tremont.
EVERETT, EDITH M.—Assistant English, Erasmus Hall H. S.; 68 Buckingham Rd., Brooklyn. Tel. 3708-J Flatbush.
EVERSON, ANNA—Assistant Biology, Manual Training H. S.; 2100 Albemarle Rd., Brooklyn. Tel. 3991-W Flatbush.
EVERY, ELIZABETH—Assistant English, Flushing H. S.; 72 Whitestone Ave., Flushing, L. I. Tel. 1526-W Flushing.
EVINS, DORA R.—Assistant Mathematics, Manual Training H. S.; 116 Hawthorne St., Brooklyn. Tel. 585-M Flatbush.

F

FAIRCHILD, RALPH P.—Assistant Physical Training, Boys' H. S.; 1035 E. 94th St., Brooklyn.
FAIRLEY, WILLIAM, Ph.D.—Principal (History), Commercial H. S.; 195 Kingston Ave., Brooklyn. Tel. 5593 Bedford.
FAIRLEY, EDWIN—First Assistant English, Jamaica H. S.; 282 Quincy St., Brooklyn. Tel. 6482-W Bedford.
FALION, GEORGE M.—Assistant Latin, Bushwick H. S.; 78 Seventy-second St., Brooklyn. Tel. 2232-W. Bay Ridge.
FALK, LOUIS J.—Assistant Commercial Branches, Washington Irving H. S.; 622 W. 137th St., Manhattan.
FALK, MRS. ANNA A.—Assistant English, Morris H. S.; 1043 Trinity Ave., The Bronx, N. Y. C.
FANNING, GRACE M. W.—Assistant History, Manual Training H. S.; 97 Clark St. Brooklyn. Tel. 4718 Main.
FARRANT, LOUISE G.—Assistant Latin, Girls' H. S.; 62 Montague St., Brooklyn.
FARRAR, PRESTON C.—First Assistant English, Erasmus Hall H. S.; 421 E. 18th St., Brooklyn. Tel. 3588-M Flatbush.
FAULKNER, EUNICE F.—Assistant Drawing, Eastern District H. S.; 50 W. 9th St., Manhattan. Tel. 1412 Gramercy.
FAULKNER, EUNICE F.—Drawing, Eastern District H. S.; 50 W. 9th St., Manhattan. Tel. 1412 Gramercy.
FAUST, CHARLOTTE C.—Assistant German, Bay Ridge H. S.; 1025 Lincoln Pl., Brooklyn.
FAY, CHARLES R.—Assistant Economics and History, Erasmus Hall H .S.; Crescent Athletic Club, Brooklyn. Tel. 3803 Main.
FEDTER, BRUNO—Assistant Modern Languages, H. S. of Commerce; 223 Bedford Park Blvd., The Bronx, N. Y. C.
FELDMAN, DANIEL D.—Principal, Curtis H. S.; 255 Hamilton Ave., New Brighton, N. Y. Tel. 1537 Tompkinsville.
FELTER, DR. WILLIAM L.—Principal, Girls' H. S.; 996 Sterling Pl., Brooklyn. School Tel. 372 Bedford.
FENNEBRESQUE, LOUIS—Assistant French, Jamaica H. S.; Floral Park, L. I.
FERGENSEN, ETHEL—Clerical Assistant, Eastern District H. S.; 37 Edward St., Ridgwood, N. J.
FERRIS, MARY D.—Assistant Drawing, Jamaica H. S.; 31 W. 11th St., Manhattan. Tel. 635 Chelsea.
FERRIS, LAURA C.—Art Department, Washington Irving H. S.; 54 Morningside Drive, Manhattan.
FERRO, HELENE—Assistant English, Washington Irving H. S.; 170 W. 89th St., Manhattan. Tel. 6237 Riverside.
FERRY, ALICE M.—Assistant Greek, Flushing H. S.; 201 Sanford Ave., Flushing, L. I. Tel. 270 Flushing.
FERRY, ORLANDO E.—Assistant English, Erasmus Hall H. S.; 1609 Nottingham Rd., Brooklyn. Tel. 7653-J Midwood.
FETTE, ELIZABETH W.—Assistant German, Washington Irving H. S.; 535 W. 135th St., Manhattan. Tel. 4357 Morningside.
FINCH, MRS. ANNA OGDEN—Assistant Physics, Bryant H. S.; 345 W. 70th St., Manhattan. Tel. 2223 Columbus.
FILFUS, NATHANIEL—Assistant Commercial Branches, Julia Richman H. S.; 1690 Lexington Ave., Manhattan. Tel. 3661 Harlem.
FINNEGAN, WILLIAM E.—Assistant Stenography, Commercial H. S.; 1199 Bergen St., Brooklyn.
FISCHER, PHILIP—Assistant Freehand Drawing, Stuyvesant H. S.; 137 W. 141st St, Manhattan. Tel. 7480 Audubon.
FISH, ALANSON L.—Assistant Physical Training, Flushing H. S.; 51 Burling Ave., Flushing, L. I.
FISHER, WILLIAM W.—First Assistant English, Boys' H. S.; 828 Lincoln Pl., Brooklyn. Tel. 6250-J. Bedford.
FINK, FREDERICK W.—Assistant German, Stuyvesant H. S.; Hastings-on-Hudson, N. Y.
FINNEY, ARTHUR E.—Assistant Spanish, Commercial H. S.; 66 Livingston St., Brooklyn.
FINNIGAN, JAMES J.—Assistant French, Richmond Hill H. S.; 256 Greenway South, Forest Hills Gardens, Elmhurst, L. I. Tel. 6214-W Forest Hills.
FIRMAN, ARTHUR B.—Assistant Biology, H. S. of Commerce; Saratoga Ave., Yonkers, N. Y.
FISH, ALANSON L.—Assistant Physical Training, Far Rockaway H. S.; 51 Burling Ave., Flushing N. Y.
FISHER, RUTH B.—Assistant Biology and Physiography, Curtis H. S.; Hotel McAlpin, Manhattan (winter). Tel. Greeley 5700. 136 Stuyvesant Pl., New Brighton, N. Y. (summer). Tel. 194 Tompkinsville.
FLANAGAN, WILLIAM—Assistant Stenography, Curtis H. S.; 316 E. 50th St., Manhattan.
FLANDERS, ADDIE E.—Assistant Latin and German, Far Rockaway H. S.; 292 Broadway, Far Rockaway, N. Y.
FLATOW, JACOB—Assistant Modern Languages, H. S. of Commerce; 234 St. James Pl., Brooklyn. Tel. 3225 Prospect.
FLEISCHER, EDWARD—Mathematics, Bushwick H. S.; 490-A Jefferson Ave., Brooklyn.
FLEISSNER, GUSTAV L.—Assistant Chemistry, De Witt Clinton H. S.; 1175 Wyatt St., Bronx.
FLINT, ARTHUR H.—Assistant Drawing, Richmond Hill H. S.; 92 Beechknoll Rd., Forest Hills, L. I. Tel. 6369 Forest Hills.
FLINT, GEORGE C.—Assistant Music, Boys' H. S.; Union Ave., Little Falls, N. J. N. Y. Tel. Co. 48-W.
FLINT, THOMAS.—Teacher Latin, Boys' H. S.; 515 Clinton Ave., Brooklyn. Tel. 5735 Prospect.
FLYNN, OSCAR C.—Assistant Chemistry, H. S. of Commerce; 43 William St., East Orange, N. J. Tel. 686-W Orange.
FOLEY, HENRY J.—Assistant Commercial Branches Bushwick H. S.
FOOTE, CARLTON A.—Assistant Latin, De Witt Clinton H. S.; 32 W. 123d St., Manhattan.
FOOTE, EDMUND W.—Assistant History, De Witt Clinton H. S.; 93 Lincoln St., Montclair, N. J. Tel. 2685-W Montclair.
FONTAINE, ANDRE C.—Assistant French, Boys' H. S.; Roslyn, L. I. Tel. 176 Roslyn.

FORBES, ABBEY BEAL—Assistant English, Richmond Hill H. S.; 161 Lefferts Ave., Richmond Hill, L. I. Tel. 2829-W Richmond Hill.
FORCIER, L. ETHEL—Assistant English, Erasmus Hall H. S.; 34 Maple Court, Brooklyn.
FORD, CELIA—First Assistant Latin, Girls' H. S.; 1228 Pacific St., Brooklyn.
FORD, JESSIE FRANCES (MRS.)—First Assistant and Head of Department of English, Wadleigh H. S.; Hastings-on-Hudson, N. Y. Tel. 757 Hastings.
FOSTER, EDWIN W.—Assistant Boys' Shop, Manual Training H. S.; Central Park, Nassau Co., N. Y.
FOSTER, HAROLD E.—Assistant English, Morris H. S.; 434 E. 4th St., Mt. Vernon, N. Y. Tel. 1330-J.
FOSTER, OSCAR R.—Assistant Physical Science, Manual Training H. S.; 203 8th Ave., Brooklyn.
FOSTER, SARAH P.—Assistant Stenography, Erasmus Hall H. S.; 815 Ocean Ave., Brooklyn.
FOSTER, WALTER E.—First Assistant Classical Languages, Stuyvesant H. S.; 611 W. 158th St., Manhattan. Tel. 5600 Audubon.
FOSTER, W. L.—Assistant Physical Training, H. S. of Commerce; 454 McDonough St., Brooklyn.
FOX, ETTA B.—Teacher in Training, Latin, Wadleigh H. S.; 581 W. 161st St. Tel. 500 Audubon.
FOX, MRS. ALICE E.—Assistant Drawing, De Witt Clinton H. S.; 175 Claremont Ave., Manhattan. Tel. 5750 Morningside.
FOY, ROSE L.—Assistant Domestic Art, Wadleigh H. S.; 24 W. 75th St. Tel. 4584 Columbus.
FOX, S. WORDSWORTH—Assistant Commercial Branches, Washington Irving H. S.; 418 W. 130th St., Manhattan. Tel. 8500 Morningside.
FOUNTAIN, EMMA A.—Assistant English, Flushing H. S.; 91 Prospect Ave., Flushing, L. I.
FRAME, RACHEL M.—Substitute Declamation Department, Washington Irving H. S.; 27 S. 13th Ave., Mt. Vernon, N. Y.
FRANCE, SANFORD D.—Assistant Mathematics, Boys' H. S.; 256 Lefferts Ave., Brooklyn.
FRANCIS, CAROLYN LOUISE—Assistant Mathematics, Bushwick H. S.; 1151 Dean St., Brooklyn. Tel. 5100 Bedford.
FRANK, CHARLES L.—Assistant Phonography, Washington Irving H. S.; 537 W. 149th St., Manhattan. Tel. 2040 Audubon.
FRANK, COLMAN D.—First Assistant French, De Witt Clinton H. S.; 3115 Broadway, Manhattan. Tel. 3943 Morningside.
FRANK, MAUDE—Assistant English, De Witt Clinton H. S.; 50 Morningside Drive, Manhattan.
FRANKE, CLARA E.—Assistant German, Morris H. S.; 423 W. 118th St., Manhattan. Tel. 2530 Morningside.
FRASER, EFFIE—Assistant Latin, Morris H. S.; 436 Ft. Washington Ave., Manhattan.
FREEBORN, FRANK W.—Assistant Latin, Boys' H. S.; 306 Halsey St., Brooklyn. Tel. 2834-R. Bedford.
FREEBERG, SIGRID C.—Assistant Mathematics, Manual Training H. S.; 1226 Atfield Ave., Richmond Hill, L. I.
FREEMAN, BENJAMIN—Assistant Commercial Branches, Washington Irving H. S.; 897 Beck St., The Bronx, N. Y. C. Tel. 3452 Melrose.
FREEMAN, MARY L.—Assistant Commercial Branches, Washington Irving H. S.; 262 W. 99th St., Manhattan. Tel. 5324 Riverside.
FREESTON, MARY C.—Assistant Physical Training, Morris H. S.; 405 W. 118th St., Manhattan.
FRENCH, LINDA M.—Assistant German, Curtis H. S.; 26 Stuyvesant Pl., New Brighton, N. Y.
FRERICHS, HARRISON—Assistant Freehand Drawing, Manual Training H. S.; 408 W. 150th St., Manhattan. Tel. 6410 Audubon.
FRITZ, HENRY E.—Assistant Freehand Drawing, Stuyvesant H. S.; 29 2d Ave., North Pelham, N. Y.
FROST, MADELINE A.—Assistant Elocution, Erasmus Hall H. S.; 397 Park Pl., Brooklyn. Tel. 4685-M Prospect.
FUESLEIN, IRMA—Assistant Domestic Arts, Washington Irving H. S.; 888 E. 176th St., The Bronx, N. Y. C. Tel. 3260 Tremont.
FULLER, ROBERT W.—First Assistant Chemistry, Stuyvesant H. S.; 947 Woodcrest Ave., New York City.

G

GAGE, STANLEY A.—Assistant Manual Arts (Metal Work), Stuyvesant H. S.; 110 Mt. Joy Pl., New Rochelle, N. Y. Tel. 456-W New Rochelle.
GALLAGHER, ELLEN M.—Assistant Latin, Curtis H. S.; 332 W. 56th St., Manhattan.
GALLAGHER, MARGARET F.—Assistant Commercial Branches, Washington Irving H. S.; 168 W. 81st St., Manhattan.
GALLOWAY, IDA GRAY—First Assistant History, Washington Irving H. S.; 609 W. 127th St., Manhattan. Teel. 6204 Morningside.
GAMBIER, LOUISE M.—Assistant French, Bryant H. S.; 351 Lexington Ave., Manhattan. Tel. 2437 Murray Hill.
GAMMON, MONTAGUE—Assistant Physical Training, Richmond Hill H. S.; 680 Hamilton Ave., Richmond Hill, L. I.
GANO, LINA E.—Assistant History, Wadleigh H. S.; 401 W. 118th St. Tel. 198 Morningside.
GARDNER, FRANK A.—Assistant Machanical Drawing, Stuyvesant H. S.; 415 W. 118th St., Manhattan. Tel. 511 Morningside.
GARDNER, GERTRUDE—Drawing, Newtown H. S.; Flushing, L. I.
GARDNER, MAUDE—Assistant Drawing (chairman), Girls' H. S.; 602 Franklin Ave., Brooklyn.
GARRITY, JULIA F.—Assistant Mathematics, Bryant H. S.; Hotel McAlpin. Tel. 5700 Greeley.
GARRIGUES, ELLEN E.—First Assistant English, De Witt Clinton H. S.; 609 W. 114th St., Manhattan. Tel. 7814 Morningside.
GASTON, CHARLES ROBERT—First Assistantl English, Richmond Hill H. S.; 215 Arlington Rd., Richmond Hill, L. I. Tel. 1469 Richmond Hill.
GAUVRAN, ETHEL H.—Assistant English, Manual Training H. S.; 5 Hillcrest Ave., Jamaica, L. I.
GAVINS, HELEN—Assistant Biology, Wadleigh H. S.; 28 W. 97th St. Tel. 3883-J Riverside.
G Y, LAURA S.—Assistant Mathematics, Jamaica H. S.; The Franklin, Jamaica, L. I. Tel. 385 A Jamaica.

GAYLORD, HARRIET E.—Assistant English, Morris H. S.; 205 W. 94th St., Manhattan.
GAYNOR, CARRIE.—Assistant Sewing, Bay Ridge H. S.; 165 Prospect Park West, Brooklyn.
GEISS, M. PAULA—Assistant German, Manual Training H. S.; 457A Halsey St., Brooklyn. Tel 8592-W Bedford.
GEMSON, IRVING.—Assistant Physical Training, Boys' H. S.; 1975 Seventh Ave., Manhattan.
GENUNG, INA E.—Latin, Eastern District H. S.; 1236 Pacific St., Brooklyn. Tel. 6256 Bedford.
GENUNG, INA E.—Assistant Latin, Eastern District H. S.; 1236 Pacific St., Brooklyn. Tel. 6256 Bedford.
GEORGE, AUGUSTE—Assistant French, Wadleigh H. S.; 100 St. Nicholas Ave. Tel. 5899 Morningside.
GERMANN, CHARLES C.—Assistant Physical Science, Manual Training H. S.; 1529 75th St., Brooklyn.
GERE, L. B.—Assistant English, Washington Irving H. S.; 435 W. 119th St., Manhattan. Tel. 8200 Morningside.
GERMANN, SUSAN M.—Assistant Mathematics, Girls' H. S.; 66 Midwood St., Brooklyn.
GERMANN, AARON—Clerical Assistant, Stuyvesant H. S.; 974 Union Ave., The Bronx, N. Y. C.
GERSCHANEK, CELIA—Teacher in Training, Mathematics, Wadleigh H. S.; 458 Manhattan Ave.
GERSTEIN, ROSE—Commercial Subjects, Bushwick H. S., Annex 129; 468 Monroe St., Brooklyn. Tel. 1035-W Bedford.
GILBERT, CLARA M.—Assistant English, Bushwick H. S.; 52 Livingston St., Brooklyn. Tel. 1000 Main.
GIBSON, J. STEWART—Assistant Chemistry and Physics, Wadleigh H. S.; 22 Clinton Ave., Montclair, N. J. Tel. 582-J Montclair.
GILMOUR, EMILY J.—Assistant Mathematics, Morris H. S.; 37 De Kalb Ave., White Plains, N. Y. Tel. 484-W White Plains.
GILLILAND, ALICE M.—Assistant Mathematics, Bay Ridge H. S.; 118 Montague St., Brooklyn.
GILSON, CHANNING W.—Assistant Shop, Manual Training H. S.; 424 4th St., Brooklyn.
GIOVANOLY, MAX F.—Assistant German, De Witt Clinton H. S.; 522 W. 147th St., Manhattan. Tel. 2090 Audubon.
GITTAL, ETHEL F.—Placement and Investigation, Washington Irving H. S.; 597 Putnam Ave., Brooklyn. Tel. 5416-M Bedford.
GLASSBERG, BENJAMIN—Assistant History, Manual Training H. S.; 143 Christopher Ave., Brooklyn.
GLUCK, EMIL.—Assistant Commercial Branches, Bay Ridge H. S.; 1590 Amsterdam Ave., New York.
GNADE, AGNES—Assistant English, Manual Training H. S.; 212 Passaic Ave., Rutherford, N. J.
GOATE, WILLIAM B.—Assistant Music, Commercial H. S.; 459 Tompkins Ave., Brooklyn.
GOERTNER, MRS. ROSE—Assistant History, Washington Irving H. S.; 307 W. 98th St., Manhattan. Tel. 3964 Riverside.
GOERTZ, MATILDA—Teacher in Training in Mathematics, Wadleigh H. S.; 343 E. 58th St.
GOLDENBERG, IRVING—German, Eastern District H. S.; 590 Jefferson Ave., Brooklyn. Tel. 7344 Bedford.
GOLDBERG, ISRAEL—Assistant French, De Witt Clinton H. S.; 763 Elton Ave., Manhattan.
GOLDBERGER, HENRY H.—Assistant English, Stuyvesant H. S.; 535 W. 151st St., Manhattan. Tel. 1642 Audubon.
GOLDBERGER, LOUIS—Assistant Commercial Branches, Bushwick H. S.; 188 Martense St., Brooklyn.
GOLDE, MARGARET D.—Assistant German, Richmond Hill H. S.; 886 Putnam Ave., Brooklyn. Tel. 521 Bushwick.
GOLDSMITH, ELIAZABETH—German, Bushwick H. S.; 66 St. James Pl., Brooklyn. Tel. 2241 Prospect.
GOLDSMITH, MORGAN J.—Assistant, Washington Irving H. S.; 27 W. 94th St., Manhattan. Tel. 1534 Riverside.
GOLDSTEIN, ALEXANDER.—Assistant English, Bay Ridge H. S.; 493 12th St., Brooklyn.
GOLDSTEIN, SAMUEL—Assistant English, H. S. of Commerce; N. Y. University, University Hts.
GOLLER, GRATIS—Assistant Commercial Branches, Julia Richman H. S.; 60 W. 10th St., Manhattan. Tel. 3460 Stuyvesant.
GOMBARTS, GEORGE K.—Assistant Drawing, De Witt Clinton H. S.; 945 Fox St., Brooklyn.
GOMPT, ANNA M.—History, Newtown H. S.; 8 Ithaca St., Brooklyn.
GOODE, ELIZABETH—Assistant Latin, Curtis H. S.; 371 Tompkins Ave., Tompkinsville, N. Y. Tel. 1460 Tompkinsville.
GOODMAN, ANNIE E.—Assistant Commercial Branches, Washington Irving H. S.; 523 W. 121st St., Manhattan. Tel. 5271 Morningside.
GOODMAN, ARTHUR—Assistant Mathematics, Bushwick H. S.; 53 Seventh St., Manhattan.
GOODWIN, W. GRANT—Assistant History, Curtis H. S.; 1464 Lexington Ave., Manhattan.
GOODRICH, CHARLOTTE—Assistant Biology, Girls' H. S.; 350 Washington Ave., Brooklyn.
GOODRICH, FOSTER—Assistant Joinery, Stuyvesant H. S.; 345 E. 15th St., Manhattan.
GOODRICH, MARTHA M.—Assistant French, Wadleigh H. S. Annex; 470 W. 146th St. Tel. 2910 Audubon.
GORDON, JOHN J.—Assistant Mathematics, Erasmus Hall H. S.; 263 Vernon Ave., Brooklyn.
GORSCH, RUDOLPH V.—Substitute Physical Training, De Witt Clinton H. S.; 3332 Decatur Ave., Bronx.
GOUDAL, EMILIE, Assistant French, Washington Irving H. S.; 225 W. 14th St., Manhattan.
GRANT, ABEL J.—First Assistant Biology, Curtis H. S.; 226 Third St., New Dorp, N. Y. Tel. 49-W New Dorp.
GRANT, ALICE C.—Assistant Latin, Bay Ridge H. S.; 21 Laurence St., Yonkers, N. Y. (189 St. Marks Ave., Brooklyn).
GRANT, ALMA M.—Domestic Art, Newtown H. S.; 59 Gerry Ave., Elmhurst, L. I.
GRANT, EVA M.—Assistant Mathematics, Curtis H. S. (Tottenville Annex); 7426 Amboy Rd., Tottenville, S. I.
GRANT, FORREST—Assistant Drawing (Chairman), H. S. of Commerce; 5 Whittier St., East Orange, N. J.
GRAY, JAMES E., JR.—Teacher Mathematics, Boys' H. S.; 123-A Halsey St., Brooklyn.
GRANT, ROSCOE A.—Assistant Latin, Jamaica H. S.; 530 Carlton Ave., Brooklyn.
GRANT, WILLIS H.—Assistant Biology, H. S. of Commerce; Jamaica, L. I.
GRAY, J. NEWTON—Assistant Physical Science, Manual Training H. S.; 5918 Bay Parkway, Brooklyn.

GREDITZER, M. MORITZ—Assistant German (chairman German department), Evander Childs H. S.; 1370 Prospect Ave., The Bronx, N. Y. C. Tel. 2578-W Tremont.
GREEN, BERNARD I.—Assistant Drawing, De Witt Clinton H. S.; 1112 Forest Ave., Bronx.
GREEN, FLORENCE—Assistant Shop, Manual Training H. S.; 165 Prospect Park West, Brooklyn. Tel. 3423 South.
GREEN, JOHN C.—Assistant Shop Work, Mechanical Drawing, Bushwick H. S.; 478 W. 159th St., Manhattan. Tel. 2348 Audubon.
GREEN, HELEN—Assistant German, Flushing H. S.; 56 W. 112th St., Manhattan. Tel. 6244 Harlem.
GREEN, MARY P.—Assistant Physical Training, Bushwick H. S.; 27 Madison St., Brooklyn. Tel. 577-J. Prospect.
GREENBERG, ABRAHAM B.—Junior Teacher Mechanical Drawing, Stuyvesant H. S.; 214 Haven Ave., Manhattan. Tel. 6650 Audubon.
GREENBERG, HENRY—German, Eastern District H. S.; 756 Jefferson Ave., Brooklyn.
GREENBERG, JACOB—Junior Teacher French, Stuyvesant H. S.; 212 Cortelyou Rd., Brooklyn. Tel. 5320 Flatbush.
GREENBERG, MICHAEL—Clerical Assistant, De Witt Clinton H. S.; 744-A Lafayette Ave., Brooklyn. Tel. 8530 Bedford.
GREENBERG, MORRIS—Assistant Drawing, Commercial H. S.; 1006 Flushing Ave.
GREENBURG, SOPHIA—Clerical Assistant, Far Rockaway H. S.; Mayer Cottage, Far Rockaway, N. Y. Tel. 250 Far Rockaway.
GREENE, RUSSEL T., JR.—First Assistant Commercial Branches, H. S. of Commerce; 33 E. 83d St., Manhattan.
GREENE, LILLIAN L.—Music, Richmond Hill H. S.; 1223 Pacific St., Brooklyn. Tel. 2977-R Bedford.
GREENSTEIN, MAX B.—Assistant Commercial Branches, Washington Irving H. S.; 860 E. 161st St., The Bronx, N. Y. C. Tel. 5516 Melrose.
GREIFF, LOTTI—Laboratory Assistant Physics Department, Wadleigh H. S.; 202 W. 79th St. Tel. 7766 Schuyler.
GRIFFITHS, ANNA B.—English, Eastern District H. S.; 5 McDonough St., Brooklyn. Tel. 3326 Bedford.
GRISWOLD, CLIFFORD B.—Assistant Forging, Stuyvesant H. S.; 16 Ocean Ave., New Dorp, Staten Island, N. Y. Tel. 161-R New Dorp.
GRISWOLD, MRS. CAROLYN—Clerk, Curtis H. S.; 16 Ocean Ave., New Dorp, N. Y. Tel. 161-R New Dorp.
GRISWOLD, EDWARD D.—Assistant Manual Arts (Joinery), Stuyvesant H. S.; Hastings-on-Hudson.
GROSS, HENRY I.—Mathematics, Eastern District H. S.; 93 Buffalo Ave., Brooklyn.
GROSS, IRENE—English, Newtown H. S.; 59 Gerry Ave., Elmhurst, L. I.
GROSSMAN, LENA M.—Assistant German, Bay Ridge H. S.; 190 Bay 23d St., Brooklyn.
GROVE, MARGARET—Clerical Assistant, Wadleigh H. S.; 60 W. 162nd St. Tel. 6256 Melrose.
GROW, FREDERICK S.—Assistant Mathematics, De Witt Clinton H. S.; 27 Mountain Ave., Maplewood, N. J.
GRUBMAN, A. J.—Assistant Mechanical and Topographical Drawing, Forging, Machine Shop Practice, Commercial Law, Bryant H. S.; 868 Whitlock Ave. Tel. 7013 Melrose.
GRUENBERG, BENJAMIN C.—First Assistant Biology, Commercial H. S.; 230 W. 107th St., Manhattan. Tel. 23 Riverside.
GULDNER, C. M.—Assistant Commercial Branches, H. S. of Commerce; 22 Lawrence St., Yonkers, N. Y.
GULLIVER, BARBARA A.—Clerical Assistant, Washington Irving H. S.; 40 Gramercy Park, Manhattan. Tel. 2310 Gramercy.
GUNNISON, W. B.—Principal, Erasmus Hall H. S.; 77 Wilson St., Brooklyn.
GURNEE, BLANDINA H.—Mathematics, Eastern District H. S.; 1040 82d St., Brooklyn.
GURNEE, MARIE E.—Assistant Drawing, Washington Irving H. S.; 1040 82d St., Brooklyn. Tel. 852-W Bath Beach.
GUTHRIE—Assistant French, Washington Irving H. S.; 182 Monroe St., Brooklyn. Tel. 1531-M Bedford.
GUTHRIE, GRACE—Assistant Latin, Washington Irving H. S.; 526 Riverside Drive, Manhattan. Tel. 1776 Morningside.

H

HAAS, ARTHUR—Assistant Mathematics, De Witt Clinton H. S.; 539 W. 141st St., Manhattan. Tel. 4357 Audubon.
HABERMEYER, LOUISE C. M.—Assistant German, Erasmus Hall H. S.; 180 Hawthorne St., Brooklyn.
HACKEDORN, MARION—Assistant German, Manual Training H. S.; 117 St. Johns Pl., Brooklyn.
HAEFELIN, FANNY J.—Assistant German, Wadleigh H. S.; 106 Morningside Ave., West. Tel. James Court.
HAGAR, ETTA M.—Assistant Stenography, Morris H. S.; 430 W. 119th St., Manhattan.
HAGENS, FRITZ—Assistant German, Commercial H. S.; 54 Slocum Crescent, Forest Hills, L. I.
HAHN, CLARENCE W.—Assistant Biology, H. S. of Commerce; 567 W. 186th St., Manhattan. Tel. 6840 Audubon.
HALE, AGNES L.—Assistant Mathematics, Girls' H. S.; 10 St. Charles Pl., Brooklyn.
HALEY, JESSE H.—Assistant English, Evander Childs H. S.; 2833 Valentine Ave., The Bronx, N. Y. C. Tel. 1037 Fordham.
HALWARD, WM. R.—Assistant Commercial Branches, Washington Irving H. S.; 186 Hamilton Ave., New Brighton, N. Y. Tel. 304-R Tompkinsville.
HALL, CAROLINE D.—Assistant History, Washington Irving H. S.; 138 W. 111th St., Manhattan. Tel. 6020-R Morningside.
HALL, HENRIETTA—Assistant Stenography and Typewriting, Bushwick H. S.; 325 Decatur St., Brooklyn.
HALL, HENRY M.—Assistant English, H. S. of Commerce; 139 Washington Pl. West.
HALL, GAMBLE—Assistant Economics, H. S. of Commerce; 357 W. 29th St., Manhattan.

HALL, MARGARET WOODBURN—Arristant French, Evander Childs H. S.; 202 W. 81st St., Manhattan. Tel. 8810 Schuyler.
HALL, MARY A.—Assistant History, Manual Training H. S.; 597 West End Ave., Manhattan. Tel. 1869 Riverside.
HALL, MARY E.—Librarian, Main Bldg., Girls' H. S.; 587 Lafayette Ave., Brooklyn.
HALLORAN, WILLIAM M.—Assistant Commercial Branches, Curtis H. S. (Rosebank Annex); 414 Richmond Terrace, New Brighton, N. Y. Tel. 1649 Tompkinsville.
HAM, GEORGE—Assistant History, De Witt Clinton H. S.; 176 Lefferts Ave., Brooklyn.
HAMILTON, ALMA L.—Assistant Drawing, Bay Ridge H. S.; 362 Senator St., Brooklyn.
HAMILTON, CHARLES A.—Assistant Mathematics, Boys' H. S.; 36 Park Ave., Jamaica, N. Y. Tel. 1520-J. Jamaica.
HAMILTON, MARY SCHUYLER—Assistant Commercial Branches, Washington Irving H. S.; Elmsford, Westchester County, N. Y. Tel. 1818-W Elmsford.
HAMPSHIRE, JOHN W.—Assistant English, Manual Training H. S.; 523 Monroe St., Brooklyn.
HANCE, WILLIAM—Assistant Physics, H. S. of Commerce; 180th St. and Fort Washington Ave., Manhattan.
HANCOCK, JOHN—Assistant Chemistry, Erasmus Hall H. S.; Douglas Pl., Brooklyn. Tel. 6263-J Hollis.
HANDRICH, PAUL—Assistant German, Bushwick H. S.; 941 Greene Ave., Brooklyn.
HANEY, JENNIE POMERENE—Assistant History, Wadleigh H. S.; 468 Riverside Drive. Tel. 6645 Morningside.
HANFORD, CLARENCE D.—Assistant Manual Arts (Joinery), Stuyvesant H. S.; Hastings-on-Hudson, N. Y. Tel. 852 Hastings.
HANKS, LENDA T.—Assistant Biology, Girls' H. S.; 950 Marcy Ave., Brooklyn.
HANNA, ALBERT S.—Assistant Biology, Boys' H. S.; Cherokee Ave., Hollis, N. Y.
HANNAH, FLORENCE—Assistant English, Bushwick H. S.; 350 Washington Ave., Brooklyn.
HANNAN, WALTER SHERLOCK—Assistant Physics, Evander Childs H. S.; 121 Mt. Hope Pl., The Bronx, N. Y. C.
HANSON, GEORGE C.—Substitute English, Boys' H. S.; 518 Jefferson Ave., Brooklyn.
HARARIS, LENA—Assistant Mathematics, Manual Training H. S.; 404 W. 116th St., Manhattan. Tel. 4940 Morningside.
HARDING, HELEN E.—Assistant English, Bay Ridge H. S.; 15 Kenmore Pl., Brooklyn.
HARDY, ANNA L.—Assistant Latin, De Witt Clinton H. S.; 418 W. 118th St., Manhatan. Tel. 6656 Morningside.
HARDY, RUTH G.—Assistant History, Girls' H. S.; 157 Willow St., Brooklyn.
HARKNESS, MME. A. de B.—Assistant French and German, Curtis H. S.; 55 Wall St., St. George, N. Y. Tel. 152-M Tompkinsville.
HARLEY, WALTER S.—Assistant Latin, Erasmus Hall H. S.; 498 Rugby Rd., Brooklyn. Tel. 2267-J Flatbush.
HARMAN, GEORGE W.—Assistant Accounts, Commercial H. S.; 779 E. Second St., Flatbush. Tel. 373-W Flatbush.
HARMON, ESTHER—German, Eastern District H. S.; Wolcote Bldg., 14 Irving Pl
HARRIS, GERTRUDE B.—Assistant German, Wadleigh H. S.; 540 W. 143rd St. Tel. 3313 Audubon.
HARRIS, MARY E.—Assistant Mathematics, Wadleigh H. S.; 281 Edgecombe Ave. Tel. 3593 Audubon.
HARRIS, MARY O.—Assistant French, Girls' H. S.; 104 Columbia Heights, Brooklyn.
HARRIS, SADIE—Assistant Mathematics, Wadleigh H. S.; 404 W. 116th St. Tel. 4940 Morningside.
HARRISON, EARL STANLEY—First Assistant Spanish, Commercial H. S.; 107 Queens Rd., Queens, L. I. Tel. 6130-J Hollis.
HARRINGTON, AGNES M.—Assistant Drawing, Erasmus Hall H. S.; 407 E. 18th St., Brooklyn.
HART, CLARA AVIS—Assistant Mathematics and French, Wadleigh H. S.; 163 W. 105th St. Tel. 1841-J Riverside.
HARTER, EUGENE W.—First Assistant, Erasmus Hall H. S.; 121 Marlborough Rd., Brooklyn.
HARTON, AMY M.—Clerical Assistant, Erasmus Hall H. S.; 591 Park Pl., Brooklyn. Tel. 7739-W Prospect.
HARTUNG, ERNEST—Assistant Modern Languages, H. S. of Commerce; 2041 Washington Ave., The Bronx, N. Y. C. Tel. 1261 Tremont.
HARTWELL, CHAS. S.—English, Eastern District H. S.; 234 Willoughby Ave., Brooklyn. Tel. 6418-W Prospect.
HARTWELL, CHARLES S.—First Assistant English, Eastern District H. S.; 234 Willoughby Ave., Brooklyn. Tel. 6418-W Prospect.
HARTWELL, F. W.—Assistant Biology, H. S. of Commerce; 17 Schermerhorn St., Brooklyn. Tel. 2857 Main.
HASTINGS, ADA L.—Assistant Drawing, Julia Richman H. S.; 137 E. 18th St., Manhattan. Tel. 2243 Gramercy.
HASTINGS, ELINOR S.—Assistant English, Washington Irving H. S.; 7 E. 87th St., Manhattan. Tel. 3796 Lenox.
HASTINGS, GEORGE T.—Assistant Biology, De Witt Clinton H. S.; 7 Robbins Pl., Yonkers.
HATHAWAY, BERTHA F.—Librarian, Morris H. S.; 419 W. 119th St., Manhattan.
HAUG, EMANUEL—Assistant Physical Training (Chairman), De Witt Clinton H. S.; 463 W. 159th St., Manhattan. Tel. 4510 Audubon.
HAYES, HELEN M.—Assistant German, Girls' H. S.; 564 Jefferson Ave., Brooklyn.
HAYNER, BURTON A.—Assistant Physical Science, Washington Irving H. S.; 751 W. 180th St., Manhattan. Tel. 6434 Audubon.
HAZEN, ANNAH P.—Biology, Eastern District H. S.; 68 Washington Sq. South, Manhattan. Tel. 1021 Spring.
HAZEN, CHARLOTTE—Assistant Physical Training, Julia Richman H. S.; 87 Hamilton Pl., Manhattan. Tel. 1200 Audubon.
HAZEN, UISE C.—Assistant Mathematics, Morris H. S.; 68 Washington Sq., Manhattan. Tel. 1021 Spring.
HAZEN, ELLA M.—Librarian, Manual Training H. S.; 512 5th St., Brooklyn.

HAZEN, ANNA P.—First Assistant Science, Eastern Distric H. S.; 68 S. Washington Square, Manhattan. Tel. 1021 Spring.
HEALY, MARGARET E. G.—Clerical Assistant, Evander Childs H. S.; 6 Melrose Ave., Mt. Vernon, N. Y. Tel. 192-J Mt. Vernon.
HEALEY, HORACE—Assistant Stenography and Typewriting (Chairman), H. S. of Commerce; 777 Prospect Pl., Brooklyn.
HECHT, ANNA—Biology, Erasmus Hall M. S.; 71 Leonard St., Brooklyn.
HEERMANCE, EMMA W.—Assistant English, Bryant H. S.; 242 Cypress Ave., Flushing, N. Y.
HEERMANS, FLORENCE—Assistant Physics, Wadleigh H. S.; 714 W. 179th St. Tel. 6450 Audubon.
HEIKES, IRVING A.—First Assistant Mathematics, Morris H. S, 1061 Clay Ave., The Bronx, N. Y. C.
HEIN, HENRY EMMO—Assistant English, Stuyvesant H. S.; 2433 Southern Blvd., The Bronx, N. Y. C. Tel. 2392 Tremont.
HELMUTH, LORE—English, Eastern District H. S.; 39 E. 27th St., Manhattan. Tel. 5427 Madison Square.
HELLER, HARRY—Assistant Mathematics, De Witt Clinton H. S.; 146 W. 111th St., Manhattan. Tel. 5253 Morningside.
HELLER, MAXWELL L.—Assistant Drawing, Evander Childs H. S.; 911 Simpson St., New York. Tel. 6657 Melrose.
HELLIN, LILLIAN—Assistant German, Washington Irving H. S.; 530 Manhattan Ave, Manhattan. Tel. 3927 Morningside.
HENOCH, STELLA S.—Drawing, Eastern District H. S.; 409 Throop Ave., Brooklyn.
HENIN, BENJAMIN L.—Assistant Modern Languages, H. S. of Commerce; 38 W. 68th St, Manhattan. Tel. 1141 Columbus.
HENDRIAN, E. W.—Assistant Physical Training, H. S. of Commerce; 121 W. 83d St., Manhattan.
HENRIQUES, MAURICE C.—Assistant Mathematics, Stuyvesant H. S.; 1753 W. 9th St., Brooklyn. Tel. 1300-W Bath Beach.
HENDERSON, ROYAL L.—Assistant Biology, Richmond Hill H. S.; Box 292, Huntington, L. I.
HENRY, MARGARET Y.—Assistant Latin, Wadleigh H. S.; 30 Tonnele Ave., Jersey City, N. J. Tel. 2148-M Bergen,
HERENDEEN, JANE E.—Assistant English and Elocution, Julia Richman H. S.; 435 W. 199th St., Manhattan. Tel. 8200 Morningside.
HERMANN, ADOLPH F.—Assistant German, De Witt Clinton H. S.; 3750 Broadway, Manhattan.
HERMANN, HATTIE—Assistant Mathematics, Wadleigh H. S. Annex; 58 E. 124th St.
HERRMANN, ANNA L.—Assistant German, Evander Childs H. S.; 1224 Union Ave., New York. Tel. 2971 Tremont.
HERTZFIELD, LEONORE H.—Clerical Assistant, Manual Training H. S.; 247 W. 111th St., Manhattan.
HERVEY, MARY BABCOCK—Assistant Physical Training, Wadleigh H. S.; 527 W. 121st St. Tel. 5271 Morningside.
HERZOG, CHARLES—Assistant German, De Witt Clinton H. S.; 550 W. 157th St., Manhattan. Tel. 402-D Audubon.
HEUERMANN, HELENA F.—Assistant German, Evander Childs H. S.; 1230 Amsterdam Ave., Manhattan. Tel. 4590 Morning.
HEUROCH, S. STELLE—Assistant Drawing, Eastern District H. S.; 409 Throop Ave., Brooklyn. Tel. 313-W Bedford.
HEWINS, NELLIE P.—Science, Newtown H. S.; Clermont Terrace, Elmhurst, L. I.
HEWITT, GEORGE E.—Assistant Biology, De Witt Clinton H. S.; 2353 Davidson Ave., Manhattan.
HEWITT, HELEN F.—Assistant English, Erasmus Hall H. S.; 268 Argyle Rd., Brooklyn. Tel. 9039 Flatbush.
HEYDRICK, BENJAMIN A.—First Assistant English, H. S. of Commerce; 900 Summit Ave., The Bronx, N. Y. C.
HEYER, ELLA G.—Assistant Latin, Manual Training H. S.; 166 Decatur St., Brooklyn.
HICKS, CLARA K.—Assistant Biology, Wadleigh H. S.; 400 Manhattan Ave. Tel. 846 Morningside.
HIERHOLZEN, CARL O.—Assistant Physical Training, Manual Training H. S.; 224 Seeley St., Brooklyn.
HIGBEE, MRS. ANNA M.—Physical Training, Eastern District H. S.; 357 Sterling Pl., Brooklyn. Tel. 5455 Prospect.
HIGBEE, MRS. ANNA M.—Assistant Physical Training, Eastern District H. S.; 357 Sterling Place, Brooklyn. Tel. 5455 Prospect.
HIGGINS, ALICE—First Assistant French, Girls' H. S.; 401 Macon St., Brooklyn.
HIGHAM, JESSIE W.—Assistant English, Eastern District H. S.; 61 Quincy St., Brooklyn. Tel. 1391-W Prospect.
HILBORN, RITA—Teacher in Training in French, Wadleigh H. S.; 11a W. 94th St. Tel. 9979-J Riverside.
HILL, GROSVENOR B.—Assistant English, De Witt Clinton H. S.; 247 Barclay St., Flushing, L. I. Tel. 63-J Flushing.
HILLS, CAROLINE M.—Commercial Branches, Newtown H. S.; 11 E. 87th St., Manhattan.
HILLMANN, MERCY ANNE—Assistant Art Department, Washington Irving H. S.; 2303 Clarendon Rd., Brooklyn. Tel. 2481-R Flatbush.
HILLYER, J. BLAKE—Assistant Physical Training, Curtis H. S.; 259 Hamilton Ave., New Brighton, N. Y. Tel. 1058-M Tompkinsville.
HINCKEN, ELSIE O.—English, Eastern District H. S.; 272 Berkeley Pl., Brooklyn. Tel. 553-W Prospect.
HINDS, GEO. K.—Assistant, Washington Irving H. S.; 128 W. 103d St., Manhattan. Tel. 5068 Riverside.
HINGSBERG, THOMAS—Assistant Manual Arts (Woodturning), Stuyvesant H. S.; 2359 Southern Blvd. The Bronx, N. Y. C. Tel. 1846 Tremont.
HIRSCH, JAMES A.—Assistant German, De Witt Clyinton H. S.; Huntington, N. Y. Tel. 292-F 13 Huntington.
HIRSCHBERG, ARTHUR—Physics, Eastern District H. S.; 660 W. 180th St., Manhattan. Tel. 3375 Audubon.
HIXON, KATE B.—Assistant Biology, Morris H. S.; Pleasantville, N. Y.

HOADLEY, HARWOOD H.—Assistant Latin, Jamaica H. S.; 133 W. 11th St., Manhattan. Tel. 6318 Chelsea.
HOBBS, ALICE E.—Assistant Art, Wadleigh H. S.; 171 Willoughby Ave., Brooklyn. Tel. 1920 Prospect.
HOBSON, GEORGE P. F.—Teacher Latin, Boys' H. S.; 1 Villard Ave., Hollis, L. I. Tel. 6347-J. Hollis.
HOCHDERFFER, MRS. M.—Assistant English, Jamaica H. S.; Harbor Haven, L. I. Tel. 1813 Springfield.
HOCHHEIMER, RITA—Assistant German, Washington Irving H. S.; 1311 Madison Ave., Manhattan. Tel. 43 Lenox.
HODGDON, KATHERINE I.—Assistant Mathematics, Erasmus Hall H. S.; 468 E. 21st St., Brooklyn. Tel. 1528-J Flatbush.
HODGETTS, ABBIE S.—Assistant English, Julia Richman H. S.; 1175 Madison Ave., Manhattan. Tel. 833 Lenox.
HODGK, ARCHIBALD L.—First Assistant Greek and Latin, Wadleigh H. S.; 414 W. 120th St. Tel. 8760 Morningside.
HODGKINS, GEORGIANA—Assistant English, Washington Irving H. S.; Great Neck, L. I. Tel. 149-R Great Neck.
HOFFMAN, MARGIE E.—Assistant Biology, Girls' H. S.; 354 Henry St., Brooklyn.
HOFFMAN, ALFRED—Assistant German, Commercial H. S.; 342 President St., Brooklyn.
HOFFMAN, MARK—Assistant English, Manual Training H. S.; 1143 Vyse Ave., The Bronx, N. Y. C. Tel. 7134 Melrose.
HOLLANDER, EDWARD—Assistant Mathematics, Stuyvesant H. S.; 401 Gregory Ave., Weehawken Heights, N. J. Tel. 2546-W Union.
HOLLY, HAROLD A.—Assistant Physical Science, Manual Training H. S.; 53 Sherman St., Brooklyn.
HOLMAN, MABEL L.—Assistant English, Girls' H. S.; 1068 Park Pl., Brooklyn.
HOLMES, ABBY B.—Assistant English, Girls' H. S.; 136 Cambridge Pl., Brooklyn.
HOLMES, ELLA A.—Assistant Biology, Jamaica H. S.; 4 John St., Jamaica, L. I.
HOLMES, DAVID H.—Latin, Eastern District H. S.; 630 W. 141st St., Manhattan. Tel. 7610 Audubon.
HOLMES, MARY H.—First Assistant German, Erasmus Hall H. S.; 180 Hawthorne St., Brooklyn.
HOLRAN, ROSE A.—Assistant Bookbinding, Washington Irving H. S.; 382A Clinton St., Brooklyn. Tel. 662 Hamilton.
HOLT, HENRY L.—Assistant Physics, Girls' H. S.; 64 Avalon Ave., Jamaica, L. I.
HOLZMAN, ABRAHAM—Assistant Physical Science, Manual Training H. S.; 506 12th St., Brooklyn. Tel. 2424-W South.
HOOK, EDWARD A.—Assistant Mathematics, Commercial H. S.; 1321 Lincoln Pl., Brooklyn. Tel. 8726-W Bedford.
HOOKS, DAVID M.—Assistant Physical Training, De Witt Clinton H. S.; 392 St. Marks Ave., B'klyn.
HOPKINS, FRANCES L.—Assistant Latin, Washington Irving H. S.; 9 8th Ave., Brooklyn. Tel. 669 Prospect.
HOPKINS, RUPERT H.—Assistant Physics, Curtis H. S.; 103 College Ave., W. New Brighton, N. Y. Tel. 373-J West Brighton.
HOPKINS, WALTER D.—Assistant Latin, Boys' H. S.; 815 E. 14th St., Flatbush, Brooklyn.
HOPKINS, WILLIAM C.—Assistant Manual Arts (Joinery), Stuyvesant H. S.; New Dorp, Staten Island, N. Y. Tel. 319-R New Dorp.
HORD, EDWARD C.—Assistant Biology, Flushing H. S.; 50 Hawthorne Ave., Flushing, L. I. Tel. 1238-W Flushing.
HORNER, CHARLESANNA—Assistant French, Wadleigh H. S.; 609 W. 177th St. Tel. 5568 Audubon.
HORWITZ, BENJAMIN—Substitute English, De Witt Clinton H. S.; 446 E. 49th St., Manhattan.
HORWITZ, LILLIAN—Assistant Stenography, Morris H. S.; 500 W. 149th St., Manhattan.
HOULEY, ELIZABETH C.—Assistant Commercial Branches, Bushwick H. S.; 554 Jefferson Ave., Brooklyn. Tel. 8585 Bedford.
HOUSTON, JESSIE F.—Assistant Mathematics, Wadleigh H. S.; 518 William St., East Orange, N. J. Tel. 3438-R Orange.
HOVEY, HORACE M.—Teacher Assistant, Wadleigh H. S.; 410 W. 115th St. Tel. 8378 Morningside.
HOWARD, CHARLOTTE B.—Assistant Latin, Wadleigh H. S. Annex; 1878 7th Ave.
HOWE, ALICE C.—Assistant Greek, Erasmus Hall H. S.; 815 Ocean Ave., Brooklyn.
HOWELL, LOGAN D.—Assistant English, Morris H. S.; 1115 Boston Rd., The Bronx, N. Y. C.
HOWES, EMILY—Assistant English, Julia Richman H. S.; 656 St. Nicholas Ave., Manhattan. Tel. 6770 Audubon.
HOY, ELIZABETH R.—Assistant Latin, Eastern District H. S.; 46 E. 21st St., Manhattan. Tel. 4662 Gramercy.
HOY, ELIZABETH R.—Latin, Eastern District H. S.; 46 E. 21st St., Manhattan. Tel. 4662 Gramercy.
HUBBARD, MARION L.—Assistant French, Evander Childs H. S.; 135 W. 71st St., Manhattan. Tel. 1762 Columbus.
HUBBARD, RUTH E.—Assistant Commercial Branches, Richmond Hill H. S.; 1130 Bergen St., Brooklyn. Tel. 8811-W Bedford.
HUBERT, MARIE R.—Assistant English, Washington Irving H. S.; 414 W. 121st St., Manhattan. Tel. 7830 Morningside.
HUGENIN, CHARLES—Assistant French, Wadleigh H. S.; 430 W. 119th St. Tel. 3350 Morningside.
HUGHAN, JESSIE W.—English Eastern District H. S.; 61 Quincy St., Brooklyn. Tel. 1391-W Prospect.
HUGHES, ANNIE R.—Assistant Physical Training, Girls' H. S.; 44 Westminster Rd., Brooklyn.
HUGHES, C. CARL—Assistant Commercial Branches, H. S. of Commerce; 550 W. 157th St., Manhattan. Tel. 4021 Audubon.
HUGHES, CHARLES E.—Assistant Biology, Boys' H. S.; 465 Fourth St., Brooklyn. Tel. South 2271.
HUGHES, FRANCIS T.—Assistant Biology, Boys' H. S.; 303 E. 5th St., Brooklyn. Tel. 5423-R. Flatbush.
HUGHES, THOMAS H.—Assistant English, Evander Childs H. S.; 705 W. 179th St., Manhattan. Tel. 3070 Audubon.
HUMASON, THOMAS A.—First Assistant Mathematics, Bushwick H. S.; 235 Brooklyn Ave., Brooklyn. Tel. 2407-J. Bedford.

HUMMEL, F. M.—Assistant German, Curtis H. S.; 53 Wall St., St. George, N. Y. Tel. 338-J, Tompk.
HUMPHRIES, GEORGE F.—Assistant Commercial Branches, Bushwick H. S.; 319 Lenox Rd., Brooklyn. Tel. 3567-W. Flatbush.
HUNT, ARTHUR E.—First Assistant Biology, Manual Training H. S.; 82 Hawthorne St., Brooklyn. Tel. 5054-R Flatbush.
HUNTER, GEORGE W.—First Assistant Biology, De Witt Clinton H. S.; 2238 Audubon Ave., Bronx. Tel. 2661-J Tremont.
HUNTINGTON, BELLE—Assistant Physical Training, Girls' H. S.; 187 Madison St., Brooklyn.
HUNTINGTON, F. W.—Assistant Physics, Erasmus Hall H. S.; 1801 Dorchester Rd., Brooklyn.
HURLBUT, MARTHA A.—Assistant Drawing, Washington Irving H. S.; 426 E. 26th St., Teel. 8350 Madison Sq.
HURLY, KATHREN E.—Assistant Biology, Erasmus Hall H. S.; 608 E. 17th St., Brooklyn. Tel. 6548-J Flatbush.
HUTCHINSON, HELEN SIMPSON—Drawing, Bushwick H. S.; 58 Madison St., Brooklyn.
HYDE, C. W.—Assistant French, De Witt Clinton H. S.; 526 W. 123d St., Manhattan.
HYDE, ISABELLA—Assistant French, Julia Richman H. S.; Hotel Holley, 36 Washington Sq., Manhattan. Tel. 3309 Spring.

I

IKELHEIMER, MINNIE—Domestic Science, Eastern District H. S.; 117 E. 56th St., Manhattan. Tel. Plaza 2546.
IHLKER, HEDWIG, W. D.—Assistant German and Study Hall, Wadleigh H. S.; Manhattan Ave., Crestwood, Westchester Co., N. Y. Tel. 759 Tuckahoe.
ILTLICH, LOUIS L.—Chemistry, Eastern District H. S.; 715 Tilden St., The Bronx, N. Y. C.
INGALLS, MARGARET L.—Assistant Mathematics, Girls' H. S.; 432 Macon St., Brooklyn.
ISAACSON, GERTRUDE E.—Substitute, Washington Irving H. S.; 343 E. 85th St., Manhattan. Tel. 822 Lenox.

J

JABLONOWER, BENJAMIN—Laboratory Assistant, Morris H. S.; 1390 Clinton Ave., The Bronx, N. Y. C.
JACKSON, ALICE R.—Assistant English, Wadleigh H. S. Annex; 70 Morningside Ave. Tel. 1100 Morningside.
JACKSON, EUGENE—Assistant German, De Witt Clinton H. S.; 672 E. 21st St., Brooklyn. Tel. 4133-W Flatbush.
JACOBIA, SPENCER P.—Assistant Commercial Branches, Morris H. S.; 303 E. 161st St., The Bronx, N. Y. C.
JACOBS, LEO.—Assistant History, Boys' H. S.; 28 Second Pl., Brooklyn. Tel. 837-J. Hamilton.
JACOBS, OLIN M.—Assistant Physics, Stuyvesant H. S.; 634 Crotona Park South, The Bronx, N. Y. C. Tell 3943 Tremont.
JACOBSEN, WALTER J.—Assistant Commercial Branches, Eastern District H. S.; 680 Beck St., Bronx. Tel. 8251 Melrose.
JACOBSON, HARRY—Assistant Mechanical Drawing, Manual Training H. S.; 594 Park Pl., Brooklyn. Tel. 5755-W Prospect.
JACOBSON, WALTER—Commercial Branches, Eastern District H. S.; 680 Beck St., The Bronx, N. Y. C. Tel. 8251 Melrose.
JAFFE, ISIDORE.—Clerical Assistant, Boys' H. S.; 214 Henry St., Manhattan.
JAMES, ARTHUR L.—Assistant Latin, Boys' H. S.; 60 Herkimer St., Brooklyn. Tel. 4711-R. Bedford.
JAMESON, JENNIE D.—Assistant Domestic Science, Washington Irving H. S.; 119th St. and Broadway. Tel. 1400 Morningside.
JAMIESON, EMILY M.—Assistant Mathematics, Far Rockaway H. S.; 1445 Pacific St., Brooklyn. Tel. 4243-R Bedford.
JEFFORDS, C. R.—Assistant Latin, Boys' H. S.; 19 Union Park Ave., Jamaica, N. Y. Tel. 1416-M. Jamaica.
JEFFS, EVA E.—Assistant Mathematics, Erasmus Hall H. S.; 607 New Lots Ave., Brooklyn.
JENKS, PAUL R.—First Assistant Latin, Flushing H. S.; 41 Mitchell Ave., Flushing, L. I. Tel. 689-W Flushing.
JENNER, WILLIAM A.—Assistant Latin, Boys' H. S.; 511 W. 122d St., Manhattan. Tel. 4670 Morningside.
JENKINS, ANNA S.—Assistant Latin, Girls' H. S.; 427 Nostrand Ave., Brooklyn.
JENKINS, MANFORD M.—Assistant Physics, Girls' H. S.; 120 Warwick St., Brooklyn.
JENNESS, JENNIE M.—Assistant Chemistry and Physics, Girls' H. S.; 602 Franklin Ave., Brooklyn.
JESCHKE, Martha L.—Assistant German, Far Rockaway H. S.; Greyloch Hall, Far Rockaway, N. Y. Tel. 93 Far Rockaway.
JEWELL, EDITH—Assistant Mathematics, Girls' H. S.; 126 Willoughby Ave., Brooklyn.
JOANNES, JULES S.—Assistant Music (Chairman), Girls' H. S.; 541 Decatur St., Brooklyn.
JOHNSON, ESTELLE M.—Assistant Latin, Richmond Hill H. S.; Lefferts and Stewart Aves., Richmond Hill, L. I. Tel. 1349-W Richmond Hill.
JOHNSON, HARRIET M. B.—Assistant Domestic Arts, Washington Irving H. S.; Hotel Grenoble,
JOHNSON, JULIUS M.—First Assistant Biology, Bushwick H. S.; 77 Herkimer St., Brooklyn.
56th St. and 7th Ave., Manhattan. Tel. 909 Columbus.
JOHNSON, LESLIE A.—Assistant Physics, Stuyvesant H. S.; Mountain Ave., Murray Hill, N. J. Tel. 524-R Summit.
JOHNSON, MARY HOOKER—Assistant English, Washington Irving H. S.; 509 W. 121st St., Manhattan. Tel. 7800 Morningside.
JOHNSON, MARION—Clerical Assistant, Erasmus Hall H. S.; 26A New York Ave., Brooklyn.
JOHNSON, WALTER R.—Assistant. English, De Witt Clinton H. S.; 165 W. 129th St., Manhattan. Tel. 1429 Morningside.

JOHNSTON, HENRY—Assistant English, Boys' H. S.; 1036 E. 10th St., Brooklyn.
JOHNSTON, INA W.—Assistant Drawing, Girls' H. S.; Milburn, N. P. P. O. Box 214.
JOHNSTON, WM. H.—Assistant Mathematics, Erasmus Hall H. S.; 996 Lafayette Ave., Brooklyn.
JONAS, J. B. EDWARD—Assistant German, De Witt Clinton H. S.; 164 W. 64th St., Manhattan.
JONAS, LOUIS—Assistant Commercial Branches, H. S. of Commerce; 248 Audubon Ave. Tel. 3513 Audubon.
JONES, EMMA A.—Assistant Drawing, Girls' H. S.; 749 Eastern Parkway, Brooklyn.
JONES, FLORENCE I.—Substitute History, Erasmus Hall H. S.; 676 Delamere Pl., Brooklyn.
JONES, FRANCES E.—Assistant English, Bryant H. S.; 345 W. 70th St., Manhattan. Tel. 2223 Columbus.
JONES, L. B.—Assistant Latin, Boys' H. S.; 135 Warwick St., Brooklyn.
JONES, W. R.—Assistant Mathematics, Manual Training H. S.; 415 W. 118th St., Manhattan.
JOQUISH, BEN M.—Assistant Chemistry and Physics, Erasmus Hall H. S.; 782 E. 18th St., Brooklyn.
JOSCLYN, ROSAMOND—Librarian, Jamaica H. S.; 413 Hillside Ave., Jamaica, L. I.
JOSEPH, MYRTLE J.—Assistant German, Bryant H. S.; 514 W. 122d St., Manhattan. Tel. 3632 Morningside.
JOSLIN, JENNIE M.—Assistant Mathematics, Morris H. S.; 540 E. 76th St., Manhattan. Tel. 2629 Lenox.
JUDD, SAMUEL E.—Assistant Latin, Wadleigh H. S.; 180 S. Oxford St., Brooklyn. Tel. 929-M Prospect.
JUDGE, ANNA G.—Assistant Music, Wadleigh H. S.; 140 W. 69th St. Tel. 3996 Columbus.
JUMNEFSKY, SIMON J.—Assistant Commercial Branches, Julia Richman H. S.; 952 Tiffany St., The Bronx, N. Y. C.
JUNGE, ANTOINE—Assistant German, Girls' H. S.; 247 New York Ave., Brooklyn.

K

KAHN, JEANETTE—Junior Stenography and Typewriting, Julia Richman H. S.; 860 E. 161st St., The Bronx, N. Y. C. Tel. 5516 Melrose.
KAHN, JOSEPH—Assistant Mathematics, H. S. of Commerce; 860 E. 161st St., The Bronx, N. Y. C. Tel. 5516 Melrose.
KAINE, JOSEPH M.—Assistant Biology, Boys' H. S.; 185 Lefferts Pl., Brooklyn.
KANE, THOMAS F.—Assistant Mathematics, Curtis H. S.; 5 Castleton Park, New Brighton, N. Y. Tel. 139-J Tompkinsville.
KAPHAN, LUDWIG—Assistant History, De Witt Clinton H. S.; 463 Eleventh St., Brooklyn. Tel. 670 South.
KATZ, HENRY D.—Assistant Commercial Branches, Washington Irving H. S.; 301 W. 122d St., Manhattan. Tel. 7620 Morningside.
KATZ, SAMUEL—Assistant Eng., Manual Training H. S.; 751 Howard Ave., Brooklyn. Tel. 2641-J East New York.
KATZ, SIDNEY F.—Librarian, Eastern District H. S.; 76 W. 82d St., Manhattan. Tel. 9126 Schuyler.
KAVENY, MARTIN—Substitute Clerk, De Witt Clinton H. S.; 70 W. 92d St., Manhattan.
KAUFFMAN, WILLIAM A.—Assistant Science, Eastern District H. S.; 15 Union Park Ave., Jamaica, N. Y.
KAUFFMAN, WILLIAM A.—Physics, Eastern District H. S.; 15 Union Park Ave., Jamaica, N. Y.
KEARNEY, MAURICE W.—Assistant Physics-Chemistry, Bay Ridge H. S.; 155 Sixth Ave., Brooklyn.
KECK, FRED R.—Assistant Mathematics, Erasmus Hall H. S.; 352 Argyle Rd., Brooklyn.
KEEN, J. R.—Assistant English, Wadleigh H. S.; 207 W. 56th St.
KEENER, ROBERT H.—First Assistant Modern Languages, Bushwick H. S.; 557 W. 124th St., Manhattan. Tel. 5780 Morningside.
KEIGWIN, HENRY W.—Assistant Mathematics (in charge of Williamsbridge Annex), Evander Childs H. S.; 24 N. 9th Ave., Mt. Vernon, N. Y. Tel. 215-R Mt. Vernon.
KELLER, FRANKLIN J.—Assistant English, De Witt Clinton H. S.; 243 E. 200th St., Manhattan. Tel. 5324 Tremont.
KELLER, HERMINA H.—Assistant English, Washington Irving H. S.; 1522 Bryant Ave., The Bronx, N. Y. C. Tel. 5284 Tremont.
KELLEY, FRANK B.—Assistant History, De Witt Clinton H. S.; 455 Madison Ave., Elizabeth, N. J. Tel. 1106 E. 113 Elizabeth.
KELLOGG, RAYMOND N.—Assistant Elocution, Morris H. S.; 2395 Walton Ave., The Bronx, N. Y. C.
KELLY, D. F.—Assistant Mathematics, De Witt Clinton H. S.; 215 E. 238th St., Manhattan. Tel. 1049-T Woodlawn.
KELLY, WILLIAM H.—Assistant Mathematics, Eastern District H. S.; 301 E. 68th St., Manhattan. Tel. Plaza 3770.
KELLY, WILLIAM H.—Mathematics, Eastern District H. S.; 301 E. 68th St., Manhattan. Tel. 3770 Plaza.
KELLNER, ANNA T.—Assistant German, Girls' H. S.; 179 Hancock St., Brooklyn.
KELSEY, LOUISE H.—Assistant Mathematics, Wadleigh H. S.; 128 W. 11th St.; Tel. 661 Chelsea.
KELSEY, LUCILE F.—Assistant English, Wadleigh H. S. Annex; 106 Morningside Drive. Tel. 8905 Morningside.
KEMNA, CHARLOTTE—Assistant Domestic Arts, Washington Irving H. S.; 353 W. 57th St., Manhattan. Tel. 6929 Columbus.
KENNEDY, ANNA J.—Assistant History, Far Rockaway H. S.; 207 8th Ave., Brooklyn.
KENNEDY, AGNES—Assistant Stenography and Typewriting, Julia Richman H. S.; 424 E. 17th St., Manhattan.
KERN, ALBERT T. W.—Assistant German, Manual Training H. S.; Jamaica, L. I.
KERR, FRANK E.—Assistant Commercial Branches, Curtis H. S.; 51 Grace Church Pl., Port Richmond, N. Y.
KETCHUM, DAISY T.—Assistant Drawing, Girls' H. S.; Hotel St. George, Brooklyn.
KEYES, ROWENA K.—Assistant English, Girls' H. S.; 27 Monroe St., Brooklyn.

KILBURN, FLORENCE M.—Assistant Commercial Branches, Richmond Hill, H. S.; 359 Jefferson Ave., Brooklyn. Tel. 1102 Bedford.
KILLEN, ARTHUR H.—Assistant, Flushing H. S.; 47 Busling Ave., Flushing, L. I.
KING, CYRUS A.—First Assistant Biology, Erasmus Hall H. S.; 387 E. 5th St., Brooklyn.
KING, ELIZABETH EDWARDS—Assistant in English, Wadleigh H. S.; 537 W. 121st St. Tel. 5120 Morningside.
KING, HELEN L.—Assistant Latin, Eastern District H. S.; 68 S. Washington Square, Manhattan.
KING, HELEN L.—Latin, Eastern District H. S.; 68 Washington Sq. South, Manhattan.
KING, MELVILLE S.—Assistant Commercial Branches, H. S. of Commerce; 932 Teller Ave., The Bronx, N. Y. C.
KINGSBURY, MARY A.—Librarian, Erasmus Hall H. S.; 117 St. Johns Pl., Brooklyn.
KINGSBURY, GEO. H.—Science, Newtown H. S.; 47 Lamont Ave., Elmhurst, L. I.
KINNAN, MADELINE—Assistant Phonography, Washington Irving H. S.; 414 W. 149th St., Manhattan. Tel. See Carolyn Court.
KIRBY, J. ALBERT—Assistant Penmanship, Bushwick H. S.; 713 Eastern Parkway, Brooklyn.
KISO, FREDA—German, Eastern District H. S. 63 Arondale St., Woodhaven, N. Y. Tel. 2495 Richmond Hill.
KIVLEN, MAUDE D.—Assistant English, Washington Irving H. S.; 22 St. Nicholas Pl., Manhattan. Tel. 2604 Audubon.
KLAFTER, SIMEON H.—Assistant German, Stuyvesant H. S.; 340 E. 15th St., Manhattan.
KLEES, C. MATHILDE—Assistant Stenography, Washington Irving H. S.; 347 W. 55th St., Manhattan. Tel. 8466 Columbus.
KLEIN, ANTHONY W.—Assistant Commercial Branches, Evander Childs H. S.; 931 Fox St., New York. Tel. 5871 Melrose.
KLEIN, JOSEPH J.—Assistant Commercial Branches, Richmond Hill H. S.; 56 W. 115th St., Manhattan. Tel. 4843 Harlem.
KLEIN, MARGARET A.—Assistant Elocution, Flushing H. S.; 40 Morningside Avenue East, Manhattan. Tel. 3447 Morningside.
KLEIN, MORRIS G.—Assistant Drawing, De Witt Clinton H. S.; 826 Hewitt Pl., Manhattan. Tel. 8329 Melrose.
KLOCK, CLAUDE W.—Assistant Latin, Eastern District H. S.; 123 Elmwood St., Woodhaven, L. I.
KLOCK, CLAUDE W.—Latin, Eastern District H. S.; 123 Elmwood St., Woodhaven, L. I.
KNOX, JAXON—Assistant English, De Witt Clinton H. S.; 195 Claremont Ave., Manhattan. Tel. 5100 Morningside.
KNOX, CHARLOTTE G.—Assistant English, Morris H. S.; 828 St. Nicholas Ave., Manhattan.
KNOPFMACHER, IDA—Assistant German, Julia Richman H. S.; 107 W. 64th St., Manhattan.
KONHEIM, JEROME—Assistant Accounts, Commercial H. S.; 548 W. 164th St., Manhattan. Tel. 6810 Audubon.
KOCH, ERNEST H., JR.—Assistant Mathematics, H. S. of Commerce; 71 E. 87th St., Manhattan.
KOOPMAN, BERNARD S.—Assistant Commercial Branches, H. S. of Commerce; 96 W. 163d St., The Bronx, N. Y. C. Tel. 5816 Melrose.
KOREY, ABRAHAM J.—Assistant English, Stuyvesant H. S.; 334 E. 25th St., Brooklyn.
KOUERMAN, HELENE V.—Assistant French, Morris H. S.; 2676 Morris Ave., The Bronx, N. Y. C.
KNAPP, ANNIE M.—Assistant History, Richmond Hill H. S.; 4651 Fulton St., Richmond Hill, L. I. Tel. 1518-J Richmond Hill.
KNICKERBOCKER, EDWIN VAN B.—Assistant English, H. S. of Commerce; 36 St. Nicholas Pl. Tel. 6009 Audubon.
KNOWLSON, WALTER S.—Assistant History, Erasmus Hall H. S.; 455 E. 4th St., Brooklyn. Tel. 7279-R Flatbush.
KNOWLTON, MARY E.—Assistant English, Morris H. S.; 168 W. 121st St., Manhattan. Tel. 6713 Morningside.
KNOX, T. HARRY—Assistant Mechanical Drawing, Stuyvesant H. S.; 243 Washington St., Glen Ridge, N. J. Tel. 1218-W Glen Ridge.
KRAKER, GOLDIE—Clerical Assistant, Washington Irving H. S.; 288 W. 147th St., Manhattan. Tel. 2284 Audubon.
KRAMER, BENJAMIN J.—Laboratory Assistant, Eastern District H. S.; 232 Henry St., Brooklyn.
KRAUSE, ARTHUR K.—Assistant Mathematics, De Witt Clinton H. S.; 2316 Andrews Ave., Bronx. Tel. 4621 Tremont.
KRAUSE, CARL A.—First Assistant Modern Languages, Jamaica H. S.; 1087 Prospect Pl., Brooklyn. Tel. 7379 Bedford.
KRELLENSTEIN, RAY—Physical Training, Eastern District H. S.; 969 Trinity Ave., The Bronx, N. Y. C. Tel. 7132 Melrose.
KRETSCHMAR, MADGA—German, Eastern District H. S.; 212 Pennsylvania Ave., Brooklyn. Tel. 3039 East New York.
KRITSCHMAR, MAGDA—Assistant German, Eastern District H. S.; 212 Pennsylvania Ave., Brooklyn. Tel. 3039-W E. N. Y. (discontinued).
KROEBER, ELSBETH—Assistant Biology, Morris H. S.; 151 W. 80th St., Manhattan. Tel. 5294 Schuyler.
KUHN, ADELINA—French, Eastern District H. S.; 2730 Broadway, Manhattan. Tel. 10461 Riverside.
KUHN, ADELINA—Assistant Modern Languages, Eastern District H. S.; 2730 Broadway, Manhattan. Tel. 10461 Riverside.
KUHN, MINA D.—Assistant Music, Curtis H. S.; 414 Richmond Terrace, New Brighton, N. Y. Tel. 1649 Tompkinsville.
KUPFER, ELSIE M.—First Assistant Biology, Wadleigh H. S.; 44 W. 97th St. Tel. 8839 Riverside.

L

LACEY, BERTHA J.—Assistant Drawing, Washington Irving H. S.; 100 Morningside Drive, Manhattan. Tel. 6272 Morningside.
LADEN, JAMES E.—Assistant Mathematics, Erasmus Hall H. S.; 419 W. 115th St., Manhattan.
LAGERWALL, CHAS. J.—Assistant Mathematics, H. S. of Commerce; 419 E. 144th St., The Bronx, N. Y. City.

LAMB, WILLIAM W.—First Assistant German, Manual Training H. S.; 952 E. 13th St., Brooklyn. Tel. 5807-T Midwood.
LANCASTER, BERTHA—Assistant English, Julia Richman H. S.; 376 E. 7th St., Brooklyn. Tel. 2444-J Flatbush.
LANDAU, LAURA—Assistant Mathematics, Morris H. S.; 307 W. 98th St., Manhattan. Tel. 3964 Riverside.
LANDERS, LELAND L.—Assistant Mathematics, Richmond Hill H. S.; 2992 Orchard Ave., Richmond Hill, L. I. Tel. 1079 Richmond Hill.
LANE, MARY C.—Assistant Latin, Flushing H. S.; 102 Jagger Ave., Flushing, L. I. Tel. 322-W lushing.
LANGDON, AMANDA—Assistant Commercial Branches, Washington Irving H. S.; 157 W. 123d St., Manhattan. Tel. 3786 Morningside.
LANGDON, RUTH J.—Assistant Stenography, Washington Irving H. S.; 157 W. 123d St., Manhattan. Tel. 3786 Morningside.
LANDSMAN, CHARLES M.—Assistant Mathematics, De Witt Clinton H. S.; 547 W. 157th St., Manhattan.
LANDSMAN, MORRIS J.—Substitute Commercial Branches (license), Bushwick H. S.; 21 W. 111th St., Manhattan.
LAMBERT, MARCUS B.—Assistant German, Richmond Hill, H. S.; 5 Maxwell Ave., Jamaica, L. I.
LAMBERT, SOPHIA W.—Assistant Biology, Washington Irving H. S.; 12 Bainbridge St., Brooklyn. Tel. 5972-W Bedford.
LANZ, IDA B.—Assistant French, Morris H. S.; 1224 Pacific St., Brooklyn. Tel. 3400 Bedford.
LANZ, JEANNE M.—Assistant French, Eastern District H. S.; 1224 Pacific St., Brooklyn. Tel. 5480
LANZ, JEANNE M.—French, Eastern District H. S.; 1224 Pacific St., Brooklyn. Tel. 5480 Prospect.
LANZ, LEA B.—Assistant French; Far Rockaway H. S.; 1224 Pacific St., Brooklyn. Tel. 3400 Bedford.
LAPATNIKOFF, PAULA—Assistant German, Wadleigh H. S.; 929 Whitlock Ave. Tel. 5435 Melrose. Prospect.
LAPOLLA, GARIBALDI M.—Assistant English, De Witt Clinton H. S.; 29 W. 129th St., Manhattan.
LARKINS, CHARLES D.—Principal, Manual Training H. S.; 225 Argyle Rd., Brooklyn. Tel. 355-W Flatbush.
LARSH, CHAS. H.—Commercial Branches, Newtown H. S.; 38 Cook Ave., Elmhurst, L. I.
LASHER, WM. R.—Assistant Mathematics, Erasmus Hall H. S.; 825 Argyle Rd., Brooklyn.
LASSWELL, ARTHUR C.—Assistant Biology, Manual Training H. S.; 392 15th St., Brooklyn.
LAUDER, MARY A.—Assistant English, Erasmus Hall H. S.; 1395 Dean St., Brooklyn. Tel. 2641-W Decatur.
LAW, FREDERICK H.—First Assistant English, Stuyvesant H. S.; 472 Argyle Rd., Brooklyn. Tel. 1316-M Flatbush.
LAWRENCE, ANTOINETTE—First Assistant History, Jamaica H. S.; 25 McDonough St., Brooklyn. Tel. 5240 Bedford.
LAWTON, MARY A.—Assistant English, Washington Irving H. S.; 50 Nevins St., Brooklyn.
LAWTON, MAXWELL F.—Assistant Latin-History, Bay Ridge H. S.; 2255 83d St., Brooklyn (1749 W. Bath Beach).
LAY, WILFRID—Assistant Latin, Flushing H. S.; 20 Neff Pl., Flushing, L. I. Tel. 1347-W Flushing.
LEAVITT, WILLIAM M.—Assistant Latin, Stuyvesant H. S.; 229 34th St., Woodcliff-on-Hudson, N. Y.
LE BEL, EMILIE M.—Clerical Assistant, Washington Irving H. S.; 4368 Richardson Ave., The Bronx, N. Y. C.
LEE, JOSEPH B.—Assistant Mathematics, Commercial H. S.; 942 St. Marks Ave., Brooklyn. Tel. 7846 Bedford.
LEE, MARGUERITE T.—First Assistant Biology, Girls' H. S.; 66 W. 95th St., Manhattan. Tel. 3562 Riverside.
LEETE, GERTRUDE M.—Assistant History, Richmond Hill H. S.; Central Ave., N. of Myrtle, Richmond Hill, L. I. Tel. 2567 Richmond Hill.
LEGGETT, BLANCHE C.—Assistant Greek, Erasmus Hall H. S.; 412 Ocean Ave., Brooklyn.
LEHRER, I. D.—Substitute Physical Training, De Witt Clinton H. S.; 1485 St. Marks Ave., Brooklyn.
LEIBOVITZ, NATHAN—Assistant Commercial Branches, Bushwick H. S.; 13 E. 112th St., Manhattan.
LEONHARD, THEODORE S.—Assistant Mechanical Drawing, Stuyvesant H. S.; 696 Decatur St., Brooklyn.
LEIGHTON, MARGARETTE M.—Assistant Mathematics, Morris H. S.; 435 W. 123d St., Manhattan.
LELAND, GENEVIEVE M.—Clerical Assistant, Girls' H. S.; 129 Lafayette Ave., Brooklyn.
LEMAN, GEORGE W.—Assistant Mathematics, Erasmus Hall H. S.; 55 Park Pl., Brooklyn.
LEMOWITZ, NATHAN H.—Commercial Branches, Eastern District H. S.; 38 W. 113th St., Manhattan.
LEMOWITZ, NATHAN H.—Assistant Commercial Branches, Eastern District H. S.; 38 W. 113th St., Manhattan.
LENFEST, BERTRAM E.—Assistant Boys' Shop, Manual Training H. S.; 152A 76th St., Brooklyn. Tel. 1455-R Bath Beach.
LENT, SUZANNE B.—Assistant English, Richmond Hill H. S.; 524 N. Lefferts Ave., Richmond Hill, L. I. Tel. 527-J Richmond Hill.
LENZ, GEORGE J.—Assistant German, Wadleigh H. S.; 357 W. 117th St. Tel. 8337 Morningside.
LEONARD, HOWARD C.—Assistant German, Curtis H. S.; 381 Dean St., Brooklyn.
LEONARD, MRS. NINA V.—Assistant Elocution, Julia Richman H. S.; 106 W. 130th St., Manhattan. Tel. 2035-W Morningside.
LEPERE, BERTHE B.—Assistant French, Girls' H. S.; 19 E. 128th St., Manhattan.
LE ROY, WALTER I.—Assistant Joinery, Manual Training H. S.; 255 Stuyvesant Ave., Brooklyn. Tel. 1493 Bushwick.
LEUCHS, FRITZ A. H.—Assistant German, Morris H. S.; 600 E. 164th St., The Bronx, N. Y. C. Tel. 560 Melrose.
LEVENE, HARRY—Assistant Mathematics, De Witt Clinton H. S.; 43 W. 112th St., Manhattan. Tel. 2009 Harlem.
LEVENTHAL, MURRAY J.—Assistant Mathematics, Stuyvesant H. S.; 3 Attorney St., Manhattan.
LEVINE, MAURICE—Assistant Mathematics, Evander Childs H. S.; 87 Taylor St., Brooklyn. Tel.

LEVINE, HERMAN B.—Assistant English, Boys' H. S.; 150 Hooper St., Brooklyn. Tel. 4150 Wmsbg. 3353-W South.

LEVINS, JULIA MARY—Assistant Domestic Arts, Washington Irving H. S.; 1785 Topping Ave., The Bronx, N. Y. C. Tel. 4886 Tremont.

LEVY, HARRY A.—Laboratory Assistant, Erasmus Hall H. S.; 607 Water St., Brooklyn.

LEVY, HENRY—Assistant Commercial Branches, Washington Irving H. S.; 116 Saratoga Ave., Yonkers, N. Y. Tel. 1319 Yonkers.

LEVY, ROSE ADELAIDE—Junior Stenography and Typewriting, Julia Richman H. S.; 216 W. 84th St., Hotel Bonta, Manhattan. Tel. 9500 Riverside.

LEWENTHAL, REBECCA—Assistant Drawing, Julia Richman H. S.; 2412 7th Ave., Manhattan. Tel. 2120 Audubon.

LEWIS, ALFRED H.—Assistant Mathematics, H. S. of Commerce; Congers, Rockland Co., N. Y. Tel. 75-J Congers.

LEWIS, ARTHUR C.—Assistant Mathematics, Morris H. S.; 1024 Boston Rd., The Bronx, N. Y. C.

LEWIS, ERNEST D.—Assistant History, H. S. of Commerce; 507 W. 113th St., Manhattan. Tel. 8420 Morningside.

LEWIS, FREDERICK Z.—First Assistant Biology, Boys' H. S.; 845 E. 34th St., Brooklyn. Tel. 5230 Flatbush.

LEWIS, EDWARD F.—Assistant Commercial Branches, Bryant H. S.; 14 Sanford Ave., Flushing, L. I. Tel. 127-M. Flushing.

LEYENBERGER, HARRY W.—Assistant Commercial Branches, Bushwick H. S.; Floral Park, L. I.

LIEBERMAN, ELIAS—Assistant English, Bushwick H. S.; 10 Bleecker St., Brooklyn.

LINDEN, MARY V.—Assistant Stenography, Washington Irving H. S.; 226 W. 75th St., Manhattan. Tel. 7265 Columbus.

LINDLAR, WILLIAM—Assistant Physical Science, Manual Training H. S.; 2725 Albemarle Rd., Brooklyn.

LINDSEY, FREDERICK B.—Assistant English, H. S. of Commerce; Waldwick, N. J.

LINGG, AMALIE S.—German, Bushwick H. S.; 303 St. Paul's Ave., Tompkinsville, Richmond Bor.

LINKER, JOHN—Assistant Commercial Branches, Julia Richman H. S.—157 W. 111th St., Manhattan. Tel. 3229 Morningside.

LINVILLE, HENRY R.—First Assistant Biology, Jamaica H. S.; 60 Sewall Ave., Jamaica, L. I. Tel. 1139-J Jamaica.

LIPPE, ADOLPH A.—Assistant Mathematics, Evander Childs H. S.; 940 Fox St., New York. Tel. 6644 Melrose.

LIPPERT, MARIE P.—Assistant German, Morris H. S.; 1153 Boston Rd., The Bronx, N. Y. C.

LIPPNER, SIMON L.—Assistant German, Bay Ridge H. S.; 302 Throop Ave., Brooklyn.

LIPSCHUTZ, BERTHOLD—Assistant Commercial Branches and Economics, Evander Childs H. S.; 162 W. 144th St.

LIPSKY, ABRAM—Assistant German, Stuyvesant H. S.; 1001 Faile St., Manhattan.

LISCOMBE, MRS. ESTHER A.—Additional Teacher Music, Girls' H. S.; 619 11th St., Brooklyn.

LITTIG, M. JOSEPHINE—Assistant Drawing, Bushwick H. S.; 296 Lafayette Ave., Brooklyn. Tel. 3791 Prospect.

LIVERMORE, HARRIET L.—Assistant Physical Training, Flushing H. S.; 550 Eastern Parkway, Brooklyn. Tel. 3143-R Bedford.

LIVERMORE, H. LOUISE—Assistant Physical Training (Girls), Far Rockaway H. S.; 550 Eastern Parkway, Brooklyn. Tel. 3143-R Bedford.

LOCKE-HENRY, ANNA W.—Assistant Physiology, Wadleigh H. S.; 44 Morningside Drive. Tel. 252 Morningside.

LOCKWOOD, CORNELIUS W.—Assistant Physics, Stuyvesant H. S.; 920 President St., Brooklyn. Tel. 5716 Prospect.

LOEW, JOSEPH—Assistant English, De Witt Clinton H. S.; 410 Central Park West, Manhattan. Tel. 7568-T Riverside.

LOEWINTHAN, ALBERT—Assistant English, De Witt Clinton H. S.; 339 E. 79th St., Manhattan. Tel. 3584 Lenox.

LOFTUS, JOHN J.—Assistant English, Commercial H. S.; 516 Sixty-first St., Brooklyn.

LOGUE, ANNIE E.—Assistant Domestic Arts, Washington Irving H. S.; 608 Lexington Ave., Manhattan. Tel. 2615 Plaza.

LONG, LESLIE O.—Assistant History, De Witt Clinton H. S.; 417 Riverside Drive, Manhattan.

LONG, R. L.—Assistant Commercial Branches, H. S. of Commerce; 2358 University Ave., The Bronx, N. Y. C.

LONGNECKER, ANNA B.—Clerical Assistant, Washington Irving H. S.; 565 9th St., Brooklyn. Tel. 1075 South.

LOOK, SAMUEL M.—Assistant English, Morris H. S.; 3875 Broadway, Manhattan. Tel. 3010 Audubon.

LORING, JACOB M.—Assistant Commercial Branches, Washington Irving H. S.; 58 S. 17th St., Flushing, L. I. Tel. 1860-R Flushing.

LOOS, RICHARD F.—Assistant German, Washington Irving H. S.; 150 Franklin Place, Brooklyn. Tel. 420 Flushing.

LOUGHRAN, AGNES M.—Assistant Commercial Branches, Eastern District H. S.; 142 Rutledge St., Brooklyn. Tel. 4179-W Williamsburgh.

LOUGHRAN, AGNES M.—Commercial Branches, Eastern District H. S.; 142 Rutledge St., Brooklyn. Tel. 4179-W Williamsburgh.

LOUGHRAN, JOHN—Assistant English, Commercial H. S.; 195 Kingston Ave., Brooklyn. Tel. 1352 Bedford.

LOVE, HARRY M.—Assistant English, Commercial H. S.; 970 Eastern Parkway, Brooklyn.

LOVELL, KATHERINE A.—Assistant Drawing, Erasmus Hall H. S.; 260 Cumberland St., Brooklyn.

LOW, CLARA L.—Assistant Domestic Science, Evander Childs H. S.; 312 W. 112th St., Manhattan. Tel. 2944-W Morningside.

LOW, J. HERBERT—First Assistant History, Manual Training H. S.; 177 Woodruff Ave., Brooklyn. Tel. 1381 Flatbush.

LOWD, EMMA F.—First Assistant English (Chairman), Washington Irving H. S.; 52 Irving Pl., Manhattan. Tel. 3827 Stuyvesant.

LUDWIG, AUGUSTUS—Assistant English, Manual Training H. S.; 170 Mortense St., Brooklyn. Tel. 8918-W Flatbush.
LUCEY, MICHAEL H.—Assistant History, De Witt Clinton H. S.; Emerson Hill, S. I Tel. 594-M Tompkinsville.
LUMLEY, ELEANOR P.—Assistant Latin, Girls' H. S.; 154 Halsey St., Brooklyn.
LUNDY, E. S.—Commercial Branches, Bushwick H. S.; 170 Highland Boulevard, Brooklyn.
LUPTON, OLIVE MOORE—Assistant English, Julia Richman H. S.; 107 W. 64th St., Manhattan.
LUTHER, E. M.—Assistant English, Manual Training H. S.; 481 6th St. Brooklyn. Tel. 2370 South.
LYLE, EDITH K.—Assistant History, Girls' H. S.; 132 Remsen St., Brooklyn.

M

McAULIFFE, ANNA E.—Science, Newtown H. S.; 154 E. 91st St., Manhattan.
McARDLE, JOHN PHILIP—Assistant Mathematics, Manual Training H. S.; 104 72d St., Brooklyn. Tel. 844-M Bay Ridge.
McBRIDE, ELINOR—Assistant Latin, Wadleigh H. S.; 449 W. 123rd St. Tel. 973 Morningside.
McCAIN, BLANCHE—Assistant Commercial Branches, Washington Irving H. S.; 574 Belgrove Drive, Arlington, N. J. Tel. 76-J Arlington.
McCAIN, MAUDE—Assistant Commercial Branches, Washington Irving H. S.; 574 Belgrove Drive, Arlington, N. J. Tel. 76-J Arlington.
McCALL, CARLETON C.—Assistant Boys' Shop, Manual Training H. S.; 1323 74th St., Brooklyn.
McCARTHY, JOHN D.—Assistant Biology, De Witt Clinton H. S.; 2337 Andrews Ave., Manhattan.
McCARTY, MARIA C.—Assistant Latin, Girls' H. S.; 38 Clinton St., Brooklyn.
McCARTNEY, HOGE—Assistant English, Boys' H. S.; 1155 Dean St., Brooklyn. Tel. 4100 Bedford.
McCONVILLE, LILLIAN M.—Physical Training, Bushwick H. S.; 25 Madison St., Brooklyn. Tel. 577-J. Prospect.
McCORMACK, THOS. H.—Assistant Mathematics, H. S. of Commerce; 1362 Fulton Ave., Brooklyn.
McCREA, ANNIE—Assistant Drawing, De Witt Clinton H. S.; 526 W. 114th St., Manhattan.
McCREARY, HERBERT J.—Assistant Mathematics, Manual Training H. S.; 784 President St., Brooklyn. Tel. 848-W Prospect.
McCUTCHEON, LOUISE H.—Assistant French, Washington Irving H. S.; 519 W. 121st St., Manhattan. Tel. 8790 Morningside.
McDERMOTT, ANNIE—Commercial Branches, Eastern District H. S.; 160 Hewes St., Brooklyn.
McDONALD, H. ROSABEL—Substitute Drawing, Evander Childs H. S.; 209 Dyckman St., Manhattan. Tel. 1127 Audubon.
McDONALD, JOHN J.—Assistant Latin, Manual Training H. S.; 132 Berkeley Pl., Brooklyn.
McDONALD, MILO F.—Assistant English, Bushwick H. S.; 1459 Dean St., Brooklyn.
McDOWELL, FLORENCE—Assistant English, Wadleigh H. S.; 504 W. 112th St. Tel. 1095 Morningside.
McDOWELL, JOHN D.—Assistant Mathematics, Boys' H. S.; 77 Lefferts Pl., Brooklyn. Tel. 1895 Prospect.
McDOWELL, MARY S.—Assistant Latin, Manual Training H. S.; 20 Crooke Ave., Brooklyn. Tel. 1379-J Flatbush.
McGILL, BEATRICE SHAW—Assistant French, Erasmus Hall H. S.; 432 Westminster Rd., Brooklyn.
McGILL, FRANKLIN CLARK—Assistant Latin, Erasmus Hall H. S.; 432 Westminster Rd., Brooklyn.
McGINN, CATHERINE A.—Substitute English, Erasmus Hall H. S.; 220 79th St., Brooklyn.
McGOWIN, MARGARET O.—Assistant Domestic Arts, Washington Irving H. S.; 106 Morningside Drive, Manhattan. Tel. 8905 Morningside.
McGRATH, WILLIAM J.—Assistant English, H. S. of Commerce; 561 W. 180th St., Manhattan.
McGUIRE, MARGUERITE E.—Substitute Algebra, Bushwick H. S.; 167 Himrod St., Brooklyn.
McGWIREY, MABEL—Substitute German, Washington Irving H. S.; 789 West End Ave., Manhattan. Tel. 9923 Riverside.
McINTYRE, EDITH A.—Assistant Cooking, Bryant H. S.; 347 W. 55th St., Manhattan. Tel. 8466 Columbus.
McINTIRE, RUBY C.—Assistant English, Washington Irving H. S.; 414 W. 121st St., Manhattan.
McKECHNIE, ELIZABETH M.—Clerical Assistant, Erasmus Hall H. S.; 1164 Pacific St., Brooklyn. Tel. 1677-J Prospect.
McKEE, LOUISE—Stenography and Typewriting, Eastern District H. S.; 205 Park Pl., Brooklyn.
McKENNA, MARY E.—Assistant Mathematics, Washington Irving H. S.; 155 W. 91st St., Manhattan. Tel. 7486 Riverside.
McKINNEY, MAY—Assistant Latin, Bryant H. S.; 68 E. 77th St., Manhattan. Tel. 1871 Lenox.
McLANE, FANNIE MOULTON—Assistant Biology, Julia Richman H. S.; 229 W. 126th St., Manhattan.
McMAHON, M. MABEL—Assistant Latin, Bryant H. S.; 7 W. 82d St., Manhattan.
McMAHON, KATHRYN—Physical Training, Newtown H. S.; 1234 Pacific St., Brooklyn.
McMILLEN, FLORENCE—Assistant Mathematics, Wadleigh H. S.; 1 W. 101st St. Tel. 6942-J Riverside.
McMILLEN, H.—Assistant Chemistry, Curtis H. S.; 1647 Richmond Tpke., W. New Brighton, N. Y. Tel. 975-R West Brighton.
McNALLY, EDWARD—Assistant English, Commercial H. S.; Lynbrook, L. I.
McQUADE, ROSE—Assistant Mathematics, Washington Irving H. S.; 370 Convent Ave., Manhattan.
McTIERNAN, THOMAS—Assistant Elocution, De Witt Clinton H. S.; 117 E. 39th St., Manhattan.
MAC COLL, GRACE BEATRICE—Assistant History, Erasmus Hall H. S.; 359 E. 21st St., Brooklyn.
MAC COLL, ROBERT J.—Assistant Mathematics, Manual Training H. S.; 616 W. 184th St., Manhattan.
MACKBY, JULIUS C.—Assistant Mechanical Drawing, Manual Training H. S.; 427 St. Johns Pl.,
MACKAY, ALFRED—Assistant Physical Science, Manual Training H. S.; 519 8th Ave., Brooklyn. Tel. 2796 South.
MACKAY, CATHERINE—Office Assistant, Newtown H. S.; 7 Chicago St., Elmhurst, L. I.
MACKAY, DAVID L.—Assistant Mathematics, Bay Ridge H. S.; 86 Woolsey St., Astoria, L. I.
MACKEY, ARTHUR J.—Assistant Commercial Branches, Bay Ridge H. S.; 187 Joralemon St., Brooklyn. Tel. 7388 Prospect.

Mac LAREN, DONALD C.—Assistant Mathematics, De Witt Clinton H. S.

MAC LEAN, DONALD CHARLES—Assistant Mathematics, Erasmus Hall H. S.; 1567 Brooklyn Ave., Brooklyn.

MacVAY, ANNA PEARL—Teacher Latin and Greek, Wadleigh H. S.; 7 W. 49th St. Tel. 3785 Plaza.

MAEDER, EMILY L.—Assistant Cooking, Julia Richman H. S.; 123 W. 121st St., Manhattan. Tel. 703 Morningside.

MACFARLANE, HAZEL P.—Substitute English, Erasmus Hall H. S.; 289 Clermont Ave., Brooklyn. Tel. 5969-W Prospect.

MAGEWORTH, J. OTIS—Assistant German, Manual Training H. S.; 902 President St., Brooklyn. Tel. 3161 Prospect.

MAGINN, ELIZABETH M.—Assistant French, Manual Training H. S.; 117 Montague St., Brooklyn. Tel. 7559 Main.

MAHAN, LUCY N.—Assistant English, Bushwick H. S.; 117 First Pl., Brooklyn. Tel. 1815 Hamilton.

MAHER, ADELAIDE E.—Substitute Latin, Bushwick H. S.; 72 E. 121st St., Manhattan. Tel. 4611 Harlem.

MAIER, AUGUSTUS—Assistant Physical Training, Stuyvesant H. S.; 254 Vanderbilt Ave., Brooklyn.

MALE, ROY R.—Assistant Accounts, Commercial H. S.; 3811 Avenue I, Brooklyn. Tel. 6974-R Midwood.

MALONEY, KATHERINE E.—Assistant Drawing, Julia Richman H. S.; 235 W. 138th St., Manhattan. Tel. 7746 Audubon.

MALOUBIER, HENRIETTE B.—Assistant French, Bushwick H. S.; 800 E. 14th St., Brooklyn. Tel. 4481 Flatbush.

MANAHAN, MARY G.—Drawing, Eastern District H. S.; 34 Jefferson Ave., Brooklyn. Tel. 3300 Prospect.

MANAHAN, MARY G.—Assistant Drawing, Eastern District H. S.; 34 Jefferson Ave., Brooklyn. Tel. 3300 Prospect.

MANFRED, MAUD E.—Assistant German (Chairman), Richmond Hill H. S.; 47 Hancock St., Brooklyn. Tel. 6072-W Bedford.

MANGUSE, WILLIAM P.—Assistant Mathematics, De Witt Clinton H. S.; 541 W. 124th St., Manhattan.

MANGUSE, WIILLIAM P.—Assistant Mathematics, H. S. of Commerce; 541 W. 124th St., Manhattan. Tel. 2669 Morningside.

MANKIEWICZ, FRANK—Assistant German, Stuyvesant H. S.; 2711 Decatur St., The Bronx, N. Y. C.

MANN, J.—Teacher in Training, Latin, Jamaica H. S.; 1302 67th St., Brooklyn. Tel. 3516 Bath Beach.

MANN, PAUL B.—Assistant Biology (head of department), Evander Childs H. S.; 6 W. 98th St., Manhattan. Tel 7600 Riverside.

MANNHARDT, E. G.—Assistant German, Jamaica H. S.; 235 E. 57th St., Manhattan.

MANTEL, HERMAN E.—Assistant German, Stuyvesant H. S.; 2374 University Ave., The Bronx,

NAPIER, FRANCES E.—English, Erasmus Hall H. S.; 1421 Pacific St., Brooklyn. Tel. 8537-J Bedford.

N. Y. C. Tel 5186 Tremont. Stamford, Conn., R. F. D. 29. Tel 1015 Ring 4.

MARGOLIES, FRED B.—Clerical Assistant, De Witt Clinton H. S.; 1459 Forty-seventh St., Brooklyn. Tel. 2503 Borough Park.

MARKS, LAZARUS E.—Assistant English, Stuyvesant H. S.; 112 E. 10th St., Manhattan.

MARSDEN, NELLE SMITH—Assistant Biology, Erasmus Hall, H. S.; 186 Prospect Pl., Brooklyn.

MARSH, BESSIE K.—Assistant Physical Training, Wadleigh H. S. Annex; 473 W. 145th St. Tel. 5175-R Audubon.

MARSHALL, ADELAIDE—Assistant English, Washington Irving H. S.; 166 W. 79th St., Manhattan. Tel. 7830 Morningside.

MARSHALL, AGNES M.—English, Newtown H. S.; 9 Toledo St., Elmhurst, L. I.

MARSTON, JAMES P.—Assistant English, Stuyvesant H. S.; 345 E. 15th St., Manhattan.

MARTIN, HARRIET—Assistant English, Wadleigh H. S.; 457 W. 123d St. Tel. 5280 Morningside.

MARTIN, PAUL J.—Assistant Music, Eastern District H. S.; 276-A Quincy St., Brooklyn. Tel. 2526-R Bedford.

MARTIN, PAUL—Music, Eastern District H. S.; 276A Quincy St., Brooklyn. Tel. 5357-J Bedford. Brooklyn.

MARQUARD, EDWARD G.—Assistant Music, Far Rockaway H. S.; 333 W. 85th St., Manhattan.

MARQUARDT, FLORENCE—Assistant History, Manual Training H. S.; 369 8th St., Brooklyn. Tel. 1473-J South.

MARQUARD, EDWARD G.—Assistant Music, Flushing H. S.; 114 Jamaica Ave., Flushing, L. I. Tel. 1582-W Flushing.

MARVIN, ROBERT B.—First Assistant German, Commercial H. S.; 826 Marcy Ave., Brooklyn. Tel. 8055-W Bedford.

MASCHMEDT, MARIE—Substitute German, Bushwick H. S.; 72 Hanover St., Elmhurst, L. I., Queens. Tel. 706-M. Newtown.

MASON, LUCIUS J.—Assistant Biology, De Witt Clinton H. S.; 188 Wadsworth Ave., Manhattan. Tel. 385 Audubon.

MASSONNEAU, ROBT. J.—Clerical Assistant, Manual Training H. S.; 12 E. 19th St., Brooklyn.

MASTIN, FLORENCE JOSEPHINE—Assistant English, Erasmus Hall H. S.; 359 E. 21st St., Brooklyn.

MATTES, MAX H.—Assistant Music, Girls' H. S.; 742 Lexington Ave., N. Y. C.

MATTFELD, WILHELM—Assistant Music, Washington Irving H. S.; 324 W. 51st St., Manhattan. Tel. 3817 Columbus.

MATTHEWS, ARCHIBALD J.—Assistant English, Morris H. S.; 425 W. 160th St., Manhattan. Tel. 4153 Audubon.

MATTUCK, J. A.—Assistant Physical Science, Manual Training H. S.; 628 E. 5th St., Brooklyn. Tel. 8975-W Flatbush.

MAY, ALFRED A.—Assistant English, H. S. of Commerce; 302 W. 22d St., Manhattan.

MAYER, ANNA S.—Assistant Mathematics, Wadleigh H. S. Annex, Highland Boulevard and Miller Ave., Brooklyn, N. Y.

MAYERS, LENA—Stenography and Typewriting, Bushwick H. S.; 678 Greene Ave., Brooklyn. Tel. Bedford 4449.

MAYFORTH, VALENTINE—Substitute Laboratory Assistant (Chemistry), De Witt Clinton H. S.; 856 Bushwick Ave., Brooklyn.
MAYNARD, ERNEST A.—Assistant Science, Eastern District H. S.; 17 Union Park Ave., Jamaica, L. I.
MAYO, MARION J.—First Assistant Mathematics, Eastern District H. S.; 179 Marcy Ave., Brooklyn. Tel. 3800 Williamsburgh.
MAYO, MARION J.—Mathematics, Eastern District H. S.; 189 Lincoln Rd., Brooklyn. Tel. 4733-W Flatbush.
MEDALIE, CARRIE K.—Assistant Latin, Bay Ridge H. S.; 51 E. 129th St., New York City.
MEEHAN, WILLIAM—Assistant Accounts, Commercial H. S.; 828 Walnut St., Richmond Hill. Tel. 605-W Richmond Hill.
MEHRTENS, HENRY E.—Assistant Manual Arts (Joinery), Stuyvesant H. S.; 115 Sickels Ave., New Rochelle, N. Y.
MEIGS, KATHERINE H.—Assistant Science, Eastern District H. S.; 70 Herkimer St., Brooklyn. Tel. 1713-R Bedford.
MEIGS, KATHERINE H.—Biology, Eastern District H. S.; 70 Herkimer St., Brooklyn.
MELSON, GEORGE W.—Assistant Stenography, Commercial H. S.; Hotel Chelsea, West 23d St., Manhattan.
MELVIN, FLOYD J.—Assistant English, Commercial H. S.; 939 St. Johns Pl., Brooklyn.
MENDUM, GEORGIANA—Assistant English, Morris H. S.; Greenridge Park, White Plains, N. Y.
MENEELY, JOHN H.—Assistant English, Manual Training H. S.; 220 6th Ave., Brooklyn. Tel. 129 Prospect.
MERAS, ALBERT A.—French and Spanish, Newtown H. S.; 9 Elmhurst Ave., Elmhurst, L. I.
MERCADO, JULIAN—Assistant Spanish, Commercial H. S.; 211 W. 121st St., Manhattan.
MERCHANT, ISABEL L.—Assistant Biology, Evander Childs H. S.; Scarsdale, N. Y. Tel. 248 Scarsdale.
MERCHANT, MANTON E.—Assistant Drawing, Erasmus Hall H. S.; 7 Linden Ave., Broolkyn.
MERRIAM, BETSEY G.—Assistant History, Girls' H. S.; 163 Lefferts Pl., Brooklyn.
MERINGTON, RUTH, Head of Drawing Department, Bushwick H. S.; 1408 Bushwick Ave., Brooklyn.
MERSEREAU, SAMUEL F.—Assistant Manual Arts (Woodturning), Stuyvesant H. S.; 26 Walnut Terrace, Bloomfield, N. J.
MESEROE, ELIZABETH E.—Assistant Biology, Wadleigh H. S. Annex; 20 High St., Glen Ridge, N. J. Tel. 3123-R Montclair.
MESERVE, MARTHA C.—Assistant English, Manual Training H. S.; 20 High St., Glen Ridge, N. J. Brooklyn address: 512 5th St.
MESSENGER, JOHN—Assistant Manual Arts (Joinery) Stuyvesant H. S.; 58 Woolsey St., Astoria, L. I. Tel. 376 Astoria.
MESSENGER, LESLIE—Joinery and Mechanical Drawing, Newtown H. S.; 103 Woolsey Ave., Astoria, L. I.
MEYENBERG, AMELIA—Assistant Stenography, Washington Irving H. S.; 102 W. 80th St., Manhattan.
MEYER, FLORENCE E.—Assistant German, Eastern District H. S.; 482 Bedford Ave., Brooklyn. Tel. 3163 Williamsburgh.
MEYER, FLORENCE E.—German, Eastern District H. S.; 482 Bedford Ave., Brooklyn. Tel. 3163 Williamsburgh.
MICHAELS, NORRIS H.—Assistant English, De Witt Clinton H. S.; 946 St. Marks Ave., Brooklyn.
MIDDLETON, FLORENCE—Assistant Biology, Wadleigh H. S. Annex; 366 St. Nicholas Ave. Tel. 4121 Morningside.
MILES, DUDLEY H.—Assistant English, De Witt Clinton H. S.; 1120 Amsterdam Ave., Manhattan. Tel. 1400 Morningside.
MILLER, CHARLES—Assistant Commercial Branches, Bushwick H. S.; 97 Rodney St., Brooklyn. Tel. 844 Williamsburgh.
MILLER, CHARLES A.—Assistant Physiography, Morris H. S.; 1042 Trinity Ave., The Bronx, N. Y. C.
MILLER, FRANK H.—First Assistant History, Flushing H. S.; 9 Bullard Pl., Flushing, L. I. Tel. 1636-J Flushing.
MILLER, GRACE HELENE—Assistant Commercial Branches, Bushwick H. S.; 126 Herkimer St., Brooklyn. Tel. 2583 Bedford.
MILLER, MABEL—Assistant English, Girls' H. S.; 189 Sterling Pl., Brooklyn.
MILLER, MAUD—Assistant Mathematics, Girls' H. S.; 81 Decatur St., Brooklyn.
MILLER, MAUDE E.—German, Newtown H. S.; 3d St., Woodside, L. I.
MILLER, MYRTLE H.—Assistant Mathematics, Morris H. S.; 582 E. 165th St., The Bronx, N. Y. C.
MILLS, EMILY WELCH—Assistant English, Washington Irving H. S.; 212 Quincy St., Brooklyn. Tel. 3813-J Bedford.
MILLS, JOSEPH S.—First Assistant Chemistry, H. S. of Commerce; 572 Van Cortlandt Park Ave., Yonkers. Tel. 1305 Yonkers.
MINNICK, JOHN D.—Assistant Mathematics, H. S. of Commerce; 2731 Broadway. Tel 10129 Riverside.
MINOR, MARIE L.—Assistant Biology, Wadleigh H. S.; 131 E. 31st St. Tel. 7495 Mad. Sq.
MIRSKY, ISRAEL—Assistant Mathematics, De Witt Clinton H. S.; 808 E. Parkway, Brooklyn.
MITCHELL, MARGUERITE F.—Assistant Stenography and Typewriting, Julia Richman H. S.; 349 W. 145th St., Manhattan. Tel. 7696 Audubon.
MITCHELL, THEODORE C.—Principal, Jamaica H. S.; 325 W. 56th St., Manhattan. Tel. 6744 Columbus.
MODEL, CHARLES—Assistant Physical Training, Eastern District H. S.; 366 Hewes St., Brooklyn.
MODEL, CHARLES—Physical Training, Eastern District H. S.; 366 Hewes St., Brooklyn.
MOHAN, LUCY F.—Assistant English, Bushwick H. S.; 117 First Place, Brooklyn. Tel. 1815 Hamilton.
MOLWITZ, ERNESTINE J.—Assistant German, Washington Irving H. S.; 88 E. 165th St., The Bronx, N. Y. C. Tel. 758-R Melrose.
MONTROSS, CHARLES G.—Assistant German, H. S. of Commerce; 120 W. 46th St., Manhattan.
MONTESER, FREDERICK—First Assistant German, De Witt Clinton H. S.; Van Cortlandt Park Ave., Yonkers.
MOONEY, LAWRENCE—Assistant Music, Washington Irving H. S.; 214 Lenox Ave., Manhattan. Tel. 3036 Harlem.
MOORE, SABRA MAUDE—Assistant English, Erasmus Hall H. S.; 101 Halsey St., Brooklyn.

MORGAN, A. S.—Assistant Mathematics, De Witt Clinton H. S.; Box 143, Tenafly, N. J.
MORREY, WILLIAM T.—First Assistant in History, Bushwick H. S., and Teacher in Charge of Annex in P. S. 75; 535 W. 111th St., N. Y. C. Tel. 3877 Morningside.
MORRILL, FRANCES U.—Assistant French, Bay Ridge H. S.; 296 Ryerson St., Brooklyn.
MORRIS, CONSTANCE—Assistant Physical Training, Bay Ridge H. S.; 650 10th St., Brooklyn.
MORRIS, EUGENE C.—Assistant Music, Bay Ridge H. S.; 813 Putnam Ave., Brooklyn.
MORRIS, MARY F.—Science, Newtown H. S.; 620 W. 116th St., Manhattan.
MORRISSEY, F. A.—Assistant Commercial Branches, Jamaica H. S.; Hollis Court Blvd., Queens, L. I.
MORROW, JULIE MATHILDE—Assistant English, Wadleigh H. S.; "The Brockholst," 101 W. 85th St. Tel. 3880 Schuyler.
MORSE, ELIZABETH E.—Assistant Drawing, Morris H. S.; 416 W. 118th St., Manhattan.
MORSE, CHARLES F.—Assistant Biology, De Witt Clinton H. S.; 230 Keap St., Brooklyn.
MOSCOVITZ, BERTHA J.—Assistant French and German, Julia Richman H. S.; 114 W. 79th St., Manhattan. Tel. 7140 Schuyler.
MOTT, HOWARD M.—Assistant Applied Mechanics and Electricity, Stuyvesant H. S.; 728 W. 181st St., Manhattan. Tel. 5700 Audubon.
MOULTON, FRANCES—Assistant Physical Training, Wadleigh H. S.; 400 Manhattan Ave. Tel. 846 Morningside.
MOYER, FAYETTE E.—Assistant History (Chairman of Dept.), De Witt Clinton H. S.; 2 Grove Terrace, Montclair, N. J. Tel. 2506-M Montclair.
MUELLER, ERNEST G.—Assistant German, Manual Training H. S.; 600 Hackensack St., Carlstadt, N. J.
MUFSON, THOMAS—Assistant English, De Witt Clinton H. S.; 17 E. 118th St., Manhattan.
MUHLEMAN, HARRIET P.—Assistant English, Washington Irving H. S.; 20 Mitchell Pl., East Orange, N. J. Tel. 3812-R Orange.
MULCAHY, MARY A.—Clerical Assistant, Julia Richman H. S.; 53 W. 106th St., Manhattan. Tel. 9141 Riverside.
MULHOLLAND, M. ESTELLE—Assistant Latin, Bushwick H. S.; 1109 Park Pl., Brooklyn.
MULLIGAN, MARY C.—Assistant Music, Erasmus Hall H. S.; 227 Macon St., Brooklyn.
MULLEN, LORING B.—First Assistant Mathematics, Girls' H. S.; 917 Rugby Rd., Brooklyn. School Tel. 372 Bedford.
MULLEN, ROSEMARY F.—Assistant, Washington Irving H. S.; 420 E. 84th St., Manhattan. Tel. 488 Lenox.
MULLER, ADA H.—Assistant English, Morris H. S.; 562 W. 150th St., Manhattan. Tel. 4745-W Audubon.
MUNRO, KATE M.—Assistant English, Morris H. S.; Court Rebelle, 420 W. 122d St., Manhattan.
MUNROE, HARRY K.—First Assistant English, Bryant H. S.; 54 Woolsey St., Astoria, L. I. Tel. 1710-W. Astoria.
MUNSON, DANIEL G.—Assistant English, Boys' H. S.; 1052 Lincoln Pl., Brooklyn.
MURPHY, MARGARET, Assistant Free Hand Drawing, Manual Training H. S.; 149 Steuben St., Brooklyn. Tel 7394-J Prospect.
MURRAY, JENNIE ERSKINE—Teacher Elocution, Wadleigh H. S.; 540 Manhattan Ave. Tel. 5770 Morningside.
MUSSEY, DELA P.—Assistant Drawing, Morris H. S.; 672 St. Nicholas Ave., Manhattan. Tel. 4312 Audubon.
MYERS, WILLARD L.—English, Eastern District H. S.; 788 Eastern Parkway, Brooklyn. Tel. 337-W Bedford.

N

NACHEMOV, MORRIS—Substitute Clerk, De Witt Clinton H. S.; 1764 Hoe Ave., Bronx. Tel. 574(Tremont, Ext. B-6.
NAHON, ZARITA—Junior French, Julia Richman H. S.; 24 W. 111th St., Manhattan. Tel. 200 Harlem.
NAMMACK, ELIZABETH F.—Assistant Latin, Wadleigh H. S.; 110 Morningside Drive. Tel. 98 Morningside.
NANES, PHILIP—History, Bushwick H. S.; 473 Hancock St., Brooklyn.
NATELSON, RACHEL.—Assistant English, Bay Ridge H. S.; 1280 53d St., Brooklyn.
NATHAN, ARTHUR—Assistant Accounts, Commercial H. S.; 1413 Pacific St., Brooklyn.
NEARING, ELENA P.—Assistant Mathematics, Flushing H. S.; 100 Jaggar Ave., Flushing, L. I Tel. 322-W Flushing.
NEHB, FRED W.—Substitute Laboratory Assistant (Chemistry), De Witt Clinton H. S.; 506 E. 162 St., The Bronx, N. Y. C.
NEIDLINGER, WILLIAM—Assistant Music, Washington Irving H. S.; 305 W. 97th St., Manhattan Tel. 7380 Riverside.
NEISWENDER, Ada B. C.—Assistant Latin, Erasmus Hall H. S.; 358 Sterling Pl., Brooklyn.
NELSON, WILLARD B.—Assistant Physical Science, Manual Training H. S.; 539 4th St., Brooklyn Tel. 472-W South.
NEUMARKER, JOHN—Assistant German, Stuyvesant H. S.; 876 W. 180th St., Manhattan. Tel 665 Audubon.
NEVINS, NANNIE R.—Assistant Stenography and Typewriting, Bushwick H. S.; 116 Hawthorne St. Brooklyn.
NEWCOMER, HARVEY—Assistant Physics (First Assistant in Physical Science), Bushwick H. S. Yonkers, Lattin Drive (Lowerre). Tel. 757-R.
NEWCOMB, FLORENCE A.—Assistant Art Department, Washington Irving H. S.; 114 Morningsid Drive, Manhattan. Tel. 320 Morningside.
NEWMAN, CHARLES—Assistant History, De Witt Clinton H. S.; 958 Prospect Ave., Bronx.
NEWMAN, JOSEPH—Assistant Chemistry, Commercial H. S.; 266 W. 139th St., Manhattan. Tel 5254-M Audubon.
NICHOLS, EDA L.—Assistant Elocution and English, Curtis H. S.; 14 Castleton Park, New Brighton N. Y. Tel. 1377 W. New Brighton.

NICHOLS, CLYDE B.—Commercial Branches, Newtown H. S.; 112 Cook Ave., Elmhurst, L. I.
NIGHTINGALE, ELEANOR M.—Assistant Declamation Department, Washington Irving H. S.; 202 Lefferts Pl., Brooklyn. Tel. 3071-W. Prospect.
NIGHTINGALE, IDA E.—Substitute Declamation Department, Washington Irving H. S.; 202 Lefferts Pl., Brooklyn. 3071-W Prospect.
NOBLE, HELEN G.—Assistant Sewing, Bryant H. S.; 432 Hoboken Ave., Jersey City, N. J.
NOCHKES, ADOLPH, Substitute, Stuyvesant H. S.; 420 Grand St., Manhattan. Tel. 6299 Orchard.
NOLAN, GRACE—Clerical Assistant, Washington Irving H. S.; 335 Clinton St., Brooklyn. Tel. 1077-R Main.
NORDEN, N. L.—Assistant Music, H. S. of Commerce; 301 Lafayette Ave., Brooklyn. Tel. 2404 Prospect.
NORMILE, MARY—Assistant English, Morris H. S.; 4260 Broadway, Manhattan. Tel. 4040 Audubon.
NORR, HENRY I.—Assistant Mathematics, Evander Childs H. S.; 896 Fox St., The Bronx, N. Y. C. Tel. 8071 Melrose.
NORRIS, JOHN S.—Assistant German, Stuyvesant H. S.; 255 W. 92d St., Manhattan. Tel. 5921 Riverside.
NORTHROP, CORA E.—Assistant English, Washington Irving H. S.; Scarsdale, N. Y.
NORTON, GEORGE W.—Reg. Assistant Joinery, Bushwick H. S.; 164 Franklin Pl., Flushing, Queens. Tel. 599-R. Flushing.
NORWOOD, CLARETTE—Assistant Mathematics, Wadleigh H. S. Annex; 529 W. 141st St. Tel. 5075-J Audubon.
NYE, BERTHOLD H.—Substitute English, De Witt Clinton H. S.; 118 Locust Hill Ave., Yonkers, N. Y.

O

O'BRIEN, CHARLOTTE E.—Junior Teacher Mathematics, Curtis H. S.; 1324 Lexington Ave., Manh.
O'BRIEN, WILLIAM J.—Junior Mathematics, Stuyvesant H. S.; 36 Wellington Court, Brooklyn. Tel. 7311-J Flatbush.
O'CONNOR, JOHN P.—Clerical Assistant, De Witt Clinton H. S.; 3599 Bainbridge Ave., Brooklyn.
ODELL, LOUIS S.—Assistant Mathematics, Manual Training H. S.; 505 6th St., Brooklyn. Tel. 2253 South.
O'DONNELL, AGNES T.—Assistant German (Latin), Bushwick H. S.; 2681 Briggs Ave., N. Y. C. Tel. 2028 Tremont.
O'DONNELL, EMMETT—Assistant English, Manual Training H. S.; 36 72d St., Brooklyn.
O'DONNELL, MARGARET M. A.—Assistant German, Bushwick H. S.; 2681 Briggs Ave., Bronx. Tel. 2028 Tremont.
O'DONNELL, MARJORIE V.—Substitute Library Assistant, Washington Irving H. S.; 2870 Briggs Ave., Bedford Park, The Bronx, N. Y. C. Tel. 1945 Fordham.
O'KEEFE, DAVID H.—Assistant Stenography and Typewriting, Jamaica H. S.; 179 Marcy Ave., Brooklyn. Tel. 3800 Williamsburg.
OLIVER, JOS. W.—Assistant Joinery, Manual Training H. S.; 154 S. Elliott Pl., Brooklyn.
OLLER, MARIE—Assistant English, Washington Irving H. S.; 70 Morningside Drive, Manhattan. Tel. 1100 Morningside.
O'NEIL, M. ALICE—Assistant Commercial Branches, Washington Irving H. S.; 175 Claremont Ave., Manhattan. Tel. 5750 Morningside.
O'NEIL, W. R.—Assistant Modern Languages, H. S. of Commerce; 175 Claremont Ave., New York.
O'NEILL, EDITH F.—Assistant Commercial Branches, Washington Irving H. S.; 407 Pleasant Ave., Manhattan. Tel. 3260 Harlem.
OPDYCKE, JOHN B.—First Assistant English, Julia Richman H. S.; 65 Broadway, Manhattan.
O'ROURKE, ANNE F.—Clerical Assistant, Morris H. S.; 148 W. 98th St., Manhattan.
ORMONT, ROSALIE—History, Erasmus Hall H. S.; 558 9th St., Brooklyn. Tel. 1493-J South.
ORR, ELLA J.—Assistant Stenography, Washington Irving H. S.; 128 W. 13th St., Manhattan. Tel. 6650 Chelsea.
O'RYAN, WILLIAM P.—Assistant Stenography, Commercial H. S.; 1051 Prospect Pl., Brooklyn.
ORLIARSKY, JOSEPH B.—Substitute Latin, De Witt Clinton H. S.; 49 Nelson Pl., Newark, N. J. Tel. 3345 Harlem.
OSBORN, RALPH—Assistant Biology, De Witt Clinton H. S.; 71 E. 87th St., Manhattan.
OSBORN, L. H.—Assistant English, Wadleigh H. S. Annex; 71 E. 87th St. Tel. 2054 Lenox.
OSBORNE, MABEL E.—Biology, Eastern District H. S.; 411 Greene Ave., Brooklyn.
OSTRANDER, AGNES—Assistant Drawing, Curtis H. S.; 12 Woodruff Ave., Brooklyn. Tel. 1194-W Flatbush.
OSWALD, FREDERICK W., JR.—Assistant German, Manual Training H. S.; 166 Martense St., Brooklyn. Tel. 8918-M. Flatbush.
OTTEN, HENRY L.—German, Bushwick H. S.; 58 Chichester Ave., Jamaica, Queens. Tel. 709 Jamaica.
OVERHOLSER, CHARLES E.—First Assistant Modern Languages, Boys' H. S.; 171 Kingston Ave., Brooklyn. Tel. 2877-R. Bedford.

P

PAINE, FREDERICH H.—First Assistant History, Eastern District H. S.; 285 Quincy St., Brooklyn. Tel. 268 Bedford.
PAGE, DONALD T.—Assistant Mathematics, Stuyvesant H. S.; 215 W. 23d St., Manhattan. Tel. 23d St. Y. M. C. A.
PAINE, FREDERICK H.—History, Eastern District H. S.; 285 Quincy St., Brooklyn. Tel. 268 Bedford.
PALMER, ANNA M.—Assistant Music, Morris H. S.; 605 W. 181st St., Manhattan.
PALMER, MAY T.—Assistant Mathematics, Flushing H. S.; 100 Jaggar Ave., Flushing, L. I. Tel. 322-W Flushing.
PARELHOFF, BERNARD M.—Assistant Mathematics, De Witt Clinton H. S.; 676 Beck St., Manhattan. Tel. 8251 Melrose.

PARKER, G. A.—Assistant Stenography and Typewriting, Jamaica H. S.; Compton Ter., Jamaica, L. I.
PARKER, JACOB—Assistant Physical Training, Morris H. S.; 1125 Boston Rd., The Bronx, N. Y. C. Tel. 8351 Melrose.
PARKER, MARGARET B.—Assistant Drawing, Morris H. S.; 1 W. 127th St., Manhattan. Tel. 5770 Harlem.
PARKER, S. RIDLEY, Library Assistant, Boys' H. S.; 28 Ormond Pl., Brooklyn.
PARMELEE, WILLIAM J.—Assistant Biology, De Witt Clinton H. S.; Bayside, L. I.
PARROTT, ALFRED F.—Assistant French, Stuyvesant H. S.; Plandome, L. I. Tel. 348-W Manhasset.
PARSONS, EDWARD B.—First Assistant Mathematics, Boys' H. S.; 488 Macon St. Tel. 3017-R. Bedford.
PARSONS, HERBERT H.—Assistant History, Boys' H. S.; 488 Macon St., Brooklyn. Tel. 3017-R. Bedford.
PASTERNAK, JESSE—Substitute Biology, Boys' H. S.; 303 President St., Brooklyn. Tel. 1186 Hamilton.
PASTERNAK, NATHANIEL—Chairman Art Department, Boys' H. S.; 303 President St., Brooklyn. Tel. 1186 Hamilton.
PATTERSON, MABEL L.—Clerical Assistant, Girls' H. S.; 20 St. James Pl., Brooklyn. Tel. 730 Prospect.
PATTERSON, SAMUEL W.—Assistant English, De Witt Clinton H. S.; 343 W. 23d St., Manhattan.
PAYNE, F. O.—Assistant Biology, H. S. of Commerce; 1819 Dorchester Rd., Brooklyn. Tel. 635-R Flatbush.
PEABODY, JAMES E.—First Assistant Biology, Morris H. S.; Scarsdale, N. Y. Tel. 158-J Scarsdale.
PEABODY, SUSAN P.—Latin Assistant, Erasmus Hall H. S.; 177 Woodruff Ave., Brooklyn.
PEACE, LILLIAN B.—Assistant Biology, Erasmus Hall H. S.; 194 Park Pl., Brooklyn.
PEACOCK, DANIEL L.—Substitute Economics, H. S. of Commerce; 469 Waverly Ave., Brooklyn.
PECK, MRS. ELIZABETH DU BOIS—Substitute Latin, Curtis H. S. (Rosebank Annex); Evelyn Lodge, Tompkinsville, N. Y.
PECK, EMILY S.—Assistant English, Manual Training H. S.; 515 Clinton Ave. Brooklyn. Tel. 3546-W Prospect.
PENHOLLOW, HARRY B.—Assistant Mathematics, De Witt Clinton H. S.; 122 W. 114th St., Manhattan. Tel. 632 Morningside.
PERKINS, FANNIE D.—Assistant Cooking, Girls' H. S.; 537 1st St., Brooklyn.
PERKINS, HELEN L.—Assistant German, Erasmus Hall H. S.; 537 1st St., Brooklyn.
PERRINE, CHARLES—Assistant Latin, Manual Training H. S.; 104 Lincoln Pl., Brooklyn. Tel. 607-W Prospect.
PERRY, MABEL L.—Clerk, Bryant H. S.; 16 Ash St., Flushing, L. I. Tel. 532-W. Flushing.
PERRY, E. O.—Assistant French, De Witt Clinton H. S.; 26 Jones St., Manhattan. Tel. 5809 Spring.
PERRY, OROLI R.—Assistant Girls' Shop, Manual Training H. S.; 163 Cumberland St., Brooklyn. Tel. 8324 Prospect.
PETERS, FRED'K A.—Assistant German, Manual Training H. S.; Holbrook, L. I.
PETERSON, A. EVERETT—Assistant History, Evander Childs H. S.; 2293 Sedgwick Ave., New York. Tel. 4752 Tremont.
PETRIE, JEAN DeELTE—Assistant Physical Training, Wadleigh H. S.; 540 W. 122nd St. Tel. 4880 Morningside.
PHILBRICK, MAX P.—Assistant French, De Witt Clinton H. S.; 153 Manhattan Ave., Manhattan.
PHILLIPS, JULIA TRACY—Librarian, Curtis H. S.; 4424 Sixth Ave., Brooklyn. Tel. 4711 Sunset.
PHILLIPS, SARA J.—Assistant English, Bay Ridge H. S.; 4424 Sixth Ave., Brooklyn.
PHILLIPS, ANNA L.—Teacher in charge Commercial Annex, Havemeyer, N. 6th and N. 7th Sts. (P. S. 143), Eastern District H. S.; 253 Steuben St., Brooklyn. Tel. 4033 Prospect.
PHILLIPS, ANNA L.—Teacher in Charge, Eastern District H. S.; 253 Steuben St., Brooklyn. Tel. 4033 Prospect.
PHILP, MARY I.—English, Eastern District H. S.; 126 Macon St., Brooklyn. Tel. 3853-W Bedford.
PICHEL, MARGARET—Assistant Mathematics, Girls' H. S.; 600 W. 183d St., N. Y. C.
PICKELSKY, FRANK—Assistant Mathematics, De Witt Clinton H. S.; 123 W. 115th St., Manhattan.
PICKENS, ROSE K.—Assistant Stenography, De Witt Clinton H. S.; 425 Park Ave., Manhattan.
PIERCE, ALICE R.—Assistant English, Washington Irving H. S.; 215 E. 15th St., Manhattan. Tel. 2934 Stuyvesant.
PIGNOL, GERTRUDE A. M.—Assistant German, Manual Training H. S.; 520 5th St., Brooklyn.
PIKE, KATHERINE G.—Assistant Latin, De Witt Clinton H. S.; 223 W. 21st St., Manhattan.
PINCH, MINNIE E.—Latin, Eastern District H. S.; 132 Cambridge Pl., Brooklyn.
PINGREY, (Mrs.) CORA E.—Assistant Biology, Evander Childs H. S.; 152 1st Ave., Mt. Vernon N. Y. Tel. 1918 Mt. Vernon.
PINTLER, HARRIET A.—Assistant Biology, Washington Irving H. S.; 968 E. 180th St., The Bronx N. Y. C.
PINKHAM, MARTHA G.—Assistant Declamation Department, Washington Irving H. S.; 139 W. 69th St., Manhattan. Tel. 4359 Columbus.
POKORNEY, RUDOLPH C.—Assistant Mathematics, De Witt Clinton H. S.; Box 353, Tenafly, N. J
POLK, ELLERY CHANNING—Assistant History, Commercial H. S.; 1320 Bergen St., Brooklyn. Tel. 1829-W Bedford.
POLLY, BRITON—Assistant English, H. S. of Commerce; 1163 Washington Ave., New York.
POND, PEARL F.—Assistant Drawing, Eastern District H. S.; 1395 Dean St., Brooklyn.
POND, HARRIET—Assistant Domestic Science, Washington Irving H. S.; 136 Irving St., Jersey City, N. J.
PORTER, GEORGE H.—Assistant History, H. S. of Commerce; 54 Morningside Ave. Tel. 4905 Morningside.
POTTER, MARY GODDARD, M. D.—Assistant Physical Training, Wadleigh H. S.; 39 W. 60th St Tel. 5755 Columbus.
POWERS, MINNIE M.—Mathematics, Newtown H. S.; 208 Maple St., Richmond Hill, N. Y. C.
POWNALL, EDYTHE M.—Assistant English, Washington Irving H. S.; 545 W. 148th St., Man
PRATT, MARION—Assistant Latin, Greek and English, Curtis H. S.; 19 Fort Pl., New Brighton, N. Y
PRATT, WINIFRED—Assistant Drawing, Washington Irving H. S.; 296 Lafayette Ave., Brooklyn Tel. 3791 Prospect.

PRENTIS, HALLY M.—Assistant English, Manual Training H. S.; 8415 13th Ave., Brooklyn. Tel. 1423-M Bath Beach.
PRESCOTT, LUCY M.—Assistant Latin, Far Rockaway H. S.; 186 Franklin Ave., Far Rockaway, N. Y. Tel. 95 Far Rockaway.
PRESTON, HELEN C.—History, Newtown H. S.; 8 Ithaca St., Elmhurst, L. I.
PRICE, ANNA G.—Assistant Drawing, Bryant H. S.; 145 Greenway South, Forest Hill Gardens, Queensboro, N. Y.
PROCTOR, ROBERT H.—Assistant English, Commercial H. S.; Hollis, L. I.
PROPER, EMBERSON, E.—First Assistant History, Bay Ridge H. S.; 1075 Prospect Pl., Brooklyn.
PUGH, ALEX. L.—First Assistant Economics, H. S. of Commerce; Pomona. Tel. 49-F2 Spring Valley.
PUIG, LOUISE M.—Assistant History, Manual Training H. S.; 1270 Carroll St., Brooklyn.
PULVERMACHER, DOLORES—Assistant Physical Training, Morris H. S.; 24 Manhattan Ave., Manhattan.
PULVERMACHER, WM. DEAN—Assistant Biology, Flushing H. S.; 24 Manhattan Ave., Manhattan. Tel. 1954 Riverside.
PUORRO, MICHAEL—Assistant Biology, Commercial H. S.; 95 Kingston Ave., Brooklyn.
PUTNEY, EDITH M.—Mathematics, Newtown H. S.; 45 Maurice Ave., Elmhurst, L. I.
PUTZ, EDWARD H.—Assistant Commercial Branches, Bay Ridge H. S.; 152 E. 80th St., New York City.
PYLE, WILLARD R.—First Assistant Physics, Morris H. S.; 125 Franklin Ave., Mt. Vernon, N. Y. Tel. 304-R Mt. Vernon.
PYLES, MARIAN—First Assistant Vice-Principal, Girls' H. S.; 1112 Dean St., Brooklyn. Tel 7371 Prospect.
PYNE, HENRY R.—Assistant Latin, Morris H. S.; 1115 Boston Rd., The Bronx, N. Y. C. Tel. 8296 Melrose.

Q

QUICK, OSCAR—Assistant Physics, Jamaica H. S.; 14 Burdett Pl., Jamaica, L. I. Tel. 738-J Jamaica.
QUIGG, HELEN TOWNSEND—Assistant English, Washington Irving H. S.; 417 W. 120th St., Manhattan. Tel. 5282 Morningside.
QUIMBY, ERNEST S.—Assistant English, Evander Childs H. S.; 244 E. 86th St., Manhattan. Tel. 412 Lenox.
QUINN, EDW. J.—Assistant Commercial Branches, Washington Irving H. S.; 501 W. 182d St., Manhattan.
QUIRK, CECILE—Assistant French, Bay Ridge H. S.; 117 Bay 28th St., Brooklyn.

R

RADIN, MAX—Latin, Newtown H. S.; 242 W. 112th St., Manhattan.
RAE, ANNE M.—Assistant Biology, Girls' H. S.; 415 Washington Ave., Brooklyn.
RAIMAN, ROBERT INSALL—Assistant English, Boys' H. S.; 492 Madison St., Brooklyn. Tel. 1017-J. Bedford.
RATNER, C. HYMAN—Assistant Biology, Commercial H. S.; 856 Nostrand Ave., Brooklyn.
RAUBICHECK, C. W.—Assistant English, De Wit Clinton H. S.; 2397 Concourse, Bronx.
RAYNOR, GEO. C.—Assistant Shorthand, Erasmus Hall H. S.; 199 Sterling Pl., Brooklyn.
RAYNOR, GILBERT J.—Assistant Accounts, Commercial H. S.; 1199 Bergen St., Brooklyn.
RAY, MEDORA L.—Assistant French, Washington Irving H. S.; 119 W. 71st St., Manhattan. Tel. 8615 Columbus.
READ, EDITH—Assistant Biology, Morris H. S.; 1350 Fulton Ave., The Bronx, N. Y. C. Tel. 5816 Tremont.
READ, WARREN W.—First Assistant English, Flushing H. S.; 4 Cedar Court, Flushing, L. I. Tel. 1573-W Flushing.
REED, MARY A.—Assistant Physical Training, Eastern District H. S.; 42 Macon St., Brooklyn. Tel. 237-J Bedford.
REINHOLD, ALIDA R.—Clerk, Bushwick H. S.; Great Kills, Staten Island. Tel. 133-R New Dorp.
RELPH, MARION F.—Assistant Mathematics, Richmond Hill H. S.; 1414 52d St., Brooklyn.
REMY, ALFRED.—Assistant Modern Languages, H. S. of Commerce; Bronx Manor Park, Bronxville, N. Y. Tel. 143-J Bronxville.
REYNOLDS, MRS. ALICE R.—Assistant Domestic Arts, Washington Irving H. S.; 117 W. 79th St., Manhattan. Tel. 7763 Schuyler.
REYNOLDS, FRANK H.—Assistant Latin, Stuyvesant H. S.; 5 W. 125th St., Manhattan.
REYNOLDS, GERALD—Assistant Music, Evander Childs H. S.; 238 W. 56th St., Manhattan. Tel. 9380 Columbus.
REYNOLDS, IONE A.—Assistant Mathematics, Wadleigh H. S.; 2071 Fifth Ave. Tel. 6015 Harlem.
REYNOLDS, JAMES I.—Assistant Latin, Boys' H. S.; 513 Park Pl., Brooklyn. Tel. 4955-M. Prospect.
REYNOLDS, LEWIS G.—Assistant German, Boys' H. S.; 103 Herkimer St., Brooklyn. Tel. 2775 Bedford.
REXFORD, FRANK A.—Assistant Chemistry (teaching Miology), Erasmus Hall H. S.; 445 3d St., Brooklyn.
RIBBER, EMMA—Assistant Commercial Branches, Eastern District H. S.; 325 Lenox Rd., Flatbush. Tel. 3567-J Flatbush.
RIBLET, MARY V.—Assistant English, Bryant H. S.; 106 E. 52nd St., Manhatttan.
RICE, WINFIELD S.—Assistant History, H. S. of Commerce; 55 Pierrepont St., Brooklyn. Tel. 3389 Main.
RICHARDS, ELLEN L.—Assistant Domestic Arts, Washington Irving H. S.; 68 Irving Pl., Manhattan.
RICHARDSON, MARION G.—Assistant Stenography and Typewriting, Richmond Hill H. S.; 336 Jefferson Ave., Brooklyn.

RICHARDSON, ROY S.—Assistant Biology, Boys' H. S.; 387-A McDonough St., Brooklyn.
RICHARDSON, WM. C.—Assistant Latin, Manual Training H. S.; 500 E. 18th St., Brooklyn. Tel. 2640 Flatbush.
RIESS, ERNST—First Assistant Classics, Boys' H. S.; 221 W. 113th St., Manhattan. Tel. 2832 Morningside.
RIEGGER, ELISABETH—German, Bushwick H. S.; 735 Greene Ave., Brooklyn.
RIORDAN, ELIZABETH A.—Assistant Stenography, Washington Irving H. S.; 65 E. 93d St., Manhattan.
RITTENHOUSE, HAWLEY O.—Mathematics, Eastern District H. S.; 392 Jefferson Ave., Brooklyn. Tel. 3797-L Bedford.
RITT, HAROLD L.—Assistant English, H. S. of Commerce; 253 Liberty Ave., Brooklyn.
ROBINS, FLORENCE F.—Junior Teacher English, Curtis H. S. (Rosebank Annex); 425 Madison St., Brooklyn.
ROBINSON, EVA A.—Assistant German, Bay Ridge H. S.; Clinton Court, 480 Clinton Ave., Brooklyn.
ROBINSON, L. ARCHIBALD—Assistant Physiography, Bay Ridge H. S.; 1916 Cropsey Ave., Brooklyn.
ROCHE, MICHAEL P.—Assistant Drawing, Commercial H. S.; Lynbrook, L. I.
ROGERS, WILLIAM W.—Assistant History, Boys' H. S.; 1421 Sterling Pl., Brooklyn. Tel. 4949 Bedford.
ROSMARIN, MICHAEL.—Assistant Stenography and Typewriting, Bay Ridge H. S.; 1332 46th St., Brooklyn.
ROSENBLUTH, HENRY.—Assistant Commercial Subjects; 145 Stanton St., Manhattan. Tel. 8013 Orchard.
ROTHHOLZ, META—Assistant Mathematics, Bryant H. S.; 13 Halsey St., Brooklyn.
ROLLINS, FRANK—Principal, Bushwick H. S.; 175 Amity St., Brooklyn.
ROBERTS, ALFRED S.—Assistant History, H. S. of Commerce; 107 Teller Ave., The Bronx, N. Y. C.
ROBINSON, ALFRED I.—Assistant Shop, Manual Training H. S.; 636 Westminster Rd., Brooklyn. Tel. 3543-J Flatbush.
ROBINSON, ALICE M.—Assistant Mathematics, Wadleigh H. S. Annex; 70 W. 164th St. Tel. 4573-W Melrose.
ROBINSON, DEBORAH P.—Assistant Phonography, Washington Irving H. S.; 70 W. 164th St., The Bronx, N. Y. C. Tel. 4573-W Melrose.
ROBINSON, F. D.—Assistant Mathematics, Manual Training H. S.; 1562 76th St., Brooklyn. Tel. 249-W Bath Beach.
ROBINSON, JOHN T.—Assistant Boys' Shop, Manual Training H. S.; 945 E. 34th St., Brooklyn. Tel. 4669-J Flatbush.
ROCHE, ELIZ. A.—First Assistant Stenography and Typewriting, Washington Irving H. S.; 2 St. Nicholas Pl., Manhattan.
ROCHESTER, M. MURIEL—Assistant English, Washington Irving H. S.; 845 Lexington Ave., Manhattan. Tel. 2573 Plaza.
ROCHOW, JOHN P.—Assistant Modern Languages, H. S. of Commerce; 269 E. Kingsbridge Rd., Fordham Station, New York.
RODMAN, BAYARD B.—Assistant Chemistry, Stuyvesant H. S.; 347 Manhattan Ave., Manhattan. Tel. 5411 Morningside.
RODMAN, HENRIETTA—Assistant English, Wadleigh H. S.; 315 E. 17th St. Tel. 2242 Stuyvesant.
ROE, ADA—Assistant Domestic Science, Washington Irving H. S.; 10 S. Arlington Ave., East Orange, N. J. Tel. 3656-R Orange.
ROESSLER, ERWIN W.—First Assistant Modern Languages, H. S. of Commerce; 411 W. 155th St., Manhattan. Tel. 3386 Morningside.
ROESSLER, NELLIE LLOYD—Assistant Latin, Wadleigh H. S.; 411 W. 115th St. Tel. 3386 Morningside.
ROETH, NATALIE—Assistant Biology, Manual Training H. S.; 598 6th St., Brooklyn. Tel. 3498 South.
ROGERS, CHAS. E.—Assistant Commercial Branches, H. S. of Commerce; University Ave. and Brandt Pl., The Bronx, N. Y. C.
ROGERS, CORA M.—English, Newtown H. S.; 71 Lamont Ave., Elmhurst, L. I.
ROLL, ROSE—Assistant Mathematics, Washington Irving H. S.; 201 E. 82d St., Manhattan.
ROMAINE, S. HELEN—Assistant English, Girls' H. S.; 213 Jefferson Ave., Brooklyn.
ROOT, MINNIE R.—Assistant English, Jamaica H. S.; 621 11th St., Brooklyn.
ROOT, LYDIA F.—Assistant Latin, Jamaica H. S.; 97 Hardenbrook Ave., Jamaica, L. I.
ROOT, EVA R.—Assistant English, Richmond Hill H. S.; 524 N. Lefferts Ave., Richmond Hill, L. I. Tel. 527-J Richmond Hill.
ROSENBLUM, ABRAHAM—Assistant Stenography and Typewriting, H. S. of Commerce; 61 W. 69th St., Manhattan.
ROSENSTADT, BERTHA—Assistant Modern Languages, Jamaica H. S.; 4 John St., Jamaica, L. I.
ROSENTHAL, DANIEL C.—Assistant French, De Witt Clinton H. S.; 961 St. Nicholas Ave., Manhattan.
ROSENTHAL, TERESE R.—Assistant Mathematics, Evander Childs H. S.; 223 W. 12th St., Manhattan. Tel. 2289 Morningside.
ROSS, ANNIE—Assistant Teacher French, Flushing H. S.; 659 Sanford Ave., Flushing, L. I. Tel. 145-W Flushing.
ROSS, A. FRANKLIN—Assistant History, Stuyvesant H. S.; 65 Kenilworth Pl., Ridgewood, N. J. Tel. 977-M Ridgewood.
ROSS, HELEN—Assistant Drawing, Wadleigh H. S. Annex; 166 W. 122nd St.
ROSTETTER, ALICE L.—Assistant English, Washington Irving H. S.; 468 W. 153d St., Manhattan. Tel. 5834 Audubon.
ROTHERHAM, PHILIP—Assistant Physical Training, H. S. of Commerce; 472 W. 147th St., Manhattan.
ROWE, MRS. EMMA L. H.—Clerical Assistant, Girls' H. S.; 130 W. 123d St., Manhattan.
ROYCE, S. GRACE—Assistant Latin, Wadleigh H. S.; 439 Manhattan Ave. Tel. 5127 Morningside.
RUBENSTEIN, JACOB.—Assistant History, Bay Ridge H. S.; 586 74th St., Brooklyn.

RUGGERI, AGNES C.—Assistant Stenography and Typewriting, Julia Richman H. S.; 1297 Lexington Ave., Manhattan.
RUSSELL, HELEN GERTRUDE—Assistant Biology, Wadleigh H. S.; 547 W. 123rd St. Tel. 5280 Morningside.
RUSSUM, RUTH E.—German, Eastern District H. S.; 76 St. Paul's Pl., Brooklyn. Tel. 3676 Flatbush.
RUSSELL, WARREN L.—Assistant Latin, Manual Training H. S.; 645 E. 4th St., Brooklyn.
RYAN, ANNA—Assistant English, Curtis H. S.; 14 Castleton Park, New Brighton, N. Y. Tel. 1377-W Tompkinsville.
RYAN, ELIZABETH G.—Assistant Declamation Department, Washington Irving H. S.; 141 St. Marks Pl., New Brighton, N. Y.

S

SACKMAN, GILBERT R.—Assistant Mechanical Drawing, Stuyvesant H. S.; 598 W. 177th St., Manhattan. Tel. 3800 Audubon.
SAGE, LILLIAN BELLE—First Assistant Biology, Washington Irving H. S.; 503 W. 121st St., Manhattan. Tel. 5010 Morningside.
SALMOWITZ, ROSE LILLIAN—Assistant Commercial Branches, Bushwick H. S.; 23 Broome St., Brooklyn. Tel. 1723-J. Greenpoint.
SALZANO, FRANCIS—Assistant Mathematics, De Witt Clinton H. S.; 1336 New York Ave., Rosebank, S. I.
SALZMAN, ANNA—Assistant Commercial Branches, Julia Richman H. S.; 54 W. 113th St., Manhattan.
SALTZBERG, FLORENCE B.—Assistant English, Wadleigh H. S.; 1045 Tinton Ave., The Bronx. Tel. 7880 Melrose.
SAN GIOVANNI, EDUARDO—Assistant Latin, Manual Training H. S.; Hollis, L. I. Tel. 503 Jamaica.
SAN, LOUIS JAMES—Assistant Chemistry, Stuyvesant H. S.; 606 W. 115th St., Manhattan.
SANDS, MARY E.—Clerk, Flushing H. S.; Flushing P. O. Tel. 1097-J Newtown.
SANFORD, CLARENCE H.—Assistant Applied Mechanics and Electricity, Stuyvesant H. S.; 27 W. 129th St., Manhattan. Tel. 2168 Harlem.
SANIAL, MARIE L.—Assistant Biology, Wadleigh H. S. Annex; 2141 Honeywell Ave., The Bronx. Tel. 5268 Tremont.
SANTEE, ELOISE B.—German, Eastern District H. S.; 1236 Pacific St., Brooklyn. Tel. 6256 Bedford.
SAPHIER, CONRAD J.—Assistant Stenography and Typewriting, Bay Ridge H. S.; 92 Bay 32d St., Brooklyn.
SAUL, GERTRUDE E.—Substitute German, Bushwick H. S.; 429 Ninth Ave., Astoria, L. I., Borough of Queens. Tel. 1169-J. Astoria.
SAUTEE, E ISE B.—Assistant German, Eastern District H. S.; 1236 Pacific St., Brooklyn. Tel. 6256 Bedford.LO
SAWYER, GEORGE A.—Assistant English, Commercial H. S.; 183 Steuben St., Brooklyn. Tel. 3391-R Prospect.
SAXTON, MARGARET D.—Assistant German, Julia Richman H. S.; 40 W. 34th St., Bayonne, N. J.
SAYMON, IGNATZ—Assistant English, Manual Training H. S.; 92 Woodruff Ave., Brooklyn. Tel. 6865-W Flatbush.
SCHACHTEL, ELSIE—Assistant German, Bryant H. S.; 911 Summit Ave., Bronx, N. Y. Tel. 2148 Melrose.
SCALES, CARRIE LOUISE—Assistant Physical Training, Washington Irving H. S.; 2053 7th Ave., Manhattan. Tel. 4108 Morningside.
SCARBOROUGH, ANDREW J.—Assistant Accounts, Commercial H. S.; 557-A Halsey St., Brooklyn.
SCHAMAHAN, WILLARD D.—Assistant Latin, Morris H. S.; 1956 Bogart Ave., The Bronx, N. Y. C. Tel. 843-J Westchester.
SCHAIBLE, G. C.—Assistant German, Manual Training H. S.; 355 St. Johns Pl., Brooklyn.
SCHAMUS, JOHN B.—Assistant Elocution, Evander Childs H. S.; 1057 Hoe Ave., The Bronx, N. Y. C. Tel. 8107 Melrose.
SCHAPIRO, BARNET—Assistant Physical Training, Evander Childs H. S.; 280 14th St., Brooklyn.
SCHARFF, VIOLETTE E.—Assistant French, Morris H. S.; 111 St. James Pl., Brooklyn. Tel. 3062 Prospect.
SCHAUMLOEFFEL, JOHN H.—Laboratory Assistant, Morris H. S.; 235 Stanhope St., Brooklyn.
SCHEIBE, ELIZABETH—Clerical Assistant, Wadleigh H. S.; 82 Morningside Ave. Tel. 7290 Morningside.
SCHEIB, RICHARD—Assistant German, Morris H. S.; 957 Teller Ave., The Bronx, N. Y. C.
SCHLANCH, WILLIAM S.—Assistant Mathematics, H. S. of Commerce; 219 Division St., Hasbrouch Heights, N. J.
SCHLOSBERG, SAMUEL—Assistant English, Morris H. S.; 855 Hunts Pl. Ave., The Bronx, N. Y. C.
SCHMALHAUSEN, SAMUEL—Assistant English, De Witt Clinton H. S.; 1069 Boston Rd., Manhattan.
SCHMIDT, CARL G.—Assistant Music, Erasmus Hall H. S.; 246 Hancock St., Brooklyn.
SCHMIDT, CLARA E.—Assistant German, Bay Ridge H. S.; 314 State St., Brooklyn.
SCHMIDT, MABEL PEARSON—Assistant English, Morris H. S.; 400 W. 118th St., Manhattan. Tel. 4769 Morningside.
SCHNEER, A. HENRY—Assistant Mathematics, De Witt Clinton H. S.; 1420 Fifth Ave., Manhattan. Tel. 3440 Harlem.
SCHOEDDE, EMMA J.—Assistant German, Morris H. S.—1350 Fulton Ave., The Bronx, N. Y. C.
SCHOENFELDT, EUGENIA—Substitute German, Washington Irving H. S.; 346 E. 20th St., Manhattan. Tel. 534 Gramercy.
SCHOENROCK, HEDWIG—Assistant German, Morris H. S.; 309 E. 162d St., The Bronx, N. Y. C.
SCHONBERG, MAX—Assistant German, Evander Childs H. S.; 888 Fox St., New York. Tel. 3310 Melrose.
SCHRADIECK, HELEN E.—Assistant German, Eastern District H. S.; 535 Washington Ave., Brooklyn.
SCHRADIECH, H. E.—Assistant German, Manual Training H. S.; 535 Washington Ave., Brooklyn. Tel. 3977 Prospect.

SCHREIBER, EMMA F.—Teacher in Training in German, Wadleigh H. S.; 155 E. 90th St. Tel. 3419 Lenox.
SCHROEDER, MRS. ANITA—Assistant Spanish (teaches German also), Bryant H. S.; Douglaston, L. I.
SCHRYVER, GEORGE ORIN—Assistant Latin, Manual Training H. S.; 315 8th Ave., Brooklyn. Tel. 2600 South.
SCHULZ, BERTHA—Assistant French, Wadleigh H. S.; Hicksville, L. I.
SCHUMER, JACOB H.—Assistant Physics, Girls' H. S.; 311 8th St., Brooklyn.
SCHUYLER, ELMER—First Assistant Mathematics, Bay Ridge H. S.; 87 71st St., Brooklyn.
SCHWAGER, HARRY—Substitute Commercial Branches, Washington Irving H. S.; 517 W. 144th St., Manhattan. Tel. 2770 Audubon.
SCHWARZENBECK, PETER A.—Assistant Drawing, De Witt Clinton H. S.; 143 W. 16th St., Manhattan.
SCHWARTZ, EDWARD E.—Assistant German, Manual Training H. S.; 157 Wyona St., Brooklyn.
SCHWARZKOPF, ERNST—Assistant Forge Work, Stuyvesant H. S.; 348 E. 87th St., Manhattan.
SCOTT, COIRA A.—Assistant Mathematics, Morris H. S.; 188 Wadsworth Ave., Manhattan.
SCOTT, IZORA—Assistant Latin, Erasmus Hall H. S.; 2015 Bedford Ave., Brooklyn. Tel. 6368-W Flatbush.
SCOVILL, FLORENCE M.—Assistant English, Erasmus Hall H. S.; 177 Woodruff Ave., Brooklyn Tel. 2426 Flatbush.
SCUDDER, JOHN O.—Assistant Physics, Morris H. S.; 441 Dunham Ave., Mt. Vernon, N. Y.
SCULLY, TERESA M.—Clerical Assistant, Morris H. S.; 137 W. 95th St., Manhattan. Tel. 4712 Riverside.
SEAMANS, MARY A.—Commercial Branches, Eastern District H. S.; 1395 Dean St., Brooklyn.
SEAMAN, MARY E.—Assistant German, Bushwick H. S.; 21 Van Buren St., Brooklyn. Tel. 2509-J Bushwick.
SEEBER, ELIZABETH—German, Newtown H. S.; 62 Montague St., Brooklyn.
SEELMAN, H. ELIZABETH—Assistant English, Girls' H. S.; 410 4th St., Brooklyn.
SEIDENSTICKER, CLARA—Assistant German, Wadleigh H. S.; 65 Montrose Ave., South Orange N. J. Tel. 340-W South Orange.
SEYMOUR, MACY I.—Assistant English, Girls' H. S.; 339 Lenox Rd., Brooklyn.
SEMPLE, LEWIS B.—First Assistant English, Bushwick H. S.; 229 Jefferson Ave., Brooklyn. Tel 5252-J. Bedford.
SESSO, PAULINE M.—Assistant German, Wadleigh H. S.; 303 E. 161st St. Tel. 4476 Melrose.
SHARPE, RICHARD W.—Assistant Biology, De Witt Clinton H. S.; 158 Parkside Ave., Brooklyn.
SHANLEY, MARY E.—English, Newtown H. S.; 139 Madison St., Flushing, L. I.
SHAW, ADELE M.—English, Newtown H. S.; Forest Hills, L. I.
SHAW, M. EDNA—Assistant Mathematics, Bryant H. S.; 520 W. 122d St., Manhattan. Tel. 3545 Morningside.
SHEA, JOHN A. J.—Assistant Stenography, Commercial H. S.; 1516 Bedford Ave., Brooklyn.
SHEARER, ROBERT J.—Assistant Stenography, Commercial H. S.; 1320 Avenue I, Brooklyn. Tel 7196-W Midwood.
SHEEHAN, MARY J.—Assistant Physical Training, Erasmus Hall H. S.; 520 Ocean Ave., Brooklyn
SHEELY, JANE VAN DEMARK—Assistant History, Wadleigh H. S.; 560 Washington Ave., Brooklyn. Tel. 4987-W Prospect.
SHEILS, FRANCES B.—Clerical Assistant, Bay Ridge H. S.; 528 Chauncey St., Brooklyn.
SHEPHERD, FLORENCE D.—First Assistant German, Curtis H. S.; 4 Castleton Park, New Brighton N. Y. Tel. 1193-R Tompkinsville.
SHEPPARD, J. J.—Principal, H. S. of Commerce; 27 W. 44th St., Manhattan.
SHERMAN, ROSE ELIZABETH—Assistant English, Bushwick H. S.; 142 Columbia Heights, Brooklyn
SHINN, VICTOR I.—First Assistant Drawing, Manual Training H. S.; 26 Waldorf Court, Brooklyn Tel. 2912-W Flatbush.
SHIPLEY, JAMES H.—Assistant Mathematics, Curtis H. S. (Rosebank Annex); 453 W. 152d St., Manhattan. Tel. 1857 Audubon.
SHIMBERG, JEANNETTE—Assistant Mathematics, Manual Training H. S.; 209 Rutledge St., Brooklyn. Tel. 4067-R Williamsburgh.
SHUMWAY, EDGAR—First Assistant Latin, Manual Training H. S.; 472 E. 18th St., Brooklyn.
SHULMAN, MORRIS A.—Assistant Commercial Branches, Washington Irving H. S.; 1044 E. 13th St. Brooklyn. Tel. 6931-W Midwood.
SHWITZER, MYRTLE—Clerical Assistant, Julia Richman H. S.; 1931 Madison Ave.; Manhattan. Tel 1735 Lenox.
SIEDLER, CHARLES W.—Assistant Latin, Evander Childs H. S.; 2316 Andrews Ave., The Bronx N. Y. C. Tel. 2121 Fordham.
SILBERSTEIN, NATHAN—Assistant Mathematics, Stuyvesant H. S.; 160 Manhattan Ave., Manhattan. Tel. 7861 Riverside.
SILVERMAN, HENRY—Assistant Physical Training, Jamaica H. S.; 153 Willett St., Jamaica, L. I.
SIMMONS, ISABEL—Assistant English, Erasmus Hall H. S.; 167 Joralemon St., Brooklyn. Tel. 4115 Main.
SIMMONS, KATE C.—Assistant Drawing, Girls' H. S.; 167 Joralemon St., Brooklyn.
SINAGNAN, LEON—Assistant, Modern Languages, H. S. of Commerce; 5000 Broadway, Manhattan. Tel. 6821 Audubon.
SINDELAR, CHARLES—Assistant Mathematics, Stuyvesant H. S.; 1421 Crotona Ave., Manhattan 5264 Tremont.
SKEELE, OTIS C.—Assistant Physical Training, Morris H. S.; 2293 Sedgwick Ave., The Bronx, N. Y. C. Tel. 4752 Tremont.
SKILHEIMER, MINNIE—Assistant Domestic Science, Eastern District H. S.; 117 E. 56th St., Manhattan. Tel. 2546 Plaza.
SKINNER, HERBERT C.—Assistant Modern Languages, H. S. of Commerce; 2430 Aqueduct Ave.,
SKINNER, E. MABEL—Assistant Commercial Branches, Washington Irving H. S.; 28 W. 97th St., Manhattan. Tel. 5531-J Riverside.
SKIPP, H. J.—Assistant Modern Languages, H. S. of Commerce; 1120 Amsterdam Ave, Tel. 1400 Morningside.

STRONG, WM. M.—Assistant Latin, Erasmus Hall H. S.; 725 E. 12th St., Brooklyn. Tel. 6568-J Flatbush.
STROUT, GEO. M.—Assistant English Erasmus Hall H. S.; 327 E. 18th St., Brooklyn.
STRUM, NELLIE AUGUSTA—Assistant English, Washington Irving H. S.; 105 E. 15th St., Manhattan. Tel. 120 Stuyvesant.
SUGARMAN, ARTHUR M.—Assistant Stenography and Typewriting, Bay Ridge H. S.; 1078 E. 14th. St., Brooklyn.
SULLIVAN, BESSIE—Assistant Mathematics, Girls' H. S.; 292 Clermont Ave., Brooklyn. The Bronx, N. Y. C.
SULLIVAN, MARY—Mathematics, Eastern District H. S.; 292 Clermont Ave., Brooklyn. Tel. 4661-J Prospect.
SULLIVAN, MARY—Assistant Mathematics, Eastern District H. S.; 292 Clermont Ave., Brooklyn. Tel. 4661-J Prospect.
SUNDERLAND, FLORENCE—Assistant English, Bryant H. S.; 414 W. 118th St., Manhattan.
SURREY, FRANK M.—Assistant Physics, Morris H. S.; 505 W. 122d St., Manhattan. Tel. 8709 Morningside.
SWARTOUT, CAROLINE H.—Assistant German, Morris H. S.; 839 W. 179th St., Manhattan. Tel. 2798 Audubon.
SWEENEY, HELEN M.—Assistant English, Wadleigh H. S.; Pearl River, N. Y. Tel. 48 Pearl River.
SWENSON, CELESTE C.—Latin, Newtown H. S.; 87 Locust St., Flushing, L. I.
SWENSON, JOHN A.—Assistant Mathematics, Boys' H. S.; 1323 Lincoln Pl., Brooklyn.
SWETT, CAROLYN P.—Assistant Biology, Bryant H. S.; 345 W. 70th St., Manhattan. Tel. 2223 Columbus.
SWICK, MARY S.—Assistant Drawing, Flushing H. S.; 54 S. Parsons Ave., Flushing, L. I.
SYMS, LOUIS CHARLES—Assistant French, Wadleigh H. S.; 11½ E. 87th St. Tel. 2148 Lenox.

T

TACKER, CHARLES R.—Assistant Physics (in charge of Tottenville Annex); Curtis H. S.; 90 Third St., New Dorp, S. I. Tel. 922-J Tottenville (Ext. of P. S. 1).
TAILOR, I. N.—Principal, Richmond Hill H. S.; 523 Maple St., Richmond Hill, L. I. Tel. 439-R Richmond Hill.
TALBOT, A. MARY—Assistant Mathematics, Erasmus Hall H. S.; 1312 Caton Ave., Brooklyn.
TAMBOISE, MADELEINE—Assistant French, Washington Irving H. S.; 26 W. 97th St., Manhattan. Tel. 2968 Riverside.
TAUSK, ALFRED A.—Assistant German, Boys' H. S.; 339 Bridge St., Brooklyn. Tel. 554 Main.
TAYLOR, ALBERT S.—Assistant English, De Witt Clinton H. S.; 1421 University Ave., Manhattan. Tel. 5656 Tremont.
TAYLOR, ARTHUR M.—Assistant Music, Bushwick H. S.; 776 Lafayette Ave., Brooklyn. Tel. 519-R Bedford.
TAYLOR, EDWARD F.—Assistant History, Commercial H. S.; Chester Ave., Hollis, L. I.
TAYLOR, JANE I.—Assistant History, Wadleigh H. S.; 53 W. 126th St. Tel. 3464 Harlem.
TAYLOR, JEANNETTE S.—Assistant English, Girls' H. S.; 934 Sterling Pl., Brooklyn.
TAYLOR, MIRIAM L.—Assistant Physiography, Wadleigh H. S.; 67 W. 126th St. Tel. 937 Harlem.
TAYLOR, NETTIE—Assistant English, Manual Training H. S.; 770 Halsey St., Brooklyn. Tel. 372-R Bushwick.
TEETER, CHARLES H.—First Assistant Mathematics, Commercial H. S.; 4123 Eighteenth Ave., Brooklyn. Tel. 1974-W Flatbush.
TEFFT, MARY BIDEMORE—Assistant Physiography, Wadleigh H. S.; 186 S. Columbus Ave., Mt. Vernon, N. Y. Tel. 760 Mt. Vernon.
TENNANT, GEORGE BREMMER—Assistant English; Stuyvesant H. S.; 217 E. 27th St., Manhattan. Tel. 1331 Madison Square.
TERRELL, LILLIAN A.—Assistant Girls' Shop, Manual Training H. S.; 515 5th St., Brooklyn. Tel. 3440 South.
THAYER, ANNIE M.—Librarian, Bryant H. S.; 373 W. 116th St. Tel. 6620 Morningside.
THEOBALD, JACOB, JR.—Assistant Mathematics, Morris H. S.; 203 W. 108th St., Manhattan. Tel. 2529 Riverside.
THOMAS, HARRISON C.—Assistant History, De Witt Clinton H. S.; 26 Jones St., Manhattan. Tel. 5809 Spring.
THOMAS, LULU E.—Assistant English, Julia Richman H. S.; 54 Morningside Ave., Manhattan. Tel. 4905 Morningside.
THOMPSON, ANNIE S.—Assistant History, Morris H. S.; 78 Livingston Ave., Yonkers, N. Y. Tel. 1103-R Yonkers.
THOMPSON, CHRISTINA M.—Assistant Domestic Arts, Washington Irving H. S.; 503 W. 121st St., Manhattan. Tel. 1050 Morningside.
THOMPSON, DORA ROUNDS—Assistant English, Washington Irving H. S.; 405 W. 118th St., Manhattan. Tel. 1051 Morningside.
THOMPSON, K. W.—Assistant Physical Sciences, Jamaica H. S.; 54 Columbus Ave., Woodhaven, L. I.
THOMPSON, LOUISE—Assistant German, Wadleigh H. S. Annex; 78 Livingston Ave., Yonkers. Tel. 1103-R.
THOMPSON, MARTHA.—Assistant Biology, Bay Ridge H. S.; Morsemere, Bergen Co., New Jersey.
THOMSON, MYRTLE E.—Assistant History, Wadleigh H. S.; 419 W. 119th St. Tel. 7700 Morningside.
THORNE, FREDERICK—Joinery and Mechanical Drawing, Bryant H. S.; 408 W. 150th St., Manhattan. Tel. 1530 Audubon.
THORNDIKE, MILDRED L.—Assistant English, Washington Irving H. S.; 251 W. 261st St., The Bronx, N. Y. C. Tel. 532 Kingsbridge.
THORP, BENJAMIN H.—Assistant English, Jamaica H. S.; 99 Madison Ave., Flushing, L. I. Tel. 1635-M Flushing.
TIETZ, JOHN W.—Substitute Laboratory Assistant Biology, De Witt Clinton H. S.; 429 Johnson Ave., Richmond Hill.
TILDSLEY, JOHN L.—Principal, De Witt Clinton H. S.; Spuyten Duyvil. Tel. 132-W Kingsbridge.

TILLEY, LYDIA L.—Assistant German, Morris H. S.; 611 W. 156th St., Manhattan.
TIMMERMAN, CHARLES E.—First Assistant Physics, De Witt Clinton H. S.; 269 N. Grove St., East Orange, N. J. Tel. 3878-R Orange.
TOBIN, JAMES L.—Assistant History, De Witt Clinton H. S.; 505 Kosciusko St., Brooklyn.
TOMLIN, STELLA M.—Assistant Mathematics, Eastern District H. S.; 1320 Bergen St., Brooklyn. Tel. 1829-W Bedford.
TOMLIN, STELLA M.—Mathematics, Eastern District H. S.; 1320 Bergen St., Brooklyn. Tel. 1829-W Bedford.
TOMPKINS, ELIZABETH W.—Assistant Biology, Erasmus Hall H. S.; 2015 Bedford Ave., Brooklyn. Tel. 6369-W Flatbush.
TOPP, EMILY—Assistant Biology, Julia Richman H. S.; 428 W. 20th St., Manhattan. Tel. 5618 Chelsea.
TOPPER, MRS. ANNA—Assistant Stenography and Typewriting, Julia Richman H. S.; 574 St. Nicholas Ave., Manhattan.
TORTORA, ALBERT—Laboratory Assistant Physics, De Witt Clinton H. S.; 620 Lexington Ave.
TOWNSEND, ARTHUR M.—Assistant Latin, Erasmus Hall H. S.; 2181 Bedford Ave., Brooklyn.
TOWNSEND, CHARLES W.—Assistant Commercial Subjects, Bushwick H. S.; 20 Glenada Pl., Brooklyn. Tel. 2246-J. Bedford.
TOWNSEND, MAY E.—Junior Teacher English, Bushwick H. S.; 272 Troy Ave., Brooklyn. Tel. 6376-M Bedford.
TRACY, EDWIN S.—Assistant Music, Morris H. S.; 1400 Clinton Ave., The Bronx, N. Y. C.
TRACY, HOWARD M.—Assistant Commercial Branches, Curtis H. S.; 35 Havenwood Rd., Tompkinsville, N. Y. Tel. 1497 Tompkinsville.
TRACY, MARY L.—Assistant English, Evander Childs H. S.; 503 W. 121st St., Manhattan. Tel. 5010 Morningside.
TRAUTSVETTER, IDA—Assistant German, Julia Richman H. S.; 118 W. 73d St., Manhattan. Tel. 413 Columbus.
TRIMBLE, LOUISE M.—Assistant English, Morris H. S.; 405 W. 118th St., Manhattan. Tel. 1051 Morningside.
TREADWELL, FLORA G.—Assistant Physical Training, Girls' H. S.; 294 Cumberland St., Brooklyn.
TREDICK, HELEN F.—Assistant Biology, Erasmus Hall H. S.; 2015 Bedford Ave., Brooklyn. Tel. 6369-W Flatbush.
TRENCH, RUTH—Assistant English, Bay Ridge H. S.; 1815 Newkirk Ave., Brooklyn.
TRESSLER, JACOB C.—Assistant English, Boys' H. S.; 49 New York Ave., Brooklyn.
TROWBRIDGE, CORNELIA B.—Assistant Science, Eastern District H. S.; 63 Groton St., Forest Hill, L. I. Tel. 6335-R Forest Hill.
TROWBRIDGE, CORNELIA—Biology, Eastern District H. S.; 63 Groton St., Forest Hill, L. I.
TROWBRIDGE, CORNELIA R.—Assistant English, Richmond Hill H. S.; 161 Lefferts Ave., Richmond Hill, L. I. Tel. 2829 Richmond Hill.
TRUCKENBRODT, LEWIS—Assistant Stenography, Washington Irving H. S.; 159 E. 178th St., Manhattan.
TUFTS, ANNE BLANCHARD—Assistant English, Bushwick H. S.; 1-A Fifth Ave., Manhattan. Tel. 5520 Spring.
TURNER, KATE E.—Assistant Principal Erasmus H. S.; 2022 Beverly Rd., Brooklyn.
TUTHILL, MARY E.—Assistant Drawing, Washington Irving H. S.; 881 Lafayette Ave., Brooklyn. Tel. 1839-R Bushwick.
TUTTLE, EDITH M.—Assistant English, Washington Irving H. S.; 267 Hamilton Pl., Paterson, N. J.
TWEEDY, GRACE B.—Second Assistant French, Wadleigh H. S.; 7 W. 83nd St.
TWEEDY, MARY T.—Laboratory Assistant Biology, Wadleigh H. S.; 930 West End Ave. Tel. 3928 Riverside.

U

UHLIG, WILLIAM C.—Assistant Chemistry, Stuyvesant H. S.; 143 N. Clinton St., East Orange, N. J.
UNDERHILL, MARY—Assistant Mathematics, Julia Richman H. S.; 87 Hamilton Pl., Manhattan. Tel. 1200 Audubon.
UNDERWOOD, E. S.—Assistant Mathematics, Wadleigh H. S. Annex; 127 Crary Ave., Mt. Vernon. Tel. 954-R.
UNGER, GERTRUDE N.—Stenography and Typewriting, Eastern District H. S.; 1206 Cortelyou Rd., Brooklyn.
URDANG, HARRY—Assistant English, Commercial H. S.; 1478 Union St., Brooklyn. Tel. 8439-W Bedford.

V

VAIL, CLARENCE W.—Assistant English, Manual Training H. S.; 238 Garfield Place, Brooklyn.
VALENTINE, CHAS. I.—Music, Newtown H. S.; 1036 Bloomfield St., Hoboken, N. J.
VALENTINE, HENRY D.—Assistant English, Erasmus Hall H. S.; 2324 82d St., Brooklyn. Tel. 2307 Bath Beach.
VALENTINE, MORRIS C.—First Assistant Biology, Richmond Hill H. S.; 1200 Pacific St., Brooklyn. Tel. 6232-R Bedford.
VAN ALLEN, KATHERINE C.—Assistant Drawing, Morris H. S.; 419 W. 119th St. Tel. 7700 Morningside.
VANDERBILT, GRACE W.—Assistant Biology, Morris H. S.; 135 W. 123d St., Manhattan. Tel. 3109 Morningside.
VAN DEUSEN, EDWIN W.—Assistant Commercial Branches, H. S. of Commerce; Hollis, L. I.
VAN DUSEN, ELDON M.—Assistant Commercial Branches (Stenography and Typewriting), Far Rockaway H. S.; 43 State St., Far Rockaway, N. Y.
VAN LEEUWEN, MARY—Clerk, Bryant H. S.; 21 Second St., Woodside, N. Y.
VAN OLINDA, JAMES E.—46 St. John's Pl., Brooklyn. Tel. 4495 Prospect.
VAN SANTVOORD, MRS. ALICE G.—Clerical Assistant, Morris H. S.; 65 W. 127th St., Manhattan.

VAN TUYL, G. H.—Assistant Commercial Branches, H. S. of Commerce; 711 W. 180th St., Manhattan. Tel. 3602 Audubon.
VAN VLIET, JESSIE L.—Assistant Latin, Wadleigh H. S.; 405 W. 118th St. Tel. 1051 Morningside.
VEDDER, ESTELLA M.—Assistant Biology, Erasmus H. S.; 661 Flatbush Ave., Brooklyn.
VERMILYA, MABEL—Assistant Mathematics, Julia Richman H. S.; 115 W. 96th St., Manhattan.
VIDAUD, NATHALIE L.—Assistant Latin, Erasmus Hall H. S.; 194 Clinton St., Brooklyn.
VINCENT, BLANCHE E.—Assistant French, Wadleigh H. S. Annex; 203 W. 78th St. Tel. 993-J Schuyler.
VINCENT, CHARLOTTE M.—Assistant German, Bryant H. S.; 53 E. 88th St., Manhattan.
VLYMEN, WILLIAM T.—Principal, Eastern District H. S.; 379 Front St., Hempstead, L. I.
VLYMEN, DR. WILLIAM T.—Principal (Latin when he teaches), Eastern Dist. H. S.; 379 Front St., Hempstead, L. I.
VOGT, CHARLES A.—Assistant Mechanical Drawing, Joinery and Wood Turning, Bryant H. S.; 65 Elm St., Flushing, N. Y. Tel. 987-M. Flushing.
VOLENTINE, MARY F.—Assistant Latin, Erasmus Hall H. S.; 370A Grand Ave., Brooklyn.
VOLKAERTO, MARIE—Assistant French, Manual Training H. S.; 411 6th St., Brooklyn.
VOLKHAUSEN, WILLIAM—Assistant Commercial Branches, Morris H. S.; 433 W. 163d St., The Bronx, N. Y. C.
VON NARDROFF, ERNEST R.—Principal Stuyvesant H. S.; 397 Madison St., Brooklyn.
VOORHEES, SOPHIA—Assistant Latin, Richmond Hill H. S.; Baldwinsville, N. Y. Tel. 1065 Richmond Hill.
VOSBURGH, CHARLES H.—First Assistant Physical Science, Jamaica H. S.; Central Ave., Richmond Hill. Tel. 274 Richmond Hill.

W

WAGENSCHUTZ, ANNA—German, Eastern District H. S.; 64 Montague St., Brooklyn, The Harbor View.
WAGNER, JULIA A.—Assistant German, Washington Irving H. S.; 243 E. 68th St., Manhattan. Tel. 6930 Plaza.
WAGNER, LORA M.—Assistant German, Curtis H. S. (Tottenville Annex); 1 Aspinwall St., Tottenville, S. I.
WAHL, EMANUEL M.—Assistant German, Morris H. S.; 456 W. 165th St., The Bronx; N. Y. C.
WAIT, HORACE C.—Assistant Latin, De Witt Clinton H. S.; 256 W. 21st St., Manhattan. Tel. 2841 Chelsea.
WAITE, CHARLOTTE AUGUSTA—Assistant Sewing and Dressmaking, Julia Richman H. S.; 501 W. 120th St., Manhattan. Tel. 4590 Morningside.
WAKEMAN, SUSAN E.—Assistant Latin, Girls' H. S.; 133 Bainbridge St., Brooklyn.
WALDMAN, MARK—Assistant German, Bryant H. S.; 1876 Belmont Ave., Manhattan.
WALES, ALMA E.—Assistant Mathematics, Girls' H. S.; 1224 Pacific St., Brooklyn.
WALKER, ALICE J.—Assistant English, Manual Training H. S.; The Montreaux, Cor. 9th St. and 9th Ave., Brooklyn. Tel. 3846 South.
WALKER, CLAUDE—Assistant Chemistry, H. S. of Commerce; 60 W. 162d St., The Bronx, N. Y. C. Tel. 6256 Melrose.
WALKER, CLAUDE—Assistant Chemisary, H. S. of Commerce; 60 W. 162d St., The Bronx. Tel. 6256 Melrose.
WALKER, RUTH N.—Assistant Biology, Manual Training H. S.; 145 Prospect Park West, Brooklyn. Tel. 3846 South.
WALLACE, MINOT L.—Assistant Latin, Stuyvesant H. S.; 941 Simpson St., The Bronx, N. Y. C. Tel. 6644 Melrose.
WALLIE, PHOEBE M.—Assistant English, Washington Irving H. S.; 417 W. 121st St., Manhattan. Tel. 6886 Morningside.
WALSH, DANIEL O'C.—Assistant Stenography and Typewriting, H. S. of Commerce; 1124 Prospect Pl., Brooklyn.
WALTER, M. LOUISE—Assistant Sewing and Dressmaking; Julia Richman H. S.; 136 W. 120th St., Manhattan. Tel. 2238-W Morningside.
WALTON, GEORGIANA C.—Assistant Mathematics, Manual Training H. S.; 166 Prospect Park West, Brooklyn. Tel. 563 South.
WARD, A. W.—Assistant Elocution, Jamaica H. S.; 32 Union Ave., Jamaica, L. I.
WARD, MERCEDES—Assistant Physical Training, Bay Ridge H. S.; 281 E. 161st St., New York.
WARNER, ELMA L.—Assistant Physical Training, Erasmus Hall H. S.; 230 Fennimore St., Brooklyn. Tel. 1805-M Flatbush.
WARR, LOUISE—Assistant German, Washington Irving H. S.; 333 W. 57th St., Manhattan. Tel. 4054 Columbus.
WARREN, JAMES P.—English, Eastern District H. S.; 596 Bedford Ave., Brooklyn.
WARREN, JAMES P.—Assistant English, Eastern District H. S.; 596 Bedford Ave., Brooklyn.
WATROUS, LOUISE E.—Assistant Mathematics, Girls' H. S.; 15 South Oxford St., Brooklyn.
WATSON, ALICE D.—History, Eastern District H. S.; 234 78th St., Brooklyn.
WATSON, ALICE D.—Assistant History, Eastern District H. S.; 234 Seventy-eighth St., Brooklyn.
WATSON, MARY H.—Assistant English, De Witt Clinton H. S.; 3 Fifth Ave., Manhattan.
WATT, HELEN S.—Assistant Biology, Wadleigh H. S.; 615 Jefferson Ave., Elizabeth, N. J. Tel. 451-J.
WAY, ABNER P.—Assistant Physical Training, Stuyvesant H. S.; 619 W. 179th St., Manhattan. Tel. 6790-J Audubon.
WAY, MARY J.—Assistant History, Girls' H. S.; 1284 Pacific St., Brooklyn.
WEAVER, ELI W.—Assistant Mathematics, Boys' H. S.; 25 Jefferson Ave., Brooklyn. Tel. 1377-W. Prospect.
WEDGE, ALFRED H.—Assistant Latin, Stuyvesant H. S.; 701 W. 178th St., Manhattan. Tel. 3780 Audubon.
WEED, HENRY T.—First Assistant Physical Science, Manual Training H. S.; 176 Prospect Park West, Brooklyn. Tel. 1919-M South.
WEEKS, MARION I.—Assistant Elocution, Bay Ridge H. S.; 55 Clifton Pl., Brooklyn.

WEHL, HANNA—Assistant German, Julia Richman H. S.; 203 W. 117th St., Manhattan. Tel. 3930 Morningside.
WEINBERGER, GEORGE G.—Assistant English, H. S. of Commerce; 200 W. 1134th St. Tel. 9097 Morningside.
WEISS, ALMA—Assistant German, Washington Irving H. S.; 633 E. 168th St., Manhattan. Tel. 2980 Tremont.
WEISER, SAMUEL—Assistant German, Stuyvesant H. S.; 1378 Webster Ave., The Bronx, N. Y. C.
WEISNER, HARRY—Assistant German, Washington Irving H. S.; 130 E. 16th St., Manhattan.
WEIRICH, CLARENCE L.—Laboratory Assistant, H. S. of Commerce; 111 E. 127th St., Manhattan. Tel. 4064 Harlem.
WELCH, ALBERTA M.—Assistant Mathematics and German, Bryant H. S.; 15 E. 71st St. Tel. 3404 Lenox.
WELLS, NELLIE P.—German, Newtown H. S.; 110 Cook Ave., Elmhurst, L. I.
WELLWOOD, ELIZABETH—Elocution, Eastern District H. S.; 100½ W. 130th St., Manhattan.
WELLWOOD, ELIZABETH—Assistant Oral Language (Elocution), Eastern District H. S.; 100½ W. 130th St., Brooklyn. Tel. 2035-R Morningside.
WELSH, JOHN C.—First Assistant Commercial Branches, Curtis H. S.; 60 Marion Pl., Tompkinsville, N. Y.
WELSH, WM. WALLACE—Assistant Latin, Erasmus Hall H. S.; 967 Argyle Rd., Brooklyn.
WENDELL, Assistant Latin, Erasmus Hall H. S.; 419 16th St., Brooklyn. Tel. 1725-M South.
WENDELL, MAY GODFREY—Assistant German, Julia Richman H. S.; 281 Edgecombe Ave., Manhattan. Tel. 3593 Audubon.
WENDT, CORDELIA—First Assistant English, Girls' H. S.; 135 Halsey St., Brooklyn.
WESSA, IDA—Assistant Latin, Washington Irving H. S.; 527 W. 121st St., Manhattan. Tel. 5271 Morningside.
WESTON, CAROLINE R.—Substitute Physical Training, Erasmus Hall H. S.; 205 W. 113th St., Manhattan. Tel. 3060 Riverside.
WHARTON, WM. P.—Assistant English, H. S. of Commerce; 207 W. 95th St., Manhattan.
WHEAT, FRANK M.—Assistant Biology, De Witt Clinton H. S.; 2456 Bedford Ave., Brooklyn.
WHIFFEN, EDWIN T.—Assistant History, H. S. of Commerce; 24 Hill St., Sycamore Park, New Rochelle, N. Y.
WHITE, ARTHUR E.—Laboratory Assistant Chemistry, De Witt Clinton H. S.; 74 Diamond St., Bklyn.
WHITE, BESSIE R.—Assistant English, Girls' H. S.; 132 Remsen St., Brooklyn.
WHITE, CORNELIA B.—German, Newtown H. S.; 56 Baxter Ave., Elmhurst, L. I.
WHITE, CORNELIA F.—Assistant Physical Training, Bryant H. S.; 2 E. 97th St., Manhattan. Tel. 4157 Lenox.
WHITE, ELIZABETH M.—Assistant French, Erasmus Hall H. S.; 20 Crooke Ave., Brooklyn. Tel. 1379-J.
WHITE, EMMA W.—Assistant English, Wadleigh H. S.; 420 W. 118th St. Tel. 3477 Morningside.
WHITE, EMORY E.—Assistant Music, De Witt Clinton H. S.; 504 W. 131st St., Manhattan.
WHITE, FRED C.—Assistant History, Morris H. S.; 1018 E. 163d St., The Bronx, N. Y. C. Tel. 4600 Melrose.
WHITE, ISABELLE D.—Assistant French, Julia Richman H. S.; 1445 Pacific St., Brooklyn. Tel. 4243 Bedford.
WHITE, MABEL M.—Assistant Stenography and Typewriting, Julia Richman H. S.; 316 W. 102d St., Manhattan. Tel. 6673 Riverside.
WHITE, RUTH E.—English, Newtown H. S.; 56 Baxter Ave., Elmhurst, L. I.
WHITE, WALTER C. L.—Teacher and Assistant Drawing, Boys' H. S.; 268 McDougal St., Brooklyn.
WHITEHALL, FRANK M.—Assistant English, Stuyvesant H. S.; 438 Quincy St., Brooklyn. Tel. 282-R Bedford.
WHITMORE, CLARA H.—Assistant English, Curtis H. S.; Tompkinsville, N. Y. Tel. 86-J Tompk.
WHITNEY, N. BELLE—Assistant Mathematics, Erasmus Hall H. S.; 11 Linden Ave., Brooklyn. Tel. 873 Flatbush.
WHITNEY, CLARA—Substitute Drawing, Washington Irving H. S.; 3604 Broadway, Manhattan.
WHITSIT, JESSE E.—First Assistant Chemistry, De Witt Clinton H. S.
WICKS, HELEN D.—Assistant English, Bay Ridge H. S.; 62 Montague St., Brooklyn.
WIGHT, WALTER A.—Assistant French (acting chairman of department), Erasmus Hall H. S.; 34 Stratford Rd., Brooklyn.
WIKEL, HENRY H.—Assistant Physical Training, Manual Training H. S.; 201 Warren St., Brooklyn.
WILDER, GEORGE F.—Assistant Mathematics, Erasmus Hall H. S.; Hollis Court, Queens, L. I. Tel. 6252-J Hollis.
WILFORD, HERBERT E.—Assistant Latin, De Witt Clinton H. S.; 107 Third St., Elmhurst, L. I.
WILKES, EDNA M.—Assistant Science, Eastern District H. S.; 49 St. Nicholas Terrace, Manhattan. Tel. 8500 Morningside.
WILKES, EANA M.—Physics, Eastern District H. S.; 49 St. Nicholas Terrace, Manhattan.
WILKIN, JOSEPHINE D.—Assistant Mathematics, Jamaica H. S.; 5 Park View Ave., Jamaica, L. I. Tel. 1152 Jamaica.
WILKINS, LAWRENCE A.—Assistant French, De Witt Clinton H. S.; 598 W. 191st St., Manhattan. Tel. 2150 Audubon.
WILLARD, FLORENCE, Assistant Domestic Science, Washington Irving H. S.; 16 Mead Ave., Passaic, N. J. Tel. 1532-M Passaic.
WILLARD, GLADYS—Assistant Latin, Girls' H. S.; 273 Martense St., Brooklyn.
WILLARD, MERIEL W.—Assistant Domestic Arts, Washington Irving H. S.; 16 Mead Ave., Passaic, N. J. Tel. 1532-M Passaic.
WILLIAMS, EDWARD M.—Assistant Commercial Branches, Morris H. S.; 794 E. 169th St., The Bronx, N. Y. C.
WILLIAMS, JOSEPH S.—Assistant Latin, Evander Childs H. S.; 1018 E. 163d St., The Bronx, N. Y. C. Tel. 4600 Melrose.
WILLIAMS, LEWIS C.—Assistant Physics, Erasmus Hall H. S.; 27 Linden Ave., Brooklyn. Tel. 357-W Flatbush.
WILLIAMS, MARGARET—Assistant Cooking, Bay Ridge H. S.; 62 Pierrepont St., Brooklyn.
WILLIAMS, S. E.—Assistant French, Washington Irving H. S.; 351 St. Nicholas Ave., Manhattan.

Tel. 5670 Morningside.
WILLIAMS, SARAH P.—Assistant English, Morris H. S.; 1153 Boston Rd., The Bronx, N. Y. C.
WILMOT, MABEL E.—Assistant English, Bryant H. S.; 391 Dean St., Brooklyn.
WILSON, AGNES W.—Assistant Physical Training, Manual Training H. S.; 489 6th St., Brooklyn. Tel. 2730 South.
WILSON, BESSIE D.—Assistant French, Girls' H. S.; 346 Westminster Rd., Brooklyn. Tel. 2824-W Flatbush.
WILSON, GEORGE W.—730 E. 229th St., Bronx.
WILSON, HENRY E.—Assistant Latin, Boys' H. S.; 27 McDonough St., Brooklyn.
WILSON, JAMES F.—First Assistant History, Boys' H. S.; 1337 Teller Ave., Bronx.
WILSON, STUART—Mathematics, Eastern District H. S.; 226 2d Ave., Manhattan.
WILSON, ZADA J.—Assistant Mathematics, Girls' H. S.; 1228 Pacific St., Brooklyn.
WILSON, RAUDOLPH C.—Substitute English, De Witt Clinton H. S.; 618 W. 138th St., Manhattan.
WILT, IDA—Assistant Academic, Washington Irving H. S.; 101 W. 109th St., Manhattan.
WINSLOW, ISABEL G.—Assistant Mathematics, Morris H. S.; 1051 Tinton Ave., The Bronx, N. Y. C.
WINSLOW, JULIA E.—Assistant Latin and History, Girls' H. S.; 132 Remsen St., Brooklyn.
WINWARD, L. E.—Substitute Art Department, Washington Irving H. S.; 610 W. 139th St., Manhattan. Tel. 4537 Audubon.
WIRTH, CHARLES A.—Assistant Biology, Evander Childs H. S.; 2063 Mapes Ave., The Bronx, N. Y. C.
WISTHALER, JOHANNA S.—Assistant German, Girls' H. S.; 771 Lincoln Pl., Brooklyn.
WITHERBEE, RETA—Assistant English, Girls' H. S.; 1406 Union St., Brooklyn.
WITHERS, SAMUEL C.—Assistant Mathematics, Evander Childs H. S.; 417 W. 120th St., Manhattan. Tel. 5282 Morningside.
WOHLFARTH, AMELIA—Assistant German, Morris H. S.; 1350 Fulton Ave., The Bronx, N. Y. C.
WOLCOTT, HENRY—Assistant Biology, Manual Training H. S.; 786 President St., Brooklyn. Tel. 4457-J Prospect.
WOLLASTON, CAROLINE M.—Assistant Physical Training, Girls' H. S.; 47 Hancock St., Brooklyn.
WOOD, ELIZABETH C.—First Assistant History and Civics, Wadleigh H. S.; 150 E. 35th St. Tel. 6262 Murray Hill.
WOOD, GEORGE C.—Assistant Biology, Boys' H. S.; 798 Lincoln Pl., Brooklyn.
WOOD, HAZEL R.—Assistant Science, Flushing H. S.; 129 Union St., Flushing, L. I.
WOOD, MARY M.—Assistant English, Washington Irving H. S.; 505 W. 124th St., Manhattan. Tel. 6802 Morningside.
WOODBURY, ELLA A.—Assistant English, Bushwick H. S.; 607 Carlton Ave., Brooklyn.
WOODMAN, IRVING L.—Assistant Commercial Branches, H. S. of Commerce; 215 W. 23d St., Manhattan. Tel. 1984 Chelsea.
WOODMAN, SOPHIE P.—Assistant History, Evander Childs H. S.; 561 W. 186th St., Manhattan.
WOODRUFF, FRANK E.—Mathematics, Newtown H. S.; 88 Cook Ave., Elmhurst, L. I.
WOODWARD, ADELE M.—Assistant French, Wadleigh H. S.; 419 W. 22nd St. Tel. 5128 Chelsea.
WORKS, AUSTIN M.—Assistant German, De Witt Clinton H. S.; 2425 Valentine Ave., Bronx.
WORNACK, MARY D.—Assistant Biology, Wadleigh H. S.; 511 W. 112th St. Tel. 3583 Morningside.
WORTH, WILLIAM A.—Assistant Manual Arts (Joinery), Stuyvesant H. S.; 93 Sickles Ave., New Rochelle, N. Y.
WORTMANN, JOHANNA C.—Assistant German, Richmond Hill H. S.; 469 Waverly Ave., Brooklyn.
WRIGHT, GRACE LATIMER—Assistant Drawing, Far Rockaway H. S.; Forest Hills Inn., Forest Hills, L. I.
WRIGHT, HELEN L.—Assistant Freehand Drawing, Manual Training H. S.; 513 5th St., Brooklyn. Tel. 4031 South.
WRIGHT, H. H.—Assistant Mathematics, De Witt Clinton H. S.; Plandome, L. I. Tel. 341-J Manhasset.
WRIGHT, KENNETH W.—Assistant English, De Witt Clinton H. S.; 2776 Morris Ave., Bronx. Tel. 2340-M Tremont.
WRIGHT, MABEL—Assistant Mathematics, Girls' H. S.; 560 Washington Ave.
WYCKOFF, HARRIET E.—History, Eastern District H. S.; 523 W. 121st St., Manhattan. Tel. 5271
WYCKOFF, HARRIET E.—Assistant History, Eastern District H. S.; 523 W. 121st St., Manhattan. Tel. 5271 Morningside.
WYLIE, STELLA M.—Assistant English, Evander Childs H. S.; Sunnyside Park, Bronxville, N. Y. Tel. 307-W Bronxville.
WYMAN, WILLIAM T.—Assistant Foundry Practice, Stuyvesant H. S.; 345 E. 15th St., Manhattan.

Y

YARRINGTON, ADRIAN—Assistant History, Manual Training H. S.; 173 Steuben St., Brooklyn. Tel. 6327-W Prospect.
YERBURY, CHAS. S.—Assistant Music, Manual Training H. S.; 215 McDonough St., Brooklyn. Tel. 844-M Bedford.
YODER, ARTHUR L.—Assistant Physics, Boys' H. S.; 520 Garfield Ave., Richmond Hill, N. Y. Tel. 2823-R. Richmond Hill.
YOKEL, ARTHUR—Assistant Latin, De Witt Clinton H. S.; 68 Kosciusko St., Brooklyn.
YOUNG, CHARLOTTE SPENCER—Assistant Biology, Erasmus Hall H. S.; 2123 Caton Ave., Brooklyn.
YOUNGHEM, EDITH—Teacher in Training in History, Wadleigh H. S.; 220 W. 107th St. Tel. 5041 Riverside.
YOUNG-HIGH, (Mrs.) CAROLINE, M. D.—Assistant Biology, Evander Childs H. S.; 814 Suburban Pl., The Bronx, N. Y. C. Tel. 5646 Tremont.
YOUNG, UISE ARMSTRONG—Assistant Mathematics, Erasmus Hall H. S.; 912 E. 18th St., Brooklyn.
YOUNG, MABEL A.—Assistant Biology, Erasmus Hall H. S.; 2123 Caton Ave., Brooklyn.

Z

ZAISSER, MATILDA—Substitute German, Washington Irving H. S.; 506 W. 168th St., Manhattan.

ZACHARIE, JEAN B.—Assistant French, De Witt Clinton H. S.; 9 Mitchell Pl., Manhattan.

ZAGAT, LILLIE—Assistant Mathematics, Washington Irving H. S.; 973 Summit Ave., New York.

ZARN, FREDA—Assistant German (Main Bldg.), Bushwick H. S.; 55 Chauncey St., Brooklyn.

ZASLAW, MYER—Assistant Mathematics, Manual Training H. S.; 211 Schermerhorn St. Brooklyn.

ZEINER, ED RD J. A.—Assistant Music, Commercial H. S.; 1068 Park Pl., Brooklyn. Tel. 8291-R Bedford. WA

ZERBAN, ALEX. H.—German, Newtown H. S.; 723 Union Ave., Brooklyn. Tel. 6583-J Audubon.

ZICK, HENRY—First Assistant Modern Languages, Wadleigh H. S.; 672 St. Nicholas Ave.

ZINMAN, MEYER—Assistant Stenography and Typewriting, Bay Ridge H. S.; 147 Fountain Ave., Brooklyn.

ZOLLINHOFER, SOPHIE—English, Eastern District H. S.; 141 Gates Ave., Brooklyn. Tel. 6554-W Prospect.

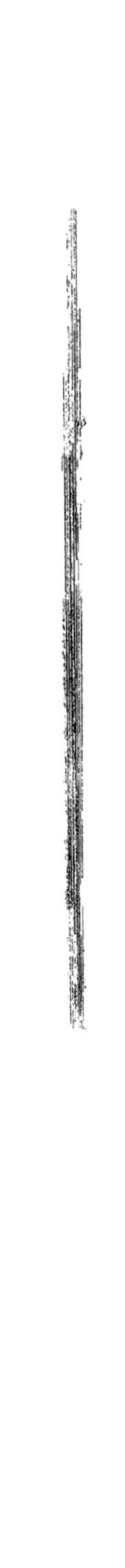

OFFICIAL BULLETIN

of the High School Teachers' Association of New York City

No. 46 DECEMBER 1914

REPORT ON A TRIP TO SOUTH AMERICA

MADE TO THE

BOARD OF EDUCATION OF NEW YORK CITY

By WILLIAM T. MORREY,

President of the High School Teachers' Association,
New York City.

TO THE BOARD OF EDUCATION OF NEW YORK CITY,

LADIES AND GENTLEMEN: I hereby transmit this Brief Report on my visit to South America as the Guest of the Pan-American Division of the American Association for International Conciliation in compliance with your action of May 27, 1914, that:

"William T. Morrey, of Bushwick High School, be granted a Leave of Absence with Pay from May 29, 1914, to June 30, 1914, for the purpose of studying and reporting upon high schools, commercial schools, trade conditions, etc., in cities in South America."

The general plan of the Pan-American Division is to encourage the exchange of visits between persons distinguished in various callings and professions in order to develop closer intellectual and cultural relations. In this way will be developed that common knowledge and experience that are fundamental to good understanding and friendly relations between the republics of America, North and South.

The immediate object of this particular visit was to form acquaintances with some of the leading men and women in the countries visited; to know some of the more important institutions; to become familiar with the method and material of instruction in geography, history, economics, Portuguese and Spanish, and to collect information and materials.

For making it possible for me to accept the invitation, I renew my thanks to President Thomas W. Churchill and to the Members of the Board of Education; to Chairman Arthur S. Somers and to the Committee on High Schools; to City Superintendent William H. Maxwell, to Associate Superintendent Clarence E. Meleney, and to the Board of Superintendents; to District Superintendent Darwin L. Bardwell, in Charge of High Schools, and to my Principal, Dr. Frank Rollins, of Bushwick High School.

For first suggesting that I be invited, I thank Dean Frederick W. Keppel, of Columbia. He knew me as President of the High School Teachers' Association. When, in addition, he learned, incidentally, of my knowledge of Spanish, my researches at Washington in the Archives of the Department of State on certain phases of United States and Colombian diplomatic history, and my studies in Spanish-American history, trade, and commerce, he suggested my name to President Nicholas Murray Butler and secured his endorsement.

I wish to thank Dr. Harry Erwin Bard, Director of the Pan-American Division of the American Association for International Conciliation, for my invitation to become the guest of the Association, for his many favors and courtesies, and for the many and great opportunities the trip afforded.

Very respectfully,

WILLIAM T. MORREY.

535 West 111th Street, New York City.
December 9, 1914.

CONTENTS OF THIS BULLETIN, No. 46

NOTICE.

Copies of this BULLETIN, *free to members of the High School Teachers' Associatic of New York City, are not for sale by Mr. Morrey, but can be obtained, postage prepaid, t non-members for 20 cents per copy on application to any of the following officers*:

ALEXANDER L. PUGH, President, High School of Commerce, 155 W. 65th St., New York City.

MISS ANNA E. STANTON, Secretary, Bushwick High School, 400 Irving Ave., Brooklyn, N. .

DR. LORING B. MULLEN, Treasurer, Girls' High School, Nostrand Ave., Brooklyn, N. Y., or

THE SENIOR REPRESENTATIVE OF THE H. S. T. A. in each High School.

ITINERARY

May 30—Left New York on "Vandyck."
June 5—Six hours in Barbadoes.
" 13—Eight hours in Balia.
" 16-21—Five and one-half days in Rio de Janeiro to Sao Paolo.
" 21—Railroad ride, 12 hours; Rio de Janeiro to Sao Paolo.
" 22—Sao Paolo, one day.
" 23—To Santos, five hours; in Santos; embarked on "Araguaya."
" 25-28—Three days in Montevideo.
" 29-July 4—Six days in Buenos Aires.
July 5-14—Ten days on "Orduna."
" 10—Two hours ashore at Punto Arenas in Strait of Magellan.
" 14—Coronel and Lota, Chile.
" 15—Concepcion, Chile.
" 16—Train to Santiago.
" 16-19—Three days in Santiago.
" 19-21—Valparaiso, two days.
" 21-27—On board "Orduna."
" 24—Antofagasto, three hours.
—Iquique, Chile.
" 25—Mollendo, Peru.
" 27-28—Callao and Lima, Peru.
" 28-Aug. 2—On board "Orduna," seven days. In Quarantine, Panama, three days.
Aug. 3-4—Panama, fifteen hours; Canal, Colon.
" 4-11—On board "Calamares," eight days.
" 11—Disembarked at New York City.

(SEVENTY-FOUR DAYS' ABSENCE—About 30 days on shore and 44 days at sea.)

PERSONNEL OF THE PARTY

The party of fourteen, including the Director, Secretary and Tour Manager, contained eight college and university professors, two high school men and two interested in school supervision and general school work.

Eight of our party spoke Spanish and three were slightly acquainted with Portuguese. Two more of the party acquired Spanish on the trip. Our party was favorably compared with previous delegations, few of whose members used Spanish.

My own tastes led me to attempt to visit general, commercial, and trade high schools, their feeding elementary schools, and the higher institutions to which they led; to note the teaching, text-books, and map and other equipment for history and geography; to attend the law-making bodies where possible, to visit the markets and to see how the workingman lived.

BAHIA

From the *Journal de Noticias* de Bahia, de 14, de Junho de 1914, under the title: Scientific Commission we learn that hardly had the "Vandyck" dropped anchor when special launches went out to her carrying Sr. Dr. Arlindo Fragoso, Secretary of State, and his aid, Captain Alcino Cerqueira, the Consul of the United States; a deputation from the Medical College, composed of Doctor Caio Moura, Aquiar Costa Pinto, Alfredo Magalhaes, Piraja Martins, Coronel Alfredo Carvalhal Franca, Director Carlos F. Stapp, of the American College, and others.

Everyone said there was no more danger from yellow fever, and easily persuaded the party to go ashore.

"The party and their hosts took five automobiles, rapidly visited the lower city, and then ascended to the upper city, going to Rio Branco Palace to visit Sr. J. J. Seabra, governor of the State, who received the visitors most courteously.

"Over a cup of champagne his Excellency saluted the illustrious excursionists. Dr. Harry Erwin Bard responded, expressing his pleasant impressions on reaching this capital,

"Colonel Alfred Carvalhal Franca courteously offered to serve as interpreter.

"Next the party went to the Medical School, where they were received in the Convocation Hall by the whole body of faculty and students.

"After a short rest, Dr. Guilhermo Rebello, in an eloquent discourse in English, saluted the renowned visitors. He was answered by Senhor Harry Erwin Bard, Presiden of the Committee and Director of the Pan-American Division of the American Associa tion for the International Conciliation.

"In addition to the medical body, there took part in the function Dr. Carneiro d Rocha, Director of the Law School; Amancie de Souza, Director of the Commercia School; Dr. Alfred Devoto, Secretary of the Municipal Intendencia; pupils of variou schools and others. A band of fifty of the Caçadores played during the reception.

"After meeting Dr. Deocleciano Ramos, Director of the Institution, the Illustration Commission passed through the whole building, manifesting the good impression they ha received.

"After the visit they took special street cars. They went to the Normal Institute where they were received by the Teaching Force, and shown the whole institution takin away with them the highest opinion of it.

"Accompanied by the Director and members of the Faculty, and students, they mad their way to the Maternity Hospital de Climerio de Oliveira.

"They were received by the Doctor Director and staff; they visited the institutio for the excellent organization of which the Illustration Professor expressed high praise.

"From here, about 3:30 in the afternoon, they rode to Graca, where they alighte at the residence of Senhor Dr. Arlindo Fragoso, Secretary of State.

"Dr. Arlindo Fragoso offered the illustrations excursionists a light breakfast, wit menu as follows:

"Peskles, azeitonas, Rabanetes, Galatine de volaille Truffee, Peixe Moqueea, Peix de forno a Brasileira, Omelette au jambon, Filet aux petit pois, Sorvete a la Vanille Fructas de bahia, Vinhos Sauterne, Pommara Champagne, Cafe.

"For dessert, Dr. Arlindo Fragoso raised his glass and made a toast to the America professors, a toast fitting to the circumstances. Dr. Harry Bard responded with thanks.

"In the evening the excursionists embarked, being accompanied by a committee o the Faculty of Medicine."

(Then follows a list of the professors with their titles and addresses.)

RIO JANEIRO

From a Noticia, of June 16th, we learn "The Program of Visits of the America Professors."

"By agreement of Senor Dr. Herculano de Fretias, Minister of Justice, and wit Senor Edwin Morgan, American Ambassador, Sr. Dr. Fresilio Machado, President o the Superior Council of Instruction, after a conference with the Directors of the variou Institutes of Higher and Elementary Instruction, and with the Director General of M nicipal Instruction, have planned the following program for the visits of the North Ame can professors:

JUNE 16—Visit to the National School of Fine Arts and to the National Libra

JUNE 17—At 9 in the morning visit to the Astronomical Observatory, and at 2 in the afternoon to the Polytechnic School and to the Electro-Technical Institute of Rio de Janeiro.

JUNE 18—At 7 in the morning a visit to the Oswaldo Cruz Institute. At 2 in the afternoon to the Faculty of Medicine.

JUNE 19—At 10 in the morning to the Duke of Caxias Model Professional Practice School and to the College of Pedro II.

JUNE 20—At 10 in the morning to the Practice Kindergarten School of the Republic. To the Pedro II College (Boarding School Department). To the Professional Institute for Women.

"On the visit to the Oswaldo Cruz Institute and to the Faculty of Medicine of Rio de Janeiro the North American delegation will be accompanied by Doctors Nascimento Silva, Director of the Faculty, and Professors Nascimento Bittencourt and Leitao da Cunha; on the visit to the Polytechnic Institute, to the Electro-Technical Institute and to the Astronomical Observatory by Doctors Nerval de Gouvea, Director of the Polytechnic School; Ortiz Monteiro, Vice-Director, and Professors Drs. Henrique Morize, Director of the Astronomical Observatory, and Daniel Henninger, Professor of Industrial Chemistry; on the visit to Pedroll College, Drs. Raja Habaglia, Director of the College, and Professors Hastroo Ruch and Carlos Americo Dos Santos."

In addition to the thirteen visits originally planned, many others were arranged for, as, for examples, a visit to the world-renowned Botanical Gardens, a reception at the Historical and Geographical Institution, a luncheon at Pedro II College, a luncheon at the Central Club by United States Ambassador Morgan, an automobile ride over the mountains and through the tropical forests of Tejuca, back of Rio; a trip to top of Sugar Loaf, 1,295 feet high, with the thrill of being suspended on two wire ropes 700 feet above the trees; with the incoming clouds from the sea and, after dark, with the lights of Rio; and on our last afternoon the wonderful trip to Corcovado, from whose 2,333 feet we could look down on Rio in the midst of its hills and the beautiful harbor with its many islands and surrounded by high mountains.

Each one of the twenty institutions and trips deserves an illustrated article longer than I am here able to devote to all Rio. Perhaps elsewhere I can go more fully into details. One sample, translated from the *Gazeta de Noticias*, 20 de Junho, 1914, must suffice:

THE MILITARY COLLEGE

"Coronel Barreto, the officers, and the teaching body, received the visitors most courteously and took them through the large departments of the establishment, taking part in various theoretical and practical recitations, which were continued as usual. Among the recitations we may mention that in English, conducted by Captain Pereira Pinto, and that in physics, by Major Pereira de Mello, which furnished interesting experiences in methods of teaching.

"They watched also the fencing exercises, directed under the instruction of Captain Valerio Falcão; the riding lessons, under Lieutenant Castello Branco, in the Riding School, and Swedish exercises, under the past master of that discipline, Captain Graduate Lieutenant Sr. Miguel Hoerhann.

"The American professors praised highly all teachers whose rooms they were able to visit.

"After visiting the various branches of the institution, which, as usual, showed itself in excellent condition, the members of the delegation were offered by the illustrious Director of the College a table profusely covered with sweetmeats, and various toasts appropriate to the occasion were exchanged over the champagne. The first speaker was the chief of the delegation, Sr. Harry Erwin Bard, who congratulated Brazil in the person of the illustrious President of the Republic, and designated Professor Frederick Bliss Luquiens, of Yale University, to respond in the name of his colleagues to the director and officers of the Military School. The toast, which was eloquent and fraternal, was pronounced in Portuguese.

"At its conclusion Colonel Alexandre Barreto, raising his glass, expressed his appreciation of the honors conferred upon them by the distinguished North American teachers and ended with a toast to the North American nation in the person of its conspicuous president, Mr. Wilson.

"The members of the delegation were eloquent and enthusiastic in their opinions of the manner of living in the institution, which they praised with every step, not only the devotion to instruction in general, in which they saw realized the most modern methods of teaching, but also the military part, which attracted their especial attention.

"The Secretary of the College, Captain Rodolpho Vossio Brigido, in the name of the directors, gave to the members of the delegation various publications of the institution, such as albums, books used in instruction, an interesting history of the college from the foundation, etc."

TRIP FROM RIO TO SAO PAULO

Nearly everybody had warned us against the daylight trip from Rio to Sao Paulo and had advised travel by night in the sleeping cars, but our party decided on the day trip.

All day Sunday we traveled at first through the low lands near Rio to Sao Paulo, with their tropical vegetation, bamboos, bananas and market gardens, then slowly our elevation increased until we were at least 2,000 feet above the level of the sea. Our ride was an agreeable surprise. Most of the day we were going up the valley of the Parahuyba River. My roommate said this part of Brazil reminded him very much of the cattle range country of his own state of Nebraska. The nearer we approached Sao Paulo the fewer cattle were seen and the more of farming, especially of coffee farming.

SAO PAULO

Ambassador Morgan had written of our visit to Sr. Jose Custodio Alves de Lima and requested him as the best qualified to take care of us. The next morning we were taken in automobiles over the city and through the finest residence sections. We visited the Faculty of Law, where Professor Reynaldo Porchat conducted us over the building. We were taken to the Normal School and to the Barra Funda School, which we found in fine buildings well equipped. It being vacation time we could see no teaching.

The Senate and the House of Deputies were visited, and the President of the House, Carlos de Campos, showed the visitors around.

Some of the party made an all-too-hurried visit to the Geographical Institute. Some visited the Secretary of Agriculture and his department and tried to learn how this most enterprising and most wealthy state was encouraging immigration and establishing its colonists.

Others in the office of the Dictator General of the Instruction were received by Dr. Joao Chrisostomo, who told how the state of Sao Paulo is grappling with the problem of education.

We could profitably have spent as many weeks as we did days in this state. We feel that this state studies its problems, attacks them with German thoroughness and energy, and has the men and the money to carry them to success. We shall study and watch Sao Paulo.

SANTOS

We had reached Sao Paulo, July 21st, their winter solstice, and, although it is close to the tropic of Capricorn, we wore our overcoats for comfort. It seemed strange to see the sun at noon in the north and but half-way between the horizon and the zenith.

Between the 48th and 57th kilometers from Sao Paulo we descended from 799 to 20 meters above sea-level—a change of 2,600 feet in five and one-half miles, and from a cool to a hot climate.

Consul Summers met us at the station in Santos and took us to the Consulate. We then in automobiles visited San Vicente Beach, the docks where most of the coffee of the world is handled, and finally the McLaughlin Coffee Shipping Building, where coffee was stacked in bags twenty-four high over several acres of space, and where there was machinery for weighing, mixing and sacking.

We left Santos on the evening of July 23rd, on the "Araguaya," for Montevideo, Uruguay.

MONTEVIDEO, URUGUAY

The official program called for:

JUNE 26, 1914

2 P.M.—Visit to the Kindergarten.

3 P.M.—Normal Institute for Girls, the Practice School, Pedagogic Museum, the Atheneum of Montevideo.

JUNE 27, 1914

9 A.M.—Visit to the Veterinary School.

10 A.M.—Visit to the Agricultural School.

11 A.M.—Visit to the Trade School.

2 P.M.—Visit to the Office for Expositions.

3 P.M.—Visit to the Faculty of Mathematics.

4 P.M.—Visit to the Faculty of Medicine.

5 P.M.—Visit to the Law Faculty, to the Section of Secondary Instruction, to the School of Commerce, and to the Headquarters of the University Council.

JUNE 28, 1914

Visit to the Cerro (the mountain that overlooks Montevideo and gives the city its name).

Trip through the parks and around the city.

Visit to the races.

I shall not here attempt to describe these visits. It would be impossible to do justice to the kindness, courtesy and interest displayed by our hosts.

Every school has so much to show, and our time was so short that it was difficult to adhere to the exact time schedule. One expected result of this was that, when we reached the Girls' School at Pocitos it was nearly dark. The location was excellent; the building was well ventilated, roomy and well lighted. Various pupils read addresses of welcome. Postal-card photographs of the school with appropriate good wishes to the visitors written by different pupils were presented as momentos. There was no hurrying or impatience even from the very little tots, although they had been kept waiting for possibly two hours at the end of a dark winter day in late June. Their self-control was admirable, their poise was perfect.

Of our visit to the Kindergarten of the Normal School, *El Siglo* of June 27th says:

"That institution, as beautiful as it is modest, produced the greatest effect on the delegates, who did not leave its school until they had seen hundreds of little tots, who sat during this unexpected visit maintaining the composure of old folks."

"Oh," said one delegate, full of admiration: "This is a university in miniature." And for a moment those grave gentlemen became tender and smiling and sympathetic while they contemplated the miniature phalanx which filed by as a battalion of pigmies."

How full a half-day was may be judged from *El Tiempo* of June 28th:

"According to the program, the North American delegates continued yesterday to make visits. They visited all departments of the Veterinary School accompanied by the Director of that educational establishment, by members of the Council of Administration, by the Mr. Grevstad, North American Minister among us; by Senor Yeregui, Introducer of Diplomats, and by many other persons, among them the ranking official of the Ministry of Industry and Public Instruction.

"Next they betook themselves to the Agricultural School, staying long enough to visit all branches, taking notes and points on the working and plan of studies unfolded in the same.

"One group continued visiting the other offices, laboratories, and the remainder of the delegates betook themselves to the Trade School (Escuela de Artes y Oficios), where they were received by its Director, Engineer Carlos Bonasso, and by the teaching body of that institution of learning.

"They visited every part, entering the various machine shops, where they were attended by the professors and instructors, who discussed every kind of detail and described the working out of their plans at this center.

"The guests were invited to pass to the principal salon, where they were served a lunch.

"Engineer Bonasso gave a toast of welcome to the embassy. He was answered for his comrades by Professor Chester Lloyd Jones, Professor in the University of Boston. Dr. Harry Erwin Bard, President of the Pan-American Division, toasted to the triumph of American con-fraternity."

BUENOS AIRES

The steamer trip from Montevideo to Buenos Aires took all night. We had our first taste of Argentine sincerity of welcome by being wakened early next morning, before daylight. The committee, on this rainy, cold winter morning had come to greet us and to find out what we wished to do.

The chairman of the committee, Dr. Ernesto Nelson, Director General of Secondary Instruction; Professor Wilmart, of the Law School, and Mr. Ewing belong to the Roosevelt type of strenuosity.

The Program

MONDAY, JUNE 29

12 M.—Photograph at the Palace Avenida Hotel. Meeting of the Commission in Room 201.

1 P.M.—Lunch.

(*Afternoon free for individual use*)

(EVENING—National Opera House, in box of Mayor. Opera "Aida.")

TUESDAY, JUNE 30

9 A.M.—Visits to schools—a Secondary, a Commercial and an Industrial.

2 to 4 P.M.—Visit through the city, including the Zoological and the Botanical Gardens.

Wednesday, July 1

9:00 A.M.—Visit to the National University of La Plata (taking the train at Constitution Station at 9 A.M., returning to Buenos Aires at 6 P.M.)

7:30 P.M.—Annual Banquet of the United States Universities Club.

Thursday, July 2

9:00 A.M.—Visit to a Primary School, to a Normal School, and to Normal School for Professors.

4:00 P.M.—Reunion in *El Musee Social Argentine*, with Professors specialists in various departments.

(Evening—Opera, "Madame Butterfly," in National Opera House, as guests in box of the President of the Republic.)

Friday, July 3

9:00 A.M.—Visits to the Faculties of Medicine, of Social Sciences and of Law.

12:30 P.M.—Breakfast in the Jockey Club by the Minister of Public Instruction.

3:00 P.M.—Visit to the Immigration Bureau.

4:00 P.M.—Visit with Senator Frers to the Capitol and to the Session of the Senate.

5:00 P.M.—Visit to the Rector of the University and to the Faculty of Philosophy and Letters.

Many monographs would be needed to describe the various phases of our visits in Buenos Aires. I may discuss elsewhere such topics as "*El Internado*," "*El Profesorado*" and Director Derqui and *El Colegio Nacional* "*Mariano Moreno*." Here I shall describe first the "Living Language School," and then give the report of July 3rd as published next day in *La Prensa*, one of the great newspapers of the world.

The Modern Language Normal School

"This institution for the preparation of teachers of foreign language is located at the capital, and forms a part of the national system of education.

"Modern languages occupy a most important position in all schools of secondary grade, *Liceos and Normal*, commercial and industrial institutions.

"As far as the practical side is concerned, they are excellently taught, but in order to improve still more the practical teaching of foreign languages the Government founded this special school and decreed a course of study that is as efficient as it is unique.

"The institution comprises two schools—a primary and a secondary.

"In the first is given a regular primary education, with the addition of one or two foreign languages—French and English. The language instruction is eminently practical, and the pupils learn to understand and speak as well as to read and write.

"On entering the upper school the student elects the language she expects to teach. It is a school for girls only. And from this time on all instruction in all subjects of curriculum, except Spanish, is given in the language which the student is preparing to teach, and usually by teachers for whom this language is the mother tongue. In other words, the high school is an English School for one section and a French School for the other.

"The curriculum varies somewhat for the different sections. For example, history in the French section means especially history of France and of the French; in the other section the stress is laid on English history. The same is true of geography and civics, and necessarily the studies in literature are totally different.

"The study of the language itself is also continued, so that by the time the girl finishes her high school course she is admirably grounded in the foreign tongue, and at the same time has studied the people, their history, literature and customs, society and politics. In addition, she has studied methodology, and has been trained in the art of teaching the language by means of practice lessons in the primary department.

"The curriculum of the preparatory school covers three years, and that of the high school four years.

"For the preparation of foreign language teachers a better method could scarcely be devised."—E. E. Brandon in Bulletin 504, U. S. Bureau of Education.

NORTH AMERICAN PROFESSORS VISIT THE FACULTIES AND CONGRESS BREAKFAST IN THE JOCKEY CLUB

"The North American professors, guests in this capital, dedicated yesterday morning to visiting the Faculties of Medical Sciences and Law.

"They were received in the first by Doctor Luis Guemes and a group of professors and physicians, who accompanied them during their visit to the establishment.

"Then they passed to the Faculty of Law, where they were attended by Doctors Bidau, Oliver, C. Saavedra Lamas, Wilmart, J. J. Diaz Arana, H. Larguia, C. de Tezanos Pinto and H. Quirno Costa.

"They were for a few minutes in the class on finance, in which Doctor Saavedra Lamas discussed the progressive income tax.

"The passages in the discussion by Doctor Saavedra Lamas were listened to attentively by the North American educators, especially when the speaker referred to the work of Seligman, whose conclusions he studied and analyzed.

"At 12 noon breakfast was served in the Imperial *salon* of the Jockey Club.

"The Minister of Public Instruction took his seat facing the delegates.

"The table, in the form of a circle, was adorned with güides and branches of flowers in different colors.

"The seat of honor was occupied by the president of the delegation, Doctor Bard, who had at his right the Minister, Dr. Cullen, and at his left the Municipal Intendent.

"Facing them was seated Dr. Percy Bently Burnett, who had at his right the Minister of Foreign Relations, and at his left Dr. Uballes."

[Mr. Morrey was seated between Dr. Wilmart, Professor of Political Science in the Law School, and Dr. Emilio Frers, Lawyer, Senator, President of the *Music Social Argentino*, who succeeded in inducing President Roosevelt to visit Argentina.]

"The other places were occupied by the delegates, scattered among professors of our faculties and National Colleges.

"The breakfast passed in the midst of a frank expression of desires for closer intellectual relations between the United States and Argentina.

"With the dessert, there was a brief discourse by Dr. Cullen, to whom Dr. Bard replied on *behalf of* his companions.

"In the afternoon the delegates were a few moments in Congress, during the Session of the Chamber of Deputies, and then they went to the Hotel for Immigrants, whose building and equipment impressed them very much.

"At 5:30 they were received by the Rector of the University of Buenos Aires, Doctor Uballes; then they visited the Faculty of Philosophy and Letters, and last assisted in a reception offered by the Young Men's Christian Association.

"The president of the delegations, Doctor Bard, was honored last night by a banquet by Doctor Francisco P. Moreno.

"The delegates will visit this morning the estancia of Senor Leonardo Pereyra.

"For this purpose they will have a special coach, placed at their disposal by the Government.

"In the afternoon there will take place in one of the parlors of the Avenuida Palace Hotel the reception, which the delegates offer in return for attentions shown them.

"There have been specially invited the members of the Executive Power, the Mayor, the Rectors and Deans of the Universities and some Professors of the Secondary Schools. Schools.

"The number of invitations distributed is very limited.

"It has been announced that the delegates leave to-night on the steamer *Londres* for Montevideo, where they will embark on the steamer that will take them to Chile."

PATAGONIA

July 10th, in the midst of heavy seas and in a storm of snow, sleet and rain, about half of our party landed at Punta Arenas, 53° 10′ S. Lat., Southern Chile, midway in the Strait of Magellan and in plain sight of Terra del Fuego.

Our party was met by a representative of the University of Chile, and in the name of the University welcomed to the Republic and shown the sights of the town.

I missed the representative, for I had found a boys' school near the post-office. Here I was cordially welcomed by Director Luis E. Zelada M., who said the Chilean plan was six years of Elementary Schools, six years of Superior or High Schools, preparatory to the University or to the Professional Schools.

As soon as the director would open the hour to enter a class room, the teacher and pupils stood quietly and respectfully until he left the room or until ordered to be seated. (This was the custom in all South America.)

The desks were good, the apparatus and maps good and abundant and excellent. For teaching anatomy this elementary school had a manikin similar to the one I used in college.

LOTA

From Coronel we went to the mining town of Lota. Here I had an opportunity to visit for a few minutes the parochial school, the only one I visited in Chile. I enjoyed the good spirit between pupils and teachers and towards the good *Padre* who welcomed me.

I was just in time to see the dismissal of the public school boys across the Plaza. They were boys all right, interesting and lively. The excellent maps here showed the same fostering influence of the central government that I had seen in Patagonia.

CONCEPCION

We arrived at 11 A.M., and visited the various sights of the city. In the afternoon we visited the Liceo, under the guidance of Professors Hopson, Stevenson and Saez. The new building will be one of the best in South America.

SANTIAGO, CHILE

THURSDAY, JULY 17.—Morning free until 11 A.M. Call from Rector of University and others. Photographs for *El Mercurio*. Excursion around city.

Afternoon—Trip around city to Santa Lucia Hill. Visit the cemetery.

The program for Juy 18th was thus described in *El Mercurio* of next day:

"The university professors from the United States, who have been our guests since last Thursday, continued their program of work as planned. Divided into two groups, they visited the principal institution of public education in this capital, accompanied by the Secretary of the Pedagogic Institute, Professor Don Eliodoro Flores.

"One of the groups, compsed of seven professors, visited the National Institute, Girls' *Liceos* No. 2 and No. 3 and the Professional School, located on the Alameda, at the corner of Santa Rosa.

"The other members of the delegation visited the model tenements for working men, built under the patronage of the Government, in San Eugenio and Santa Rosa, and then they visited the Hospital of San Salvador, and afterwards the Providencia Home for Orphans.

"Everywhere the distinguished guests were surrounded with attentions, as well as with facilities to accomplish the purpose of their visit.

"After the morning visit, at mid-day we met them in their quarters in the Grand Hotel, in order to obtain the opinion of the members concerning the impressions they had received during their trip.

" 'We have come back indeed highly pleased with the great progress in this country, and on a scale so vast, especially in the matter of technical training for girls,' Mr. Chester Lloyd Jones replied, 'for the school we have just visited merits nothing but praise.'

"Just then there approached us Mr. J. Byrne Lockey, in the midst of the other group, when we also requested him to give us his impression of the morning.

" 'To sum it up, everything we have seen to-day is admirable,' he answered wit enthusiasm, 'especially the Salvador Hospital, with perfect conditions technically and fo comfort. Believe me that I did not expect to be so enthusiastic in praise, but,' said he 'in its class there is no superior to that in this capital.

" 'With reference to the Home for the Little Orphans,' he added, 'if I may judg it from the passing view I had of it, it is a splendid institution, well maintained, and comparatively speaking, at a very low cost.'

"His judgments showed us that he had examined what he had seen with the spirit o the true observer.

"When we spoke of the homes for workingmen, his remarks about them aroused i us the justest interest.

" 'The flourishing state of these centers,' he declared to us, 'is the more noteworth in my opinion if we consider that they are built and maintained in this country at th expense of the State. This work of the Chilean treasury shows us what can be accom plished in small nations, considering the difficulties that their administration presents. I my country we have them in satisfactory conditions, but founded by private enterprise.'

"Following the schedule previously made, in the afternoon the delegation continued it visit to educational institutions and to other public buildings. Among the first were th Pedagogic Institute, Jose Abelardo Nunes Normal School, Girls' Normal School No. and the Institute of Physical Education.

"In each one of these state-supported educational establishments, and especially i the Pedagogic Institute and in the No. 3 Normal School for Girls, the North America professors were the object of sympathetic manifestations on the part of the teachers an pupils. In the last the arrival of the delegation was saluted by the students with grea ovations to the United States and with the Yankee hymn sung in correct English by th girls of the upper grades.

"The professors, as they made known to me after their visit, have greatly admire the high grade of every department of every public educational institution that they hav had occasion to visit.

THE RECEPTION AT THE UNIVERSITY

"At the reception offered by the Rector of the University of Chile, Don Doming Amunatequi Solar, in the reception rooms of our first nursery garden of higher educatio in honor of the North American professors who are visiting there, took part yesterday th teaching body, the Under-Secretary of the Ministry of Foreign Relations, the Unde Secretary of the Ministry of Public Instruction, and the Section Chiefs of this last depart ment. By special invitation there was also present the Minister from the United States his Excellency, Mr. Henry P. Fletcher.

"The members of the delegation were accompanied through the University by the Rector, Secretary and Pro-Secretary of the Institution. In their honor was served *una copa de champagne*. They then visited the class rooms and the Laboratories of the Engineering School. A few minutes after seven the professors left the University.

TO-DAY'S PROGRAM

"The distinguished travelers will visit to-day, in company with some of our university professors, the following public institutions: Museum for Fine Arts, School of Fine Arts, and National Museum.

VISIT OF COURTESY

"The president of the delegation made yesterday a ceremonial visit to the Ministers of Instruction and of Foreign Relations. This visit had for its object the thanking of Senores Rodriguez and Villegas for the attentions that they had bestowed upon the members of the delegation during their stay in Santiago.

DEPARTURE OF THE DELEGATION

"The delegation will leave at noon to-day for Valparaiso in a special car. They will remain until Tuesday in the neighboring port before embarking to sail north. It is their intention, as we have already given notice, to visit Peru and Panama."

ESCUELA PROFESIONAL SUPERIOR DE NINAS DE SANTIAGO

On this Industrial High School for Girls of Santiago, I have much valuable material, thanks to Senorita Dona Albina Bustos, its charming Directora.

It will be interesting to all of us to know what our Chilean co-workers prohibit as not conducive to the good manners of girls. Pupils are forbidden:

(*a*) To use the *manto*.
(*b*) To leave the room during hours of recitation, except in case the teacher permits it for urgent necessity.
(*c*) To speak in a loud voice, or to promenade at recess arm in arm or holding hands.
(*d*) To carry to school any work strange to the course, or newspapers, or books for reading, or letters,
(*e*) To offer any present whatever to teacher, or to superior officers.
(*f*) To go upstairs, or to enter the room before the bell rings, indicating time to begin work. To remain within when the bell rings, to leave or to take out her work at recess time.
(*g*) To cease promenading during recess time.
(*h*) To begin conversation with the Mozos (servants or "boys").
(*i*) To spit on the floor in the rooms or in the courtyard.
(*j*) To take work out of the school without the permission of the professor.
(*k*) To form groups in the toilets. To visit them more than one pupil at a time. To leave them in disorder.
(*l*) To bring fruits to eat during recess.
(*ll*) To wait in front of the door of the building and form groups.
(*m*) To wear a skirt that touches the ground in walking.
(*n*) To wear costly jewels, clothes, or hats, or to use rouge or rice powder on the face.
(*o*) To write initials on desks or on the walls of the school.

"Punctuality is the first duty of a worker."
"Silence is the rule of the School."

VALPARAISO

On account of the very heavy rains, and because of the public military funeral of Admiral Uribe, there were no school functions in Valparaiso. We had an opportunity of seeing what fine soldiers Chile has. The next day we visited the very interesting Naval School, the Annapolis of Chile.

IQUIQUE, CHILE

In this west coast desert town I embraced an opportunity to visit a school in a rented warehouse facing the public square. There were four classes in the four corners of the large room. I saw only the opening exercises. The marching and the singing were very good, and the teachers courteous.

LIMA, PERU

Because of the July 28th National Holiday Celebrations we could see only the outside of the various educational buildings in our drives around the city. But in one of the private schools we had a splendid opportunity to see and hear how a Peruvian school observes Independence Day.

Next day some of the delegation called on the President. All attended the formal Military and Naval Parade and the Solemn High Mass in the Cathedral.

PANAMA

We lay three days in quarantine in the bay of Panama, so that we had just a few hours for the Isthmus. We were met at the pier by our Ambassador, by the representative of the Consul, by the President of the National Institute of Panama, and by representatives of the Normal School and the Department of Education of the Republic. We took automobiles through Panama and down to the ruins of old Panama.

That evening many of us visited the National Institute of Panama, and caught, I hope, some of the enthusiasm of its Rector, Dr. Edwin G. Dexter. May his dream of a Pan-American University at Panama come true with him as guarding spirit.

Next morning, led by our indefatigable Ambassador, William J. Price, we climbed Ancon Hill in time for sunrise. We caught an early train to the entrance to the Culebra Cut, where we took a launch through the cut and into the lake caused by damming the Chagres River. We then boarded a train for Colon, where we embarked on the Calamares, pleased with our trip, but all more or less homesick.

ON TRADE CONDITIONS IN SOUTH AMERICA

Although the purpose of the Pan-American Division in sending the party of eleven college and school men to South America was to cultivate closer cultural and intellectual relations rather than to foster trade relations, yet the purpose of several in the party was, if possible, to obtain, in addition, some idea of the economic ideas obtaining and of the trade conditions.

But one member of the party was under orders to observe to report on trade conditions. When the Board of Education of New York City granted Mr. Morrey leave of absence with pay he was so requested. This party, unlike most preceding parties, was composed of men trained in history and economics, several of them professors of those subjects. In addition, most of the men read and talked Spanish and three of them Portuguese. All but three had been in South America, in Spain, or had lived among Spanish and Spanish-American people and had learned, at least in part, to understand them and to appreciate them. It was this friendly, sympathetic, appreciative attitude that made the visit as a whole a real success.

The long sea trips, the numerous travelers (South Americans returning from the United States or going there; American agents, engineers, officials, etc.), the desire to learn made it easy for us to make many acquaintances and under conditions more favorable to confidential exchanges of opinion than around some festal board. Many of the party had college friends, who had been many years in South America so that an intimate knowledge was available to many of us.

There was a general complaint of "hard times." The causes were given as three. The cause, most frequently heard on the east coast—in Uruguay and Argentine, and also in Chile—was poor crops, resulting from the abnormally excessive rains. This failure of crops diminished the purchasing power of the agriculturists.

Great stocks of imported articles could not be sold. Some of our party were driven by miles of storehouses along the docks of Buenos Aires, said to be filled with such unsalable imported articles. This great mass of merchandise must be reckoned with in all of our plans to obtain a foothold and obtain the trade of the Argentine Republic.

Another great cause of hard times is the optimism of the Latin-American. His leaders are well trained, broad-minded, widely traveled, and ambitious to show their ability and pride of country and city. Their great cities can proudly invite comparison not only with our own great cities, but also with the best in Europe. This is a fact that we are beginning to learn and to appreciate, thanks very largely to ex-President Roosevelt's visit and his subsequent enthusiastic advertising. When in conjunction with this optimism of the South American you consider his strongly centralized government, you can see that when an aggressive, ambitious, forceful President, or Governor, or Mayor, or all together, in many cities, many states, and in several republics—when they all at the same time inaugurate very desirable public improvements—there is a very great demand for credits. New public buildings, libraries, legislative halls, municipal theatres, street-car lines, electric light and power plants, railways—all are very much in evidence. New streets, avenues, and boulevards, grading down of immense hills and the filling of deep valleys—all very desirable, but all very expensive, especially if done by or for the government.

In addition to the poor crops, and the optimistic everborrowing for governmental and for public utilities, there is the third cause of curtailment of credits. Although there has been more or less of this going on for some time, yet we found that at Buenos Aires, for example, there has been going a steady calling in of credits given by German banks and firms. This strong, steady, persistent demand for money, for gold, made by the Germans had a very depressing effect on South American trade. For it must be remembered that the Germans do a very large share of South American business. There is close supervision and direction, probably governmental, of German foreign trade activities. The Germans deal with Germans, and when a German merchant does business as agent for a North American firm, he probably has inducements made to him to direct the trade so as to further German interests. Many of the electric industries are owned largely by Germans, who, of course, insist that equipment be purchased in Germany. In these and in other ways German money has been scattered over the world, and especially in Spanish-America and Brazil. The Germans in South America have probably been by far the best supplied with proper banking facilities. For this reason the curtailing of credits by the Germans had a very great effect financially. It also had a very great psychological effect, for the Germans had been underbidding the English by granting extremely long credits as well as good rates. The Germans very deservedly won success by catering to the tastes, manners, and customs of the country.

The Germans learn the language of the country. They grant the long credits asked for. They try to find out the pattern, size, colors, and shapes of the articles wanted. They then try to fill the specifications furnished, pack securely, exactly as ordered.

We, of course, have heard directions for packing, crating and securing machinery, sewing machines, for example, sent abroad. It is worth the cost of the trip to send packers of such goods down the West Coast of South America to see how freight has to be handled in getting out of the hold and into lighters or upon the wharves while the waves are seemingly mountains high.

The South American knows his business. He knows what his customers desire to buy, consequently he knows what he can sell. He may very naturally resent it when a bumptious *Yanqui* tries to persuade him that he needs something better. We cannot expect to make South America a dumping ground for our surplus products, if those products do not happen to suit the taste of the South American. He knows that his customers are slow to change long-established tastes and that

Entre gustos—no hay disputos. ("In matters of taste there can be no disputes.")

Our South American is first a gentleman, and then a merchant. He must be first approached as a gentleman. In this way respect and confidence and friendship arise. A great deal of business is based on friendship and mutual esteem. They know us and our country better than we know them and their country.

He who is going to South America to capture trade should be first a born gentleman at heart. He should become conversant with the languages that he is to use and with the manners, customs, history, geography and traditions of the people he is to meet. With the proper knowledge of his own business and with a sympathetic and appreciative attitude towards the people he meets he is, with all these qualities, bound to succeed; but let him make haste slowly.

GENERAL OBSERVATIONS AND CONCLUSIONS

Our hosts in South America, in order to bring us into true cultural and intellectual relations, very properly insisted upon showing us those institutions that are basic in any civilization. They showed us all stages in the evolution of a citizen, from the cradle, through school and college and professional or trade school, into public life, or in case of the weak or poor into places of charity—the hospitals.

We were shown kindergartens, primary schools, elementary schools, high schools, trade schools, day schools and boarding schools, colleges and universities, law, medical, and dental schools, orphan asylums, hospitals, maternity wards, morgues, agricultural colleges, bacteriological and biological experiment stations and prize stock farms, importing houses, banks, hotels for immigrants, and model government tenement houses, botanical and zoological parks and gardens, race tracks and jockey clubs, municipal theatres and opera houses, art museums, with their accompanying trade and art schools.

Everywhere automobiles were placed at our disposal, so that we were able to see the most in the least time. We were always under expert guidance. On entering an institution we were escorted to the rooms of ceremony and properly presented to the supreme authority, conducted through the offices of the directing and administrative bodies and then over the institution, generally accompanied by students and professors who could talk English.

Most of the party were surprised at the high degree of excellence in buildings, equipment and management. Our hosts were everywhere proud of their institutions and anxious to show them to us.

THE TEACHERS

The men and women we met were ladies and gentlemen of the world, of culture, refinement and good breeding. They were not only part of the best society, but they were also men and women of affairs.

Many of the teachers were also practicing lawyers, doctors, and engineers. The schoolmaster and the professor are welcomed in politics and are consulted in affairs of state. This is distinctly an advantage. I heard no intimation that the South American teacher is looked upon as theoretical rather than practical, or that he is ever characterized as a "highbrow."

The availability of the teacher for public service is increased by the device of appointing a man as professor of a chair requiring his services but three or four or five hours per week. He may be appointed to several chairs, either in the same or in different institutions. There may in this way be a much larger faculty for a student body of 500 than there would be with us. There may be less of the strictly professional teacher's point of view; less attention to the best methods of instruction, and more of a tendency to talk and to lecture. Over against these disadvantages may be placed the greater number of sincere supporters of the institution, the contact of the students with men of affairs, and the greater public service and the higher social standing of those teaching.

ADMINISTRATION

The more centralized form of government in the South American governments makes school administration more easily regulated by the state, especially with reference to high schools, colleges, and universities. This was particularly noticeable in Chile, where there was a central storehouse at Santiago, well filled with excellent equipment for schools. The school I visited at the most distant city in the republic, Punta Arenas, in the Strait of Magellan, was exceedingly well supplied with excellent maps and charts, with abundant demonstrative materials, and with a very costly manikin for teaching anatomy.

The number of administrative officers was large for the number of professors, viewed from the point of view of most of city school authorities. For example, in one school of perhaps 350 students, there were 19 teachers under eight administrative officers, whose titles were director, sub-director, general inspector, inspector of teachers, storekeeper, first and second assistant, and an accountant. The office of the accounting force was everywhere in evidence, it seemed to me.

I have heard in times past intimations from some of our North American teachers, instructing in some large public high school with much clerical and statistical work to do, that occasionally they had some time in which to do a little teaching. Such teachers might envy their fellow-teachers in Dom Pedro II. College in Rio, where, in addition to the 38 professors in the Day School (*Externato*) and the Boarding School (*Internato*), there were in the administrative force 1 director, 1 secretary, 1 sub-secretary, 1 treasurer, 2 librarians, 5 clerks, 2 chiefs of discipline, 2 preparers, 2 beadles, 20 inspectors of students, 2 caretakers of cabinets, 2 library caretakers, 2 porters, 1 storekeeper, 1 doctor, 1 nurse, 1 tailor, 1 assistant, and cooks, helpers and necessary servants.

BUILDINGS

The schools were not only well officered, but they were well housed and with plenty of room space. They were generally, though not always, abundantly lighted, although we visited them during their winter season. Nearly every city school building was two stories high.

They were built around one or more inner courts called *patios.* The patios were generally paved, though occasionally they contained a small flower garden, a collection of ferns, or other shrubbery. Around the patio were an upper and a lower corridor, into which opened the recitation rooms. Unlike our New York City school buildings, there is no inside hall into which the class rooms open. Occasionally we came across a patio with a roof that could be moved aside in fair weather, as, for the best example in the

United States, at the Pan-American Building in Washington, D. C. Sometimes the patio was permanently covered, as, for example, in the beautiful Hispanic Society Building, 155th Street and Broadway, New York City (a building which no New Yorker interested in Spanish America or in Spain can afford to be unacquainted with).

There were always numerous, large, handsomely-furnished quarters for the administrative officers. In comparison with the few small, over-crowded office rooms of some of our largest New York City high schools it was quite a transition to enter large, light, high-ceilinged, richly-furnished rooms, with privacy for director, secretary, accountant, faculty and board of trustees.

BOARDING SCHOOLS

Outside of West Point, Annapolis, and some charitable and penal institutions we have few boarding schools supported by public money. But they are relatively numerous in Brazil, where they are called *Internatos*, and in Spanish America *Internados.*

They seem to indicate that, although these governments may not do so much foı every child and every youth as is done in Europe and in North America, yet when these governments do help they help the fewer selected earlier, longer and more per pupil.

In the Internado of La Plata University there were private bedrooms for very small groups of students. Elsewhere the rule was the large sleeping halls with many cots.

In many, if not in all, Internados there were Dentists' Offices for gratuitous care o the teeth of the students.

EQUIPMENT

The equipment for the teaching of biology (botany, zoology and anatomy), physic and chemistry was abundant—almost excessive at times. The apparatus was generall for demonstration by the teacher rather than for individual laboratory work by the pupil This is in line with the more recent trend or fashion in science teaching in the seconda schools of the United States, where there is less intricate, mathematical, quantitativ laboratory work and more qualitative work and demonstration. This elimination of excessive mathematical work tends to infuse interest in the practical.

Many of the institutions had large libraries. Of the books not in the language of th country French books were generally far in the lead, especially in Brazil, where man of the text-books used in the higher schools were in French.

HIGH SCHOOL COURSES

One great lesson impressed upon me by my trip is that we in the United States ar away behind our South American friends in the arrangement of our primary and secondary school work. We have an eight-year elementary school with the same instructio common to all children in the community, followed by a four-year high school wi some differentiation.

In New York City we are more or less vaguely recognizing the unwisdom of this b endeavoring to differentiate in the seventh and eight years, and within the last few week there has arisen the question of whether it may not be wise to change the elementary schoo course from eight to seven years

In Brazil and Spanish America six years elementary school work is followed by si years of high school work. The schools, called *colegios* in Argentine and Brazil, an *liceos* in Chile, are divided into four and two years' work.

Colegio Nacional "Mariano Moreno," Director Manuel Derqui, Buenos Aires, Argentina, four and two years' course.

Gymnasio Nacional, or *Collegio Pedro II.*, Rio de Janeiro, Brazil, four and tw years' course.

Liceo del Instituto Nacional de Panamá, Rector Edwin G. Dexter, Ph.D. Three and three years' course, based on Lycées of France. Planned by a man conversant with educational problems of United States, Europe and Porto Rico.

Horace Mann School for Boys, Private School, New York City.

New York City High School, General Course. DeWitt Clinton High School for Boys, Principal Francis H. J. Raul, and P. S. No. 40, Manhattan, Principal Joseph K. Van Denbury. (*Comparative table showing courses of study on pp. 362-363.*)

The advantages are that the *Foreign Languages are begun two years earlier* than in our high schools, and at an age when pupils can memorize words and can learn to pronounce strange sounds much more easily than later.

Algebra, General History and Sciences begun two years earlier and the pupils particular bent entered early, but not too early.

If the six and six plan should be introduced here pupils desiring to take Commercial, Manual Training, or other Industrial or Vocational Work could do so much more easily and also earlier. How this problem has been solved in Chile for commercial students appears under heading "Commercial Education."

In the Table of Courses of Study electives are put in dark-faced type. It will be noted that in Panama there is a choice between French and Latin; in Horace Mann between French and German, and in DeWitt Clinton between Latin, French, German and Spanish as first foreign language, and also between them and Greek (and Italian) for the second or third foreign language.

COMMERCIAL EDUCATION

Commercial education is carried as a part of university work in Uruguay, and as we do in New York University. In the Argentine the commercial *liceos* are of high school rank with some studies for general culture introduced into their five-year course. A foreign language is begun the first year, with a choice of English, French, German or Italian; bookkeeping, 4 hours per week, and stenography and typewriting, 2 hours per week, begin in the second year, the commercial rank proper. The third type, based on less than an equivalent to our eight-year elementary school course, is illustrated in Chile.

Some elementary schools in Chile do not have the complete six grades and can give in their three or four or five years only the rudiments of the common branches.

El Instituto Comercial de Valparaiso, Chile, maintains one preparatory year, three superior years, and also night courses of at least two years. From its last available annual report (1911) we have an interesting statement of the ages of pupils:

Years.	10	11	12	13	14	15	16	17	18	19	20	
Number of pupils......	18	25	57	113	97	102	46	25	3	2	2	=490

In Buenos Aires in the *Instituto Superior de Estudios Comerciales* there are five years of preparatory work. Of these the first three lead to diploma of *Bookkeeper;* if two more years are taken the degree *Bachiller* or *Perito Mercantil* (office expert). The four more years in the course for *Licenciado en Ciencias Economicas* are omitted in the table.

For New York City the three years' Commercial Course as given in Bushwick High School. Subjects given but a half-year are given half-credit.

For the four years' course that offered in the Commerical High School.

COMPARISON OF GENERAL COURSES OF STUDY IN HIGH SCHOOLS OF LATIN AMERICA AND NEW YORK CITY

	Argentina Colegio						Brazil Gymnasio						Panama Liceo						Horace Mann H. S.						P. S. No. 40		DeWitt Clinton			
Year.	1	2	3	4	5	6	1	2	3	4	5	6	1	2	3	4	5	6	1	2	3	4	5	6	7	8	1	2	3	4
Mother Tongue	6	3	3				3	3	3	3			5	5	5	5	5	5	5	4	2	4	4	4	11	11	6	3	3	3
Literature				3	3	3																								
Foreign—																														
English		4	4	3				3	3	3			**33**																	
French	4	3	3	3			3	3	3				**4**						**4**	**4**	**4**	**4**	**4**	**4**			**5**	**5**	**5**	**4**
German																			**4**	**4**	**4**	**4**	**4**	**4**			**5**	**5**	**5**	**4**
Spanish																											**5**	**5**	**5**	**4**
Italian					2	2																						**5**	**4**	**4**
Latin					6	6					5	5	**4**							5	5	5	5	5			**5**	**5**	**5**	**4**
Greek											3	3																**5**	**4**	**4**
Mathematics	5	2	4	4	4	2	4	4	4	6			**3**						**55**					5	5	5	5	4	**4**	**4**
Bookkeeping or Accounts.		2												2	3														**3**	**3**
History	4	4	4	3	3	4					4	4	2	2	2	3	2	2	**55**						2	2		3	2	3
Civics				2		2						3		1	1	1	1	1							1	1				1
Economics																													**3**	
Geography	2	3	4	2	2	1	3	3	3				2	2	2	3			3		3	3			4	4		**4**		
Science, Natural	**33**										6	3	2	1	3	2	2	2						5	2	2	5	**4**	**4**	**4**
Physics					3	3					3	3		3	3	3							5						5	
Chemistry					4	3					*	*		*	*		3											5		
Philosophy				3	2	3											3	3												
Manual Training													2	2	2	**2**	**2**	**2**	1	1	1				2	2				
Stenography																													**3**	**3**
Fine Arts																			1	1	1									
Music													2	**22**											**11**					
Drawing	2	2	2	2			3	3	2	4			2	2	2	2	2	2	1	1	1				**21**					
Physical Training	2	2	2				**33**						**22**												**22**				2	2
Military Drill				1	2	1																								
	28	28	29	29	31	30	19	19	21	19	21	21	29	34	37	34	32	29	25	26	24	26	?	?	33	33	26	25	25	25

Black type indicates an elective between Latin and French at Panama, between French and German at Horace Mann and between French, German and Spanish at DeWitt Clinton.

* Physics and Chemistry are combined in Brazil and Panama.

COMPARISON OF COURSES OF STUDY IN COMMERCIAL SCHOOLS OF SOUTH AMERICA AND NEW YORK CITY

	Valparaiso				Buenos Aires					Bushwick			Commercial High School				High School of Commerce				
Year	P	1	2	3	1	2	3	4	5	1	2	3	1	2	3	4	1	2	3	4	5
Mother Tongue and Commercial Correspondence	5	4	3	..	4	4	3	2	2	6	6	3	5	3	3	3	4	3	3	3	3
Foreign—																					
English	6	6	6	6	3	3	3	3	3	..	..	..	..	..	..	..	..	..	..	..	..
French	..	..	..	..	3	3	3	3	3	..	..	..	..	..	..	..	4	4	4	4	4
German	..	4	3	3	3	3	3	3	3	5	5	5	5	5	5	4	4	4	4	4	4
Spanish	..	..	..	..	..	..	..	..	..	..	..	..	5	5	5	4	4	4	4	4	4
Mathematics (Pure)	..	..	..	..	..	..	3	3	3	..	..	..	..	..	..	4	4	3	3	4	4
Commercial Arithmetic	5	5	5	3	5	5	..	..	..	5	..	..	..	..	..	..	1	..	..	..	..
Bookkeeping, Accounts	..	3	4	8	..	4	6	4	4	3	2, 4	5, 0	..	4	5	..	..	3	3	4	4
Office Practice and Organization	..	..	..	..	..	..	..	..	..	..	..	0, 3	5	..	..	..	..	..	..	4	4
Geography	3	3	4	4	3	3	2	2	..	..	2, 3	..	2	..	..	..	1	1	2	..	4
History	..	..	..	..	3	3	2	2	..	..	..	..	..	3	4	..	..	3	3	4	4
Civics (Religion)	2	..	..	..	..	..	..	..	1	..	..	..	..	..	..	..	1	..	..	..	..
Law, Commercial, etc.	..	..	3	3	..	..	..	..	3	..	..	2, 3	..	..	..	3	..	..	..	4	4
Economics	..	..	..	..	..	..	..	..	3	..	..	..	..	..	3	..	..	..	..	4	3
Banking and Finances	..	..	..	..	..	..	..	..	..	..	..	..	..	..	..	..	..	..	..	..	4
Sciences	4	4	3	5	..	..	3	6	6	1	..	..	3	4	..	4	4	4	5	12	8
Stenography	..	5	5	4	..	..	..	2	2	..	5	5	..	3	5	..	..	3	2	4	..
Typewriting	..	..	*	*	..	..	2	..	..	..	3	5	..	..	..	5	..	..	1	..	..
Penmanship	4	..	..	..	3	3	..	..	..	2	2, 0	2, 0	..	..	..	..	3	..	..	..	..
Manual Training	..	..	..	..	..	..	..	..	..	..	..	..	..	..	..	3	..	..	..	..	..
Drawing	..	..	..	..	..	..	3	3	..	2	..	..	2	..	..	3	1	2	3	4	4
Music	..	..	..	..	..	..	..	..	..	1	1	..	1	1	1	1	1	..	..	..	..
Physical Training	2	2	2	2	..	..	..	..	..	2	2	2	2	2	2	2	2	2	2	2	2
	37	36	38	38	24	28	30	30	30	27	28	28	25	25	25	25	26	28	28	25	?

* At Valparaiso Typewriting is included under Stenography.
Black Type indicates electives. In Buenos Aires any two languages. In Commercial High School either language.
In High School of Commerce any one of three languages.
In Bushwick High School in second year 2, 3 means 2 for the first half-year and 3 for the second half-year.

ON THE STUDY OF PORTUGUESE

What has been said of Spanish applies also to the study of Portuguese—the mother tongue of 20,000,000 Brazilians.

They, in their immensely wealthy republic with an area greater than that of the forty-six states of our union, have more virgin soil, more undeveloped waterpower, more mineral wealth, more timber, and in general more undeveloped natural resources than any other South American republic, if not more than all together.

Their language is so little studied in our universities, if it is studied at all, that at the present there would appear to be more chance for a well-trained man in any given line of work if he knew Portuguese than if he knew Spanish. Although there may be in all of the Americas four Spanish-speaking persons to every one speaking Portuguese, there are in the United States twenty who speak Spanish to one who speaks Portuguese.

ON THE STUDY OF SPANISH

The most important conclusion of our visit is the great value and importance of the study of Spanish in our high schools, and, as soon as possible, in our elementary schools.

The 100,000,000 people of the United States will have more and more to do with the 80,000,000 people in Spanish America in business, science, arts, literature and politics. The opening of the Panama Canal and the great European war have tended to bring the two great peoples much closer together. They are looking to us for credits in the financial world, manufactured articles, raw products, machinery, books, just as they have looked in the past for political examples.

They have been reaching out towards us much more than we towards them. They offer their high school pupils English for three or more years in Brazil, Argentina and Chile. They send an increasingly larger percentage of their best students to continue their education in the United States. They everywhere teach more of the history and geography of the United States than we teach of Spanish America, so that the average Latin American is not so ignorant of the United States as we are of his country.

The changing business conditions, as Professor Snider, of City College, points out, demand that more Spanish-speaking agents be sent from the United States to introduce our wares. Heretofore we have had so excellent a home market that we have not felt the necessity of going out and fighting for our share of the markets of the world. We have relied too much on selling our goods through great commission houses, who in turn sold to smaller houses and jobbers, who in turn sold to the native merchants. This method of doing business required few or no agents using Spanish.

But more and more must we do what some of our great firms have already begun so profitably. We must have agents who can sell directly to the merchants, creating in them, if necessary, new demands that we alone can supply. All this will require more and more agents trained in Spanish.

In the petition to the Members of the New York State Examinations Board, to restore Spanish to its position of equality with other modern languages, the following reasons were given:

1. *The country as a whole and this State in particular has in the past year or so seen a marked renascence of interest in the study of Spanish.* Present conditions in Europe and South America, the success of Pan-American diplomacy in the Mexican crisis, and the opening of the Panama Canal are daily accentuating this interest. Commissioner Claxton of the United States Bureau of Education has recently, October 1, 1914, issued a circular letter to high school principals urging the formation of classes to study South American history and geography, and the Spanish and Portuguese languages. The Pan-American Union of Washington, D. C., is actively encouraging the study of Spanish.

Universities and colleges agreeing to accept Spanish on a par with French and German are Brown University, The College of the City of New York, Washington Square

College of New York University, Princeton University, University of Pennsylvania, Columbia University, Colgate University, Hamilton College, Cornell University, Syracuse University, Amherst College, Dartmouth College, Stevens Institute of Technology, Rensselaer Polytechnic Institute, Massachusetts Institute of Technology, Lehigh University.

Some New York City High Schools having Spanish courses: Bay Ridge High School, Commercial High School, 1,200 students in a four-year course; High School of Commerce; Newtown High School. In DeWitt Clinton High School, New York, *not a commercial school,* the Board of Education of New York City has established this fall a separate department of Spanish, and opened up Spanish to first term boys. Practically all of the Evening High Schools offer Spanish.

2. The study of Spanish has, in the opinion of those best equipped to know, a disciplinary value fully equal to that of, say, a study of French. A study of Spanish will develop as many brain loops as the study of any other modern language. Intricacy of idiomatic expression and a great wealth of vocabulary make Spanish a subject of study worthy of the best mental effort.

3. The older Spanish literature has given to the world some of the great writers of all times. Modern Spanish literature, both in Spain and Spanish America, is notable for its high development of the novel and short story. Such things make for the *high cultural value* of a knowledge of Spanish letters.

4. The *commercial* value of a knowledge of Spanish cannot be too strongly emphasized. The acquirement of the language for such practical purposes does not, of itself, detract from the general educational benefits involved in such acquirement. *The state should not refuse credit for this acquirement.*

5. What may be called the *social value* of a knowledge of Spanish is becoming increasingly important as our relations with South America daily become closer. Commissioner Claxton says: "A further reason for teaching Spanish more than we do is that it is the language of one-tenth of all the people claiming protection under the American flag, as well as of one of the culture nations of Europe." Of the three major national languages spoken in the western hemisphere, English, Spanish and Portuguese, Spanish is the tongue of over sixty million people. With the future of these people our destiny is inextricably interwoven. That the peace, prosperity and mutual understanding of the Americas, now being auspiciously promoted, may not fail in the future, the first duty of educated North Americans is to encourage all efforts to teach the tongue of our neighbors, neighbors whom, up till now, we have more or less neglected. Just as they have everywhere in their secondary and higher institutions courses in English, so should we provide in all high schools an opportunity for the study of Spanish equal to those opportunities already offered for study of other modern languages.

Along with this knowledge of Spanish there must be training in the geography, history, manners, customs, literature, and art of our Latin American brethren.

When a person knows these he will be in an appreciative and sympathetic attitude. He will then be *muy simpático.*

"It will not be possible," says President Butler to the trustees of Columbia University, "for the people of the United States to enter into close relation with the peoples of the other American republics until the Spanish language is more generally spoken and written by educated persons here, and until there is a fuller appreciation of the meaning and significance of the history and civilization of those American peoples which have developed out of Spain.

"It will not be enough to teach Spanish literature and to teach students to read Spanish. They must also be taught to speak it in order that in business and in social intercourse they may be able to use it with freedom as a medium of expression."

MINUTES OF GENERAL MEETING OF HIGH SCHOOL TEACHERS' ASSOCIATION, MAY 2, 1914

The meeting was called to order by President Morrey at 11:25 A. M. The minutes of the previous meeting were read and accepted as read. The President asked for Directory material not yet furnished, and made a very brief report, which was accepted by the audience with approval. The Treasurer reported 897 members, the largest enrollment in the history of the Association, and a balance of $945 in the treasury.

The business of the morning was the election of officers for the year, September, 1914-June, 1915.

By unanimous vote in each case the members of the Association present elected the following to serve for this period:

PRESIDENT—Alexander L. Pugh, High School of Commerce.

VICE-PRESIDENT—Jesse H. Bingham, DeWitt Clinton.

SECRETARY—Anna E. Stanton, Bushwick.

TREASURER—Loring B. Mullen, Girls' High School.

MEMBERS OF EXECUTIVE BOARD—William T. Morrey, Bushwick; Aaron I. Dotey, De Witt Clinton; Fred C. White, Morris.

Principal Mitchell, of Jamaica, suggested that in some way the Dove of Peace should be represented upon the minutes of this meeting, as for the first time since the founding of this Association complete harmony had prevailed in the election of officers.

Mr. Bryant, of De Witt Clinton, moved that it be the sense of this meeting that expression of approval and appreciation of the work of President Morrey be placed upon the minutes of this meeting. Carried.

Moved by Mr. Oberholser that in view of the balance in the treasury the dues of this Association be reduced from $1.00 to 75 cents.

This motion was seconded, but as it involved a change in the constitution it remaine as notice of proposed change to be discussed at the first meeting of next year.

Meeting adjourned at 12 M.

Signed,
AGNES CARR, *Secretary Pro Tem.*

WILLIAM T. MORREY, *President.*

MINUTES OF MAY 26, 1914, MEETING OF REPRESENTATIVES

The meeting of the representatives on May 26th was called to order at 4:20 P. M. with Mr. Pugh in the chair in the absence of the President.

The Secretary's report was omitted. The Treasurer reported a balance of $892.36 i the treasury.

Reports from Standing and Special committees were called for.

Mr. Dotey spoke of the double session plan. It was voted that we pay for publishin a questionnaire and co-operate with the Principals' Association.

Mr. White asked whether our Anti-Noise Resolutions had ever been acted upon by th Board. He also spoke on the question of interest in regard to Sabbatical Year's Leave o Absence, etc.

Mr. Morrey took the chair.

Mr. Pugh moved that copies of our BULLETINS be bound and furnished to the Hig School, College and Public Libraries of the City. Carried.

It was voted on motion of Mr. White that we urge the Teachers' Council to give earl and sympathetic consideration to the report of the Committee of the High School Teachers Association on teachers' absences and Sabbatical Year.

The meeting adjourned.

MARY J. BOURNE, Secretary.

THIRD ANNUAL REPORT OF WM. T. MORREY AS PRESIDENT

Policy

The President has tried:

First. To bring about as friendly relations as possible between the men and women in the high schools.

Second. To find out who wanted to do some valuable piece of work, to help form their committees, to support them financially, and, finally, to give full credit to whom credit is due.

Third. To devote the three years to an examination of the Principles of Scientific Management and their application to High School Problems.

Purpose

This purpose has been carried out along three lines—in the general meetings, in the department meetings, and in the work of the various committees of the Association. This purpose has influenced other associations also, for Dr. Feldman said to the Schoolmasters' Association in January, 1913: "As far as I know, every gathering of secondary teachers in New York City, this school year, has had for its topic of discussion 'Efficiency' in some form or other."

The General Meetings

The general meetings have served as a forum for the discussion of school problems and and as a source of inspiration. If the reports of these meetings should be published as a book its title might well be "Efficiency Studies of New York City High Schools," with the following chapters, most of which were discussed in general meetings:

I. The Principles of Scientific Management. By Mr. Harrington Emerson, Consulting Engineer.

II. What is this School System for? By Prof. Paul H. Hanus.

III. Efficiency in Administration, by Association Superintendent Edward L. Stevens, Principal James Sullivan; First Assistant Alfred C. Bryan, Grade Adviser Miss H. Elizabeth Seelman, and Class Teacher Miss Maud E. Manfred.

IV. Efficiency in Type of High School—Large vs. Small, and Specialized vs. Cosmopolitan, by Mr. Frederick H. Paine and Mr. Clarence D. Kingsley.

V. The Efficiency of Factory Methods as illustrated in Double and Triple Sessions of our large High Schools, by Principals Rollins and Denbigh and Messrs. Avent, Gruenberg and Hartwell.

VI. Efficiency in the Recitation, by District Superintendent Darwin L. Bardwell.

VII. Efficiency in the Various Departments. Address by Alfred C. Bryan on Duties of First Assistants.

(a) Efficiency in Mathematics, by Daniel D. Feldman.

(b) Efficiency in History, by Arthur M. Wolfson.

(c) Efficiency in Biology Department, by James E. Peabody.

VIII. How to Test Pupils—a Means of Judging Efficiency of Teaching, by Prof. Charles H. Judd, of University of Chicago.

IX. The Efficient Teacher: "What Constitutes the Teacher of Superior Merit?" A Discussion by Examiner George H. Smith, Superintendent Edward L. Stevens, and Principals Clark, Denbigh, Fairley, Felter, Larkins, McAndrew, and Tildsley.

X. High Schools and Moral Efficiency. Addresses by Hon. Frank Moss, Assistant District Attorney of New York City, and Examiner Walter L. Hervey.

Relations With Other Associations

The President has tried to bring about friendly relations with the other associations.

Each Association has its own legitimate field, but there are many questions in which all are interested. This Association planned to take up the study of the relations between High Schools and Elementary Schools, a vital topic, but this was abandoned out of courtesy to the Women's High School Teachers' Association. In a similar way this Association did not prosecute its studies in Programs and Program Making, out of deference to the High School Principals' Association.

Relations to the National Educational Association

The work of Mr. Clarence D. Kingsley for this Association and his work along similar lines for the National Educational Association have brought the two associations into close relations.

Finances

The finances of the Association for many years have been carefully attended to by the Treasurer, Dr. Loring B. Mullen, who reports that Mr. Morrey began with a net balance of $13.39.

The first year the receipts were $740.78, the expenses $531.06, the balance during the year was increased $209.72.

The second year the receipts were $858.85, the expenses $568.69, the balance was increased $290.16.

The Organization

The 850 members are represented by about seventy-seven representatives in the Board of Representatives, which meets on the last school Tuesday of every school month, excepting September and June, with "power to act upon all matters affecting the Association."

The Executive Committee consists of the President, Vice-President, Secretary, Treasurer, and three other elected members. It has the power to "approve all appropriations of funds and shall audit and direct the payment of all bills."

Standing Committees—Teachers' Interests and Secondary Education, each with nine members, including the President.

President's Appointing Power

He was empowered by Board of Representatives on October 31, 1911, to appoint a Committee on Efficiency and such other committees as he sees fit to call. [Bulletin No. 3, p. 3.] May 28, 1912, power to appoint was renewed and power to remove was added. [Bulletin No. 35, p. 3.] These powers were again renewed by the Board of Representatives on October 28, 1913.

Committees on Principles of Scientific Management as Applied to High School Problems

This committee was organized with Dr. Edward H. Fitzpatrick as Chairman. He gave an excellent preliminary address to the Board of Representatives, and later prepared a report that was tabled. He did not prepare, as requested, a systematic report as to the best methods to be adopted. Dr. Fitzpatrick's suggestive Annual Report before he left to take part in Wisconsin State School Inquiry may be found in Bulletin No. 36 p. 43.

Of the report on Teaching of Stenography, by Mr. Edward J. McNamara, galley proof copies were used as a basis of a Section Meeting. By the time it was to be published many of the criticisms no longer held, and at Mr. McNamara's request its publication was held up.

A report on Typewriting, by Mr. David H. O'Keefe, of the Jamaica High School, was promised, but never delivered.

The work of the Hanus Committee occupied several of the fields that it had been planned to enter.

Bulletins and Bound Volumes

The policy of issuing BULLETINS instead of Year Books has been continued. It is more expensive, but it publishes addresses and reports in a comparatively short time after they are ready.

By printing more BULLETINS than were distributed, it will be possible to bind up enough to send the whole Efficiency Series to every high school library in New York City for reference.

Superior Merit

The Association on March 24, 1912, took formal action through its Executive Committee, ratified also by the Board of Representatives at the March 28, 1912, meeting, asking the Committee on High Schools of the Board of Education:

(1) To rate as of Superior Merit all teachers whose marks are B+ or higher; *superior* being a comparative term and not a superlative, not equivalent to supreme.

(2) To rate as of Superior Merit those receiving the maximum salaries of their grade, prior to January 1, 1912.

(3) To rate as approved for twelve years, such as have been approved for nine years and have in addition received credit for three additional years in the adjustment of the Junior Teacher Question.

First Assistants

This position, at first a salary grade, is the most available avenue to increase salary for the efficient teacher. It is his Door of Hope. On May 23, 1911, the Board of Representatives recommended:

1. That first assistants be appointed on the grounds of efficiency in teaching and administrative work without regard to chairmanship of a department.

The Board of Representatives endorsed, February 25, 1913, the following amendments to the By-Laws: (a) Amend Section 52, paragraph 3, by striking out words "First Assistant." Insert:

(b) Every assistant teacher in high schools who has been granted a license as first assistant teacher shall be entitled to the rank and pay of a first assistant teacher without further examination or appointment, and said rank shall become effective, and said salary shall be paid from the first day of January of the year next following that in which the license as first assistant teacher is granted, provided that no first assistant shall receive on becoming a first assistant teacher a salary less than he would have received if he had remained an assistant teacher.

(c) Examinations for the license as first assistant teacher in high schools shall be held at least biennially in all subjects for which the license as first assistant teacher is provided in the By-Laws.

Dr. Henry R. Linville's Committee

Dr. Linville's painstaking and valuable report on the Mortality in High Schools represents much hard work, careful investigation, and temperance in statement. It well deserves most careful consideration.

Laboratory Note Books

Mr. George H. Kingsbury, of Newtown High School, organized a committee and made a careful study of the question.

New High Schools

Studies were made of high school conditions in Brownsville and East New York portions of Brooklyn for three terms for graduates of Public Schools in January, 1912, and for January and February, 1913. (See Bulletin No. 39, p. 117.)

Committee on Students Aid and Employment

The committee co-operated with other associations in the movement for systematic efforts in vocational guidance, and as all the high schools had committees in operation this committee confined its activities to the extension of its list of vocational bulletins. The sale of the Bulletins paid for their printing so that no demands were made upon th treasury of the association. The financial statement promised by the chairman to th President, and announced in his last Annual Report, November, 1913, (Bulleti No. 41, p. 130), has not yet been received, December 1, 1914.

Vocational Instruction

The Board of Representatives, May 28, 1912, directed the Secretary to urge tha the New York City members of Congress consider the Page Bill in support of an appropriation of $14,000,000 for Vocational Education.

Committee on Conference With Colleges

The Report of the Committee of Nine was favored by five out of six members o the committee. Dr. Sullivan believed that both mathematics and a foreign languag should be required for entrance to college.—Meeting of Representatives, October 31 1911. (See Bulletin No. 31, p. 3.)

Teachers' Absences

Mr. Charles R. Fay, of Erasmus Hall, formed a committee whose report was approved by the Board of Representatives on April 30, 1912, and by the Board recommended to the Board of Education. The report is printed in full, Bulletin No. 34 pp. 31-46.

Sabbatical Year

The most important of Mr. Fay's recommendations is that a sabbatical year fo study or travel be allowed on half-pay.

These recommendations were taken up by Mr. Fay and his committee with a Committee of the Board of Education; but no action has been taken by the Board.

The subject was later taken up by our Teachers' Advisory Council and again lai before the Board of Education.

Pension Legislation

The logic of events is showing the soundness of the contention of Mr. Frederick H Paine that the city should pay an increasingly larger share into the fund.

The pension of a retired teacher plus the salary of a beginning teacher may amoun to less than the full salary received by the pensioner just before he was pensioned.

In addition to thus saving money, there is also an increased efficiency from younge and more enthusiastic teachers.

It is good business policy to retire the weak.

Pensions are looked upon by some as simply deferred payments on inadequate salaries

Hanus Committee

A committee was formed by the President, to represent the High School Teachers' Association before the Hanus Committee.

The preliminary draft of the report of the sub-committee was read to the Board of Representatives, amended, and adopted by the committee.

It recommends that the Course of Study in New York High Schools have (1) greater flexibility; (2) the introduction into the general course "under proper restrictions, such subjects as may be demanded by a reasonable number of students, and for which there are qualified teachers in the school; (3) greater concentration upon fewer subjects; (4) the five-subject plan per week, each subject allotted four hours per week of prepared work, enabling those desiring to specialize to take two-fifths of their work vocational and three-fifths academic. (Report in full in BULLETINS No. 33 and 36, p. 48.)

The Central Council to Study Hanus Reports

The President planned to devote much of the energy of the Association to the study of the Hanus Reports during 1912-1913; but when they appeared those relating to High Schools showed so much evidence of consultation and conference with High School principals, first assistants, and teachers that it seemed better that these reports should be studied preferably by the Central Council.

The weekly conferences participated in by both elementary and high school teachers and principals did much to promote a better understanding and a mutual respect.

Men and women that had been antagonistic on salary questions found that they could work harmoniously on purely professional questions.

Teachers' Advisory Council

The President was asked by President Churchill to give his suggestions with reference to the formation of an Advisory Council. He served on the Committee of Organization.

Recommendations

This Association has submitted several recommendations to our school authorities: A sabbatical year; first assistant, a salary grade; that Teachers' Records be consolidated and kept in one place in the Hall of the Board of Education; that all adverse ratings and reports be made in writing, and that the teacher be furnished with a copy of such ratings and reports.

McKee Bills

Though the Association has ventured to make certain suggestions along purely professional lines, it has carefully refrained from entering, as an Association, into the field of school politics.

An adroit effort to place it on record on the McKee Bills resulted merely in passing a resolution that the President notify the President of the Board of Education, the Mayor, the Governor, the President of the Senate, and the Speaker of the Assembly that "The High School Teachers' Association has taken no action on the McKee Bills, either for them or against them."

BUREAU OF REFERENCE AND RESEARCH

Director Shiels not only addressed the Association on the work of his bureau, but he also had prepared for the High School Directory complete lists of all persons holding licenses to teach in the high schools. The bureau in return was supplied with copies of the Directory.

ELIGIBILITY TO THE ASSOCIATION

November 25, 1913, the Board of Representatives voted that "eligibility to the High School Teachers' Association is limited to teachers and supervisors in the public day high schools of New York City and in the high school departments of Normal College and City College."

DOUBLE SESSIONS

The General Meeting of May 2, 1914, was devoted to Factory Methods in Education as illustrated in the Double and Triple Sessions of our large High Schools.

The following resolution was passed with but two dissenting votes:

"Resolved, That the High School Teachers' Association, after full discussion of the matter, places itself upon record as strongly opposed to the plan of double and triple sessions for high schools."

This, I believe, represents in general the attitude, *in theory* at least, of those who know most about Double Session, which is Part Time under another name.

"It is not a theory, but a condition that confronts us." Under present financial conditions, with the rapidly increasing high school population, and with the present inability to build high schools rapidly enough, part time and double or triple sessions are bound to come. I believe that the attitude of every loyal teacher is to make the very best of the circumstances.

DIRECTORY

As the result of calls upon the Senior Representatives, beginning December 6, 1913, materials for a directory were prepared by them and forwarded to the President. Galley proofs of lists were sent back to the Senior Representatives for revision and correction. Most responded promptly and carefully. Eastern District was kind enough to send an extra list of the High School Teachers' Association members, many of whom have their names appearing twice. Principal Dillingham, of Newton, and a few others had their names omitted. Some changed their addresses after their first cards were made out and did not notify the Directory people. The President regrets that mistakes were made.

The linotype material is still at the printers. Those who desire a change in the next edition of the Directory should notify President Alex. L. Pugh at High School of Commerce. Kindly use library cards of the standard size.

ACKNOWLEDGMENTS

He believes that members of the Association have felt free to give him advice and counsel. He has felt just as free about accepting, modifying, or rejecting it.

The success of this Association, as of all organizations, depends upon the spirit of mutual helpfulness between members and officers. An executive needs (1) a few good ideas of his own, (2) with the ability to recognize good ideas of others; (3) the ideas of many others, and (4) the help of others in carrying out ideas.

The President has thoroughly enjoyed his work. He has done much of his thinking and planning during the two hours per day he spends in traveling to and from his school work. He believes that it is restful to change work.

December 5, 1914. WILLIAM T. MORREY.

INDEX TO H. S. T. A. BULLETINS 29-46

Lightning Source UK Ltd.
Milton Keynes UK
UKHW020122090119
334943UK00005B/591/P

9 780656 681884